Lyons'

NIPPY TARTLETS

Wholesome goodness and perfection of quality are revealed in these tartlets. They are famed for their crisp pastry and the pleasing variety of jams or lemon curd with which they are filled.

9 for 7D.

IN CARTONS.

Lyons'

COCONUT TOASTIES

The chief ingredient of these delightful cakes is pure shredded coconut toasted to a golden brown. They are simply delicious.

1D. EACH.

Or in Cartons of 6 for **6d.**

Also
PICCANINNY CAKES

1D. EACH.

Or in Cartons of 6 for **6d.**

J. LYONS & CO. LTD., CADBY HALL, LONDON, W.14

THE FIRST FOOD EMPIRE

A History of
J. LYONS & CO.

This image of a Lyons waitress predates that of 'Nippy'. Before 1925 Lyons waitresses were known as Sallys and these cardboard cutouts were distributed to retailers to display in their windows. Smaller metal replicas were mounted on some of the company's vehicle raidator caps.

THE FIRST FOOD EMPIRE

A History of
J. LYONS & CO.

Peter Bird

Phillimore

2000

Published by
PHILLIMORE & CO. LTD.
Shopwyke Manor Barn, Chichester, West Sussex

ISBN 1 86077 132 7

Printed and bound in Great Britain by
BUTLER & TANNER LTD.
London and Frome

This book is dedicated to those employees of J. Lyons and Company Ltd who gave their lives in two world wars.

Their names are recorded in Appendix 5.

These memorials were erected by the directors.

'Who Stands if Freedom Falls Who Dies if England Lives'

Contents

ACKNOWLEDGEMENTS

Throughout its history J. Lyons & Co. has been relatively secretive about its affairs, publishing only that which management felt necessary or legally bound to report. In 1924, the thirtieth anniversary of the opening of the first teashop, management did commission Sir Basil Clarke, journalist and war correspondent for the *Daily Mail*, to write a brief history of the company which he called *Two Great Undertakings*. Produced in the style of a small booklet, comprising some thirty-six pages, it is the only known unrestricted publication covering the firm's history and activities. There is, therefore, a paucity of historical record, and that which survives, in the London Metropolitan Archives, can only be described as ephemeral. Thus my research has concentrated on a wide range of other contemporary sources. Primary amongst these are the official annual trading accounts between 1894 and 1978, reports of the directors 1894–1978, official minutes, miscellaneous financial departmental reports, the John Simmons papers, management memoranda, company reports, press reports and other ephemeral documents, begged, borrowed or donated. Some information has been obtained from Parliamentary Publications issued by H. M. Stationery Office (now the Stationery Office) and the Office for National Statistics.

I am grateful to librarians and archivists who have helped in my quest for information, particularly the staff of the British Newspaper Library at Colindale; the records at Companies House, Cardiff; the Public Record Office, Kew; Reading University Library; the British Library; the British Architectural Library; the British Consulate General, Istanbul; the Supreme Court Library; Circus World Museum, Wisconsin; the City of London Public Relations Office; the Church Missionary Society; the Royal Society for the Prevention of Cruelty to Animals; Hammersmith Reference Library; the Theatre Museum; the Imperial War Museum Library; the London Metropolitan Archives; Greenwich Maritime Museum Library; the Hotel and Catering International Management Association; *Jewish Chronicle*; the Office for National Statistics; the Salvation Army International Heritage Centre; the Royal Air Force Museum, Hendon; the Turkish Embassy, London, and several other reference libraries including those in the County of Avon, Birmingham, Canterbury, Ealing, Leeds, Liverpool, Manchester, Merton, Newham Council, Norwich, Wandsworth, Wolverhampton, Plymouth and Portsmouth. The *Lyons Mail* and *Lyons Journal*, internal magazines published for employees of J. Lyons & Co., have also been useful in identifying events and dates. With fragmented documentation I have relied heavily on personal accounts from some members of the Salmon and Gluckstein families, other technical, managerial and administrative personnel – mainly former employees –

whose collective knowledge about the firm and its activities proved substantial. Their accounts of events were corroborated, independently, with other sources wherever possible.

To all I would now like to take this opportunity to express my indebtedness for their patience and personal memories. To mention all by name would not be possible. However, I would like to give special thanks to: Len Badham (deceased), Harold Boon, Mary Cakebread, John Crahart, Arthur Christian (deceased nephew of Joseph Lyons), John Dick CBE (deceased), Ken Gillard, David Gluckstein, Roy Gluckstein, John Hutchinson, Hugh Joseph (deceased), Lorna Josey, John Lampitt, Ray Mears, Ralph Morhaim, Marius van Oorschot, Les Pavitt (deceased), Jack Pennell, Anthony Salmon, Ivor Salmon, Jeremy Salmon, Robin Salmon, George Stevens, David Stringer, Fred Vine and Dick Watson for their expert, knowledgeable advice. Some former employees, anonymous and otherwise, have previously set down their own accounts of events past. In this respect I am particularly beholden to S. D. Harris, one-time Finance Director of Henry Telfer Ltd, for his typewritten account of that company and for the account of the Jersey-based firm, Overseas Trading Corporation, supplied by Bob Gallicham but written anonymously.

Most importantly I would like to thank my editor, Linden Stafford, for her meticulous attention to detail. There is no doubt that her advice, constructive criticism, suggestions and enthusiastic encouragement, at all stages, have turned my manuscript into a coherent book.

Finally I would like to thank my wife, Sylvia, for her unswerving support and patience during the six years it has taken to research this work. She has given me encouragement and the space and time to dedicate myself to this task.

Every effort has been made to identify photograph and other illustration copyright. The name 'Lyons' is a trademark, and J. Lyons & Co. a trading name of J. Lyons & Co. Ltd.

I am grateful to the following organisations and individuals for permission to publish pictures and illustrations in their possession: Hammersmith & Fulham Archives and Local History Centre; Hamptons International; Liverpool Record Office; London Metropolitan Archives; Museum of London; Royal Borough of Kensington and Chelsea, Libraries Department; Tetley (GB) Limited; The Public Record Office, Kew; Thistle Tower Hotel; Waldegrave Films, Twickenham; John Bishop; Florence Bonard; Mary Cakebread; Arthur Christian (deceased); Cedric (Bill) Doe; Michael Grant; Tony Hawthorne; Raymond Hicks; Jack Jolliffe; John Lampitt; Alice Lewis; Tony Morgan; Ralph Morhaim; Peter Murch; Wynn Simmons; Denis Toombs (deceased). All other illustrations are from the author's private collection.

FOREWORD

I am the oldest living male member of a family which founded J. Lyons & Company Ltd and managed it for over one hundred years. My grandfather, Barnett Salmon, married Helena Gluckstein in 1863 and although he had doubts about forming a catering concern with the Glucksteins and Joseph Lyons in 1887 he would have been astonished to see how it flourished to become one of the largest food manufacturers in Europe, employing more than 30,000 people. My father, Alfred Salmon, who was chairman when he died in 1928, was one of the original directors, along with Joseph Lyons and my great-uncles Montague and Isidore Gluckstein, when the company sought limited status in 1894. Since that time no fewer than sixteen Salmons and eleven Glucksteins have served in a directorship capacity. There is no doubt that our family have dedicated themselves to this endeavour. Like others of my family I started my career in a modest way by serving an apprenticeship in the firm's Trocadero restaurant kitchens in 1929. After the Munich crisis of 1938 I enlisted in the Territorial Army, joining the Army Catering Corps when it was formed in 1941. After the war I returned to Lyons and took over the managing directorship of Henry Telfer, the meat pie subsidiary. Subsequently I assumed responsibility for all the firm's non-food businesses, except for property, until my retirement in 1972.

This chronicle records the major achievements of the fortunes and traditions of a great catering and food enterprise which earned and retained an enviable reputation for over a hundred years. It is the very stuff of history. Throughout this book we are presented with a remarkable variety of people and events, from the early tobacco beginnings, through two world wars, to the supremacy and eventual decline of the company. Peter Bird describes each of the major events – the teashop development, the tea and coffee production, the Corner House and super-restaurant catering, hotel building, mass food production and the non-food activities – in chronological sequence, providing an extraordinary, vivid and accurate picture of the business as it unfolded, peaked and declined.

Having read the book with great pleasure and interest, I find it a splendid, meticulous and entertaining account. Peter Bird has told this story with skill and accuracy, interweaving the separate themes of company activities with political and social history. His knowledge of Lyons, my family and company developments over the years is wide-ranging. During the two or more years I have known him we have met on a number of occasions to discuss personalities, events and more specifically my own activities within the company. I am confident that his book, which is the result of much painstaking research, will serve as a reference source on the activities of J. Lyons & Company Ltd which hitherto has never been recorded. Above all it is a record of achievement and endeavour by all those associated with this great company from the modest clerk to the senior manager. In commending this book, I congratulate Peter Bird for recording this part of our history in such a readable manner.

Ivor Salmon
Inkpen, Hungerford
December 1998

INTRODUCTION

The history of J. Lyons & Company has its origins in the nineteenth century, when two brothers, Isidore and Montague Gluckstein, decided to break away from a profitable tobacco business, and embarked on an exhibition catering enterprise. The business quickly developed so that by the middle of the twentieth century Lyons was one of the largest catering and food-manufacturing companies in the United Kingdom.

Established in 1887 as exhibition contract caterers, the firm required large quantities of equipment from marquees and furniture to napkins and toothpicks. Most of these supplies remained in store at Olympia when not in use, so they formed the Hire Department, which became one of Lyons' first business diversifications outside catering. As the catering business developed, management became increasingly concerned with the mediocre quality of food that was supplied to them by other firms for their catering contracts. Therefore they began to produce, in a small way, some of the food and drink themselves.

In 1894 Lyons initiated their second major business diversification when they opened their first teashop in Piccadilly. By the turn of the century the ubiquitous Lyons teashop had become famous and remained a familiar sight in London's high streets for another seventy years. Since all teashops were supplied with their food and other commodities from a central point – to ensure continuity of standards and hygiene – it became necessary for the company to develop its own extensive kitchen and food-manufacturing processes. As a consequence Lyons became inextricably connected to food production to the extent that this would eventually be more important than catering.

Restaurants, in varying styles, sprang up throughout London and provincial towns, and they became the company's most important generator of revenue during its formative years. The teashops placed a heavy burden on the central kitchens and food-manufacturing plants at the firm's headquarters, Cadby Hall. All cooked and uncooked food sold in the teashops was supplied from this central point and transferred by an efficient transport system. Bread manufacture began first, followed by cakes and other confectionery, tea blending and then ice-cream.

With the evolution of door-to-door selling of bread and other goods from handcarts and horse-drawn vehicles, an even greater demand was placed on food manufacturing, which could only be met by substantially enlarging the production facilities. This immense operation was supported by sophisticated accounting services followed in time by laundries, printing works, building and maintenance teams, wine companies, transport systems and box-making departments. Later, hotels became a significant business activity which also made use of the food-manufacturing and service units within the company.

For most of its 108-year history (1887–1995) J. Lyons & Company was a household name and for ninety of those years enjoyed independence as a public limited company, with shares quoted on the London and New York stock exchanges. It had grown into one of Britain's largest catering and food-manufacturing conglomerates, employing over 33,000 staff at its peak. Few people in the country were unaffected by Lyons' catering or food products: the famous Lyons teashops were everywhere, and Lyons tea, coffee, bread, cake and ice-cream were sold by virtually every food store in Britain. West Londoners and others were familiar with Cadby Hall, an 'architecturally drab' complex of factory buildings and offices sprawled along the Hammersmith Road between Olympia and Brook Green.

From these headquarters the company's operations spread throughout the world. Dominating the catering scene in London for many years, Lyons provided banqueting facilities to such well-known annual events as the royal garden parties, the Chelsea Flower Show, the Wimbledon Lawn Tennis Championships, the Lord Mayor's Banquets and many more. They were innovators too, laying claim to being one of the first British companies to manufacture and market frozen food. Surprisingly, they also built and operated the world's first commercial computer in 1951 because nothing else was available at the time to handle their increasingly complex accounting routines. A 'mechanical shop' (a vending machine) opened in 1932 at a teashop in Camberwell; from this over sixty Lyons products could be bought twenty-four hours a day.

Growth and success were achieved within the context of family ownership, management and control. Throughout its independent history, which lasted until 1978, the Salmon and Gluckstein families dominated. Joseph Lyons was the only non-family member ever to hold the position of Chairman. The Salmons and Glucksteins had started out as small-time cigar makers but through astute business skills they soon became the world's largest retail tobacconists, owning 140 shops by 1901. In 1887 they turned their attention to exhibition catering and invited Joseph Lyons to head up the new business. From these early beginnings the gigantic Cadby Hall food factory evolved. The food business continued to flourish until the 1960s, when for a variety of reasons the company went into decline.

This account of the firm's history is not intended to be exhaustive. Moreover, lack of space has prevented me from recounting, with a few exceptions, other food business developments occurring elsewhere. Nevertheless, the factual information has been gathered from a wide range of sources, and the broader social and political background to Lyons' own history has been outlined throughout the book. Some of the material in the appendices lacks dates and other details, but it seemed worth including at least that which was known. In this way others may be inclined to take the research further.

The main body of this history covers the period 1887–1978, after which Lyons lost its independence. Where relevant, some of the company's history since 1978 has been briefly sketched in, to record the last period of the Lyons supremacy which came to a close in 1995 when the directors reported: 'The company is in the process of disposing of its remaining assets and it is likely that it will become a dormant company during 1996.'

SUBSCRIBERS

Gordon Adair, known in the trade as Joe Lyons
John Adams
Edward Akehurst
Stella M.E. Alick
Andy Anderson
Derek (Andy) Anderson, Lyons Maid
Mr. P.G. Anderson
Sheila Anderson, Sol Café
Jan Attree, daughter of George Edward Talbot
Joyce Badham
A.J.V. Baker
Elizabeth Rosina Baker
Jack Banyard
Ray Barby
Eric Barker, engineer, Cadby Hall, tea
    department, Greenford 1953-1989
Mrs. Queenie Barker, forewoman, Swiss Roll,
    Cadby Hall 1937-1967
George F. Barnett
Ken Baugh, bakery sales rep
Reginald Stuart Beaney
Tony Bedford
Stuart David Beese, J. Lyons tea division 1969-1997
Ronald Benneworth
Marshall Benson
Kurt Berger
Bert [Mr. A. Lee]
Alan J. Betts
Lilian Billows
Mrs. Peggy Bilton
Tom Birch, heavy transport, May 1951-May 1981
Ivy Bird
Mary Biscardi
Roy Blackbee, tea factory, Greenford 1958-1994
Mr. Tony Blackburn
W.H. Blake
John J. Blanche, OBE CA
Inge Blanks (formerly Kitson)
James Bolt, Vienna doughmaker
Harold A. Boon
Martin C. Booth
Colin Botting
William G. Box
Jack and David Brandon
Norman Brayshaw, Lyons computer services

C.M. Brazier
John Bretton 1946-1984
Graham Briscoe
Mr. J.L. Bristow, maintenance engineer, Lyons
    grocery, Greenford
Frank Brooker
Peter Brookes, ex-Packing Development
    Manager, Lyons Bakery
Tom Brooks, Wimpy International Marketing
Iris Broom
A. Brown
David Brown
Gordon Richard Brown
Tony Buckingham (1936-1987)
Montague Burroughs
Mrs. K. Bush, née Evans, Manageress Teashops
    1934-1969
Josephine Butcher
Clive Butler
Mrs. Butler
Phyllis Byatt
T.J. Cahill, M.ChemA, C.Chem, FRSC
David Caminer
Frank Carstairs
Joyce Chilvers, Housekeeping WX block 1964-91
Eve Clark
John Clemes
Gladys Coker
Mrs. Helen Coleman
Mr. and Mrs. A.T. Conn
Elsie Cooper
George W. Cooper, 1937-1982
Mrs. P.M. Coopland
Joan D. Cox, ex-Teashops
Trustees of W.S. (Bill) Cox, F.C.C.A., A.T.I.I.
John F. Crahart, FCMA
Mr. Thomas Crane, Tea Dept. 1939-1983
Albert Cruse, Lyons bakery
Bill and Lucille Cullin
Keith Dalton, Symbol biscuits
Dr. F.S. Davidson
Dennis Davies
Harold Davies, Registrar Allied Domecq and
    J. Lyons Ltd
Keith Davies, former Group Food & Drink law adviser

'Deller', Cadby Hall 1935-1973
Gerald P. Diamond
Mr. Cedric A.F. (Bill) Doe
Lily Downer
Gordon Duff
Frank Dyer
Philip S. Dyer
David F. Eastland
The Evans family
Jack Evans (Lyons Maid)
Joyce Evans, wife of late Cyril Evans, employee for
    51 years
Mrs. M.I. Evans (née Forbes)
Ron Exley, Packaging Engineer, Wakefield Bakery
Ronald F. Fagioli
Barrie Faircloth
Henry Fearn
W.P. Fenton, J. Lyons Glasgow, manager -
    distribution centre
Patricia Rose Fisher
Miss G. Fitch
Mrs. Fittock (known as Miss Kenny), wholesale tea
Derek R. Fitzhenry
Charles W. Fordham
S.C. (Bill) Foy, Lyons Tetley Catering Supplies
Brian Freehold, Estates Department
Bob Freeman (Normand Ltd)
Gordon Frosdick
Mr. John K. Gadsby
A.M. Gardner
John S. Garner, F.C.A.
Leonard Gasson
Ian Gazzard
Phyl Van Gelderen
Elizabeth Gerred
Charles Giblett
Ken Gillard, Director of Lyons Maid Overseas Ltd
A.J. Gillett
Peggy Gluckstein
Thomas E.L. Goldsmith
Tom Goswell
Alfred L. Gould
Bill Grange, Lyons Maid
Ann Rosemary Grant
Margaret A. Grant
Michael C. Grant
A. James Green
Melvyn Greene, OBE
Bob Gridley, HR manager, J Lyons
Dirck Gunning
Brian Haigh
Alan R. Hames
Phil Hamilton, Personnel & Training Director,
    Strand Hotels Ltd
E. Hamm
Michael Hammond
Joan F. Hanbury
Fred Hannington, ex-J. Lyons & Co. Ltd, Cadby
    Hall & Normand Ltd (1938-1987)
Mr. M.W. Harley
Lily Harrill
Miss Nell Harris

Charles Edward Hart
Alf Hawes
Harry and Mavis Hawes, Greenford Tea dept.
Charlie Hawker
Olive Hawkins (Sally)
Tony Hawkins
Tony Hawthorne
John Hayman, Allied Domecq Pension Funds
P.E. (Pat) Hearse
Joe Heath, Wakefield driver HGV (32 years)
Leonard Hemson, ice-cream sales 1922-1969
Derek C. Hemy
William James Hendle
Ray Hicks
Jimmy Hilditch
John G. Hill
Frederick C. Hilling
Alan W. Hinkins
Usha and Brian Hobson
Joan Hodge (Mrs.)
Michael Thomas Hodge
Bill Hodgson, driver drayman (retired)
    Warrington
Iris B. Hollman
Keith R. Holloway
Richard Holman, Works Dept., Cadby Hall
Bill Holsman (C.A.O. and Henry Telfer)
Stan Holtorp, Managing Director, Food
    Management Ltd
Colin Hornblower
Jack Horne
Peter Horsfield
Kenneth Howel
Mrs. D. Howes, née Eveleigh
Mrs. V. Howkins, née Cottol
Jim Hubner, '56-'94
Louisa Humphries, supporter and tea shops
    nostalgic
Hilda Grace Hutchin (daughter of J. Lyons
    employee F.E.D. Barnes 1927-1963)
John P. Hutchinson
Kenneth Richard Hutchinson
Mike Isaacs, Lyons Bakery 1951-1990
Peter Iveson
Mr. Basil Jackson
Sid Jago, driver, 10 years Cadby Hall, 17 years
    plus, Greenford HT
Helen Jaworski
B. Jeffery, ex-Oxford Corner House, CHCS,
    Strand Corner House, CHSE (pastry)
Mrs. Ivy Jenn, payroll section Cadby Hall
Peggy Grace Jessup
Dorothy A. Jones
Sidney M. Jones
Lorna Josey
Ernest Kaye
David R. Keen
Malcolm Kellas, Business Analyst Leo Computers
Simon Kester, Chairman Sol Café Ltd
Mark E. Kimber, Chief Cashier of J. Lyons & Co.
    (Manager of Treasury)
Michael P. Kimber, Tech. Dir. D.C.A. Industries Ltd

A.R. King
Alan King, Systems Consultant 1959-1988
George E. King
Jack Kitchingman W/TEA
Ivan Knowlson
Alan Lacy
John Lamb
John L. Lampitt
Professor Frank Land
C.G.W. Law
A.J. Lawrence, Joe
Gerry Lawrence
Eileen Lee
Jethro Lee-Mahoney
John Leeder
Kathleen Leeds
Frank Leicester, Cadby Hall electrician
Alice and Raymond Huntley Lewis
Michael Lindsay-Bush
Godfrey Linnett
Mr. David W. Llewellyn
Dennis Long (Works Department)
Patrick Lowe, Alpine Refrigerated Deliveries
Susan Maby
Peter Mackay, Depot Manager, Alpine
    Refrigerated Deliveries
Michael Major
Arthur Mansfield (50 years)
Tony Marcus
Bill Marshall, driver (ice cream)
Major A. (Tom) Martin
Doreen Martin, ex-Lyons Tetley, Greenford
The late Charlie Martin, E&S Cadby Hall
Marie McCulloch
Jimmy McGuire, J.L. Catering, 1949-85
Ken McLean
Ray Mears
G.W. Medway
Barry Menzies
Jean Metcalf
Cecil Milner
Mr. Charles W. Mitchell, Lyons Maid
David Mitchell
Christopher Moloney, tea buyer for J. Lyons &
    Co.
Charles A. Moore
Ralph Morhaim
Mary Moriarty
Richard W. Morley, M.B.E.
John Mortimer
Tony Morton
Eric A. Moss (deceased 1996) who worked for J.
    Lyons in 1953
Patrick Moules
Marilyn Mulley, née Martyn
Mr. Thomas W. Mullins
Violet Munns
Mr. John Murphy (Normand Fleetways)
    Stockport
William George Murray, C.E.RA RN
Bill Nash, Total Refrigeration Ltd
George and Frances Neave

Mike Neville, central buying
George R. Niblock
Paul Nicholls
Mr. T.J. and Mrs. M.J. Nightingale
Bill Nixon
Lacon Robert Noad (choc sales) Wholesale
    Round (bakery)
Anthony J. Noble, employee Cadby Hall 1966-73
    (maintenance)
Edward Noble, C.Eng. M.I. MECH E., M.I. Mgt,
    Chief Eng., Carlton Project
Ethel Norris, retired clerk, Barnsley
Arnold George Nyburg, D.S.C.
G.M. Oddie
P.D. O'Doherty
Mike O'Donovan
Philip Oexle, Lyons Maid Overseas Ltd., Bridge
    Park
Catherine B. O'Higgins
Maurice Oldfield
Fred Oliver, royalty messenger
John O'Sullivan
Jay Outhwaite, Lyons Maid
Geoffrey F. Page
E.V. Palmer (Lyons, Greenford)
Alfred Parnes, Director, Overseas Hotels
Ronald G. Parsley
Jeff Parsons
Edeltraut R.H. Partridge, Group Manager, 30
    very happy years with J. Lyons & Co.
James W. Paton
Derek Patterson
Mrs. George Patterson
The Pavitt family
Vic Paynter
Mrs. Nellie Peek
Percival Charles Pellowe
Peter S. Penman
Claudio Petrassi
Nenad Petrovic, Clerical Supervisor, Lyons Maid
Lewis Philipp, Senior Commodity Buyer, 1933-
    1982
Mrs. Hannah Phillips
John Piper
Ken Plimmer
Patricia and Peter Pocock
Roy W. Poole, ex-J.L. Catering Ltd
George Potter (deceased) 36 years service with J.
    Lyons & Co.
Walter John Pountney, Maintenance Electrical
    Engineer
Mr. R.J.R. Price
Pritchard, dental surgeon at Lyons Tetley, Cadby
    Hall
Charlotte (Peggy) Pugsley
Gurmit Singh Rai
Mrs. Rosslyn Randall
Vera I. Read
A.S. Reynolds, Legion d'Honneur
Bert Reynolds, former ASM Blaydon Depot
Robin Richards
Miss Evelyn M. Richardson

Jack Ridge, Accounts Manager
E. Robbins, C.H.E.S.
Mrs. June Roberson
John Roberts
Ian A. Robertson
Len Robinson
Bill Rodgers, Lyons Bakery 1969-1980
Brian M. Rodmell
Raymond Rogers 1944-84
Sybil M. Rose
Margaret Ross
O. de Rousset-Hall
Alan Russell
Mrs. B.D. Sallows
Anthony Montague Lawson Salmon (grandson of
    Montague Gluckstein)
Giles Pollock Salmon
Ivor Salmon, Company Director 1950-1972
R.E.A. Salmon
Paul J. Sands
Mrs. J. Saunders
L.W. Savage
Betty Saxton
Lilian Scriven, manageress, Importers Retail Sales
    Rooms Ltd., wholesale dept.
Alec Semark
Richard and Sue Serafinski
Raymond Shaw
Judith P. Shelford
R.D.C. Shimell, son of Reginald (sales) & Florence
    (nippy) Shimell
Henry G. Simon, B.Sc., MIET, D.Oenolgique (Gp.
    Wine Exec.)
George R. Sivyer
Mr. L.C. Smith
Mrs. M.E. Smith
Sylvia Smith, ex-Teashop Nippy (née Rivière)
Jenny Smith-Hayes
Alan F. Southcott
Thomas Frederick Spenceley
Herbert W. Spencer, Central Laboratories
Edith Spilsbury
John Spittle
Mr. F.R. Squance
Bob Stackhouse, rtd Sales Manager, Grocery
    Division
John Staunton, from 1954 Cadby despatch to
    1995 Carlton despatch
Mr. A.E. Steadman, soft drinks
Roy Steinke
Mrs. Enid S. Stephenson
Mr. A.N. and Mrs. J. Stevens
Mr. G.F. Stevens, F.C.I.S., F.I.A.C., comptroller
    bakery division
V.T. (Tom) Stevens, driver 1932-1974
Mrs. Jo Stockley, née Scrine
David Stringer
Peter J. Stubbs
Andy Sutherland
Barbara Sutton
R.J. Sutton

Mrs. M. Szczyglowski
Mrs. Iris Taylor
Tessie Taylor, née Elmy
Victor John Taylor
Miss Dorothy Team
Eileen Telford, Central Laboratories 1941-1978
Doris Tennant
Ron Thomas (heavy transport)
A.R. Thompson
Anthony and Denice Tinson
G. Torkington, Eng. and loyal employee
Harold W. Trill
Mr. Leslie Trimmer
William (Tommy) Tucker
Mr. Morrison Tweedle
Roy Tydeman
John R. Tyrrell
Bob Vass
Eve Velluet
Fred Vine
Richard Vivian
Yvonne A. Walker
Mr. George A. Waller
Alan Wallwork, Company Secretary 1987-1995
Mrs. Joan D. Warcup, née Sexton
Keith Warwick, J. Lyons & Co. 1961-1992
John Watkins
R.M. Watson
Terry Weathers (ex employee), Waldegrave Films
    (photo credits)
Ken Wells, 1944-1982
Leonard Wells, Building Surveyor, J. Lyons Estates
    Dept.
David J. Welsh
Kenneth Westoby
David B. White, Chartered Engineer and P.I.U.
Ian B. White
Hubert R. Whiteman
Christina Whitmore, née O'Neill
Struan Wiley
Bill Williams
Mike Williams
Wᵐ Williamson, of Ready Mix & Lyons Maid,
    Bridge Park
J.D.N. Wilson, '56-'96
Alan and Jean Wise
Dorothy Wood
E. Wood, née Bartram, teashops
Dr. Keith N. Wood
Tom Wood
D.F. Woodroffe
Evelyn Wright
John A.P. Wright
Ronald A. Wright, Lyons Bakery
Walter Wrigley
Mary Wyatt (laboratories)
Harold G. Young, CVO and family
Eugenie Zam, secretary, 1941-1976, Strand
    Corner House

Part 1
ORIGINS OF THE LYONS EMPIRE
(1887–1914)

1821	Samuel Gluckstein born in Rheinberg (4 January).
1829	Barnett Salmon born (24 May).
1841	Samuel Gluckstein arrived in England.
1845	Samuel Gluckstein married Julia Joseph (25 May).
1846	Helena Gluckstein born (15 February).
1847	Joseph Lyons born (29 December).
1851	Isidore Gluckstein born (13 August).
1854	Montague Gluckstein born (18 July).
1861	Samuel Gluckstein naturalised (10 August).
1863	Helena Gluckstein married Barnett Salmon (24 June).
1864	S. Gluckstein & Co. incorporated (15 October).
1868	Alfred Salmon born (20 July).
1870	S. Gluckstein & Co. dissolved (25 March).
1873	Samuel Gluckstein died (23 January).
1873	Salmon & Gluckstein (tobacco) incorporated.
1881	Harry Salmon born (23 August).
1885	Maurice Salmon born (9 December).
1886	Major Montague Gluckstein born (13 October).
1887	J. Lyons & Company incorporated (first Lyons company).
	First catering contract, Newcastle Exhibition (May).
1888	Glasgow Exhibition catering contract.
	Imperial Institute (workers) catering contract (11 October).
1889	Paris Exhibition.
	J. Lyons & Company Ltd registered (second Lyons company) (16 March).
	Caterers to Barnum & Bailey Circus, Olympia.
1891	*Venice in London* opened at Olympia (26 December).
1893	*Constantinople* opened at Olympia.
1894	J. Lyons & Company Ltd registered (third Lyons company) (10 April).
	Cadby Hall acquired (August).
	First teashop opened at 213 Piccadilly (20 September).
	The Orient, opened at Olympia (December).

1895	Salmon & Gluckstein acquires limited status (15 March).
1896	Trocadero restaurant opened (5 October).
1897	Death of Barnett Salmon (founding member) (11 February).
1899	Prince of Wales awards first Royal Warrant.
1900	Throgmorton restaurant opened (15 October).
1902	Imperial Tobacco Co. acquire controlling interest in S&G (January).
1903	Cadby Hall Athletic Club formed (March).
	First tea & coffee production statistics.
1904	Popular Café, Piccadilly, opened (10 October).
	Tea Retail Sales commence under Michael Pezaro.
1905	George Pollard joins tea sales department.
1908	Caterers to Franco-British Exhibition, Shepherd's Bush (May).
1909	Coventry Street Corner House opened (4 January).
	Strand Palace Hotel opened (14 September).
	First cocoa and chocolate production statistics.
	Interests of Ceylon Café Ltd acquired.
1912	Maison Lyons, Oxford Street, opened (21 November).
1913	First issue of *Lyons Mail* (April).
1915	Strand Corner House opened (8 April).
	Regent Palace Hotel opened (26 May).
1916	Maison Lyons, Oxford Street (second) opened (18 September).
1917	Death of Joseph Lyons (founding member) (22 June).

TOBACCO BEGINNINGS

TOWARDS THE END of the nineteenth century, Britain could, with reason, consider herself most fortunate among nations. By 1830 she had undergone the transition from being primarily agricultural to becoming the first modern industrial state in the world, with the City of London acknowledged as the hub of world commerce. At this time Britain had no rivals in either commerce or industry. Her colonies in Australia, Canada, India and South Africa supplied the necessary raw materials to guarantee dominance, with the trade routes protected by a powerful navy.

Britain's pre-eminence in commerce was partly a result of its communication systems (telegraphic and telephonic) including the coastal signal stations that gave Lloyds an unrivalled grasp on the shipping intelligence of the entire world, partly through access to high-quality commercial intelligence, its accumulated expertise in insurance, legal, brokering and labour markets and its rapid transport facilities to all parts of the world. Paul Reuter had established his international news agency in 1851, taking full advantage of the new communication systems, even to the extent of using carrier-pigeon post in those areas where links had not been completed. London too housed the world's leading stock exchange, which traded in a wide variety of stock and bonds. It was here also that speculative forward dealing evolved, using the telegraph to trade in futures, rather than actual delivery of commodities, in the great Baltic, metal, shipping and other exchanges that matured in London.

Britain had been at peace with her European neighbours for several decades, and her export trade with the Continent and the rest of the world, aside from the effect of foreign protectionism against manufactured goods, created a prosperous society at home. By 1856 the textile factory barons had reduced their working week to 60 hours. The railways had welded the small nation into one economic unit and provincial towns flourished. Vast sums of money were accumulated for investment both at home and overseas. With almost a quarter of the world's land mass, the British Empire was one of the largest empires ever known, reaching its territorial zenith during the reign of George V. Competition among shipping companies kept down the cost of imported goods and the mid-century marked the start of a revolution in retailing.

The transport of goods within the United Kingdom took full advantage of the reliable railways. At the end of the train journey customer goods were off-loaded into public sidings, from where they could be transported by the many cartage companies. Where costs could be justified, some large organisations built their own railway sidings to handle their specific needs. Once the main trunk system was complete, the railways soon eclipsed road transport, even though this was increasingly rapid and efficient. The railways eventually spelt doom for the canals, which along with rivers had provided a network of inland waterways that had served the industrial revolution, connecting the great ports with inland factories, bringing in raw material and taking out finished product.

Industrial and technological innovations in the late nineteenth century facilitated the supply of a wider and cheaper range of food and drink. Manufactured foods lent themselves to branding, creating a mass market for items such as biscuits, cake, tea, chocolate, confectionery and preserves. As the wholesale price of food fell by 30 per cent, consumers were able to buy more food with a less than proportionate increase in expenditure. This led to a transformation in retailing.

Firms such as James Sainsbury, the Maypole Dairy and Thomas Lipton introduced new styles of marketing. By 1914 the Home and Colonial Stores (which had merged with the Maypole Dairy) and Lipton Ltd each had over 500 branches and became household names by the turn of the century. As advertising grew, the names of company products were emblazoned everywhere; many of the enamel signs used for this purpose are now collectors' items. Shopfronts became more decorative and products began to be attractively packaged. Coupons and trade cards formed an important part of marketing, enticing consumers to buy branded products. It was in these prosperous times that Lyons had its beginnings, but its roots lay much earlier. The achievement of becoming Britain's largest catering and food-manufacturing company was still several years away.

The Salmons and Glucksteins

The earliest events that led to the formation of J. Lyons & Co. can be traced to 1841, when two brothers, Samuel (1821–73) and Henry (1832–1905) Gluckstein, arrived in England with their parents and six other siblings, as immigrants from Europe. Their father, Lehmann Meyer Gluckstein (1794–1859), who was born in Jever in the Duchy of Oldenburg, near Bremen, was a linguist and professor of languages who had written a work in Flemish and French that he called *A Simple and Sure Guide to Learn the Gender of French Substantives in Ten Rules*. He had married Helena Horn (1797–1854) in Rheinberg, Prussia, on 25 August 1819, and the couple lived variously in Lippe and Rheinberg, as well as Arnhem and Rotterdam in the Netherlands. Samuel was born in Rheinberg on 4 January 1821 and Henry in Arnhem on 10 May 1832.

On his arrival in England the twenty-year-old Samuel Gluckstein lodged with his aunt, Julia Joseph (1792–1868), in the impoverished Spitalfields district of London. Four years later he married her illiterate daughter Hannah (1819–85), on 25 May 1845, at the Great Synagogue in Duke's Place, Aldgate; the synagogue, having been built for Spanish and Portuguese Jews, was destroyed by fire in the winter of 1940–1 during the ferocious blitz on London. Between 1846 and 1862 Samuel and Hannah Gluckstein had ten children, five of whom married consanguineously – an accepted custom among Jews at that time. As the tendency towards intermarriage was repeated through more than one generation, many offspring were direct descendants of Samuel Gluckstein. Such was Samuel Gluckstein's aura in family circles that his name continues in his descendants today. Although Samuel and Hannah had ten children, it was Helena, Isidore (1851–1920), Montague (1854–1922) and to a lesser extent Joseph (1856–1930) who became the key players in the story of Lyons.

Samuel Gluckstein wasted no time in finding employment in his new country (he was naturalised on 10 August 1861) but we cannot be sure what form this took. From the documentary evidence available it would be safe to assume his activities centred on the tobacco industry. Samuel Gluckstein's wedding certificate gives his profession in 1845 as 'dealer'. On the birth certificate of his first children (twins Julia and Helena) in 1846 his profession appears as 'general dealer'. Later, in similar records, his occupation is variously listed as 'cigar dealer', 'tobacconist' and 'cigar merchant'. It seems, therefore, that his original occupation was that of a tobacco salesman and that he progressed to become a self-employed trader in cigars, as his knowledge, wealth and business proficiency developed. Henry Gluckstein was only nine years old when he arrived in London, but he too became involved with the tobacco trade.

By 1854 the Gluckstein brothers felt they had sufficient knowledge of the tobacco industry and had accumulated enough wealth to start their own business. With their cousin, Lawrence

Abrahams, they took their first step towards becoming businessmen by forming a partnership from Samuel Gluckstein's home at 35 Crown Street, in the Soho district of London. A year earlier there had been a serious outbreak of cholera in Soho and many wealthier people had moved out of the area. As property prices fell, immigrant families began to move in, among them numerous fortune seekers. This period is distinguished by the number of hospitals built in the area: no fewer than six between 1850 and 1875 including the Hospital for Women (1852), the Royal London Homeopathic Hospital (1850) and the Royal National Throat, Nose and Ear Hospital (1862) as well as a French and Italian hospital.

Like other small traders of those times, the Gluckstein family occupied accommodation over the working area of their business. The informal understanding between Samuel and Henry Gluckstein and their cousin was that any profit resulting from the enterprise should be shared equally. Theirs was, arguably, an ideal partnership. Lawrence Abrahams and Henry Gluckstein devoted their expertise to cigar manufacturing and administration while the entrepreneurial Samuel Gluckstein assumed the role of travelling salesman. It was in this capacity that Samuel befriended another young cigar salesman called Barnett Salmon (1829–97). Their friendship grew and in 1863 Barnett married Samuel's twin daughter Helena. Although there was a seventeen-year age difference, and Helena was only seventeen, Samuel was delighted with the match. The couple had fifteen children, although heartbreakingly six died in infancy of scarlet fever; yet the survival of so few from a marriage was not unusual in the nineteenth century. However, neither Samuel Gluckstein nor Barnett Salmon could have foreseen the eventual importance of this marriage.

Ten years later the Gluckstein brothers and Lawrence Abrahams decided to formalise their business arrangements. Documents at the Public Record Office indicate they formed a company under the title S. Gluckstein & Company, which they registered on 15 October 1864. The choice of name probably arose from Samuel Gluckstein's

greater contribution of capital at formalisation, although there is no evidence to support this. Shortly thereafter the company relocated to 43 Leman Street, in the Aldgate district of London. The reason for this move may have been due in part to the planned roadworks at Crown Street (it became Charing Cross Road) and a desire to be nearer their family and the larger tobacco industry existing in Aldgate at that time. On the other hand it may have been a compelling desire to leave one of the most notorious slums areas of central London, the so-called 'St Giles rookery'. Crown Street marked the western border of this district where some 54,000 people lived a wretched existence.

After the firm's incorporation, a good deal of family feuding started, allegedly because of the irascibility of Samuel Gluckstein, who felt he was putting more into the business than the other two. This may have been the case; he certainly

The wedding certificate of Barnett Salmon and Helena (Lena) Gluckstein, 24 June 1863. This marriage cemented a business partnership between the Gluckstein and Salmon families which endured for over 100 years.

seemed more adventurous and with hindsight we know he was an extremely gifted businessman. However, the one-sided naming of the company may have exacerbated family tensions. Quarrels, sometimes violent, became more frequent, continuing until 1869, when Samuel Gluckstein notified the others that the business owed him £2,000 and demanded payment. Henry and Lawrence objected and the disagreements were eventually aired on 25 March 1870 in the Chancery Court, where, after hearing evidence, Sir Richard Malins made an order that the business be dissolved and the assets, amounting to tons of tobacco, be divided among the three, with Samuel Gluckstein's share to be greater than those of the other two.

Their antagonisms now resolved, Henry and Samuel established new and separate tobacco firms in close proximity to each other. Henry's traded as Abrahams & Gluckstein from 26 Whitechapel High Street and although it did moderately well it did not feature further in the story of Lyons. Little is known of the enterprise but records at Companies House show that Abrahams & Gluckstein became a limited company on 9 April 1920 and in the 1970s changed its name to P. Arthur Lewis & Company before changing it back to Abrahams & Gluckstein Unlimited in November 1980. The company was dissolved in December 1993.

Samuel Gluckstein, on the other hand, formed a partnership with his two sons, Isidore and Montague, and his son-in-law, Barnett Salmon. A few years later his fourteen-year-old son, Joseph, joined the firm. They registered their business at 34 Whitechapel Road, where Barnett Salmon had a warehouse. Post Office directories for 1871 list the occupants merely as 'Gluckstein, Samuel, cigar manufacturers'.

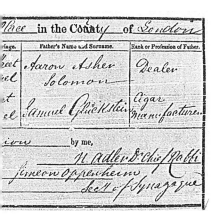

Samuel Gluckstein's new tobacco undertaking was, like Henry's, moderately successful. However, two years later, in 1873, Samuel died of diabetes mellitus at the early age of fifty-two. In those days, before the discovery of insulin, diabetes was a fatal illness. Samuel had been a sickly man nursed by his devoted wife Hannah, and the years of family bickering may have taken their toll. Indeed, his illness may have given rise to his alleged aggressive manner, which appears to have been one of the causes of family disunity.

Meanwhile his three young sons, Isidore, Montague and Joseph, now faced the prospect of becoming breadwinners. Although only twenty-two, nineteen and seventeen years of age respectively, all three were mature and intelligent, and had been privately educated at Hartog's Academy in Camden Town and the Whitechapel Foundation School. Their first priority was the rebuilding of family relationships, and in order not to become embroiled in another damaging feud they had the wisdom or perhaps good advice, or both, to form a family fund based on the principle of equal shares. Underpinning the equal distribution of wealth was an unyielding moral code of family loyalty, respect, educational achievement and, not least, hard work. The strong willingly supported the weak, each member originally withdrawing what he required. Later, as the members increased, a more orderly system evolved which always had regard for the ideals of the founding members. The fund, instituted when the family had little money, held together even when prosperity was achieved, and has now lasted for 100 years as an internal method, within the tax laws, for ensuring mutual support.

After Samuel Gluckstein's death, Montague assumed responsibility for managing the business. He had inherited his father's appetite for hard work and innovative skill and developed an astute business acumen. The fledgeling company faced intense competition from the many small cigar businesses operating in the area, including Henry's. The greater opposition, however, came from two other sources: the larger manufacturers, who had enough capital to adopt mechanisation; and the increasing number of imports from other parts of the world which threatened not only the small manufacturer but the whole United Kingdom tobacco industry. Cheaper labour in other countries together with low freight charges, assisted by the rapid construction of railways in the United States, meant that tobacco products could be shipped to, and sold in, the United Kingdom at prices that domestic manufacturers could not match. This led several companies to merge their interests as a way of surviving this onslaught.

Montague Gluckstein had already realised the firm could not compete with the low-priced imports and the larger home-based manufacturers such as Wills, Players, Lambert & Butler and so on. In his view, diversification was the answer, and in 1873, a few years after Sainsbury and Lipton had opened their first shops, Isidore and

Montague Gluckstein opened their first retail tobacconist's shop at Barnett Salmon's home address of 251 Edgware Road (263 in 1881 census). Initially the shop traded under the name of Barnett Salmon but some time thereafter changed to Salmon & Gluckstein to reflect both families' interests. The diversification into retailing enabled business economies to be exploited, since not only did the Salmon & Gluckstein shop secure a ready outlet for their own products but they were able to sell other smoking apparatus and gentlemen's needs such as pipes, tobacco pouches, wax vestas, cut tobaccos, walking-stick mounts and snuff as well as cigars and cigarettes from other manufacturers, while still maintaining control of their own branded manufacturing and distribution. Although the Glucksteins' interests were primarily connected with the tobacco trade, they did operate subsidiary trades as goldsmiths and silversmiths and were importers of amber.

Notwithstanding the economies of the tobacco diversification, the augmentation of the Salmon & Gluckstein retail trade depended on the slow accumulation of capital. Yet by 1886 six shops had been opened in London selling not only branded Salmon & Gluckstein goods but an increasing number of other manufacturers' products as well. At first Montague Gluckstein anticipated that other manufacturers would recognise the significance of the retail sector and try to put them out of business. He was so concerned this might happen that he gave serious consideration to other, more radical business alternatives. His ideas, controversial as they were, eventually took root, and this period marked the beginning of the Lyons catering empire.

Tobacco Price Wars

The Salmon & Gluckstein manufacturing and retailing strategy was not unique. Several other companies had entered this field – A. Baker & Company, Wm Clarke & Son, A.I. Jones & Co. and Singleton & Cole Ltd – but Salmon & Gluckstein became the largest and most aggressive tobacco retailer with a fierce reputation for price-cutting. At first the large manufacturers, such as W.D. & H.O. Wills, were glad to supply their own branded products at discount prices, but soon they found themselves under fire from thousands of small tobacconists who claimed that Salmon & Gluckstein were driving them out of business with their relentless underpricing. Although, collectively, Salmon & Gluckstein, Baker, Clarke, Jones and Singleton & Cole only accounted for approximately 2 per cent of total retail sales, their market influence was greater, being concentrated in the London and Midlands conurbations. What was of concern to the large manufacturers was the way in which the bigger retailers were vigorously extending their retail chains; most active in this field was Salmon & Gluckstein.

The large manufacturers, such as Wills, tried to control retail prices and in 1889 drew up an agreement, binding on customers who signed it, not to sell their products below the list prices. Their scheme was introduced first in Sheffield and then in Nottingham, but by 1891 the bigger retail companies unilaterally started a price-cutting campaign. Salmon & Gluckstein cut the price of Woodbine and Cinderella cigarettes by passing on to smokers part of the sum it received from large-purchase discounts. As a consequence profits soared, so that by 1894 enough capital had been set aside to open some thirty shops in the London area. In March 1896 Wills gathered together some of the largest manufacturers in the country at the Gresham Club, in London, specifically to discuss a common policy on Salmon & Gluckstein's price-cutting campaign, especially in view of their recent forays into the provinces. In spite of their misgivings each manufacturer was keen to continue supplying Salmon & Gluckstein, who, fully realising their pivotal role, exploited the situation by playing one manufacturer off against another in order to maximise any discount terms.

In March 1897 Salmon & Gluckstein reported a profit of £78,503 – 50 per cent up on the previous year – and the addition of thirty-two new shops to their chain. The attempts to fix cigarette prices failed, mainly because branded goods were growing in number and being taken up by the established retailers. Lipton and Kearley & Tonge, for example, had a fearsome reputation for selling cigarettes at almost wholesale prices, probably to tempt customers into their shops in order to sell them higher-value groceries. Their shops, like Salmon & Gluckstein's, traded in the busier, more prosperous areas and the companies began extending beyond their traditional territories. Salmon & Gluckstein even opened a shop in Bristol, to the great embarrassment of Wills, whose main production centre was situated in the same city. Needless to say, Wills were bombarded with complaints from local tobacconists who, until now, had not experienced such competition. Both manufacturers and retail tobacco chains knew they could not do without each other but this did not stop Salmon & Gluckstein omitting Wills products from their window displays when relationships soured, as they did from time to time. Incentives too, were offered by Salmon & Gluckstein for customers buying their unlikely named Raspberry Buds cigarettes. For each 100 cigarette cards from the packs, returned to their Clerkenwell Road offices, Salmon & Gluckstein supplied either: a Saddler's leather cigarette case, a ladies or gentleman's purse, a sovereign case or a Meerschaum and amber cigarette tube in a case. As a result of this offer few of these cigarette cards have survived and those that have fetch over £100 at auction.

Economically priced machines for making cigars and cigarettes were becoming more widely used. In 1883 Wills had installed their first Bonsack cigarette-making machine, which was capable of producing 200 cigarettes per minute. The Baron, one of the leading machines of the period, had the capacity to make 450 cigarettes per minute in either round or oval shapes. The Richards Cigarette Machine Company claimed in an advertisement of 1896 that its machine, powered by steam, was so simple that it could be operated by children and calculated wage costs to be 11d. per thousand cigarettes. While many manufacturers converted to mechanised methods in the 1890s, they nevertheless realised the importance to the consumer of handmade cigarettes and continued to claim their products were hand-produced, even though they had been made by machine. Salmon & Gluckstein maintained this deception until 1898, when a dispute arose between Salmon & Gluckstein and

Nathan Kershenboim, of Glasgow, who claimed the public were being misled. He argued that a packet of ten cigarettes, which he had bought for 2¼d. from a Salmon & Gluckstein shop and which was labelled 'guaranteed hand-made by experienced workmen', had in fact been made by a Baron cigarette machine. The usual price for ten handmade cigarettes of the same-quality tobacco would have been 2¾d. – nearly 20 per cent more. Kershenboim admitted that he bought the cigarettes for the purpose of ascertaining whether the cigarettes were handmade or not, with a view to eventual legal proceedings. During these proceedings Salmon & Gluckstein admitted that the cigarettes Kershenboim had purchased were not handmade but it was not their intention to deceive. The magistrate found that the cigarettes 'were as pure and clean in point of material and as proper in point of construction for all smoking purposes as they could have been if hand-made. In using the remaining stock of old labels containing the words "guaranteed hand-made" the respondents were actuated merely by a spirit of petty economy to save the cost of printing new ones [packets] with the words "hand-made" omitted and that in so using the labels there was no intention to deceive the buyer.'

However, Salmon & Gluckstein were eventually found guilty under the Merchandise Marks Act and were fined 5 shillings, with £5 5s. costs, for selling machine-made cigarettes as handmade. The judgment brought about a review of the marketing practices of the cigarette-manufacturing companies.

With turnover increasing from the growing number of Salmon & Gluckstein shops, management were able to obtain even larger buying discounts and continued their aggressive price-cutting methods. The profit of ¼d. or ½d. on a large turnover was sustainable for long periods, but such tactics were naturally detrimental to the majority of tobacconists who largely were single-family businesses. Although customers were glad to embrace this practice, the small traders feared they would be put out of business because they could not afford to sell at such low prices. As far as London was concerned, A. Baker & Company with its twenty-two retail outlets did just as much to demoralise the tobacco trade as Salmon & Gluckstein, but the trade overlooked this. Instead their wrath was poured out on Salmon & Gluckstein. *The Cigar and Tobacco World*, a monthly trade journal, regularly reported the fate of bankrupted businesses, providing comprehensive details of their creditors and final 'arrangements'. Whether these failures were due to competitive forces or just bad management will never be known. The large manufacturers, although sympathetic to the small traders' predicament, were reluctant to introduce price controls for fear of losing market share. Salmon & Gluckstein was, after all, the largest retail tobacconist in Britain as well as having manufacturing capacity of its own. With such a vast outlet for tobacco products, Salmon & Gluckstein played manufacturer against manufacturer to ensure the best possible terms.

Nevertheless, the management realised that low prices with marginal profits could not be a permanent basis for the ongoing prosperity of the business, even though the quantity of tobacco cleared at the Custom House for consumption in the United Kingdom increased from 35½ million pounds in 1861 to 65½ million pounds in 1895. With tobacco sales so buoyant, Salmon & Gluckstein decided on a massive expansion of their business by offering shares to the public and in so doing converted the company from private to public status. Their prospectus issued on 15 March 1895 was aimed at raising £400,000, of which £300,000 would go to the former owners by way of shares and cash – said to be for property, stock and trademarks – and £100,000 as a fund for future expansion. Such was the company's reputation that the share issue was oversubscribed and there was no objection from the new shareholders to Messrs Salmon and Gluckstein continuing as directors. Salmon & Gluckstein Ltd, as it became, wasted no time in tightening their grip on the market, much to the consternation of the retail trade. New shops were carefully planned and refurbished, and flamboyant window displays became a feature of their branches.

Twelve months after flotation, the Whitechapel factory was producing 1½ million cigarettes per week, mostly of the Sunshine brand that had been introduced as a cheap label to help counteract the criticism of underselling. Nevertheless, continued trade criticism of their tactics caused the management to write to the editor of the *Daily Telegraph* in September 1896, setting out their case under the title 'Salmon and Gluckstein's Appeal to the Public':

Sir, – It is satisfactory to be able to state that we have arrived at a settlement of what has been termed 'The Tobacco War', which at one-time threatened to seriously affect the interests of smokers generally. ... The original proposition was that we should raise the prices of all packet tobaccos sold throughout the whole of our establishments to a minimum standard, which was put forward by certain manufacturers at the instigation of the small retailers. This was strenuously resisted, because we did not see why the consumer should be called upon to pay a larger price than that to which, for a score of years past, he had been accustomed, and because we felt that the right of a private company to decide on the way in which its business should be conducted – provided it was carried on in an honorable [*sic*] manner – was both morally and legally unquestionable. At the same time we had no desire to enter into a warfare with firms with whom we have long had friendly relations. A protracted discussion took place between our directors and the houses concerned, and eventually we have come to an agreement which was definitely decided upon this evening, under which the prices of proprietary brands of tobacco stocked throughout the whole of our London shops will remain as heretofore, while those in the provinces will be raised to the standard mentioned above. In no case, however, will the prices of our own proprietary or loose tobaccos be raised. We are bound to say that we do not agree with this policy of hampering free trade in an article which is no longer the luxury of a few, but the solace, and almost the necessity, of the million. At the same time, we are a company, and are bound to protect the interests of the public consistently with those of our shareholders. We have deemed it prudent to make this concession rather than to enter into a warfare the result of which might have proved injurious to our business, but which would certainly have been disastrous to the great reputation of the manufacturers with that important section of the public who indulge in tobacco. We fear that our provincial customers will resent this differential treatment as between themselves and our London clients, but that question, which inevitably will be raised, must be answered by the manufacturers, who have allowed themselves to be used as a lever by the small retailer for artificial inflation of prices. Their policy, which is entirely indefensible, is bound to meet with its own reward. We venture to express the opinion that this scheme will never work. In justice to the manufacturers, we must point out to you that it has been arranged that the prices of packet tobaccos sold in London by us shall be increased when a plan has been devised under which it can be proved that no underselling can take place. – We are, Sir, your obedient servants, Salmon & Gluckstein (Limited). London September 4th. [1896]

New alliances: the Imperial Tobacco Company

At this time Salmon & Gluckstein's production was centred on four sites – Whitechapel, Clerkenwell and Aldgate for cigarettes and Rosebery Avenue for cigars. As this fragmentation required expensive supervision as well as additional costs for transit, by 1897 plans were made to bring all the factories under one roof. It was originally intended to have a factory built in the vicinity of Aldgate, since Her Majesty's Customs, at that time, stipulated that bonded factories should be within half a mile of the Custom House. Intense negotiations with HM Customs eventually resulted in their waiving the half-mile regulation and they subsequently issued a licence for a bonded factory in the vicinity of St Luke's in Clerkenwell, very close to the City of London. A freehold site measuring 28,900 square feet bounded by four important streets – namely, Lever Street, Hull Street, Clarence Street and York Road – was obtained and plans were

A Salmon & Gluckstein tobacco price list dated early 1890s.

SALMON & GLUCKSTEIN

········ THE ········

SMOKERS' PROVIDERS.

PACKET TOBACCOS.

	1-ounce Packet	2-ounce Packet		1-ounce Packet	2-ounce Packet		1-ounce Packet	2-ounce Packet
WILLS'—			LAMBERT & BUTLER'S—			SUNSHINE—		
Gold Flakes	4d.	8d.	Bird's Eye	4d.	8d.	Virginia		
Westward Ho!	4d.	7½d.	May Blossom	4½d.	9d.	Bird's Eye		
Bird's Eye	4½d.	8½d.	Light Cake	4½d.		Golden Flakes } Special Value	4d.	8d.
Three Castles	5½d.	10½d.	Jessamine		10d.	Mixture		
ARCHER'S—			Sun-Dried Honeydew		8½d.	PLAYER'S Navy Cut	4½d.	8½d.
Virginia		8d.	GALLAHER'S—			Sweet Yankee Pride. 5d.		
Bird's Eye		8d.	Harlequin Flakes	5½d.	10d.	SMITH'S Mixture		1/6
Returns		8d.	TADDY'S—			MURRAY'S Mixture		1/6
BRANKSTON'S —			Myrtle Grove	4½d.	9d.	MORRIS'S Gold Flake		1/6
Red Virginia		8d.	GODWIN'S Old Judge		1/1½			

WE SELL, WE MAY SAY WE GIVE,

We Sell, we may say we Give, } at **3d.** per oz., All Tobaccos sold usually at 4d., Mixture, Bird's Eye, Returns, Virginia, Fine and Coarse Cut Cavendish, &c.

We Sell, we may say we Give, } at **4d.** per oz., All Hand-cut Tobaccos sold usually at 5d., such as Mixture, Bird's Eye, Turkish Returns, Gold Flakes, Latakia, Monopoly, and Virginia.

We Sell, we may say we Give, } at **3d.**, All the noted Havana Brands, such as Henry Clays, Larranagas, Intimidads, Carolinas, Murias. &c., &c.

We Sell, we may say we Give, } at **4½d.**, All the usual 6d. Havanas. Every Cigar guaranteed sound and sweet.

We Sell, we may say we Give, } at **2d.**, Splendid Manila Cigars and Cheroots, large No. 2 size, first quality; also La Unions, Trichinopoly's, &c., &c.

We Sell for **2d., or 7 for a 1/-**, All the Cigars usually sold in the trade at 3d.

We Sell for **1½d., or 9 for a 1/-**, All the Cigars usually sold in the trade at 2d.

And we offer, at **5d.** per oz., Cigarettes sold in the trade at 8d. per oz.

	Packet of 10	Packet of 20	EGYPTIAN CIGARETTES—			ORMOND'S SWISS SEGARS —		
CIGARETTES—			Viceregals ... for 25		1/9	Vevey Fins ... for 25		1/4
Sweet Sunshine	3½d.	7d.	Isabellas... ... „		1/6	„ Sans ... „		1/11
Sweethearts (Pres'd)	3½d.		Exquisitos ... „		1/3	„ Longs ... for 20		1/10
Ivory Virginians	4d.		Rosettas... ... „		1/2	Charles Macintosh's Fyfe Pouches		
Tunis		4d.	Dongolas ... „		1/-	(Improved Horsey),		
Richmond Gems	4½d.	8½d.	Majors ... „		11d.	No. 2 No. 3 No. 4 No. 5 No. 6		
Ohancellors	4½d.		Rosettas... ... for 16		10½d.	4½d. 6d. 6d. 7d. 8d.		
Sweet Caporals	4½d.		MELACHRINOS—			Prince of Wales Pouches, 6d. & 9d.		
French Vizirs		7d.	No. 4		7/-	Hooper's Cachous, 3d.		
„ Caporals		4½d.	„ 5		6/6	Evans' Concinnum Machines, 2/6.		
„ Elegantes		7d.	„ 8		5/6	Tobacco Jars, Vesta Boxes, Briar		
Algerians ... for 25		5½d.	„ 10		5/-	and Meerschaum Pipes, Cigar and		
Oxford & Cambridge „		1/-	Plantagenat Whiffs ... for 12		8½d.	Cigarette Tubes and Cases, and		
Paganini... ... for 24		1/-	LAMBERT & BUTLER'S—			every class of Smoker's Requisite,		
NESTOR GIANACLIS—	For 25	For 100	Brilliantes ... for 13		8½d.	at Factory Prices.		
Petit Formet	1/9	6/9	THE COMBINATION—					
Formet Minces	1.6	6/-	Case and 20 Cigarettes for		7½d.			

ONE PRICE ONLY.

ALL GOODS MARKED IN PLAIN FIGURES.

FACTORY AND STORES: 34, WHITECHAPEL ROAD, E.

drawn up by William James Ancell (1852–1913), an architect who from 1896 until his death was principally engaged in building hotels and restaurants for Lyons. The £80,000 needed for land, buildings and equipment was raised by the issue of 4.5 per cent debenture stock with an additional £45,000 for the further development of the business – an issue of £125,000 in total. Shareholders were informed that the bonded factory would 'prove a great revenue source to the company, and will place us in a position to conduct a foreign and colonial business the fringe of which we have only just touched'. In 1898, helped by a reduction in tobacco duty, Salmon & Gluckstein recorded a profit of £53,646 15s. 10d.

By the early 1890s America had become the largest tobacco-growing country in the world, annually harvesting almost 500 million pounds from 205,862 plantations whose total area, excluding those of less than an acre, exceeded 1,000 square miles. A large quantity of their tobacco-related products, which came from forty-two of its states and territories, found its way to the United Kingdom market. By 1899, however, tobacco imports into Britain were slowed, partly because of British import duties on American products. This displeased the American manufacturers and in September 1901 James Buchanan Duke, president of the American Tobacco Company, having already ruthlessly bought up many of the independent American tobacco businesses, stunned the British tobacco industry when he purchased Ogdens of Liverpool for £818,000. As a result of Duke's acquisition of Ogdens, which had been expected for some time, thirteen British tobacco manufacturers came together under the name of the Imperial Tobacco Company to counteract this force. The name had been chosen instead of the British Tobacco Company, since Duke had foreseen some kind of amalgamation of British manufacturers and had registered 'British Tobacco Company' himself. The thirteen companies that formed the Imperial Tobacco Company continued trading under their own names, fiercely resisting Harry Wills's suggestion that Salmon & Gluckstein should also join the group.

The first public announcement of the formation of the Imperial Tobacco Company, December 1901.

The presence of Duke in the United Kingdom market had enormous implications for the retail trade. Tobacconists who had suffered from pricing differentials for many years saw they had an opportunity to extract more favourable terms from the British manufacturers by threatening to buy from the Americans. To strengthen their case, they formed the United Kingdom Tobacco Dealers' Association (UKTDA) to represent their views. This caused Salmon & Gluckstein to reconsider their practices which, up till now, had been at variance with the small tobacconist. Accordingly they entered into an agreement with the UKTDA which enabled them to affiliate with small traders. This alliance allowed Salmon & Gluckstein to manufacture tobaccos, cigars and cigarettes, including other companies' private brands, to agreed terms. Salmon & Gluckstein undertook not to open further shops of their own if this was likely to cause trading difficulties with others, and they agreed, in advance, generous discounts and pricing structures. Old animosities were forgotten, and it did not seem to occur to retailers that Salmon

& Gluckstein's plan was to promote a third combination of own-label retailers under their control. Not all retailers were in favour of an association with Salmon & Gluckstein but, faced with the changes taking place in the tobacco industry, liaison with the largest trader, who was also able to provide manufacturing capacity, was inevitable.

By the turn of the century Salmon & Gluckstein had become the world's biggest retail tobacconist, with 140 shops. There were some who believed that the agreement with the UKTDA was a ploy by Salmon & Gluckstein to absorb the small tobacconists. However, they did not have an opportunity to discover whether their views were correct, since another wave of price-cutting by Duke, in 1901, concentrated the minds of those running the Imperial Tobacco Company. To maintain their markets, they realised it would be imperative to have some influence over the retail trade and consequently they initiated discussions with Salmon & Gluckstein. Besides, Harry Wills judged that Salmon & Gluckstein might fall into the hands of the Americans, a scenario he could not contemplate. He had only just secured, by a whisker, their supply of cigarette papers from Braunstein Frères of Paris and cigarette-packaging paper from Sweden a few days before Duke had offered them more in an attempt to control supplies. By January 1902 the Imperial Tobacco Company had acquired a controlling interest in Salmon & Gluckstein for £400,000. The Salmon & Gluckstein management persuaded the new owners to leave them in charge and they succeeded in increasing the company's share capital to £600,000, thus allowing further expansion of the business. The new Articles of Association, which enabled the directors to convert their original preference shareholdings to fixed cumulative preferential shares, entitled them to fixed dividends of 10 per cent per annum in the new company.

As cigarettes became cheaper after the First World War (when they were given away free to soldiers) cigarette smoking was taken up on a mass scale. Film stars showed cigarettes to be glamorous for women as well as men. With the emancipation of women, tobacco usage in the United Kingdom increased to the extent that by 1928 Britons were regarded as the most prolific smokers in the world. Tobacco consumption had grown from 2.4 lb per head in 1917 to 3.4 lb in 1927. The pipe, which had been a favourite with the working class a few years earlier, declined in popularity, as did cigars, with more of the population now smoking cigarettes. At this time Southern Rhodesia was exporting 75 per cent of its tobacco leaf to the United Kingdom, and Nyasaland 80 per cent. Britons could, with some justification, be acknowledged as 'votaries of the weed', a title adopted by the cigarette manufacturer Gallaher Ltd for a set of cards issued in 1916.

Although some of the Salmon and Gluckstein family members continued to act as directors of the new company, new interests began to occupy their business talents. In particular more of their time was increasingly directed to the development of the catering business, which had been founded fifteen years before the two families disposed of their tobacco interests.

Chapter

EXHIBITION CATERING AND SHOWMEN

MOST CONTEMPORARY ACCOUNTS, including recent company records, claim that J. Lyons & Company was founded in 1894, the year in which the firm opened its first teashop in Piccadilly. This notion was reinforced in 1994 when J. Lyons & Company celebrated its official centenary. Apart from presenting its employees – and, after strong representations, several thousand pensioners – with a small crystal bowl commemorating the occasion, the firm gave little publicity to this event. Quite why Lyons dates its beginnings to 1894 remains a mystery, since documents in the Public Record Office clearly indicate there were two earlier companies, of the same name, from which the 1894 company evolved. Indeed, in the 1954 Report of the Directors the Chairman at that time, Major Montague Gluckstein, stated that the company was established in 1887. One possible explanation for the confusion is the dimorphic status of the different organisations. On the one hand the first two were private companies within the definition of the Companies Act, with shares therein restricted, whereas the company of 1894 traded as a full limited liability company able to raise money from investors and City institutions. From a management point of view, however, the two were identical: the directors of the 1894 company had been directors of the earlier companies, and management control, style and ownership were virtually unchanged.

Towards a New Enterprise

By 1886 the Salmon and Gluckstein families, having substantially increased in numbers, had decided their tobacco business was not enough of a challenge to occupy the ambitions and energies of the younger generation. There seemed few long-term prospects in tobacco retailing and manufacture. With little scope to reduce overheads, profitability became increasingly dependent on the turnover of cigars and cigarettes. In effect, manufacturers had over-supplied and increasingly used every stratagem to ensure brand loyalty in their particular market niche. For a few years, however, well up to the turn of the century and beyond, the tobacco business flourished. One of the most startling examples of growth during this depressive period was the rise in the number of tobacconist's shops: between 1911 and 1939 they increased by almost two-thirds. Nevertheless, compared with other large tobacco-manufacturing businesses the Salmon & Gluckstein manufacturing capacity seemed modest. It was so modest in fact that the firm did not even get a mention in 'One Hundred Heads of the Tobacco Trade', a supplement portrait plate published in the *Cigar and Tobacco World* of May 1896.

Many grand plans and ideas took root in the final years of the nineteenth century, which were characterised by rapid industrial and social change, both at home and abroad. With the empire almost at its peak, the period was marked by the many grand exhibitions that the Victorians were so fond of creating. Captivating the public imagination, such spectacles provided not only a showcase for British industry and empire but a feast of entertainment, the like of which most citizens had never seen. Exhibition organisers

Clockwise from top left: the founders, Isidore and Montague Gluckstein, their brother-in-law Barnett Salmon, and Joseph Lyons who gave his name to the enterprise.

had no difficulty in attracting millions of visitors; the Manchester Exhibition of 1887, for example, recorded nearly five million visitors and a year earlier the Liverpool Exhibition two million.

Such large attendances gave caterers enormous opportunities to make huge profits, especially when they enjoyed a monopoly of catering rights. Under these circumstances many charged such extortionate prices that some visitors, especially the less well-off, were deterred from buying any refreshments at all. In some cases exhibition organisers complained that the high cost of refreshments had even prevented many working-class citizens from attending their events. These exorbitant costs were in fact a consequence of the tendering methods employed to sell the lucrative catering contracts. For example, it was not unusual to charge catering contractors £25-40,000 for exclusive rights. Understandably there

was fierce competition and if a contractor had paid too much he would tend to raise prices and reduce quality in order to recover his investment.

Montague Gluckstein's experiences at these exhibitions, which he patronised to market the Salmon & Gluckstein tobacco products, revealed to him their dismal, unappetising catering. These unacceptable standards caused him to examine the possibilities of venturing into exhibition catering. After some preliminary calculations he went to his brothers and other members of the family and outlined his ideas. He had not counted on their apathy. Appalled with the proposition, they all felt it beneath their dignity to involve themselves in such a discredited business as catering and would have nothing to do with it. Undeterred by their lack of enthusiasm, Montague Gluckstein tirelessly worked to win them over. After a great deal of discussion they agreed to allocate funds on the understanding that the name of Salmon & Gluckstein be dissociated from the enterprise and some other person be employed to head the business. It is believed that this condition was proposed by the fifty-eight-year-old Barnett Salmon, and it is therefore ironic that his eldest son, Alfred (1868–1928), played such an active role in managing some of the new company's earliest and most important catering contracts when only twenty-one years of age.

Enter Joseph Lyons

Montague Gluckstein, having agreed to find someone else to front the new business, at once thought of Joseph Lyons (1847–1917), a relative of Rose Gluckstein (née Cohen), the wife of his brother Isidore. In the absence of official documents the precise relationship is difficult to establish but it may not be a coincidence that Joseph's mother's maiden name as well as his wife's was Cohen. In any event it is believed that Joseph Lyons was running a successful market stall in the Liverpool area when Montague Gluckstein approached him. Some have suggested that it may have been a coffee stall but there is

Joseph Lyons, in smoking jacket, at home in West Kensington.

no evidence to support this. Given Joseph Lyons' artistic qualities and the fact that he was a watercolour artist at that time, it is more likely that he would have been involved in selling his paintings and artists' supplies. His wedding certificate, dated 24 August 1881, lists his profession as 'artist' and that of his father as 'picture dealer'. By 1887, when he was thirty-nine, his pleasant personality and persuasive manner – together with the fact that he had cultivated important commercial friendships and had knowledge of exhibition procedures – had not escaped Gluckstein's notice.

Joseph Nathaniel Lyons, affectionately known throughout his life as Joe, was born in Lant Street, Southwark, on 29 December 1847 of humble parents. His father, Nathaniel Joseph Lyons, born in 1820, had married Hannah Cohen in 1847. According to the 1881 British Census three children were living at the family home in Fentiman Road, Lambeth, namely Laurence Lyons (b.1858), Isaac Lyons (b.1860) and Kate Lyons (b.1854). Joseph Lyons was lodging at 31 Drury Lane at the same time. Joseph's father died, as a 'gentleman', of heart failure on Bishopsgate railway station on 15 October 1888, just after the first Lyons company had been established.

Joseph Lyons was educated at the South London Jewish School in Heygate Street, Walworth (Isidore Salmon and later his son Sir Samuel Salmon both served as governors of the school in later years), and at an unknown private academy. He developed a great love of beauty and the arts, but he began his career as apprentice to an optician and invented a device he called a chromatic stereoscope that he hawked around exhibitions and fairgrounds. It sold for 1s. 6d. and comprised a telescope, binoculars, micro-scope and magnifying glass all in one. As he did not see any future in making spectacles, he turned his hand to watercolour painting. Several of his works were exhibited with the Royal Institute of Painters in Water Colours; in later years, when he was well known, he sold some pictures to eminent people of the period including Sir Spencer Wells, private secretary to the Chancellor of the Exchequer, and Rear-Admiral Sir Cecil Eardley-Wilmot.

As a young man Joseph Lyons had written music-hall sketches and songs which he sold to theatregoers in the vestibule of the Pavilion Theatre, Whitechapel, and it was there that he first met Sarah Psyche Cohen (1860–1948), whom he married in the New Synagogue, London, on 24 August 1881. She was always known as Psyche and has two separate official entries of death in the registers, one under Sarah and the other under Psyche. Both her parents were associated with the theatre: her mother was an actress who used the stage name Fanny Harrison (born Frances Harris); her father, Isaac Cohen, was a theatrical comedian who became the Pavilion's manager in September 1894. The Pavilion Theatre had opened in November 1828 and was rebuilt in 1874 after being destroyed by fire in 1856; major alterations were made in 1894, the year that Isaac Cohen became manager. By the time it finally closed for entertainment in 1934, the Pavilion had become the home of Jewish drama in the East End.

Like other new playhouses that opened in the East End in the nineteenth century, it catered for a local clientele, with its own plays and play-wrights. The Pavilion specialised in melodramas, many with a nautical flavour which presumably reflected the interests of those East Londoners whose livelihood was associated with the river and sea. It was the first theatre in London to stage a dramatisation of Charles Dickens's *Oliver Twist* after the Theatre Regulation Act of 1843 deprived Covent Garden and Drury Lane of their mo-nopoly on staging plays using only the spoken word, which had restricted other theatres to 'il-legitimate' drama – defined as melodrama, panto-mime, spectacle, burlesque and anything with some musical accompaniment and a few songs.

The Whitechapel Pavilion gained a reputa-tion for pantomime and, under the management of Isaac Cohen, for melodramas in Yiddish, since many of the Jews living in the area were unable to speak English. Yiddish theatre had first come to Whitechapel in the 1880s when a Russian actor, Jacob Adler, gave performances at clubs, meeting halls and later theatres.

Victorian melodrama in general echoed the society's emphasis on acquisitiveness and business enterprise, the pulse of city life, the sense of teeming humanity in ceaseless motion. By the late nineteenth century, the growing taste for realism and sensation meant that all the paraphernalia of living had to be transposed to the stage, but new developments in stage machinery enabled remarkable illusions to be achieved. By the 1880s exact reproductions of familiar street scenes, squares, bridges and public buildings as well as domestic interiors could be seen in the theatre. After the 1843 Act, even the legitimate theatre had made increasing use of spectacle, and all classes enjoyed the blend of conventional plays interspersed with orchestral music, songs, dances, processions and pageants. In providing inside knowledge of a popular London theatre, therefore, Joseph Lyons' connection with the Pavilion and the theatrical Cohen family was to prove enormously useful to the showmanship that characterised the business of J. Lyons & Company.

Joseph Lyons also turned his hand to writing detective stories and co-authored *The Master Crime* and *Treasures of the Temple* with Cecil Raleigh, one-time drama critic of *Vanity Fair* (copies of both are held by the British Library). During the First World War he wrote a recruiting song titled 'Shoulder to Shoulder', but one of his earliest patriotic efforts in verse was 'A Tragedy of the War', which he wrote during the South African campaign of 1899–1902.

Outside his business interests Joseph Lyons was a keen member of the Territorial Army and played an active part in introducing athletics into its training curriculum. In June 1909 he was largely responsible for organising the first Territorial Athletic Meeting at Stamford Bridge, which attracted 1,700 entries. It was proclaimed such a success that a national event was held the following year at the Crystal Palace.

Joseph Lyons' knighthood, which he received from George V on 23 February 1911 at St James's Palace, brought him congratulations from all over the country, and he especially cherished those from the less well-known people he had befriended. Indeed, he took a particular interest in the less fortunate members of society, frequently giving assistance to the homeless who adopted the Embankment benches for their beds, as well as actively supporting the Little Sisters of the Poor. Later in life he encouraged Hannah Gluckstein, the artistic daughter of Joseph Gluckstein, when she was a child; once he gave her a miniature silver-gilt box of water colours. Hannah Gluckstein eventually became a full-time artist, assuming the name of Gluck, and her life is told in Diana Souhami's biography *Gluck*.

The First Lyons Company: Newcastle and Glasgow exhibitions

When he was approached by Montague Gluckstein in 1887, the idea of venturing into exhibition catering appealed to Joseph Lyons. As often happened in arrangements of this kind, in classic romantic style they agreed business terms at a single meeting, said to have been on a train, the terms being handwritten on a single sheet of paper which regrettably is now lost. Little other documentary evidence of the company for the period 1887–9 has survived but it is assumed that the partnership was a private company with the shares, if any, in the names of the Salmon, Gluckstein and Lyons family members who collectively originated the enterprise. It must also be assumed that Joseph Lyons had agreed to his name being used for the firm, for it was registered as J. Lyons & Company.

The formal characteristics of a private company are that the transfer of shares is restricted and invitations to the public are prohibited. Originally such restrictions were compensated by the privilege of not having to make public certain financial information about the company's affairs. This rule changed in 1967, when the publication of accounts and a balance sheet became mandatory for all private companies. Another significant difference between a public and private company is that a private company is generally owned and controlled by its directors and subject to different tax rules. These have been the subject of legal exploitation over many years and continue to occupy the minds of tax specialists.

So in 1887 Isidore, Montague and Joseph Gluckstein, with their brother-in-law Barnett Salmon and Joseph Lyons, started their exhibition catering enterprise from the tobacco business address at 34 Whitechapel Road. During the same year Queen Victoria celebrated her Golden Jubilee, and the Lyons company's formation at this time could not have been coincidental, given the exhibition catering opportunities that were likely to occur during that year. All over Britain there were festivities and exhibitions to celebrate not only the past successes of the empire's soldiers but also the high expectations for future national prosperity and enterprise. Joseph Lyons' imagination, entrepreneurial talents and logistical ability together with Montague Gluckstein's business expertise helped them to secure their first catering contract. They were invited to manage the catering facilities at the Newcastle Jubilee Exhibition, to be held in May 1887.

To influence the exhibition organisers, a number of special features were included in the Lyons tender. Salmon & Gluckstein themselves mounted a large tobacco display, including demonstrations of cigar making; Joseph Lyons had designed a shooting gallery; and Montague Gluckstein planned to engage the Blue Hungarian Band to play in the refreshment area. The band's fee alone was £150 per week – then without precedent. With such commitment from caterers, it was hard for the organisers to ignore the fledgeling firm's overtures.

Joseph Lyons' shooting gallery was the first of its type in the world – the first in which animal targets moved across realistic scenic effects to make it more difficult to obtain a 'kill'. Now commonplace in fairgrounds and amusement arcades, albeit in inferior imitations, it caused a sensation in 1887, principally among the visiting soldiers who were eager to demonstrate their prowess at weaponry to their accompanying ladies. This idea was sufficiently interesting for the Admiralty later to invite Joseph Lyons to one of their training establishments in Portsmouth to advise on the setting up of a torpedo-firing range.

At their first exhibition, J. Lyons & Company were responsible for three main areas: a reproduction of Newcastle's fourteenth-century Carliol Tower, where fruit and flowers were sold; a replica of the entrance to Alnwick Castle, which

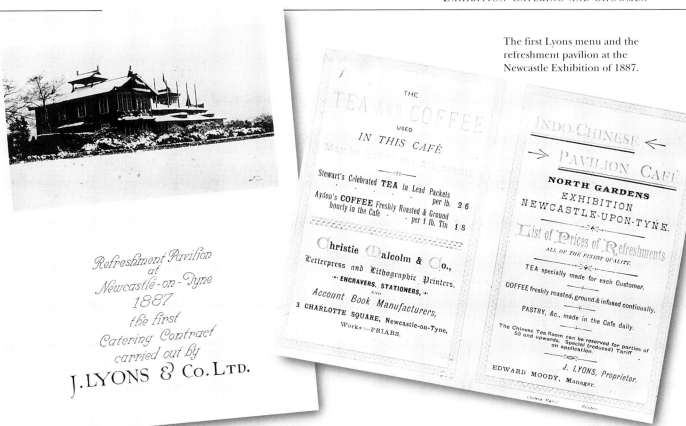

The first Lyons menu and the refreshment pavilion at the Newcastle Exhibition of 1887.

Refreshment Pavilion at Newcastle-on-Tyne 1887 the first Catering Contract carried out by J. LYONS & Co. LTD.

was used as the archery and shooting gallery, depicted as an Indian jungle with animals and birds; and the Indo-Chinese Pavilion Café for the sale of tea, coffee and light refreshments. Inside the pavilion, tea was 'specially infused and served in a teapot for each customer', and charged at 3d. per pot; the brand, Stewart's Celebrated Tea, could be bought in lead packets at 2s. 6d. per pound. Aydon's freshly roasted and ground coffee was made every hour, and all pastry was baked daily in the café. Among the light refreshments were bread and butter, jam, scones, Bath buns, Scottish shortbread, Huntley & Palmer's biscuits, jam tartlets, Russian cake, cream sandwiches, éclairs and ices, and apart from tea and coffee the drinks available included Fry's chocolate, milk, mineral waters and iced fruit drinks. The manager of the Indo-Chinese Café was one Edward Moody, and catering, administrative and other staff were specially hired for the event. No expense was spared in providing catering facilities on a far grander scale than in the past, to ensure maximum publicity for Lyons' first catering contract. The Salmon and Gluckstein families had

made a huge investment in design, construction, furnishing and decoration, creating an extraordinary impact on everyone who visited the exhibition.

With their innovative combination of freshly brewed tea, a first-rate orchestra playing in the refreshment area and a shooting gallery, Lyons received generous praise from the public and media alike. Indeed, the refreshments were so successful that after the exhibition closed the tea pavilion continued to operate. Before the event the *Newcastle Daily Chronicle* of 9 May 1887 reported extracts of exhibition plans from the *Jubilee Chronicle of the Newcastle Exhibition*, mentioning 'a stand of goodly dimensions belonging to Messrs. Lyons & Co. of London, where cigars, pipes and cigarettes will be made'. The newspaper continued:

> The first building, which the visitor reaches on leaving the North Court, is a representation of the old Carliol Tower, which has been produced at the instance of Mr. Lyons, a London gentleman who, after Messrs. Gibson & Co., is the largest

speculator in the Exhibition. The model of the familiar building that used to grace New Bridge Street will be utilised for the sale of English and colonial fruits and flowers. The Indo-Chinese Pavilion, which also belongs to Mr. Lyons, was designed by Mr. J. S. Fairfax of London, and has been constructed under the superintendence of Mr. Charles Brooks. Light and elegant, it will be recognised as one of the handsomest buildings on the ground. Externally it is decorated in the Indian style, and the combined appearance of domes and minarets, with a profusion of bright colours, produces a very fine effect. Downstairs there is an Indian court, and upstairs a Chinese court, in both of which light refreshments will be sold. The building is almost ninety feet long and forty feet wide, and it is estimated to seat about 1,200 persons.

In 1888 the Glasgow Exhibition followed, with similar tea and music combinations. This was the largest exhibition held anywhere in the British Empire since the London Exhibition of 1862 and it attracted over six million visitors. Joseph Lyons and his partners took over the Bishop's Palace Tea-Rooms, giving them a thorough renovation before opening them to the public. Dressed in expensive costumes and Mary Stuart caps, the attractive Scottish waitresses were a splendid advertisement for the company. As it was a good summer, Joseph Lyons busied himself trying to feed the crowds that deluged the restaurants. On the last day stocks of food were low. Using his organisational skills, Lyons chartered almost every spare horse-cab, handcart and any other vehicle in the vicinity to bring in extra supplies of food and tea by scouring every retailer in the city.

The Glasgow Exhibition proved to be as successful as the Newcastle Exhibition, resulting in twenty smaller contracts during the year. A contract to cater for the builders of the Imperial Institute at South Kensington in London which was agreed on 11 October 1888 continued until its opening in 1893. As part of the catering arrangements, and for which they were paid £300, Lyons had an agreement with the Ceylon Association in London to ensure that none other than Ceylon tea would be served. Apart from its tower, the building was demolished when the Imperial College of Science was expanded. Emboldened by these successes, Lyons took their catering to Paris for the exhibition of 1889, setting up their Franco-English Café in the Hotel Piccadilly in the Avenue Sufferen. Unlike the earlier events the Paris experiment was not altogether a financial success; but the experience gained, Montague Gluckstein later observed, 'was helpful in modelling the home business'.

The Second Lyons Company

The Public Record Office preserves the first official evidence of the second Lyons company on a document dated 16 March 1889, when J. Lyons & Company sold its contracts to the newly formed J. Lyons & Company Ltd. The share capital for the new company was £5,000, all issued in £1 shares and held by Joseph Lyons (1,249), Isidore Gluckstein (1,249), Montague Gluckstein (1,249), Barnett Salmon (1,249), Joseph Gluckstein (2), Abraham Joseph (1) and Julius Koppenhagen (1); these last two being family members by marriage. In the Memorandum of Association (the governance regulations for conducting a limited company's business) it is worth recording that the company's main objectives included:

(a) To carry on the business of Contractors for the supply of Refreshments, Restaurateurs, Entertainment Contractors, Theatre and Music Hall Proprietors, Contractors for supplying Public Exhibitions, Theatres, Music Halls, and other places of public or private entertainment with refreshments, Hotel Proprietors and General Merchants and Commission Agents.

(b) To tender for and acquire shops, stalls, places and buildings in Exhibitions and other places for supplying entertainment's [sic] and refreshments, and for the sale of all goods and merchandise …

(d) To carry on the business of a Hotel and Restaurant, and Circus Proprietor and Manager and a Theatre Proprietor and Manager at Paris, France and to carry on a business as a Shooting Gallery Proprietor at Brighton and elsewhere,

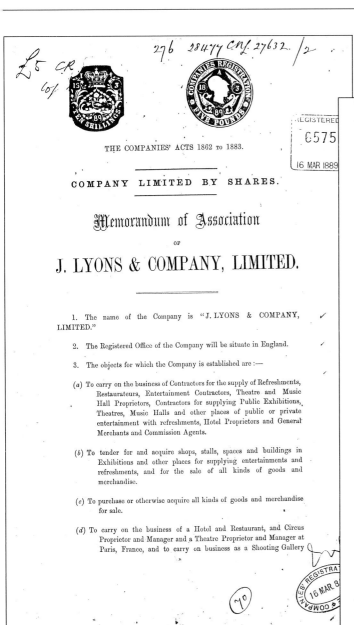

The earliest documentary evidence of J. Lyons & Co. Ltd, dated 16 March 1889. An earlier, unlimited company had been formed in 1887. Unlike today's business trends, the company never changed its name. *By kind permission of the Public Record Office.*

and to enter into or acquire a contract or contracts for supplying refreshments at the Imperial Institute, South Kensington, London.

The Articles of Association of the 1889 company also stated: 'Directors shall act without remuneration and each shall be entitled to continue in office so long as he holds capital of the nominal amount of £1,200 at the least.' Isidore Gluckstein was appointed Director and Joseph Lyons Managing Director, a position he held until his death in 1917. By this time evidence indicates that relationships had become strained, to the extent that Joseph Lyons' death was, shamefully, not even reported to shareholders – the only time in the company's history that a death in service of a director went unreported.

When these articles were drawn up, the founding members obviously had plans for a number of new business ventures and it seems that a version of the shooting gallery, so successful at Newcastle, was to be introduced at Brighton, although there is no record that it actually happened. Writing in the *Jewish Chronicle* of 26 October 1906, Joseph Lyons did outline his ambitions for building and operating music halls, and clearly the Memorandum of Association had anticipated these desires. Reportedly with unlimited capital he aimed to build beautiful variety theatres offering refined entertainment for the middle class hitherto not properly addressed in the popular music halls of the period. His intention was to run them as temperance houses with attached winter gardens and other attractions. Primarily sponsored by Joseph Lyons himself, the theatre project came to nothing, but music and entertainment did feature strongly in many of the company's future restaurants.

Teashops and restaurants were also part of the company's plan. Coincidentally, Montague Gluckstein had recently been taken for the first time, by a businessman called Harold Hartley (1851–1943), to Buszard's tearoom in London's Oxford Street, where Gluckstein was astonished at its popularity. William Buszard, described in *Kelly's Directory* as a 'bride cake manufacturer, baker and pastrycook', catered mainly for the aristocracy. His success highlighted the need for good light refreshments in London at this time.

Olympia

Following the incorporation in 1889, Lyons were appointed caterers to the first Barnum & Bailey Circus at Olympia, with the 21-year-old Alfred Salmon managing the event. Alfred Salmon had been educated at Archbishop Tenison's School in Leicester Square and at thirteen had joined the tobacco business before serving an apprenticeship in the restaurant of a West End hotel company, enabling him to learn the catering business thoroughly from the point of view of the kitchens and of the markets where meat, vegetables and other supplies were purchased. Just three years earlier, in October 1886, the National Agricultural Hall Company Ltd had issued a prospectus to raise capital for their new National Agricultural Hall in Kensington. They had purchased twelve acres of freehold estate set aside for buildings and a garden.

Part of the property had been a vineyard before Lewis Kennedy and James Lee turned it into a famous nursery in about 1745. James Lee was no ordinary nurseryman: he had translated the works of the Swedish naturalist Carolus Linnaeus and had written *An Introduction to the Science of Botany*, a book for laymen and professional botanists which explained Linnaeus' natural history classification for the first time. He had also befriended the botanist Joseph Banks, who sent him seeds from Australia, and Lee became the first nurseryman to grow plants in England from Australian stock. Lee's name is most often linked to the fuchsia, since he was the first nurseryman to make it available. Banks' association with Lee ensured that their Royal Vineyard Nursery (variously called the Hammersmith Vineyard Nursery and Vineyard Nursery) became a famous rendezvous for other botanists, and it was here that the immensely talented Sydney Parkinson, often referred to as 'Mr Banks' natural history painter', first met Joseph Banks. Parkinson accompanied Banks and Captain James Cook on their voyage to the South Pacific aboard the *Endeavour* to observe the transit of the planet Venus across the sun on 3 June 1769 – an event which provided a rare opportunity to calculate the distance of the sun from the earth and which would not occur again until 1882, and then not again until 8 June 2004.

The National Agricultural Hall's buildings in Kensington together covered an area of four acres and became popularly known as Olympia. The Grand Hall, 2½ acres in extent, was the largest in the country when built and covered by one span of iron and glass to the design of James Edmeston. The open gardens, comprising 5½ acres, were immediately adjacent to the hall and intended for fashionable gatherings, garden and floral fêtes, musical promenades and outdoor sports: later they became known as the Gardens of Olympia. Refreshment licences had been secured with Bertram & Company for a term of seven years at a fixed minimum rental of £1,500 per annum. The first event to be staged at the Agricultural Hall when it opened on Boxing Day 1886 was the Paris Hippodrome Circus. With 400 animals, a stag hunt and chariot race, it was remembered for its magnificence and splendour. In spite of the rush for shares – at £10 each – the National Agricultural Hall Company did not appear to have been very successful, for by 1893 it had gone into receivership (as we shall see later in this chapter).

The Barnum & Bailey Circus catering contract had been secured by Joseph Lyons himself after searching out Barnum's principal, George Oscar Starr, whose wife, Lazel, was the 'human cannon-ball'. Lyons had explained to Starr that he regarded refreshments as a vital part of the overall entertainment. This idea pleased George Starr so much that in consequence he not only granted catering rights for the many visitors to the circus but also contracted Lyons to provide for the 500 circus staff and performers who took their meals in the Pillar Room before and after the daily performances. There is nothing on record to suggest that Lyons also had the task of feeding the animals!

For events such as these, temporary staff were hired to supplement the chefs, head waiters, banqueting and other administrative personnel. Senior management were responsible for setting policy, standards and procedures; they negotiated prices and terms with the drinks suppliers and bought most of their raw foodstuffs from wholesalers or London markets. Some items of food such as biscuits, butter and sauces were bought direct from manufacturers (Huntley & Palmer, Carr's, HP Sauce, Idris minerals, etc.), but wherever possible the middleman was eliminated. Senior management inspected every operation in detail, sometimes on a daily basis, to ensure that their instructions were being rigidly adhered to. Any difficulties reported by lower managers or supervisors, who had a great deal of responsibility themselves, were acted upon immediately.

When Barnum & Bailey's appearance at Olympia closed, Joseph Lyons entered into discussions with Harold Hartley. Hartley was an entrepreneurial businessman who became a successful publisher and was a partner in Emmott, Hartley & Company. Joseph Lyons had first met him in 1888 after Hartley had bought at auction, for £100, the Pure Water Company. Hartley had heard that Lyons had just been successful in securing a contract – managed by Alfred Salmon, who was then only just of age – to cater for the workers who were building the Imperial Institute in London and had approached them to sell his aerated water. Thereafter Harold Hartley would often meet Joseph Lyons in one of the Olympia bars for a drink. During their meetings they invariably discussed using Olympia to stage a big show that would be characterised by novelty and flamboyance, both men confident there was money in it. Their ideas ranged from 'Olde London' to the Orient, including the possibility of a Dutch or Scandinavian show. Both were convinced that water or snow should form part of the attraction. Finally they decided to exploit the increasing Victorian popularity of exotic settings and ingenious spectacle by combining these elements in a theatrical entertainment. Joseph Lyons had, of course, always been passionately interested in the theatre. His enthusiasm and the late Victorian public's appetite for theatrical spectacle knew no bounds, and what emerged from his discussions with Hartley, in 1890, was a privately staged extravaganza called *Venice in London*.

Events moved fast, after an agreement to rent Olympia for £300 per week for an extended period. Joseph Lyons then set out to re-create in wood and plaster, inside the Olympia building, the famous landmarks of ancient and modern Venice. After huge endeavours he eventually raised £18,000 from a consortium of business colleagues and friends – including the Salmon and Gluckstein families. All agreed that for the spectacle to succeed it would be necessary to secure the services of a well-known professional showman. Sir Augustus Harris (1852–96), actor, impresario, dramatist, and producer of a succession of highly popular melodramas, operas and pantomimes, was approached but after prolonged negotiations he lost interest. Finally Harold Hartley suggested they contact Imre

Kiralfy (1845–1919), with whom Joseph Lyons had previously worked in connection with Barnum & Bailey's Circus, and who was in New York at the time. Hartley cabled him with the message: 'Will you come over and produce *Venice in London* at Olympia and if so on what terms.' The reply that came from Kiralfy the next day was: 'I am leaving by the next boat.'

Upon his arrival in the United Kingdom, Kiralfy listened intently to the ideas proposed by Joseph Lyons and other members of the consortium; then he came up with an estimate of £17,000 for the production. After some hard bargaining in respect of his fees, it was agreed that he would take 40 per cent of the profits. This seemed extravagant, but, since Kiralfy's reputation was legendary and time was slipping away, the consortium had no alternative but to acquiesce. They formed themselves into a company, named Imre Kiralfy Ltd and registered on 16 July 1891. By the time all the work had been completed in preparation for the opening, Hartley, in his biography *Eighty-Eight Not Out* (1939), reported that expenditure had increased to £60,000, and 'Were it not for the generosity of a sympathetic bank manager the project would have failed.'

Notwithstanding Kiralfy's association with the event, many potential exhibitors viewed Joseph Lyons' overtures with suspicion and were reluctant to become involved with the event. Thanks to the assistance of the Italian Chamber of Commerce, however, some seventy Italian exhibitors eventually occupied space made available to them. Joseph Lyons had travelled to Venice, with Hartley and their wives, to persuade tradespeople and others to participate in their show. Lyons desired Italian support, believing their attendance would add authenticity to the spectacle. While in Venice, Hartley and Lyons stayed at the Grand Hotel, where the proprietor, Alphonse Pianta, on hearing about their venture, insisted on investing £500 of his own money in the project. Pianta thereby became one of the larger individual shareholders, with the Gluckstein brothers and Joseph Lyons taking only one £50 share each. By contrast, Samuel Lewis, a known money-lender of Savile Row, London,

Programme cover of *Venice in London* 1891. *By kind permission of Hammersmith & Fulham Archives and Local History Centre.*

who also happened to be staying at the hotel, decided that buying shares in the venture was too speculative and declined Joseph Lyons' advances.

During his stay in Venice, Joseph Lyons purchased fifty gondolas at £40 each. Transporting these to London caused a major problem. To send them by freighter would have meant shipping them as uninsurable deck cargo and risking the added uncertainty of late arrival, which Joseph Lyons could not contemplate. Instead he dispatched them by train to the Channel ports and thence by road from Dover; although this proved more expensive, he felt reassured by an overland transit. Inside Olympia, waterways had been ingeniously constructed using soft, ductile lead, which the astute Montague Gluckstein had rented. Concrete would have been too expensive

An undated photograph of Isidore Gluckstein (centre) with Joseph Lyons seated to his right (bowler hat) and other managers at an early, unknown, exhibition. The big man in the back row (white hat) is J. Fraser, formerly a ticket writer with Salmon & Gluckstein.

The Grand Hall of Olympia, measuring 450 feet by 250 feet with an outer parade of 40 feet, contained an immense stage and an arena seating 10,000. An elaborately painted backdrop depicted historical Italian scenes representing love, warfare, festivities and marriages. The magnificent costumes worn by the 1,400 performers were said to be historically accurate. Passing on from a replica of the Grand Canal, with its limpid water, one entered modern Venice and the myriad smaller canals – collectively equal to a water surface 1¼ miles long – on which plied a number of gondolas and barges for hire. For those preferring to walk there were ample promenades, and thirteen bridges criss-crossed the canals, which were lined with simulated marble palaces, picturesque houses and shops selling Italian glass and leather goods. Adjacent to one of the bridges was a replica of the Café Florian, a house on the Piazza San Marco famous for its hospitality. Here light refreshments and special dinners were served by waitresses dressed in Venetian costumes. Decorated by Campbell Smith & Company, the Café Florian had been constructed with a new building material known as 'Ligomur' – a thick, embossed, fireproof card lending itself to the most decorative painted effects. With their normal forethought Lyons provided a number of other refreshment facilities. Besides the bars, where snacks were available as well as drinks – including drinks for children – a large dining hall and grill room had been built. The dining hall, used during the Barnum & Bailey Circus show, had undergone a complete refurbishment: the walls had been panelled with Venetian pictures and floral designs, all executed by Italian artists. The dining hall

to purchase and to remove after the show. To add greater authenticity Joseph Lyons had engaged Italian gondoliers, with their traditional dress, billeting them in London for the duration of the event.

Opening on 26 December 1891, *Venice in London* ran for thirteen months. There were two daily performances, with admission fees ranging from 1s. 6d. to 5s. 6d. For many months every performance was fully sold out, and the show became so successful that ticket touts began buying advance bookings and selling them on at inflated prices. When the swindle was discovered the touts' tactics were frustrated by making tickets available on the day of issue only, one hour before the performance started.

offered an à la carte menu, while the Café Florian allowed customers to order exclusive 'refection' to their particular taste. There was a selection of Italian wines, and the table ornaments, designed and crafted by Price's Patent Candle Company of Battersea (pioneers of oil-based candle manufacture), were in the form of graceful gondolas with a light in the centre surrounded by natural flowers. At any one time, over 300 waiting and kitchen staff laboured to provide the services, with an additional 100 employed as barmaids.

Venice in London attracted many distinguished visitors, including the Prince of Wales, who dined there one evening in a private box. When the Prince congratulated Joseph Lyons on the 'table' and the event generally, he happened to remark, 'Why don't you do "Constantinople" when "Venice" fails to attract?' His advice was apparently taken: *Constantinople at Olympia* opened eight months after *Venice* closed in 1893, but not before a host of obstacles had been overcome.

A representative had been dispatched to Turkey to negotiate trade deals and to obtain other items needed for the spectacle. Furnished with the highest credentials supplied by Rüstem Pasha, the Turkish Ambassador in London, the representative persuaded Sultan Abdul Hamid II to grant a special trade mandate allowing nationals to leave Turkey to participate in the London show. Meanwhile, at the Gaiety Theatre in London's Strand, the Turkish Sultan was being depicted as an undignified character in a burlesque comedy that naturally displeased the embassy staff and the rulers in Turkey. This unfortunate incident caused the Sultan to rescind the trade agreement and he refused permission to any nationals to leave Turkey to participate in the event. Faced with a major crisis, Joseph Lyons found himself coercing various Turkish nationals to leave Turkey surreptitiously – which caused serious concern to the management, who believed diplomatic action might follow if the matter were exposed. Fortunately, enough Turks were able to leave without any serious consequences and the show proceeded.

Constantinople at Olympia had been produced by Imre Kiralfy's brother Bolossy Kiralfy (1847–

1932), and when it opened in 1893 it became as successful as *Venice* and was widely acclaimed. No fewer than forty artists were employed to mould the pillars, built over wire-netting frames, and other imitation stonework. Lending an air of authenticity were caiques gliding through the two-million-gallon artificial waterways. A harem scene, which also offended members of the Turkish government in London, was so popular with the Victorian public that it remained despite protestations.

This was not the last of the company's extravaganzas. *The Orient* followed *Constantinople* one month after it closed, in November 1894. Again Joseph Lyons excelled himself. Elephants, camels, donkeys and entertainers dressed as Nubian slaves were among a whole range of devices used to create his realistic depictions of Egyptian street scenes, the Sphinx, snake worship and, surprisingly, 'A Chronicle of Henry V'. As the watercourses had been retained from the previous two shows, *The Orient* featured a subterranean hall through which the public could sail in hired boats. Over 2,500 performers took part in the stage show, and on the opening day the attendance of 34,537 broke all records for Olympia. Yet the initial public interest in *The Orient* waned during the winter months of 1894–5 and the last of the theatrical spectacles closed in July 1895.

The Olympia Property Deal

Some time between 1889 and 1892, J. Lyons & Company Ltd moved their head office from Whitechapel Road to basement premises at Olympia (formally used by Bertram & Roberts), where on 4 August 1892 the private shareholders met for their Annual General Meeting. 'A most successful year' was how they reported the last financial period. Little further is known of the company's activities until 1894, except for a legal case, arising from a property deal, which eventually went to the Court of Appeal.

High Court records reveal that in 1893 the National Agricultural Hall Company Ltd was 'in chancery' and being wound up by the official liquidator. The National Agricultural Hall property, known as 'Olympia', was for sale, but

An early invoice for wine supplied to Alfred Waterhouse, architect of the Natural History Museum, South Kensington. The letter heading shows that Lyons had both a telephone and telegraphic address in 1893.

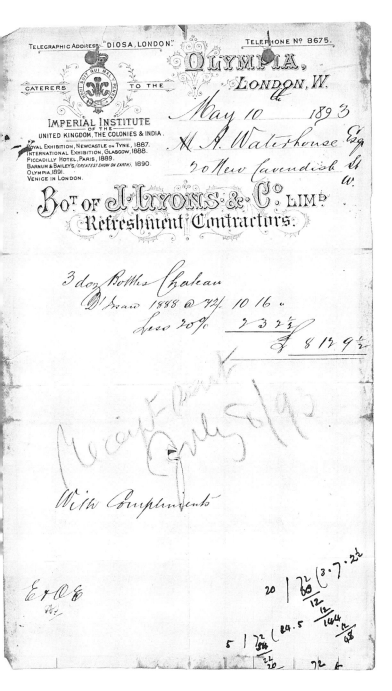

secretary for the syndicate, whose objective was to buy the National Agricultural Hall from the official liquidator and sell it to a new company being formed for that purpose. In February 1893 the Freehold Syndicate paid £27,220 for the debenture mortgage, which afterwards realised £42,358, and they gave £500 for the additional mortgage, which later realised £6,096. The profit on the transaction amounted to £20,734. About the same time, in January 1893, the syndicate agreed to buy the property for £140,000 and on 8 February 1893 a formal contract for the sale to the trustees was executed. With a deposit of £20,000 the purchasers agreed to a completion date of 8 May 1893.

The judge who had ordered the sale took the unusual step of hearing bids in his chambers; £140,000 was the highest bid and this secured the property for the syndicate. The last bid was £8,000 more than the previous one, although no other bid had exceeded the one before it by more than £1,000. Such apparently irrational behaviour was a strong indication that the syndicate meant to acquire the property at any cost.

By 20 March 1893, before the syndicate had finalised the purchase of Olympia, all necessary arrangements had been made by the syndicate trustees for the registration of a new company, Olympia Ltd, bound by its articles to buy the property from the syndicate for £180,000 – that is, £40,000 more than the trustees paid for it. On 20 March 1893 an agreement to form the company was made between the syndicate trustees (vendors) and a person called Close, a trustee for the intended company (purchaser). That agreement cites the contract of 8 February 1893, by which the vendors had promised to buy the property for £140,000. It also mentions that a company was about to be formed for the purchase of Olympia, and that the memorandum and articles of that company had been prepared with the privity of the vendors. The Articles of Association specified that the directors should adopt and carry out that agreement. It was then confirmed that the company, Olympia Ltd, should buy the property known as Olympia, subject to, and with the benefit of, two contracts of 18 January 1893 with J. Lyons & Company Ltd for

it had certain financial encumbrances, a debenture mortgage of £100,000 and another mortgage of £10,000. In 1893 the Freehold Syndicate was created, consisting of thirty-three persons for whom Montague Gluckstein and Messrs Lyons, Hart and Hartley acted as trustees. John Hart, who had been the second largest shareholder in Imre Kiralfy Ltd and described himself as an advertisement contractor, was made

refreshments and with John Hart for advertising. The price for Olympia was to be £180,000. It was by this method that Montague Gluckstein and John Hart respectively secured a catering and advertising contract for Olympia in which the directors who eventually purchased the property had no involvement, and which they could not influence. Montague Gluckstein, Joseph Lyons and others were also directors of Olympia Ltd.

The catering contract with Olympia lasted for sixty years, but local licensed houses and temperance deputations frequently objected to applications for liquor licences for the great exhibitions. The neighbouring licensed houses had every cause to complain of loss of trade to themselves. Olympia bar records show that total drinks takings – alcoholic and non-alcoholic – for the Ideal Homes Exhibition, Horse Show, Motor Show and Bertram Mills' Circus in the years 1929, 1930 and 1931 were £103,931, £112,271 and £98,259 respectively, some of which must have been at the expense of the local publicans. However, in the case of Bertram Mills' Circus, the revenue from non-alcoholic drinks accounted for 70 per cent of sales, reflecting the very young clientele; therefore, since children were not allowed in public houses, publicans could not realistically claim loss of potential earnings during the circus show.

The prolonged litigation over Olympia initiated by the appellant and official liquidator, Thomas Abercrombie Welton, under section 10 of the Companies Acts 1862 and 1867, was eventually heard on 26 May 1898 in the Court of Appeal by Nathaniel Lindley, Master of the Rolls, assisted by Lord Justices Rigby and Collins. No attempt was made to conceal the price the syndicate had paid for the property, and no one complained about that. The case focused on the secret profits which the syndicate was alleged to have made on the mortgage transactions in 1893. In the agreement for the sale of the National Agricultural Hall by the syndicate to Olympia Ltd, a clause was inserted to the effect that the validity of the agreement should not be impeached on the ground that the vendors as promoters – or as persons standing in a fiduciary position to the company – should not be required to account for

Share certificate No. 2 issued to Joseph Lyons on 7 May 1894

any profit made or to be made by them by the purchase of any debentures of the National Agricultural Hall Company. This clause was assumed by the defendants to afford a complete answer to their case. The directors of the new company were Montague Gluckstein, Joseph Lyons, John Hart and Harold Hartley, but the only person with whom they had now to deal was Gluckstein. Being members of Olympia Ltd, they had certain fiduciary duties laid upon them by statute, and the question was whether they had performed those duties or not. The conclusion reached by the appeal judges was that 'no proper and sufficient disclosure of the profits made by the syndicate had been made'. Abercrombie Welton's appeal succeeded and an order was made for the repayment, by the syndicate, of the amount mentioned in the summons, that is £6,341.

Although he received several open letters of support in the national press following the Olympia judgement, the adverse publicity was deeply wounding to Montague Gluckstein's pride, since by now he held directorships in the

Westminster Electric Supply Corporation, the Guardian Assurance Company, and the Pall Mall Electric Light Company. At the age of forty-four, he retreated from public life, channelling his energies instead into the Lyons business, which did not seem to suffer unduly from this case, although it was widely reported by all the leading newspapers of the day. Generally, the company received excellent press coverage. This was due in part to the extrovert personality of Joseph Lyons (now a member of the Eccentrics Club), who was frequently seen entertaining journalists in London's fashionable restaurants.

Catering for the troops

Although diversification of the Lyons company activities began in 1894, catering was still a principal source of revenue and the firm continued to tender for contracts both large and small. Outdoor catering, in particular, frequently required the use of marquees, furniture and other paraphernalia and for these Lyons had already built up a comprehensive inventory under the

Aldershot in 1899 where Lyons undertook the baking for all the troops stationed there during the Boer War. The team was managed by Henry Lane Edwards, who had joined Lyons as an assistant manager of the bakery in 1898. He became a director in 1934.

auspices of the Hire Department, one of the first departments established after the Newcastle Exhibition.

One of the most unusual contracts the company was granted during this time was to provide catering to the officers of a British Army regiment while they were on a six-week manoeuvre in 1894. The catering staff joined the Duke of Connaught and Lord Methuen's army units in the field at Hounslow Heath, travelling across country with them to the New Forest via Aldershot. Bivouacking at frequent intervals with the army units, the catering team was equipped with four horse-drawn vehicles and a dozen or so men who were responsible for all the catering tents. These were quite luxurious by current army standards, and all were lit by four oil-lamps whenever food and drink were needed at night. Isidore Salmon regularly visited the travelling ensemble from his office at Hammersmith to ensure that standards were maintained, but how he knew where the troops were located is bewildering, unless he had been provided with maps as part of the contract. Some accidents with the catering wagons did occur en route. On one occasion a horse-drawn van had to be abandoned when it became bogged down during a very wet spell, but it was later retrieved.

In 1908, having just completed the contract at the Dublin Exhibition of 1907, the firm were successful in tendering for the catering rights to the prestigious Franco-British Exhibition held at Shepherd's Bush in London.

The Franco-British Exhibition

The French Chamber of Commerce first conceived the idea of an exhibition in which both France and Britain would display and promote their respective industrial achievements. After the appointment of Imre Kiralfy as Director-General, and once the committees had agreed on finance, a 140-acre site north of Shepherd's Bush Green, roughly bordered by the present West Cross Route and Wood Lane, was allocated. The architects were Marius Toudoire and John Belcher, a partner in his father's practice who had previously designed the Victoria and Albert Museum and the Institute of Chartered Accountants in the City.

The exhibition buildings were fireproofed and designed to a high safety standard of steel frames and concrete shrouding.

The company formed to oversee the construction – the International & Colonial Commercial Co. Ltd (later Shepherd's Bush Exhibition Ltd) – employed their own staff, with 4,000 contractors working by day and 2,000 by night. In total they built twenty palaces and 120 exhibition buildings, waterways, bridges, roads and other structures. The visitor's first impression of the all-white construction soon earned it the nickname of 'The White City' – which, of course, has remained. The location had been carefully chosen for its access to good communications: the main entrance adjoined the new Central London Railway (underground) and was close to several other stations, tramways and bus routes.

For the exhibition organisers a Garden Club had been specifically built, facing the sunken bandstand. Both ladies and gentlemen were eligible for membership, entitling them to unlimited admission to the exhibition at all times and the use of the many boxes and spacious verandas serving luncheons. For those unable to afford the expenditure of three guineas, Lyons catered in the same liberal style in their aptly named Grand Restaurant situated on the north-west side of the gardens. Luncheons could be obtained for three shillings, and dinners at 5s., 7s. 6d. and 10s., depending on one's pocket. Afternoon teas were available for a shilling and if these were too expensive there were a number of other restaurants, tearooms and buffets. An example of the tariffs is illustrated.

During the period of the exhibition, which ran from May to October 1908, the Olympic Games were staged in the specially constructed stadium. On this occasion Great Britain won fifty-six gold medals, the highest number of any

nation. The 1908 games are credited with having extended the marathon to its current distance of 26 miles 385 yards. Queen Alexandra, who attended the finish of the marathon in 1908, asked if the finishing line could be placed in front of the royal box to give her a better view, which meant extending the race by 385 yards. This act of folly accounts for the unusual distance which all marathons are run today in order to maintain the race standard throughout the world.

Twenty years of exhibition catering had passed by 31 October 1908, when the Franco-British Exhibition closed, but the great exhibitions were becoming less fashionable and thus more risky to mount. Several other exhibitions were held on the same White City site after the Franco-

The Olympic Café at the Franco-British Exhibition of 1908.

The Grand Restaurant, probably the finest at the Franco-British Exhibition of 1908, was staffed and managed by Lyons.

British Exhibition closed – approximately one per year up to 1914, when the buildings were taken over by the government for troop training. Lyons, however, did not tender for any catering contracts, preferring instead to concentrate on their prospering teashop trade.

The contract catering years of 1887–1908 had been prosperous ones for Lyons. Requiring no large-scale capital investment – apart from the theatrical events at Olympia – they had broken the traditional influence of the brewing and licensed trades on exhibition catering. As a result the Lyons name received legitimacy in the domain of catering. Profitable though these years had been, exhibition catering was, by its very essence,

no more than a temporary excursion, and in that respect it mirrored the philosophy of the Salmon and Gluckstein families of an earlier era (from small-time cigar making to retail tobacconists). Contract catering lacked permanency, and therefore could not become the foundation on which to build a sound trading base. Since management had learned the need for efficiency, vital to the success of the next business phase, they sought a more permanent solution to their catering aspirations. J. Lyons & Company turned their energies to becoming restaurateurs supported by food manufacture – two spheres in which they became internationally prominent.

Chapter

Lyons of Cadby Hall

Charles Cadby and his second wife, Harriet Mary. These paintings hung in the Lyons boardroom for many years. *By kind permission of Waldegrave Films.*

Until the middle of the nineteenth century most industrial development in the United Kingdom had been carried out by one-man or family businesses. Expansion was limited by modest earnings; in barren years no growth occurred, but in good years owners could divert some of their profits to capital or other expenditure to improve their production. Fresh changes in the law in 1856 and 1862 made it easier for businesses to raise capital by converting to limited-liability status and many small undertakings attracted new shareholder investment. These new investors expected accountability and financial reporting from directors or owners, as well as receiving a share of the profits; and more serious investors could spread their risks over more than one investment. The new legislation also enabled dissimilar companies to combine or merge and thereby iron out fluctuations in trading. These companies became known as combinations. The sewing thread company of J.P. Coats, for example, took over so many businesses that by the late 1890s it had become the largest firm in manufacturing industry with a market value of over £20 million; it was also monopolistic. Other examples are the Distillers Company, formed in 1877, and the Nobel Dynamite Company a year earlier. Originally concentrated in the industrial sector, these super-companies progressively spread throughout industry but did not affect the food trade until later.

With several exhibitions and contracts to their credit, Montague Gluckstein's growing reputation for shrewdness and business ability and Joseph Lyons' imagination, it seemed an opportune time for the company to 'go public' in order to raise capital to greatly expand the business on a large scale. On 24 March 1894 a Special Resolution of Members (effectively Messrs Lyons, Gluckstein and Salmon) confirmed that the 1889 company should be wound up voluntarily and reconstructed using the old company name, J. Lyons & Company. A 'Notice of Consent to Take the Name of a Subsisting Company' – a device under section 20 of the Companies Act 1862 – was the instrument used to achieve this. With share capital of £120,000 (increased to £200,000 in January 1895) the reconstructed company, although trading from 1 April 1894, did not officially register until 10 April 1894. The purchase price of the old company was set at £70,000, half paid in cash and the balance in shares: 8,750 each to Joseph Lyons, Barnett Salmon, Montague Gluckstein and Isidore Gluckstein. Edwin Levy, a businessman of independent means, with printing and stockbroking interests, took up 60,000 shares and was appointed a director for a short period until his untimely death in February 1895. Little is known of him, and, although a substantial shareholder and director, he played no part in the day-to-day administration of the company other than in providing Lyons with printing services including menus, price lists and stationery. Private investors contributed additional capital but it was not until May 1897 that directors made an application to the Committee of the Stock Exchange for an official quotation of the company's shares.

On 11 April 1894 the Lyons board met to appoint bankers (Parr's Banking Company), a

Secretary (George Booth) and a Treasurer – Isidore and Montague Gluckstein's younger brother Joseph, who handed over to the youngest brother, Henry, in 1895 in order to devote more time to the tobacco interests. At the same meeting the board passed a resolution confirming Olympia as the company's head office; it remained so until

shareholders and the 1 per cent to Joseph Lyons. In addition all directors, including Joseph Lyons, were paid 10 per cent of the balance, if any, of net profits remaining after the aforesaid payments. Thus all benefited financially in three separate ways: by the distribution of profit to shareholders, which they were entitled to in their own right;

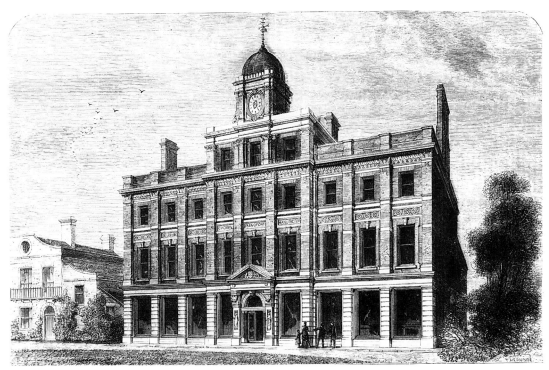

This architectural drawing of 1874 shows the original Cadby Hall piano showrooms built for Charles Cadby to the design of Lewis Isaacs. Much of the building survived as part of Lyons' food factory until it was demolished in 1984.

August, when the administration transferred to the newly acquired premises of Cadby Hall. Within the company's Memorandum and Articles of Association, dated 10 April 1894, the directors had predetermined their remuneration. For his services as Managing Director Joseph Lyons would be paid 1 per cent per annum of the nominal capital of the company after and when 10 per cent on the paid-up capital in any one year had been distributed among the shareholders. The other directors collected 3 per cent each for their services after the 10 per cent had been paid to

by their percentage remuneration (1 and 3 per cent accordingly) of net profits after shareholder distribution; and by their 10 per cent appropriation of outstanding net profit after other disbursements.

In 1873 the piano manufacturer Charles Cadby had bought 8½ acres of the land along High Road (later Hammersmith Road), known as the Croften Estate, where two houses had been demolished. He had been required to vacate his factory and warehouse at 38 Liquorpond Street by the Metropolitan Board of Works for street improvements. With a frontage of over 100 feet towards the Hammersmith Road, Charles Cadby allocated 1½ acres for his new piano factory and showrooms, the remainder being set aside for smaller building plots. Four distinct blocks were built along with showrooms, which were approached by a carriage drive to the entrance porch. Built to the design of Lewis Henry Isaacs, Cadby Hall was faced in red Fareham bricks and Portland stone with terracotta panels over the first floor windows, the keystones of which contained nine carved portraits of celebrated composers. The royal arms decorated the tympanum of the porch with bas-reliefs on the sides of the entrance doorway depicting music and poetry. Above the three floors of showrooms were rooms occupied by the housekeeper. Administration and private offices for use by members of the firm were situated at the rear of the building.

Set back forty feet from the rear of Cadby Hall itself was a five-level factory in which the finer portions of the pianos were crafted and assembled. Behind the factory block was a five-level mill where most of the sawing, planing and heavier tasks associated with piano-making were executed. Towards the rear of the property were additional timber stores, a packing-case shop, stables and a coach-house. The arrangement of buildings had been designed principally with the object of preventing the spread of fire by confining it to one building should such an accident occur. Building costs totalled £26,024, some £824 more than the original quotation, since Cadby decided to have a fifth floor added to the mill block during the building programme.

Charles Cadby died on 22 October 1884 leaving the bulk of his estate to his second wife, Harriet Mary, and eight children (one by his first marriage). He was buried in the same vault as his first wife, Valencia, in Highgate Cemetery. The factory and its stock including 170 pianofortes were sold on Charles Cadby's instructions. Charles Henry Cadby, the oldest male heir, inherited £1,000 (plus a share of the business after its sale) and because he suffered poor health he moved to the warmer climate of South Africa on the advice of his doctor. In 1931 Muriel Cadby,

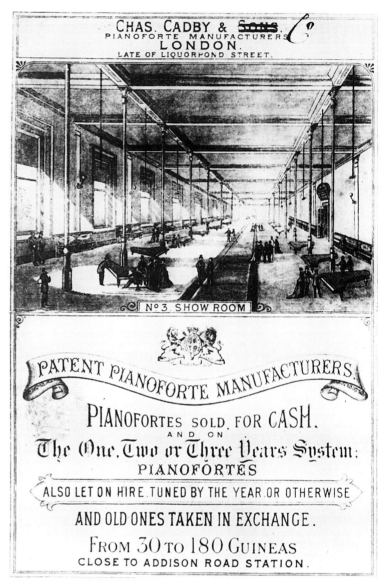

Charles Cadby's advertising brochure illustrating his No. 3 showroom.

Charles Cadby's granddaughter, visited Cadby Hall on her first trip to England to see the former family piano premises.

Between 1886 and 1890 the Cadby Hall estate was occupied by a variety of businesses, and the local rating record shows that by 1890 the building had been taken over by the Kensington Co-operative Stores, who carried out further reconstruction and revived the name of Cadby Hall (which had been dropped during the intervening period). Apparently Kensington Co-operative Stores subdivided the property before

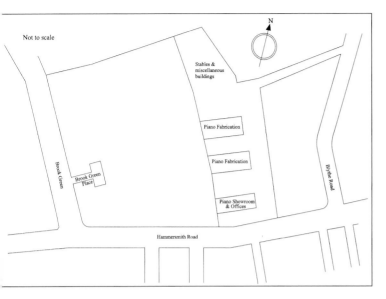

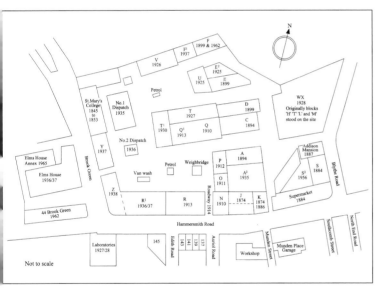

Top. A plan showing the approximate placement of Charles Cadby's buildings when Lyons took occupation. Access was via a narrow entrance onto Blythe Road.

Bottom. This plan gives an indication of how Cadby Hall's factory buildings evolved between 1894–1965. The operations spread to the south side of Hammersmith Road and the whole complex consisted of approximately 13 acres. Building 'J' is Charles Cadby's original piano showrooms.

subletting parts of it to the Schweppes Mineral Water Works until the end of 1893. In July 1894 Lyons discerningly bought two acres of the original Cadby property, including the Cadby Hall showrooms and piano factory blocks behind, for £10,050 – less than half its original cost – from Francis Drake Leslie, receiver and manager for Woodhouse & Rawson United Ltd. Confusingly, the Lyons name appears in the rating records as early as 1 January 1894 as occupying '3rd. block No. 74'. Although there is no evidence to support the view, it is possible that a small block had been bought earlier, in anticipation that Cadby Hall itself would soon be acquired.

Because Schweppes controlled the frontage to Hammersmith Road, access to the old Cadby property was via a narrow roadway at the rear leading into Blythe Road. By 1899, however, Lyons were occupying No. 62 Hammersmith Road and, in agreement with the Kensington Co-operative Stores, built a new entrance on to Hammersmith Road which provided easier access to and from the factories behind. On taking over the premises the directors decided to retain the original name of Cadby Hall, pretentious though this may have sounded for a factory complex. Nevertheless the name became widely known, especially by people in West London. In time it became one of the largest food factories in the country, eventually covering more than thirteen acres.

The nomenclature adopted to identify the factory buildings subsequently occupied and built by Lyons seems idiosyncratic and remains puzzling. Equally bewildering is the sequence of land acquisitions as the business expanded. It started from a central point, the original Cadby Hall, spreading in all directions but mainly along the Hammersmith Road in an east-west direction. Because Lyons occupied the site for over seventy years, old buildings were modified or demolished and new ones erected to accommodate new food-processing mechanisation and to meet increasing consumer demand. Regrettably, no known complete plan or delineation of the factory buildings from 1894 has survived. From available data it appears that the first block brought into use was the original piano-manufacturing block known to Lyons as A Block. It housed the early

bakeries when production moved from Olympia as well as a basement kitchen and a top-floor tea-packing department. The old mill block, forty feet to the north-west and identified as C Block, accommodated a variety of departments. Initially providing storage for the Hire Department, it came to be used for boiling hams and then for clerical staff from the Checking Department in 1896 before they moved to Addison Mansions and eventually Spike House (once the home of Edward Latymer, founder of Latymer School). In 1899 Blocks E and F replaced what is believed to have been B Block, originally used as stables between 1894 and 1899. Cadby Hall itself, the old piano showrooms, became known as J Block and remained largely intact until the factory's demolition in 1983. Its longevity was a tribute to the Victorian builders.

Hand carts and horse-drawn vehicles lined up at Cadby Hall in 1900. The tall chimney in the background is that of the Post Office Savings Bank; its foundation stone was laid on 24 June 1899. The buildings to the right are the directors' offices. The stables are at the far end.

An inspection of the factory in 1904 by Hammersmith Borough Council recorded in their annual report:

Messrs. Joseph Lyons & Company Limited were operating three underground bakehouses. The bakehouse in D block is used for fancy pastry and as a kitchen for outdoor catering. ... The area was ventilated by three windows and there were three tables for making pastry and one long bench. The tables were raised one foot ten inches from the floor, so as to be easily accessible for cleaning under. ... There was a proper covered receptacle for refuse, no animal was found in the bakehouse, there was no coal. The water supply was drawn direct from the rising main. There were two brick ovens and one iron oven.

A teashop opened in 1903 providing an important frontage on to Hammersmith Road at this time. Buildings on the western side of Cadby Hall numbered N, O, P and Q were built in 1910–12 together with the roadway that connected with the old yard in 1914. In 1928 a large factory and dispatch (a central reporting point for loaded vehicles entering or leaving the factory area with goods) with offices above was erected on the northern side of the estate, replacing four earlier blocks known as H, T, L and M. Built to a high standard for factory use and having a large ground-floor dispatch, the new block, numbered WX, became offices for a number of departments as well as the administrative headquarters of the company. This building was the only one identified by two letters, W for the factory part and X for the clerical. In 1928 the original street-level administrative offices, situated in the eastern part of the old Schweppes Mineral Water Works, were demolished to make way for a larger yard and garaging. Buildings belonging to St Mary's Roman Catholic Training

College became part of Cadby Hall in 1925, and one of the two-floor stable blocks nearby was knocked down to make a second road connecting with the main factory estate. Blocks T, U, V, F^1 and T^1 were constructed at this time. R block, which housed the ice-cream department, was built in 1913 and R^1 in 1936–7.

Within twenty-five years of taking over the piano factory and its showrooms, Lyons had progressively acquired properties in the immediate vicinity whenever they came on the market, including shops, private houses and apartments, laundries and in one case a seminary. This allowed for the rapid expansion of the factories as the business grew; and the complete block of land along the Hammersmith Road between Blythe Road and Brook Green (and beyond) soon became one vast heterogeneous manufacturing enclosure where over 30,000 workers toiled 24 hours a day 365 days a year. Some parts of the organisation never closed. No. 219 dispatch (a small clerical office, so called because of its telephone extension number, providing a focal point for urgent and private orders – mainly family) and the telephone exchange, for example, were always manned so that any call from any part of the world could always be taken.

After 1894 the factories at Cadby Hall had been progressively enlarged to satisfy the phenomenal expansion of business in all departments. However, by the end of the First World War there was little scope to extend facilities at Cadby Hall sufficiently to cope with demand, and management's plans for a massive increase in production were threatened. Accordingly a decision was taken to purchase a large piece of land at Greenford in Middlesex, where a new tea and coffee factory was built to alleviate the pressures on Cadby Hall. The factory at Greenford also underwent many extensions, becoming almost as famous as Cadby Hall. Nevertheless, Cadby Hall remained a highly productive unit for cake, bread and ice-cream. At a time when public transport buses employed 'clippies', Cadby Hall was frequently shouted out for those wishing to alight, and the name remained part of West London's local history for many years.

THE RESTAURANT REVOLUTION

SOME ECONOMIC HISTORIES refer to the period 1850–1914 as the Second Industrial Revolution. Associated with it were great advances in scientific knowledge followed by science-based inventions which found their way into manufacturing and agricultural industry. Unfortunately some did not come about without cost. Farmers, who had enjoyed a time of plenty – brought about by advances in mechanisation and fertilisers – suffered a collapse in fortunes in 1878, first through a bad harvest and secondly through cheap imports of grain from North America. During the following ten years, grain prices fell by almost one-third as a direct result of these cheap imports and improvements in farming methods. Coincidentally, the development of refrigeration enabled meat to be imported from Argentina, Australia and New Zealand, further harming British agriculture.

These two events brought about an agricultural depression that encouraged a movement of population from the rural areas to the towns. For manufacturing industry this created a source of low-cost labour at a time when many firms were expanding. Manufacturing also benefited from mechanisation and the standardising of parts, enabling mass production of commodities on a very large scale. The food industry especially gained from these developments, and the Cadby Hall factories took advantage by equipping with large kitchens and automatic baking facilities for the next phase of Lyons' expansion: the supply of food to consumers both directly and through catering outlets.

Between 1887 and 1894 the two private Lyons companies had been almost exclusively involved in contract catering and by 1894 they virtually dominated the main exhibitions and public events. Having consolidated their reputation soon after the Newcastle Exhibition of 1887, they had strengthened their position enormously when several other smaller contracts were won in quick succession. Montague Gluckstein and Joseph Lyons had made names for themselves by paying attention to detail, by planning each operation meticulously and, in particular, by giving good value. No catering function seemed beyond their capability; few organisations, if any, had their expertise, and in less than a decade they became world leaders in mass catering. This must have come as a surprise to some of the Salmon and Gluckstein family members who had earlier expressed their misgivings about forming a catering enterprise at all.

Refreshments for the workers

As the movement of labour from the land to the cities fuelled industrial expansion, during the second half of the nineteenth century a new middle class or, more accurately, a series of social classes developed. With changes in production methods and the emergence of service industries there was rapid growth of white-collar occupations – lower management, clerks, technicians and commercial travellers – and of the female workforce, in factories, offices and shops. In an attempt to escape the shoddy housing conditions of the cities, whose population had swollen through the influx of agricultural workers, many members of the new middle and lower-middle classes began to occupy the suburbs. With the railway network now complete, people could travel, inexpensively, into the cities for both work and shopping – with the consequence that many men and women were away from home for long periods of time. Their need for light refreshment during the day fuelled the increase of shabby, rudimentary restaurants such as those owned by the Aërated Bread Company (ABC), which opened its first teashop in the Strand, London, in 1861.

Foremost among the lower-middle-class restaurants in London in the late nineteenth century were Pearce's Coffee Bars. The founder of the business, John Pearce, had started his working life at the age of nine as an office boy and by nineteen had become a porter in Covent Garden market. While working in the market he hit on the idea of running a coffee stall, and accordingly opened one with capital of £1. Later he and his wife built their own stall which Pearce named 'The Gutter Hotel'. In 1880 he opened a coffee bar in Aldersgate Street in the City after buying a derelict house and setting up there. He handed over this first coffee bar to his brother Joseph in 1883, then opened another branch in Farringdon Street in the same year. His business was advertised as Pearce & Plenty, a name John Pearce later used when he formed a limited company. The aim of Pearce's Coffee Bars was to satisfy the needs of his less well-off customers, who also frequently brought their own food and simply ordered a mug of coffee or cocoa for a halfpenny. Apart from the bare necessities, Pearce did provide a smoking room and free newspapers for his clientele, but the smoky atmosphere deterred most women. Notwithstanding these deficiencies, Pearce's Coffee Bars did serve their purpose and were moderately successful.

Around this time Lockhart's Cocoa-Rooms offered strong competition to Pearce. Lockhart was operating twenty-three rooms in London by 1884, having already made a name for himself in Liverpool, where he had opened sixteen similar outlets. Served from five in the morning until twelve o'clock at night, Lockhart's meals and snacks were more numerous and varied; they included light refreshments such as confectionery – for example, a large cheesecake selling for a penny.

Walter Harris was another less-well-known caterer for the lower classes at this time. A pork sausage manufacturer based in Smithfield, he was operating at least three so-called restaurants as well as two retail shops by the 1890s. His system of management differed from those of Pearce and Lockhart in that he provided no tables at which to sit. There were a few stools, but customers usually had to stand against a narrow ledge, with only enough space to swallow their food quickly before leaving immediately to make room for the next customer. Harris offered little choice, his fare consisting mainly of sausages, pork chops and beefsteaks served every day, with no drink of any kind. Since it cost only 6d. to stand and eat a pork chop, onions and potatoes, Harris obviously saw no need to provide extras.

George Sims, an influential journalist of the day, described London's tea-rooms in the nineteenth century in the *Daily Mail* of 5 October 1921:

> The coffee house had disappeared long before my time, but I have vivid memories of the coffee shops. They were mostly dingy places with high-backed boxes and a slip-shod waiter or an untidy handy girl to attend to your wants.
>
> You might sit in a time-worn, boxed-in compartment, and under a dim gas jet take your cup of tea – it was generally served slopped over into the saucer – and have your hot buttered toast or your muffin, if your means would allow, and glance at a greasy magazine or periodical that had as great a variety of thumb marks as the Scotland Yard collection.
>
> In some of the coffee shops in the midday hours you could get a chop and potatoes, but as a rule the menu was limited to eggs and bacon and the humble bloater.
>
> In the days before the Lyons establishments had sprung up in every part of the Capital it was apparently the

generally held opinion that woman's place was the home, and that was where she should take her meals.

The coffee shops and the eating houses did not cater for her. In one or two of the City houses was a room on the top floor to which a lady being in the City at lunch time, and feeling hungry might climb, and where if she were patient and rang the bell persistently she might eventually get something to eat.

If a woman in those days found herself from home at the hour of tea she might, if she were fortunate, find a pastrycook's shop where she could be 'obliged' in a little back room. But there was no announcement of tea in the window and no suggestion of it on the counter. As a rule the only liquid refreshment displayed on a pastrycook's counter was a glass urn filled with cherry brandy with the cherries in it, and nearby were two decanters, one of sherry and one of port.

Another critical report appeared in *The Caterer and Hotel-Keepers' Gazette* of 15 September 1894 – just five days before Lyons opened their first teashop:

> The now old-fashioned coffee and cocoa houses will really have to improve their style of service and the quality of victuals they sell if they are to keep pace with the more modern cafés. The latter have taught them a good lesson – that people do not mind paying a little more to have their tea and coffee served in good china, and their other beverages in a good quality of glass. The days of the thick granite cup and saucer and the dull, heavy German moulded tumbler are fast being numbered. Education is gradually refining the general public, and caterers must march with the times or be left behind in the race.

The Lyons Teashop Revolution

Against this background Lyons entered the teashop trade. With the experience of exhibition catering behind them and with a large injection of capital, Lyons began what must be acknowledged as their greatest achievement: the creation of their famous teashops. Now that the lower-middle classes were demanding higher standards in catering, Lyons' timing could not have been surpassed. The Aërated Bread Company (ABC), the British Tea Table Company, Lockhart's, Pearce & Plenty and many more had been running teashops and coffee houses for several years – in the case of the ABC for thirty-three years. All seemed to suffer from dull, unimaginative menus, second-rate food, bad presentation and prices which prohibited their widespread use by office workers, the new lower-middle classes.

Having studied the competition, Montague Gluckstein reckoned he could capitalise on his rivals' limitations not only by providing light refreshment facilities to a wider section of the public but at the same time vastly improving their quality and value for money. He passionately believed it was essential that prices be lowered. According to his calculations, if the volume of business could be increased, with rigid financial controls along lines similar to those that had been applied to the Salmon & Gluckstein tobacco firm, then the economies of scale would create the necessary conditions for competitive retail pricing. Expansion, in turn, would generate additional business and the cycle would be self-perpetuating. The essential ingredients, therefore, in Montague Gluckstein's plan turned out to be conformity of pricing – copied from Lockhart's, as it happens – in all Lyons teashops wherever they might be located, and a commitment to giving the public what they wanted. This he perceived to be good temperance fare at economic prices, in attractive surroundings and with a polite and dignified service – factors missing or neglected by other refreshment providers of the period.

The acquisition of a lease on part of Ellam's harness-maker's shop at 213 Piccadilly heralded the first phase of the teashop revolution. Minutes of the company record that Edwin Levy, the printer and stockbroker who was briefly a Lyons shareholder and director, negotiated through

The first teashop at 213 Piccadilly which opened on 20 September 1894. The premises were formerly occupied by a harness-maker. *By kind permission of Waldegrave Films.*

solicitors a price of £35,000 for the lease with an annual rental of £1,000, having first established with the vendors that there would be no objection to carrying on a refreshment business on the premises. The Salmon and Gluckstein families' long experience as tobacco retailers had taught them the importance of shop design and careful siting, ideas carried forward into the teashops' common visual identity. Under Lyons' building surveyor, Charles Wake Oatley, the property was extensively redesigned, both inside and out. On 20 September 1894 it opened as a teashop with a strict temperance policy.

From the very first day it caused a sensation. Queues formed early and customers waited outside on benches thoughtfully provided by the management. At times the crowds became so excited that police attendance was required. On the inside there was no sawdust on the floor – a practice still current in many of the so-called 'slap-bangs' in and around London. Tea, instead of being brewed in the morning and kept hot for much of the day, was freshly made for each customer, yet realistically priced. Contemporary

reports indicate that the public were amazed at the interior décor in the eighteenth-century French style of the Louis XVI period, with red silk-panelled walls and elaborate gas chandeliers. There were marble tables, red plush chairs instead of benches and dainty china. On the outside over the top of the teashop the name of J. Lyons & Co. Ltd was embossed in pure gold leaf on a white background. Although the gold leaf alone cost £15, this design remained virtually unchanged for more than sixty years. Samuel Gluckstein himself had decided to use real gold because he felt it would be too expensive for others to imitate. The letters in the name were individually cut from American white wood and bevelled by hand before priming and gilding. After the name had been assembled on the shop front, an elaborate Victorian swag in the form of a garland of leaves, fruit and ribbons was added to each end. This work took a full week to prepare and the swags too were finished in gold leaf. Later, a duplicate name in pearwood embellished the stall-boards which ran along the bottom of a teashop's main window. The distinctive gold and white appearance became easily recognisable among the drab colours of Victorian London, although London's grime made it necessary to repaint shop fascias and replace the gold leaf every four years.

From the outset management had decided that all food supplied to the teashop, and the others which followed, should be prepared first at Olympia and then at Cadby Hall by their own bakers, chefs and cooks. In this way it only became necessary to employ servers and waiting staff, supervised by a manageress, at the teashops. Some modest cooking facilities were made available at subsequent teashops (for frying eggs, making toast, etc.) and the food delivered from Cadby Hall was kept on hot plates or in ovens while cold food was chilled or kept in refrigerators. Special facilities were installed to provide boiling water for making tea and coffee on site. After Cadby Hall had been acquired in August 1894, and a large kitchen capacity became available, the Cadby Hall kitchens and bakeries prepared all the teashop food which was then distributed by Lyons' own transport system (described in a later chapter). This not only enabled management to economise on labour but also made it easier to maintain hygiene and food standardisation, made efficient use of labour and equipment at Cadby Hall, minimised storage and food-handling equipment in teashops and allowed management to implement simple but sound financial controls (also discussed later in this book).

One of the favourite dishes on the menu was mutton pie, a traditional London delicacy, priced at 7d. At first only two desserts were available, apple tart (hot or cold) and prunes and cream. French pastries, priced from 2d., were introduced to the majority of the working-class public for the first time. Other items on the menu were iced Bovril and soda, egg rissoles and truffled foie gras sausage at 3d. per portion. Customers had a choice of sixty-six items, a far greater selection than offered by competitors. Menus carried the notice: 'In case of incivility or inattention please report giving number of employee (originally worn around the neck as a brooch) to Head Office, Kensington. Postage will be refunded.' After a few months more items were added to the menu including éclairs – a novelty in

London – and the fashionable drove up to order them.

As theatre matinées were fashionable at this period, the Lyons teashop at 213 Piccadilly became a popular rendezvous for many theatrical personalities and quite a number of patrons were carriage customers who arrived with their own equipage. Initially the Piccadilly teashop seated 200 but by the end of the year the remaining part of Ellam's shop became available, enabling seating capacity to be doubled. The day of the office secretary had not yet arrived and the teashop had a greater appeal to the actor and actress (Sir John Martin Harvey, Ada Reeve and Mabel Love are known to have been frequent customers), student or man about town. In the late 1890s most customers were male, with a sprinkling of married women, but by the turn of the century Wednesdays and Saturdays had become 'matinee days', when large numbers of women and children visited the teashop. During the First World War a rapid increase of female labour in offices reversed this trend and it became commonplace for young women to enter such premises unescorted.

Surprisingly, Lyons' plans for teashop expansion did not depend on the success of the Piccadilly, although management must have been confident that it would succeed. Rather than wait to see how it performed, they pressed ahead with preparations for two further 'depots' (the quaint name given to these early establishments in the company accounts). In October and November 1894, Lyons teashops opened at 17 Queen Victoria Street and at 76a Chancery Lane. Adjustments were made as experience indicated aspects that needed improvement. Joseph Lyons and Montague Gluckstein frequently lunched on a little balcony in the Piccadilly teashop where they could observe events below.

In the following year twelve new teashops opened. This must have placed a heavy strain on the Lyons' Estate Department, which had to negotiate purchases of property and lease arrangements. Plans were brought to an abrupt end by 1896, when only one new teashop opened. Overspending on the Trocadero restaurant had brought about a financial crisis, but by 1898 this

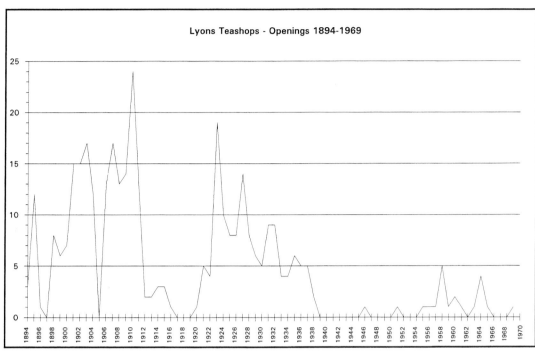

Lyons Teashops - Openings 1894-1969

Peter J Bird. September 1994

This graph dramatically illustrates the growth of teashop openings in the period before the First World War and the inter-war years. In 1910 a new teashop opened approximately every fortnight. Their decline after the Second World War is also obvious.

had passed and the familiar pattern of openings was resumed, with eight in that year. This expansion continued for many years, the most dramatic growth occurring in 1910. Some mistakes were made in siting, and where teashops did not perform to acceptable criteria they were closed. For example, the Chancery Lane teashop, which opened in 1894, closed seven years later. A full list of teashops with their opening and closing dates can be found in Appendix 4.

At the completion of the first trading year J. Lyons & Company Ltd announced a profit of £11,404 6s. 4d., which made it possible to pay a 10 per cent dividend to shareholders. At the first Annual General Meeting held at the *Cannon Street Hotel* on Monday 20 May 1895 the Directors' Report announced:

> During the year the Company has acquired the following seventeen properties for the sale of light refreshments: Piccadilly; Queen Victoria Street; Chancery Lane; Ludgate Circus; Bishopsgate Street; Wallbrook; Budge Row; Aldersgate Street; Chapel Street, Westminster; Oxford Street; Fore Street; Fenchurch Street; Gracechurch Street; Strand; Cheapside; Paternoster Row; St. Paul's Churchyard.

> … Your Directors have the pleasure to inform you that the shops now opened are doing exceedingly well, and they are therefore confirmed in their views that the system of trading introduced by this Company supplies a public want. … Negotiations are in progress for the acquisition of several other premises for the sale of light refreshments. …

> In addition to the retail refreshment businesses, various other sources of revenue exist. The Company has just undertaken the house-to-house supply of Bread manufactured by the Company, which the Directors believe will result in a valuable addition to the Company's income, and it has the honour of supplying bread to many of the Royal households.

Teashop Expansion

In just ten years Lyons established themselves as one of the major restaurateurs in the capital and made good progress in some provincial cities. This success is extraordinary, given that many other restaurant operators were and had for many years been in direct competition. Of course Lyons were by no means the inventors of teashops, which had grown slowly out of the coffee houses. In 1894 Lockhart's, Pearce & Plenty, ABC and the Spiers & Pond chain were well entrenched in London, but Lyons appeared to have the necessary capital to develop a unique style of teashop where prices were standardised and where good food was served by smart waitresses in pleasant, hygienic surroundings. This combination was lacking in some other teashop chains which struggled to bring their premises up to the standards of Lyons, who remained always one step ahead.

By the turn of the century thirty-seven Lyons teashops had been opened in London. Fifteen more teashops opened in Liverpool (4), Manchester (6), Leeds (2), Sheffield (2) and Bradford (1) when Lyons acquired the interests of the Ceylon Café Company Ltd in 1909. Under the management of Jack Joseph, who subsequently joined Lyons as a director, the new acquisition produced a rapid expansion of trade in the north of England. The two great periods of teashop expansion were 1905–12 and 1920–30, reaching a peak in 1910, when no fewer than twenty-four new teashops opened, nineteen in London and one each in Southport, Birmingham, Nottingham, Liverpool and Brighton. During this time Lyons teashops became especially popular with working women, who found that the atmosphere suited them admirably. Some competing businesses such as Lockhart's and Pearce & Plenty, whose trade had been built around 'working-class' breakfasts and dinners, were increasingly challenged by the variety and excellence of lunchtime choices offered by Lyons. Lady Angela Forbes, writing in the *Daily Mail* of 5 October 1921, observed:

> To-day the Lyons teashop is everywhere. For the business girl, not only in the City but in every part of London, the nearest teashop is not far away. The girls who crowd into the teashops at midday no longer need the protection of a room reserved for their sex alone. They share a table with men as naturally as they take a seat – or a strap – in tram and tube.
>
> Nothing, perhaps, has had a greater influence towards the sensible and natural intermingling of the sexes than the management – the revolutionary management, as it was once regarded – of the Lyons teashop.
>
> Men have formed the habit of sharing the teashop with the women for whom it was originated. They have broken away from the bad old tradition that a man's restaurant must of necessity be a public-house into the bargain, and the change has done them good. From every point of view, and most emphatically from a woman's, London has changed for the better during the past 25 years; in that metamorphosis the teashops have played a meritorious part.

Appropriately enough, Lyons also acted as midwife to the best-selling book *Married Love*, written by the birth control pioneer Marie Stopes. As her biographer June Rose records in *Marie Stopes and the Sexual Revolution* (1992), no major publisher was willing to risk printing this controversial work. A small firm was interested but required financial backing. One of Stopes's supporters, Dr Binnie Dunlop, had found a prospective backer – a flying officer and former aircraft manufacturer, Humphrey Roe. Dr Dunlop invited both Marie Stopes and Humphrey Roe to lunch at the Lyons teashop at 213 Piccadilly on 6 February 1918. 'Humphrey had pictured Marie as a stout German *Frau*. … He met, instead, a youthful woman with softly waved chestnut hair, luminous eyes, immensely alive, dressed in flowing feminine clothes. She saw a tall, handsome officer in khaki in the uniform of the Royal Flying Corps.' That evening Humphrey Roe wrote a letter which began, 'Dear Dr Stopes, I am very glad indeed you have allowed me to take a hand in publishing your book, it is very good of you' – and sent a cheque for £200. Marie and Humphrey were married three months later, in May 1918, and *Married Love* was published that spring.

Lyons Waitresses

When the Piccadilly teashop opened in 1894 twenty-six young women, supervised by the twenty-seven-year-old manageress Maria Davies, were taken on as waitresses. As there was an initial seating capacity of 200, each waitress became responsible for approximately eight customers, a standard used for all Lyons' banqueting and catering events. At that time waitresses were selected for their poise and deportment as much as for their waiting talents, and apparently all were unmarried and in their late teens or twenties. Originally, any women with waists measuring more than seventeen inches failed in their applications for employment as waitresses, but these anatomical requirements soon collapsed when insufficient numbers of 'correctly' shaped girls could be found. Tall women were also preferred and the first waitresses were chosen by stature as well as by appearance and efficiency. As the first recruits were all young and single, it was customary for their father or brothers to wait outside the teashop at closing time to conduct them safely to their homes.

All waiting staff received complete outfits comprising dresses, aprons, cuffs, collars, caps, head-dresses, brooches, chatelaines, ribbons for caps and hat-pins. The dresses at the time were extremely expensive and made from estamin, a worsted cloth of coarse, loosely woven yarn with a short nap; the material cost 2s. 2d. a yard. Parisian costumiers made hundreds of dresses for Lyons under a special contract until Lyons established their own dressmaking department a few years later. Each waitress's issue amounted to four dresses a year and the complete outfitting cost £15 a year plus £5 towards cleaning and repairs. Lyons had decided to control laundering costs themselves to ensure cleanliness, tidiness and uniformity. As one manageress put it at the time:

> We have to supply our customers with food instead of coals, we are bound to have all our waitresses look as clean and fresh as newly-gathered flowers. The Company, therefore, arranged to pay one half of the cost of each girl's washing, and

This early sketch of an 1895 Lyons waitress was mailed to Lyons in 1934. It clearly shows a crescent and star emblem on the front bib. No original photographic or documentary evidence has survived to confirm this early uniform design but it is unlikely to be artistic licence.

Many teashops, particularly those situated in London's finance and business centres, had a masculine club-like atmosphere. Dominoes, draughts, newspapers and magazines were made freely available to customers occupying the smoking room as businessmen and merchants had done in the coffee house era. In Lyons' Hatton Garden teashop, for example, jewellers would congregate; in Cannon Street the furriers; in Bishopsgate the bankers; and in Fleet Street the newspaper journalists and writers. Lyons teashops soon became a British institution: there was hardly a high street in Greater London without one; at one time no fewer than nine traded concurrently in London's Oxford Street alone. Teashops soon became known as 'Joes', after Joseph Lyons, and this endearing name now seems to have entered our language as a term for a restaurant or café specialising in light refreshments.

this proposal was hailed with delight by all because the frilling on the aprons, collars, cuffs and head-dresses were, and are, expensive and difficult to do up.

Clothed in their high-necked, ankle-length, dark grey dresses, early teashop waitresses, for reasons lost in time, became known as 'Gladys'. Over their boned bodices they wore an apron consisting of a heart-shaped bib with a continuation piece extending down to the bottom hem of the dress. Paintings of some early designs bewilderingly show that a star and crescent symbol was originally embroidered on the bib front but this embellishment had been discontinued by May 1895. From time to time modifications were made including the replacement of the worsted cloth in 1897 with a slightly shorter cashmere dress which incorporated a bib apron fastened at the shoulders, then in 1916 a waist apron with wide straps over the shoulders. Since Lyons was operating fifteen teashops by the end of 1895, waitresses' uniforms alone had cost nearly £6,000.

Working hours for waiting staff were long – often seventy-four hours per week. The recognised method of payment for the catering trades in the 1890s was the commission system, and at first Lyons saw no justification for changing this practice. Lyons waitresses received 5 per cent commission plus any gratuities the customers felt inclined to leave. As a consequence they were totally dependent for their living on the measure of business done and on customers' generosity in giving tips. On the one hand, if teashop trade prospered, then waitresses would benefit by getting more commissional take-home pay, with a corresponding loss of revenue to the company. Poor trade resulted in less take-home pay. Since Lyons teashops were a spectacular success, waiting staff tended to receive good take-home pay. Staff turnover nevertheless remained high. This was probably due to the long hours standing or walking, and the stern working conditions which included the occasional use of 3d. fines against staff who were persistently late for work. On average waitresses earned 30 shillings per week (more than some family incomes at that time) made up of 12 shillings commission plus 18

Right. Waitresses dressed in replica costumes of 1894. Any evidence of the crescent and star, if it ever existed, has been omitted here.

Below. Nell Bacon, the most famous of all Lyons' waitresses, posing with a customer in the Piccadilly teashop in 1897. A more modern bib has replaced the original heart-shaped version but the dress is still ankle length.

Below. The dress-making department where all waitresses uniforms were made while they underwent training. Seen here at Orchard House in about 1952.

shillings in tips. Since each woman's laundry expenses amounted to 3s. 5d. per week, the company deducted 1s. 9d. from their earnings.

In October 1895, perhaps simply to maximise profits, Lyons decided to reduce waitresses' commission from 5 to 2.5 per cent. The new rates appear to have been introduced furtively: individual waitresses were dismissed, for the slightest misdemeanour, and their replacements were immediately recruited at the lower rate of commission. When challenged by staff, management explained that new waitresses would be recruited on 2.5 per cent commission, graduating to 5 per cent as they became proficient. In this way management had hoped to prevent staff from leaving before completing their training period. Whatever Lyons' excuses for the reduction in pay, the waiting staff at the Piccadilly and Strand teashops withdrew their labour on 23 October 1895 and held a meeting in the St Andrew's restaurant in St Andrew Street, to plan tactics. Present at the meeting was the trade-unionist Tom Mann, one of the leaders of the great London dock strike of 1889. Tom Mann suggested that a deputation should be formed to go to see Alfred Salmon, and it was then decided to ask him if he would take them back on the old terms of 5 per cent commission. A prominent feature of the dispute was the part played by the newspaper industry. Under the slogan 'The Lyons and the Lambs' many talented writers took up the waitresses' cause. When the resulting publicity began to damage Lyons' reputation, the company responded after a few days by introducing salaries and abolishing the commission system for good. The changes were introduced on 11 November 1895 and at the same time the directors decreed that the grey dresses hitherto worn by waitresses would be changed to black ones.

Although this was seen by some staff as a positive concession, in fact take-home pay was drastically reduced, equating with a 2.5 per cent commission had it been retained. Other staff regarded it as a defeat, even though their take-home pay would be guaranteed rather than being dependent on business done and the goodwill of customers. In reality the new pay structure made earnings dependent on the numbers of staff employed in each teashop, with a sliding scale from 10 to 15 shillings per week. For example, in teashops employing ten staff, 50 per cent would be earning 10 shillings per week, 40 per cent 12s. 6d. and 10 per cent earning 15 shillings. In teashops employing twice that number, again only 10 per cent would be paid 15 shillings a week, but 45 per cent would receive 12s. 6d. and the remaining 45 per cent 10 shillings. Such a system aimed to encourage staff to stay longer in order to benefit from promotion and the higher levels of salary that brought. (See Appendix 1 for a complete analysis.) Customer tipping was discouraged: all teashops had 'No Gratuities' signs painted on entrance doors to reinforce this. Of course the company had no power to stop customers from tipping if they so desired, but they did insist that any gratuities be placed in a 'Provident Fund Box'. These funds were to be spent on employees in such manner as the directors might from time to time think best, the principal object being to give relief in cases of sickness. As a gesture of goodwill, the company contributed a starting float of £11 to all Provident Fund Boxes. In 1899 they set up a Provident Fund whereby employees could contribute 8d. per week in return for monetary benefits in the event of their sickness or death. The scheme continued up to the start of the Second World War, when it had over 1,000 members.

A Life in Lyons Management

Alice Eleanor Bacon – known throughout her career as Nell – took up employment at the Piccadilly teashop in 1897 and remained associated with Lyons for more than 60 years. This is thought to be a record unbroken period of service within the company for a female employee. The longest-serving male employee is believed to have been George Seaton, who started in the Checking Department in 1902 and worked until his death in 1976, a period of seventy-four years.

The youngest of three sisters (Flora, Lillian and Alice), Nell was born in the *Butcher's Arms*, a fifteenth-century inn, in the Suffolk village of Nayland on 18 November 1879. Her father, James

Bacon, who had converted his butcher's shop to an inn, had been landlord before he contracted smallpox from one of the overnight guests and died at an early age, leaving the family almost destitute. At seventeen years of age Nell Bacon travelled to London with her sister Lillian for Queen Victoria's Diamond Jubilee celebrations; the first time either of them had been on a railway journey. During this visit they both successfully applied to become temporary waitresses at the Piccadilly teashop, taking up their appointments on 31 May 1897. Both were attractive, hard-working young women and were taken on to the permanent staff. Nell's country charm and Suffolk accent endeared her to many, and her tables at the teashop were the most popular. Meanwhile Lillian married Edwin Jones, a teashop inspector, and afterwards resigned her position.

Nell, on the other hand, quickly progressed to become a teashop manageress in 1903 and chief superintendent of all teashop staff in 1909. On 25 November 1922, at the age of forty-three, she secretly married the divorcee Frank Andrew, a jeweller's manager. Nell Bacon was reticent about her private life and few people within Lyons knew of her marriage. This was not entirely for personal reasons but through a desire not to draw unnecessary attention to her changed status, since management attitudes then were less tolerant to career women than today. There were no children of the marriage (Frank Andrew had two daughters from his former marriage) and Nell Bacon continued to work. Insisting on high standards within the teashop administration, she expected obedience from her subordinates. She was well respected by both management and staff but did not suffer fools gladly. There is no doubt, however, that her management proficiency played a significant part in the Lyons teashop success story.

After the two Bacon sisters had gone to London, the eldest sister, Flora, travelled to Finchampstead, Berkshire, where she worked for a friend who was landlord of the Greyhound public house in the village. Flora Bacon subsequently married Fred Goswell and they had two daughters, Marjorie and Nellie. Nellie Goswell herself took a job as a Lyons waitress in 1927 and became the manageress of the Guildford teashop some time later. She retired in 1945 to marry Graystone Bird, a widower and professional photographer from Bath. They lived in a thatched cottage in Finchampstead and Nellie ran her parents' village shop next door. Nell Bacon visited her niece frequently, travelling down from London in her chauffeur-driven car. On these occasions, as Nellie Bird recalled, there was always something special for tea, while the driver was sent to the local pub to fend for himself. She remembers Nell Bacon as strong and austere, with rigid Victorian discipline, although with warm qualities, but Nellie was always glad when her aunt had left.

During her employment with Lyons, Nell Bacon was responsible for more than 10,000 staff at any one time and over half a million waitresses passed through her charge. She occupied a company flat over the teashop in Streatham High Road, where for a while she employed her mother (Alice née Eagle, who lived for ninety-two years) as housekeeper. She died on 28 June 1961.

As Nell Bacon's career progressed and the teashops became increasingly popular with Londoners, restaurants of another kind were developing. Of more lavish design, these establishments were characterised by their sumptuous interiors and high-class cuisine.

The Trocadero Restaurant

Shortly after the opening of the first teashop, Lyons embarked on a hugely ambitious project to build a restaurant rivalling anything in the country. In October 1894 the company bought, by private treaty, a property near Piccadilly Circus on the corner of Shaftesbury Avenue and Great Windmill Street for £4,750, having first successfully extended the lease from nineteen to ninety-nine years. This was the first stage of an exceptionally shrewd property investment, for in 1917 an adjacent 35,000-sq. ft. property known as the Arundel Estate was purchased for a record price of £250,000, allowing the two to be linked. The freehold for the original Trocadero property became available in 1921 from the Commissioners of Crown Lands, and when in 1967 Lyons disposed of its interests in the site, which by then included the Coventry Street Corner House, the

whole property realised £7.4 million.

The first reference to the Trocadero's site can be found in Lord Clarendon's *History of the Rebellion*, published posthumously in 1704. Situated in Windmill Street and before the construction of Shaftesbury Avenue, the place had a chequered history, being used variously as a tennis court and a circus until about 1832, when it became known as the Royal Albion Theatre. Between 1833 and 1846 it became in turn the New Queen's Theatre, then the Theatre of the Arts, the Royal Albion Subscription Theatre, Dubourg's Theatre of Arts and the Ancient Hall of Rome, throughout this time functioning as a subscription club to avoid infringing the theatre licensing laws. The property eventually came under the proprietorship of Robert Bignell, a wine merchant, who opened it under the name of the Argyll Rooms for music and dancing in the 1870s. Close to Laurents's Dancing Academy, the Argyll Rooms became famous for their masquerade balls attracting both the nobility and the *demi-monde* of the period. Since it was considered rather vulgar to dance, the more aristocratic clients loitered in the gallery above, observing the antics of those below. On one occasion it was reported that Lord Hastings provided a memorable evening by emptying a sack of rats on to the dance-floor among the whirling crinolines of the respectable and not so respectable ladies. Because of the Argyll Rooms' growing notoriety, however, Bignell's licence was not renewed, and the place was closed in 1878. Hugh Didcott and Albert Chevalier, singer and songwriter, then reopened it as a music hall under the various names of the Trocadero Palace, the Royal Trocadero and the Eden Theatre, then simply the Trocadero. Some time between 1883 and 1891 the lease became available again and the Trocadero came into the ownership of Samuel Adams until 1894, when Lyons acquired it.

The building of the Trocadero restaurant almost bankrupted Lyons before it had properly established itself. Because of unsound professional advice the building took much longer to construct than anticipated and costs spiralled out of control. After a few months of construction, independent experts advised that an extra £100,000 would be necessary to complete the job. This almost quadrupled the original estimate. Considering the Albert Hall had cost only £200,000 to build in 1870, the Trocadero project had clearly run out of control, and the consequences of overspending were disastrous. So serious was the burden of expenditure that no shareholder dividend was allocated in 1896 and, as has been noted, only one teashop opened between September 1895 and February 1898 compared with twelve during 1895 and eight in 1898. As the financial crisis of 1895–6 deepened, it became clear that the astronomical building costs for the project could not be met from company earnings. After Lyons' predicament had been explained to the shareholder and director Edwin Levy, he agreed to take up debenture stock to enable construction work to continue, but in February 1895 he died suddenly of heart failure at his West Hampstead home before the legal financial arrangement could be completed. Since he had died intestate, his estate, amounting to £261,578, was eventually granted to his widow, Marion, and the company directors had no alternative but to call an Extraordinary General Meeting of shareholders to discuss the financial plight.

The meeting was held in the incomplete Grill Room among a mass of iron girders and bricks. Montague Gluckstein later remarked that 'there was uproar when the need for further capital was explained to them but after a time, much to my surprise, I was able to soothe them.' The grumbling shareholders, however, subscribed only £100 towards the £100,000 needed to complete the work, leaving Montague Gluckstein the task of securing a loan. With the co-operation of other members of his family and Joseph Lyons, he managed to raise £63,200, allowing the main work to proceed. Perhaps some shareholders may later have felt they had missed an opportunity, since the restaurant subsequently became one of the finest and best-known in the world.

Having been pushed to the brink of bankruptcy, Montague Gluckstein took a firm stance against the architects and builders alike, establishing a building committee to monitor contractors' costs and schedules. Further funding

A CORNER IN THE GRAND SALOON.

did become necessary, despite the controls, but by 5 October 1896 the first phase had been completed and the Trocadero restaurant opened to a blaze of glory.

Thousands gathered at Piccadilly Circus to watch the fireworks display and to spot the many celebrities arriving for the inaugural dinner. A total of 399 guests sat down to a ten-course meal consisting of oysters, hors-d'oeuvre, fish, saddle of lamb, game, two roasts, sweets, savouries and five wines, ending with nuts and brandy. Joseph Lyons himself presided, with the former Lord Mayor of London beside him. Among the diners were many of the best-known figures of Victorian society including a naval officer called John Rushworth Jellicoe, who eventually became First

A pen and ink drawing of the Trocadero Restaurant's Grand Saloon as it appeared in the *Penny Illustrated Newspaper* of 1896.

This photograph, of the foyer of the Trocadero Restaurant, clearly shows the lavish splendour of an age now past. The murals depict scenes from King Arthur.

Sea Lord at the Admiralty during the First World War. Other celebrities included Sir Hiram Maxim, inventor of the singled-barrelled water-cooled quick-firing machine-gun, and the famous cartoonist Phil May. On the opening night, Katherine (Katie) Christian of the D'Oyly Carte Opera Company, who was sister to Joseph Lyons' wife Psyche, sang the National Anthem at the opening ceremony – a custom followed each night thereafter at closing time. For a period subsequently, the uniformed Band of the Scots Guards played from the balcony, much to the delight of the clientele, and music became a main attraction at the Trocadero.

In the style of Louis XIV, the restaurant was decorated in red with a gilt balcony, where the band played. The height of the cream-and-gold ceiling provided the necessary ventilation in the days before air conditioning. Electric lighting, only just becoming available, had been chosen by the architects in preference to gas. Brocades and silks decorated the walls and panels, floors were tessellated and there was an abundance of Moroccan leather chairs. Waiters wore gold-braided collars and sported side whiskers. Curry was served by Indian waiters dressed in traditional costumes, and a waiter with fez and bolero jacket served Turkish coffee. The famous Long Bar, with its variegated marbles in the neo-classical style, opened in 1901. It was a strictly male preserve, and its visitors' book, first instituted at the request of overseas visitors so they could trace friends with whom they had lost touch, bore addresses ranging from Tooting Bec to British Guyana, Waziristan, Fiji and the French Cameroons. In December 1937 it changed its name to the Salted Almond cocktail bar, where women were welcome. During the two world wars it was a rendezvous for British and Allied officers, some of whom must have said hopefully: 'Meet you in the Long Bar ...'.

Situated below the main restaurant was the Grill Room, decorated in the style of the Flemish Renaissance and approached by a staircase built over a staircase, the original being too steep and impracticable to remove. Off the Grill Room were billiards, smoking and reading rooms. From the ground floor a grand marble staircase led to the Empire Room, used for banqueting, and where several other ante-rooms and private suites were situated. The grand staircase gave an air of elegance, luxury and respectability, an atmosphere that Lyons strove to create in many of the subsequent restaurants and buildings the company designed and erected.

In 1896 and for several years afterwards, a nine-course meal at the Trocadero, with sorbet in the middle, cost half a guinea, but lunch was 3 shillings and less expensive dinners could be obtained for 5 shillings and 7s. 6d. Apart from the table d'hôte, diners could choose from an à la carte menu containing a couple of dozen hors d'oeuvres, at least a dozen soups and numerous entrées, roasts, entremets, pastries, savouries and desserts. Another feature of the Trocadero was the telephone dinner whereby customers could place their order by telephone, for a given time, perhaps specifying the price they were prepared to spend. Alternatively they could give a general idea of the meal they required leaving the details to be decided by the *maître d'hôtel*. For example, customers could order a dinner for 12s. 6d. per head, specifying partridges and a Japanese salad and leaving the rest to be chosen by the *maître d'hôtel*. Trocadero prices remained unchanged for many years, since management were reluctant to increase them, even though the rise in the cost of raw materials would have justified higher prices. Later, when overheads increased – brought about by the high cost of entertainment – the

policy of price fixing became detrimental to profits.

The concert tea also had its beginnings at the Trocadero. During the First World War the banqueting rooms were under-utilised, and in 1916 tea was served for the first time in the Empire Hall along with a full concert programme. It was not long before fashionable London realised that with its music, its delightful teas, and the pleasant atmosphere the Empire Hall held attractions that were too good to miss. Indeed the Trocadero's concert teas became so popular they were soon copied by many other hotels and restaurants across London.

In the mid-1920s cabaret was introduced and continued every night until the start of the Second World War. Marjorie Robertson, later known as Dame Anna Neagle, started her career as a dancer at the Trocadero in 1926 when she joined one of Charles Blake Cochran's late-night cabarets, called *Supper Time*, in the Grill Room. *Supper Time* later merged into *Merry-go-Round* and then into *Champagne Time*. In all she spent three years at the Trocadero between 1926–9. Cochran, a leading theatrical impresario of his time, presented many successful shows there during the 1920s including a midnight performance of Delibes' ballet *Coppélia* in 1924.

The restaurant's international chefs were famed for their talents and the wine cellar, supplied from Lyons' own wine premises in Regent Street (until 1905 under St Philip's Chapel until it had to be vacated under authority of an

XMAS NIGHT
Gala
DINNER DANCE
(from 7.30 p.m.)
Dancing to 12 midnight
ONE GUINEA

NEW
In the
EMPIRE HALL :
DINUIT *with* MAURI
(from 9 p.m.)
Dancing to 2.30 a.m.
TWO GUINEAS
Dancing — Surpris
TROC
J. Lyons & Co. Ltd.

A typical Art Deco-style menu cover of the 1930s. Talented graphic artists were used for this stylistic work of the period. Beevor's name is associated with many of Lyons' menu covers.

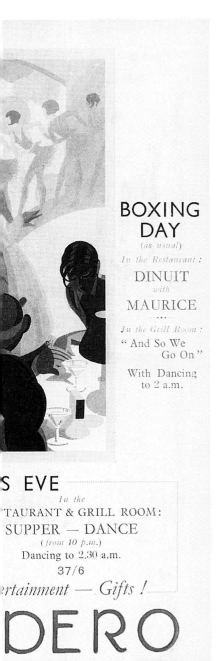

BOXING
DAY
(as usual)
In the Restaurant :
DINUIT
with
MAURICE
...
In the Grill Room :
" And So We
Go On "
With Dancing
to 2 a.m.

S EVE
In the
TAURANT & GRILL ROOM :
SUPPER — DANCE
(from 10 p.m.)
Dancing to 2.30 a.m.
37/6

rtainment — Gifts !

DERO
Proprietors

Act of Parliament obtained by the Ecclesiastical Commissioners) and Southwark Street, was equipped to please the most exacting tastes. The 1920 wine list had no fewer than 560 varieties and none had spurious labels. So much wine was consumed at the Trocadero, and the other Lyons restaurants and hotels that developed, that it became necessary to employ a full-time buyer who regularly travelled to France to secure huge quantities of the best vintages. During the years 1895–1916, Lyons purchased, among others, the entire output of Château Belair St Emilion. As to price, in 1921 an excellent Château Lafite of 1906 vintage cost 14s. 6d. The Château Mouton Rothschild 1905 was marginally cheaper at 14 shillings. The Trocadero became the home of the gourmet, and a journalist of the period observed:

Go into the Trocadero any evening or night! Guests are waiting for one another in the comfortable, well-furnished hall; you can book your box or stalls at the theatre or music hall; flowers are prepared to decorate button holes or charming dresses; you can dine with music or without, richly or plainly, and with the ease and grace of those invited to a country house or London mansion. Up the grand staircase you are escorted by liveried servants to the balconies, the private rooms, the special dinners, the

Masonic banquets and to various friendly gatherings of guests, often followed by a concert or ball.

The Trocadero restaurant set new standards in catering. It became a popular topic of conversation for London's Victorian and Edwardian glitterati and attracted the most discerning customers from home and abroad. Here, women could take luncheon alone without having to leave the country afterwards! Children too were welcomed and 'bribed' with little gifts, many of them returning as adults with their own children – the gifts being a clever form of long-term investment. One of the restaurant's most sparkling nights, according to Francis Maltby (one-time page-boy at the Trocadero), was in May 1900, 'when London went riotously mad and the Trocadero was packed with the gayest, smartest throng the West End had ever seen and many beautiful women gathered him in their arms and kissed him soundly, whispering in his ear, "Darling boy, isn't it wonderful. Mafeking has been relieved."' News of the relief of Mafeking, besieged during the Boer War, had been announced from the restaurant's balcony by Joseph Lyons himself, who frequently entertained friends and business acquaintances in the main restaurant.

From the very first year the Trocadero made a profit of £200 per week, increasing to £800 by the turn of the century – nearly twice as much as all the teashops put together and a third of Lyons' profits – but by the 1930s its revenues declined, for reasons already explained, despite its continuing popularity. Uniquely placed, at what many believed to be the hub of the British Empire, it was used from 1896 to 1962 as the venue for the shareholders' Annual General Meetings, during which they were frequently reminded by the Chairman to use its facilities for their own business or private entertaining needs.

The Trocadero closed on 13 February 1965 but before Lyons disposed of the entire site (which included the Coventry Street Corner House) they leased it for two years in two separate blocks. For many years the future of the island site occupied the attention of Walter Davies (town planning manager, Lyons' Estate Department) and other professional advisers, who eventually put forward outline plans for a 1,000-room hotel. However, management were undecided on the vast project. Some felt it would undermine the takings at the Regent Palace Hotel on the other side of Piccadilly Circus. There was also some uncertainty about the whole redevelopment of the area by Westminster Council. These doubts led to the sale of the entire property in 1967 to the Electricity Supply Nominees Ltd, the Pension Fund Trustees of the electricity supply industry.

The Throgmorton Restaurant

Meanwhile Lyons had been opening other upmarket restaurants. In 1897, against intense competition from the British Tea Table Company and others, Lyons secured an eighty-year building lease in Throgmorton Street in the City of London from the Worshipful Company of Drapers. This was achieved largely through the services of Sir Henry Isaacs (1830–1909), who had had been a co-director of Salmon & Gluckstein Ltd but, more importantly, was a member of the Corporation of London, a former alderman, Sheriff of London and Lord Mayor. With these credentials he managed to acquire for Lyons the Drapers' Company property for a ground rental of £8,000 per annum. Situated in a most prestigious position, at the heart of London's financial centre, the property had a frontage of 115 feet and faced the London Stock Exchange on the opposite side of the street. Reporting to shareholders in 1898, Lyons announced it intended building another high-class restaurant as well as providing 'capacious light refreshments and handsome suites of offices which would provide additional earning power for the company'. In the proceedings of the Eleventh Ordinary Meeting of the company, held at the Trocadero restaurant on 6 June 1905, Joseph Lyons was able to announce that the rental from the offices not only paid for the entire ground rent but also yielded a reasonable interest on the cost of building.

Construction work was carried out day and night, at a cost of some £30,000. On 15 October 1900 the Throgmorton restaurant opened. Enjoying the same location as the coffee shops of an earlier era, the restaurant partly contributed to the demise of London's so-called chop-houses with their dirty kitchens, cracked china, discoloured pewter and cubicles resembling horse-boxes. The Throgmorton's main dining areas, which were mostly below street level, the Grill Room being 40 feet below ground, were fitted out with oak panelling and expensive furnishings, and the restaurant became highly popular with businessmen, who sometimes used the Oak Room for dinners, smoking concerts and private evening soirées. Unusually, among the items on one of its menus was a starched linen napkin priced at one penny. Management must have felt that customers would be prepared to pay to protect their expensive pinstripe trousers and tailcoats, which were widely worn by the bankers and stockbrokers.

The *Building News* of 1900 described the Throgmorton restaurant as 'providing first-class refreshments, dinners, &c., on a very complete scale, built, lighted, ventilated, and drained entirely below the level of the street'. It continued:

> Entering from Throgmorton-street through a spacious lobby, we descend by a marble staircase, lined with gold mosaic, semicircular in shape, or by a lift, to the level of a large handsome restaurant adorned with oak panelling, marbles, a decorative frieze and ceiling, and paved with mosaic. ...The coloured modelled frieze in low relief depicts an old German story – the Legend of the Magic Ring ... Beyond this apartment we enter the dining-room ... its marble-lined walls of Devonshire spar with coupled pilasters of verde antique, with bronze Ionic capitals and frieze and rich red marble dado. Bevelled mirrors, enclosed in the marble background ... adorn each bay of this room, and give it a brilliant appearance.

An area called the saloon, which was used for private dinners and other functions, was 'an oak-panelled and handsome apartment'. The verdict of *Building News* was that 'for complete-

A menu from the Throgmorton Café for 4 July 1927. Note the price of a serviette under the heading 'Sundries'.

J Lyons & Co. Ltd. Proprietors.

THE Throgmorton Café

Caterers by Appointment to H.M. The King.

Menu

SOUPS

| Tomato.. | .. | .. | .. | .. | 6d |
| Consommé Villageoise | | | .. | .. | 6d |

FISH

Fried Fish Croquette and Sauce	..	5d
Whitebait and Lemon	..	10d
Grilled Herrings, Mustard Sauce	..	1/-
Fresh Haddock, Parsley Sauce	..	1/2
Fried Fillets of Fish ..	..	1/2
Fried Sole and Lemon..	..	1/9
Boiled Salmon, Cucumber,		
Hollandaise Sauce	1/9

COLD

Fish Mayonnaise	..	..	1/-
Fried Fillet of Fish, Tartare Sauce	1/4
Salmon & Cucumber, Mayonnaise Sce	1/9
Mayonnaise of Salmon	..	1/9

EGGS

Poached Egg on Spaghetti	..	8d
Curried Eggs ..	..	1/1
Eggs Berey	..	1/6
Scrambled Eggs on Toast	..	1/3
Omelette, Plain	..	1/4
„ Fines Herbes	..	1/5
„ Cheese	..	1/7
„ Jam..	..	1/7
„ Ham	..	1/8
„ Tomato	..	1/8

ENTRÉES

Steak and Kidney Pudding	..	8d
Curried Mutton and Rice	..	9d
Chicken & Veal Cutlet Milanaise	10d
Braised Sweetbreads and Peas	..	1/1
Braised Beef Niçoise ..	..	1/1
Chicken poêlée Demidoff	..	2/4

VEGETABLES

Cabbage	..	..	..	3d
Macaroni and Tomato Sauce ..	..	4d
Spinach..	..	..	5d
Cauliflower au Gratin	..	6d
New Peas	..	..	6d
Fried Potatoes ..	..	4d
New „	..	5d

HOT JOINT

| Roast Beef and Yorkshire Pudding | .. | 11d |
| Horseradish Sauce | .. | 2d |

BRAND'S "A1" SAUCE

COLD BUFFET

Egg Mayonnaise	..	..	..	8d
Tongue ..	..	..	..	10d
Ham ..	..	..	..	10d
Roast Beef	..	..	..	10d
Pressed Beef	..	..	..	10d
Veal and Ham Pie	..	..	11d
Tongue and Ham	..	..	1/-

SALAD

Beetroot	..	..	..	4d
Lettuce ..	..	4d	Potato	..	4d
French ..	..	6d	Tomato	..	6d
Cucumber	..	..	..	6d

GRILLS

Tomatoes	..	..	..	6d
Mutton Cutlet ..	..	..	8d
Bacon (two Rashers) ..	..	9d
Sausage..	..	(1) 5d	..	(2) 10d
Loin Chop	..	..	1/-
Chump Chop	..	..	1/-
Rump Steak	..	..	1/1
Kidneys	..	(1) 7d	..	(2) 1/2
Kidneys on Toast (2) ..	..	1/5
Mushrooms	..	..	1/6
Fillet Steak	..	..	1/7
Mixed Grill :—Kidney, Sausage,		
Tomato and Cutlet	1/9

Early Morning Coffee
served in the
LONG ROOM
from
10 a.m.

Afternoon Tea
is served in
The OAK ROOM
and
The LONG ROOM
from
3 p.m. to 5.30 p.m.

SWEETS

| Gâteau Special.. | .. | .. | .. | 5d |

HOT

Rice Custard Pudding..	..	..	4d
Gooseberry Tart	..	..	4d
Apple Pie	..	..	4d
Date Pudding ..	..	..	4d
Open Peach Pie	..	..	4d
Jam Tart	..	..	4d
Baroness Pudding	..	..	5d
Bread and Butter Pudding	..	5d

COLD

Stewed Prunes or Figs..	..	..	4d
Sliced Pineapple	..	..	4d
Meringue Chantilly	..	..	5d
Caramel Custard	..	..	5d
Preserved Ginger	..	..	5d
Trifle and Custard Powder Sauce	..	5d
Stewed Cherries	..	..	6d
Stewed Gooseberries ..	..	6d
Stewed Peaches	..	..	6d
Apple Flan	..	..	7d
Compôte of Fruit	..	..	8d
Custard Powder Sauce..	..	2d
Cream (Preserved)	..	3d

ICES

Strawberry	..	..	..	3d
Vanilla ..	..	..	3d
Meringue Glacé	..	..	6d
Coupe Montreuil	..	..	1/-
Pear or Pêche Melba ..	..	1/3

CHEESE

Cheddar	..	3d	Little Wilts	3d
Gorgonzola	..	5d	Gruyère ..	5d
Double Swiss Cream	5d	Camembert	5d

SUNDRIES

Eggs, soft or hard boiled	..	..	4d
„ Poached	..	..	4d
Welsh Rarebit ..	..	..	6d
Sardines on Toast (2) ..	..	7d
Buck Rarebit ..	..	..	10d
Eggs, Poached on Toast (1) 7d ; (2)	11d
Butter ..	..	..	per pat	1d
Blackberry Jelly	..	..	2d
Jam (various) or Marmalade ..	..	2d
Chutney	..	2d	Pickles	..	2d
Sardine ..	..	2d	Honey	..	2d
Virol ..	..	..	per portion	2d
Pickled Walnuts	..	..	2d
Apple ..	..	..	..	3d
Banana..	..	..	..	3d
Serviette	..	..	..	1d

LYONS' TEA

All Cream served in this Establishment contains Boric Acid Preservative not exceeding 0·4 per cent.

Will you kindly report to the Superintendent or write on the back of the bill in any case of incivility or inattention.

Throgmorton Café—W/C—4/7/27

ness in the arrangement of the cuisine, lavish expenditure in costly fittings, in marbles and mosaics, decorations, and sanitary appliances, these new premises leave little to be desired.'

The Popular Café and the State Restaurant

The simultaneous openings of the teashops, with their fixed-price menus, and the speciality restaurants for higher-spending customers, continued into the early part of the century. On 5 October 1903 Lyons' first expensive restaurant outside London opened in Manchester under the name of Victoria Mansions. Being a business restaurant it opened between noon and 9 p.m. This was followed in 1904 by two new London restaurants: the Birkbeck Café, Holborn, on 9 June (known as the businessman's café), and the Blenheim Café, New Bond Street, on 5 September – both licensed restaurants. Although the Birkbeck remained open until 1923 and the Blenheim until 1921, compared with other establishments they were not considered successful.

With the opening of the Popular Café in Piccadilly, London, on 10 October 1904, another 'super-restaurant' was ushered in. It enjoyed instant success by offering a four-course luncheon for 1s. 6d. with the benefit of musical accompaniment. It was here that Victor Sylvester, the famous bandleader and broadcaster, started his show-business career. The Popular Café, situated opposite St James's Hall, had seating capacity for 2,000 and remained open until the start of the Second World War. By this time it had been considerably extended after Lyons had purchased Crown Lease property adjoining the restaurant for £54,000 in 1906 from a Mr Lorden. A correspondent writing in the *Jewish Chronicle* in October 1904 described the 'huge new' restaurant that 'will be opened by Messrs. J. Lyons & Co., Ltd, next Monday':

> There will be no charge for attendance, and gratuities will not be expected by the waiters as it is the desire of the management to abolish all fees. The place is of palatial proportions, consisting of a very large ground floor restaurant, an

enormous grand hall, a commodious banqueting hall, spacious lobby entrance, cloak rooms, service rooms &c. In the main floor café, the treatment of the wall is in hand-painted panels of small design with satin wood panelling and gilded enrichments, let in and supported by linked pilasters of sienna [*sic*] and Sky ross [*sic*] marble. The ceiling exhibits Pergolesi enrichments picked out with delicate tints of greys, gold-browns, heliotrope, and green, with gilded mouldings running round. The ceiling light is cloisonné glass in colours out-lined in gold wires to show up the design. A marble staircase leads to the balcony, which has a Greek marble balustrade with gilded enrichments. The lighting arrangements consist of four large electroliers and forty smaller ones, suspended from the ceiling, with ormulu [*sic*] mountings filled with wedgwood [*sic*] placques [*sic*] and cut glass. …This is one of the largest cafés in the world. It has marble-lined walls and arched recesses supported on columns of sienna [*sic*] marble. The spandrils [*sic*] of the arches are filled in with dull red Venetian mosaic, with designs outlined in gold and filled in with various shades of mother-of-pearl, and each recess contains a mirror framed in green bronze.

The lobby entrance had a Roman-style mosaic floor and coloured panels; and the entrance hall contained white statuary. Each floor had a separate kitchen service with pneumatic tube connections and electric lifts. The kitchens and offices were lined with white glazed tiles. The *Jewish Chronicle* added:

> Afternoon musical teas will be among the special features of the establishment. The main floor café and balcony will be exclusively utilised for this purpose from 3 to 6 p.m., and it is hoped that ladies out shopping will appreciate the arrangements which have been made to please them. Silver tea services and daintiness in every detail are the key-notes of these afternoon

teas, and the band will play continuously during the afternoons.

Following the success of the Popular Café in Piccadilly, Lyons opened the State Restaurant in Liverpool's Dale Street in January 1905, then a Maison Lyons in Church Street in 1911 and another Popular Café in Manchester in January 1906. Although both cities had world-famous hotels, their restaurants did not quite meet the needs of the middle-class resident or shopping public. Although no records have survived describing these two provincial restaurants, they achieved the same instant success as the Piccadilly restaurant. The service was similar to that of the London establishments and they were supported by a miniature Cadby Hall in Liverpool complete with bakeries, kitchens and all the necessary equipment for the teashops in the north of England. Music too formed part of the service and this was expanded to include vocal concerts in the early 1920s. Another popular restaurant which received little publicity within Lyons was the Arcade Café in Leeds. Opened in October 1903, it was originally more upmarket than the teashops but a few years later it converted to a teashop and closed as such in July 1938. The Popular Café, Manchester, closed in July 1938 followed by the State Restaurant, Liverpool, in July 1949.

These larger restaurants, which catered for the middle and upper classes, were in a league of their own, setting new standards in catering. On the one hand some were used by business-men, while others catered for shoppers who frequently used the restaurants as a rendezvous or a special treat at the end or during a shopping spree. Music had certainly been an attraction: it made lunchtime more an event than just an occasion for eating. These large restaurants were, however, a precursor of the famous establishments to come: the Corner Houses and Maison Lyons.

CADBY HALL'S STEAM BAKERY

FOOD MANUFACTURE had been a necessary component of Lyons' extensive catering business since its beginnings. Limited bread and baking activities had been undertaken at Olympia (the company's first headquarters) to satisfy the early catering requirements. Some preparation, especially for the outdoor catering events, had been undertaken in field kitchens – a skill which helped Lyons secure the contract for feeding the troops while they were on their manoeuvres between Hounslow Heath and the New Forest just before the Boer War. When Lyons took over Cadby Hall in 1894, baking capacity was greatly enlarged, not only to meet the continuing demand for outdoor catering but to supply the teashops and to some extent the restaurants as their popularity rapidly grew.

There was, however, another reason why the bakeries expanded as quickly as they did. When local people began calling at the factory gates to buy fresh bread, Lyons saw an opportunity to deliver their products from handcarts, on a door-to-door basis, to the middle-class community occupying high-density terraced housing close by. These deliveries started in a small way, in parallel with the growth of the teashops, from as early as 1894. Local needs could easily be accommodated from the plant already in place, but bread prices were politically sensitive and little profit flowed from bread deliveries on such a small scale.

From a survey carried out by the *Morning Post* and published in the *Baker and Confectioner* in October 1894, it appeared the price of bread in the London area varied considerably and was much higher than many provincial prices with

which it was compared. The London prices varied from 3d. to 6d. per quartern (a 4lb loaf measuring four inches square), although a small baker in Deptford was selling a quartern loaf for as little as 2½d. With such big discrepancies it is no wonder the public were so critical. Bread delivered to the door tended to carry a higher premium and some bakers, characteristically those in central London, allowed credit, which they recovered in their higher price. The bread delivered from Cadby Hall's handcarts sold for 2½d. per half-quartern (a 2 lb loaf); this represented the mid-range price in London. As the profit from the standard quartern loaf was so meagre, many bakers, including Lyons, supplemented their income with a variety of other loaves. Being more elaborate, the special loaves carried a higher premium. At one time Lyons were prepared to bake almost anything to order for delivery the next day, providing the order was received by 7 p.m. The price of bread remained stable in those days; a decision by the full board, not taken lightly or frequently, was required in order to raise its price by as little as a farthing, since any increase would draw the wrath of the newspapers. The comments of *The Caterer and Hotel-Keepers' Gazette* in 1895 about the Aërated Bread Company, a dominant competitor, give some idea of the public's feelings:

> A good deal was said at Friday's meeting about the Aërated Bread Company's patents. We presume the company attaches some value to them. We confess that we don't. The company does not owe its success to its bread and its cakes. It has

The first bakeries at Cadby Hall in about 1895. The building is one of the original piano workshops which has been converted into a bakery. Electric light has been installed. Some twenty-three bakers appear in the photograph.

been successful not because, but rather in spite, of its special methods of manufacture. Really good bread, such as the Londoner seldom or never gets, but which any competent North Country housewife would show him how to make, would be an attraction to such place as the ABC shops; but the plaster-of-Paris-like compound which the Aërated Bread Company provides is a repellent rather than otherwise. We are therefore of the opinion that the company need not trouble about its patents. In our judgement most of them are worthless.

The Vienna rolls, pastries and cakes first introduced into the teashops also became popular with the growing clientèle of bread buyers. Such a heavy demand was placed on the Cadby Hall bakeries that by 1899 it became necessary to expand their capacity. At a cost of £900 six new ovens were installed and formed part of what became known as the Vienna Bakery. Vienna bread was produced in static ovens with sloping soles (surfaces), enabling the dough to be loaded under a ceiling of steam. Sufficient steam condensed on the cool surface of the dough to keep it moist and allowed for maximum expansion of the dough; the steam also gelatinised starch on the outside of the loaf or roll. When the steam was withdrawn, the dry heat of the oven baked the starch, thereby producing the characteristic high glaze and thin crusts of Vienna bread and rolls. Undoubtedly it was this method of baking which prompted Lyons to lay claim to a 'steam bakery', a term which appeared on a hoarding outside the factory entrance. Joseph Lyons referred to the new steam bakery in his report to shareholders in May 1899 as 'One of the most modern and replete bakeries in the United Kingdom'. Prices had also fallen so that by 1901 a London loaf was cheaper than it had been in any year since 1762.

The new baking ovens operated day and night to meet the additional demand from the catering establishments and their associated retail outlets. Door-to-door sales had grown progressively, and the handcarts were soon augmented by horse-drawn vans able to operate within a wider radius from the factory. By 1900 the local door-to-door delivery fleet numbered eleven handcarts and five horse-drawn vans of the type where the driver was exposed to the weather on an outside 'dickey' seat. By 1905 the number of journeys from Cadby Hall had grown to thirty, all operating within a five-mile radius. Introduced in 1911, the first covered van became the classic vehicle of the delivery system known as the bakery rounds. To meet the increasing demands from the suburbs, bakery depots opened at Crystal Palace, Brixton, Highbury and Croydon. From these centres the rounds developed with similar success, and soon tea and coffee were added to the inventory of bread and cakes.

By 1913 demand again outstripped capacity and it became necessary to build another bakery block housing what was known as a Titanic travelling oven, which displaced the draw-plate method in use up to this time. The draw-plate method had gone some way towards automating the production of bread in that the whole baking surface of the oven could be withdrawn to allow bread tins to be loaded or unloaded very much faster. This replaced the earlier static oven system in which bakers manually loaded or unloaded bread tins into the baking chamber by use of peels or spatulas.

Incorporating a continuous-belt action, the Titanic oven enabled bread to be made on true production-line principles. Prepared dough was placed on the steel belt, in sandwich tins, and taken mechanically, at the appropriate pace, through the heated chamber, appearing as cooked bread at the other end of the production line, where the loaves were discharged down chutes into a packing area ready for dispatch. This was a more efficient process than the conventional draw-plate system, and when a second Titanic oven was added, with automatic machines for weighing and cutting dough, the output from the bakery increased to 10,000 loaves an hour.

The rapid growth of the bakeries, and other manufacturing departments, came at the time of the second Boer War of 1899–1902, which exacted a strenuous effort from the whole British Empire to defeat what was regarded in military circles as a guerrilla army. As well as providing catering logistics and tented accommodation for troop manoeuvres stationed at Aldershot and elsewhere during this campaign, the Baking Department at Cadby Hall found time and money in 1899 to prepare and dispatch 10,000 Christmas puddings for the troops already serving in South Africa.

The period between 1914 and 1920 was notably gloomy. Britain's post-Victorian economy crashed in ruins and did not fully recover until 1935. Between these years prices rose so steeply as to merit the term 'inflation', forcing the government to introduce price controls. The government bought raw materials in bulk and released them at fixed prices, any loss falling on taxpayers, who were, by September 1915, paying 40 per cent if their earnings exceeded £130 per annum. Prices nevertheless continued their relentless upward spiral with bread prices reaching an all-time high of 10d. per quartern in October 1916. King George V suggested that the population should cut back their consumption of bread and pastry by a quarter. His proclamation, no doubt initiated by the government, was read out from church pulpits throughout the land on four successive Sundays in 1917. Coming from the monarch, and effec-

Some Cadby Hall bakers of *c.*1904. The Royal Warrant was bestowed by King Edward VII on 1 February 1904 which helps date this photograph.

Loaves being automatically discharged from the baking ovens and attended to by female staff.

tively the church, the proclamation was no doubt felt by the government to be more effective in persuading the population to curb their intake of bread and other flour-based foods. Only one part of the economy seemed briefly to resist the collapse: the City of London, source of the world's capital and international trading centre. Since central London had become a stronghold of Lyons teashops, they too remained insulated from the general downturn in the economy, and as a consequence profits remained satisfactory.

As the First World War intensified, labour shortages became more critical, and this put pressure on many catering companies. Expenditure on food dropped continuously as the government imposed absolute control on the bread trade. Flour mills were heavily regulated: the price and quality of bread were determined by statutory order. The government calculated that bread makers should be allowed 23 shillings per 280-lb sack of flour to cover all expenses and profit, with the government providing a subsidy of 3d. per quartern loaf. Even though the controls were rigidly applied, bakers such as Lyons enjoyed considerable prosperity during this period. There continued a steady market for bread, production costs were stable, and labour costs were reduced owing to the number of female workers who had come into the factories, on lower wages, for the war effort. It was not until 1920 that wartime controls affecting the baking trade were changed in any way and not until 1921 that millers were again allowed to sell flour of varying qualities and grades at competitive prices. The only regulation retained was one requiring bakers to sell loaves weighing a pound or multiples of a pound. This was unpopular with the trade for a long time, since bakers could not introduce new weights to improve profitability as the price of flour fluctuated. By September 1921 the price of the quartern loaf was cut to one shilling in the Liverpool area, at a time when there were over a million unemployed nationwide. Of these 368,000 were ex-servicemen.

Numbered at more than a hundred at the start of the war, bakery rounds salesmen did not hesitate to volunteer for the armed services and with some apprehension on the part of directors their jobs were taken over by women. The women kept the bakery rounds not only functioning but secure for the men returning after the war. Their success can be judged by the fact that there were 140 rounds by 1922 and the service continued to grow. The prosperity enjoyed during 1914–18 was not entirely due to the support given by the female drivers; statutory control of raw materials and absence of competition would at least have guaranteed profits at pre-war levels.

There is some doubt as to the exact date when the next phase of bakery distribution started, that of the wholesale sales. It has been suggested that agents had first contacted Lyons before 1914 to buy bread in bulk to sell on to their customers. Other evidence suggests the process did not start until 1914. In any event the real transition from door-to-door sales to part-wholesale selling did not properly begin until 1922. Then, two vans with a nucleus of some ten dealers started to build from the East End of London and from there the service extended to cover the whole of outer

A typical bread salesman of the 1920s. Most salesmen appeared to wear bowler hats and had a 'boy' accompanying them.

This 1899 photograph shows two carts, loaded with Christmas puddings, just before their departure from Cadby Hall for the troops in South Africa. They caused much interest at the time decorated with patriotic flags and bunting. They were a gift from the directors to the troops. *By kind permission of Waldegrave Films.*

London by the start of the Second World War. Meanwhile, the traditional horse-drawn vans continued to ply their routes radially from Cadby Hall, but this service declined as the wholesale and retail trades matured through agents and the teashops. Nevertheless, by 1920 each morning 200 horse-drawn vans, of varying sizes, were radiating from Cadby Hall and returning later to the extensive stabling facilities. The 'carmen', as they were originally called, earned £1 15s. per week in 1915 depending on seniority. Forage for the animals worked out at a little over £2 per week per horse, partly compensated by the sale of manure to many of the local market gardeners. The cost of shoeing, harness repair and veterinary expenditure, together with forage, made this form of transport expensive – delightful as they must have been trudging the streets in their dark-blue and grey livery, gold-and-white edging and colourful Royal Warrant transfers.

As the teashops and restaurants continued to increase in numbers, so did the demand on the bakeries. Bread-wrapping and bread-slicing machines were introduced and yet more ovens installed. With the introduction of motorised transport the wholesale trade expanded outside London, distributing from provincial catering establishments. The first of these had been set up in Sheffield in 1900 and afterwards at Liverpool, Bristol, Brighton and Margate.

Despite the many disruptions to trade and cost in human life on the battlefields of northern France, the Cadby Hall bakeries were transformed between the years 1894 and 1920. In that short time the steam bakeries became one of the largest baking operations in the country. From a modest start in 1894, the baking capacity of the factories had been massively enlarged to satisfy the almost insatiable appetite of those using the teashops and to provide for the wider distribution of bread and cake to the wholesale and retail trade. Automation and other innovative ideas came in the guise of the Titanic travelling oven and automatic dough-handling machinery. These alone lifted production to a staggering 10,000 loaves per hour, freeing other equipment for the more specialised task of cake confectionery. In the twenty years since Queen Victoria's death the country witnessed major changes in its social structure, and businesses were poised to take advantage of the new-found wealth sweeping the country.

Chapter

Tea – The Nation's Drink

THE ORIGIN OF TEA is obscure and many legends about its discovery have been handed down. For example, the Chinese claim that it was discovered by the Emperor Shen Nung in 2737 BC. Others believe that Buddhist priests first took tea seeds to Japan in about AD 806 after Darma, a Buddhist, had devoted seven years to sleepless contemplation of Buddha. After five years he felt sleep was about to overcome him and chewed some leaves idly picked from a bush nearby. He was so invigorated that he was able to complete the two remaining years.

Whatever the myths, the tea plant is an evergreen shrub (*Camellia sinensis*) now cultivated in many tropical and subtropical regions of the world, the chief producing areas being India, Pakistan, Sri Lanka (formerly Ceylon), East Africa, Indonesia, China (including Taiwan) and Brazil. The name is derived from the Chinese word *t'e* as is the slang word 'char' (*ch'a*). The leaves of the tea plant are stiff, shiny and pointed, and the flowers, which resemble buttercups in shape, are white with golden stamens. Requiring an acid soil, the plant grows at varying altitudes up to 7,000 feet and needs 50 inches of rain every year. The bushes have an economic life of between 40 and 100 years depending on type.

Tea comes in many forms and varieties according to country of origin, altitude grown, soil, seasonal variations in climate and the methods of drying and storing by the tea gardens. Not only does the grade of tea differ between the gardens themselves but variations in grade and crop occur within the same garden at different seasons. Sampling and grading these teas was the task of brokers, who tended to specialise in one or two gardens only and thus knew their standards. The blender's task, an even more specialised operation, involved mixing as many as thirty teas to achieve the required blend. Because tea is easily contaminated by other aromas its shipment from country of origin to blenders' warehouses required special care by shipping companies. It could not be handled in bulk, like grain or sugar, but instead was individually boxed in tea chests which had been lined in foil and tissue paper, each chest individually coded from garden to factory. The small circular metal discs sometimes seen in tea chests are the repair points in the plywood chest from which sampling was taken when the tea arrived in the United Kingdom to enable the brokers, buyers and blenders to compare the contents with samples previously sent by the garden growers to check that no contamination or deterioration had taken place during transit. The London buyers had set a fair price for tea at their weekly auctions from about 1679 and apart from disruptions caused by the world wars their industry continued until 29 June 1998 when London's last tea auction was held.

Tea drinking became the subject of elaborate ceremonies in both China and Japan centuries before ships of the Dutch East India Company brought the first tea cargoes to Europe from Macao in about 1610. The use of tea spread throughout Holland and their ships became important carriers of tea cargo from the Far East. The Chinese regarded tea more as a medicine than as a refreshing drink and this notion continued when the first shipments arrived in England in the 1650s. In 1660 HM Customs imposed a duty of 8d. per gallon on all makes of tea, putting it beyond the reach of most, and it remained expensive until 1784, when the duty was removed. Until then the evasion of tax was rife and smuggling became a lucrative industry involving a wide spectrum of society from downright villains to clergymen, some of whom were reported to have put their church crypts at the disposal of the smugglers. The continuing high price of tea meant that it was purely an upper-class luxury and led to the widespread practice of adulteration, which continued into the twentieth century until packet tea transformed the market.

In 1823 the tea plant was discovered growing wild in Assam and in 1839, after the British had conquered Assam and developed a plantation economy there, Indian tea was auctioned for the first time in Britain. Sri Lanka, known as Ceylon and owned by the British from 1796, was also transformed into a plantation colony, and Ceylon tea was first auctioned in Britain in 1875. By October 1878 Ceylon tea had made its mark on the London tea market. The finest quality (Golden Tips) was made from young leaf buds, hand-sorted, and possessed a rich flavour hitherto unknown to tea drinkers. As a consequence it became enormously expensive. On 10 March 1891, in the Mincing Lane auction rooms, the Mazawattee Ceylon Tea Company trumped all other bids with one of £25 10s. per pound which they intended using as a centre-piece for their stand in the Great Chicago Exhibition of 1893. Generally though, the arrival of Indian and Ceylon teas from the British Empire in the mid-1840s caused tea prices to fall, making tea affordable as a national drink.

Lyons' Tea

T.C. Bridges in his *Kings of Commerce* reported that Joseph Lyons had first met Thomas Lipton, a well-known tea merchant, during the Glasgow Exhibition of 1888 when additional supplies of tea were purchased from him to satisfy the unexpectedly huge number of visitors who had turned out on the last day of the exhibition. From their beginnings in catering, Lyons had always insisted on using high-quality tea, which in those days of course was leaf tea; the tea-bag had not been invented. Of equal importance was the method of infusion – freshly drawn boiling water, warming the teapot, leaving the tea to stand for three minutes and so on. It was the quality of the tea which first brought Lyons to public notice at the early exhibitions. Whether or not Lyons had previously bought Lipton's tea is not known, but there is no doubt that Lipton's was of excellent quality. Lipton's credibility suffered a temporary setback, however, in September 1914, when Lyons were granted an injunction restraining Lipton's from speaking or writing words to the effect that J. Lyons & Co., or the directors, were Germans and that by buying their commodities the public was assisting the enemies of Britain. Publicity issued by the directors prior to the case being heard said that 'J. Lyons & Co. Ltd (by Appointment to His Majesty the King) was an all-British company with all-British directors, had 14,000 all-British shareholders and 160,000 all-British shopkeepers selling Lyons Tea'. Their case was based on 'imputation of anti-social behaviour' and the courts found that 'It is defamatory to state of a man, in time of war, that he is an alien enemy.'

By 1894 Lyons' use of fine blended tea had grown enormously and continued to do so during their teashop and restaurant revolution. Throughout the eighty years the Lyons teashops reigned, their cup of tea was widely acknowledged as best value. During 1895 the company began blending and packaging a tea which they sold to teashop customers under the name of 'Maharajah'; they were more reluctant to sell to the public their own teashop blend which always remained a classified secret; indeed it was a very high-class blend with choice Darjeeling leaf as its base. Sold from the retail counters of the fifteen teashops which had opened during 1894–5, Maharajah became so popular that by 1897 nearly one ton per annum of this tea was being blended at Cadby Hall for sale through these outlets although it must be said that some customers complained it was not the same as that served in the teashop, a claim Lyons never made.

Situated above the Vienna bakery and known originally as the Tea Room, a four-man team consisting of George Percy (supervising), Arthur Webb, William Gray and in 1899 the 15-year-old L.J. Ashdown, took delivery of about 20 chests each week and packed sample teas, by hand, for distribution to grocers initially in the London area. The large grocers were reluctant to take this packet tea, partly because they were able to make more profit from blending and packing their own tea, and also because they did not like to have to pay cash on delivery, as Lyons insisted. Lyons therefore approached the small side-street retailers and produced small packets of tea to meet their limited needs and resources. From these modest beginnings retail packaging commenced in about 1898, but no records survive to show under what name it was marketed. Again the tea was weighed and packed by hand for distribution to the grocery trade. The first official factory production statistics appear in a handwritten ledger started in 1903. During that year nearly 280 tons of packet tea left the factory, with Carter Paterson distributing it on a cash-on-delivery basis to dairymen in the London area. The following year, output almost doubled, leading to the creation of a tea-selling department. By 1909 tea factory output had increased by a massive 2,204 per cent.

Lyons' Coffee

In 1903 Lyons began to sell packaged ground coffee, to complement the packet tea trade. Coffee sales, however, did not achieve such high volumes as tea. From 117 tons in 1903 coffee sales had only increased to 332 tons by 1909. The coffee trade in Britain was centred on the London Commercial Sale Rooms (built in 1815) in Mincing Lane but it took twenty or more years before trade moved from its cosy, traditional home of the Jerusalem Coffee House. It was from the Mincing Lane auction rooms that Lyons obtained their coffee supplies. Coffee is grown in more than fifty countries of the world; Brazil is by far the largest exporter but even Yemen and the Cape Verde Islands export small quantities.

The origins of coffee, like tea, are lost in time. Legend has it that the drug nepenthe, which made people carefree and happy and which Helen of Troy brought out of Egypt, was probably a mixture of coffee and wine – an early coffee liqueur perhaps! The habit of brewing the dried seeds inside the berries of the coffee plant – *Coffea arabica* is the most widely cultivated – most probably started in Arabia in the fourteenth century when a pious sheikh brought the plant from Abyssinia (now Ethiopia). At first it was classed as an intoxicant by Muslim religious leaders and therefore forbidden by the Koran, but doctors declared it harmless. Its use extended to many parts of the Middle East and Africa. By 1570 coffee was firmly established as the most popular beverage in the Arab regions that belonged to the Ottoman Empire, and from Turkey it spread to Europe. The Turks supported their long vigils on the battlefield by drinking coffee and when their armies pushed towards Vienna they carried with them hundreds of

MONTH	CONSUMPTION in LBS.	OVER	SHORT	PERCENTAGE OVER	PERCENTAGE SHORT	REMARKS
JANUARY	36112	332		·9		
FEBRUARY	34083	559		1·6		
MARCH	37038	282		·8		
APRIL	40265	590		1·4		
MAY	47019	1308		·9		
JUNE	47151		454			
JULY	57015	1819		1·2		
AUGUST	49328		520			
SEPTEMBER	59967	420		·7		
OCTOBER	68703	686		1·0		
NOVEMBER	82039	1445		1·7		
DECEMBER	67288	1523		2·3		
TOTAL FOR YEAR	626,011			Average 1·28 for 12 months OVER		

TEA 1903

Although tea was packaged in small quantities before 1900, official production figures did not start until 1903.

wagons loaded with coffee. After they laid siege to Vienna and were defeated in 1683 by Jan Sobieski, the Polish king, they left behind large quantities of coffee which led, it is said, to the opening of Vienna's first coffee house.

Around 1714 the Dutch – who for some years had been trading in coffee from their own colonies in the East Indies (now Indonesia) – sent a coffee seedling from Java to Louis XIV of France, who had it planted in the Jardin des Plantes in Paris. Eventually seedlings from this plant were shipped to the then French colony of Martinique, with a view to establishing an industry, but only one plant survived which a young French naval officer had managed to nurture on the long journey. From this plant, however, legend has it that a sizeable coffee industry developed in the area, but the French and Dutch were anxious to prevent other countries from obtaining the plant. They failed when, according to the legend, the wife of the Governor of French Guiana fell in love with the Governor of Brazil and smuggled a coffee seedling to him in a bouquet. This seedling is supposedly the ancestor of all the coffee trees now growing in Brazil. Nowadays the world's largest producers of coffee beans are Brazil, Colombia and the Ivory Coast as well as Indonesia, Ethiopia and other countries.

There are many celebrated accounts of how coffee-houses were first established in England but it is generally accepted that the first English coffee-house opened in 1650 in Oxford, where students and dons soon became frequent patrons. Coffee gave them the energy to fight sleep and tiredness because of the stimulant of caffeine, while its agreeable flavour was a change from wine, which had a depressant and soporific effect. Daniel Edwards is credited with being the first merchant to bring coffee into London from Smyrna, where it had long been established as a fortifying beverage. Some accounts suggest that he trained a Greek servant, Pasqua Rosee, to make his coffee, and that Daniel Edwards then left the country to resume his travels. In 1652 Rosee founded the London Coffee House in St Michael's Alley, Cornhill, which became known as the Pasqua's Head, where it is claimed coffee

beans were first publicly sold. Coffee was enormously expensive and some early street stalls sold an alternative beverage infusion known as saloop made originally with powdered salep, then from sassafras oil, mixed with hot milk and sugar. When coffee became more affordable the aromatic saloop lost favour. The most famous London coffee-house is probably that of Edward Lloyd which originated in Tower Street in the 1680s and from 1692 in Abchurch Lane on the corner of Lombard Street in the City of London. Jonathan's Coffee House in the City was also popular and it is said that securities-trading first began here. Coffee-houses became the rendezvous of the shipping fraternity; news of shipping movements was exchanged and business conducted there. It was from Lloyd's coffee house that two great institutions emerged. Here, insurance underwriters first established their unique insurance market which had no shareholders and accepted no corporate liability for risks insured. All underwriters accepted insurance risks for their personal profit or loss and were liable to the full extent of their private fortunes to meet their insurance commitments. Then as now, Lloyd's provided only the premises, intelligence and other facilities. Similarly, from the same coffee house, Lloyd's Register of Shipping appeared. This organisation was wholly responsible for the classification of ships and their technical standards on which the insurance market depended. In spite of popular confusion, however, Lloyd's Insurance and Lloyd's Register of Shipping were, and continue to be separate organisations, each with their individual history.

The success of the coffee, and chocolate, houses became hugely popular as businessmen, scholars, politicians, newsmongers or just wits regularly met to exchange gossip in amiable surroundings. As they developed some acted as doctors' consulting rooms, matrimonial agencies, post offices, masonic lodges, gambling rooms and in some cases brothels. In time many converted to clubs such as the St James's Coffee House for Whigs and they spread throughout the capital. This idea fuelled the growth of London club building such as those of Boodle's and Brooks' and this continued into the middle of the nineteenth century when the Baltic Coffee House in Threadneedle Street became a members club in 1823.

Lyons' Cocoa and Chocolate

Cocoa production at Lyons started in about 1908, closely followed by chocolate. Its name derives from the small evergreen cacao tree (*Theobroma cacao*) from whose seeds it is obtained. Being native to tropical America, cocoa was unknown to the people of Europe until the discovery of America, and the Spanish conquistador Ferdinand Cortez is linked with the importation of cocoa beans from Mexico and the introduction of cocoa as a drink into Europe in the sixteenth century. It was once so valuable that native people of Central America used the cacao seeds as currency. Nowadays the cocoa bean is grown chiefly in West Africa, the Ivory Coast being the principal exporter (in Ghana cocoa is the largest single source of revenue), Brazil and East Africa.

Chocolate was first made from cocoa beans according to much the same methods as those used by the Indians of Central America. After roasting, the beans were passed through a winnowing machine, whose steel plates cracked the tough outer shell into fragments (which were then blasted away by air jets) and continued to break up the kernel. Then the pieces were put through a grinding machine, where they were rapidly passed through a series of heated grinding stones, to emerge as a brown liquid known as pate.

For cocoa powder production, some of the cocoa butter had to be extracted, and so the hot liquid was subjected to high pressure in hydraulic presses to squeeze out, through filter pads, part of the cocoa butter. The residue was cocoa powder, which was then poured into a pulverising machine and sieved through fine meshed silk to produce household cocoa powder.

Drinking chocolate followed much the same production process as cocoa except that the butter content was not extracted. In fact more butter was added together with sugar, making the powder, when mixed with milk, smoother and richer in taste. The high butter content enabled the milk and chocolate powder mixture to be

whisked and frothed, thus giving an added sophistication to the drink.

In the case of hard chocolate production, again cocoa butter was not extracted from the pate as it left the grinding process; instead more butter was added after the pate had been combined with sugar and milk. The ingredients were then thoroughly mixed and refined further by additional grinding before being placed for several days in heated rooms where it underwent a slow cooking process which further developed its characteristic flavour. After cooking, the concoction was put into continuous mixing machines where more butter was added and the liquid chocolate was slowly stirred. This 'conching' process lasted for forty-eight hours, although in the case of Swiss chocolate it continued for a week. Once out of the mixing 'conch' the chocolate was cooled, and at this stage nuts or fruit could be added before it was poured into polished metal moulds which were vigorously shaken to remove air bubbles and ensure that the liquid flowed into the corners of the moulds.

Lyons' diversification into coffee in 1903 and cocoa in 1909 seems to have been part of a general trend among the large tea suppliers of the period. Coffee was sold as a luxury to the wealthy, whereas cocoa was intended for working-class customers who could not afford tea. Thus revenues were obtained from each end of the class spectrum without jeopardising tea sales. There was, however, another reason for the diversification. Between 1898 and 1901 crippling tea duty had bankrupted several small tea firms and so the survivors adopted diversification as a contingency against rising duties; the Mazawattee Ceylon Tea Company, for example, which had been trading from an eight-storey warehouse in Great Tower Street from about 1865, opened a vast new cocoa and chocolate factory at New Cross in October 1901.

The first tea motor van crossing the river at Fowey, Cornwall, in 1908. The folk of Fowey had cause to remember the incident as the local council had to put sixpence on the rate for the year to cover compensation.

From a base of 99 tons of cocoa in 1909 rising to 1,462 tons in 1918 (outselling coffee by 100 per cent in that year), Lyons' factory cocoa output fell dramatically in the 1920s and cocoa became a marginal product. Between 1908 and 1913 the cocoa and drinking chocolate departments only operated a packing facility; cocoa and chocolate production proper did not start until 1913. Drinking chocolate too never fulfilled its expectations, rising only to a maximum of 40 tons in 1915 (see Appendix 2).

Satisfying the National Thirst

These four beverages – tea, coffee, cocoa and drinking chocolate – are all refreshing, despite being dissimilar. The first two are stimulants containing caffeine, which raises blood pressure, stimulates the brain and temporarily averts fatigue (as well as acting as a diuretic), while the latter two when sugar and milk are added have the nutritional properties of a food, mainly carbohydrate, fat and protein which provide energy (although the alkaloid present in cocoa – theobromine – can trigger attacks of migraine in sufferers). Their importance in British consumption is very different: the consumption of tea in the period between the two world wars was, by weight, roughly ten times that of either coffee or cocoa. Once it had become a cheap drink tea grew more popular with the working class; coffee seems largely to have been drunk at this period by the more or less well-off, while cocoa also appears to have been consumed mainly by the working class, especially manual workers. Perhaps its nutritional properties were found to make cocoa more sustaining as a refreshment. As well as being sold in ¼lb, ½lb and 1lb tins, Lyons packed cocoa in 2d. drums and 1d. packets so they could be included in workers' lunch packs, the hot water (or milk) being obtained from their braziers: a common sight with large groups of manual workers (day and night) at the beginning of the twentieth century.

Although tea and coffee were first put on the market around the same time, more emphasis was placed on tea, where volume sales were greatest. It is not surprising, therefore, that the department formed in 1904, under the supervision of Michael Pezaro, to develop the retail sales of tea and coffee, became known as the Tea Agents' Department. The following year, under the management of George Pollard, a Provincial Tea Agents' Department was added, but because of overlapping sales territories – frequently two travellers would be competing for the same business – the two departments amalgamated under the common name of Tea Agents' Department.

Consumption of tea *per capita* had risen strikingly during the nineteenth century, as Indian and Ceylon output soared, and continued to do so until the early 1930s, after which it settled and even began to decline. At its height in 1931 tea consumption per head amounted to 9.6 lb per annum. Assuming that in domestic use a pound of tea makes approximately 190 cups, this rate of consumption equated to about five cups of tea per day per head. The phenomenal increase of packet tea sales within Lyons is largely attributed to the efforts of Michael Pezaro and notably George Pollard.

George Pollard and the Tea Agents

George Arthur Pollard was born in 1863 in Heckmondwike, Yorkshire, of a comfortable Congregationalist family. After attending one of Bramwell Booth's meetings in London in 1881, he joined the Salvation Army. Originally rejected for 'officership' on the grounds of his frail physique, he quickly demonstrated his qualities and by the time he was nineteen years of age held the rank of captain. When he was only twenty the Salvation Army selected him to journey to New Zealand, their furthest outpost, to take control of Salvation Army operations there. He was accompanied by Lieutenant Edward Wright from Runcorn in Cheshire, who, it is reported, was only nineteen years old at the time. (Chancellor Pollard, writing in *All the World* in

One of Jules Pettit's distribution vans in Paris where he had the tea contract up until 1910. The translation of the lower side reads: 'The most important seller of tea in the whole world'.

April 1902, put Wright's age as 'a few months older' than himself.) Together with three colleagues they sailed from London on the Cunard steamship *Cephalonia* on 12 January 1883, suffering many privations during the voyage in the poor steerage accommodation. They travelled by way of Suez and Adelaide and arrived on 5 March 1883 in Melbourne, where they were met by three other Salvation Army pioneers. After a brief stay Pollard and Wright continued their journey on the steel screw schooner *Manapouri* (the world's first merchant ship to be equipped with incandescent electric lighting throughout and to accommodate her saloon passengers amidships), arriving in Port Chalmers (Dunedin) on 27 March 1883 with only £1 between them to keep themselves and form the New Zealand Salvation Army. Pollard returned to England in 1895 when he was thirty-two and became a commissioner and the Salvation Army's first chancellor. Said to have been a remarkably talented young man, he became the closest confidant of both William and Bramwell Booth between 1894 and 1904.

While involved with complex arrangements for the Salvation Army's International Congress in 1904, Pollard suffered a nervous breakdown and on medical advice took a long furlough. He and his wife sailed for New Zealand again, and during the return voyage he became acquainted with Montague Gluckstein, who was returning to England with his wife and son, probably joining the ship at Colombo. Pollard had earlier been responsible for the Crystal Palace Congress, a gathering of 60,000 Salvationists, and had demonstrated his negotiating proficiency when Isidore Salmon approached him about the catering contract. Familiar with these discussions himself and now having an opportunity to learn more about George Pollard, Montague Gluckstein became impressed with his personal and persuasive qualities as the voyage passed. On his return to England, Gluckstein offered Pollard a job, to set up a tea sales operation and take charge of it.

George Pollard started work with Lyons in 1905 with unfettered responsibility for developing a network of provincial tea agents or retailers and he set off towards Bristol with a horse-drawn van loaded with half a ton of White Label tea priced

A tea salesman calling on a typical rural shop (this one also has a post office attached) somewhere in England. *By kind permission of Waldegrave Films.*

at 1s. 6d. per pound. This was more than the predominant prices being paid for tea across the United Kingdom in 1905, but it compared favourably with the mid-range prices; the average price of tea in London was marginally over 1s. 4d. per pound. Pollard soon established a small office in Bristol, engaging his son as a clerk, and quickly appointed his first tea agent (retailer) there. Later that year the Provincial Tea Agents' Department merged with the former Tea Agents' Department of Michael Pezaro and both were appointed joint 'Chiefs'. They toured the country in a De Dion car, painted in the company's blue, grey and white livery, to supervise the district centres they set up.

White Label tea became the first of many coloured-label tea brands marketed by Lyons, the most successful being the famous Green Label, still produced and selling from a Dublin factory nearly 100 years on. No definitive record of brand introduction has survived but by 1922 four standard blends were being sold, Red Label (3s. 4d. per lb), Green Label (3s. per lb), White Label (2s. 8d. per lb) and Blue Label (2s. 4d. per lb). Later these were augmented with Orange, Yellow,

Striped-Green, Mauve and Buff. Early teas sold in 1d., 2d., 2 oz., ¼ lb, ½ lb and 1 lb packets. This packaging style had first been used by John Horniman in 1826 from his factory on the Isle of Wight, and many had copied his idea. John Horniman originally had difficulty in marketing his packet tea, since the grocery trade preferred loose tea, which they could adulterate to make more profit, and he was forced to sell through confectioners' and chemists' shops. The public, however, reacted with enthusiasm to packaged tea and Horniman's system soon became accepted and the smaller measures, adopted by Lyons, were discontinued. Loose tea became less popular with consumers as time passed.

Lyons' sales methods differed from those of other tea traders because of their insistence on cash on delivery and their imposition of a maximum profit margin of 2d. per pound for the agent (retail shop). As with all their other operations, Lyons wanted control of quality and a standard selling price. Any fluctuations in price, which were rare in those times, were passed on to the customer. Retailers' 2d. profit on Lyons' tea was a full penny less than they could receive from other tea packers, and it is a measure of Pollard's competence that he persuaded them to buy Lyons' tea at all. In an open letter to all tea agents, published in the *Lyons Mail* house journal in December 1921, he suggested it was far better for the shopkeeper to sell 6 lb of tea at 2d. profit per pound (the 1921 margin) than one pound of a competitor's tea at 3d. profit, since he would earn a shilling instead of only 3d. Shopkeepers were also well aware of the price sensitivity of food and, quality being equal, the consumer would usually choose the lower price. A similar strategy had been used by Salmon & Gluckstein in selling cigarettes – likewise a cash business – and they were able to maintain high turnover with modest profit on each sale.

George Pollard's open letter in the *Lyons Mail* constituted one of many editorial pieces aimed specifically at the tea agents; explanatory articles were written in such a way as to make the agent feel part of the Lyons organisation and believe he was gaining an insight into the workings of the grocery operation within the firm. Since the journal was also widely available to the public through the main newsagents, the public too were subtly being exposed to Lyons' branding. Pollard's first letter began: 'The object of these lines is to give a hearty greeting to our Agents throughout the whole of the United Kingdom who are engaged in selling the Tea, Cocoa, Coffee and other special commodities produced by this Company.' He went on: 'A criticism recently levelled at us from various quarters was that the "*Mail*" is "too high-class." If it be so, that is surely not a fault calling for an apology. Our Agents are accustomed to receiving the best from us, and in offering them the *Lyons Mail* we are only following our usual practice.' Pollard then set out his position:

> We have asked for your help, and now offer you our co-operation. Many of you will have read in the *Daily Mail* of October 5th, an account of the origin, growth, extent and prospects of this Company, and will have formed some idea of its resources. It is those resources which we place at your disposal as our Agents. ... Whilst it will be long before the prosperity

of the country is re-established on a pre-war basis, there are many signs which warrant us in being optimistic, and the encouragement of co-operation and of cordial relations between all classes is surely one of the most helpful and necessary ways of assisting in this recovery. ... We feel that we can rely upon your continual and increasing support until every one of our Agents becomes a regular and enthusiastic subscriber to the *Lyons Mail*.

In 1919 George Pollard was one of a few individuals to be appointed an employee director, a reward reserved by the Salmons and Glucksteins for exceptional service. None the less the recipient had to retire every three years for reselection by shareholders. George Pollard died on 20 March 1939 at the age of seventy-six.

With Isidore Salmon as General Manager of the tea factory (followed by his younger brother Harry in the 1920s, his youngest son Julian in the mid-1930s and Kenneth Gluckstein in the late 1940s) the amount of tea cleared for home consumption increased from just over 1,000 tons in 1905 to nearly 14,000 tons in 1914. The volume increases were not due entirely to the effort of Pezaro's and Pollard's sales teams, who by now numbered over 200, but also to the expanding catering and exhibition trade. Mass production was also assisted by automation in about 1910 when William Coyte, who subsequently became Chief Engineer and a director, successfully installed a mechanised tea-filling machine which replaced the hitherto hand-filling method. Consumption in the teashops alone soared to 10,000 lb per week.

Tea exporting had started in 1910 when it was first sent to Holland from an address at Butler's Wharf, on the south bank of the Thames in what was known as the Pool. Situated between London Bridge and Tower Bridge, on both north and south banks, the Pool of London's warehouses held virtually the whole of Britain's tea stocks. Not only that but importers, buyers and brokers were but a short distance away and nearly a half of the tea landed was blended and packed within a radius of two or three miles. By

1911 Lyons' tea vans were operating in Rotterdam, Amsterdam, Paris and in Germany. When the tea firm of W.H. & F.J. Horniman was acquired in 1918 (see chapter 2) much of Lyons' export tea business was handled from their packing centre at Shepherdess Walk in Islington, North London. During 1913 just 310 tons had been exported from Butler's Wharf but the First World War put a stop to this trade so that by 1918 the volumes had dropped back to seventy-eight tons. Nevertheless, Pollard remained enthusiastic. On one occasion he suggested Lyons should abandon their unsatisfactory association with Jules Pettit, their tea agent in Paris, and establish their own sales team in much the same way as in London, except that the French salesmen should use tricycles instead of the traditional horse-drawn van in use in Paris at that time. Pollard's idea was not taken seriously; perhaps as a consequence the French export market for tea was never adequately developed.

Market Gains and Losses in Wartime

With the nation at war in 1914 tea shortages had a devastating effect on the amount of tea Lyons could distribute. Their factory output fell by nearly a half between 1914 and 1917, as did their own consumption. Most worrying of all, the tea shortages led to a loss of market share in the north of England, from which Lyons never recovered. As the war intensified, more working men answered the call to arms and proportionally more men were drawn from the poorer communities in the industrial north of England. Much of the Tea Department's sales force, which between 1905 and 1914 had penetrated the traditional northern territory of Brooke Bond (established by Arthur Brooke in Manchester in 1869), was lost to the armed services. Those few who were left, largely unmanaged, sold almost all their tea allocation to a handful of preferred agents, causing alienation among the rest. This allowed Brooke Bond to re-establish themselves again in their traditional stronghold, and, with the co-operatives likewise entrenched in the north, Lyons found they were virtually locked out of this territory when hostilities with Germany ceased.

Throughout the First World War, under the Defence of the Realm Act (a power originally introduced in August 1914 to help deal with espionage and other defence matters and not rescinded until 31 August 1921), the government had progressively introduced dozens of statutory rules and orders affecting the prices, allocation, manufacture and distribution of food. Many of these government orders were designed to conserve supplies, reduce profiteering and, not least, raise revenue for the war effort, which by July 1917 was costing the country £7 million per day. In his budget of September 1915 the Chancellor of the Exchequer, Reginald McKenna, raised customs duties on tea and tobacco by 50 per cent, and later a government order specified that 40 per cent of all imported tea had to be retailed for not more than 2s. 4d. per pound. By April 1917 the supply of tea had been interrupted by the severe loss of shipping and a scheme had been introduced by which 40 per cent of the tea up for auction was sold at a fixed price, the other 60 per cent being free of restrictions. In July the government raised the percentage of tea under price control to 90 per cent and divided tea stocks into three grades, each at a fixed price. The scheme became unworkable because astronomical prices were fetched on the uncontrolled tea and there was a collapse of tea stocks.

In February 1918, for the first time in Britain's history, rationing was introduced. Paradoxically, this revolutionary step was not really necessary, since the German U-boat supremacy – which had so severely reduced Britain's food imports – had been ended. Nevertheless, from February 1918 all tea was sold at 2s. 8d. per pound as a single government blend known as National Tea. To strengthen the rationing arrangement, retailers were permitted to register their choice of supplier. Under this procedure Lyons were able to consolidate much of their market in the south but, because of their neglect of the northern agents, they lost out to Brooke Bond and the co-operatives. Although tea consumption fell by only 15 per cent nationally during the war, Cadby Hall's tea production suffered a loss of over 36 per cent – an agonising indicator of the business

lost to competition. At one stage Brooke Bond offered to loosen their hold on the tea markets in the north if Lyons undertook reciprocal action in the south.

Lyons rejected this idea and instead responded by purchasing a controlling interest in W.H. and F.J. Horniman & Co. Ltd who by now had moved their operation from the Isle of Wight.

William Henry and Frederick John, John Horniman's sons, gave their initials to the company name when it was incorporated in 1899. Horniman's markets were strong in Yorkshire and Lancashire and they had an appreciable export trade supplied from their Shepherdess Walk packing centre and Wormwood Street factory close to Liverpool Street in the City of London. At the

A retailer's commitment to Lyons' Tea, August 1910.

same time Lyons bought outright the business of Black & Green Ltd, a tea blender and retailer with sixty shops, who had a strong presence in the Manchester area. Expansion by acquisition was unconventional for Lyons, who hitherto had preferred to develop their tea business organically, but such was the weakness of their northern operation that it became essential to put in place some means to expand quickly in the north, when the relaxation of tea regulations permitted. As it happened, packet tea became more widely available to consumers after the war by the entry into the market of a number of smaller suppliers who took advantage of the more efficient distribution systems such as road and rail. The anticipated titanic struggle between Lyons and Brooke Bond did not materialise as some had predicted. It seemed everyone was a winner, including Ty·phoo, with its catchy Chinese-sounding name, and its claim that 'Tea relieves indigestion for which many doctors recommend it'. Started in 1903 by John Sumner, who sold just 30 chests in that first year from his grocery store in Birmingham, it registered as John Sumner's 'Typhoo' Tea Ltd in July 1905. His sister, Mary Augusta, had been given some special small-leaf tea to help cure her indigestion and was so impressed with the result that she persuaded her brother to sell it to his customers. After careful consideration he decided to call his tea Ty·phoo Tipps.

Under the direction of Harry Salmon, his older brother Isidore having left to take charge of the Lyons Works Department and pursue political interests (he became Member of Parliament for Harrow), the period 1900-20 saw a rapid growth in the tea business. Harry Salmon's high standards were reflected in all departments and during this period the Green Label brand became the promoted blend and consumers' all-time favourite. At the same time, though less well documented, Lyons was developing its coffee, cocoa, chocolate and other grocery lines, all the responsibility of the Tea Agents' Department.

Lyons' best-quality tea for the consumer market became known as Maison Lyons. Blended from the finest Darjeelings and Assams from India, and characterised by its unique 'Muscatel' flavour, it required longer infusion to bring out the full flavour of the leaf. Then came Orange Label, a blend of high-grown Ceylons and peak-quality Indian teas selected for their balance of flavour. Red Label arrived next, distinguished as a strong blend, followed by many others including the budget and Dividend teas. Blue Label was a blend of predominantly whole-leaf grades requiring five minutes' infusion to obtain its full flavour, whereas Green Label was a blend of whole-leaf and small-leaf teas capable of giving a good second cup.

With more space required for tea storage, cocoa and chocolate production transferred to new premises at St John's Square, Clerkenwell, in 1912. By 1918, however, it had become obvious that Cadby Hall lacked the space and facilities to support all the food-manufacturing needs if business expansion continued. The West London factories, which had been progressively enlarged by the acquisition of properties along Hammersmith Road, eventually encompassed 13 acres. By the 1920s it was clear that, although Cadby Hall could be expanded marginally, the inability to extend it massively threatened the existence of some crucial departments. It was no longer a question of finding alternative accommodation for some sections but a matter of revolutionary transformation. This diversity, centred on the hamlet of Greenford, is covered in chapter 11.

7

HOTEL BUILDING

THE RAPID DEVELOPMENT of the hotel industry in London was assisted by the growth of the railway networks in the middle of the nineteenth century. With the great railway trunk lines one after another planting their termini in London, the railway companies built hotels to provide accommodation for their long-distance travellers, pioneering the vast hotel industry which began at Euston in 1838. The Euston Hotel was the first of many to grace a London terminal and it was followed by the Gothic magnificence of the Midland Grand Hotel at St Pancras and the Great Northern, Great Western, Charing Cross, London Bridge and Cannon Street hotels. After a further interval came the Holborn Viaduct, the Great Eastern and the Great Central hotels. Soon hotels were established in other large railway centres, eventually extending to seaside and inland holiday resorts. Said to be one of the largest hotel empires in the world, the railway hotels established themselves throughout Britain and Ireland, with over 140 properties at their peak.

Although these facilities benefited the new travelling public, the upper class visiting London still preferred the small select establishments in Mayfair and Belgravia. Nevertheless, the middle class and businessmen visiting the metropolis eagerly availed themselves of the new palatial railway hotels. Some even took advantage of their low prices to use them as permanent residences for months on end. The large companies encouraged this by allowing residents to switch from one hotel to another without incurring any financial penalty. In this way the big hotels created

a fashion and the old order of small hotelier was relegated to the background.

As more American and wealthy colonialists began to visit London, far-seeing capitalists realised that a new wave of hotel building seemed inevitable. The construction of Northumberland Avenue led directly to the building of the Grand, Metropole and Victoria hotels. When in 1886 the Hotel Cecil – dubbed Hobb's Folly after the name of its builder, whom it brought to financial ruin – opened on the Embankment (at what is now Shell Mex house), it had the distinction of being Europe's largest hotel. In quick succession the Royal Kensington Palace, the Hyde Park, the Savoy, the Carlton and the Russell hotels opened their doors. In 1855 William Claridge, who had bought a small hotel in Brook Street, acquired the adjoining Mivart's Hotel and combined them into a single hotel he named Claridge's. It is still one of the most fashionable in the world.

At the beginning of the twentieth century a chain of hotels was established by Felix Spiers and Christopher Pond. Both had travelled to Australia in the middle of the nineteenth century as 'lads' to seek their fortunes in the gold-fields. With little success in this venture they took up railway catering and returned to England, securing their first railway contract, at Farringdon Street, London, in about 1888. They went on to become the leading railway caterers and by 1925 had contracts for over 200 refreshment rooms. Simultaneously they built their famous Spiers & Pond chain of restaurants and provision shops well before Lyons became established. In 1900 they opened the Empire hotels at Lowestoft, Bath and Buxton. By 1908 twelve hotels had been opened and Spiers & Pond introduced a scheme whereby a man or woman could live in any of their hotels, transferring from one to another at will, for £168 a year, £95 for six months or £50 for three months. At this time the company had four hotels in London, one in Manchester, four at seaside resorts and three in the country and the prices covered room, service, bath, breakfast, lunch, tea and dinner. Both Felix Spiers and Christopher Pond were keen cricketers, organising the first matches between England and Australia, which became the Test games; the first Test match was played in Melbourne in 1877.

The Strand Hotel Ltd

Lyons was associated with hotels as early as 1903, when the company briefly ran the Challis Hotel which had come into its possession by way of a property acquisition. It was demolished to make way for the building of the Coventry Street Corner House which opened in 1909. On 31 October 1907 the company known as the Strand Hotel Ltd was incorporated by the Salmon and Gluckstein families. The new hotel company had no legal association with Lyons, although they did share common directors (on incorporation these were Joseph Lyons, Montague Gluckstein and Alfred Salmon). The hotel company had been financed by public subscription to acquire long leases on Crown land in London's Strand but it was not until August 1922 that Lyons bought an interest in this hotel business when Isidore Gluckstein and others sold 4,500 deferred ordinary hotel shares to Lyons for £225,000. Eventually, on 1 July 1968, the Strand Hotel Ltd changed its name to Strand Hotels Ltd following a board resolution.

Official documents record that Montague Gluckstein and Joseph Lyons had entered into an agreement with the Crown to pay a £6,000 deposit for the existing leases of the estate on which stood Exeter Hall and St Michael's Church in the Strand. These agreements, including a building agreement dated 11 September 1907 between the King's Most Excellent Majesty and John Fortescue Horner, were later transferred to the Strand Hotel Ltd for an exchange of 5,000

£1 deferred ordinary shares. The principals in this contract, Montague Gluckstein and Joseph Lyons, had also entered into a number of other agreements (in December 1906, May 1907 and July 1907) with those who had interests in the property including William Ancell, the architect whose association with the Salmon and Gluckstein families had begun in the days of their tobacco business.

With the architectural and building arrangements concluded before the issue of the public prospectus, the projected expenditure on the development had been estimated at £200,000, including the cost of acquiring the site, the demolition and clearance of which amounted to £28,500. Salmon and Gluckstein family funds were probably used to pay the interest on the 130,000 £1 participating preferred ordinary shares before they were taken up by public subscription. The conditions for transfer of the agreements by Messrs Lyons and Gluckstein for capital investment in the company ensured that shares were quickly assigned. Not only did the Strand Hotel Ltd undertake to pay 5 per cent interest to shareholders on their investments while the hotel was being built, but the participating preferred ordinary shares carried a non-cumulative 7 per cent dividend, commencing from the date of the hotel's opening. All shares were entitled to 7 per cent dividend with each class of share receiving an additional 50 per cent allocation of the remaining profits. Because the deferred shares were much fewer in number than the participating preferred ordinary shares, the profit allocation always favoured the deferred shares over the participating preferred ordinary shares, sometimes by as much as 200 per cent. This disproportionate allocation of profit became the source of much acrimony from shareholders for many years after.

The Strand Palace Hotel

With its medley of hotels, theatres and shops, the Strand is one of the most famous thoroughfares in Europe but sadly lacking in architectural grandeur. In Elizabethan times, and long afterwards, it was bordered by aristocratic mansions, with gardens extending down to the riverside. The names still survive in, for example, Burleigh Street, Villiers Street, Bedford Street and Exeter Street. Earlier still the Strand had been the site of the Savoy Palace – home of John of Gaunt, younger son of Edward III and father of the future Henry IV – until it was burned down during the Peasant's Revolt of 1381. From Charing Cross to Temple Bar, where the famous griffin marks the western City boundary, the Strand is almost a mile long. It connects the fashionable West End to the financial axis of the City of London via Fleet Street, once famous the world over for journalism.

On 14 September 1909 the Strand Palace Hotel, with 470 rooms, opened. Although it was a few months behind schedule, it was an immediate success. From the outset the hotel was managed by twenty-one-year-old Julius Salmon (1888–1940), the youngest son of Barnett Salmon. He had joined Lyons straight after leaving school, and, in accordance with the company's usual practice, his apprenticeship began in the kitchens of the Trocadero restaurant. In September 1921 he became a director of the Strand Hotel Ltd (along with his elder brother, Maurice Salmon, who was in charge of the Cadby Hall factories). Julius Salmon took a keen interest in architecture, becoming engrossed with plans for the Cumberland Hotel, which was to open in 1933, and he was renowned for his 'hands-on' style of management. With a vivid imagination, often inventive and always smartly dressed, he even opened a clothing shop in 1934 in Oxford Street, near to the Cumberland Hotel, intending to compete with Marks & Spencer; but his clothing business was unsuccessful, and it was eventually sold to a Canadian firm. Similarly, his attempts to introduce innovative marketing methods at the Cadby Hall bakery in the mid-1920s foundered. He married Montague Gluckstein's daughter Emma, his cousin, and died in January 1940, aged only fifty-one. After his period managing the Strand Palace Hotel, he was put in charge of Lyons' Corner Houses, where his direct management skills were put to good use.

Originally the Strand Palace Hotel comprised 450 bedrooms, but during construction additional property, which included a bridge arch and

Left. The Strand Palace Hotel soon after it opened in 1909 with Haxell's Family Hotel embarrassingly positioned on both sides of Strand Hotel's entrance.

Right. This photograph shows Oliver Bernard's Art Deco entrance to the Strand Palace Hotel. *By kind permission of the Museum of London.*

connecting passage, had enabled extra bedrooms to be built. The management, however, did seem to miss an opportunity by not incorporating private bathrooms into the design; even after major extensions in 1928, private bathrooms were not added. By contrast many American hoteliers were increasingly providing such luxuries after the Mount Vernon Hotel at Cape May, New Jersey, opened in 1853 as the first hotel in the world to offer private bathrooms.

Although there was an entrance on to the Strand, the frontage of the Strand Palace Hotel at this point was relatively narrow, but the building widened out towards the rear. Embarrassingly, Haxell's Family Hotel occupied two separate frontages each side of the new hotel's entrance, giving the designers no alternative but to place the main entrance and lobby to the Strand Palace

Hotel round the corner in Exeter Street. In 1928, however, Haxell's property was acquired, enabling management to carry out major extensions that doubled the hotel's accommodation to 1,000 rooms as well as creating new retail outlets along the main thoroughfare of the Strand.

For the design of the hotel's new foyer, management had commissioned one of the most innovative British Art Deco architects of the period, Oliver Percy Bernard (1881–1939). Although he had no formal architectural training, Bernard's life was filled with adventure. After he left school in 1897 at sixteen he spent a short time in repertory theatre before signing on as a cabin boy on the tramp steamer *Manchester Commerce* and afterwards as a seaman on the Norwegian barque, *Naja of Arendal.* He studied stagecraft and became an assistant artist at Covent Garden. After briefly working in New York as principal scenic artist for Klaw & Erlanger, Oliver Bernard returned to England on the Cunard liner *Lusitania*, narrowly escaping drowning when the ship was torpedoed off southern Ireland on 7 May 1915. Commissioned in the Royal Engineers during the First World War, he was wounded and awarded the Military Cross. After demobilisation in March 1919 Bernard returned to the theatre as technical director for the Grand Opera Syndicate. Later he was placed in charge of the displays for the British Empire Exhibition of 1924. He was blown up while producing *Air Attack on London* in the Admiralty Theatre but survived to supervise the entire interior decoration and lighting for the Oxford Corner House in 1928 including the first mural landscape executed in marble. He began his work for the Company, however, in 1924 by designing the Lucullus Restaurant at the British Empire Exhibition of that year.

His superb masterpiece at the Strand Palace Hotel became known as the 'Bernard lobby' where, with his use of marbled walls, geometric carpet, leaded ceiling lights and ashtrays on stands, he created a design considered by many to be at the leading edge of the Art Deco movement. Styles change, however, and in 1968–9, in yet another refurbishment (this time by Dennis Lennon and Partners), the foyer was dismantled, 'in an act of incomprehensible vandalism' (from a memorandum by Steven Brindle held by the London Metropolitan Archives), and carted away to the Victoria and Albert Museum, where it remains in store and out of sight to visitors.

The 1928 programme of renovation at the Strand Palace Hotel included equipping every room with a telephone extension to bring the hotel in line with the trend in America. This was costly, however: with nearly 1,000 extensions required after the enlargement, the hotel company had to pay the same annual rental as 1,000 single subscribers. Furthermore, the telephone company insisted upon a permanent deposit of a sum equal to two-thirds of the quarterly account for call fees, so that the more the residents used the telephones, the more the Strand Palace Hotel was penalised. This reversal of the usual order of business methods served to discourage British hotels from installing telephones, and many hoteliers avoided this for years.

When the Strand Palace Hotel opened in 1909 it set new pricing standards for the industry. Rooms cost as little as 6 shillings per night (double rooms cost 11 shillings), including a table d'hôte breakfast, electric light, running hot and cold water in every room, second servings of dishes in the restaurant without charge and a no-tipping policy. Baths were included in the charge and, at extra cost, a private sitting room could be had. As an extra luxury fires could be lit in sitting rooms for an additional payment of 9d. per evening. Public rooms consisted of a 'handsome winter garden, luxurious dining and refreshment rooms, a drawing room, smoking and billiards rooms and lounges, bathrooms, domestic offices and kitchens with every modern facility'. A doctor's consulting room was made available for two hours every weekday evening and rooms 178 and 180 were used as ladies' and gentlemen's hairdressing saloons.

One of the hotel's most infamous guests was Fernando Buschmann, the First World War German spy who was executed in the Tower of London on 19 October 1915. Buschmann, a traveller in musical instruments who was always short of money, had been staying at the Piccadilly Hotel in April 1915 but had been advised by his friend, Emil Franco (who was involved in communicating information about naval and military matters to the enemy), that the Strand Palace Hotel was less expensive. He signed the register there on 25 April 1915. Even with the lower prices, money was still a problem and so he moved out in May, taking rooms with Franco in South Kensington.

The low prices opened up a new market for those of modest means, making the Strand Palace Hotel immediately popular. Confuting predictions that the hotel market in London was saturated, and in spite of the fact that the hotel was built right next door to the established Haxell's Family Hotel, the intuition of Joseph Lyons and Montague Gluckstein proved once again to be extraordinarily accurate. A profit of £41,727 was returned in the first year of operation.

The Regent Palace Hotel

Within a year, encouraged by the early success, the Strand Hotel Ltd embarked on an even more audacious plan by securing an eighty-year lease, again from the Crown, on an island site at the bottom of Regent Street bordered by Sherwood Street, Glasshouse Street, Brewer Street and Air Street. Waiting for the expiry of existing leases had delayed demolition and given the company valuable time to secure the necessary finance of £500,000. This was raised by the issue of additional stock in the hotel company which again was quickly taken up, probably from existing shareholders. When the Regent Palace Hotel opened on 26 May 1915 the 1,028-bedroom hotel,

An advertisement announcing the opening of the Regent Palace Hotel, taking up the whole front page of the *Daily Mail* on Saturday 22 May 1915.

with only public bathrooms, became the largest in Europe. It occupied a position near Piccadilly Circus where Joseph Lyons and Montague Gluckstein had existing interests – the first teashop, in Piccadilly, and the Trocadero restaurant in Shaftesbury Avenue.

By the outbreak of war in 1914 most of the construction work on the Regent Palace Hotel had reached completion and government officials allowed the interior decoration to proceed. Many hoteliers believed that the war would seriously damage their trade – partly through the loss of foreign visitors – and many had planned to close or reduce the number of rooms in use; yet it did not have the serious effect they had feared. Although the Regent Palace Hotel opened in the

midst of war, it attracted huge numbers of guests and all accommodation was fully occupied from the first day. Loss of tourist trade seemed to be outweighed by the fact that those who normally took their holidays in France spent them in London instead. Moreover, the huge influx of personnel from the armed services who spent their leave in London helped to fill rooms and increase bar takings. Further, as former domestic servants went to work in the factories, where they enjoyed higher pay, more middle-class families were eating out and so hotel restaurants benefited. Although from October 1914 licensed restaurants were ordered by government statutes to close one hour earlier at 10 p.m. instead of 11.00 p.m. (later, meatless days were introduced), this restriction did not affect hotel restaurants.

As the war progressed, the hotel trade received a further stimulus when the government appropriated fourteen of London's largest hotels, including the Hotel Cecil, to accommodate the increase in civil servants that wartime circumstances created. Many of these people remained in government occupation until the end of 1919, and during that time the fourteen hotels housed staff from the War Office, Ministry of Munitions, Air Ministry, Ministry of Labour, Board of Trade, Ministry of National Service and Reconstruction, War Savings Committee and US Army headquarters which were costing the government £782,000 per annum in rent. Some hotels, such as the Great Central at Marylebone, were requisitioned to accommodate the increasing number of wounded troops returning from the front. However, the Strand Palace and Regent Palace hotels were not commandeered, and so were able to profit substantially from the hotel famine that government requisitioning had created.

The acute shortages greatly benefited those hoteliers who had escaped the government's clutches. Hotels were so fully booked that during a criminal trial in April 1919 at the Old Bailey it was found impossible to secure beds for the jury in any hotels within a reasonable distance of the court. Likewise businessmen from the Midlands and the north with urgent matters in London found it difficult to obtain rooms, since hotels 'were sheltering a small army of more or less useless clerks', as one editorial put it. With almost 100 per cent of rooms occupied for most of the war it goes without saying that hotel restaurants also did well. Net profits of the Strand Hotel Ltd increased by 142 per cent between the start and end of the war, and shareholders received 9 per cent dividends during the same period. Before the requisitioned hotels were able to be brought back into general use, in order to benefit from the brief post-war boom, they needed extensive refurbishment because of damage caused by the wartime occupants. Some hoteliers even found it necessary to take action in the courts to obtain compensation from the government when they were eventually returned to normality (see Appendix 3).

Occupying an awkward, triangular-shaped site, the Regent Palace Hotel posed a challenge to the architects, Henry Tanner, Frederick Wills and William Ancell. They designed all the principal apartments to be aligned on an axis from the apex of the triangle, the hotel's main entrance. Rising to a height of 126 feet from the basement level, the hotel comprised nine floors above ground level and two basement storeys 20 feet below containing an immense grill room, a smoking room and a reading room, a small palm court and a billiards room as well as the hotel's services below. During excavation of the underground areas, part of Brewer Street subsided into the workings and a disaster was narrowly avoided when several of the business properties along Brewer Street almost fell into the abyss. The whole structure, when completed, required no less than 6,000 tons of steelwork. Glazed terracotta facings were used externally and the roof was covered with green slates. The nine upper floors formed a curtain around a large central light well, from which the ground-floor reception rooms on the main axis were top-lit.

Immediately after passing through the main entrance to the Regent Palace Hotel, which had a pavilion roof and faced Piccadilly Circus, the visitor arrived in a circular lounge lined with marble whose shallow dome was richly embellished. This led to the inner hall, where the stairs and three lifts to upper floors were

situated. Beyond the inner hall there was a spacious winter garden with a large domed roof containing over 70 feet of stained and leaded glass. From the winter garden, guests and visitors had access to a big coffee lounge. Most of the interiors of the public rooms were decorated in the manner of Louis XVI or with Adam-style plasterwork of great refinement. An annexe to the Regent Palace Hotel added a further 102 rooms in 1934, but it was not until the 1950s that some private bathrooms were installed.

The Royal Palace Hotel

With an eagerness to expand further their hotel interests, Montague Gluckstein entered into talks with the Metropolitan Railway Company in 1912. The railway company planned to build a hotel at Baker Street station and had already arranged finance from their sponsor for the building work. It had been agreed that the Strand Hotel Ltd would lease the hotel – uninspiringly named The Terminus – from the railway company for 2s. 6d. per square foot for eighty years. This was a perfect arrangement for the Strand Hotel Ltd, since by then they were already financially committed to the building of the Regent Palace Hotel, and a long lease with the Metropolitan Railway Company for a cash-generating business seemed ideal. However, leasing negotiations became delayed and work did not start until 1914, by which time war had broken out in Europe and the government terminated all new construction. When war ended the railway company had difficulty in raising new capital to proceed with building its hotel and, although discussions between the Strand Hotel Ltd and the Metropolitan Railway continued for many years, agreement could not be reached on a number of issues, principally the increase in costs, resulting in the abandonment of the project in 1919.

Undaunted by the loss of the Baker Street development, the Strand Hotel Ltd acquired a controlling interest in the Palace Hotel Company Ltd in August 1919. Built on the old site of the King's Arms Tavern, the Royal Palace Hotel had been designed by Basil Champneys in a grand Renaissance style. Champneys had laid out a series of rooms as self-contained apartments and when

The Royal Palace Hotel next to Kensington Palace driveway entrance. *By kind permission of the Royal Borough of Kensington and Chelsea, Libraries Department.*

Hall on the site of the present-day Royal Garden Hotel. The Royal Palace Hotel had been commandeered during the war years but its location, away from the main theatre centre, railway termini, clubs and exclusive shopping areas of the West End prevented it benefiting from the post-war hotel boom. Burdened with poor management, and in a somewhat run-down state, its profitability slumped. By the start of 1919 its financial situation had become critical and in May the Strand Hotel Ltd made an offer to buy a controlling interest which was quickly accepted. The directors were replaced by the nominees of Strand Hotel Ltd after having received a 'golden handshake' of £5,000.

Acquisition of the Royal Palace Hotel was extraordinary in a number of respects. First, its name uncannily matched the Strand Palace and Regent Palace hotels. Second, it deviated from the company's policy of building their own large units and operating them at popular prices – being pseudo-luxury, the Royal Palace Hotel's prices were two or three times higher than those of the Strand or Regent Palace hotels – and, third, the hotel did not occupy the central position so favoured by the Salmons and Glucksteins. Nevertheless, the Royal Palace Hotel did provide additional accommodation when the availability of hotel rooms in London was outstripped by demand. Since up to a hundred people were being turned away daily at some central hotels, this new capacity enabled management to transfer guests from their central London sites to Kensington. In February 1919 *The Caterer* reported that 'People have flocked to the metropolis from all parts of the country on business and pleasure bent. Army officers have come to town in battalions and foreign visitors have swelled the multitude of those besieging the hotels for accommodation.'

With good omnibus communications to the West End, and once Kensington High Street had become a fashionable shopping area with the Derry & Toms and Barker's department stores, the hotel prospered. Its popularity was enhanced in some measure by its non-residential activities, such as its famous tea dances and dinner dances for every occasion from St Patrick's Night to Leap

the Royal Palace Hotel opened in 1894 it had 350 bedrooms. The public rooms were most elaborate, with extensive use of carved walnut and red Moroccan leather. In 1897 a new elegant Empress Ballroom was opened with its own elaborate canopied entrance from Kensington High Street. It became popular for its Sunday evening dinners, served in the ballroom itself, and from the gallery diners were entertained by the same Blue Hungarian Band who had played so well at the Newcastle Exhibition.

The hotel occupied a prime position in a fashionable part of London just west of the Albert

Year. During the inter-war period the Royal Palace Hotel came under the control of Isidore Gluckstein's youngest son, Montague (1886–1958), who claimed that most crowned heads and virtually every member of a royal family in exile had visited the hotel. With Kensington Palace on one side, and the embassies lining Kensington Palace Gardens on the other, the hotel might well have been a magnet to these unfortunates.

The Cumberland Hotel

Although the shortage of London hotel rooms continued up to 1921, it gradually declined as the government progressively released hotels they had requisitioned during the war years. In the few years after the armistice, hotels and restaurants experienced a prosperous period peaking perhaps in 1919, the year of the Peace Celebration Parade in London. Needless to say the huge profits they were enjoying led to accusations of profiteering which on the bald evidence appeared justified. For example, the income of the Strand Hotel Ltd in 1914 had been assessed at £65,507 and by 1919 this had increased to £121,405 – a growth of over 185 per cent (see Appendix 3). However, a Ministry of Labour study (reported in *The Times*, 2 February 1920) found that the level of retail prices of food and other items of working-class family expenditure was 130 per cent above pre-war levels. Such increases would probably have been greater in the case of hotels and restaurants, which tended to use more luxurious items whose prices would have risen even higher. Butter for example had risen 300 per cent, carpets 250 per cent, linen 600 per cent and labour 130 per cent. A separate survey at this time by the Incorporated Association of Hotels and Restaurants found that hotels had seldom increased their costs beyond 50 per cent of pre-war levels. Their profitability was attributed to the lack of immediate maintenance during and after the war together with the general shortage of hotel rooms brought about by government commandeering.

Hoteliers continued to enjoy their brief period of prosperity up to and during the Wembley Exhibition of 1924–5, after which trade went into decline again throughout the

depression of the 1930s. To the bewilderment of some observers, the Strand Hotel Ltd seemed insulated from these barren trading circumstances and its hotels remained universally popular. Their central locations, high standards and reasonable prices no doubt helped. Therefore the hotel slump did not deter the management from planning new hotels and they used the Lyons AGM of 1922 to promote shareholder participation in the hotel industry for the first time. The formal bonding came during 1922, when Lyons acquired, from Isidore Salmon and others, 4,500 deferred shares (valued at £225,000) in the Strand Hotel Ltd by issuing 450,000 'B' proportional profit shares and exchanging them. From this point the two companies began sharing costs in a hotel-building programme which led to the magnificent Cumberland Hotel and the Maison Lyons restaurant at Marble Arch. Although hotel building continued after the Second World War this particular project probably marks Lyons' pinnacle of hotel building, but much was still to come.

On 18 June 1921 the Strand Hotel Ltd had secured a building agreement with the Right Honourable Henry Berkeley, Viscount Portman. The agreement itself was relatively straightforward, but before work could begin a series of complex discussions took place with the aim of obtaining other leases in the immediate and abutting properties. Lyons themselves complicated matters by acquiring an adjacent site for another Corner House development (the first Corner House having opened in 1909) when on 7 April 1922 they paid Viscount Portman £99,938. The Marble Arch acquisition was so enormous in its complexity that no fewer than seventeen insurance companies were associated with mortgage arrangements as well as the chocolate firm of Cadbury. Building work did not commence until the late 1920s, partly because of the £500,000 extension to the Strand Palace Hotel.

Negotiations for the Marble Arch site were largely secretive. It was nearly ten years since Lyons had become a shareholder in the Strand Hotel Ltd and in 1931 all shareholders were notified that a new company, Cumberland Hotels

The Cumberland Hotel opposite Marble Arch. Built by Lyons' own Works Department, it had raised floors, cavity walls and other special sound insulation properties. The bell-boys were forbidden to call out names.

personnel representing all trades and skills from its own large Works Department based at Cadby Hall. The architect for the overall design was Frederick Wills, and Oliver Bernard was responsible for designing the public rooms. Meticulous attention had been given to comfort, including innovative sound-proofing measures. For example, all the bedroom walls were cavity-constructed, floors were raised above their concrete bases and covered in sound-insulating rubber, large motors in the hotel were secured to insulated foundations and pageboys' cries were replaced by a system of lights. Each of the 900 bedrooms had its own bathroom, yet prices were as low as 11s. 6d. per night including breakfast. Amilcare Proserpi, manager until his death in December 1948,

Ltd, would be incorporated, the capital of which would be divided equally between J. Lyons & Co. Ltd and the Strand Hotel Ltd. Although Lyons had intended to build a Corner House on the property it had acquired at Marble Arch between Old Quebec Street, Oxford Street and Portman Street, 'after mature consideration' management decided that complications would probably arise from the close proximity of their other restaurant (located in Oxford Street) and the new hotel, with its planned restaurant facilities.

Cumberland Hotels Ltd registered on 6 November 1931 and shortly thereafter raised £750,000 from debenture issues and mortgages. The two parent companies contributed towards the loans, with Lyons' share standing at £781,500 by March 1934. Building costs, which had been rising during the 1920s, were kept to a minimum. Lyons allocated to the project large numbers of

accompanied King George V and Queen Mary when they visited the hotel two days before it opened on 12 December 1933 in time for the Christmas trade. With such heavy bookings, which continued into 1934, many disappointed hotel guests had to be accommodated at the Strand Palace and Regent Palace hotels.

The opening of the Cumberland Hotel in 1933 marked the end of Lyons' first phase of hotel building and there were no significant new developments until 1960. There were several reasons for this pause. The large loans which funded the Cumberland Hotel project had to be repaid and £200,000 of this remained outstanding twenty years later. Further building work was also prevented by the outbreak of war in 1939. Some hotels suffered temporary staff shortages when Italy entered the war in June 1940. Many Italians had worked in the restaurant or hotel trade in

Britain and during anti-Italian demonstrations in Soho the windows of their restaurants were smashed.

One of the most important elements in the cessation of hotel building, however, was the indecisiveness of General Management – a consortium, at the highest level within Lyons, composed almost exclusively of members of the Salmon and Gluckstein families, some of whom were directors. General Management could not agree on policy and had no clear vision of how the hotel business should be developed. During the first phase strong leadership had been given by Julius and Harry Salmon but Julius died in 1940 and Harry in 1950. The unseasoned younger General Management members, although holding individual and sometimes passionate views, could not agree on a common strategy. Discussions on hotel plans were long and unstructured and the one which evoked the most passion was the idea of redeveloping the Trocadero restaurant and Coventry Street Corner House site. This controversial project, known as the 'X' Scheme, called for the replacement of the Trocadero and Corner House restaurants with a 1,000-bedroom hotel. The plan, first proposed in 1944, was exhaustively discussed for fifteen years with numerous variations on style, size and facilities, but it eventually came to nothing.

The Pioneers of the Lyons Empire

The period leading up to and including the First World War, when the first phase of hotel building began, was particularly momentous for Lyons. At the time that the Lyons company was established, less than a generation had elapsed since the Gluckstein family had arrived in London from Europe in 1841. In conjunction with the Salmons they had set up a successful tobacco retail and manufacturing business which had grown from nothing to become the largest retail tobacconist in the world and a profitable quoted company. This had been accomplished largely by individuals who did not have the benefit of further education but had a strong family bond which endured for many years. With their accumulated wealth the second generation of the families ventured into exhibition catering with

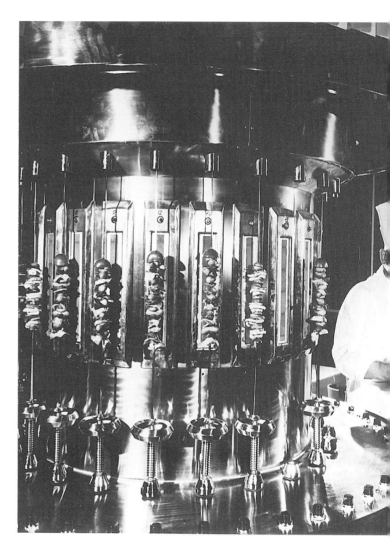

the assistance of an artistic entrepreneur, Joseph Lyons. For several years both tobacco and catering interests were run simultaneously and although the catering company had been funded by the Salmon and Gluckstein families its figurehead was Joseph Lyons, whose name the new enterprise adopted.

Many of the characteristic methods used in advancing the tobacco undertaking were translated to catering: meticulous planning, high standards, resourcefulness, value for money and boldness. These qualities and the untiring ambition of all, helped by the economic mood of the country, ensured that the catering experiment prospered. Once Lyons had established a reputation for contract catering, there followed a diversification into retail trading,

The Brochette (revolving grill) in Cumberland Hotel's L'Epée d'Or Restaurant. By kind permission of Ralf Morhaim

as Salmon & Gluckstein had done with the tobacco business. This came about in 1894 when the consortium opened their first teashop and retail outlet in Piccadilly. With persistent vigour the teashop chain was greatly enlarged between 1895 and 1920.

When the Salmon and Gluckstein families disposed of their tobacco interests in 1902 to the Imperial Tobacco Company, they concentrated on catering and food manufacture, which had meanwhile evolved to satisfy the teashop and catering needs. Door-to-door sales of bread and other food augmented sales in the teashop retail outlets. A modest tea and coffee packaging operation, which had been started to gauge the market, grew phenomenally so that by the 1920s Lyons tea could be bought throughout Britain, in the face of strong competition. The first provincial teashops were brought into the group in 1909, although they had opened earlier, when the Ceylon Café's interests were acquired. Meanwhile, after an inauspicious start, huge restaurants had been opened in London. All these activities flourished under a competent management, largely of Jewish origin.

Although the hotels that had been built were not officially part of the Lyons empire until later, the twenty-five years since the company was incorporated had been extraordinary, and by the First World War Lyons were ready for the next phase of their development.

Sadly, by the 1920s those three far-sighted individuals who had made it all possible were dead. Barnett Salmon, who had befriended Montague Gluckstein and married his daughter Helena thus starting the Salmon and Gluckstein dynasty, died in 1897. Sir Joseph Lyons died on 22 June 1917 at the Hyde Park Hotel in London. He was sixty-nine years of age and had been suffering from Bright's disease, the name given to an acute inflammation of the kidneys. He left no children and his wife, Sarah Psyche, died at Grosvenor House in Park Lane, London, on 27 November 1948 aged eighty-eight. She had outlived him by thirty years, having had the unenviable experience of living through two world wars. In her will Lady Lyons, as she had become, bequeathed over £20,000 to no fewer than fifty-six members of her family, mainly cousins, nieces, nephews and sisters as well as to friends. In addition, a number of charities and other institutions benefited. Among these was Sir Joseph Lyons' old school in Heygate Street, St Dunstan's (a charitable organisation founded in 1915 to care and rehabilitate those blinded in the service of their country), the Jewish Soup Kitchen of Whitechapel, the Society for the Distribution of Bread, Meat and Coals to the Jewish Poor of Lyncroft Mansions, the Boot Fund of the Jewish Borough Schools and many more. £1,000 was bequeathed to the Jewish Cemetery at Willesden for the upkeep of Sir Joseph and Lady Lyons' and his parents' graves and £400 for the upkeep of Lady Lyons' parents' graves at the Jewish Burial Ground in Ramsgate. Instructions were left that fresh flowers should be placed on the graves every fortnight in summer and every four weeks in winter and that they should not be allowed to fall into disrepair, nor should the lettering on the gravestones become illegible. In 1933 Daphne du Maurier wrote her novel *The Progress of Julius*, and it has been suggested that she modelled her character Levy on Joseph Lyons. One of the finest compliments Joseph Lyons ever received was from King Edward VII who reportedly said of him, 'I like Mr Lyons, he feeds my people well.'

Isidore Gluckstein died three years after Joseph Lyons, on 10 December 1920. He was sixty-nine years old and was the financial genius behind the Lyons success. It was through his wife's family that Joseph Lyons had been asked to join the 'catering experience'. Rose Gluckstein had died in 1908, leaving six children, of whom Samuel and Montague, and also their children, would play important roles in the Lyons story.

Montague Gluckstein died on 7 October 1922 aged sixty-eight. In February 1884 he had married Matilda Franks, who played an active role in staff social affairs and lived until 1950. Their two sons, Samuel and Isidore, became directors of Lyons, Samuel in 1914 and Isidore in 1925. Although he was the second son of Samuel Gluckstein, Montague was largely responsible for shaping the company's policy and direction. Among his great qualities was his foresight; he was seldom taken

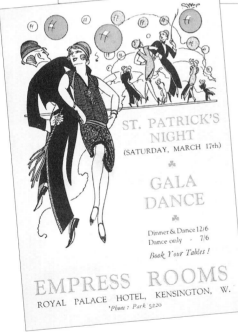

Royal Palace Hotel, event menu covers.

Alfred Salmon, the first son of Barnett Salmon, died at the relatively young age of 60 in 1928. He had been a director since 1894 and took charge of the hugely successful British Empire Exhibition in 1924. His brothers Isidore, Montague, Joseph, Harry and Maurice, as well as their children, all played their parts in the Lyons story.

Deaths, too, of another kind had occurred. Mostly volunteers, 238 former Lyons employees did not return from the battlefields of France. Their deaths were deeply deplored but they would not be forgotten; as will be seen later in this book, management purchased a large parcel of land at Sudbury Hill, Middlesex, and turned it into a magnificent sports ground in their memory, erecting a granite memorial obelisk there.

However, once the war ended, Lyons' catering would scale new heights, as the company took advantage of a final flourish of the British Empire.

by surprise and his inspirational leadership was undoubtedly one of the reasons for the company's success. Such was his popularity that no fewer than ninety British newspapers reported his death, some carrying extensive obituaries. They included such diverse publications as the *Stage*, the *Electrician*, the *Policy Holder* and the *Referee*.

Part 2

LYONS' HEYDAY BETWEEN THE WARS
(1918–1945)

1918	Interest in W.H. & F.J. Horniman Ltd acquired.
	Black & Green Tea Company, Manchester, acquired.
1919	Sudbury sports ground opened (2 August).
	Royal Palace Hotel acquired.
	First Royal Garden Party.
1920	Overseas Trading Corporation Ltd formed (31 January).
	Death of Isidore Gluckstein (founding member) (10 December).
1921	Greenford Factory opened (18 July).
	Normand Garage Ltd registered.
1922	Death of Montague Gluckstein (founding member) (7 October).
1924	British Empire Exhibition catering contract (23 April).
1925	Bakery Rails Service (delivery by railway) started.
	Nippy waitress created (1 January).
	Largest banquet, Masonic Festival held at Olympia (8 August).
1926	Lujeri Tea Estate bought (February).
	Henry Telfer commenced trading (7 June).
	James Hayes & Sons Ltd acquired.
	First full-time medical officer appointed.
1927	First ice-cream ammonia freezers installed.
1928	Oxford Corner House opened (3 May).
	New laboratory opened.
	Strand Palace Hotel enlarged with Art Deco entrance.
	Death of Alfred Salmon (11 October).
1929	Construction of Lujeri tea factory completed (August).
1931	Cumberland Hotels Ltd registered (6 November).
1932	First Deed of Trust of pension scheme signed (20 December).
1933	Cumberland Hotel opens (12 December).
1934	First modern car park opens at Marble Arch (November).
1935	Staff swimming pool opened at Sudbury sports grounds (2 June).
1936	Catering at Wimbledon Lawn Tennis Championships started.
1937	Sir Isidore Salmon becomes Catering Advisor to War Office.
1938	Lyons buys 54 per cent of Bee-Bee (Symbol) Biscuits.
1939	Popular Café, Piccadilly, closed (15 September).
1940	Jersey tea company (OTC) occupied by German troops (1 July).
	Teashop damaged by first air attack on London (25 August).
	Blitz feeding.
1941	Lyons appointed managers of Elstow munitions factory.
	Teashop self-service introduced.
	Normand Garage Ltd renamed Normand Ltd (19 June).
1942	WW II Food Orders imposed (June).
	American Red Cross take over Maison Lyons, Shaftesbury Av.
1943	Catering Wages Act introduced.

Chapter

THE LAST OF EXHIBITION CATERING

THE COLOSSAL SCALE of the First World War was underpinned by a world-wide belief in imperialism. While Britain, Russia and France had already created vast colonial empires, Germany belatedly aspired to conquer the few remaining unclaimed territories. In 1914 imperialism reached a peak, when nearly 80 per cent of the world's land was under the control of a few colonial powers. By this time the internal stability of the great nations depended strongly on access to raw materials and successful competition in international markets. During the First World War, the USA replaced Britain as the world's major industrial power. It was therefore to its empire that Britain looked for markets to replace those lost to the United States and other powers.

A million of the British Empire's men were killed during the war and two million more were wounded. Shipping tonnage loss exceeded 7.5 million, with the Royal Navy losing 207 of its capital and support ships. The economic damage was immeasurable, and Britain and its empire bore nearly 30 per cent of the cost of the war. Inevitably, the vitality and enterprise of the nation suffered. During 1918–19 Britain's trade benefited from a post-war boom resulting from world-wide efforts to rebuild the economy, but the recovery was short-lived. From 1920 the nation's staple export industries – coal, iron, textiles and shipbuilding – sank into a long period of stagnation and decline with high unemployment, leading to the depression of the 1930s. However, the general economic climate for caterers was more favourable, especially once food was released from government controls in June 1920.

During the war the business of outdoor catering had in large measure been suspended and it did not revive fully until the 1920s. The restrictions placed on caterers in the aftermath of the war were severe. As well as shortages of every commodity, outdoor caterers had to contend with enormous increases in the cost of erecting marquees, rail fares, wages and food and lodging for staff. Even the expense of replacing broken tableware had soared to four times that of pre-war years. Every article of food and furnishing used by caterers had risen in price; by 1920 the estimated average increase in the price of commodities was 128 per cent. The cost of sugar was up by 400 per cent, milk 350 per cent, eggs 200 per cent, poultry 250 per cent, tablecloths 450 per cent, glass tumblers 360 per cent and dinner plates 200 per cent; even the outlay on waiters' cheque pads had risen by 600 per cent.

The British Empire Exhibition

The war, which had been so extravagant of human life, is said to have been 'a triumph for the Empire'. In London, Australia House was completed in 1918 followed by India House in 1928 to complement Sir Edwin Lutyens' New Delhi capital which had been started in 1911 and took seventeen years to complete. As well as providing goods of all kinds for the United Kingdom, the British Empire served another purpose. The high level of unemployment at home prompted thousands of dejected Britons to sail for the Dominions, all hopefully seeking new opportunities. Between 1921 and 1925,

635,000 people emigrated from Britain. Most knew little of the countries to which they were going except perhaps that Canada had mounted police and Red Indians and South Africa was the land of the Zulus and diamonds. To combat this ignorance of the empire at home the government conceived of a British Empire Exhibition at Wembley in what was then rural Middlesex. For the first time the empire came to Britain rather than the other way around. Being only seven miles from the capital, Wembley Central station had been connected to the London Underground system in 1917, but before the exhibition opened considerable road construction had been necessary; this subsequently facilitated the rapid growth of residential building in the area.

At a cost of £4.5 million Wembley's 220 acres incorporated fifteen miles of streets, the centrepiece being the great Empire Stadium, which had opened a year before the main exhibition for its first major sporting event, the Football Association Cup Final between Bolton Wanderers and West Ham United on 28 April 1923 (Bolton won 2-1). The stadium was designed to hold 100,000 spectators, but owing to a miscalculation at the turnstiles 126,000 football fans were let in. An estimated 75,000 more people managed to scale the inadequate boundary walls to gain free admission. A crowd disaster was narrowly averted by the effort of a solitary mounted policeman who coaxed the good-humoured crowd back on to the terraces single-handed. The stadium is the only structure remaining and continues in use for major sporting and entertainment events to this day although it is now due for replacement. Biggest of all, however, was the Palace of Engineering, the largest concrete building in the world in its day, six and a half times the size of Trafalgar Square. So many flags flew from this and the other structures that it was difficult to pick them all out. In the Canada building Niagara Falls had been reproduced, while the gardens throughout the site contained 100,000 tulips and 5,000 delphiniums. As the whole exhibition, which was floodlit at night, was impossible to see in one day, season tickets were made available for the earnest.

Despite a strike in early April, the British Empire Exhibition opened as planned on St George's Day, 23 April 1924. At the opening ceremony Sir Edward Elgar conducted massed bands and choirs in the intensely patriotic 'Land of Hope and Glory', while King George V, whose speech was relayed to millions of people on the radio by the British Broadcasting Company, was heard by his subjects for the first time from Land's End to John O'Groats. As a piece of theatre, to demonstrate the nations' technological achievements, the King sent a telegram to himself routed from London to London via the British Empire, passing through Canada, New Zealand, Australia, South Africa, India, Aden, Egypt and Gibraltar. Taking just one minute and 20 seconds to complete its journey before being returned to the King, the 'electric message' was delivered by a telegram boy, Henry Annals, in front of the 50,000 people at the opening.

From the outset only Lyons could satisfy the requirements of the exhibition organisers, who wanted the catering plan to be in the hands of a single supplier who could provide a range of catering alternatives. Those enterprises that had tendered for the business on the basis of sub-contracting were rejected. Quite apart from providing chefs, waiters, porters and other catering staff, Lyons brought dozens of clerks and statisticians from their administrative head-quarters to supervise and control the thirty-three different restaurants scattered across the 400 acres of exhibition space. Everything had to be produced on a vast scale: tens of thousands of cups, plates and cutlery, tables, seating, menus and every possible item associated with mass catering, right down to cash tills. It was probably the largest catering contract ever undertaken in this country over such a long period of time, and it is doubtful whether any organisation could have mounted – or could now mount – such an operation.

In an 'Agreement for and Relating to Catering and Other Rights and Services', the British Exhibition Company had appointed J. Lyons & Co. Ltd as sole and exclusive refreshment caterers. The signatories to the agreement were Alfred and Isidore Salmon for Lyons and

J. Stevenson and Travers Clarke for the British Empire Exhibition. Lyons were bound by an undertaking that the refreshments sold should be of 'sound, wholesome and merchantable quality' and that unless authorised in writing by the British Empire Exhibition, all food and beverages supplied were to be the produce of the British Empire. As well as supplying refreshments to the public, Lyons were to provide not only staff canteens, at usual canteen prices, for the exhibition staff but tea-rooms and a licensed bar at the press club.

The interiors of the refreshment premises were equipped and decorated by the exhibition organisers at their expense according to Lyons' plans, including the stoves, boilers, washing-up services, cellar, lighting, water closets and fixtures. Costs were submitted by Lyons and accepted by the exhibition authorities. Special rail excursion rates and privileges were obtained for Lyons staff by the exhibition company from railway companies. Details of the cost of the contract have been lost but from a copy which survives in the London Metropolitan Archives it would appear that the exhibition organisers settled on a commission system, calculated from cash receipts, based on a five-tiered scale.

The restaurant fronts were painted red, for in those days maps always showed the British Empire in red so that schoolchildren as well as adults could easily identify the extent of the empire's bounds. Even the 1d. commemorative postage stamps issued by the Post Office were red.

The Lucullus Restaurant, situated near the Raglan Garden, became the exhibition's showpiece and the most exclusive restaurant. Adjoining this Lyons had built a beautiful dance-floor with entertainment provided by famous musicians. The Lucullus Restaurant could also be reserved for private functions. The Grand Restaurant, on a huge scale, was also very chic but there were many other restaurants including a Grill Room and Popular Cafés to satisfy all tastes and pockets. The cost of meals ranged from 3s. 6d. to 5 shillings for luncheon, to 5s. 6d. to 10s. 6d. for dinner and 2s. 6d. for a set tea.

The staff requirements for the Grill Room and associated kitchens alone numbered 380,

and are set out in the table on page 91. Of these there were 155 waiters with forty associated aides who assisted the waiters away from the customers' tables. Many of the waiting staff were seconded from the Trocadero and other restaurants, while others were recruited specifically for the exhibition. Copious instructions were prepared for all levels of staff. For example, all waiters and aides were warned that every customer must be treated with the utmost courtesy and promptness. Soliciting or touting for tips would be severely dealt with. The waiter's place was at his station, near his tables facing the customer, and the aides were instructed to stand near their respective sideboards when not having other duties to perform. No conversation whatsoever, especially in a foreign language, was allowed during the service. Fourteen washers (plus two others for glass) were employed in the Grill Room alone, and there were six cheese men responsible for ensuring that waiters were provided with the correct brands and portions. Instructions to all members of staff, including superintendents, covered every aspect of catering from the correct procedures for taking an order to dealing with a complaint. Every member of staff from the humble lavatory attendants to the superintendent in charge had his or her respective instructions, which in all cases were extremely detailed. There was no room for ambiguity. The cigar and liquor butlers, for example, were reminded that packets of cigarettes could not be sold after 8 p.m. (9 p.m. on Saturdays) but single cigarettes and cigars could be sold. There were over sixty different job definitions covering chefs, carvers, vegetable cleaners, poulterers, fishmongers, butchers, fish fryers, sauciers, plongeurs, porters, linen room maids, cellermen, cocktail butlers, cashiers and many more. All had to sign in well before their work started so they could take their own meals and be ready to begin their duties, properly attired, in good time.

When complete, the total catering plan gave an estimated seating area of 10 acres where 30,000 individuals could eat simultaneously; in a single day Lyons could produce 175,000 meals and, if necessary, increase the numbers at short notice.

It is reported that during the first year of the exhibition 8 million meals were served and at its peak seventy van deliveries were required each day to keep demand satisfied.

Not only were the catering supplies brought in by road but a special railway siding had been built to assist with the weekly delivery of 75 tons of meat, 260 tons of bread and cakes, 1,500 cases of colonial dried fruit, 2,000 colonial pineapples, 3,000 tins of sardines, 2,000 gallons of soup, 40 tons of potatoes, 6 tons of tea and milk, and half a million bottles of mineral water. Catering staff in attendance numbered 7,000, plus support staff from headquarters, and it has been estimated that over 100,000 cubic feet of gas per hour was used in the kitchens and 20,000 gallons of water in food preparation and cleaning. The exhibition was one of the most successful ever held in this country, attracting 27 million visitors over a two-year period.

One innovation at the Wembley Exhibition was the United Kingdom's first rodeo, brought from Mexico by the impresario Charles Blake Cochran. He had learned many of his theatrical skills while working in various touring companies in America in the 1890s. Cochran had first come to the notice of Lyons in 1902, when he put on a show called *The Miracle* at Olympia, subsequently using this venue to promote boxing and other entertainment. In the meantime he had promoted and managed entertainments ranging from circus and wrestling to Diaghilev's Russian ballet. In 1924, having been warned by animal protection societies in America of the undoubted cruelties entailed by rodeos, the Royal Society for the Prevention of Cruelty to Animals (RSPCA) protested to the exhibition authorities and tried to have the show stopped. In this they were unsuccessful, but severe injuries to many steers at the rodeo subsequently drew the wrath of the

Grill Room

Superintendent in charge	1	Superintendent (assistant)	1
Superintendents	8	Waiters	155
Aides	40	Cigar & liquor butlers	4
Cocktail butlers	4	Goods clerk in charge	1
Goods clerk assistants	1	Cellerman in charge	1
Cellerman assistants	3	Storeman in charge	1
Storeman in charge	1	Storeman assistant	1
Watchman (day & night)	2	Cashiers	4
Counterhands, steam	4	Still room maids	2
Supply wine barmaids	4	Cheesemen	6
Porters on dirties	8	China washers	14
Platemen	10	Glass washers	2
Linen room maids	3	Goods porters	7
Desk attendants	4	Door attendants	2
Lavatory attendants (M&F)	2		

Grill Kitchen

Chef	1	Sous chef	3
Garde manager	1	Garde manager commis	6
Saucier	1	Saucier 1st commis	2
Saucier commis	4	Entremetier	1
Entremetier 1st commis	1	Entremetier commis	6
Rotissier	1	Rotissier commis	3
Patissier	1	Patissier commis (F)	3
Hors d'oeuvier	1	Hors d'oeuvier commis (F)	3
Grill cooks	8	Carvers	4
Checkers (F)	2	Checkers	4
Fishmongers	2	Poulterers	1
Butchers	4	Vegetable cleaners (F)	6
Fish fryers	4	Plongeurs	2
Porters (larder)	1	Porters (pastry)	1
Porters (grill)	2	Porters (kitchen)	2
Kitchen Clerks	4		

press, and the RSPCA, the public, the police and finally the exhibition authorities demanded the withdrawal of part of the programme. The RSPCA issued summonses against Cochran, the manager and one of the cowboys for cruelty to the animals, and the police also took out summonses. The hearing of the RSPCA and the police's cases took three days and finally, by a majority of one, the bench of twelve judges dismissed them.

Nevertheless the resulting bad publicity and legal costs almost bankrupted Cochran, who was no stranger to insolvency, having built his reputation on extremely lavish productions. However, Major Montague Gluckstein (1886–1958), younger son of Isidore Gluckstein and a Lyons director since 1919, threw him a lifeline by engaging him, at considerable expense, to present cabaret at the Trocadero restaurant grill. During the later 1920s Cochran had a successful collaboration with Noël Coward in the musical theatre and was responsible for producing the English première of the Russian opera, *Mozart and Salieri*, by Rimsky-Korsakov. Cochran was knighted in 1948 and remained a close friend of Major Gluckstein, attending the Trocadero restaurant's jubilee celebrations in 1946 even though he was seriously ill at the time and could hardly walk.

The British Empire Exhibition closed on 1 November 1924, but after much speculation it reopened at the beginning of the following May and continued until the end of October 1925. Some changes were made for the second year, including new flower beds, new attractions in the amusement park and, in particular, new catering structures. Since Lyons had enjoyed a catering monopoly during the 1924 season, they were less inclined to share catering arrangements with others as required by the new contracts and refused to tender. Lyons' management felt that the goodwill earned during the first twelve months might be put at risk if other caterers failed to adopt the same high standards. The first year's revenues had been so gratifying that Lyons management were able to concentrate on extending and re-equipping the factories and replacing ageing transport fleets. They had also gained immeasurable benefits from the exposure

of their products to a world audience; but the exhibition had been a great strain on the company.

Outdoor Catering and Banquets

Although Wembley was the last important exhibition for which Lyons undertook the catering, general outdoor and contract catering remained important revenue-earning activities. These had started in the company's formative years following their success with the Newcastle and Glasgow exhibitions. Although small in comparison to many private banquets which followed, one of their most important must have been the banquet given to His Excellency Li Chung Tang, a diplomat in the service of the Emperor of China, on 14 August 1896 when he visited the Telegraph Construction & Maintenance Company works at Enderby Wharf

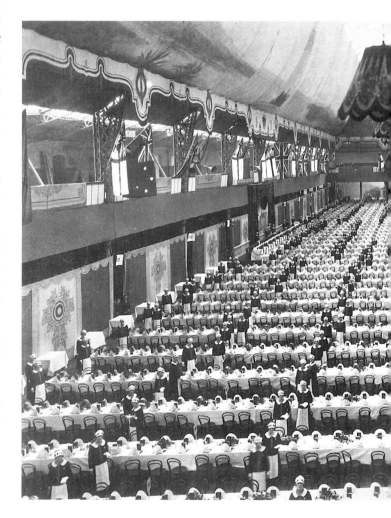

A banquet for the World Cotton Conference held in Liverpool's St George's Hall on 15 July 1921.

Waitresses take up their positions for an official photograph just before 7,250 Freemasons take their seats for the largest banquet ever, the Masonic Festival, given at Olympia on 8 August 1925.

on the River Thames. With the Marquis of Tweedsdale just 141 Admirals, Vice-Admirals and other important guests sat down to a six-course lunch which started two hours late due to the late arrival of Li Chung Tang.

It was the experience of outdoor catering that led Lyons to undertake banquets. Lord Strathcona, the Scottish-born fur trader and financier who built the Canadian Pacific Railroad, had commissioned Lyons to cater for 2,400 guests in 1906. All supplies, waitresses included, had been sent to Aberdeen by special train from London, the food having being cooked in field kitchens. An even larger event was a house garden party for 3,000 guests which King Edward VII had given at Windsor Castle in 1904; catering for both this and the event in Aberdeen had been arranged at very short notice.

The responsibility for the garden parties and banquets fell to the Outdoor Catering Department, which for many years was managed by Bertie Joseph, son of Samuel Gluckstein's nephew Abraham Joseph and his first cousin Sarah Gluckstein (daughter of Samuel Gluckstein). Born in 1886, Bertie Joseph started work at Lyons in 1900 at the age of fourteen. He underwent a long apprenticeship in all departments before becoming manager of the Throgmorton restaurant. In due course he was put in charge of the Outdoor Catering Department, which included Olympia. For a brief period he was responsible for the waitress training school. His name, however, is usually associated with the direction of some of the main events handled by the Outdoor Catering Department, particularly the Dublin Exhibition of 1905, the grand banquets, the royal garden parties, the Wimbledon Lawn Tennis Championships and the Chelsea Flower Shows.

When Bertie Joseph died in February 1948, his outdoor catering responsibilities were taken over by his second cousin Norman Joseph, a Lyons director who, unlike Bertie, had a quick temper and frequently displayed an intolerant, aggressive attitude towards his staff. He served as a major in the Army Catering Corps during the Second World War and afterwards in 1948 was appointed an honorary adviser to the Home

Office, advising on catering for the Metropolitan Police and HM Prisons, work which earned him a CBE in 1953. He was knighted in 1963; in 1969, in recognition of his services to the royal household, the Queen made him a Knight Commander of the Royal Victorian Order.

During Bertie Joseph's time, Lyons' expertise in catering for large numbers was typified by their preparation for a banquet commemorating the 25th anniversary of the *Daily Mail* newspaper on Sunday 1 May 1921, the largest banquet ever held in the United Kingdom up to that time. Only eight days' notice was given for the Outdoor Catering Department to plan and prepare a party for 7,000 persons. The meal, which was hot, was designed to take one hour. It was actually served in one hour and two minutes without a hitch. The part which aroused most favourable comment from Viscount Northcliffe, the newspaper's proprietor, was that 'in every part of the hall the soup was served hot'. Even at such a vast event as this Lyons' high standards dictated that each waitress was responsible for no more than eight guests, and staff were brought in from all parts of the country; no other firm could have catered for such large numbers within the limits of their own resources. One of Lyons' largest catering events took place in 1921 when 15,000 people, including King George V, commemorated the completion of the Royal Albert Dock, the last of several which had been started in 1802. In the same year they catered for the World's Cotton Conference in Liverpool.

By far the largest indoor banquet ever undertaken by Lyons, however, was the Masonic Festival held to mark the Freemasons' Peace Memorial Fund and the raising of over £1 million towards the erection of the magnificent Grand Lodge in Great Queen Street. It was put on at Olympia as a luncheon on Saturday 8 August 1925. Some 7,250 Freemasons sat down to nearly one and a half miles of banqueting table; one meal was entirely salt-free for a guest on a special diet. The original estimate had been for 7,093 people with a guarantee of 6,600, but during the planning stages further interest in the banquet had been shown. The Masonic brethren, who were entertained by a forty-five-piece ensemble

from the Welsh Guards, were served by 1,253 waitresses, some of whom were brought to London from all over the country, 940 for food and 313 for wine, supported by 700 cooks and porters. More than 188,000 table appointments were required simultaneously including some 50,000 plates, 30,000 glasses, 30,000 knives, 37,000 forks and 15,000 spoons, with an additional 12,000 cutlery items used by the waiting staff. The requirements were so colossal that the Hire Department was unable to provide all the necessary equipment and some silverware had to be borrowed from teashops after they had closed on the Friday evening. Everything had to be returned by 6 p.m. on the day of the banquet, just two hours after the lunchers had departed. Records show that more than 3,500 items were broken.

A banquet of this size had never been attempted by anyone before, and its planning had started a year earlier when the first scheme and menus were submitted. Negotiations continued for some months and by November 1924 a price had been agreed after Grand Lodge had requested a reduction of 2 shillings per head on the original quotation; regrettably there are no records of the full price paid.

Nothing was left to chance for this prestigious banquet; copious instructions on twenty typed pages of foolscap were drawn up by Arthur Christian, one of the senior managers responsible for the detailed planning. All participating staff underwent rigorous training in banqueting technique, since many had not experienced any event like this before.

Tables had been decorated with fresh flowers, which had taken forty-five florists fourteen hours to arrange. The banquet area inside Olympia had been divided into seven sections, each assigned a distinctive colour – yellow, mauve, green, pink, red, blue or white, corresponding to guest tickets. Though no division was apparent, each section was entirely self-contained, with its own kitchens, staff dressing rooms, chefs and superintendents. The waiting staff were all informed of the colour indicating the section in which they would be working. Arrangements were made with the local constabulary to have four detectives on hand to

Above. Buckingham Palace garden party, July 1949. Looking down from the Corps Diplomatique buffet. *By kind permission of Arthur Christian (deceased).*

Below. HM Queen Elizabeth with Nippies at the Buckingham Palace garden party on 19 July 1951. Note that waitresses are not wearing their coronet caps. *By kind permission of Florence Bonard.*

deal with any disturbances and a number of other constables were on duty with representatives of Grand Lodge, to inspect each member's entry ticket.

The banquet was directed with military precision by Bertie Joseph from what he referred to as the 'conning tower'. This had been erected above the banquet area and camouflaged with bunting and drapes to disguise its purpose. From the conning tower Bertie Joseph controlled the entire assembly, instructing in the idiosyncratic ways of banqueting etiquette with a system of bells and coloured lights designed to minimise speaking between members of staff. In fact, for the Freemasons' Festival staff had been forbidden to speak to each other, even in the kitchens, in order that guests would not be unduly disturbed. After everyone had been seated the 1,300 impeccably and identically dressed waitresses simultaneously took up their allotted serving positions for the first course. This caused the entire ensemble to rise to their feet as one, cheering and waving their napkins and menu cards. As Arthur Christian later recorded: 'It was a never-to-be-forgotten sight.' Indeed, such a sight was never seen again nor perhaps ever will.

The Outdoor Catering Department of Lyons was renowned for providing a truly professional service, whether for royalty or merely for public schools such as Wellington College, Crowthorne. Each contract was considered special and great efforts were made to make it so. For example, in September 1931 Lyons went to the trouble of having the menus for the Iron and Steel Institute banquet held at the Drill Hall, Swansea, printed in colour on sheet metal.

The Royal Garden Parties

The first royal warrant had been bestowed on Lyons by HRH The Prince of Wales (later King

Edward VII) in 1899. This was repeated in 1902, when the new Prince of Wales (later King George V) appointed Lyons as 'bakers'. King Edward VII issued a further warrant commissioning Lyons as 'refreshments contractors' in 1904, and King George V did likewise in December 1910.

As far as the royal events were concerned, the one strict principle always adhered to was that of no publicity, even to the extent of not correcting errors in press editorials which occurred with alarming frequency. Records for the garden parties do not start until 1919 and in that year five were held, the largest for 10,000 persons. The greatest number ever catered for at Buckingham Palace was 15,000 just before the Second World War but when the garden parties restarted after the war the guest numbers were reduced to approximately 8,000.

The length of the buffet table for these fewer numbers stretched to 357 feet (three tables of 119 feet) in one straight line in a splendid marquee with wooden flooring. A special tented enclosure was made available for ambassadors and members of the Diplomatic Corps, with a third and even more ornate tent for use by the royal party itself. Tent fronts were decorated with trellis-work and on the lawns stood an array of garden tables, each with four green canvas garden chairs. The superintendents appointed to the main buffet had to inspect every chair in their section to ascertain that all seats and backs were correctly fitted and they had to sit upon each chair to ensure its stability. It became common practice to choose at least one waitress from each of the firm's teashops and restaurants to assist with the heavy load the garden parties generated. After 1945 Queen Elizabeth, both as George VI's consort and later as Queen Mother, always found time to be photographed with them. Although the garden parties were organised as buffets, the waitresses attending were especially well trained and underwent rigorous inspections for dress and general appearance by senior management before being allowed on duty. They were prohibited from talking to each other during the event unless necessary in the line of duty and even then were allowed to address each other only as 'Miss', not

by Christian names. 'Sir' or 'Madam' had to be used when addressing guests. Waitresses were also forbidden to stand in pairs or lean against counters. In the case of royal weddings such as that of Mary, Princess Royal, to Henry, Viscount Lascelles, 6th Earl of Harewood on 5 March 1922, staff regulations were even more stringent.

In addition to these special events Lyons were appointed to supply bread and other bakery items to the royal household on a daily basis. For many years bread was also provided for the pink flamingos which occupied the Buckingham Palace gardens lake, an item that was entered separately in the Lyons accounts! During the Second World War, Queen Mary, mother of George VI, was evacuated to Badminton in Gloucestershire and her bakery order was sent down every day by train at Lyons' expense. Although Badminton had its own station, trains stopped only on request, and it was therefore necessary for Lyons to inform the railway company officials on which train the goods had been loaded so that the driver could be instructed to stop the train as he passed through.

When Montague Gluckstein first engaged the Blue Hungarian Band to play in the refreshment pavilion at the Newcastle Exhibition in 1887, it must have seemed improbable that the company just formed would be regularly catering for the royal household less than forty years later. Although exhibition catering had enabled the Salmons and Glucksteins to break away from cigar and cigarette manufacturing, at the time it had seemed a risky venture. Nevertheless, their bold approach and excellence of service soon endeared them to all levels of society and the Lyons name became synonymous not only with exhibition and contract catering but with catering *per se*. They had been responsible for some of the greatest catering challenges this century, from their phenomenal success at the 1924 British Empire Exhibition to the largest banquet ever undertaken in the United Kingdom. However, by the mid-1920s the British public's appetite for large exhibitions had waned, and Lyons turned their attention to building new restaurants.

A typical banquet venue. This one is for the Prudential Insurance Company's centenary dinner held at Olympia on 2 June 1949. This was the largest banquet since pre-war days when over 1,300 male only guests were served by 300 waitresses and 40 chefs. It was in a complete tented enclosure.

Chapter

The Corner Houses

THE OUTBREAK OF WAR in 1914 had brought the problem of home-grown food to the fore. Agriculture passed under the direct control of the state and prices increased by 30 per cent. Under the Defence of the Realm Act the Public Meals Order of December 1916 had restricted restaurants to two courses for daytime meals and three courses for evening meals. On 25 January 1918 further controls were introduced whereby caterers had to introduce meatless days. This Public Meals Order comprised no fewer than eighteen paragraphs which became effective from 3 February 1918.

Shortly after this Order was issued it was varied to take account of a meat ration coupon, based on alternative monetary weight value, which came into force with butter and margarine rationing in London and the Home Counties on 25 February 1918. Dozens of statutory rules and orders in respect of food were issued between 1914 and 1918 but, astonishingly, general rationing only began in June 1918, just five months before the signing of the armistice in the Forest of Compiègne. With food shortages increasing, the government promoted a National Kitchens movement which continued into 1919, when an attempt was made to turn them into National Restaurants. This proved a failure and by the 1920s the government's Kitchens Department declined. Food shortages continued throughout 1919, but, with the lifting of the blockade, Germany became an active competitor. The disbandment of the 1,850 local food offices on 30 June 1920, which had been instituted at a critical period of the war, had secured the co-

operation of trade interests so as to maintain an equitable distribution of the available supplies. The economic improvements for caterers were short-lived, however, as they began to experience subtle changes to their trade. During these unsettled times, Lyons nevertheless continued to expand their most prestigious restaurant developments, for which the company became justifiably renowned.

Before the First World War, Lyons' expertise in operating large exhibition catering contracts had already been systematically employed in the building of new large restaurants, each new establishment excelling the previous one. Following the success of the Popular Café in Piccadilly, Lyons had opened their State Restaurant in Liverpool in January 1905 and another Popular Café in Manchester one year later. These restaurants attracted not only middle-class customers who were beginning to have more disposable income but also increasingly some of those who previously had frequented Gatti's Adelaide Gallery at Charing Cross, the St James's Restaurant in Piccadilly, the Café Monico in Shaftesbury Avenue, Spiers & Pond's Gaiety Theatre Restaurant in the Strand and, most notably, the Holborn Restaurant. Originally the Holborn Casino on the corner of Kingsway and Holborn, this had opened as a restaurant in 1873–4 in a rich Renaissance style and survived until April 1955. Apart from an ornate terracotta Empire Grill and Grand Restaurant with cabaret and dancing, it boasted three Masonic temples, fourteen smaller restaurants and a number of private dining rooms. Lyons, however, were about to unleash their most ambitious restaurant project ever, the building of the super-restaurants which became known as the Lyons Corner Houses. The first of these was erected in Coventry Street between London's Leicester Square and Piccadilly Circus.

The Coventry Street Corner House

Lyons had shown interest in the Arundel Estate property in Coventry Street many years earlier (during the Trocadero restaurant era). The firm had waited patiently until 1903–4 when they were able to purchase the Challis Hotel and adjoining property for £96,000 – £74,000 in cash and the remainder by way of a mortgage. For a brief period after acquiring the property, Lyons continued to operate the Challis Hotel, which stood on the corner of Rupert Street, before it and the adjoining properties of Messrs Lambert, goldsmith's (said to be the oldest in London), Norden's, costumier's, Murdie's the bookseller's and a large slum area were demolished. These made way for the building of the Coventry Street Corner House which opened as a licensed restaurant on 4 January 1909.

Designed, like the Strand Palace and Regent Palace hotels, by William Ancell, the exterior façade was built partly of Carrara marble in a baroque style and as usual Lyons had spared no expense on the internal décor. Going in from the street, customers had the impression of entering a vast ballroom decorated with immense chandeliers which hung level with a cream and gold balcony above the entrance foyer. There small boys, dressed up as chefs, wheeled trolleys of sandwiches, pastries and confectionery to the tables. The name 'Corner House', chosen to be deliberately neutral, became universally recognised as a brand name and consequently contributed to revenues.

Originally seating 2,000 customers, the Corner House was enlarged in 1922 to accommodate 4,500 after the purchase of an additional part of the Arundel Estate in June 1915 for £250,000. In 1919 the company acquired a further 34,000 square feet of property, between Shaftesbury Avenue and Coventry Street, including the Hotel Previtali, the Hotel Mathis

and the dubious West End Hotel, all of which were demolished. This enabled the Trocadero Restaurant and the Coventry Street Corner House to be joined. The extensions were carried out by Sir Frederick T. Wills, an articled pupil to William Ancell who took over his architectural practice after his death in 1913. Throughout its life after 1922 the Corner House gained a number of other facilities starting with the All-night Café in July 1923, the basement Brasserie in September 1936, the Old Vienna Café in February 1940, the Sandwich Meal Counter in September 1942, the Vita Sun Café in October 1942, the Salad Bowl (Brasserie) in April 1943 and many more including the Wimpy Grill in May 1955. After an all-night service had been introduced, as many as 25,000 meals could be served in a single 24-hour period. The operational immensity required over 400 staff, more than the average industrial enterprise of that period. In the Corner House, unlike the teashops, every meal was cooked on the premises and managed to convey the impression that it had been specially made for the customer. The vast operation created opportunities for economies of scale and this catering for 'commonplace' people proved highly successful.

The construction of large restaurants in London had started in the second half of the nineteenth century after an influx of rich and leisured foreign visitors, especially Americans, French, Germans, Indians and others from British colonies and the European continent. The Grand Hotel and Brasserie de l'Europe on the north side of Leicester Square bears testimony to this with its lager-beer hall in the basement serving German dishes such as Berliner rollmops, Wiener schnitzels and Frankfurter sauerkraut. On the ground floor was the Grand Café, its name being continental in flavour, and above it was the Italian Room. These new restaurants allowed for the architectural and decorative expression of Victorian ingenuity that was also reflected in the designs of the Corner House super-restaurants. Their multi-storeyed structure of carefully segregated eating-rooms – each with its own menu and price range – was an invention by Lyons which brought to the less well-off the same dining

This 1953 photograph shows the Coventry Street Corner House, opened in January 1909, decorated with flags for the coronation of Elizabeth II.

experience enjoyed by more wealthy society of an earlier era.

On the ground floor of the Coventry Street Corner House, with easy access from the street, Lyons had positioned an extensive food shopping hall, where cooked meat, chocolate, confectionery, biscuits, wine, cakes and other items could be purchased. There were luxury hairdressing salons, a shoe-shine parlour, a theatre ticket booking office and a telephone bureau. In the early 1930s picnic luncheon boxes could be ordered and delivered to the customer's door for as little as one shilling – a service which had been available from most of the teashops in 1921. Deliveries were made three times a day anywhere in London to arrive before 1 p.m., 4 p.m. or 7 p.m., with one delivery on Sunday.

Although the Corner Houses attracted middle-class customers, they nevertheless catered for everyone, and the less well-off frequently used the facilities if only on special occasions. Homely dishes such as steak and kidney pie and suet pudding could be obtained alongside others bearing French names. These 'super-cafés' became meeting places or restaurants for treats, especially for those on shopping sprees into London. So many services were available at Corner Houses that it was said people could do almost anything there. It even became popular to propose marriage at a Corner House. Many people still remember their first visit with parents or grandparents, each able to recall some particular aspect of their experience. Several more Corner Houses were opened, although strictly speaking only three were officially known as Corner Houses: the original at Coventry Street, the Strand Corner House, which opened in April 1915, and the Oxford Corner House, which opened in May 1928. The Maison Lyons at Marble Arch, although in the same style as the Corner Houses, came under the management of the Cumberland Hotels company.

Major Montague Gluckstein and the Band Office

In the Corner Houses, as in all Lyons' more expensive catering establishments, management continued to place a strong emphasis on combining the provision of food and drink with musical entertainment. More than one promising young musician was talent-spotted while performing at a Corner House. Such was Lyons' appetite for orchestras and musicians that there was a special Band Office, which operated from the teashop headquarters in Shaftesbury Avenue. Its sole *raison d'être* was to administer the supply of performers not only for the restaurant work but also for the many regular and *ad hoc* events in hotels.

In overall charge of the Band Office was Major Montague ('Monte') Gluckstein, who had offices on the third floor of the Trocadero restaurant. Born on 13 October 1886, Monte Gluckstein was the younger son of Isidore Gluckstein and a nephew of the first Montague Gluckstein, two of the firm's founders. He had joined Lyons in 1900 after leaving the City of London School at the age of fourteen and was put to work as an apprentice in the Trocadero kitchens. Perhaps through the influence of Joseph Lyons, whom he had known since earliest infancy, Monte Gluckstein was fascinated by the theatre. During the First World War he became a private in the Artists' Rifles, a London volunteer Territorial regiment formed in 1860 by an art student, Edward Stirling. The regiment, which elected its own officers, was sent to France as a fighting unit in October 1914, but in November was called upon to send fifty selected men as officers to the British Expeditionary Force. Subsequently they formed a cadet training school supplying 10,000 officers to various arms of the Service and later were merged with the SAS. Their cap badge of Mars and Minerva is still the title of the Regimental journal. During the summer of 1916 Monte Gluckstein was commissioned as a major and sent as messing officer to the so-called 'government workshops and shipyard' at Richborough, north of Sandwich on the river Stour in Kent.

Richborough Port, managed by the Inland Waterways and Docks Directorate on behalf of the War Office, had been created in 1916 partly to relieve pressure on Dover, where the Royal Navy needed more space. Built and operated by the Royal Engineers, it rapidly became a huge transportation base and a manufacturing centre, both operating and constructing the steel barges which carried supplies across the Channel to France and were navigated through the French and Belgium canal systems up to the front line. Schools of technical instruction were also set up at Richborough to train recruits – many of them men disabled in the fighting or otherwise unfit for battle – in such skills as shipbuilding, motor mechanics, pile driving and welding, before they were drafted to a relevant area of labour. By September 1918 over 19,000 personnel were working at Richborough Port, all eventually housed in concrete or wooden huts. As most of the men (and some women) worked shifts, hot meals had to be provided throughout the day and night, but the catering facilities at first were so inadequate that the army decided to call in an expert, in the form of the thirty-year-old Montague Gluckstein. The original catering staff were found other jobs, and modern kitchen equipment was brought in. According to Major Gluckstein, when he arrived at Richborough Port in the summer of 1916 some 3,000 men were being fed in nearly a hundred different places with separate cookhouses, resulting in huge waste and poor-quality food. By the end of the war, the facilities had been transformed so as to cater for 20,000 men in three large mess halls, with central kitchens employing top-class chefs paid £10 per week – four times the salary of the most highly skilled warrant officer. Some of the officers thought it ironic that they had to pay 10s. 6d. at Lyons' Trocadero restaurant for a similar meal to the one they received for part of their 6d. daily mess bill at Richborough. As Major Gluckstein was the first specialist messing officer in the British army (assisted by Henry Atwell of the teashops organisation), it is presumed that his operation at Richborough Port – for which he was awarded the OBE – laid the foundation of the Army School of Cookery established at Aldershot after the war. In March 1941 it became the Army Catering Corps.

In 1919 Monte Gluckstein became a Lyons director, and a year later he joined the board of the Strand Hotel Ltd. He went on to play a leading role in Lyons' tremendous growth during the period between the two World Wars, promoting

The Strand Corner House, built on land which was earlier part of Hungerford Market. Being close to Charing Cross station it provided a valuable service to the public during the Second World War and was the last of the Corner Houses to close, on 28 February 1977.

the firm's image through a new publicity department. In particular, he had a talent for conceiving bold schemes that caught the public's imagination and the media's attention. Among his successful ideas in the 1920s and 1930s were the cabarets produced by Charles Cochran at the Trocadero, the invention of the Nippy waitress, and a publicity slogan which was used in a series of advertisements and became a national catchphrase: 'Where's George? Gone to Lyonch.'

In 1939 he was made honorary catering adviser to the Ministry of Food, a post he held for several years. During the Second World War he prepared secret plans for the emergency feeding of Britain, to enable the government to take immediate action if the German bombing offensive disrupted all normal food distribution. Though the scheme was never required, one consequence – described in chapter 23 – was the introduction of frozen food (known as 'Frood') in 1941. Major Gluckstein was also a director of Lyons' Pension Trust, which was formed in 1946. He spoke three languages and after his appointment as Chairman of Lyons in 1950 he played a key role in extending the company's activities to South Africa, Canada and the United States. His son Kenneth was also a director of Lyons.

Throughout his life Monte Gluckstein retained his interest in the theatre and live music, continuing the traditions established by Lyons a generation earlier. He believed in encouraging young musicians who showed promise, not only through performances at the Trocadero but generally through the operations of the Band Office.

From 1923 until his death in June 1943 the office was managed by Charles Grant, who had been trained by the army as a musician; in fact many musicians of his period were likewise taught. Grant reported to Major Gluckstein, and he was largely responsible for the engagement of musicians and entertainers working in the London area. He liaised closely with the entertainment agents of Charles Tucker Enterprises and auditioned those who had not yet developed a musical reputation, or were relatively unknown. In addition to these duties,

Charles Grant also helped with musical arrangements and supplied the music which some bands were instructed to play, much of it comprising the golden classics, tangos and other popular music of the period. On a trip to America with Monte Gluckstein in September 1937, Grant bought copyright in the song 'The Lady is a Tramp' but the London audiences of that time did not appreciate it. When Frank Sinatra sang it in the film *Pal Joey* in 1957, however, it became an instant success. Charles Grant died in 1943 and was succeeded by Arthur Burrows, who joined the management team. Throughout the war, whenever musicians could be found, Lyons establishments continued to provide music.

The Orchestral Department, or the Band Office as it was more popularly known, became one of the largest employers of freelance musicians and entertainers in the country during the first half of the century, acting as a magnet for both the up-and-coming and the established musician. For the Trocadero restaurant alone the expenditure in 1932 on bands and artists amounted to £8,428. For the company as a whole the annual expenditure on musicians and orchestras was no less than £150,000. On one memorable occasion in October 1941 the conductor Sir Adrian Boult, then Musical Director of the BBC, was invited to lunch in the Coventry Street Corner House to hear Philipowski's orchestra play a selection of his music. Boult later wrote to the management thanking them for the experience, congratulating Philipowski on his orchestra's performance and suggesting that, if it were not for the wartime restrictions, the management might consider placing rubber sheets on the trays so that the clatter of glass and cutlery did not disturb the music! He did not seem to realise that the diners were there mainly to enjoy the food and that the music was supposed to be an incidental to make the eating experience more pleasurable. Needless to say, the idea was not taken up.

The Oxford Corner House

After the opening of the Coventry Street Corner House, Lyons took a long lease on a large plot of land at the corner of Craven Street and the

Strand, between Charing Cross railway station and Trafalgar Square. Here they built the Strand Corner House, but this was never given as much publicity as the other Corner Houses. Before Charing Cross station was constructed in 1863, Hungerford market stretched from the Embankment to the Strand and incorporated the land which Lyons leased. Craven Street was formerly an ancient thoroughfare known as Spur Alley, where, among other famous people, the American politician and scientist Benjamin Franklin and the Dutch-born woodcarver Grinling Gibbons, employed by Christopher Wren to carve choir stalls in St Paul's Cathedral and other work in London's new churches, once lived. At the time when the Strand Corner House was designed, Westminster Council planned to widen the Strand at this point and so the architects created a false front, ten feet deep, which could be removed without damaging the main structure. When it opened on 8 April 1915 many notable theatres and stores (including the Civil Service Stores and Peter Robinson) were nearby and the restaurant's close proximity to Charing Cross Station ensured a steady flow of customers. The Strand Corner House restaurant provided a valuable service during both world wars and up to 1939 was open all night. By the mid-1950s its opening hours were 7.30 a.m. until 11.30 p.m., during which time up to 13,000 customers would pass through its doors. It was the last of the Corner Houses to close when it shut its doors on 28 February 1977.

The third and final Corner House to be built was the Oxford Corner House, which was erected on the site of the old Oxford Theatre at the junction of London's Oxford Street and Tottenham Court Road. The Oxford Theatre had opened in 1861 on the site of an old inn, the Boar and Castle, and was one of the first theatres in London to be classed as a music hall. Like many theatres of its day it suffered a number of fires and was rebuilt at least twice. In 1924 Charles Cochran brought the Old Vic company to play Shakespeare for a month in the West End, for the benefit of the visitors who had flocked to London for the British Empire Exhibition, where Cochran had put on the controversial rodeo.

However, the Shakespeare season was not a success and the Oxford Theatre went into decline in 1925. It closed in 1926, at which point Lyons bought the site. By this time Cochran had been engaged by Montague Gluckstein to present cabaret at the Trocadero.

For the Oxford Corner House Lyons employed Oliver Bernard to design the interior and he used 550 tons of finest marble imported from the quarries of France, Italy, Greece, Switzerland and Ireland to create the restaurant's most striking feature – the 20-foot-high pictures decorating the walls. They ran for hundreds of feet around the walls depicting trees, waterfalls, mountains, lakes and cypress trees and prompting the individual restaurants to be named the Niagara and Mountain View Cafés. The exterior of the building was faced in a kind of white terracotta. It claimed to be the largest restaurant in the world.

No attempt was made at uniformity in the public rooms, which were decorated in the styles of Pergolesi, Louis XIV, Empire Adam and Louis XVI, with cartouches, raised and sunken

Left. With an entrance from Oxford Street and Tottenham Court Road, the Oxford Corner House was built on the site of the Oxford Theatre. Four large bracket lamps once adorned the front between the small and large windows. The small frontage conceals a vast restaurant area. The shoe repair shop was once a Salmon & Gluckstein tobacconist. *By kind permission of Waldegrave Films.*

Below. Syd Katchki and his band playing in the Oxford Corner house c.1934. *By kind permission of Michael Grant.*

panels, architraves, scrolls, swags, consoles, dentils, aprons, columns, pilasters and sun-bursts, much of the work being carried out by G. Jackson & Sons Ltd.

Opened by the Duke and Duchess of York (the future King George VI and Queen Elizabeth) on 3 May 1928, the Oxford Corner House served 21,947 meals on the first day. It is distinguished, however, by not having made a farthing's profit during its 39-year history. With a staff of 780, of whom 260 were waitresses, the restaurant served numbers of meals which appeared to remain constant up until the start of the Second World War, averaging around 100,000 per week. At times the numbers slumped to around 90,000, but during other weeks records show that up to 151,000 meals were served. The trading loss was probably due to two factors: too low a price was levied for each meal, and far too many tiers of management and staff added unnecessarily to labour costs. Quite why this lack of profitability was allowed to continue will never be known, but pride must have played an important part. Management culture at that time was also heavily

influenced from the centre, with little or no local accountability. If the unit had been closed, not only would it have been embarrassing to management but it would have exposed overheads on the Cadby Hall factories. In other words, the vast consumption of food within the Corner House subsidised another part of the business, and the profit of the overall business seemed more important than that of individual outlets. Perhaps, above all, the enormous prestige of the Oxford Corner House contributed so much to Lyons' reputation that it was worth allowing it to trade at a loss.

Attempts were nevertheless made to make it profitable. An All-Night Café opened in October 1934, a basement Brasserie in September 1935 and the Salad Bowl in May 1944. In 1954 a detailed internal audit concluded that each restaurant within the Oxford Corner House was running at a loss of £100-200 per week. Even a new management structure with fewer levels of responsibility and greater local accountability failed to reverse the restaurant's decline and it finally closed in May 1967.

A year or so after the first-floor Salad Bowl had been opened, the Oxford Corner House became the scene of a terrible crime by a certain Jack Tratsart. Having met his family in the ground-floor restaurant, shortly after 5 p.m. he produced a Browning automatic pistol and shot five of them; his father, John Tratsart, and sister Claire were killed outright, but three others, although wounded, survived. The restaurant lighting had been influenced by Art Deco, with upturned glass bowls at the top of marble pillars directing the light upwards toward the ceiling. Tratsart, having shot his relatives, threw the gun into one of these upturned bowls, thus confusing the police as to what had become of the weapon. Several hours passed before the gun's outline was spotted through the glass when the lights were switched on. The police charged Tratsart with double murder and attempted murder but he never stood trial; suffering from insanity, he was incarcerated in Broadmoor Hospital and died two years later.

Maison Lyons and other Super-restaurants

Other grand restaurants in the Corner House style opened between 1911 and 1933. Called Maison Lyons, the first opened in Liverpool in 1911 followed by Maison Lyons in Oxford Street (1912), Maison Lyons, Shaftesbury Avenue (1915), Maison Riche, Regent Street (1915), Maison Lyons, Oxford Street (1916), Maison Lyons, Liverpool (1929), and Maison Lyons, Marble Arch (1933). The Marble Arch restaurant, and other establishments called Maison Lyons for that matter, were sometimes wrongly referred to as Corner Houses. This confusion is understandable, since both the Maison Lyons and Corner House restaurants were very similar in style. However, they had different interior designs and their prices varied. The Maison Lyons on the north side of Shaftesbury Avenue – until 1930 the headquarters of the teashop operation – closed in November 1940. The premises were taken over by the American Red Cross in 1942 and turned into a large café and lounge club for American servicemen under the name of Rainbow Corner – the name derived from the rainbow insignia of Supreme Headquarters Allied Expeditionary Forces (SHAEF) and the First World War US 42nd Infantry Division's motto: 'This Division will stretch over the land like a rainbow'. It closed in January 1946, having served over 12 million meals.

From their introduction in 1909, and during the inter-war period, the Corner Houses, with the exception of the Oxford, consistently made a profit. This had been achieved not by good management – most were grossly overstaffed and dominated by innumerable management levels – but by the fact that wage costs were low and food prices stable. After the Second World War, however, the trading circumstances in Britain changed. Corner House profits, which in 1939 were approximately £80,000 per annum, progressively decreased until 1956, when a loss of nearly £500,000 was recorded. Much of this loss can be attributed to the rising cost of catering

Proprietors :

"Mountview C
LYONS' OXFORD CORI
Oxford Street & Tottenham Court

The Mountview Café, Oxford Corner House.

labour, brought about by the Catering Wages Act of 1943 and the decline in Corner House popularity. It has been estimated that the Corner House wage bill was converted from 18 per cent of turnover before 1939 to 40 per cent by the early 1950s, an increase of over £1 million. At the same time there was new competition in the restaurant trade and price rises in the Corner Houses may also have contributed to the decline.

Having unshackled themselves from exhibition catering, in the inter-war years Lyons had seen a dramatic increase in their restaurant business but their fortunes were mixed. The Trocadero restaurant, for example, flagship of all Lyons restaurants, had undergone several refurbishments and continued to attract the wealthiest members of London's society. Music remained a central feature, as did the evening cabarets, many of which were staged by Charles Cochran. By the mid-1920s, however, the Trocadero began showing a loss which continued unchecked into the 1930s. Although its tables were always taken, management seemed reluctant

J. Lyons & Co. Ltd.

A Luncheon menu for the Popular State Restaurant, Manchester, dated 20 October 1937. The restaurant closed a year later on 13 July 1938.

to increase prices, preferring instead to provide a high level of service (with the entire musical and artistic accompaniment) at the lowest possible price. It was a very short-sighted policy, since the upper middle class whom the restaurant attracted were well able to afford any increase.

Meanwhile, the Corner House super-restaurants provided levels of service and prices which hitherto had not been available to less prosperous people; consequently they became hugely popular. At its zenith the Coventry Street Corner House had seven 12-piece bands playing from noon to midnight. Over 200 chefs backed by a waiting staff of 1,200 served 400,000 meals a week and the restaurants were capable of seating 9,000 customers at any one time arranged in a variety of restaurant themes, which were replicated in other Corner House establishments. Apart from during the war years (1914–1918 and 1939–1945) when London's population was boosted by all manner of service personnel hell-bent on having a good time, profits were mixed. Again this was caused by management's desire to provide high levels of service on razor-thin profit margins. Nevertheless, all the restaurants were taken to the nation's heart and have quite rightly passed into our social history.

Teashops – Mixed Fortunes

OF ALL THEIR RESTAURANT ventures, Lyons will probably be best remembered for their teashop chain, which gave birth to that other British institution, the Nippy waitress. Their characteristic décor and single pricing structure dominated many of the nation's high streets for over eighty years. At first the teashops benefited from the short-lived prosperity after the First World War, but there followed a period of industrial unrest when the country slid into depression in the 1930s.

As a result of the Public Meals Order of 1916, which restricted restaurant meals to two courses in the daytime and three courses in the evening, only nine Lyons teashops opened between 1914 and 1920. After the Food Control Committees were disbanded on 30 June 1920, however, the popularity of Lyons teashops revived to such an extent that many rival catering firms suffered large losses. The drastic price cuts made by their competitors, far from reducing the number of customers patronising Lyons, actually increased the teashops' turnover enormously. For some, the post-war period continued gloomily. In 1918 the Aërated Bread Company (ABC) found it necessary to amalgamate their business with that of William Buszard – whose 'posh' tea-room in Oxford Street had greatly influenced Montague Gluckstein when he was taken there by Harold Hartley in the early 1890s – but although ABC's trading improved temporarily the continued thrust of Lyons' business was too strong for them to have any impact. Under new management ABC's business was again reorganised but it was not until 1930 that the scale of their activities

remotely compared with those of Lyons, who were still the market leaders in teashop operation.

A Period of Change

In spite of the swollen labour market, created by demobilisation and the continuance of many women in the workplace, white-collar workers secured improved conditions and a reduction in their hours. At the same time transport facilities improved: between 1895 and 1920 passengers on the railways doubled and there was a 12-fold increase in motor cars between 1905 and 1920. This allowed many workers to spend less of their time away from home and so they had less need for refreshment elsewhere. Offices too started providing tea trolleys for clerical staff, encouraging them to work through their break periods. Thus the circumstances which had prompted the catering needs of the late nineteenth century were being systematically removed.

This period is also characterised by the changing fashions of the 1920s. New entertainment arrived. Silent (and talkie) movies, with their romantic heroines and dashing heroes, attracted huge audiences of all ages. Dance halls were built in working-class areas to provide regular Saturday night entertainment for the country's youth. High-class restaurants and hotels encouraged the dance craze by offering tea dances in the afternoon and early evening for as little as a shilling. Flugel soda fountains made their début and were being increasingly installed in catering establishments. Not only did they provide a continuous flow of ice-cool, flavoured, carbonated drinks but the handsome modern appearance

Right. Prepared for the International Professional Tennis Association banquet of 1939, this table plan is designed to resemble a tennis racquet. The waitresses are dressed as 1931 ball-boys and small tennis courts, with deck chairs, are part of the table design. An arrangement of flowers resembles a tennis ball in the centre of the table. *By kind permission of Arthur Christian (deceased).*

Below. A rare view of the inside of a teashop in about 1920. Situated on the corner of 321 Oxford Street and Dering Street, this teashop opened in January 1907. The cast-iron framed tables with their marble tops were discontinued soon after this picture was taken as they were found to be too heavy to move for floor cleaning. The teashop closed in December 1966.

of the apparatus itself stimulated soda-water sales in preference to more traditional soft drinks. Milk bars too took advantage of this American drinking concept, thus challenging traditional caterers, whose income became increasingly dependent on their midday service only.

Along with new forms of entertainment there was rising industrial unrest, as labour organisations demanded a greater share of post-war profits. In 1920 many teashop staff became members of the United Catering Trades Union, to the dismay of management. Although they had accepted the principle of unionisation, management remained adamantly opposed to those who flaunted their union membership publicly, since they considered this would put pressure on non-union members and would give rise to conflict in the workplace. Thus, when in August 1920 a kitchen-maid at the Brompton Road teashop was dismissed after 16 years' service for wearing the union's badge while on duty, it came as no surprise.

Inevitably an official strike developed, and the union called out their 500 members, just 10

This busy street scene shows the Lyons teashop at 20 Cannon Street, London. It opened in 1895 and closed during the blitz in December 1940. *By kind permission of the Museum of London.*

per cent of the total 5,000 waitresses employed at that time. Each side blamed the other for the dispute. The union leaders, on the one hand, felt a vital principle was at stake, that this was a management attempt to crush trade-unionism and that the sacking was a case of victimisation. Management, on the other hand, declined to enter into negotiations with the union leaders, declared that the kitchen-maid was in breach of an agreement and denied accusations of victimisation. The 500 strikers took part in demonstrations in the West End of London, with processions headed by a brass band. Several teashops were picketed, with limited success, and trade did subsequently suffer. After issuing an ultimatum, the management dismissed those who refused to return to work. There was no shortage of applicants waiting to take their places and the press reported a scramble for the 500 jobs which became vacant overnight, with large queues forming outside the Shaftesbury Avenue recruitment office. The 'Storm in a Tea-Cup' strike, as the press dubbed it, collapsed in two days, putting an end to any further similar disruptions.

There is no evidence that Lyons were especially stingy or severe in their treatment of staff or that they underpaid teashop waitresses in relation either to the rest of the catering trade or to the company as a whole. The average wage of a waitress at this time was £1 16s. 4d. per week, and they were entitled to free food, which was said to be costing the firm 10 shillings a week per person. The fact of the matter was that, because labour was so plentiful, industry generally held wages down. Montague Gluckstein, in his address to shareholders in 1920, remarked: 'The wages paid are already considerably higher than those paid in kindred establishments and whilst that is the case the company cannot and will not pay more because every time wages are increased prices must rise.'

In 1925 Isidore Gluckstein (1890–1975), younger son of the first Montague Gluckstein (and cousin of Monte Gluckstein), took over responsibility for the teashops from John (Jack) Joseph (1881–1929), who it is believed was in poor health. Isidore Gluckstein had recently been appointed a director but his father's wish was for him to become a barrister. He had attended St Paul's School, where he showed academic promise, but his education was disrupted by the First World War and in 1917 he served as an infantry officer in Flanders. At the end of the war he read Classics and Law at Cambridge University and although he was called to the Bar in 1919 he never practised. Instead he decided to join the family business and started his career, as others had before him, working in the kitchens of the Trocadero restaurant. Although his public and business life was outstandingly successful, his private life included much sorrow. His only son, Bruce, was killed in action at Anzio in Italy in 1944, and his only daughter, Cynthia, died in her early twenties. Isidore Gluckstein had the onerous task of steering the teashops not only through their greatest period of growth but through a difficult phase up to and including the war.

At this time Alan Jenkins and Nell Bacon were both key employees in the teashop hierarchy. Alan Jenkins had been employed in 1913 as a teashop inspector after answering an advertisement in the *Grocers Gazette*. In 1918, as part of his training he had been appointed manager of the teashop at 215 Oxford Street which had been opened in 1907. Very few men ever held the position of teashop manager and Jenkins was the first to do so. As an inspector, Jenkins was responsible for food quality and general development. Nell Bacon, who had started her career with the firm in 1897 as a waitress, eventually became superintendent of all Lyons teashops in 1909, responsible for personnel matters. Isidore Gluckstein depended heavily upon both individuals for the teashops' day-to-day operation. Although Nell Bacon was extremely talented and highly respected among her peers, equality for women, at least in Lyons, had not yet arrived. While Alan Jenkins became an employee director in 1946, Nell Bacon never progressed beyond superintendent – a considerable achievement nevertheless for a country girl. The highest accolade she probably received was when Harry Salmon referred to her as 'our senior woman executive' when presenting her with a silver casket, on 2 June 1947, commemorating her fifty years of employment. In fact no women were ever appointed to the Lyons board in the whole of the company's hundred-year history.

Between 1929 and 1933 prices of primary products fell sharply, with wholesale prices averaging falls of 40 per cent. The cost of tea fell by 60 per cent and of wheat products by 50 per cent. This prompted Lyons to reduce the price of items on the teashop tariff, including roast beef, one of the most popular dishes. Fluctuations of this sort made it necessary to produce teashop tariffs on a weekly basis; by the start of 1939, 40,000 copies were printed every week by the Lyons subsidiary, Hogarth Press. Originally occupying a small room in the stables block at Cadby Hall, the press took its name from its second home at Hogarth Lane, Chiswick, before moving to Willesden.

Although the teashop business had continued to be profitable during the depression years, by the mid-1930s their fortunes went into reverse. Labour costs rose steeply after the depression of 1929–33, when meagre trade had led to mass unemployment rather than wage cuts. The cost of higher salaries was further increased by overtime payments after Lyons decided to open more shops on Sunday (in the mid-1920s Sunday overtime working had been compensated by time off in lieu). In addition to the longer working week, extra staff were being recruited because many teashops were enlarged at this time.

All this happened at a period when customer numbers, and their spending, suddenly declined. Comparative analysis of the 'average spending power' before and after 3 p.m. by customers in

This picture of Old Haymarket, Liverpool, reminds us of another era. Here the provincial teashop, sandwiched between a cycle and wallpaper shop, was the eighteenth provincial teashop to open. *By kind permission of Liverpool Libraries & Information Services.*

the teashops had been meticulously carried out for many years. For the month of March-April 1914, for example, the daily average spend for the Piccadilly teashop was 6¾d. before 3 p.m. and 5½d. after 3 p.m., while for the Basinghall Street branch it was 4¾d. and 3¾d. respectively. To enable customer spending to be monitored in this way, every teashop's revenue had to be calculated twice a day and records kept of the numbers using them. The fact that only a farthing's profit was made on each meal had not been a problem when high numbers of customers

Above. Staff posing inside the Southampton teashop in 1927. It was opened by breaking a bottle of champagne on the entrance step.

Left. The 'mechanical' teashop at 21 Camberwell Green, London which could dispense 60 different items. When it opened on 30 June 1932 it was said to incorporate the first coin-operated mechanism to give change (or return money if too much was inserted) and was advertised as 'the shop which never shuts'.

ensured profitability. Once the customer base was reduced, for the first time some teashops began to make a loss. During the period 1934–9 the collective loss was £374,000. Some attempt had been made to encourage the public to buy more items and in June 1932 Lyons opened what they described as the 'first mechanical shop'. In effect it was a vending machine designed to dispense sixty or so items priced between 2d. and 2s. 6d. Installed in the teashop at 21 Camberwell Green, the 'mechanical shop' represented the latest achievement of British engineering. It was apparently the first machine to give change and, moreover, would return money if too much had been inserted. However, it must have posed some technical difficulties because no others were installed until a bread vending machine was introduced in 1970.

At this time it seemed like a good idea to gain some free publicity by celebrating the fortieth anniversary of the opening of the first teashop at 213 Piccadilly. The first teashop superintendent, Miss Day, was invited to the three-day celebrations on 20 September 1934. The original teashop was re-created as it had been forty years earlier in one half of the Piccadilly teashop, to enable customers to make comparisons and see how styles had changed. Those waitresses serving in the 1894 part of the teashop wore the original Victorian dresses and served the tariff of the period. To mark the occasion a special bronze medallion was struck in a limited edition of 100 copies. Each director received one, as did four original shareholders, customers who had patronised the teashop on its opening day and members of staff who had spent 40 years with the company.

Despite the anniversary celebrations, 23 teashops closed between 1934 and 1938 but paradoxically 19 new ones opened. This enigma can be explained by the changing circumstances of teashop locations, since over the years traffic and pedestrian movements, together with property lease problems, all affected teashop fortunes. Also, there was a belief within senior ranks that if individual teashops did not necessarily make a profit they nevertheless contributed to the overheads of the total business and a reduction in their overall numbers would expose these disbursements. This belief, artificial though it is, frequently permeates businesses which are centrally controlled and where individual units do not have financial responsibility. With profits continuing to slide, Isidore Gluckstein, on the advice of others, considered introducing self-service as a way of reducing labour costs. However, before this idea could be put into effect the country was plunged into another World War.

The Nippy Waitress

From the opening of the very first teashop in 1894 until the start of self-service in the Second World War, Lyons employed mainly female labour in their teashops, restaurants and Corner House with one or two exceptions. The hotels and grand restaurants, however, remained the preserve of male waiters. Rarely employed during the Victorian and Edwardian periods, young trained waitresses were enthusiastically accepted by the public when they were introduced and for many the Nippy waitress became an icon synonymous with the Lyons teashops and Corner Houses. Although waitresses ceased to be used in Lyons teashops at the outbreak of the Second World War, they continued in service in the Corner Houses, and at banqueting and outdoor catering events, including the royal garden parties and the Wimbledon Lawn Tennis Championships (which started in 1936), right up to the 1980s. Initially, the waitresses were referred to as 'Gladys' and did not inherit the name Nippy until 1 January 1925, when a picture of a waitress modelled by Doreen Vise appeared in most London newspapers and the public were confronted, for the first time, with the modern Nippy image.

With the active support of Nell Bacon – some have suggested the idea was hers – Major Montague Gluckstein, in co-operation with his cousin Isidore, decided to remove every emblem of servitude from the waitresses' uniforms by introducing a more up-to-date image for the teashop staff. Monte Gluckstein had already established Lyons' first publicity department, employing W. Buchanan-Taylor (known to acquaintances as 'Buckie'), a career journalist, who directed affairs from an office above the teashop at 61 Fleet Street. It was from here that much of Lyons' advertising and public relations activities was masterminded (Nippy, 'Gone to Lyonch' and Peter the Planter are examples). Buchanan-Taylor's newspaper contacts ensured that Lyons received good press coverage. He left Lyons at the start of the Second World War when the office closed. After the war it re-opened under a succession of managers including Mark Quinn, a journalist who developed the publicity

department with Jack Richards – handling advertising – and Denis Somerfield, who was responsible for artwork and design for the promotional material. A number of other changes were made between 1945 and 1961 and at one time the office employed some fifteen staff. However, post-war developments brought other changes within the Lyons group, in particular decentralisation of its business activities. In 1961 Raymond Marquis joined from the City of London Corporation and in 1962, when the centralised Fleet Street office closed, he was invited to become public relations adviser at corporate level at Cadby Hall.

The name 'Nippy' had been selected through a staff competition, but the word had been in use much earlier within the company, albeit on one of Lyons' 5-ton steam tractors. Eventually the name became almost a brand in its own right and it became necessary to protect it by registration. 'Nippy' perfectly reflected the social atmosphere of the inter-war years.

The waitress image rested not only on a change of name but, more importantly, on a fresh style of uniform. Nell Bacon had designed a new short black Alpaca frock with a white Peter Pan collar and white cuffs which were detachable for cleaning. The white square apron was worn at dropped-waist level and secured by hidden buttons so that this too could be easily removed. By now each waitress had become responsible for her own laundering. The black dress had thirty pairs (sixty buttons in total) of non-functional white pearl buttons in two rows from the neck to waist, all secured with red thread in a cross-stitch style; God help any girl who replaced a button with white thread! On the left of the bodice was pinned a medallion in the form of a JL logo set in a clover-leaf design. Dark grey or black stockings were required, and black shoes with low heels, preferably with a strap across the foot. Hair was cut fashionably short, and Nell Bacon had designed a smart white mitre-style cap with a black interwoven band to be worn low on the forehead. This band also incorporated a clover-leaf JL badge similar to that fastened on the dress. Finally a cord or strap was tied around the waist and an order pad hung from it. Each

A publicity photograph featuring Marjorie Robertson (later Anna Neagle) dressed as the new Nippy waitress when they made their debut on 1 January 1925.

uniform was individually tailored by Lyons' own dressmaking department, under the management of Henry Atwell, and presented to waitresses after they had completed their training and been assigned their teashop posting. The new flapper-style uniforms replaced an Alpaca dress which had been introduced in 1910. This Edwardian-style garment, worn at mid-calf length, had been buttoned higher at the neck and had a larger apron which was secured across the shoulders with wide straps tied at the back in a 'flying' bow. The 1925 uniform underwent a final change in 1933 when the skirt was made slightly longer and fuller and the square-shaped aprons were replaced with pleated aprons forming a 'V' or 'W' at the waist and three pointed ends at the hem.

Left. The actress Binnie Hale on the cover of *Lyons Mail* in November 1930. She died in January 1984 and in memory of her role in the theatre production *Nippy* this cover picture was reproduced in the *Lyons Mail* of February 1984.
Right. Two waitresses comparing uniforms of different eras.

It is now difficult to realise the impact created by the Nippy waitresses in pre-war Britain. Their poise, efficiency and smart appearance enchanted all levels of society from George VI's queen consort (the present Queen Mother) to the humble teashop customers. For years afterwards the Nippy's uniform was imitated, with slight variations, by others in the catering trade. With the waitress strike of 1895 now history, and the 'Storm in a Teacup' strike of 1920 having collapsed after two days, Lyons had no difficulty in recruiting new staff at a time of rising employment. Competitions were introduced as a way of improving standards and a prize of £100

was awarded each year for the highest-achieving waitress.

Systematic training had long been established, the school of instruction having been inaugurated at 396 Strand in 1912 by Nell Bacon, who felt that 'had she been able to avail herself of such an advantage in 1897 she would not have emptied a cup of tea into the upturned top-hat of one of her customers'. The first step of the training curriculum was to instil into the new waitress a thorough knowledge of the teashop tariff. Not only must she be familiar with every item upon it, so as to know the extent of the service, but she should memorise the price of every item so that she could compile a customer's 'check' or bill without delay. The trainee waitress was then taught the practical details of the art of waiting, such as the layout of items to be placed on the table, the correct position of knives and forks, the right way of serving and of holding the tray, and so forth. Every patron of every Lyons teashop would notice the uniformity of the table fittings and the tariff card. Some members of the public might consider this an unnecessary detail, but it was none the less given great emphasis in the training programme. The curriculum also included poise, etiquette, personal hygiene and, for some, soda fountain preparations.

More thorough training became necessary for waitresses employed by the Outdoor Catering Department, which provided services for many prestigious events, some of which were regular contracts and even royal occasions. These waitresses had to undergo stringent final examinations; after the Second World War, any woman achieving a mark of 70 per cent or more was awarded the coveted 'gold efficiency star', engraved with her name, which she proudly wore on her uniform. Examinations were first introduced in 1921, but the efficiency gold stars for outdoor catering were not brought in until August 1948, when six candidates successfully completed the examinations which took place in the Pillar Hall restaurant at Olympia.

Using the modern technique of film, Bertie Joseph, renowned for his achievements managing the Outdoor Catering Department, directed a training film for waitresses in 1929 which he called *Noona be Nippy*. Dorothy Wotton took the part of Noona Sloe, a young waitress who is not as nippy as her opposite number, Nora Swift. The film depicts the working lives of the waitresses, one quick and eager to get on, the other resentful of guidance and not very proficient. But the Lyons training system proves effective and Noona becomes as efficient and cheerful as Nora after completing the waitress training course. Taking six months to make, the film was a big success and afterwards the two stars were presented with gold watches from the directors.

Women employed in what were termed the 'front shops' – that is, retail counters in teashops – were, for unknown reasons, known as 'Sallys', and Nell Bacon preferred tall girls for this specific work. Lyons advertised them as: 'Sally the salesgirl sells in the shop – 550 good things to buy'. Unlike their Nippy contemporaries, sales staff did not wear coronet caps and their dresses were dark blue instead of black. These young women were given systematic training in sales technique and were also expected to maintain high presentational standards in window dressing. This formed part of their training and for this purpose a teashop window was constructed at the training centre at Orchard House, as were a cashiers' room and later a self-service counter. The Orchard House expenditure on training during the early 1930s exceeded £3,000 per annum, with staff salaries accounting for two-thirds of that figure.

Below This more than twice size model was frequently demonstrated at carnivals round the country. The Nippy appearance means that this picture was taken after January 1925. The appearance of the children suggests a poor area. Note the two black patches, below the model's bust line, through which the wearer could see out.

The window displays of the teashops were greatly improved in the Corner Houses, where they received wide praise. Their mechanised scenes evolved almost as an art form, attracting throngs of fascinated shoppers. Many of the static and animated models, assembled in the windows by Louise Gibbins between 1922 and 1963, had been devised and constructed by a small team of six women tucked away in what was described as the 'Studio' at the back of the Coventry Street Corner House, where birds, bees, mermaids, rabbits, dwarfs and chickens flowed from their agile fingers. Many of these creations were designed to run round in unending circles, swing a hammer with untiring energy or toss perpetual pancakes. In 1946 Kay Man joined the company and created the Window Display Department.

Training staff at the Clerkenwell Soda Fountain Training School in 1926.

The coveted merit star awarded to banquet waitresses who achieved a pass mark of 75% or more in their examinations. This particular merit was won by Ms S. Bright in February 1953. The broaches were blue enamel with white enamel lettering and gold coloured star points.

Teashop retail counter staff (Sally's) being trained in the art of window dressing and display at Orchard House in the 1950s.

Backed by the skill of the Corner House and Maison Lyons construction departments, whose task it had been to make in wood and fabric the figures and scenes of Kay's imagination, she contributed something quite distinctive in the London scene. Her displays astonished millions of Londoners and visitors alike who paused at the Marble Arch, Coventry Street, Strand and Oxford Street Corner Houses to admire her ingenious creations. Between 1946 and 1953, when she left with her husband to go to Uganda, Kay Man was also responsible for the designs on the front of the *Lyons Mail* Journals.

Montague Gluckstein's promotional campaign to introduce the Nippy was one of the most successful publicity ideas in the history of catering and it is the more extraordinary that it was achieved under a cloak of secrecy. On the morning of 1 January 1925 all 3,000 waitresses employed in the teashops were asked to report for duty thirty minutes earlier than usual. By the time the doors opened for business, every waitress had been transformed from the image of an Edwardian maid to that of a modern 1920s 'flapper'. Doreen Vise, the model chosen to epitomise Nippy, became a celebrity herself, receiving hundreds of letters and even offers of marriage. By the end of January 1925, once Monte Gluckstein knew he had pulled off a coup, there began a continuous marketing campaign exploiting the image at every opportunity. For example, Nippies were photographed with Chelsea Pensioners and retired taxi drivers and took part in local charity fund-raising events such as Poppy Day collections. Lyons produced a special brand of chocolates called 'Nippy'. A song about Nippies was included in a Jack Hulbert musical comedy, *By the Way*, performed in the West End. Similarly, in 1930 Binnie Hale, a popular actress of the day, played the heroine in a new musical comedy called *Nippy* at the Prince Edward Theatre. She appeared in November 1930 as the cover girl on the *Lyons Mail* magazine, which in February 1984 reported her death and remembered her by republishing the original cover. A racehorse, a railway engine, a rose and a Spitfire of the Second World War (see chapter 16) were named after the Nippy.

Blitz Feeding and Self-service

The outbreak of the Second World War caused enormous disruption to the teashop trade. In 1939 Isidore Gluckstein had overall control of 253 teashops in London and elsewhere; by the end of the war there were seventy fewer branches. Many had been destroyed by fire or blast, and only one of the London teashops escaped completely unscathed. The teashop situated at 54 Fore Street (off London Wall) was damaged by the first bomb which was dropped on the City of London in the Second World War. It reopened after hasty repairs but was gutted by fire – as was the teashop at 17 Fore Street – during the ferocious incendiary-bomb attacks of 1940 and 1941. Even the Tarmac road surfaces were on fire. With insufficient fire appliances and water, the area was evacuated from Gresham Street in the south to Golden Lane in the north, Aldersgate Street in the west and Moorgate in the east, and left to burn. As a

Taken outside Cadby Hall on 7 May 1926 during the General Strike. The Staff Stores shop can be seen to the right of the Cadby Hall entrance. Almost everyone in this orderly gathering is wearing a hat.

consequence the Barbican district was all but erased from the map of London, remaining a wasteland until after the war. The Fore Street teashops never reopened again. Provincial teashops in towns with strategic significance also suffered much destruction including those in Coventry, Southampton and Bristol.

For protection teashops were equipped with large wooden shutters which were fastened over the outside of windows not only during air raids but every day before closing. Some shops had steel shelters built into them, and these were capable of protecting any customers and staff caught during a day attack. During the whole of the war Lyons made a colossal effort to provide some semblance of service from all their teashops, despite the extreme hazards and difficulties of supply and transportation. Even when a teashop was completely destroyed, staff would try their utmost to offer refreshments from tents they pitched on pavements outside the unusable premises. On one occasion, after a particularly devastating raid on London, a temporary teashop opened from the back of a delivery van among the ruins of London's Barbican. It was a gesture of defiance but nevertheless prompted the idea of the temporary teashop. Small trailers were hastily assembled – by the Normand workshops in Park Royal – and towed to areas of distress where emergency feeding became the main priority. This service became known within Lyons as 'blitz feeding'. Frequently the 'tea and bun' services were provided free, since many of the recipients were members of the emergency services or victims who had lost their homes and possessed nothing but what they stood in. Besides, management and staff were public-spirited and knew that their efforts helped to maintain the morale of the nation in probably the darkest period of its history. It must also be remembered that Lyons' founding families had suffered privations themselves before their flight to England.

Some teashops did close during the war because of transport difficulties and food restrictions, although the catering trade fared better than other industries. Other London teashops were used by the General Post Office when their own sorting offices were damaged –

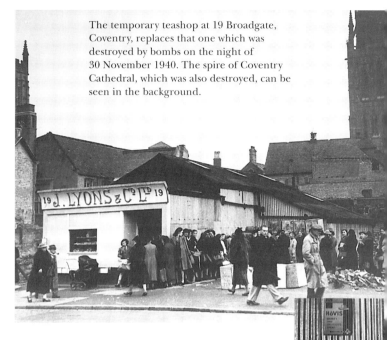

The temporary teashop at 19 Broadgate, Coventry, replaces that one which was destroyed by bombs on the night of 30 November 1940. The spire of Coventry Cathedral, which was also destroyed, can be seen in the background.

one or two were requisitioned by some of the 10,000 staff employed by the Postal and Telegraph Censorship Department to disseminate and censor the huge influx of forces' mail. Government policy at the time centred on maintaining supplies to restaurants and hotels with only limited controls on prices. Nevertheless, government orders and shortages caused food standards to deteriorate as the war lengthened; some products, such as ice-cream, were banned totally. In June 1942 a number of government orders were imposed on hotels, restaurants and other catering establishments restricting the number of courses which could be served and imposing a ceiling of five shillings on the price of any meal. These controls were not lifted until May 1950. The curtailment of road transport, resulting from the national need to conserve fuel and rubber, together with railway disruptions, made it increasingly hard to supply provincial teashops.

As women progressively replaced men in the factories, a shortage of labour in teashops intensified, and Isidore Gluckstein began to adopt self-service. In 1941 an Oxford Street branch had been successfully converted and Alan Jenkins, the teashop inspector, was instructed to go ahead with converting the rest. By the end of the war all teashops had been changed over, many having

Below. This type of emergency teashop was towed to areas of London where teashops had been destroyed, or severely damaged, to help relieve the needs of the homeless and those caring for them.

Left. Inside the temporary teashop at 19 Broadgate, Coventry during 1940. The notice reads: 'We respectfully ask customers not to retain their seats for a longer time than absolutely necessary when others are waiting to be served. Wartime conditions have depleted our staff and increased the demand for the seats available'.

Above Published in 1928, the date on this *Daily Mail* supplement is Saturday, January 1, 2000. Lyons clearly had ideas of what visiting teashops might be like at the turn of the millennium. *By kind permission of Hamptons International.*

been re-equipped over the course of a weekend, and the famous Nippy waitress disappeared from them for ever. Without self-service and the customers' ready acceptance of it, Lyons would not have been able to cater for the large numbers who continued to use their establishments. It must be said, however, that after the war the teashops never regained their former elegance. Management lurched from crisis to crisis and the lack of reinvigoration led the teashops to stagnate.

Paradoxically, wartime conditions artificially increased teashop profits in two ways. First, since no maintenance or refurbishment had been undertaken during the war years, all revenues were classified as profit. Second, as labour costs had been reduced by the introduction of self-service and of part-time staff, there was a corresponding fall in expenditure on salaries. Food shortages also meant that consumers were prepared to accept almost any quality without complaining, and so there was little wastage. After the war, food shortages became greater than at any other period in British history. Controls were not relaxed until the 1950s and some foods remained rationed until 1954, meat being the last item to be freed. By then, the teashops were being run according to an entirely different style of management.

In the period after the First World War, Lyons had moved away from their origins in exhibition catering to focus on retailing, restaurants and hotels. Yet the experience of large-scale catering had involved the company in diverse food production, and it is not surprising that food manufacture became the next main development in the story of Lyons.

THE GARDEN FACTORY

FROM NORTHOLT THE ROAD WINDS somewhat circuitously in a south-easterly direction to Greenford, a small and retired village, situate on the road towards Sudbury and Harrow and about nine miles from Hyde Park Corner. There is, in summer-time, a pleasant walk thither from the churchyard of Northolt, across the meadows, stretching away eastward, through which the Paddington canal winds its course, and which are also watered by numerous streams and bournes. The village of Greenford consists of about twenty or thirty cottages and small shops, together with a commodious school-house and other buildings. ... The hamlet of Greenford Green which lies away about a mile to the north of the village, is chiefly noticeable for the chemical works of Messrs. Perkin and Sons, which give employment to a large number of hands. The building covers a large space of ground, and its tall chimney-shafts are a landmark all around.

So wrote Edward Walford in his work *Greater London*, which he published in 1883. During the First World War there had been a growth of industries along the short section of the Grand Union Canal north-westward from Brentford Dock and it was in this mixture of idyllic countryside and industrial works that Lyons arrived in 1919. A 30-acre site at Greenford Green, consisting of meadows, fields, stables, barns, a house and pasture land known as Grove Farm,

together with six cottages and their appurtenances, had come on to the market for £20,150. Six years later, as mortgage documents show, Lyons bought an additional 'eight acres two rods and one perch' for £3,200 from Alfred Perkin, a relative of Sir William Henry Perkin, who had built a synthetic dye and chemical works at Greenford Green in 1856. It was at this factory, set up to manufacture his new coal-tar process, that Perkin created the world's first synthetic dye, which he named mauve, and which became one of the most popular colours of Victorian society.

Although it was some distance from Cadby Hall, Lyons had carefully chosen this site for the new tea factory that was to be built there. Plans for the Western Avenue roadworks, giving access to West London, had already been approved, and construction continued throughout the 1920s. Likewise the first stretch of the Great West Road, further south, immeasurably improved communications from Greenford to the west when the first section was completed in 1925. Lyons' management could not have been unaware of these important road schemes. In addition, the Grand Union Canal ran through the property, connecting Greenford with the Thames, and thence to London Docks, where tea and other imported materials were off-loaded from freighters.

George Edward Holman, principal in the firm of Holman & Goodrham, advised Lyons architecturally on the design of the single-storey, saw-tooth-style factory at Greenford which he laid out with trees, lawns and flower beds. By 1921 the first factory buildings and transport infrastructure were in place; these included

private railway sidings, which facilitated the movement of products from the factory via the Great Western and other railway networks, and a canal basin, which enabled bulk imports, transported from London Docks by river and canal, to be unloaded from several barges simultaneously. After unloading the tea was stored before being blended and fed into 72 automatic electric weighing and tea-packing machines each capable of producing one packet of tea per second complete, ready for sale.

Having officially opened on 18 July 1921, the new factory at first produced tea in parallel with Cadby Hall, whose tea facilities closed on 21 October the same year. From 1915 the Tea Factory Manager at Cadby Hall had been Gordon Stamper and when Greenford opened he assumed the same post there until his death in August 1948. From 1921–2, tea, coffee, cocoa and

other products were transported from Greenford by road, rail and water. Barges carried bulk leaf tea, coffee and cocoa beans from London Docks up the Thames to Brentford, some having stopped at Lyons' Rannoch Road wharf in Fulham to off-load supplies destined for Cadby Hall. Each of the eleven barges, managed by the subsidiary George Henry Collier Ltd from their Brentford Dock offices, could carry a maximum weight of sixty tons. Steam tugs pulled them up the Thames from London Docks to a point at Brent Creek where smaller craft took over and towed the barges through the Grand Union Canal as far as Gauge Lock. There, weights were computed and tolls paid and the barges were then pulled, in time-honoured fashion, by shire horse all the way to the Greenford basin, where their cargoes were discharged into Lyons' own bonded stores. The barge *Trial* was the first to make the voyage,

123

This unique photograph from 1924 clearly portrays the three distribution schemes adopted by Lyons' Greenford factory. This road, rail and canal arrangement come together at Windmill Lane, Osterly.

THREE WAYS TO LYONS' GREENFORD FACTORY.

The first barge to arrive at the Greenford factory after its opening in 1921. Having started its journey in the London docks it is now on the last tranquil canal passage, pulled by shire horses who seem to be resting while this picture is taken.

in October 1921. With a saving of ¼d. per lb over road transport, canal usage continued for many years.

Eventually the Greenford factory became a manufacturing showplace drawing many distinguished visitors from home and abroad; the directors even organised an inspection by King George V. The head of the Tea Agents' Department, George Pollard, personally escorted train-loads of tea agents around the estate, eager to show them the new mechanical equipment used for unloading the barges, the busy tea-loading rail and road dock and the hall for blending and packing tea. Then, after suitable tea refreshment, he sent them home, somewhat bewildered by the efficiency of it all. The opening of the factory in July 1921 coincided with an improvement in the market for tea, and by the end of 1921 tea sales equalled pre-war peaks. In the late 1920s the Greenford factory handled over 446 tons of tea per week, distributing their packaged blends to over 200,000 outlets throughout the country by road and rail.

The output of ground coffee (Lyons did not sell coffee beans) and cocoa had also grown steadily between 1903 and 1919 and in 1922 both manufacturing processes were relocated to the Greenford factory. Although production volumes slowly increased, coffee, cocoa and drinking chocolate were always less popular than tea, so that revenues from these never achieved the same levels. Nevertheless at this time Lyons claimed to be the country's largest ground coffee producer.

Coffee Essence: Lyons' Bev

In 1921 a liquid coffee essence, sold under the brand name of Lyons' Coffee & Chicory Extract, had become popular when first introduced. In the 1930s the name was changed to Bev (beverage) and throughout the period leading up to and beyond 1939 it sold well against the market leader, Camp. Before the invention of vacuum sealing in foil packets or tin containers, conventional roasted coffee suffered from one major disadvantage: once the coffee bean had been ground, up to 65 per cent of its flavour could be lost within twenty-four hours from the action of oxygen in the air. Liquid coffee and chicory essence on the other hand can be kept very much longer after being opened. In the manufacturing process, coffee beans and roasted chicory root (*Cichorium intybus*) are pulverised into a powder, which is then held in a container while steam is forced through and the resulting liquid is drawn off. This mixture is then heated under vacuum to reduce it to a concentrated liquid essence which is then sweetened. Chicory root acts as a substitute for coffee but it also adds a bitter taste which is favoured by the French.

Although 'real' coffee was popular in continental Europe and the United States, before

Part of the Great Western Railway transfer point at the Greenford factory. This saddle-back shunting engine, owned by Lyons, is called *The Lyons Mail*. Two lorries are being loaded with chocolates. The tall chimney in the background was once part of William Perkins dye works where the colour mauve was invented. It was demolished on 4 February 1926 when Lyons enlarged the factory facilities. *By kind permission of Tetley (GB) Ltd.*

Below. This 1923 group of girls knocked on doors to offer householders free samples of tea from their wicker baskets.

Right. A view of the Greenford canal basin, with several barges awaiting unloading. Notice the rural character of the adjoining property to the rear. *By kind permission of Tetley (GB) Ltd.*

instant coffee powder or freeze-dried coffee granules were available, it remained a luxury drink in Britain. Coffee essence on the other hand could be used by all social classes without the need for percolators or other apparatus and the less well-off were among its principal users. Later, when instant coffee became available (the first, Nescafé, was introduced by the Swiss firm Nestlé in 1938), coffee essence declined in popularity, though it continued in use for making iced coffee and flavouring for icings, fillings, milk shakes, cakes and so on.

During the Second World War the Ministry of Food decided that coffee essence was a wartime necessity as a morale booster for canteens, messes, wardens' posts and air-raid shelters. When Belgium and northern France were overrun, however, the supply of chicory was interrupted. Then a senior chemist at Lyons, Dr Edwin Hughes, discovered that artichokes were similar in composition to chicory. Instructions went out to the Covent Garden buyers to purchase as many artichokes as they could lay their hands on. The artichokes were then dried, under laboratory supervision, in the hopfield kilns of Kent, before being pulverised and added to the preparation of coffee extract. This ingenious idea transformed Bev into a bestseller, with sales having trebled by the end of the war. Its success can be attributed partly to its ease of preparation, just by adding hot water or milk, but perhaps more significantly to the fact that it was already sweetened. Its rapid success, however, was matched by an equally rapid decline after the war, as rationing ended and tea and coffee ingredients became more widely available.

Coffee roasting machine at Greenford. *By kind permission of Tetley (GB) Ltd.*

New Branded Lines: Jersey Lily Tomato Sauce

Although Lyons had achieved some success with coffee essence between 1921 and 1945, this was more by luck than by strategic planning. It was another coffee product which fitted neatly alongside their tea, ground coffee and cocoa manufacture. When the essence was launched in 1921, management did not understand the concept of branding, other than with the name of Lyons. Nevertheless they proceeded to introduce all kinds of new grocery and confectionery lines without proper market evaluation. With a customer base of 200,000, serviced by 250 salesmen, management judged that any new product bearing the prestige name of Lyons could be sold without difficulty and at no extra cost; the intrepid tea salesmen would do the job. Lyons' management probably did have grandiose plans for expansion, for why else would they have acquired such a large parcel of land to transfer the tea and coffee operations in 1921?

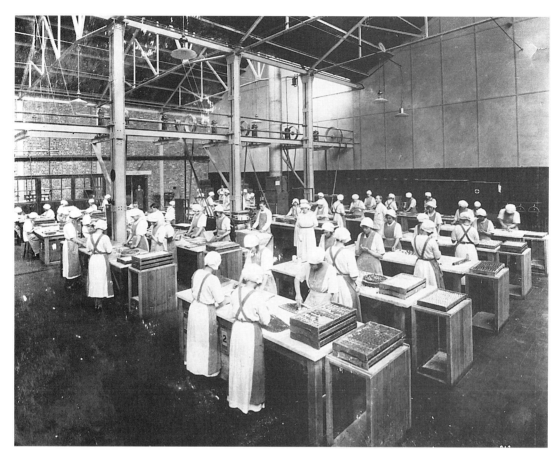

Above.   Fondant making at the Greenford factory. Note the lack of safety measures associated with the power belt drives, the first-aid box on the rear wall and the elegantly attired supervisor in the centre of the picture. *By kind permission of Tetley (GB) Ltd.*

Right.   One of the main tea packing floors at the Greenford factory. The appropriate blend was poured into hoppers from an upper gallery which then cascaded to the weighing and packing machines below. It was a dusty process and vacuum cleaners were much occupied. *By kind permission of Tetley (GB) Ltd.*

The Chocolate Sales Department was formed in 1921 and operated a traveller service with deliveries by rail from Greenford. A year later the Wholesale Tea Department started what was first known as the confectionery van sales section of that department, and in 1926 this section was transferred to the Chocolate Sales Department. The chocolate van sales gradually covered the entire country with the exception of Scotland, but although fair progress was made, it was felt that the van sales' system prevented sales through better class channels and a traveller operated service was re-introduced with deliveries from selected centres throughout the country.

This system operated until the outbreak of war, when zoning and rationing came into being. The various chocolate and sweet firms co-operated and agreed to deliver each other's goods. Many of Lyons' small depots were closed and finally only Greenford remained open. When the combined delivery arrangements ended after the war, the sweet confectionery firm of Rowntree continued to handle the bulk of Lyons' orders outside the Greenford area. In this way Lyons were able to save on manpower and packing material, since goods were sent in bulk which otherwise would have been sent to each agent separately by rail.

The first new grocery products also appeared in 1921 with the introduction of tomato sauce. Although Greenford had ample space to set up a production line for this product, Lyons instead turned to Jersey, where there was an abundance

of tomatoes and where they already had an export tea operation. In 1826 John Horniman had founded a tea-packing business in Jersey primarily for home sales. John Horniman's sons moved the business to Wormwood Street (and Shepherdess Walk), London, at the end of the nineteenth century and in 1917 Lyons took a controlling interest in W.H. and F.J. Horniman & Co. Ltd.

The first export tea-packing trade in Jersey had been established in April 1876 by Thomas Cook, an export merchant in Reading, with flourishing markets in South America and the Far East. He had arrived in Jersey with William Brett to set up a business packing and exporting tea, presumably to escape the extortionate excise duties at home. Cook rented premises in Commercial Buildings, Old Harbour, St Helier, from where his tea-packing business was launched, with William Brett in charge of the day-to-day management until November 1884, when he was

succeeded by Joseph Walker,
Cook's brother-in-law. After
Thomas Cook was killed in
a hunting accident in 1890,
the business passed to Joseph
Walker, who, with his five
sons, continued to enlarge
the business.

Most of Walker's sons
established themselves in
Buenos Aires, building up a
reputation for tea sold
throughout Argentina under
the brand name of Te Sol,
which had been registered as
a trademark by Cook himself
in 1880. The distribution
centre in Buenos Aires originally operated under the
name of Compania Te Sol
but in 1912 it converted to
a limited company known as
Walker Hermanos Limitada.

When Joseph Walker's
business rapidly outgrew its
premises in Jersey, the
company bought a large plot
of land at First Tower in 1900
and constructed a modern
factory there. As Jersey enjoyed five per cent more
sunshine annually than the
sunniest spots on the south
coast of England, Joseph
Walker appropriately named
it the Sun Works. The following year the enterprise
was converted into a limited
company – J.J. Walker & Sons
Ltd – and in 1912 it re-registered as Walkers Ltd.

While Thomas Walker (one of Joseph
Walker's sons) and William Bruce Douglas, a
director of W.H. & F.J. Horniman & Co. Ltd (now
in the hands of Lyons), were homeward bound
on the same ship from South America, they
discussed the possibility of a merger between the
two firms. This culminated in the formation of
the Overseas Trading Corporation Ltd, registered

Centre. Although a contrived photograph, this image does convey a sense of frantic activity at Greenford's tea dock. *By kind permission of Tetley (GB) Ltd.*

Bottom. Part of the Greenford factory's tea dock taken in the mid-1920s. A variety of transport systems are shown including Sentinel steam waggons, internal combustion lorries and a railway shunter. A railway box car is hoisted by overhead crane for loading on to a flat-bed rail wagon.

Right. Part of this consignment of tea, being un-loaded at Greenford in the 1950s, comes from the company's own plantation at Malangi (Mlanje) mountain, Nyasaland.

in Jersey on 31 January 1920, to acquire the tea export businesses of Horniman's, J. Lyons & Co. Ltd (subject to reservation in some of the English-speaking countries), Walkers Ltd and its Argentine subsidiary, Walker Hermanos Limitada. Lyons are believed to have had a 51 per cent shareholding in the new company but this has not been authenticated because of the rules concerning Jersey company registrations. In any

event, in 1968 Lyons bought out the remaining shareholders, the Overseas Trading Corporation Ltd became a wholly owned subsidiary and eventually the whole operation moved to the United Kingdom.

In 1921, having established an interest on the island of Jersey, Lyons decided to manufacture their new brand of tomato sauce where the raw material was both plentiful and inexpensive (few realised that the bulk of tomato puree was imported from Hungary after Lyons discovered this was less expensive). They called this product Jersey Lily Tomato Sauce, after one of the island's most famous citizens, the actress Lillie Langtry, who was known herself as the 'Jersey Lily'. This brand of tomato sauce was one of the first additional grocery items introduced by Lyons. Production in Jersey was carried out in part of the Overseas Trading Corporation's tea-packing factory during the slack summer months. Lyons regarded it as no more than a cheap alternative to supplement the income from the company's prestige tea exports. With no real commitment to the product, no evaluation of the market, inadequate advertising, mediocre packaging and, worse still, competition with the market leader, Heinz, Jersey Lily Tomato Sauce failed miserably.

In 1923 Lyons and United Dairies Ltd jointly formed Milkal Ltd, with Lyons holding the controlling shares, to develop a dried milk powder business. Produced at a factory in Hemyock, Devon, its low-volume output ended up being used in the ice-cream factories at Cadby Hall although some product was sold to the trade under the brand names of Milkal and Kookal, the former a soluble full-cream milk powder and the latter a skimmed milk powder. The joint operation ran during the years 1923–9 before Lyons sold their interests to United Dairies Ltd. Like tomato sauce it was not successful.

Similarly, Lyonaize (a salad dressing), custard powder, jelly crystals, toffee and plain chocolate were all introduced but suffered from the same problems as tomato sauce: they lacked a marketing strategy, were assigned no adequate advertising budget and were expected to compete, head on, with the strong brand leaders of Heinz Salad Cream, Bird's Custard, Chiver's and Hartley's Jellies, Palm Toffee and Cadbury's Chocolate. Nevertheless, some moderate success was achieved with custard powder and jelly, both launched in 1921, despite their being more expensive than the brand leaders. Lyons' custard powder also had a faintly almond taste and was a slightly different colour from that of its competitor. This limited success can only have been the result of tenacious selling, even though

Much favoured by tea salesmen, this Renault of 1908, with its non skid tyres, is seen here with its driver and 'boy'.

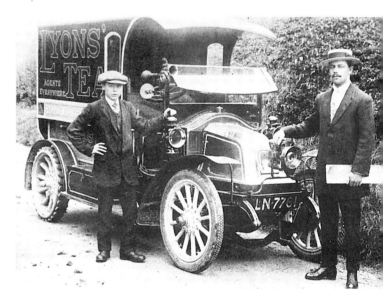

the salesmen themselves were generally uncommitted to the confectionery lines, many of them finding it impossible to make any headway in the face of strong competition from less expensive branded alternatives. Some salesmen even believed that the poor quality of these new products actually damaged Lyons' reputation. Since sales managers had not yet been introduced into Lyons, there was no mechanism to allow the salesforce properly to ventilate their opinion. Many worked away from Greenford and were not skilled in marketing techniques, nor did they have any communication channels. In the absence of any opposing views, Lyons' management continued experimenting with a whole range of new products including chocolate(s) and toffee.

These confectionery lines were also introduced in 1921 and, like the grocery products, they too had mixed fortunes, with the years

This Falke glider (piloted by Hans Kraus) took part, unsuccessfully, in a £1,000 cross-channel competition organised by the *Daily Mail* in June 1931. The picture was taken at Freshwater, Isle of Wight.

Left. Photographed in New Road, Basingstoke, this van has been decorated to participate in a local carnival to raise money for the Cottage Hospital. The 1921 Fiat appears to have spoke wheels but they are discs with emblems of tea packets on them. *By kind permission of Tetley (GB) Ltd.*

Below. A typical corner shop of the 1920s. Tens of thousands were privately owned before supermarkets replaced them. This one is in Gordon Road, Chiswick.

1924–32 showing the best performance. Lyons had invested in seven special demonstration and display vehicles which travelled the country promoting new confectionery lines to shopkeepers and consumers. Handmade chocolates, such as the Nippy and Dickens's brands, sold quite well through the food halls of the Corner Houses and high-class restaurants as well as in cinemas and other outlets. Speciality chocolates, made at the Corner Houses, were much more successful, offering over fifty different fillings from Angelica Supreme to Walnut Rock.

Over 200 staff were employed on confectionery production at Greenford. Some lines did better than others, but by the start of the Second World War most confectionery products had ceased to be manufactured, partly through supply difficulties. However, Slam (a chocolate wafer), Crispy Fingers (a chocolate wafer biscuit similar to Kit-Kat which was retailed predominantly through Woolworth's stores), American Candies and Buzz Bars (an oval chocolate biscuit bar made by Bee Bee Biscuits which Lyons bought in 1922) continued to be made for a short period as supplies allowed. After the war, further attempts were made to introduce new lines and a powdered summer drink, called Lyonzade, became fairly successful when it was launched in 1954 selling over one million packets a week. Other items, such as the Mint Choc range, were not so successful.

Bone-meal and Chicken-rearing

Until 1920 the clean bones from the butcher's shop and other meat processes at Cadby Hall were sold to trades which turned them into bone-meal for use as fertiliser and supplements in cattle-feeds. When Greenford opened, more space became available and Lyons decided to process these meat by-products themselves, presumably as a new revenue source, by opening a small facility to process bones. There is no evidence that Lyons retailed this bone-meal directly to the consumer and the output was probably sold to fertiliser producers and the agricultural trade. Although bone-meal production is perfectly acceptable, management must have felt that the practice of making it at a modern food factory

Tea blenders at work in the 1950s. Blends were tested for taste, fragrance and colour. Tea blend samples were measured into mugs and boiling water poured on them from a specially designed kettle that kept the water boiling long enough to complete a long row. It was tasted after milk was added so that taste and colour could be determined. Some wet and dry leaf from each blend sample was put at the back of the mug so the taster could compare them. Following this process blenders were then better prepared to bid at auction for tea supplies.

might create negative impressions and bone-meal production was discontinued in the mid-1920s. In any case the volume of production was too low to make the venture worthwhile.

Before the start of the Second World War, with so much under-utilised land at Greenford, chicken-rearing was introduced to provide eggs intended for cake production. Prior to this the bakeries were using frozen eggs imported from China, but supplies were curtailed when the Sino-Japanese war broke out in 1937 in China. Battery cages were imported from the United States in kit form and assembled at Greenford. At the time, Lyons were proud of having the only farm in Britain where laying birds were raised from a day old to maturity entirely in cages – a system now considered to be cruel.

In 1939 the chicken-rearing was transferred to seven acres of land at Lower Gravenhurst, Bedfordshire, where Ion Bridge Poultry Farm was built to accommodate 6,000 chickens. It had formed part of an estate owned by the company secretary George Booth, but it is not known whether the seven acres passed into Lyons' ownership by way of sale or lease. The operation never fulfilled the original purpose of producing eggs for the bakeries. After rationing was introduced in 1939, poultry became so scarce that Ion Bridge supplied chickens for the table – much needed in Lyons' hotels and restaurants.

The farm was run by Edward Lutley and his wife Daphne. Edward Lutley had joined Lyons as a chemist after graduating in 1927 and took up his first post in the Milkal factory at Hemyock in his native Devon. After Lyons disposed of their interests in the Milkal factory in 1929, Edward Lutley moved to the central laboratories at Cadby Hall, where he remained until 1937, when he agreed to take charge of the chicken-rearing at Greenford. With the transfer to Ion Bridge at the start of the Second World War, Lutley moved again. One of Edward Lutley's difficulties during the war was how to obtain sufficient feed for the growing number of birds, but he used his ingenuity to formulate what he dubbed his X13 compound. After much experimentation this had been concocted from bakery breadcrumbs, fish leavings from restaurants, the residue from soup

making and other factory waste. Everything was mixed together in an obsolete sausage-meat machine and the recipe remained in use until the early '50s, when poultry food became more widely available again. By then 10,000 eggs were being produced each week from a flock of 16,000 crossed Black Leghorns and Rhode Island Reds and by 1970 the number of eggs had increased to 50,000.

In the post-war period, with food still in short supply, mushroom farming was also carried out at Greenford. The air-raid shelters which had been built to protect the workers were now no longer required and so they were put to good use to grow mushrooms for the restaurants and hotels. This operation lasted until the mid-1950s.

Competition in the Tea Trade

Between 1920 and 1922 the national retail price of tea fell by 12–17 per cent. It stabilised and slightly rose between 1922 and 1928, when again there was a sharp fall, though less severe, continuing then to decline from year to year until a low point was reached in 1932. A year later a recovery set in and prices rose until the start of the Second World War. From Appendix 2 it can be seen that the factory output of cocoa grew dramatically from just under 100 tons in 1909 to 1,462 tons in 1918 – an increase of more than 1,300 per cent. The consumption of cocoa, however, declined thereafter, possibly because people began to buy more expensive drinks which they preferred, as real incomes grew. On the other hand, drinking chocolate sales started from a very low base and, although there was some improvement up to 1915, factory output never exceeded 100 tons and production seems to have been discontinued in 1917.

Lyons' Green Label tea enjoyed uninterrupted growth throughout the 1920s and became the firm's best-selling brand, undoubtedly with the help of massive advertising across the country. In processions and carnivals Lyons entered giant models, floats and decorated vans from which they distributed free cups of Green Label tea. The company sponsored gliding competitions, where hostesses provided tea for all spectators free of charge. At concerts, outdoor events and sponsored cinema showings, cups of Green Label would be handed out. In addition, thousands of sample packets were given away through the agents, the retailers. Some enterprising salesmen even persuaded shop-owners to display nothing but Green Label tea in their windows. With a distribution network of over 200,000 outlets, coupled with the nationally promoted Green Label brand and keen pricing, Lyons had every reason to believe that consumption of tea would continue its relentless upward surge. At the Tea Department's beginnings in 1903, factory output had been less than 300 tons. In just 21 years it had risen to a phenomenal 22,573 tons – an increase of nearly 8,000 per cent.

While much of industry enjoyed remarkable growth after the First World War, the decline of coal production, textile making and shipbuilding caused high levels of regional unemployment, especially in northern England, Wales and Scotland. Therefore the distribution of the increased national income was uneven, and labour unrest continued up to May 1926, when a government proposal to cut wages and increase the working day in the coal industry provoked a miners' strike, which in turn led to a General Strike in support of the miners. Although the Trades Union Congress called off the strike after nine days, the miners stayed out until November. Some 4,000 strikers were prosecuted for violence or incitement to violence and 1,000 were imprisoned. The following year Stanley Baldwin's Conservative government passed the Trade Disputes Act, making general strikes illegal until the Act was repealed in 1946. During this period, Lyons saw a steady increase in sales of its tea but in the few years between 1928 and 1933 sales unexpectedly declined. This decline coincided with two separate events. On the one hand, the Great Depression brought a world-wide fall in trade, reduction of industrial production and mass unemployment as well as the financial crisis of 1931 which led to the collapse of Ramsey MacDonald's Labour government, devaluation of the currency and wage cuts leading to strikes, riots and naval mutiny. On the other hand, the reduction in tea duty and falling world prices encouraged other tea packers to enter the market.

Filling tins of Quoffy in the 1950s.

The quality of many packers' teas, however, was much lower than that of Lyons and other well-established blenders. Nevertheless, inferior blending enabled them to undercut the higher-quality Lyons teas and thus widen the price gap. Brooke Bond decided to cheapen their best-selling Edglets brand in an attempt not only to maintain their market share but to capture some of the market for Green Label, which Lyons had refused to make less expensive. In the face of the price-cutting onslaught from other manufacturers, Lyons decided in early 1930 to increase their advertising in their favoured *Daily Mail* newspaper. The newspaper advertising was supported by a marketing campaign on Radio

Luxembourg using a fictitious character with the unlikely name of 'Peter the Planter' and devised by Lyons' publicity department. With an air of authority Peter the Planter elucidated the merits of Green Label tea and how best to drink it. By the late 1930s tea sales had again increased but sales of the heavily promoted Green Label continued to decline. Peter the Planter and the advertising campaign unexpectedly created a larger market for the cheaper Lyons brands at the expense of Green Label. Not surprisingly, the additional sales of lower-grade tea came mainly from areas of the country with high unemployment.

Brooke Bond and Ty·phoo continued their assault on Lyons by introducing quick-infusion teas which were made from smaller leaf and could be sold at lower prices. In November 1935 Brooke Bond also brought out their first 'dividend' tea incorporating a gummed stamp in the packet. The penny 'thrift' stamps, which depicted a beehive, could be collected and stuck on to a card marked out with sixty squares, and when it was full it could be exchanged for 5 shillings. Dividend tea became an enormous success, but Brooke Bond's tactics were initially despised by the conservative management in Lyons' Tea Department who regarded them as a desperate attempt to stay competitive. Meanwhile Lyons maintained their market position without the aid of gimmicks, even when Brooke Bond launched a new blend claiming it improved digestion – a claim they later withdrew when it was legally challenged. Thereafter, Brooke Bond resorted to naming this new blend Pre-Gest-Tea (later known as PG Tips).

Horniman, in their centenary year of 1926, had been the first Lyons company to introduce incentives by offering a box of chocolates for every forty packet labels collected. The campaign was so successful that the scheme was extended for a further year. In 1938 they copied Brooke Bond and the co-operative societies by launching first a 2d. dividend tea and then another gift scheme. Black & Green imitated Horniman's 1926 offer by bringing in a gift scheme for their Family Tea in 1928 which, apart from the war years, continued into the 1960s, when over 200 gifts were on offer. Both Horniman and Black & Green competed with Brooke Bond in the north of England, where gifts were more popular.

While many of the tea managers insisted on producing only traditional leaf tea and opposed quick-infusion tea, there were some at Lyons who felt they had missed an opportunity to regain some of the northern tea markets lost to Brooke Bond and Ty·phoo. Although Brooke Bond were beginning to capture more of the Lyons business – in both the north and the south of the country – the warning signs were still ignored. As disagreements within the company over the merits of small-leaf teas continued, sales of Green Label, and the more expensive Red Label, began to improve. Green Label had been one of Lyons'

best-selling teas for many years, yet at this time tea managers took an extraordinary decision to promote the Red Label blend and completely overlooked the need to produce their own quick-infusion tea if only to stop the encroachment of other manufacturers into their market. Largely influenced by the conventional buyers, this decision prevented Lyons from participating in the fast-growing market for quick-infusing teas, thus compounding the marketing errors made earlier. Despite heavy promotion, Red Label never achieved high sales.

Tea Controls in the Second World War

The tea trade suffered less than other food commodities during the Second World War, and government action was less drastic than in the First World War in many respects. Pre-war plans had been based on the principle that the tea trade should control itself if war broke out, and by 1937 a distribution scheme had been agreed by the Tea Buyers' Association. In essence, this meant that the tea-producing firms would share packing factories in the event of war damage. London-based firms arranged to switch their production to Greenford, while Manchester became the tea centre for the rest of the country. Provincial tea firms were encouraged to form mutual arrangements to support each other in the event of factory damage. The

Left. The Bev coffee production line at Greenford in the 1950s.

Below left. Nut milk bars of chocolate coming off the production line at Greenford.

Right. This superb picture shows the Horniman's tea packing factory at Wormwood Street, London. Compared with the modern facilities at Greenford these working conditions were far from agreeable. Child labour is still in evidence and, although the factory appears to have electric light, gas fittings can still be seen. *By kind permission of London Metropolitan Archives.*

Right. An attractive scene showing the unloading of tea chests at the Horniman factory in Wormwood Street, London. *By kind permission of London Metropolitan Archives.*

HRH Queen Mary accepting three miniature chests of India, Ceylon and China tea from Alfred Salmon following a royal visit to the Greenford factory on 27 February 1923.

Tea Buyers' Association also recommended that the two controls introduced during the First World War should again be initiated – the introduction of National Tea and registration of consumers with retailers. Thus when war came a great deal of planning had already been undertaken and the tea trade was prepared. In the event, National Tea was not introduced, nor were consumers asked to register with their retailers. At the start of the war, the government set up, under the Ministry of Food, the Tea Control Organisation, which included Headquarters, a Selling Section and a Distribution Section. Headquarters were responsible for policy and supply before tea entered the market, Selling Section transferred tea to the market and Distribution Section advised on problems that arose once it was in the market. After July 1940, when the tea supply was restricted, the Ministry of Food's rationing division also became concerned with distribution.

Controls began on 5 September 1939 when the auctions were abandoned and tea was distributed on a datum system – the datum, or base-line, being the calculated quantity of tea on which each company paid duty between 1 January 1938 and 30 June 1939. Each buyer received an equal quota of high-, medium- and low-grade tea. From September 1939 to May 1940, 100 per cent of the datum was released to blenders. An increase in tea prices was considered but soon ruled out. Rationing was also rejected – first, because of public morale; second, because there was no real shortage as yet; and, third, because it was assumed that rationing would require registration and a pooling of tea.

The dispersal of tea stocks from London's warehouses started early, but as fast as it was being moved out more tea cargoes arrived. By May 1940, though, real shortages occurred when the Mediterranean was closed to shipping and many fewer consignments arrived from the tea-producing countries. Tea allocations were cut to 90 per cent of datum and an appeal for economy was made. The rationing division of the Ministry of Food hoped that a cut in allocation would be sufficient to reduce demand but throughout May and June 1940 rationing continued to be discussed. By July the supply of tea from abroad had slumped further and allocations were at once reduced to 70 per cent. At the same time a decision was taken to introduce coupons for rationing loose tea merely as a temporary measure. Tea coupons could be exchanged at any retailer and were valid for any grade of tea. Retailers would obtain their quotas according to number of coupons collected and from only one supplier in a sixteen-week period, after which they

A delightful picture of a Sentinel steam waggon towing a flat-bed trailer in the early 1920s. Despite extensive research the location of the picture is not known.

were free to change supplier.

This system of tea allocation, with blends graded into high, medium and low, put Lyons at a disadvantage. Ty·phoo, for example, had only one blend and continued to pack all three government grades under that one label, offering large cash discounts to retailers and thereby encouraging re-registration at the end of a sixteen-week period. Brooke Bond packed two grades, PG Tips and its own dividend brand. Lyons, however, had many blends and would not devalue Green Label, which it continued to sell during the war years. Less expensive Lyons teas included Yellow Label and Black & Green's Golden Tips. As consumers soon learned that better-quality tea would go further, cheaper teas became less popular during the war. This anomaly created a market for the more expensive blends and Green Label did well. Unfortunately the quota system did not allocate sufficient quantities of the higher-grade tea to satisfy demand and, despite the anger of retailers, Lyons refused to adulterate Green Label tea. Retailers were further frustrated when Lyons insisted they take an allocation of cheaper teas to obtain a supply of Green Label.

During the Second World War, although an apportionment system operated, real rationing of tea did not occur. The main tea companies successfully resisted the introduction of a National Tea (as in the First World War), on the grounds that it would prevent poorer families from buying the cheaper tea blends which had been progressively introduced after 1918. Some Members of Parliament did, however, criticise the tea companies for their wasteful use of transport in supplying their tea to the distant towns and villages, but this charge was largely unfounded. As the war progressed, these distribution networks began to carry many other goods, thus making a considerable contribution to fuel savings.

The war years were profitable for most tea companies but during the brief six-year period between 1939 and 1945 Lyons' tea sales halved. Worse still, when supplies again began to improve in the early 1950s, Lyons were faced with increasingly strong competition from Brooke Bond, Ty·phoo and others, with their strong brand images and the premium teas that Lyons had so studiously avoided. It was a predicament from which Lyons never fully recovered.

Chapter

THE EVOLUTION OF ICE-CREAM

IN THE AFTERMATH of the First World War, as refrigeration technology developed, there was a huge expansion in the production of ice-cream, which rapidly came into vogue during the 1920s. It was probably introduced into Europe from China by the Italian traveller Marco Polo at the end of the thirteenth century, and from Italy it slowly spread to the rest of Europe. In France, the sixteenth-century court of the Florence-born queen, Catherine de Medici, started a fashion for ice-creams and sorbets. Apparently she brought the idea from Italy as a kind of wedding present for her husband, King Henri II of France. Ice was transported down from the mountains during winter and stored in ice-houses; a large ice depot in Paris gave its name to the rue de la Glacière. Its importation into England is said to have been undertaken by Gerrard Tissain, chef to Charles I, who was given a pension on condition that he kept his recipe for ice-cream entirely secret. After Charles I was executed in 1649, Tissain returned to France and sold his recipe to the Café Napolitain – hence Neapolitan ices. As techniques advanced, ice-cream desserts were enjoyed not only by the privileged few but by the middle class and eventually, through mass production, by everyone.

One of the first printed references to ice-cream in England appeared in the *London Gazette* of 1686, in a description of an official banquet where 'iced creams were also served'. London's first ice-cream shop belonged to a Swiss Italian confectioner named Agostino Gatti, who set up business on the corner of Leather Lane and Holborn. Gatti also owned the more famous shop

in Hungerford market which was demolished in 1862 to make way for Charing Cross railway station. It was then the largest restaurant in London, serving 1,000 customers at a time.

The Italian ice-cream trade in Britain appears to have been typically retail, built around family ownership, with maybe no more than a few outlets and perhaps selling from handcarts in the poorer districts, where the vendors were known as hokey-pokey men. This trade flourished after the First World War and gradually ice-cream vendors vied for pocket money from children who had up until now spent their meagre allowances on flavoured carbonated water. According to the *New Survey of London Life and Labour* (1933), ice-cream replaced much of the fizzy water business between 1925 and 1933.

The Italians developed an ice-cream which was smoother in texture than that of the mass producers. They also paid particular attention to the ornamental and artistic presentation which mass production was unable to copy. Made with only the finest ingredients, their ice-cream found a niche market right up to the start of the Second World War, when many Italian businesses were boycotted. In Britain some of the original Italian families eventually moved into large-scale manufacturing but despite the number of Italians involved in ice-cream making in the early part of the century they did not seem to dominate the trade. Some families that branched out were eventually absorbed by Lyons, including the names of Massarella, Rebori and Bertorelli, who had built an exclusive, high-quality business around shaped ice-cream desserts and sorbets.

These were specifically prepared for the hotel and high-class restaurant trade as well as exclusive food stores such as Fortnum & Mason and Harrods.

Italian immigrants had taken ice-cream to America in the eighteenth century but it did not catch on until 1816 after James Madison – architect of the Bill of Rights and fourth President of the United States – served iced custard tarts at a party for friends. The party was given wide press coverage when one of the guests complained he had been poisoned as a result of biting into a frozen tart and the chef responsible was quickly arrested. Once the incarcerated cook had explained the formula, ice-cream production soared and America soon led the world in ice-cream consumption. For reasons unknown, the state of Illinois did not initially allow ice-cream to be consumed on Sunday, but after some debate with the legislators ice-cream was considered not to be ice-cream if other ingredients, such as syrup, nuts or fruit, were poured over the top – and so the 'sundae ice' was invented. By 1855 the first wholesaler, a Pennsylvanian dairyman called Jacob Fussell, who used his excess milk to make ice-cream, was already the main competitor. It was perhaps the hotter climate, the flourishing dairy companies with their increasing mechanisation, the invention of the ice-cream cone in 1904, as well as the large Italian population, that encouraged ice-cream making to develop in America more rapidly than in Europe as a whole.

The process of ice-cream manufacture is relatively simple, lending itself to both small- and large-scale production. Ingredients are readily available, but the way in which they are mixed and frozen determines the texture and flavour of the ice-cream produced. Gelatine has been used in ice-cream manufacture for a number of years, its function being to form minute capsules around the water crystals to prevent them from growing into long, coarse spines while the ice-cream is being cold-stored. The eggs and milk in ice-cream make it a nutritious food. Cow's milk contains four essential nutrients – fat, carbo hydrates, protein and vitamins – as well as minerals such as calcium. However, milk is easily contaminated by bacteria once it leaves a cow's udder – or earlier if the animal is in ill health

or has unclean teats. In most early ice-cream processes in this country bacteria were destroyed by heating the milk to the required temperature followed by fast freezing and hygienic storage. Early ice-cream production in America tended to use fresh, untreated, milk with a result that much of their ice-cream, although of superior taste, had high bacteriological contamination.

Early Production Methods

Lyons had started making ice-cream in small quantities as early as 1894 using the turbine bowl method of mixing milk, cream, sugar, butter, gelatine, flavouring and other stabilisers. From a department next to Cadby Hall's fish shop – chosen because of the close availability of ice – milk was boiled in steam kettles together with sugar and pure vanilla beans. After the mixture had cooled, the untreated cream and any flavourings were added. Only three flavours were produced: vanilla, strawberry and pistachio, with its characteristic green colour; whole strawberries in syrup were imported in barrels from America until the late 1920s, when Lyons made their own puree from home-produced strawberries kept in cold stores for use the following season. The mixture of flavoured milk, cream and sugar was then steadily poured into a spindle-driven revolving drum, cooled on the outside by salt and ice. When it froze an operator scraped the mix from inside with a wooden spatula and scooped it into a variety of containers. The standard mix comprised three gallons of milk and one and a half gallons of cream and was known as French ice-cream. The product supplied to Buckingham Palace, termed Royalty ice-cream, also contained three gallons of milk but included three gallons of cream – twice as much as the standard blend. One mixing would make six gallons and it was a slow, low-volume process. Choc-ice was also produced at this time: ice-cream slabs were cut into small fingers and hand dipped into a chocolate-like mix known as couverture – a very messy process. The turbine method of manufacture was used until refrigeration methods improved in the 1920s, but, despite many problems, some progress was achieved in the mechanical technology before then.

Packing ice-cream bricks at the Cadby Hall factory in 1923. When the factory opened it was the largest in Europe, occupying nearly 70,000 square feet. Ice-cream output was 50 tons per day.

In 1917 the wartime government Food Controller introduced an Ice-Cream Restriction Order preventing ice-cream manufacture. It was not lifted until 22 March 1919, and even then the Cream Order prohibited its use in ice-cream manufacture. Sugar restrictions were lifted in 1919, but buyers had to apply to the local Food Officer giving proof of 1915 purchases before supplies could be obtained.

After the 1918 armistice tremendous advances were made in the application of engineering technology to the catering trades and none more so than in refrigeration. Until then the sale of ice-cream was confined to a spasmodic retail trade during the height of the summer season. Between 1920 and 1923 ice-cream consumption in the United Kingdom increased from 870,000 gallons to 1,683,000 gallons per year, while during the same period consumer expenditure on ice-cream grew from £0.9 million to £1.6 million, in each case roughly doubling in three years.

Improvements in refrigeration and a higher standard of living led Lyons to believe that ice-cream sales were poised to accelerate from 1920. Maurice Salmon (1885–1947), sixth son of Barnett Salmon, and the director responsible for all food manufacture at Cadby Hall, decided to invest in new factory processes so that Lyons

would be able to take advantage of any surge in demand as soon as it came. He engaged Fred Hesse, an American expert in ice-cream-manufacturing equipment, to conduct a study of the available processes. On his advice, in 1922 a prototype factory was built in the basement of A Block, consisting of mixing vats and vertical freezers. Fred Sealey, a confectionery salesman, joined the ice-cream department with the objective of creating a larger market. From an initial radial territory around Cadby Hall, Fred Sealey sold ice-cream to confectioners whom he had previously provided with wooden tubs to store the frozen product, having also arranged to top these up with crushed ice on a daily basis for a charge of 6d. Distribution was by horse-drawn

An early form of ice-cream transport photographed at the Normand Garage, Park Royal, London. The vehicle's maximum speed was 12 m.p.h.

Like the bakeries, the ice-cream factory functioned on the gravity system. In other words, all raw materials entered the plant at the top of the building and moved downwards as production advanced. Within the preparation room, milk powder and water were mixed and then pumped to the vats in the mixing room, where sugar, fats and stabilisers were added before heat treatment – or, more correctly, pasteurisation – which continued for a specified duration to ensure the mix was free of harmful bacteria. The pasteurised mix was then pumped over coolers to reduce its temperature while it passed to the ageing-vats, where it was held for at least 24 hours to hydrate before freezing – a process not always followed by small ice-cream manufacturers. During the freezing process, fruits and flavours were added.

After freezing, the ice-cream was conveyed to cold store and hardened. If it was intended for bulk supply, it was filled in cylindrical cans, surrounded by crushed ice and salt, and dispatched to

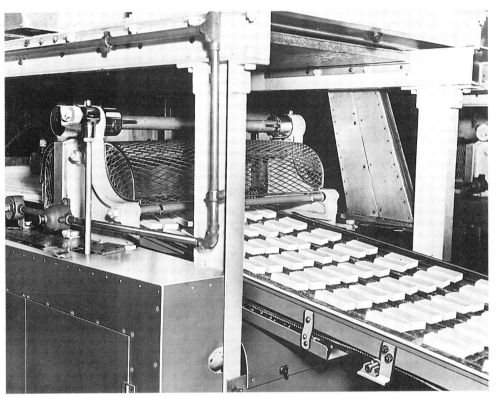

These ice-cream bars, photographed in the early 1950s, are on their way to the chocolate enrobers to become choc ices.

van and later, as sales grew, by the steam-powered vehicles bought from Sentinel Waggons to reach a wider area. Water tanks, filled with brine and crushed ice, were carried by Sentinel Waggons while the ice-cream cans were in transit.

A New Factory for the Ice-Cream Boom

In August 1922 Lyons launched into an even more ambitious project by installing a massive ice-cream plant capable of producing 50 tons of block ice-cream and 100 tons of water ice, for cooling purposes, per day. With tea and coffee production now transferred to Greenford, R Block at Cadby Hall became available. The new ice-cream plant occupied four floors, the basement and the roof – a floor area of 69,000 square feet.

the teashops and restaurants. If ice-cream was to be made into 'bricks', it was poured into long, flat containers and frozen hard. After hardening it was released by compressed air and shaped by a cutting device. The bricks passed to a conveyor, where they were enclosed in a pre-lined white box with gold printing and wrapped in parchment paper, ready for sale to the public. During this process the ice-cream was exposed to the atmosphere only for a few seconds and was never touched by hand. There were also carousel-type machines which dipped small fingers of ice-cream into couverture tanks to produce choc ices. In 1923, when the factory was fully operational, it was said to be the largest ice-cream plant in Europe.

Ice-cream manufactured from this plant was known as American-style, that is, ready for sale and uniform in composition. It was less likely to be contaminated than hand-processed products up to this time. Homogenisation, or fat dispersion, made the ice-cream smoother in texture and helped to increase its storage life. The new equipment had many advantages: the ice-cream was of a standard quality and never varied, it could be stored longer and therefore stocks could be built up for peak periods (such as bank holidays), it could be made in large batches, it was more hygienic and its packaging could be adjusted to meet a variety of marketing needs. Eighty thousand bricks a day were being produced by the summer of 1925, much of this being taken by the teashops to serve as desserts. On average 250 portions per day were sold in each of the teashops by November 1924, and those equipped with soda fountains sold even more.

Market Expansion

Having already established a large retail outlet for the sale of tea, coffee and bakery items, Lyons naturally turned to the same retail agents to sell their ice-cream. As an incentive, profit margins for the retailer were set higher on ice-cream than on other Lyons products. In 1924 bulk ice-cream was sold in one-, two-, three- and four-gallon containers at 10s. 9d., 10s. 3d., 9s. and 8s. 6d. per gallon respectively. Ice-cream bricks sold to the consumer for 1s. 6d. were wholesaled at 13 shillings per dozen, giving a profit margin of 38.5 per cent.

Despite the costly advertising campaigns, and in contrast with America, ice-cream in Britain remained a seasonal product for individual customers, and profits fluctuated widely according to weather. Since this peak-and-trough consumer demand exposed factory overheads, other more stable sales outlets were sought to iron out the fluctuations and increase winter turnover when demand was at its lowest. This started in the 1930s with a contract to supply the Odeon cinema chain and subsequently theatres and greyhound racetracks, although this last outlet was less profitable. It has often been claimed that cinema management stimulated ice-cream sales by increasing the heat in their auditoriums, but there is no documentary evidence to support this. Experience showed that cinema-goers were prepared to pay more for the ice-cream tubs specially made for cinemas, and this market helped to smooth fluctuations in sales. The price differential, however, did not improve profits for Lyons, since most of the revenue was offset by the higher discounts received by Odeon Cinemas for the contracts. Later still, hotels and passenger ships were supplied, as were sports grounds and other mass entertainment venues. All these made some contribution to maintaining sufficient winter sales.

Manufacturing Improvements

The 1929 Ice Cream Convention was for the first time held in Toronto, Canada, because prohibition was still in force in the USA where the convention traditionally met. Demonstrations were given in the Silverwood Ice Cream Factory, where the Vogt freezer was first introduced to the trade. Invented by Henry Vogt, of the Girdler Corporation of Louisville, Kentucky, for texturing fats and oils, it was modified by his son Clarence for continuously freezing ice-cream mix. Representatives from Lyons witnessing the Vogt demonstration were José Sierra, Fred Hesse and Harold Boon. The machine looked very promising, and after their return to London settlements were made to take delivery of a Vogt device. Mark Bogod, who had worked as a chemist in Lyons' food laboratories since joining the firm from the Royal College of Science, succeeded Fred Hesse as manager of ice-cream production. As with other food processes, the laboratories became heavily involved in all aspects of ice-cream manufacture, storage and transportation. Bogod became a world authority on ice-cream manufacture before he moved on to personnel and training and Harold Boon took over much of the experts' responsibility.

Vogt installed their first J1000 four-cylinder machine at Cadby Hall in 1931 but it was not a success and was returned to the American makers. Smaller single- and twin-tube (cylinder) machines followed, and by 1934 Girdler had developed a machine that produced tube-like portions of ice-

The American Cherry-Burrell machine produced these vanilla and strawberry flavoured Pola Maid ice-creams in the 1930s.

cream which they called Melo Roll. Lyons negotiated exclusive rights to use the equipment in the United Kingdom and renamed the product Pola-Maid. Two large plants, making vanilla and strawberry flavours (in 1d. and 2d. sizes), were installed on the first floor of R Block in an area previously used for making ice.

In 1936–7 the factory size had increased by 100 per cent enlarging the choc ice process through the installation of enrobers, and accommodating new packaging machinery to replace hand-wrapping. For two or three years Lyons also made special 'baby bricks' for a small company in Fulham who traded as Nysice and sold from tricycles until 1939.

From the 870,000 gallons of ice-cream purchased from all manufacturers in the United Kingdom in 1920, consumption rose to a staggering 35.5 million gallons in 1938 but by 1939, and throughout the Second World War, the government imposed restrictions which seriously disrupted manufacture. Milk production in the United Kingdom fell from 395 million gallons in 1939 to 235 million gallons in 1940

and to 145 million gallons in 1941. It is not surprising, therefore, that the Ministry of Food had already taken measures to conserve milk by restricting its use for non-essential products. The use of fresh cream in manufacturing processes had also been restricted and then in September 1940 was completely banned. Milk and synthetic cream suffered the same fate in November and December 1940 respectively. The lack of milk solids in ice-cream making caused immense difficulties for manufacturers, who turned to alternatives such as dextrinised wheat flour up until September 1942, when the government prohibited all ice-cream manufacture. Before these interdictions, however, transport problems had already arisen because of restricted fuel supplies.

After the cessation of ice-cream manufacture, the Cadby Hall factory produced dextrinised wheat flour and a sugar substitute which Lyons called Malogel, both used in bakery merchandise. The cold-storage rooms became a store for raw materials and were used for quick freezing a variety of cooked meals and bakery products – first as emergency food for the teashops but later to sell to other caterers. Malogel continued to be produced for a period after the war, since bakery management discovered it had a sweetening and texturing effect when used in some cake recipes. When ice-cream production resumed on 8 December 1944 the Malogel process transferred to Greenford, where it played an important role in the development of the successful Ready Brek cereal.

Ice-cream raw materials remained in short supply for many years after the war, and the laboratories devoted much effort to reformulating pre-war recipes. When supplies eventually returned to pre-war standards, some of the sweetener and fat substitutes were retained in ice-cream production. Not only did they simplify the manufacturing process but in some cases they were found to be more economic. This adulteration from pure to substitute ingredients is probably partially responsible for the deterioration in the taste of most mass-produced ice-cream today.

COMPETITION IN BAKING

THE CONTRACT TO SUPPLY the British Empire Exhibition at Wembley in 1924 not only brought Lyons handsome profits but placed phenomenal pressure on the Cadby Hall bakeries. Every week during that year, 260 tons of bread and cake were delivered daily by up to seventy vans. The exhibition also provided a wonderful shop window for Lyons' products. By now the factories at Greenford and Cadby Hall were among the most efficient in the country, and their collective colossal output was distributed nationally through teashops, door-to-door salesmen and several thousand grocery retailers in every town and village in the United Kingdom, not to mention the occasional exhibition.

In the *First Report of the Royal Commission on Food Prices* (1925), it was said that bread was 'generally admitted to be the most important foodstuff in British households, and is, as one of our witnesses stated, a "tremendous item" in the budgets of families which contain many children'. The committee's calculations showed that nearly five million tons of flour was consumed annually in Great Britain of which a half was used for the manufacture of bread, the remainder being used for domestic cooking and the production of cake and biscuits. At 9d. per 4lb loaf this represented an annual expenditure of over £80 million on bread alone, eight per cent of which is said to have been 'baking profits'. A big incentive, therefore, for bread producers to grab as much of this market as possible.

The last stage of automated bread making. This oven was one of three which ran twenty-four hours a day.

The Beginnings of Mass Production

Between 1920 and 1938 consumer expenditure on cake, biscuits and bread increased so enormously that by 1939 the bakeries were contributing more than a quarter of Lyons' total net profits of just over £1 million. In the south of England – where sales of Lyons' products were strongest – high employment in white-collar jobs brought about better living standards and

Isidore Howard Gluckstein (manager of the Trocadero Restaurant) talking to the Duke and Duchess of York on a tour of the Cadby Hall factory in May 1931. Leading the party is Maurice Salmon. To the immediate left of the Duchess is Sir Isidore Salmon. Isidore Howard Gluckstein was killed in a horse riding accident in Richmond Park two years after this picture was taken.

price of cake fell by 60 per cent, biscuits by 61 per cent and bread by 26 per cent.

Maurice Salmon, who was in overall charge of food manufacturing at Cadby Hall, ran the bakery like a well-oiled machine, meeting every new demand by adapting production techniques with exceptional flexibility and precision. He has been described as a 'mischievous, puckish character' who used vocabulary and expressions of his own invention, such as 'a necessitacious factor' for 'essential ingredient'. Although it was not recognised at the time, he probably suffered from dyslexia, a learning difficulty that hinders the ability to read and write, despite normal intelligence. While dyslexia may have caused problems for Maurice Salmon in properly understanding and using language – for instance, he hated public speaking – it may have given him other talents such as multi-dimensional thought, reflected in his ability to imagine and modify a new machine even before a prototype had been built. This may partly explain his extraordinary capacity for visualising and organising mass production on such a vast scale. Maurice Salmon commanded great respect from peers and subordinates alike and seemed to be highly skilled at motivating other people.

Under Maurice Salmon's management the bakeries successfully fitted into their regular day-to-day schedule the special orders – such as the two million hot cross buns which in 1922 were produced in 24 hours for Good Friday morning.

provided more disposable income for many. With a greater variety of foodstuffs in the shops, housewives tended to bake less at home, and the regular purchase of bread led naturally to the buying of biscuits and cakes. The price of raw materials plummeted up until 1936 (when the cost of butter, eggs, lard, flour, milk, cream and sugar rose). More significantly, the use of automation in large baking units enabled Lyons' prices to be held so low that housewives found it just as economical to buy cake and biscuits as to bake these themselves. The quality and diversity of new bakery products in particular stimulated the demand for cakes and biscuits. Nationally, the sales of cake (by all manufacturers) almost doubled during this period and those of biscuits trebled, although bread sales increased by only seven per cent. Correspondingly the

Cadby Hall at night where a large sign advertises Lyons' Wrapped Puriti Bread. Enclosed in waxed paper, the loaf was not sliced. 1935. *By kind permission of Mary Cakebread.*

Cooked in tunnels 40 feet long, each bun had precisely 20 currants. For the first time since the end of the war they were flavoured with unadulterated spice. Buns were sold at 16 for a shilling. Cadby Hall's breathtaking production statistics became a frequent source of comment from analysts and journalists. Two million Vienna rolls every week, 40,000 French pastries, half a million or 36 miles of Swiss rolls, three-quarters of a million muffins, a quarter of a million cream and jam sandwiches: the list was endless. Lyons' own records show that in 1939 the bakery output reached 60,000 tons, providing an annual turnover of £3½ million.

High demand for products such as cake could not be entirely satisfied by means of the machinery available in the 1920s. Unlike bread, some cake was difficult to handle when hot, and methods had to be found to transport it around the building (so as to maintain a production-line flow) until it could be removed from its tin and packaged. Lyons developed a continuous process whereby after baking and de-tinning a conveyor carried the baking tins through a cleaning system; then more mix was added and the cycle repeated. Some automated machinery had been obtained from America, but much of the technology had to be devised by Lyons' own engineers, who became highly skilled in solving many production-line difficulties.

William Isaac Brown: Mail Order Trials and Bakery Rails

During the mid-1920s Julius Salmon (Maurice Salmon's younger brother), who had successfully managed the Strand Palace Hotel and was renowned for his inventiveness, had returned

A Bakery long-distance lorry of the 1950s. The cab shows a strong American influence and is probably a Bedford.

Below. Princess Elizabeth, accompanied by Monte Gluckstein, talks to workers in the Cadby Hall cake decoration department during her visit to the factory in 1951, whilst master baker Frank Jacobs displays his extraordinary cake decoration skills.

Above. Taken from an aeroplane in October 1921, this photograph of Cadby Hall was one of several taken to commemorate the 25th anniversary of the opening of the Trocadero Restaurant. The original Cadby Hall is seen slightly to the right of centre with the words 'Lyons Tea' just below the clock level. The small properties to the left of the factory were all eventually bought by Lyons as were those in Brook Green and Brook Green Place (extreme left).

Above. Part of the vehicle loading/ reception area within Cadby Hall. The factories enclosing this area were a hive of activity both day and night. Vehicles entered from the Brook Green entrance and departed by the Blythe Road gate. A vehicle wash can be seen in operation.

Left. Layer cake production at Cadby Hall. *By kind permission of Waldegrave Films.*

This exquisite cake was presented by Lyons for the wedding of Princess Elizabeth and the Duke of Edinburgh. It was one of 12 official wedding cakes presented but was not selected as the 'official' cake.

from a visit to America fired up with a plan to introduce mail order to the British public. This, he hoped, would increase cake sales still further. While in the USA, Julius Salmon had met a British-born immigrant called William Brown, who worked as a jewellery buyer for a large department store. The two men became friendly and Julius Salmon persuaded Brown to give up his job and return to the United Kingdom, with his American wife, to take charge of a cake mail order operation.

William Isaac Brown (1888–1976) – later known as WIB – started work with Lyons in 1925 and with the help of Lyons Staff Stores (a staff shop selling company products which later opened to the public) produced a modest mail order catalogue. During the experimental trials many items ordered from the catalogue were returned, and this led Julius Salmon to conclude that the United Kingdom market was not yet ready for mail order. The project was hastily abandoned. However, since Brown had insisted on a contract with Lyons – probably the only employee then to be engaged on contractual terms – his employment could not easily be terminated. Instead he was appointed sales manager for the wholesale bakeries and later assumed responsibility for ice-cream. Within a very short time he became to sales and distribution what Maurice Salmon had become to factory production.

When William Brown introduced the Bakery Rails service in 1925, the distribution of cake took another leap forward. By making extensive use of the railway networks, Brown's initiative created a colossal surge in bakery sales. Well-trained salesmen would visit remote rural shops, persuading retailers to buy cake from a printed catalogue with the sole proviso that their orders be for no less than 12 shillings. All orders taken were guaranteed delivery within 24 hours. This was made possible by the closeness to Cadby Hall of Kensington (Addison Road) railway station with its unique interconnection to 13 railway networks which collectively linked up directly with the entire national railway system. At one time Kensington station handled nearly 500 steam trains a day. In addition, Carter Paterson and other carriers provided a local daily service from rural railway stations to the innumerable village stores in the more isolated regions. Within its first year, Bakery Rails generated so much additional trade that it became necessary to build a further bakery unit in 1926 to meet demand.

With a reputation for being super-critical, William Brown travelled throughout the railway networks, checking and improving every detail. Stationmasters were alerted to his travels and treated him almost like royalty during his trips up and down the country. Such was Lyons' influence with the railway companies that Walter Gaunt, transport director between 1942-51, was even able to arrange, on more than one occasion, to stop the 'Flying Scotsman' at his local station.

Competition and Expansion

Despite the huge output of bread and cake from the Cadby Hall factories, more than 80 per cent of the nation's bread continued to be supplied by local craft bakers. As these small operations had modest overheads, with little or no transport or labour costs, they were able to provide bread that was not only inexpensive but fresh. In urban and thickly populated areas the balance of advantage rested therefore, with the craft baker who 'established price equilibrium' during the 1920s. Since the cost of retail distribution amounted to about 16 per cent of the price paid by the consumer for bread (1923 figures), Lyons decided to open provincial bakeries in Brighton, Bristol, Liverpool and Margate in the period leading up to the Second World War.

In 1934 the Canadian manufacturer, Willard Garfield Weston, had introduced biscuit companies in Britain and expanded into bakeries a year later by purchasing a large number of small bakeries which between them had nearly a hundred retail shops. By the start of the war Weston's Allied Bakeries had acquired twenty-eight local bakeries which together operated 500 delivery rounds. His most spectacular acquisition was London's ABC teashops, which were in direct competition with those of Lyons. As his company grew, the flour suppliers, Joseph Rank Ltd and Spillers Ltd in particular, became concerned that such a large part of their business was concentrated on one customer. They feared that Garfield Weston would use his buying power to drive down the price of flour or, worse still, take his business elsewhere. He did just that after a disagreement over prices with the British millers who imported much of his flour from Canada. In response, and in order to protect their businesses, both Rank and Spillers acquired bakeries of their own in 1962. The inter-war years also saw the emergence of a large number of medium-sized local bakeries that began to challenge the more lucrative cake market dominated for so long by the small craft bakers. In 1926 Frank Hale, for example, started his business by copying one of his wife's cake recipes. His Somerset company, Hale-Trent (Holdings) Ltd, eventually became part of Lyons Bakery Ltd in 1974.

The Lyons cake catalogue for Christmas 1938 illustrated 45 different types of cake with no fewer than 21 varieties of elaborately decorated Christmas cakes ranging in price from 5 shillings to £1. One of the best-selling lines was the Swiss

The architecturally drab façade of the Cadby Hall factories dominate the north side of Hammersmith Road between Brook Green and Blythe Road. *By kind permission of Waldegrave Films.*

The power house of the Cadby Hall factories. A large team of engineers, plumbers and electricians kept the factory going twenty-four hours a day. *By kind permission of Waldegrave Films.*

Lyons' first venture into the biscuit trade occurred in 1938, when they secured nearly 54 per cent of the Bee Bee Biscuit Company, which they bought from Lesme Ltd, a couverture company founded by Leslie Atwell, who was a grandson of Isidore Gluckstein. Bee Bee Biscuits had originated in 1922 as the Blackpool Biscuit Company. Selling its brandy snap and Shrewsbury biscuits locally, it quickly expanded and in 1924 not only introduced travelling salesmen but had to move to larger premises. In 1931 Lesme, which were based in Willesden, London, acquired control of the company and, as chairman, Atwell moved the registered office to London, while production continued at Blackpool. Eight and a half acres of land was purchased in 1932 and a new factory building was erected in Devonshire Road, Blackpool, to which production transferred two years later. Bee Bee became one of the pioneers of pre-packed biscuits, which up until 1933 had largely been sold loose or in tins. In June 1944 Lyons incorporated Symbol Biscuits Ltd and on 1 April 1950 the company changed its name back to Bee Bee Biscuits Ltd. In January 1968 the sales team were fully integrated with the Tea Division salesmen and on 24 March 1969 the company name was changed again to Lyons Bakery Ltd.

Symbol manufactured approximately forty different types of sweet, dry and savoury biscuits packed and sold under the Symbol and Lyons brands. A wide variety of customers' own labels were packed for sale in stores and supermarkets both in this country and overseas. Their introduction of Maryland Cookies in 1956 brought a significant increase in revenues. In 1976, when a Viennese Whirl plant was installed, cake was added to Symbol's biscuit lines. The firm that had begun life as the Blackpool Biscuit Company had a final change of name in 1990 when it became Lyons Biscuits Ltd. It continued to trade profitably until 17 December 1994 when the business was sold to a subsidiary of Hillsdown Holdings plc as part of asset disposals.

Wartime controls on bread and cake

At the outbreak of the Second World War the government took steps to control the milling and

roll, available in three sizes and ten flavours. The least expensive were the Nippy tartlets, which were priced at nine for 7d. Kup Kakes cost 1d. each. The French Cream Sandwich, another high-selling product, cost a shilling. The ubiquitous Individual Fruit Pie, designed for lunch boxes, was priced at only 2d. and came with a choice of 14 fillings. It became so popular that by 1932 a new fruit pie factory had to be built to satisfy demand. The baking process had been invented by the chief engineer, William Coyte. Raw ingredients were lifted to the top floor and then dropped through several levels where they were cleaned, mixed, weighed, cooked and cooled before appearing as boxed pies on the ground floor ready for dispatch. Between 1936 and 1938 the Lyons Individual Fruit Pie turnover rose from £10,000 to £20,000 per week.

bread-making industry, although bread was not actually rationed until 1946. However, from October 1941 until September 1956 national bread was subsidised and its price was rigidly controlled; 8d. until October 1942, and then 9d. until 1946. On 6 May 1946 the size of the 4 lb quartern loaf was reduced to 3½ lb by government order, and in February 1956 the subsidy was halved and the controlled price of the 3½ lb loaf was increased by 2d. On 30 September 1956 the subsidy was discontinued and bread was freed from price control. By the end of the year it was selling for approximately 1s. 9d. per 3½ lb loaf; its size never returned to the 4lb quartern and indeed the standard loaf after the war weighed approximately 1¾ lb, roughly the weight of the former half-quartern (2 lb).

At the start of the war Britain was importing 60 per cent of its food requirements. The loss of imported foodstuffs and raw materials by U-boat attack was a problem dealt with by the Ministry of Food, which took control of all supplies. However, the government was also concerned with the potential disruption of bread production and distribution in the event of air-raid damage to factories or to the supply of gas, water, electricity and transport. To prepare for such eventuality, the Emergency Bread Scheme was introduced in May 1940. In the London area this was co-ordinated by Area Bread Officers (whose appointments were honorary) in collaboration with the baking industry itself. The Bread Officers, who were recruited from the baking industry, were fully acquainted with the baking capacity in their respective areas as well as the stores for maintaining flour stocks. Under the Emergency Bread Scheme, the various geographic divisions were required to support any neighbouring division in an emergency. The Bread Officers were expected to ensure that bread was produced whatever the difficulties, so as to prevent a breakdown of normal supplies which the government feared would severely damage morale. Throughout the war the public, at least in London, never lacked bread supplies except for a few hours after the heaviest air raids. The success of the scheme was partly due to the efficiency of the bakers but mainly because every

bakery had spare capacity as a result of cuts in cake production through shortages of ingredients. In November 1940 the system was comprehensively tested when the city of Coventry suffered one of the most intensive bombings of the war. All services were cut off and the transport systems crippled. Bread baking in the city was impossible. Nevertheless, no one in the city went without bread, since the bakeries in other Midlands towns, notably Leicester and Birmingham, stepped up their production to maximum capacity. These bakers worked long hours until after a few days a small bakery was again able to operate in Coventry. Similar instances occurred when Swansea, Bath and Liverpool were bombed. Two million loaves were supplied to Liverpool from outside bakeries on the morning after a heavy raid on the port.

As the war intensified, the crippling loss of shipping threatened wheat supplies from North America and it was not until 1943 that effective means were in place to counteract the menace from German U-boats. The flour shortage manifested itself in the summer of 1941, when cake queues first started to appear. At this time the government decided to increased the allocation of rationed ingredients rather than introduce cake rationing. During 1941–2 the Ministry of Food and the various food committees reporting to it debated how best to bring the production of cake under some measure of control. The Orders Committee objected to the wide variety of cakes allowed under the order, while the Food Utilisation Committee proposed that attempts be made to reduce the attractiveness

Top. Taken in the late 1920s, this lorry-load of apples, destined for the bakery department, has lost part of its consignment when turning into Brook Green. The original Elms House, from which a new office block was named in 1937, can be seen to the left, clad in ivy. The white stone buildings of St Mary's College can be clearly identified. *By kind permission of Mary Cakebread.*

Bottom. Vans being loaded with food in standard trays for delivery to the teashops. All these vehicles were of Albion make; some had pneumatic tyres and others solid tyres. The number plates of the facing lorries were registered in 1928 and 1929.

of cake. As the views of the Margins Committee, the Bakery Division and the Commodity Division caused further disagreement, it is not surprising that cake control remained unresolved for so long. The government eventually fixed a maximum retail price of 1s. 2d. per pound on all products and imposed a maximum fat and sugar content of 20 and 30 per cent respectively. However, the trade objected to these proposals, arguing for a maximum price of 1s. 6d. per pound and a maximum combined fat and sugar content of 50 per cent. Although the government conceded the former point, it refused to allow more than 45 per cent for the combined fat and sugar content, even when Lyons provided abundant evidence that Swiss rolls could not be made without more. Several other restrictions were imposed, including a ban on cake icing, but collectively the controls achieved the desired economic effect. The Ministry of Food tried unsuccessfully to encourage the use of potatoes in confectionery flour in 1943, but their ideas were not seriously considered by the trade. Nevertheless, chemists struggled in vain to find some alternative.

In January 1943 the Cake and Biscuit Wartime Alliance – a consortium of large cake and biscuit manufacturers – devised and introduced a zoning system in order to conserve road fuel. Under the scheme the Alliance arbitrarily divided the country into nine regions, and confined wholesale distribution of groceries and provisions to one region unless the total journey was less than forty miles. This meant that vast numbers of customers had to be supplied by rival manufacturers. Yet special concessions were granted to the three largest manufacturers, who were allowed to continue deliveries in their respective areas of the country. Lyons were permitted to deliver from Cadby Hall throughout the south of England and the Midlands; Scribbans of Smethwick to the Midlands, Wales and the north of England; and Lavery of Ormskirk, Lancashire, to the north of England and North Wales. These concessions caused a great deal of unrest among the smaller traders and those dealing in speciality goods, such as shortcake, who were forced to lose part of their established

trade in other regions without receiving compensation in the form of new customers in their allocated sector. Some traders ignored the scheme and continued to deliver to their old customers, while others refused to take on new trade. Despite these problems, substantial savings were achieved. Although the scheme affected the activities of only 44 firms, mainly large manufacturers, these represented one-third of the total output of flour confectioners. The scheme had meant the transfer of 35,000 tons of annual production with an estimated saving of 3.25 million tons per mile annually.

The scarcity of bakery labour and the imposition of more stringent controls on cakes by the Food Order of 1943 made it necessary to consider how much man-power would be permitted in cake manufacture. The large manufacturers like Lyons were heavily automated and the labour price per ton of cake was relatively low compared with the craft bakers and other smaller businesses. From time to time workers were lured away from cake to bread manufacture, but shortages were made up by part-time labour which at Lyons consisted mainly of women. Cake manufacture suffered the same problems as bread; as the war progressed, shortages became more acute and lasted until 1952. Occasionally the ceiling price was increased to take account of post-war inflation, but the trade did not see a freeing of all restrictions until 1954, fifteen years after they initially took hold.

The central feature of Lyons' history during the inter-war years was its transition from catering to food manufacture. Foremost among the food-manufacturing departments was the bakery. After Maurice Salmon introduced mass-production techniques to the bread and cake departments as well as to ice-cream, manufacture became more important than catering. Individual department profits were never published, but Lyons' accounts show that total profits increased from £396,000 in 1920 to over £1 million in 1939, and this was largely achieved by the colossal increase in food

A small replica of their 1899 wedding cake is presented to Major Isidore Salmon (right) and his wife Kate during a New Year party at Cadby Hall in 1931. It was baked by J. Gilkerson who made the 1899 cake. On the left is Isidore's son Samuel. Both men were eventually knighted, Isidore in 1933 and Samuel in 1960. Four and a half thousand guests attended the party and drank 500 gallons of claret, smoked 20,000 cigarettes, 1,500 cigars and consumed 22,500 sandwiches.

Their Majesties King George V and Queen Mary passing along Hammersmith Road in front of Cadby Hall on their way to Kensington Town Hall during the Royal Jubilee drive on 8 June 1935. *By kind permission of Bill Doe.*

production. Although profits continued to remain high during 1939–45, wartime restrictions prevented any new capital expenditure on factory equipment. Bakery production was geared to producing as much as possible, with the available resources, in the simplest, most economic way. Because shops were restricted to particular suppliers, everything Lyons made could be sold. The war years also witnessed an unexpected decline in the number of small craft bakers, as many answered the call to arms and others, because of rationing, found baking uneconomic. This benefited the large manufacturers by creating a wider market for their products. The Cadby Hall bakeries were fortunate in that they came through the war period unscathed. Being so close to much of the devastation in London, they were able to make a positive contribution to feeding the nation.

While the bakeries at Cadby Hall flourished from the 1920s onward, there had been some significant failures of grocery lines at Greenford. An improved market for tea had, however, enabled the tea factory at Greenford to expand production, and Lyons decided to make a big new investment.

The Lujeri Tea Estate

Quite how Lyons' interest in Africa became aroused is not clear. They had suffered a loss of business in the north of England during the First World War but by the mid-1920s trade had improved and continued to expand, partly through Lyons' acquisition of Horniman and Black & Green. Traditionally, most tea had been purchased at the London auctions in Mincing Lane, while a smaller quantity was obtained from agents in Calcutta and Sri Lanka. When in 1926 Lyons acquired the Lujeri tea estates in what is now Malawi, the company presumably intended to gain some control over tea stocks. Why buy tea from an agent in London if you can grow and ship your own more economically?

Lyons were by no means the first British company to invest in tea factories in the tea-growing areas of the world. Brooke Bond and the Co-operative Tea Company were among other British packing houses owning foreign tea estates. Their great rival, Lipton, had been running the Bunyan Estate in Sri Lanka as early as 1908 but Lyons' interests may have been the result of contact with a certain William Geddes Dickson, a director in the Mini Mini (Nyasaland) Tea Syndicate Ltd, which acquired a 1,500-acre tea estate in Nyasaland in December 1923. Nyasaland was the name given in 1907 to the former Central African Protectorate, annexed by Britain in 1891 for use primarily as a labour resource for the mines and plantations of southern Africa. Colonisation had begun before this by Scottish missionaries, in the wake of David Livingstone, pursuing a policy of 'divide and rule' – overwhelming the warriors, banishing the slave traders, building missions and opening up estates. Since independence in 1964, it has been known as Malawi.

Apart from his role in the Mini Mini (Nyasaland) Tea Syndicate, Dickson was also a director of Dickson, Anderson & Co. Ltd, an organisation specialising in providing company secretarial services which Lyons subsequently used for the purpose of anonymity in their negotiations for African land through the Chartered Bank of India, Australia & China. In 1923 – before Dickson's tea company had gained control of their own tea estate in Nyasaland – he presumably alerted Lyons to other property which had come on to the market close to his own estate and volunteered his services to carry out some inquiries. From an undated memorandum it seems the original plan was for Dickson, Anderson & Co. to act as agents for Lyons receiving a commission based on the tea produced. In August 1923 Dickson produced a comprehensive report for Lyons on what he called the Sabbatini land, which was situated close to the Mlanje mountain near the border with Portuguese-owned Mozambique to the south.

Although not mentioned in Dickson's report, the earliest conveyances for the property were dated 1892, when it was owned by Hugh Bloomfield Bradshaw, who in 1896 acquired several hundred more acres from the Commissioner and Consul-General to add to the 2,000 acres he already possessed. In the late 1930s boundary disputes arose with a neighbouring landowner and with government surveyors.

However, by July 1940 these were satisfactorily resolved. The Lujeri tea nurseries, which the Lands Department had first believed to be outside the estate's boundary, were in fact well inside it. A heavily timbered area, thought to be government forest reserve land, also turned out to fall within the estate boundary, and this helped to relieve a fuel reserve problem. It also gave control, to the estate management, of Chief Nandola and his tribe, until now native tenants who were reported to be destroying the timber and soil on the previously disputed land.

In his report, Dickson observed:

> The block of 8,140 acres is situated on the S. base of the Mlanje Mountain (which has an elevation of 10,000 feet) and gets the full benefit of the rainfall attracted to such a mountain, which is some 90 miles in circumference rising abruptly from a flat plain.
>
> The land lies to the E. end of the Mlanje Tea District, which I am confident will develop into one of the finest tea-producing countries in the world, obtaining prices quite equal to the average of Ceylon and the London Market.
>
> The area with sufficient rainfall to grow tea in this district is restricted, and cannot be much more than 60,000 acres, half of which is probably freehold, now mostly held in private hands. The Government of Nyasaland have decided that no land shall be sold outright in future, and that leaseholds only shall be granted. Freehold tea land in the Mlanje district must therefore increase greatly in value.

Dickson said he had visited most of the tea properties in the district and was satisfied that 'tea grows luxuriantly, and, with more knowledge of the cultivation, bigger yields can be expected. ... The whole of this land was at one time jungle but now consists of a very heavy growth of grass land and scrub about 10 feet high interspersed with jungle. ... The Makulanji, Lujire and Ruo rivers flow through the property with a very large and permanent flow of water and a good fall.'

He concluded:

> The whole acreage is suitable for the growth of tea. Rainfall is ample, probably 90 to 100 inches, but no records have been kept. ... From figures obtained locally the cost of opening up new land may be 230s. 6d. [£11 10s. 6d.]. I value the land at £5 per acre. There is no leasehold land in the tea area of Nyasaland to be obtained now, except what is in private hands, and S.-[Sabbatini] land is the best block in the district.

The Purchase, the Plantations and the Factories

Before Lyons committed themselves to the land purchase, there was much correspondence with Sabbatini, his agents, solicitors, banks and others. Most of the property was still 'bush', apart from a small acreage which had been cleared and in part was tea-producing. Alberto Hercolani Sabbatini was a difficult, shrewd negotiator who tried hard to persuade Lyons that several other interested parties were negotiating for his property in the hopes of getting a higher price. Correspondence sent from London by Union Castle mail ship took four weeks to reach Nyasaland via the nearest East African deep-sea port of Beira. As communications were so difficult, much of the discussion between London and the representatives in Blantyre, the country's commercial centre, was carried out using coded cablegrams. During the prolonged negotiations, Dickson's own credentials came under suspicion when a long letter was sent by Charles Lyst, the Calcutta manager of Lyons (India) Ltd. Lyst had been instructed to carry out some inquiries in Sri Lanka and to advise on the manager Dickson proposed – a man called Charles Shaw, whom Harry Salmon had briefly met – for the new estate in Nyasaland. The letter, which was undated, was addressed to Harry Salmon and sent from Colombo in March 1925. 'It is my intention,' wrote Lyst, 'and I am sure you will agree the wisdom of it, not to rely too much upon the people to whom Dickson has given me introductions, as each and all of them are, in some way or other, interested parties.' The letter continued:

The good impression which I formed of Shaw during my brief acquaintance with him here in Colombo was more than confirmed during our visit to his estate as his guest. ... He is more a planter than a man of business, which perhaps is only to be expected ... he is an ideal host and we had a very happy time indeed. ... I was much impressed on these occasions by the manner in which he was appealed to for advice at the club and elsewhere by the younger planters, and in fact also by men contemporary with himself. ... He is 49, so I think we shall have to rule him out as a candidate for our managership in Nyasaland, if the proposition goes through. However, there will be lots of time to discuss this point later on.

I have made one or two carefully placed enquiries both in Colombo and upcountry regarding Dickson, and what sort of a reputation he has in the Island. Frankly, I have been rather disappointed in the replies received. Apparently he is more of an office man than a practical planter; although he *has* planting knowledge, his experience of Ceylon [Sri Lanka] has been more or less confined to visiting work (in a supervising capacity) and more particularly on the office side of tea in Colombo. I mention this as I notice from a letter which I received from Barton that we appear to be leaving a very great deal to Dickson in the matter of the selection of a man for us to work the property in Africa, should we go into it. No one spoke actually disparagingly of Dickson, but no one enthused about him, or rather about his ability as a planter. I rather gather that he comes within the category which is known in planting circles as a 'gentleman' planter, which translated means planting in kid gloves!

Harry Salmon (1881–1950), fifth son of Barnett Salmon, had been made a director in 1909 and had taken over the management of the tea factory from his elder brother Isidore at this time. Like so many of his family contemporaries, after his education at the City of London School he entered the business at the age of 15 in the time-honoured way by serving his apprenticeship in the Trocadero kitchens. Harry was highly intelligent, modest and well read, with a passion for history. During the First World War he served as a cipher officer at the Admiralty (salvage branch) and by arranging to do his Admiralty duties at night, he was able to continue to put in a near full day's work with the Company. Afterwards, and throughout the inter-war period, Harry Salmon was consulted and took increasing responsibility for all property negotiations, a role in which he excelled until his death in 1950.

On the advice of Charles Lyst, Harry Salmon decided to employ Charles Francis Sicklemore Shaw, the 49-year-old experienced planter working in Sri Lanka, to inspect and survey the Sabbatini estate for a fee of £500 plus travel and other expenses; subsequently he became estate manager. At first it was thought that at 49 Shaw would be too old to undertake the hard work necessary to develop a new tea estate but he had a pleasant manner and won over both Lyst and Harry Salmon. Lyst had already concluded, and Harry Salmon agreed, that Shaw lacked administrative skills but he was a thoroughly practical planter and his knowledge of tea and planting methods more than compensated for this. He was also at the top of his career in Sri Lanka and Lyons had to pay more for him than would normally have been the case. After having reported on the Sabbatini property to Harry Salmon in London in July 1925, Shaw accepted the job and with the approval of Lyons, placed an order with Walker Brothers for 120 Ceylon felling axes, a dozen sledge-hammers, six land chains, four lining compasses, 60 pruners, a dozen cross-cut saws, 5 tons of galvanised corrugated sheets, guttering, ridging, pipes, roofing clips and a whole consignment of other materials.

Lyst was also in England at this time and during discussions with Harry Bennett – a Lyons company secretary – it was agreed that an assistant should be employed for Shaw. Lyst suggested J. A. Allan, who had previously worked for the Consolidated Tea & Lands Co. Ltd on their

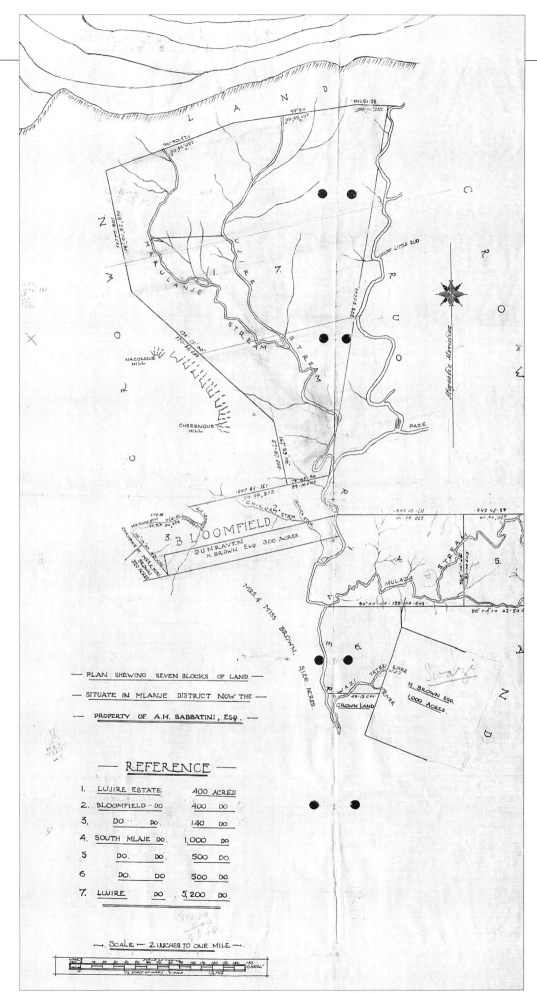

Scale land plans of the Lujeri Tea Estate, Nyasaland. The tea from this 'garden' produced only a small quantity of Lyons' total needs.

PLAN SHEWING SEVEN BLOCKS OF LAND

SITUATE IN MLANJE DISTRICT NOW THE

PROPERTY OF A.H. SABBATINI, ESQ.

REFERENCE

1.	LUJIRE ESTATE		400 ACRES
2.	BLOOMFIELD	DO	400 DO
3.	DO	DO	140 DO
4.	SOUTH MLAJE	DO	1,000 DO
5.	DO	DO	500 DO
6.	DO	DO	500 DO
7.	LUJIRE	DO	5,200 DO

SCALE — 2 INCHES TO ONE MILE

163

Phulcherra Tea Estate in India. In September 1925, Allan was sent out to Mlange to join Shaw and to undertake preparatory work on the estate.

By now the negotiations with Sabbatini were drawing to a conclusion. However, it was not until February 1926 that the land and all conveyancing transactions were finally completed and Lyons became the owner of 8,640 acres of virgin land at Lujeri. A price of £23,500 had been paid for the property, including Sabbatini's small 150-acre

Bloomfield estate, which had been partly cultivated. Harry Salmon had done exceedingly well. He had eventually paid just under £2 15s. per acre, compared to Dickson's 1923 valuation of £5 per acre.

By the end of June 1926 Charles Shaw had recruited 3,072 labourers, many from isolated rural areas, who brought their families to live in huts on the estate. He provided an allowance for food, reported his satisfaction with his team and

Filling tea chests with dried leaf from the withering lofts above at the Lujeri Tea Estate, Nyasaland. The men to the left are adjusting the weight of the full chests prior to sealing and marking.

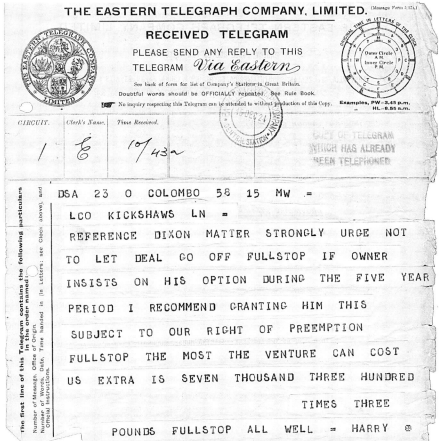

One of several telegrams sent to London from Harry Salmon in Colombo during his negotiations for the Lujeri Tea Estate in Nyasaland.

maintained that this was reciprocated by his workers and their families. A year earlier the company had ordered from India and Sri Lanka seeds for tea plants appropriate for the climate of Nyasaland, and the seeds were packed in charcoal for shipping. Experiments were made in planting out one- and two-year-old plants and also seed stakes for plants to be matured for additional seed. Saplings were planted at 2,240 per acre – slightly more than the standard

normally adopted in Nyasaland. To strengthen the plants, Shaw had them pruned down several times to within six inches of the ground. Old tree stumps were cleared and a deep trench, to prevent disease from spreading in from the adjoining jungle, surrounded the whole of the cultivated area. Over-fertilisation was avoided, since this tended to reduce the quality of the yield.

Meanwhile, work proceeded on the tea factory, which had been commissioned in

February 1928 from Messrs Guest & Thorne Chapman of Gracechurch Street, London. Under the supervision of S. Joliffe Butler, head of Lyons' engineering department, it was supplied and erected for £34,132 7s. 3d.; the factory consisted of a ground floor and four upper withering lofts with large air-circulation fans at one end. The factory's location, at one of the most exposed parts of the estate, ensured that as much withering as possible could be carried out naturally by spreading the leaves to dry on racks. Cheap labour was used, many of the workers migrating from the Portuguese colony of Mozambique on the southern border. Artificial withering, when required, was achieved by circulating air by a main air duct from the ground floor to each upper floor and then discharging it into the open through fans placed at the end walls of the building. On the ground floor were the rolling, fermenting, drying, sorting and packing rooms. At the fermenting stage the leaves absorbed oxygen before turning to a coppery-red colour. After subsequent 'firing' in a drying machine they emerged dark and crisp, ready for brewing. Dried tea was then sorted, sifted, graded and finally packed into chests, to be sent for shipment.

Harry Salmon visited the Lujeri estate in May 1928 and in his letter home, addressed to 'My dear family' (meaning the directors of Lyons and other family managers), he described his recent tour of the estate: it had been 'cleared of jungle. ... The nurseries and plantations look very healthy from a layman's point of view, and whatever contemptuous opinion I have for Shaw's commercial ability, in his particular calling there is no doubt we would have the greatest difficulty in getting his equal.' Harry Salmon continued:

> We are invited to go to the Governor to lunch next Friday. This is no nosh. It is 140 miles there and it means sleeping en route on the return journey. ... In visiting the bungalow of Shaw's assistant, Allen [sic], we find it most extravagantly constructed, so Julian [presumably Julian Salmon] suggested that we put another man in with Allen and use the vacated bungalow for Taylor [an engineer sent out

to supervise factory work], thus saving the erection of another bungalow. Allen does not relish this much, nor does the man who is going to live with him, but as far as I am concerned they can both go. Anything more diabolical to have spent so much money on a bungalow for a single man it would really have been difficult to imagine. ... We then motored to our friend Sabbatini who had a house built like a castle. He treated us splendidly. ... We left the following morning and visited the I.T.C. [Imperial Tobacco Company] factory at Limbe.

The letter was signed 'With ever fondest love in which we all unite, Your devoted Harry'.

The Landowning Companies

During Harry Salmon's visit to the Lujeri estate he had sent a coded cable to London alerting the Lyons board of pending government legislation promoted by the Colonial Office which would require all owners of land exceeding 3,000 acres to set aside 10 per cent for native reserves. The proposed compensation – an equal amount of land elsewhere in the protectorate – was unacceptable to Harry Salmon. After seeking local legal advice, he suggested that Lyons form three landowning companies so that individual company holdings would not exceed the 3,000-acre minimum. He further recommended that the companies, requiring only £10,000 each in capital, be set up without delay so they would be operational before the Act was passed. The idea was quickly approved and further discussed with the local Governor, who could see no objection, but after further consideration the holdings were divided into four blocks instead of three. Harry Bennett calculated that the cost of establishing the four companies would be no more than £750.

Unknown to Lyons when they purchased the estate, the legislation now under consideration had already been set out in Ordinances of the Nyasaland Protectorate of 1904 and 1917. The Ordinance of 1904 stated that 'Every landowner ... shall, if directed by the Governor, and from and after a date to be named by him, set aside a

This photograph is taken against the backdrop of the Victoria Memorial in Calcutta's Maidan. Built in white marble, the memorial took 15 years to complete and is a mixture of classical western influences and Mughal architecture.

location or locations for natives of a total area not exceeding one-tenth of any undeveloped land in his possession.' In 1928 the Nyasaland Planters' Association took up the landowners' cause and lobbied all estates in the Mlanje district, urging companies to use whatever influence they had to persuade the Secretary of State for Colonial Affairs to advise His Majesty King George V to exercise his power to disallow that part of the Bill, to prevent 'a grave injustice being done to his loyal subjects in Nyasaland'. The British Central Africa Company lobbied the Colonial Office so hard that, after a meeting of the Joint East African Board to discuss the Nyasaland Natives on Private Estates Bill, the British government on 17 August 1928 informed the Governor of Nyasaland that the acreage of estates subject to the ordinance would be raised from 3,000 to 10,000 acres.

While this concession was warmly accepted by Lyons, they nevertheless proceeded to register seven companies on 20 September 1928. These landowning companies were registered in England, with the bulk of the land occupied by Lujeri Tea Estates Ltd, a Nyasaland-registered company.

Before the African tea factory had been completed, tea had already begun to arrive in London in small quantities from the Bloomfield estate, which had been partly cultivated by Sabbatini. In the two years during which Lyons had owned the estate 80,048 lb of tea had been plucked and 14,000 lb of this had been dried and shipped to London. A drought during August and September 1927 had reduced the crop but the saplings which had been planted earlier were reported to be 'looking extra-ordinarily healthy'. Shaw reported in July 1933 that the tea-producing estate, by now 1,134 acres, had yielded nearly 2 million lb of green-leaf tea, out of which half a million lb of dried tea had been manufactured.

In 1934, with Kenneth Gluckstein (1911–59), son of Major Monte Gluckstein, now in charge of the Nyasaland business, Lyons turned their attention to a hydro-electric power scheme. They planned to dam the Ruo river which ran through part of their tea estate, and the British government granted them permission to use part of Crown land to pipe water and electricity. On 17 August 1934 an agreement was signed between His Excellency Kenneth Lambert Hall, Acting Governor and Commander-in-Chief of the Nyasaland Protectorate, on the one part, and J. Lyons & Co. Ltd on the other.

The Final Reckoning

The main area of the plantation did not start producing tea until 1935, by which time Shaw had retired and been replaced by Eric Guy Bohun de Mowbray. Between 1935 and 1939 ten further British employees were sent to Mlanje to assist in the expanding business. By 1935 the tea industry of Nyasaland had become of increasing importance to the wealth of the protectorate. On the basis of exports it was the second largest industry after tobacco. No exact figures for tea exportation are available for this period but the Nyasaland Tea Association estimated it to be worth 7 million lb with a total potential output, based on the acreage under cultivation, estimated at 11 million lb per year.

Prior to 1914, Chinde, north of Beira in Mozambique where the Zambesi river flows into the Indian Ocean, was the main shipping port for tea which had been transported by rail and river from Luchenza (Luchenza station was 26 miles from the Lujeri estate) at a cost of 50 shillings per ton (0·305d. per lb). In 1920 the Trans-Zambesia Railway opened and the route to Chinde was seriously threatened by the institution of inter-station rates. Rates for transporting tea rose from 0·305d. per lb to 0·97d. per lb. Protests were made to the government by the tea growers and in 1930 the dispute attracted the attention of the London Chamber of Commerce. With railway authorities reluctant to reduce their charges, and faced with a desperate situation, the tea industry in Nyasaland took action. It diverted its tea through Quelimane,

Lyons' Lujeri Tea Estate is depicted on these postage stamps issued by Nyasaland in 1938.

a small port just north of Chinde. This diversionary action forced the railways to reduce their rates to 0·715d. per lb and, although this was higher than previous railway rates, there was a return to the Trans-Zambesia Railway and tea again flowed through the port of Chinde. In 1934, however, the industry suffered another blow when a Road and Rail Act gave a monopoly to the railways. Now protected by legislation, Trans-Zambesia Railways immediately increased the rates once again to 0·97d. per lb. Despite heated discussions between the railway's chairman and the Nyasaland Tea Association, the growers received no satisfaction. In November 1935 the tea industry in Nyasaland petitioned the Governor, who not only supported the trade's argument but forwarded their petition to the Colonial Secretary in Whitehall. The Governor's dispatch to London suggested that the discontent and hardship dated from 1930 and was gathering momentum as time passed. He observed: 'The time is over-ripe for concessions, and the Colonial Office should now intervene.' However, the colonial authorities in London refused to become involved in the dispute. With little scope to reduce estate costs to compensate for the high freight rates, and faced with recalcitrant railway management, the profits of the Nyasaland tea industry were reduced compared with Kenya, India and Sri Lanka, where railway rates were all lower.

By the outbreak of the Second World War only 1,134 acres had been developed for tea production and, when de Mowbray, the estate manager, answered the call to arms in 1939, Eric Howard Gridley, one of four remaining Europeans at the plantation who had not been conscripted, was asked to take responsibility for the estate. There are no surviving records for the period 1940–56 other than information that Gridley had joined Lyons in 1932, that after three years in the Tea Department at Greenford he was appointed assistant manager at the Lujeri estate and that he died there aged thirty-five on 30 March 1946, leaving a widow and two sons. It is also known that Albert William (Bill) Bellamy, of the Lyons Works Department, was sent to Lujeri in about 1948 to supervise local labour when extensions to the factory became necessary. In 1957 John Fraser Ramsden assumed the management of the estate until his retirement in 1962, when John George Sanderson was appointed estate manager and director of each of the six UK-registered land-holding companies.

Colonial domination and the growth of the settler economy continued unchallenged until the late 1940s, when two new developments provoked enormous popular resentment. One was the formation of the Central African Federation of Rhodesia and Nyasaland – which formally came into being on 3 September 1953 and threatened to bring to Nyasaland the conditions that migrants working in the south hated so much. Federation with Rhodesia (now Zimbabwe and Zambia), which was dominated by the white minority, also conflicted with the ambitions of black nationalists in the newly formed Nyasaland African Congress. Secondly, the colonial administration decided that agricultural regulations should be rigorously enforced. Tribal farmers were made to plant and to harvest in ways and at times that the colonial agriculturalists considered to be correct, but which the local farmers themselves bitterly opposed. These grievances fermented but were not taken up until the mid-1950s, when educated young radicals, such as Henry Chipembere and Kanyama Chiume, recognised the importance of rural agriculture. They felt that the Nyasaland

The Lujeri factory in about 1930.

African Congress lacked a leader with widespread respect capable of uniting the people in their struggle for independence. So, in July 1958, Dr Hastings Kamuzu Banda was invited to return to Nyasaland, after forty years practising medicine in the USA and London, to assume leadership of the Nyasaland African Congress. Banda's oratory and his single-minded denunciation of the Federation led the colonial authorities to declare an emergency and Banda and other political radicals were jailed. After fifty-two Africans had been killed in the emergency the Colonial Office ordered the release of Banda and brought him to London for a constitutional conference. By August 1960 it was agreed that a new constitution should be written for Nyasaland, and in the first parliamentary elections in August 1961 Banda's newly formed Malawi Congress Party won all twenty lower-roll seats, gaining an overall majority in the Legislative Council. In 1963 the Federation was dissolved and replaced by self-government. Malawi finally became independent on 6 July 1964.

With land tenure becoming a subject for black nationalist political pressures, Lyons considered what steps might be taken to safeguard their interests in the colony. In 1962 the Nyasaland government asked Lujeri Tea Estates Ltd to sell them 1,500 acres, for which they were prepared to pay £1 per acre. Lujeri Tea Estates Ltd refused, since the land was owned not by them but by J. Lyons & Co., by way of the six landowning companies. The land, which Lyons had purchased freehold in 1924, had formerly been under the control of the Paramount Chiefs, from whom the previous owners of the estate had acquired the land and then registered a freehold title, now legally held by the six landowning companies.

In 1962 a study of Lujeri Tea Estates' capitalisation gave concern to Anthony Salmon, eldest son of Julius Salmon, who had taken over full responsibility in 1959 on the untimely death of Kenneth Gluckstein from cancer. He was not unfamiliar with the issues in Africa, having been involved, on and off, in a less senior position since 1944, after being discharged from the army on medical grounds. The secession of Nyasaland from the Federation would, he believed, place the country in economic difficulties and probably lead to increases in taxation. This was likely to fall on the country's biggest revenue earner – the tea industry, which in 1966 was valued at £4.4 million in export earnings – with a subsequent restriction on dividends. 'In any event, a dividend of £50,000 on a share capital of £65,000 is capable of gross misunderstanding,' he wrote. The fear of land confiscation, which had happened in other former colonies in Africa after independence, caused a revaluation of assets to 1962 values. It was suggested that the share capital should be increased from £65,000 to £350,000, or £200 per acre. However, records show that the share capital for Lujeri Tea Estates Ltd had, by 1966, been increased to £500,000.

The land-holding subsidiaries were subsequently transferred to Lujeri Tea Estates Ltd on 16 November 1966 after Lyons had cleared the transaction with the Treasury, fearing they might object on grounds of Capital Gains Tax; as they were still registered in England, annual returns had to be filed under the Companies Act. On 1 February 1963 Nyasaland assumed internal self-government under the British Crown and on 6 July 1966 it became a republic within the Commonwealth, by which time it had been renamed Malawi. In March 1970 Lyons considered disposing of Lujeri Tea Estates Ltd to the Malawi authorities. In correspondence with the Malawi Buying and Trade Agents in London the company was priced at £784,213 using financial data from the 1969 balance sheet.

Negotiations with the Malawi Buying and Trade Agents in London in June 1970 to dispose of the African interests came to nothing, as did the plan to sell the estate to the conglomerate, Mitchell Cotts Ltd, some time afterwards. Instead Lyons continued to develop the Lujeri estate through most of the 1970s but the crop was too small to satisfy the company's needs. More importantly, perhaps, it produced only one type of tea, when others were required for mixing the best blends. The yields from the Lujeri estate for the three years 1967–9 amounted to 6.8 million lb, most of which was used by the Greenford tea factory. Excess to their requirements was sold on the London markets and some to America and

Native workers on the company's Lujeri plantation in Nyasaland. Mlanje Mountain can be seen in the background.

Lyons formed a separate tea subsidiary, Lyons (India) Ltd, with offices at 11 British Indian Street, Calcutta, responsible for the marketing of packet tea to Indian retail agents while the former company, which became Heath & Company (Calcutta) Ltd, continued selling tea to other customers all over the world. By the early 1950s Lyons (India) Ltd, whose quaint telegraphic address was 'Teaspoons', were employing about forty Indian clerks responsible for invoicing and accounts. Also on the payroll at this time were three Greenford-trained tea buyers (Charles Davis, Michael Adams, and Peter Hollier) who were responsible for tasting and examining samples of the tea coming up for sale at the weekly Calcutta auctions.

With the African economies experiencing difficulties and most African colonies gaining independence from the European powers, Lyons came to the conclusion that the business should be sold, particularly since the trade at home was in decline. Brooke Bond Liebig Ltd, their old adversary, became interested, but both companies believed that the Malawi government might object to one British company selling to another. Tentative soundings were therefore made with the President, Dr Hastings Banda, but he showed no interest in the sale whatsoever. In consequence Lujeri Tea Estates Ltd was sold for an undisclosed sum to Brooke Bond Liebig Ltd on 28 July 1977.

the Irish Republic, where Lyons had a highly productive tea factory. Greenford's blending operation obtained its tea from 5,000 gardens and estates world-wide, yet most was bought at London auctions and the balance through a buying agent in Calcutta (Heath & Company), which Lyons acquired in 1921. In 1923, however,

171

15

MEAT PIES

ENRY TELFER THOMPSON began trading as a pie maker on 7 June 1926, just after the General Strike. A Scotsman by birth, he had recently returned from a failed South African venture with his wife Kate, and in desperation they put what money they had left into a meat pie business operating from a rented baker's basement in Borough High Street, Southwark. Henry and Kate Thompson decided to price their meat pies similarly to those of their main competitor, Doubleday's, but improved on them by using higher-quality ingredients. They employed a baker, Albert Edward Muteham, who had previously worked for Wheeler's of Croydon. The name they chose for their meat pie business was Ticky Snacks, 'ticky' being South African slang for 3d. Albert Muteham baked the pies, Henry Thompson sold them from a tricycle (1s. 6d. a dozen wholesale, 2 shillings a dozen retail) and Kate Thompson took charge of the financial matters.

The pies were shaped like an inverted cone with an overlapping top crust, to give the impression of greater size. No early recipes have survived but they probably included cheaper cuts of meat, gristle, flour, lard, caramel, flavourings and other questionable ingredients, with meat accounting for possibly less than a quarter of the content. Two types were produced, steak pies and steak and kidney pies, and Thompson's advertising declared they were 'Made as muvver makes 'em'. Produced in small quantities, the pies were packed in boxes for delivery – the same boxes in which Thompson had received his cooking fat ingredients, to keep costs down.

Although it was a modest operation, Ticky Snacks' pies soon began to acquire a good reputation. Henry Thompson focused his marketing strategy on the hundreds of small cafés and coffee stalls around London, claiming that his pies contained more meat than Doubleday's products and persuading his customers to buy freshly cooked pies rather than bake them themselves. Thompson realised, however, that unless Ticky Snacks could expand into a wider catering market the sales would be limited to what he could distribute from his tricycle. In a bold move he took on more staff, who operated the ovens both day and night, and planned to replace his tricycle with vans. His first big break came when he secured a supply agreement with the Mobile Catering Company, which ran numerous coffee stalls in and around London, many outside railway stations, where trade was brisk. In March 1927 these increased sales enabled Thompson to formalise his partnership and he registered Ticky Snacks Ltd as a private company, with the Thompsons and Muteham as shareholder directors. He moved to larger premises: first to Lomond Grove, Camberwell Green, and in November 1927 to 194 Garratt Lane, Wandsworth. As the company grew, many family members joined, and Thompson brought down several bakers from his home town of Jedburgh, in the Scottish border country; these formed the core of the production team.

Twelve months later the annual business turnover had increased to £30,000 and by 1929 to £47,000. By now Thompson had abandoned his tricycle deliveries, having purchased some

One of the original shop advertising signs for Ticky Snacks before the company became Henry Telfer Ltd. Made as Muvver Makes 'em' was dropped by Lyons as it created the wrong image. *By kind permission of Waldegrave Films.*

second-hand Trojan vans from the Lyons subsidiary Normand Ltd; the consequences of this were not immediately evident. Meanwhile, the business slowly expanded into the Portsmouth and Bournemouth areas but the lack of capital became a serious handicap to growth.

Ticky Snacks and the Salmon Family

In 1931 Geoffrey Salmon (1908–90) had completed his education and 'apprenticeship' at the Trocadero restaurant and was ready to take control of a Lyons department or subsidiary. Aged 23, he was the son of Harry Salmon, the Lyons director responsible for property negotiations and currently in charge of the tea factory at Greenford. Geoffrey Salmon had a particular desire to manage an independent business in order to gain more experience outside Lyons. Coincidentally, Frederick Stokes, Normand's manager, had mentioned to Harry Salmon that he was supplying Ticky Snacks with second-hand vans, and had suggested that he might consider acquiring their business, especially since they were short of investment capital. Although Lyons did not want to have other firms supply them with meat pies – because their perishable nature required the utmost thoroughness in manufacture – the idea suggested a possible opportunity for the young Geoffrey Salmon.

Discreet preliminary negotiations with Henry Thompson were opened through the intermediary, Harry Salmon's cousin, Leslie Atwell. However, Atwell was initially unaware that Harry Salmon intended his son to run the business rather than himself, and Henry Thompson too had been misled, but he welcomed the chance to receive additional capital when Harry Salmon agreed to buy 49 per cent of the equity in Ticky Snacks. The deal was finalised on 17 August 1932. Both Leslie Atwell and Geoffrey Salmon were appointed to the board of Ticky Snacks Ltd on 28 September 1932 but Atwell resigned in November 1933 when he learned of Harry Salmon's plans for his son. Nevertheless the settlement suited both Henry Thompson and Geoffrey Salmon – Thompson because he got his injection of capital and Geoffrey Salmon because he was given a part business of his own to run.

Ticky Snacks had been intentionally kept separate from Lyons, but George Booth, the Lyons company secretary, thought the compromise would lead to a conflict of interest and in 1933 Henry and Kate Thompson and Albert Muteham agreed to sell their shares in the company to Lyons, Henry Thompson because his health was failing and Albert Muteham because he could see no future with others now in control. Thus the Ticky Snacks equity was divided between Lyons (51 per cent) and the Salmon family (49 per cent). Lyons had acquired the balance of the business for £17,375 and allowed Henry Thompson to stay on as a director, until his death in July 1940. However, the production director, Albert Muteham, remained there for only six months.

During the negotiations Lyons had employed the accountancy firm of Clemetson Wood, who had reported on the business and advised on its worth. They had criticised Henry Thompson's management style, the production processes and the lack of hygiene controls. For example, pies were left to cool in a passageway which everybody used, costs had been kept low by buying second-hand equipment and maintenance was skimped. Clemetson Wood concluded that the whole factory environment was quite unsuitable for meat pie production, yet they described the business as 'very interesting' and Geoffrey Salmon had no doubts about its potential.

With such a derogatory report, Lyons distanced themselves from the operation for fear of damaging their own reputation; the letterheaded stationery referred to the director as Hamilton Salmon (Hamilton was Geoffrey Salmon's third given name) in order to confuse. The deception was replicated on some official documents where Geoffrey Salmon is listed as G. Hamilton Salmon. Production methods at Lyons were modern, hygienic and efficient, and factory management was supported by the food technology developed in the Lyons laboratories. Because Ticky Snacks operated independently from Lyons it was many years before Lyons' quality control methods were brought to bear on the meat pie business. Some investment was made in new plant, however, culminating in the delivery of a new Ericcson pie-making machine in 1933. Capable of producing 1,500 pies per hour, the Ericcson was the first new piece of equipment that Ticky Snacks had ever purchased. Yet little could be done to improve the unsatisfactory Garratt Lane factory in Wandsworth and the business was relocated to a former brewery in Lillie Road, Fulham, in 1934. At the same time Baker Perkins supplied a new travelling oven which operated on the cyclothermic principle – cooking by circulating hot air rather than by direct heat. The first of its type in the country, the oven was closely studied by Lyons' own production staff who subsequently installed similar equipment at the Cadby Hall bakeries.

A Ticky Snacks delivery van before the company changed its name to Henry Telfer Ltd. *By kind permission of Waldegrave Films.*

Henry Telfer's pie shop on the corner of North End Road and Lille Road, Fulham. *By kind permission of Waldegrave Films.*

Henry Telfer Ltd:
Diversification and the Rural Pie Scheme

Having installed new production facilities at the Fulham factory, Ticky Snacks began to increase turnover so substantially that by 1940, boosted by the government's need to feed troops returning from Dunkirk, it had trebled. However, the heavy investment in plant, rising wage costs and fluctuating prices of raw materials all contributed to keeping profit margins low. Nevertheless Geoffrey Salmon was pleased with progress and his pies continued to enjoy a reputation for quality. Although veal and ham pie was introduced with some success, few other meat products, such as sausages, were manufactured. With so many butchers' shops in the high streets, consumers had a good choice of locally made sausages and it would have been difficult to compete on quality and price. Some consideration had been given occasionally to extending the product range away from meat pies, even to such items as crisps and biscuits. Then in 1935 Ticky Snacks bought a small firm trading as the London Preserving Company Ltd, and Thompson became a director. Their pickles, sauces and a lemon drink called Elpeco were sold alongside meat pies without adding significantly

to the cost of distribution. The lemon drink has been described as a great thirst quencher, rather like a liquid acid-drop, but the Elpeco sauce, used liberally by pie stall customers to garnish their pie and mash meals, was also said to be very good at cleaning the copper tea urns! The operation was closed down after a few years and the original owner and son continued to run it, although the company name was retained by Lyons.

A more determined attempt to diversify came in 1934, when Ticky Snacks began supplying several London department stores with small pork pies known as Bachelor Buttons. Contracts with these higher-class outlets made it necessary to transform the traditional image of Ticky Snacks. Their advertising slogan, 'Made as muvver makes 'em', did not seem appropriate for Selfridge's and it disappeared from the firm's livery, which itself was changed from dark brown with yellow lettering to orange with black lettering. This remained the fleet's colours until after the war. By resolution on 14 June 1938, the directors elected to change the company's name to Henry

complained about quality. Paradoxically, in the years immediately after the war, supplies were at their lowest ebb but it was then that Telfer's enjoyed their most remarkable expansion, largely through their participation in Lord Woolton's Rural Pie Scheme. Between 1943 and 1945 Lord Woolton (Frederick James Marquis), former Minister of Food, was Minister of Reconstruction. His scheme's objective was to supply rural areas with quantities of food equivalent to those being made available to restaurants and hotels in the cities. The Ministry of Food planned to allocate flour, meat and fat to the Women's Voluntary Service (WVS) so that they could make and distribute pies in their local areas. In practice the Rural Pie Scheme was beyond the means of the WVS and thus a permit transfer was introduced. According to this, Telfer's and other pie manufacturers took delivery of the allocated raw materials, baked the pies and distributed them to the WVS, who then delivered locally.

So great was demand that Telfer's production facilities were overwhelmed, and Lyons had to set up satellite pie plants in their provincial bakeries to meet requirements and to deliver to counties from Sussex in the south to Yorkshire in the north. An empty factory in Southend covered Essex and Norfolk and a small plant even operated behind the Lyons teashop in Ipswich. The whole network was created in a very short period of time and Ivor Salmon was appointed a director in October 1945 to help with the growing work-load. Between 1946 and 1949 Telfer's turnover almost trebled to £1.1 million and profits rose from £20,500 in 1946 to £60,800 in 1949, when they began delivering pies to Buckingham Palace. With the end of meat rationing in July 1954, turnover dropped as fast as it has risen.

In 1952 Telfer's prepared to apply for a royal warrant, for which three years' consecutive service is a necessary qualification, but King George VI died suddenly in February and the present Queen came to the throne. The process had to be restarted, but in 1955 a warrant was finally issued to Telfer's as purveyors of pork pies to HM Queen Elizabeth II.

Telfer Ltd, after its founding member, but still dissociating it from the Lyons group. Sydney Harris, who compiled much of Ticky Snacks' history, was appointed a director and accountant at this time. New meat products, such as sausages and sausage rolls, and potato straws, known as 'Pommes Apéritif', were introduced, but as these proved unsuccessful Henry Telfer Ltd became dependent on meat pies alone and was thereby unable to break into mass retail marketing.

Nevertheless, Telfer's failure at diversification was no hindrance to growth. When the Second World War came, Geoffrey Salmon joined the Army Catering Corps, where he had the opportunity to influence the NAAFI and other wartime organisations which demanded huge quantities of meat pies for troops, and the government turned to Telfer's for supplies. During the war years raw materials were made readily available for food manufacture and Telfer's production doubled. As with cake production, in wartime food manufacturers could sell just about everything they produced and nobody

THE BOMB MAKERS OF ELSTOW

I N THE YEARS leading up to the Second World War Captain R.G. Leggett, the army's Inspector of Catering, began to investigate whether the Army School of Cookery was knowledgeable enough about mass catering and sought relevant statistics from the editor of *The Caterer*. As it happened he had been in discussion with Sir Isidore Salmon (1876–1941), Managing Director of Lyons, a day or two earlier. Sir Isidore was the second son of Barnett Salmon, and a brother of Harry and Maurice Salmon. When contact was made again, following Leggett's request, Sir Isidore offered to provide as much information as he could to the War Office inquiry. Leslie Hore-Belisha, the Secretary for War in 1937, believed the army were short of 20,000 men, and tried to learn about issues concerning the troops by discussing them with generals and private soldiers, often visiting barracks and kitchens and sampling food. On 10 March 1938 he announced to the House of Commons that Sir Isidore Salmon had been appointed Honorary Catering Adviser to the War Office and a member of the Quartermaster General's Committee.

Isidore Salmon had joined Lyons at its formation in 1894 after having been privately educated at the City of London School. He was made a director in 1909 and subsequently served 33 years as Chairman of Lyons. During the First World War he was a major in the army and continued to use the title until 1933, when he was knighted. As well as becoming Conservative Member of Parliament for Harrow in 1924, between 1918 and 1922 he was chairman of the London War Pensions Committee. During the

1920s and 1930s he served on a number of government and parliamentary committees covering such diverse issues as transport, the employment of prisoners, the price of building materials and public accounts. Isidore Salmon received an OBE in 1919 followed by a CBE in 1920 and eventually a knighthood in 1933 for his wide-ranging services (many not covered here) to society.

From Sir Isidore's appointment to the Quartermaster General's Committee in March 1938 until his death in 1941, he provided much advice to parliamentary committees on mass catering, drawing on the knowledge he and his staff had acquired within Lyons. He suggested, for example, that food supplied to the anti-aircraft units stationed around the country (on 24-hour standby) should be cooked in advance at central points, dispatched and then reheated at individual sites as required. These small units had previously been expected to cook for themselves in a 'boy scout' fashion which not only was labour-intensive but interfered with the units' ability to maintain their vigilance. One of his first acts as honorary catering adviser was to appoint Richard Byford, then catering manager of Trust Houses, as chief inspector of army catering. Byford recruited many of the best-known managers in the industry into his team and they became the backbone of the Army Catering Corps, which was formed in March 1941 out of the Army School of Cookery.

Lyons at War

After the fall of France in 1940 Britain was in dire peril, standing alone, with the whole might

This photograph is believed to have been taken at the Elstow armaments factory in Bedfordshire during the Second World War. Employing mostly female labour, Lyons put in a team of managers, chemists, accountants and other specialists at the request of the government.

of Germany's war machine facing her across the Channel. Already by February of that year some 2,000 Lyons employees had been conscripted or had volunteered for military service (including those joining the Mercantile Marine), and 28 of these were unmarried women from the teashops. Although over 162,000 British soldiers were killed in the war, more British civilians than soldiers died during the first three years. The Battle of Britain was an attempt by Germany to break British resistance by gaining air superiority before launching an invasion. German air operations started in July 1940 with attacks on ports, naval bases and shipping. Then in August the Luftwaffe targeted aircraft production centres and airfields in the south of England, as well as bombing coastal ports and shipping in the Thames. From 7 September onwards the offensive shifted to daylight bombing of British cities but when Hitler's invasion plans collapsed the Luftwaffe switched to night-time raids on London and provincial cities such as Birmingham, Bristol, Coventry, Liverpool and Southampton. Although

the Battle of Britain officially ended on 30 October, night bombing continued until May 1941, including two devastating attacks on Plymouth in March and April 1941, the second of five nights' duration. These air raids caused colossal destruction, creating severe hardship for the civilian population. However, instead of breaking Britain's morale, as the German high command had intended, the Battle of Britain and the Blitz had the reverse effect and strengthened the solidarity of the entire population as no other crisis has done before or since.

For many women the war years brought comradeship and independence, and they quickly replaced men in factories and other male-dominated occupations – in defiance of the politicians, whose initial belief was that women should remain at home to bring up the children. By 1943, some 17 million women of working age were in paid employment and in addition many undertook work for the Women's Voluntary Service or Civil Defence. Harsh working conditions and long hours caused immense disruption to people's everyday lives; in particular, such normal routines as shopping became irksome. For those working at Lyons, the staff shop alleviated some of these daily predicaments. Staff who could not fight helped in other ways, some by raising funds to buy war weapons, others by giving up their time to pack food parcels for distribution by the Red Cross to prisoners of war. Space at Cadby Hall was made available for tinned milk, meat and fruit – supplied by Libby's, Batchelor's, Fray Bentos and others – to be delivered and packed by volunteers, sometimes on a two-shift basis. From November 1942 until the end of the war Lyons delivered over 3½ million composite rations to troops serving in the European and Pacific theatres of war. Like the Red Cross parcels, these rations were packed at Cadby Hall and Rannoch Road (Lyons' former jam factory) in cartons bearing the distinctive 'J.L. & Co.' logo. Over half the boxes were made by Lyons' own carton-making department. Parachutes too were packed in the vast basement area of the administration block and were used specifically for supply drops to troops; the standard of assembly was not as high as for those parachutes used by personnel.

Because of the need to save petrol, deliveries to the teashops were reduced to two a day. This economy also accounted for the novel sight of wholesale travellers, in many areas, doing their journeys on bicycle. The blackout at first made a great difference to teashop and restaurant business, particularly in the West End, though many reopened later. Daily dancing was introduced to the Trocadero restaurant, the Coventry Street Corner House and the Cumberland, Strand and Regent Palace hotels. The Corner Houses, which had always been a rendezvous for couples planning to marry, witnessed a surge in marriage proposals during the first few months of the war. Staff also gave support when some 12,000 undertook to contribute weekly for the purchase of 55,000 National Savings Certificates and the company gave one free certificate per month for every fifty members.

Early in the war many well-off individuals donated their own private aircraft to the Royal Air Force and these were used for non-combat duties. At the start of the Battle of Britain other citizens started to collect money for new fighting aircraft in the most ingenious ways. For example, a ticket surcharge was made on Manchester trams, all girls with the name of Dorothy were invited to contribute to a Spitfire which would be marked with their name, a shot-down German aeroplane was taken around the country on display and people were asked to contribute sixpence to view it. The idea of presentation aircraft (those aircraft paid for by donation) was initiated by the Russians in the First World War, and they continued to adopt these measures in the Second World War, as did Japan and America to a lesser extent. The Ministry of Aircraft Production in Britain, exploiting the mood of the time, suggested that organisations might raise a nominal sum of £5,000 for the construction of a Spitfire, which, as a result of the fighter planes' exploits over Kent, had captured the spirit of the nation. By September 1940 groups, individuals – including Queen Wilhelmina of the Netherlands, who donated £216,000 on behalf of the Dutch East Indies to equip a whole squadron with 43 Spitfires – corporations and other organisations throughout the country and the British Commonwealth had raised enough money to buy one thousand Spitfires or Hurricanes. Between June and September 1940 over a thousand Spitfires came off the production lines and nearly all bore the name of donors. The staff at Lyons soon raised the necessary £5,000 for their Supermarine Spitfire numbered P8656, which was powered by the legendary Rolls Royce Merlin engine. It bore the name 'Nippy' when it left the factory. Lyons' Spitfire was attached to 234 Squadron, based at Warmwell in Dorset, and entered service in May 1941, but while providing high-altitude escort to a bombing raid over the Cherbourg peninsula it was damaged in a skirmish with Messerschmitts. Although the pilot managed to bring his damaged aircraft home, its engine failed and (in RAF parlance) it made a 'wheels-up landing' at West Knighton, Dorset, on or about 23 July 1941. The Spitfire was beyond repair and became a total loss, having flown only 17 hours before its accident.

£5,000 was raised by Lyons' staff to build this 'presentation' Spitfire during the Second World War. Attached to 234 Squadron, it was damaged by Messerschmitts over the Cherbourg peninsula and crashed in Dorset in July 1941 (before this picture was published) having flown only 17 hours.

The Lyons Mail
(WAR-TIME EDITION)

"For the bow cannot possibly stand always bent, nor can human frailty subsist without some lawful recreation."—CERVANTES

FORCES NUMBER SPECIAL

New Series   THURSDAY, JANUARY 15, 1942   No. 15

"We Wish You All . . . . . .

. . . . . health, safety and happiness during the year, for yourselves and for your families. May those families which have been scattered by the War be brought together again soon and may all those who are overseas return safe and well, with that Victory which alone can bring peace. Good luck to you all "

These words are taken from a message from the directors to the staff broadcast at Cadby Hall on New Year's Day. Through these pages it is hoped that they will reach "Lyons" men and women everywhere, whether with us at work or serving in the Forces.

★ "NIPPY" ★

★ This is the Spitfire " Nippy," the cost of which was provided ★ by the staff. It is one of the fastest and hardest hitting types of aircraft. It carries two 20 m.m. Cannon in addition to machine guns, is powered by a Rolls Royce engine and attains a speed approaching 400 miles an hour.

1

In a similar but unrelated incident Lyons again demonstrated their commitment to the war effort. In 1940, after the fall of Dunkirk, some of the trains which carried the returning troops away from the Channel ports were routed through Kensington (Addison Road) station, which was closed to passenger traffic between 19 October 1940 and 19 December 1946. Kensington station then was unique in that it provided interconnections with most of London's railway termini and the important railway junctions at Willesden to the north and Clapham to the south. The troop trains passing through were stopped just long enough to load supplies direct from the Lyons production lines at Cadby Hall to the exhausted men in transit, many of whom had not eaten for several days. The pork pies, sausage rolls, cakes and urns of tea must have tasted delicious after their evacuation ordeal. For security this incident was never publicised and remains unrecorded to this day. Teashop manageresses were never told why their orders had been so drastically reduced at this time, so they had assumed there were supply difficulties.

Apart from the top floors of the ice-cream factory, which were damaged by bombs at the height of the Blitz, Cadby Hall came though the war relatively unscathed. This was partly due to the vigilance of the fire watch that Lyons established, with observation bunkers built high on the buildings around the large complex. Fire-watch duties had been forced on businesses by the government's first Fire Prevention (Business Premises) Order, introduced on 18 January 1941. Towards the end of December 1940 the blitz on London brought home to the government the need for more widespread and organised fire-fighting teams. Although members of the public had been asked to form themselves into street fire-fighting units, it soon became obvious that business premises – in particular those associated with the war effort – were increasingly being lost to fire. The Fire Prevention Order of 1941 compelled all occupiers of business properties to make adequate arrangements to prevent fire at their premises. It also required all male employees to perform fire-prevention and fire-watch duties at their place of work, with the exception of men who were physically unfit, or over the age of sixty, or performing some other civil defence duty.

In order to satisfy these requirement Lyons established observation posts, staffed by 55 departmental heads between 6.00 p.m. and 8.00 a.m. every day between 1941 and 1945. The same personnel also played an active role in reporting German aircraft movements from their command and telecommunication facilities at Cadby Hall, which were connected by telephone to government centres. To deal with any immediate fire emergency within the factory grounds, Lyons had constructed their own fire-engine staffed by volunteers from the factories. During the whole of the war the firm's medical officer, Dr William Blood, slept every weekday night at Cadby Hall in order to assist with any medical emergency which might arise. Later in the war, in June 1944, Germany unleashed Hitler's much vaunted miracle weapon, the flying bomb, called the *Vergeltungswaffe* ('reprisal weapon') or

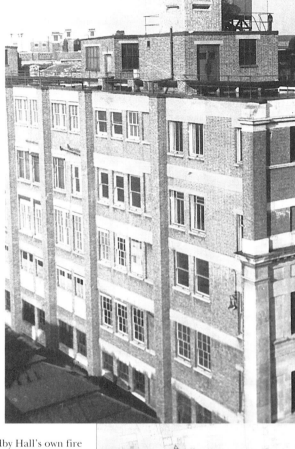

V-1, but dubbed by Britons the buzz-bomb or doodlebug. One of these fell on St Mary's church on the opposite side of the road to the Cadby Hall factories but, although completely destroying the church the V-1, caused little damage to Cadby Hall itself. The sports ground at Sudbury also suffered some minor damage when a flying bomb exploded there during the summer of 1944, when the area was being used to billet troops, whose tents provided little protection from the enormous blast.

The Elstow Ordnance Factory

From the end of 1941 Lyons managed, on behalf of the Ministry of Supply, a large munitions factory at Elstow in Bedfordshire, where shells and some larger bombs were filled. Contractors had started work in 1939, after the Munich crisis of 1938, preparing artificial earth mounds to separate each factory unit from the other for safety purposes. Individual production areas were equipped for blast with materials which included unsecured concrete slabs for roofs, designed to

Above left. Cadby Hall's own fire fighting appliance during the Second World War. *By kind permission of Mary Cakebread.*

Above right. One of several fire watch positions on top of Cadby Hall's factories during the Second World War. This one is on top of the head office building. *By kind permission of Mary Cakebread.*

Right. Cadby Hall's fire watch control room during the Second World War. A plan of the factory hangs on the back wall. Aircraft silhouettes, German and British, hung on the opposite wall (not shown). *By kind permission of Mary Cakebread.*

cushion most of the blast if an explosion occurred. At the instigation of Lord Beaverbrook (1879–1964), the Minister of Supply, the government had sought volunteers from among the better-run enterprises, believing a business-like style of management would be more productive than administration by civil servants. Accordingly, the government invited Lyons to manage the Elstow ordnance factory, near Bedford, as agents for £1 per year. Lyons loaned to the Ministry of Supply, free of charge, a senior director and several members of staff with appropriate qualifications. Maurice Salmon, who had a genius for mass production, was put in overall charge, and he established a small committee with responsibility for managing and running the works. Using Lyons' well-tried office and production-line

methods and employing the talents of other Cadby Hall specialists, Maurice Salmon and his colleagues set about establishing and running, in absolute secrecy, one of the largest ordnance units in Britain at that time. Although Maurice Salmon only visited the factory each Wednesday, under his leadership the management created an effective and cohesive team. Walter Messenger, the Lyons chemist responsible for essences, was given the job of factory manager while Redvers Dundonald Ross, a Lyons tea sales superintendent, was in charge of procurement with responsibility for obtaining all inventory from railway engines to knives and forks. Later Ross was appointed production manager and, when Messenger died in May 1943, he took over the management of the whole factory. Ross was not a well-liked person within Lyons having, it is said by some, 'a pompous disposition'. After the war Ross returned to Lyons to take charge of bakery sales which created much disquiet within the bakery team.

Working with Ross at Elstow was John Raines. He had been servicing ice-cream cabinets before the war and worked under Ross as supplies officer helping with stores ordering but more specifically with storage and distribution within the factory. He was responsible for 8,500 items of inventory including the storage of 2,000 tons of TNT and other high explosives. Raines was also responsible for the laundry at Elstow which was vital to the safety of the factory. All workers had to wear special clothing and it was essential that these clothes (15,000 items per week) were laundered within the factory compound because they were impregnated with explosive powder.

By 1942 enough of the gigantic infrastructure had been put in place for the production of explosives to commence. The eventual factory complex included 250 separate buildings, 14 miles of roads, 15 miles of railway lines, community centres, drainage, air-raid shelters, fire-fighting and medical services, heating systems, laundries and an electricity sub-station producing 2,500 kilowatts of power. The predominantly female workforce, recruited not only from Bedford but from as far away as Norwich, Lowestoft and Ireland, were extremely hard-working and consistently reached their production targets when output had to be increased to meet wartime demands. However, many of the women were reluctant to wear the prescribed safety protection for long hair, and several even used some of the chemicals to dye their hair. Since women workers often proved averse to wearing hair protection in industries during the war, the government sought the help of fashion editors to persuade women that short hairstyles were fashionable. The large numbers of so many young women billeted in the area acted like a magnet to the American forces stationed nearby. With their zest for a 'good time' there was a thriving social life.

At Elstow the labour force worked on three shifts to achieve production targets. The first task was the manufacture of two-inch mortar bombs; in 14 months over 5.1 million bombs were made using the high-explosive compound of ammonium, nitrate and trinitrotoluene known as 80/20 amatol, hot pressed. All chemicals were mixed on site in the cordite unit under tight quality control. Sample analyses made over a long period proved that the staff were achieving the correct mixture to almost 100 per cent accuracy, with the aid of Lyons' laboratory specialists. The cordite unit closed down in 1943 and was re-equipped as a shell-reconditioning depot.

Other parts of the plant were manufacturing a variety of aerial bombs of 1,000, 2,000, 8,000, 12,000 (Tallboy) and 22,000 pounds in weight. The 22,000-pound bomb, whose sobriquet was 'grand-slam', was designed by the engineer and inventor Barnes Wallis and was carried to the target in specially modified Lancaster aircraft of 617 ('Dambusters') Squadron. These bombs were used in deep-penetration raids on strategically important targets such as bridges, viaducts and underground fuel storage tanks which were destroyed by the earthquake-like movements set up after detonation. Their first reported use was on 14 March 1945 when the Bielefeld railway viaduct in Germany was bombed, causing 100 yards of the structure to collapse.

Between 1942 and 1945 Bomber Command dropped 920,276 tons of explosives on enemy territory. During the same period, 94,597 tons passed through the Elstow factory, representing more than 10 per cent of the total used by Bomber Command. Elstow also produced 3,916 mines, which were laid in enemy waters. The task of achieving this level of production while operating in total secrecy presented a tremendous organisational challenge to Lyons, and much credit must be given to Maurice Salmon.

As part of the war effort, the transport and engineering workshops belonging to the Lyons subsidiary Normand at Park Royal and elsewhere were producing canteen equipment for the services, tank transporters, aircraft generator sets, depth charges, ammunition for the Oerlikon anti-aircraft gun (used extensively by the Royal Navy), machines for washing bombs, lifting-cradles for 2,000-lb bombs, thousands of special vehicle bodies and king-pins for the famous Bailey Bridges. These had been invented by Donald Coleman Bailey (knighted in 1946), chief designer at the Experimental Bridging Establishment, Christchurch, who came up with the idea of prefabricated panels, erected in various combinations of storeys and trusses to give varying strengths. The construction of the Bailey Bridge components required 150 operations to ensure total accuracy. They were extremely important to the armed forces because their modular construction enabled them to be erected, very quickly, for virtually every load requirement. First used in the North African campaign of 1942–3, nearly 700,000 separate panels were manufactured, by small to moderately sized engineering workshops, between 1942–5. About 4,500 Bailey Bridges were used to replace demolished bridges over the rivers of Italy, France and Germany in the push towards Berlin culminating in the crossing of the Rhine, over which the first 40-ton bridge was built in thirty hours.

A teashop menu issued during the war and dated 14 October 1940.

The Sun Works under German Occupation

J. Lyons & Co. Ltd must have been one of the few British companies to have had their assets seized by Germany in the Crown dependency of Jersey during the Second World War. The Channel Islands, to which Jersey belongs, are the only portion of the Dukedom of Normandy still owned by the Crown, to which they have been attached since the Conquest. The German occupation of the Channel Islands covered a period of almost five years – from 1 July 1940 until 9 May 1945 – during which time Jersey's import and export trade – including the Lyons subsidiary tea-packaging business of the Overseas Trading Corporation – was at a standstill. In anticipation of the invasion, senior management in Jersey and other members of the Sun Works' staff on the island had escaped to London, taking with them as many of the account books and documents as possible, thereby enabling the company's activities to be undertaken from Horniman's premises at Shepherdess Walk in London.

The Sun Works sold tea to the local wholesalers on a limited scale, and for a brief period both wholesalers and retailers continued to dispose of their stocks of tea until the German authorities realised that tea was far too valuable to be left in the hands of the civil population. They soon issued instructions that all stocks of tea on the island were to be handed in at the Sun Works without delay and, together with factory stocks, placed under secure storage. Two local directors of the Overseas Trading Corporation were held personally responsible for this stock, and no issues were permitted without the signed requisite order of the German Command. The German authorities regarded tea

as a priceless commodity, so much so that whenever any of their visiting generals came over from France they would be taken to the Sun Works with an official order for a 4 oz tin of Te Sol. Permits were also sparingly issued to the occupying military forces, to the extent that stocks became finally exhausted only a week before Jersey's liberation on 9 May 1945.

The Sun Works itself remained under the Overseas Trading Corporation's control during the whole occupation, and its greatly depleted staff were employed in hand-making paper bags for the retail trade. Much of the storage facilities on the La Mielle property was requisitioned by the German Command as a repository for grain and other foodstuffs. A 24-hour guard on the stocks was maintained until liberation day, while the premises were also heavily mined to within a few feet of the roadway.

The company was nevertheless able to render a useful service to the civilian population during most of the occupation. In conjunction with a committee comprising the senior members of the legislative assembly (in Jersey, Guernsey and Alderney these assemblies are known as States), rations were put together and delivered daily to all Jersey's elementary schools, as well as to several depots in both town and country, thereby ensuring that most of the inhabitants were adequately fed. Arrangements were later made to reopen many bakehouses, where food was taken by housewives for baking – although the dishes contained only root vegetables for the most part.

The joinery department at the Sun Works was formally requisitioned by the legislative assembly and, under the supervision of Paul Dart, the highly efficient joinery manager, prepared timber to be used as fuel by the civilian population in the place of coal and oil, all of which had been consumed in the early days of occupation, as well as supplying wood for burning in the bakehouses.

The Sun Works were never requisitioned by the Germans, although this was threatened on a number of occasions. The packaging machinery and other plant were placed in jeopardy when a special German commission arrived from Paris in order to remove all available machinery to occupied France. The management of the Sun Works, however, deliberately misled the German commission by falsely expressing the view that, since Germany would inevitably win the war and therefore take possession of the island, the machinery would be invaluable for a tea export business after the war and accordingly should remain in Jersey. Having retired to a corner in a huddle, the German commission decided to accept this advice and the plant was saved.

In 1947 the Overseas Trading Corporation recommenced business in a small way by exporting Te Sol and Horniman's teas to South America and developing the Lyons brand in Europe, mainly in France, where a subsidiary, the Société Anonyme de Produits de Margue, had been formed for the purpose.

Although victory in Europe was celebrated on 8 May 1945, the formal state of war between Britain and Germany was not ended until July 1951, when the government gave notice of the ending of hostilities in the *London Gazette*; they had lasted eleven years, ten months and six days.

On the Home Front

The writer H.E. Bates said of the Elstow factory: 'It was run by people who would have been happier making, in a world of peace, prodigious quantities of Swiss rolls or ice cream, instead of mortar-shells and bombs.' Of that he can be assured, but, like so many industries of all sizes and classifications, their wartime contributions have not been fully revealed. Millions of working-class men, most of whom had never even crossed the Channel, were sent to fight all over the world, while at home men and women working in various small firms performed feats beyond their wildest aspirations.

Those with specialised skills or in reserved occupations contributed in other ways at home. Chemists, for example, were exempt from fighting but feverishly laboured to identify alternative foodstuffs to help keep the troops and home population fed. Despite their best efforts and because of the terrible loss of shipping, food rationing was introduced in 1940. Accordingly, day by day, week by week and month by month the women, the young, the middle-aged and the

old waited in long lines so they could carry home those meagre items that could be bought. For Lyons staff this time-consuming activity was at least partly alleviated by their being able to buy goods in the staff shop, and many found recreation during the summer by using the camping facilities that management provided at the Greenford sports grounds.

Some of the war's effects on the economy were favourable and hastened the end to the economic difficulties of the 1930s. Unemployment diminished and over-production in some industries disappeared as shortages began to bite. New Ministries of Supply, Home Security, Information, Aircraft Production, Shipping and Food were inaugurated. When rationing was introduced, the government provided generous subsidies to help farmers to concentrate on growing crops rather than keeping livestock. People were encouraged to invest in National Savings and large firms like Lyons made their own collections to help with the war effort. While fewer British lives were lost in the Second World War than in the First, the collateral destruction of cities and industry was much greater. Early calculations of the number of civilian deaths caused by the first air raids were put at between 200,000 and 250,000. Fortunately, the estimates proved grossly overstated but they did result in the formation of a credible civil defence force which was assisted by many large companies such as Lyons.

The physical destruction to homes, cities and industrial centres during the war was huge. To pay for reconstruction, and the loans for vital war material, Britain needed to increase its exports substantially and yet its capacity to achieve this had been damaged. Of all the 'fighting units' the Mercantile Marine, whose personnel were all volunteers, had suffered most. The ships, which had been laid up in the pre-war depression, had been sunk while trying to keep Britain's, and Russia's, sea routes open. Their casualties were higher than those of any other fighting unit (British Army, Royal Air Force and Royal Navy) as a percentage of personnel employed. The civilian population had also suffered gravely, with more than 60,000 deaths across the country,

This first issue of *Lyons Pie*, sent to Lyons employees serving in the armed forces, is thought to have been the only issue of this journal. The *Lyons Mail*, however, continued to be issued during the war but was much reduced in size. *By kind permission of Alice Lewis.*

KEEPING IN TOUCH
Page 4 carries correspondence from men in the Services. Here is an easy way of maintaining contact. One letter is read by thousands.

Published by J. LYONS & COMPANY LTD., Cadby Hall, London, W.14

No. 1 — February, 1940

PEOPLE to-day are hungry for news—send us yours, wherever you may be, on land, on sea, flying high or in the Maginot Line.
Address:
Editor, "Lyons Pie," Cadby Hall, London, W.14

INTRODUCING "LYONS PIE"

We should like "Lyons Pie" to begin its career by conveying our sincere good wishes to you all. Wherever this message finds you, we know that if there's anything to enjoy you'll be enjoying it. We can't afford space to reprint the individual good wishes which have come in from the heads and members of practically every Department, but every one of your colleagues and friends in "the Company" joins in wishing you GOOD LUCK.

What it is

Perhaps this little sheet needs some explanation. Here it is: We can't write to all of you and you can't write to all of us. Yet we are all deeply interested in anything you can tell us (Censor permitting, of course). We want to know how your new life is treating you. Many letters have reached us asking for " local news," and enquiring after comrades in arms. "Lyons Pie" sets out to give those on Active Service news about each other and about the "Home Front," and to give those at home all the news it can gather about you.

Reporters All

That makes everyone in the Company a possible contributor. Write and tell us anything you like (subject to blue pencil) and we'll print all we can. As a beginning, we're giving a fairly full list of members of the staff who are in the Forces. Help us to add to it. We're also giving extracts from letters already received. We rely on you to keep that page filled. The news from the home front is all we can gather for this issue but we hope that every reader will find something of interest. Send in your criticisms, anyway, and we'll treat this number as a trial run.

And so to Press . . . .

If we try to keep the silver lining, you'll know it isn't because we forget the cloud. You don't need to be reminded of the hardships of War. Let's all keep our thoughts on victory and happy days together again in the future, with this little link between us meanwhile. So away we go, with the very best of wishes to you all from us all—and please wish "Lyons Pie" good luck, too!

WHERE'S GEORGE?

— gone to [CENSORED]
CENSORED

HERE AND THERE

"Dr. Livingstone, I presume . . . . ?"

Our appeal for news brought in a crop of stories, tall, short and medium. One story, tall but true, is that of an Accounts man in the Army who heard a familiar voice among the newcomers to his unit. Enquiry revealed that the owner of the voice was an Ice Sales correspondent, an old acquaintance by telephone. The Army brought these two face to face for the first time!

Home Front

Our black-out is a large scale affair. Here are some figures:
4½ acres of glass blacked-out at Greenford.
4,000 special blinds at Cadby.

13,000 metal respirator containers supplied to staff.
240,000 sandbags used at Cadby.
Those sandbags, filled, are 20 inches long. End to end, they would reach from London to Margate.

"Where's George?"

The cartoon on this page should revive not-so-old memories, of the popular "Where's George?" series to which Mr. Arnold Beauvais, the artist, contributed so many amusing drawings. "George's" popularity was unique when you come to think of it: he had no distinguishing feature except the fact that he was always missing. Some day perhaps we will get Mr. Beauvais to draw the man whom everyone knew and nobody saw.

---

nearly half of those in London. Londoners had endured 354 air raids but there had been nearly four times as many alerts. In addition 2,937 pilotless bombs rained on the capital, destroying many great landmarks and an estimated 116,000 houses. Steel, railways and electricity-generating industries had been damaged or neglected, and of course major building work was required in most big cities.

With such large food-producing facilities, it is not surprising that Lyons supplied tons of commodities, to all theatres of war. These rations were painstakingly packed by the many women recruited for the job, while others packed parcels for prisoners of war and the injured. Much of this activity was carried out voluntarily by staff who had other duties but felt a need to do something more. As we have seen, the mass-production expertise built up over many years was used to great effect to run the Elstow munitions factory, while other parts of the Lyons empire undertook light engineering for the armed forces. It was Abraham Lincoln who said, 'The Lord prefers common-looking people. That is why he makes so many of them.' Common people they may have been but the consequences of the Second World War greatly speeded up the move towards a fairer society. The rich and poor, academic and uneducated, middle class and working class, skilled professional and labourer had all been thrown together in the united effort to achieve victory. The class system had not been broken but it had been damaged beyond repair.

Lyons between the Wars

Economically the period between the First and Second World Wars was one of remarkable improvement in living standards. In the twenty years leading up to 1939, however, many traditional industries such as cotton, shipbuilding and mining went into decline. Millions of men and women stumbled into unemployment and their suffering was indelibly marked with bitterness and anger which in turn gave rise to a General Strike. By contrast, light industries flourished because they were able to make use of mass-production techniques and the power of marketing. Retail distribution, for example, increased by two-thirds between 1911 and 1939, with tobacco products, confectionery (including biscuits, cake and jam), electrical goods and medical preparations selling particularly well. The consumer goods factories along the Great West Road grew rapidly at the time when Cadby Hall had reached its limits of expansion and Lyons transferred some of its production to Greenford to cope with the new consumerism. Public entertainment prospered during the 1920s, creating a proliferation of baroque cinemas, with their illuminated rising organs, and of theatres, grand restaurants and dance halls, while luxury hotels emerged to cater for the flood of foreign

The blitzed Southampton teashop, to the right of the Tivoli cinema, seen here with a fresh coat of paint and open for business in an otherwise devastated area.

visitors. It is a paradox that unemployment and economic depression during the inter-war period coexisted with rising living standards, mainly for the middle class. This contradiction reflects the changes occurring in British society between the wars.

Much of the growth of entertainment during the inter-war years benefited the Lyons empire. Restaurants, especially those with music and dancing, enjoyed increased patronage. Although the number of teashop openings peaked between 1894 and 1914 (194), a further 138 teashops opened before 1939. These, together with the Corner Houses and hotels, placed heavier burdens on the central bakeries, which then transformed themselves into mass-production units by adapting to automation. Soon, however, the huge expansion of baking and ice-cream production made it necessary to move tea and coffee manufacture to Greenford to make room for even more baking capacity. Cadby Hall had become the largest food factory in Britain.

Outdoor catering assumed less significance while management concentrated their minds on food production. The prestigious events such as royal garden parties, Wimbledon and the royal weddings continued in favour with management, even though many were loss-making, but this source of income was no longer so important. In this momentous period Lyons became a

household name. Joseph Lyons had died in 1917 and the main board members then chiefly consisted of Glucksteins and Salmons. Even though the business had changed immensely, its composition remained unaltered: there was a highly centralised structure with most of the individual departments run by a so-called 'family member'. During the early years of Lyons' development, Gluckstein directors outnumbered Salmons by two to one, but the balance shifted gradually so that by 1914 the Salmons were more prominent than the Glucksteins. This movement continued throughout the inter-war period so by the start of the Second World War the main board directors included eight members of the Salmon family but only three Glucksteins. In subsequent years many more members of the two families became main board directors, their numbers reaching a peak of thirteen, collectively, in the early 1950s, with a continuing bias towards the Salmons, who by the late 1960s outnumbered the Glucksteins by three to one. Lyons was still very much a family-run business, despite the growing number of outside shareholders.

As Lyons tried to come to terms with the aftermath of war there began to appear a number of inadequacies which were eventually to have profound consequences for the company's well-being. The story of the reconstruction and decline of Lyons is told in the next chapters.

Part 3
POST-WAR RECONSTRUCTION AND DECLINE
(1946–1978)

1946 Frozen food introduced to airlines.
Pension fund introduced (26 March).

1947 Death of Maurice Salmon (8 June).

1948 Frozen food exhibited to public at Hotelympia (January).

1949 Margaret Thatcher (née Roberts) joins Lyons laboratory (June).

1950 Death of Harry Salmon (13 October).

1951 Glacier Foods Ltd (ice lollies) bought.
First clerical job completed by programmed computer (September).

1952 First speciality restaurant (Haversnack) opened in Oxford C/H (28 April).

1953 Massarella Ice-cream Company bought.
Wimpy Hamburger introduced.

1954 Quick Brew tea introduced.
Orange Maid (ice lolly) introduced.
New frozen food plant built at Rannoch Road (Fulham) factory.
Computer manufacturing subsidiary formed (4 November).

1956 Lyons supermarket opens (February).

1957 Cereal Ready-Brek launched.
Bakery Division formed.
Death of Dr Leslie Lampitt (3 June).

1958 Bridge Park ice-cream factory (May).

1958 Major Montague Gluckstein died (25 December).

1960 First Carvery Restaurant opened in Regent Palace Hotel (1 October).

1961 Ariel Hotel (Heathrow) opened (January).
Chocolate & Confectionery business sold to Callard & Bowser (1 July).
First Steak House opened in Baker Street.

1962 Schweppes & Lyons merge their soft drinks businesses (January)
Neilson's & Eldorado ice-cream businesses acquired.
Lyons merge frozen food business with Union International and Associated Fisheries.
Robley group acquired.
Albany Hotel (Birmingham) opened (December)

1963 Lyons merge computer interests with English Electric (8 February).
Zoom ice lolly launched (May).
Fifty per cent of Celebrity Holdings acquired (September).
Bread Division formed.

1964 Traditional Tea Van Sales ended (January).
Park Lane Garage car park (under Hyde Park) opened.

1965 Trocadero restaurant closed (13 February).

1967 Oxford Corner House closed (May).
FAB ice lolly launched.
Tonibell ice-cream business bought.

1968 Frozen food business merged with Findus (Nestle).

1969 Scribbans Kemp acquired (March).
Margetts Foods acquired (Chalmar Holdings Ltd).
W. Symington & Co. Ltd acquired.
Lyons Bakery Ltd formed.
Management Share Purchase Scheme introduced.
Fifty-one per cent in Ulrich NV (Netherlands) acquired (June).
Albany Hotel (Nottingham) opened (October).
Supermarket restaurants opened (December).

1970 First Jolyon restaurant converted from teashop (Marble Arch) (March).
Bakery business of International Stores acquired (April).
Coventry Street Corner House closed (13 June).
Lyons Groceries Ltd formed.
J.L. Catering Ltd formed (December).

1971 Alpha Hotel, Amsterdam, opened (5 April).
Upper Crust (bus restaurant) enters service (May).
Queen's Award to Industry presented to Strand Hotels (4 June).
Rugby Albany Inn (Crick) opened (August).

1972 Wakefield Albany Inn opened (May).
Patrick, Grainger & Hutleys acquired.
Riunite del Panforte di Sienna acquired.
Park Hotel Marzocchi, Siena came into group.
Homburg meat business (Netherlands) bought.
Tetley Tea Company bought from Beech Nut (December).
Planning application made to develop site at Carlton, Yorkshire (December).

1973 Midland Counties Dairy Ltd acquired (1 January).
Albany Hotel (Glasgow) opened (February).
Hooimeijer en Zonen (Rotterdam) bought (March).
Havant Albany Inn opened (April).
Jb. Bussink Koninklijke acquired (24 May).
Schweppes & Lyons disentangle their soft drinks business.
Marina Kuchen (Germany) bought (May).
LSA World Travel Service bought (July).
Tower Hotel opened (September).
Park Court Hotel (Bayswater) development completed (October).
Hôtel Commodore, Paris, bought (October).
Baskin-Robbins, American ice-cream business bought (31 December).
Last Jolyon restaurant conversion completed (London Wall).

1974 Henry Telfer's production moves to Northampton.
Hale-Trent Holdings bought.
Production starts at new Carlton Bakery.
Frozen food interests sold.

1976 Albany Birmingham conference suite opened (January).
First Piccadilly teashop closed (September).
Wimpy sold to United Biscuits (December).

1977 Most hotels sold to Trust House Forte (27 January).
Strand Corner House closed (28 February).
Tower Hotel sold to EMI (15 July).
Lujeri Tea Estate sold to Brooke Bond (28 July).
Carlton factory fully commissioned.

1978 Alpha Hotel, Amsterdam, sold to Novotel Nederland (2 January).
Approach made by Allied Breweries to buy Lyons (21 July).
Terms of sale between J. Lyons & Allied Breweries agreed (4 August).
Keith Showering joins Lyons Board (September).

Chapter 17

CATERING IN CRISIS

B Y THE END of the period 1939–45 the final chapters of one phase of world history had been written. The changes wrought after this conflict signalled far more than mere adjustments to national boundaries or shifts in political allegiance. A different social order struggled to emerge from the turmoil and loss. Economic values were challenged by the theory of John Maynard Keynes that government intervention can resolve problems in the economy; and technology started to make itself felt as a primary force for change throughout society, fuelled by the great advances made from wartime research.

During the five years of war, industry was preoccupied with producing as much as possible, and this was particularly true of the food industry. At the height of the war in May 1943, hotels, restaurants and canteens in Britain were serving 180 million meals a week. With many having been conscripted for wartime service, Lyons' management were deflected from long-term business strategies, turning instead to logistical matters with the prime objective of surviving, and making as much money as possible. After 1945 came a period of stability and reconstruction. Even before hostilities had ended it was well understood that the British people would not be satisfied with returning to their existence of pre-war days. In July 1945 the Labour Party won a landslide victory in the general election.

Town and country planners were already working on the design and rebuilding of ruined cities. The housing shortage was a major concern, which eventually was resolved, now believed wrongly, by the construction of high-rise apartments. Many city centres were redesigned and new hotels built. By 1948 demobilisation and the restoration of economic equilibrium had led to one of the most conspicuous factors of this period: full employment. Many young families also emigrated to Australia and New Zealand to find a better life for their children. So when the 1948 British Nationality Act was passed, affirming that there was no colour bar to British citizenship, the government turned to the Caribbean to recruit labour for the massive building programmes, hospitals and transport systems which were taking shape in Britain. At this time many of the West Indian islands suffered from low wages, high unemployment and unprecedented population growth, and there was a flood of applicants, initially from the skilled trades. The first 492 official immigrants to enter Britain (many had come as stowaways) arrived on the *Empire Windrush*, which docked at Tilbury on 23-4 June 1948. Many West Indians subsequently settled in West London and thousands were employed in the food factories of Lyons.

As the fear of unemployment diminished, disposable income improved so that many working-class households were able to afford some of the luxuries which hitherto had been the indulgence of the middle class. With the advent of package holidays, many working-class families gradually began to travel abroad and the colossal post-war expansion of motor car production increasingly made ownership affordable to poorer households. People spent more of their income on a greater variety of foods and there was a trend to entertaining at home or eating out in moderately priced restaurants. Full employment, however, did not come without a price to be paid by British employers, and the period from 1948 to 1979 saw an unprecedented growth in the power of trade unions, with frequent disruptions to production as well as rising labour costs.

The Fading of the Teashops

The Meals Orders, introduced by the government during 1942, remained in force until 1 May 1950, when the Minister of Food announced their abolition. The government felt that, by lifting the restrictions on the number of courses, on what could be served as a main dish and on the prices charged for a meal, the catering industry, which included hotels, would be better placed to make a larger contribution to dollar earnings from tourism. Although the catering trade had pressed since the end of the war for the restrictions to be abolished, the announcement, when it came, surprised everyone. Remarkably, caterers had maintained price levels which had been in force since 1942, progressively adding variety when circumstances allowed. Food nevertheless remained in short supply and in 1951 the Labour government were forced to cut the meat ration to its lowest level ever, the equivalent of 4 oz of steak per person per week, when Argentina suspended shipments following Britain's refusal to a demand of £97 per ton. Faced with other shortages and building controls, Lyons were unable to make any significant improvements to their teashops until the second half of the decade and only then on a piecemeal basis. Some teashops had to close after the war because of the government's massive house and road development schemes. The teashop in East India Dock Road, an area of London which suffered badly from bomb damage, is an example. Poignantly the teashop fittings were left in place for the workers building the new Blackwall Tunnel.

In 1936 Felix Salmon (1908–69), son of Alfred Salmon, became responsible for teashops and returned to that department after wartime service in the Army Catering Corps. Like other members of his family, he began his career in 1926 in the Trocadero kitchens. After four years he transferred to bakery production, then ran Maison Lyons (the Corner House lookalike) at Marble Arch followed by the Oxford Corner House, and became a Lyons director in 1946. In 1961 he took charge of the Works Department central offices and from 1962 was responsible for central personnel functions. Between then and his retirement in 1969 he was closely involved in the reorganisation of Lyons' management structure, playing a key role in adapting the management style to the growing complexities of the business. He was forever telling his youngest brother, Ivor, to watch out when crossing the road and it is ironic that he was knocked down himself, and killed, by a Green Line bus in Redhill in 1969.

In an effort to brighten teashop interiors, in 1947 Felix Salmon commissioned a series of lithographs and original paintings by contemporary British artists. The artists he assembled included Barnett Freedman, whose wartime painting of a submarine interior had been greatly admired, and in the artists' presence the finished paintings were introduced to the press at the Trocadero restaurant by Sir Stafford Cripps, then President of the Board of Trade. Prints of the pictures were hung in all the teashops, overnight, ready for display to customers the next day. By special request a copy of each of the originals was retained and viewed by Queen Mary at a tea party organised by the directors.

Such were the difficulties in post-war Britain that only one new teashop opened between 1938 and 1951, and that was in Portsmouth in 1946. London, by contrast, waited another five years for its first post-war teashop to be opened. In a deviation from normal practice Lyons had commissioned Lonsdale Hands Associates, who were more familiar with packaging design and aircraft interiors, to design the teashop, which opened in Lower Regent Street in 1951.

Soon afterwards Lyons introduced a new operational style, based around management committees, and for the first time enabling middle managers to participate in the day-to-day running of the teashops. Hitherto, overall control had been in the hands of General Managers (family

The Watford Steak House with its open plan cooking arrangement.

directors) at one end and teashop manageresses at the other, with a sprinkling of other grades in between. Now Felix Salmon led a team of some seven executives with departmental responsibilities ranging from supply and distribution, sales, retailing operations at teashop counters (front shops) and personnel. This operational formula might have worked if all committee members had performed effectively but some were not up to the task and the team lacked professional cohesion. The driving force and direction of the management committee's activities came from the trading position. The trading figures, however, were only given in full to the directors, who then had the task of interpreting them in terms of day-to-day management, being advised solely by the cost accountants at Cadby Hall. The main drawback was that the cost accountants lacked any understanding of the teashops and in consequence many decisions were based on unrealistic advice from either the cost accountant or the head of an operational group. Since the cost accountant could not appreciate the problems typically faced by teashop managers,

the head of an operational group was unable realistically to assess the results of his actions and recommendations on the trading position. In effect, directors had to approve any type of expenditure, yet they gave, or denied, approval without always being able to evaluate the full effect on future trading. As heads of groups could find themselves making unsound recommendations for which they would then be held liable, some became increasingly reluctant to accept responsibility for either current or future work.

Since duties were not clearly defined, there was often an overlap of work – for example, between the front shop group and the food group, or between the food group and administration. Attempts to establish liaison between the groups and define duties were unsuccessful for any length of time because the division of responsibility had no basis in the business itself. The same problems soon reappeared at a different point in the artificially imposed borderlines, which were never static. In addition, the directors all tended to express their personal opinion on many subjects. This frustrating hierarchy not only confused the day-to-day operations but contributed to the abysmal morale of teashop staff.

Although there were some small trading improvements under the new regime (which may have been due to fluctuating consumer trends), the underlying financial position was still far from satisfactory. The introduction of self-service in 1941 had been a necessary expedient to address the acute labour shortages caused by the war, but its continuance after the war was one of the most important factors adversely affecting teashop popularity. In those days self-service catering was still fairly crude. Meals were put out on to plates and placed in small, box-like cubicles by staff behind the serving counters. Customers would pass along the front of these cubicles and lift the small glass-hinged doors to withdraw their choice of meal without having the opportunity to order more of this or that. When a box had been emptied a new meal was inserted. It was all too reminiscent of a factory canteen. As a result the teashops became unfashionable.

Quality was also regularly criticised. Food shortages during the war had made it necessary to substitute ingredients in many recipes, with a noticeably detrimental impact on the taste of the food. Because many of these substitutes were cheaper to buy – and raw material prices rose alarmingly after the war – the substitutes continued in use even when supplies became more plentiful. Paradoxically, food rationing prompted wealthier families to eat out, since the catering trade suffered less from shortages, especially when the Meals Orders were removed. In the 1950s Britain had nearly 235,000 catering establishments, serving 236 million meals and 320 million cups of tea and coffee every week. Against this competition Lyons struggled to attract customers. Their humble meat pie and sausage, which had served them so well in the past, had lost its charm as more young people increasingly favoured European dishes and were drawn to the American-style fast-food outlets which began to appear. With the deterioration in food quality, the lack of waitress service and a continuing upward trend in prices, not altogether the fault of Lyons, the public were no longer getting value for money.

Some improvements were made to the teashop retail counters when they converted to self-service in 1955–6. Several shops experimented with direct buying, to reduce transport costs, but this raised the question of quality and exposed the overheads at Cadby Hall. Even with unemployment at 1 per cent, and younger people having more disposable income than any previous generation, the Lyons catering business still lacked the profits it once enjoyed. In the period 1954–63 teashop numbers declined from 192 to 177, bringing about a loss in revenue of nearly £1 million, from both restaurant and front shop sales. This decline occurred when the average spending power increased by 45 per cent from 27½d. to 40d. over the same period.

Corner House Innovations: Birth of Themed Restaurants

With losses in all catering units, attention turned to the Corner Houses. Traditionally these had been run as independent units in which several management levels controlled individual operations within each establishment. The co-ordination of these multiple restaurants was in the hands of a General Manager, who reported to a main board director. While the Corner Houses remained profitable this style of management was acceptable, but when the ratio of turnover to customers seemed more material than profit their operation came under scrutiny in the early 1950s. The outcome of this study led to the implementation of standardised menus, a pricing policy, improved clerical services and labour planning. Neil Salmon (1921–89), the thirty-year-old son of Julius Salmon who became chairman in 1977 and is thought by many to have been responsible for the company's eventual collapse, introduced an experimental mechanical conveyor in the Coventry Street Corner House in 1952 to improve productivity. Although Neil Salmon was highly intelligent, and radical in his thinking, he was not always a good judge of people, or the events affecting them, and at times was rather callous towards employees. However, fortunately for the staff, the mechanical contraption was found to be unreliable and to the relief of many it was soon discontinued.

By the early 1950s Brian Salmon (b. 1917), the elder brother of Neil Salmon, had returned from a visit to the United States with the idea that speciality restaurants, built around themes, might help to revitalise the once thriving Corner House. He had started his career in the Trocadero kitchens, afterwards becoming a waiter in the restaurant and grill room there. He gained further catering experience in the Coventry Street Corner House and the Outdoor Catering Department, where he helped cater for Bank of England staff who had been evacuated from London to Hampshire at the start of the Second World War. In 1940 he joined the Royal Air Force, where he spent six years as catering officer, ending his service as a squadron leader in India. On his return to Lyons he went to manage the bakeries and took charge of the Strand Corner House, eventually becoming responsible for all the bakeries and all three Corner Houses.

Brian Salmon argued that if smaller restaurants were opened in the Corner Houses they could offer a much smaller menu selection and thereby lead to a dramatic reduction in wage costs. There would be no need for highly paid chefs and a vast range of foodstuffs. Many restaurants could even cook their uncomplicated 'grub' in full view of the customer. These ideas were put into practice during the 1950s, and it was found that when an individual dining room was restricted to a small menu the easy cooking and fast service enabled management to give outstanding value. Yet the cost of constructing and furnishing them was heavy; by the end of 1958 £2 million had been spent on the modernisation programme, the largest sum ever spent on a restaurant scheme. After the changes had been made, Lyons believed it was the most important development in eating out in fifty years: nothing in the world could be compared to it. Reductions in wage costs and public interest in these restaurants combined to improve turnover, so that by 1959 the financial position had improved.

The first of Brian Salmon's speciality restaurants was the Haversnack, which opened in the Oxford Corner House on 28 April 1952 and ran simultaneously with the Snack Counter,

which had been introduced in January 1951. The Bacon & Egg restaurant was launched first at the Coventry Street Corner House on 1 February 1954, taking advantage of the recent de-rationing of meat. A similar restaurant opened at the Oxford Corner House on 30 November 1955. These were followed by the Grill & Cheese, serving chops and steaks; the first of these set up in the Oxford Corner House on 14 September 1954 followed by one in Coventry Street on 16 July 1956. The Trolley, where roast meats were served, was established in the Oxford Corner House on 3 April 1956. Other small restaurants included the Chicken Fayre, the Seven Stars and the Restful Tray, which also opened in the Oxford Corner House on 5 October 1955.

The policy of creating 'themed' restaurants continued into the 1960s. 'The Piccadilly' was introduced to the Coventry Street Corner House in 1958; its principal aim was to serve those who were in a hurry but wanted something more substantial than is usual at a snack counter. In March 1968 a new pub-style bar opened, as part of a remodelling of the ground floor, called the Pub Alfresco. Besides the bar, the scheme included a self-contained front shop, a new ninety-two-seater Wimpy restaurant, a new entrance for customers and a separate entrance for the members of a casino being built on the third floor. The theme of the Pub Alfresco was, of course, a convivial, open-air style. It was capable of seating 120 people, and above the 57-foot bar was a stage where performers entertained customers in the evenings. Dividing the Pub Alfresco from the rest of the ground floor was a series of bow-windows, imitating the style of an old-fashioned inn and allowing other customers to look in.

The Trafalgar Room and the Carving Room were introduced into the Strand Corner House during the main refurbishment programme of 1962, and in January 1964 the Hamilton Room opened on the second floor. The marble mosaics on each wall were made from stones recovered from various teashops when they were modernised. A new seafood restaurant, the Fisherman's Wharf – which became very popular – opened in Brompton Road following the success of the Trident (fish) Restaurant in

The old London Wall teashop after its conversion to a Jolyon restaurant. The change of style did not revive teashop fortunes.

The Double Delight supermarket (J. Sainsbury) restaurant at Ipswich, 1970. *By kind permission of Raymond Hicks.*

the Strand Corner House, which coincidentally had opened on the same day that the Trident aircraft made its first commercial flight from Heathrow airport. Unfortunately this fact did not come to light until after the event and a potential advertising opportunity was lost. In 1966 a new theatre restaurant opened in the Strand Corner House under the name of Showboat, its theme and decor designed by Jack Fallon.

One of Neil Salmon's most radical suggestions was that all the Corner Houses should be grouped under a single administration manager and that departmental managers should be replaced with assistants. His idea was strongly opposed. Many members of his family considered it would have brought about a decline in standards, but, more importantly, they felt it would weaken the family links. The Corner Houses had, after all, been a training ground for many of the younger family members, who were reluctant to depart from tradition. Nevertheless, change was inevitable if the large restaurants were to return to profitability. After much debate it was agreed to carry out an experiment, with Harold Young (1921–89) being nominated as the manager of the Oxford Corner House. Young was the first non-family member to manage a major catering outlet and moved from here to the Strand and Coventry Street Corner Houses to carry through fundamental changes in management and reforms. Despite his earlier training in organisation and methods, his background in system research and his other considerable talents, it became obvious that the Corner Houses could not continue to trade alone with their uneconomical use of space and their elaborate construction in prime-cost sites. In 1956 Neil Salmon eventually had his way, and the Corner Houses were merged into a single entity under his control. Harold Young continued to play an active part in the catering reforms and in 1963 became the chief executive of the new Catering Division, where he was responsible for royal garden parties and other prestige events. In 1965 he was made an employee director and for his services to the royal household he was created a Commander of the Royal Victorian Order.

Brian Salmon was awarded the CBE in 1972 and became chairman in February of that year. Retiring on 30 June 1977, he was succeeded by his brother Neil, who was the last of the Salmon and Gluckstein families to head up the company before its takeover by Allied Breweries Ltd in 1978. The dynasty had lasted ninety-one years.

The Wimpy Bar

Lyons' most successful speciality restaurant was the Wimpy. Its success was so spectacular that it prompted management to develop a whole chain of franchised Wimpy restaurants.

The Wimpy hamburger was first introduced into this country by Eddie Gold in 1953. He had opened his first snack bar in Bloomington, Indiana, in 1934 to sell hamburgers, and had called it the Wimpy Grill after Elzie Segar's 1931 cartoon character in Popeye, J. Wellington Wimpy. As any scholar of Popeye knows, J. Wellington Wimpy was always stuffing himself with hamburgers. Eddie Gold came to England with a view to interesting Lyons in his product. At first the Lyons management were dismissive and adopted an elitist attitude. They did not want to create the impression of being snack bar operatives, and in any case they had no experience with serving fast food other than the Snack Counter and Sandwich Meal Counter in the Corner Houses. Eddie Gold then offered his product on a trial basis, without royalties or other payment. An experimental counter was opened in the Coventry Corner House in 1953 selling the Wimpy hamburger and an associated milk shake known as the Whippsy. The experiment was so impressive that Lyons introduced a similar snack bar at the 1954 Ideal Home Exhibition; it sold 10,000 hamburgers in one week. At this point Lyons came to an agreement with Eddie Gold based on royalty payments, the terms of which have not been recorded. However, the Bank of England would not allow the transfer of funds from the UK until the stringent currency controls, in place at that time, were eased. Disappointed at not being able to share in the profits, Eddie Gold continued to allow Lyons to develop his idea in the belief that the royalties, which were accruing, would eventually be paid. At the same

Outside Wimpy's headquarters in King Street, Hammersmith. A Green Line bus, in Wimpy livery, helps to promote the Wimpy hamburger. *By kind permission of Waldegrave Films.*

time he entered into further discussions with Lyons and in 1957 they agreed to set up a company, registered in the United States as Wimpy International Inc., to develop the Wimpy idea internationally. Lyons were granted UK rights in the Wimpy and 51 per cent of the new company equity, while Gold received a cash settlement, believed to be half a million dollars, and 49 per cent of the company equity.

Meanwhile hamburger sales continued to rocket at the Coventry Street Corner House, and the snack bar was enlarged in May 1955. During the next six weeks the number of customers averaged 42,500 per week on just 120 covers (seats) with an average seating time of fifteen minutes at the counter and twenty minutes in the banquettes. These statistics – 77 per cent occupancy between 10.30 in the morning and 12 at night – were quite unrecognisable compared with previous restaurant performance. Soon, Wimpy restaurants were operating in the Oxford Corner House (from September 1958) and elsewhere, and in the mid-1950s the first

experimental Wimpy bar opened in the basement of the teashop at 277 Oxford Street followed by another one in Hammersmith Broadway. Franchising was introduced in 1957 through a newly formed subsidiary, Pleasure Foods Ltd, which was registered on 3 May 1957 specifically to grant licences. Pleasure Foods provided advice on restaurant siting, marketing, operating ideas and all products. Within a few years the Wimpy Restaurant chain spread rapidly across the world.

In 1968, when the ground floor of the Coventry Street Corner House was redesigned, Lyons opened a new Wimpy restaurant seating ninety-two. The restaurant was situated in the self-service area of the front shop. Because business in groceries had declined after supermarkets opened in Soho, the new front shop was smaller and concentrated on selling the specialities for which Lyons were noted, such as gateaux, delicatessen, cocktail party food and the famous petit fours. The Wimpy restaurant had a colourful 1960s design including a metal-tiled ceiling sprayed with 'Wimpy poppy red'. Its walls, covered with rosewood laminate, were decorated with large gold Wimpy bun shapes. The seating comprised vinyl-upholstered banquettes and the curtains at the end of the restaurant were bright scarlet. A feature of the decor which attracted much attention was the polystyrene clouds which hung from the ceiling near the entrance. The Wimpy restaurant provided a full waitress service, the uniforms being midnight-blue dresses with red aprons.

In the late 1960s Wimpy bars were opening at the rate of one a week, somewhere in the world. By the end of 1968 new Wimpys had been opened in Frankfurt, Cologne and Rotterdam; more were set up in Lebanon, Cyprus, Luxembourg, Libya, Tanzania, Uganda and the Canaries. Wimpy's growth seemed unstoppable. The Wimpy subsidiary, Ristoranti Italiani Wimpy srl, launched Italy's first Wimpy bar on the fashionable Via Veneto in Rome; it was designed by Minale Tattersfield, Provinciali Ltd, one of Italy's most progressive firms. When Amsterdam's first Wimpy opened in November 1963 the rush of customers was so great that the doors had to be shut after an hour to allow the staff time to cope.

The Wimpy hamburger, made from minced beef, was grilled on a large flat griddle (normally in full view of the customer) and eaten with cooked onions in a toasted bun; in restaurants it was served with French fries or salad. The ingredients and style of operation enabled big economies to be made and after other trials in selected teashops a decision was taken to expand the franchise more widely. By 1969 Lyons had opened 461 Wimpy restaurants in the United Kingdom and by 1973 one thousand Wimpy restaurants overseas.

Henry Telfer – the meat subsidiary company – tooled up to produce hamburgers, which were frozen before dispatch. The exception to this were the hamburgers produced by the central butcher's shop in the Coventry Street Corner House for use in the Corner House Wimpy restaurants. The buns were produced by Lyons' own bakeries, which already had experience of producing soft buns for the US forces stationed in the United Kingdom during and after the war. Soft ice-cream used in the Whippsy milk shake was supplied by Lyons Maid.

The London Steak Houses

In the summer of 1962 Lyons took over the Liverpool-based Robley Group, a business managed by Robert Roberts, who had started his career when he left the Army Catering Corps in 1946 with a sergeant's gratuity. After a short association with the Bowler Hat Club in the Wirral, in 1949 he opened the Rembrandt Club in Liverpool which soon became one of the best-known licensed dining clubs in the north of England. Roberts teamed up with David Leach, an accountant and expert in licensing law. By 1962 their company had opened some thirty-five clubs in the Liverpool area. Lyons had paid £19,000 cash plus an exchange of 57,198 'A' non-voting shares in Lyons for the Robley business, by which they hoped to increase volume sales.

Having introduced Lyons methods into the new enterprise, management experimented with other types of food outlets such as the Golden Egg (started by Philip and Reggie Kaye, who had been running Wimpy bar franchises since 1958), the Egg & Platter – a licensed restaurant which

opened in Kingston on 18 July 1963 – Chips with Everything, Bake'n' Take and, not least, the London Steak Houses. The first of these opened in Baker Street in 1961, just before a change in the law made it easier to obtain drink licences. Catering for the higher-spending customer, the London Steak House spawned from the successful Grill & Cheese restaurants which had been introduced into the Corner Houses some years earlier. As the new scheme did not initially have the full support of the Lyons board, the catering development team judged that their Steak House initiative could not be allowed the same level of investment as the Corner House Grill & Cheeses. Therefore the Baker Street restaurant was created using in-house resources and standard catering equipment; the first 100-seat London Steak House was converted from a Lovibond off-licence for a mere £19,000. An off-licence was chosen in preference to a closed teashop because the premises had already been granted a liquor licence for its former trade and the authorities would be less likely to refuse an application for a licensed restaurant there. A proposal, initiated by the catering management, to purchase

London Steak Houses, clockwise from top left: Blackheath; King's Road, Chelsea; the Pantiles, Tunbridge Wells; Epsom; Scotland Yard; Windsor.

Lovibond's one hundred outlets as a means of guaranteeing successful application for more Steak Houses was turned down by the Lyons board.

The Baker Street Steak House became popular almost overnight and traded at a such a high level that the board rapidly embraced the further expansion with enthusiasm. Increasingly, however, people who dined out in restaurants tended to travel by car. As traffic congestion worsened and parking became more difficult in city centres, the expansion of the London Steak House restaurants developed outwards, initially within a fifty-mile radius of London, from the traditional West End to the more affluent suburbs such as Wimbledon, Harrow, Epsom and Dulwich. Eventually there were forty-seven London Steak Houses in service, including several in provincial cities and towns, such as Bristol, Birmingham, Gloucester, Cheltenham, Norwich and Southampton (see Appendix 4). Most, nevertheless, were located in Greater London, and after the run-down of the Jolyon restaurants (see later in this chapter) old teashop sites were converted into Steak Houses or Wimpy restaurants. The new

Licensing Act, which came into force in 1961, helped increase the Steak Houses' popularity and made it less difficult for companies to obtain licences for catering establishments.

The London Steak Houses were managed by Harold Young and Peter Byford, who were appointed the first directors of a new private company, London Steak Houses Ltd, which registered on 21 February 1962. Both London Steak Houses Ltd and Pleasure Foods Ltd – like the vast majority of Lyons' subsidiary companies – effectively traded as dormant companies carrying on their business without remuneration as nominees on behalf of the umbrella holding company, J. Lyons & Co. Ltd. As a consequence there was no profit and loss account; therefore the financial trading situation did not have to be declared publicly but instead was consolidated, with the other Lyons trading subsidiaries, into the accounts for Lyons.

The original Baker Street Steak House, which had seating for a hundred, had been converted at a cost of just £190 per customer. When the board decided to proceed with more London Steak Houses, however, the inevitable 'Lyons Committee' took root, headed by a family member and a professional designer – in this case Dennis Lennon – leading to a steep rise in costs. The sixty-seat Wimbledon Steak House opened next at a cost £40,000, or £667 per customer. Kensington followed with an eighty-seat restaurant costing £60,000 (£750 per customer). Each London Steak House had its own unique design. This caused a huge reduction in the return on capital which, along with other factors, eventually caused their decline after forty-seven had been opened.

Some of the centrally located Steak Houses in London, particularly those in the main shopping areas such as the West End, failed to attract enough customers in the evenings. This was true of the Clifford Street Steak House, near Bond Street. Peter Byford and Leslie Crowhurst, manager of the public houses, and Donald Coope, London Steak Houses catering manager, came up with the idea of transforming the restaurant in the evening to what was called Cliffords Bistrotheque. Every day after its opening in April

1968, the lunchtime Steak House was transformed into a bistro and discotheque, by dimming the lighting and placing candles on the tables. A small dance floor was specially introduced and was spot-lit with ultraviolet lamps. In the evenings the front of the restaurant was brightly lit and a gaily coloured placard announced, 'Cliffords Bistrotheque is now open'. A new bistro menu was introduced, with prices aimed at young executives. An eighteen-year-old actress, Jane Bethall, was employed as DJ, and the Steak House managers, both in their early twenties, put on polo-necked silk shirts, while the waiters wore colourful shirts with bow-ties. Cliffords Bistrotheque had an informal atmosphere designed to appeal to young people who frequented both French bistros, where they were introduced to Pernod, and the 1960s innovation of the discotheque, which had relatively recently displaced dancing to live bands.

A Radical Transformation: the Catering Division

Throughout the whole of Lyons' current catering empire more than three million meals were sold each week. The streamlined menus and speciality restaurants enabled economies to be made in the use of labour, equipment and space. Staff training became simplified, and, more importantly, catering staff tended to be less qualified than before. Opportunities for expansion continued with the rising standard of living. The speciality restaurants at the Corner Houses demonstrated how waitress service, counter service and self-service could be balanced and combined to meet changing needs.

By the 1960s the catering development group were intent on replacing the teashop chain. They had tried unsuccessfully to convince the board that mass catering was moving from the high streets to the new arterial roads where more people were travelling by car. Some companies had already started to establish themselves on these motor routes and a small operation consisting of approximately three units, the Little Chef, was targeted by the catering management for a possible takeover. It was proposed that a number of Little Chef-style restaurants should

An artist's impression of the Diplomat Restaurant in Mount Street, London. When it closed in 1967 Lyons' Sebastian Restaurant was renamed Dukes so that the expensive monogrammed china from the Diplomat could be re-used. *By kind permission of Waldegrave Films.*

be established, at the cost of no more than £25,000 each, furnished in a basic, unadorned style and, most importantly, incorporating a simplified administration with a high level of autonomy. The figures had been meticulously calculated with a realistic estimate of building and fitting-out costs; however, the directors then appointed Terence Conran, whose design costs more than doubled the £25,000 investment suggested by the catering development group. Furthermore, the board were unwilling to consider any form of administration other than that which existed in the teashops and Corner Houses at the time. As a consequence the project became economically unsound and eventually fizzled out.

During the same period the catering development group considered a scheme for creating quick, snack-like outlets in the emerging supermarkets which were increasingly attracting customers away from traditional high street shops. Coincidentally, Sainsbury, which had discontinued individual distribution and processing in favour of centralised commissaries, found themselves with surplus floor space in many of their supermarkets and contemplated renting it out for cafés providing low-price snacks inside supermarkets. Again Lyons directors insisted on introducing a comprehensive menu at a high price and wanted to incorporate the cafés within the existing teashop administration, with all the attendant costs. Supermarket snack bars – like the basic motor restaurants – again became an expensive idea and plans for these also faded.

During 1961 serious thought was given to merging the teashop and Corner House operations, prompting the question whether Lyons' catering should be completely reorganised. For many years the Corner Houses had been overstaffed (Coventry Street alone employed 570), with an extravagant hierarchy of managers. Working practices and staffing levels were frequently altered to satisfy the outdoor catering events such as Wimbledon, the Chelsea Flower Show and the Buckingham Palace garden parties, which, though unprofitable, were considered important enough prestige events to outweigh financial considerations. Catering at Wimbledon, for example, had made a loss for eighteen years until it was rationalised and restructured in 1962. So confused had thinking become that two studies were commissioned. John Simmons, assisted by Len Badham and Harold Young, both of whom had different kinds of experience of the Corner Houses, conducted the first study; and Stuart Dorizzi, of the recently formed Lyons Marketing Consultancy Unit, undertook the second study, which focused on marketing policies.

John Simmons completed his survey in September 1962, when he produced a report that was highly critical of Lyons' catering as a whole and in so doing did not endear himself to the catering management. He found that almost all restaurants, teashops and Corner Houses were loss-making, with no prospects of becoming profitable in the foreseeable future. Nobody had a feel for high street business with its intricate balance of shop rental, turnover and profit. In particular, General Managers had always been handicapped by their lack of overall control of the teashops. For example, while Major Montague Gluckstein had overall responsibility for the teashops' profitability, at least until 1945, Harry Salmon was responsible for Lyons property, including teashop property, and Maurice Salmon for the factory at Cadby Hall where the teashops obtained their supplies. It was Maurice Salmon who set the prices paid by the teashops, and Harry

Salmon who determined the rate of return on teashop real estate; thus Monte Gluckstein could not easily maintain control of profitability.

Simmons also criticised the anti-social effect on staff of continuous trading and suggested offering part-time jobs to overcome the problems of shift working (unfortunately this simply increased labour costs and resulted in even greater losses). He found that the London Steak House chain operated in a distinctly healthier manner, but compared with a total catering turnover of over £16 million the small Steak House profit was scant encouragement. Simmons argued that catering should be classed as entertainment and that the relationship between customer and restaurateur needed to be made more personal. Restaurants could not, therefore, mass-produce their meals, although they might make use of mass production facilities. According to Simmons's analysis a successful large catering business should be composed of a number of smaller units, either of the same type or not, depending on circumstances. In this way, he deduced, the whole business would maintain flexibility with profitable evolution. In addition, his report proposed a new costing system. Simmons's study also recommended that increased responsibility be given to line managers, who should be in charge of up to five autonomous units, supported by a modified central function. Since Simmons's brief had been wide-ranging, he also recommended that a new marketing organisation be established; but this was being considered in more detail by Stuart Dorizzi.

Simmons's most controversial proposal was that the catering business should put forward and implement its own organisation plan. This idea was far too radical for the Lyons board to accept and his detailed suggestions were rejected. Nevertheless, by November 1962 Brian and Michael Salmon (son of Barnett Salmon the younger) had studied Simmons's report carefully, and, with minor reservations, the Lyons board accepted his plan in general as showing the way ahead.

Stuart Dorizzi's report, however, had put forward even more radical proposals, although in some ways they were similar to those of Simmons. He called for a total reappraisal of the teashops' costing system, advocating, like Simmons, a self-contained organisation but with an effective marketing unit which, if implemented, would be very costly. His ideas were considered to be too ambitious and impractical and so they were politely rejected.

In order to improve management control, the Teashops Department, as it had been known hitherto, was grouped with other catering establishments into regions and became part of a newly formed Catering Division in 1963. At the same time a vast modernisation programme was undertaken in an effort to revitalise the teashops' image. Orchard House, for many years the teashop headquarters where 300 clerical staff were employed, took on a new role and became part of the enlarged Catering Division. Some members of the teashop administration moved out to the regions, but other departments, such as the London Steak Houses, moved in and the new management took over their first pub, the Lion and Lamb in Brentwood, Essex. At this time the transportation cost of supplying the London teashops alone was put at over £200,000 and so by 1966 the teashop production facilities at Cadby Hall were closed and individual teashops assumed responsibility for their own supplies and for cooking and heating all food and drink on site. By December 1970 the Catering Division had become a wholly owned subsidiary under the name, J. L. Catering Ltd – bringing together under one director all the company's catering operations. Lyons' chairman Sir Samuel Salmon (1900–80) spoke of these changes in his Annual Report to shareholders in 1967:

> The newly formed Catering Sector comprises the Catering Division (teashops, Corner Houses, restaurants and public houses) and the subsidiaries engaged in catering franchise operations. All these activities are now under the overall control of one single Director. Among the many advantages of integrating our 'own-managed' and 'franchise-managed' catering activities more closely in this way is that each division will be better placed to learn from the experience of the other.

We have continued our hard look at the nature and organisation of the Catering Division. The changes in supply arrangements to which I referred last year have been completed: many of our restaurants' food requirements are now delivered direct to them by outside suppliers, while virtually all cooking is now carried out on site. The new system has already proved its advantages in practice. We have also established new marketing and planning resources for the Division, and important managerial changes have been made with the object of delegating authority as far as possible down the line.

Experiments in Catering

Lyons' policy of treating catering as entertainment led to one of the most radical changes to a Corner House. It was decided to convert part of the Coventry Street premises into a gaming casino. The 600-seat Windsor Room, used for banquets and private parties, was moved to make space for it. Plans were laid by Harold Young, chief executive of the Catering Division, in October 1966, when in partnership with Frixos Joannou Demetriou – a naturalised Cypriot and owner of the Olympic Casino Club in Queensway, London – he incorporated Olympic Entertainment Ltd to manage the new enterprise. When it opened in March 1968, gamblers had to become members of the casino before they were allowed at the tables where roulette, baccarat, blackjack, dice, punto banco, kalouki and poker were played. A restaurant adjoined the gaming room and, like the casino, was open from 3.00 p.m. until the early hours of the following morning. Four months after the launch of the Coventry Street casino another opened at the Strand Corner House. Occupying space on the second floor, previously used for the Hamilton Restaurant, it was smaller but had similar features including a casino restaurant.

Lyons were operating 120 teashops in 1969 when they experienced their most radical transformation in one last attempt to revitalise them. Under a £2 million conversion programme it was decided, foolishly according to some, to give teashops a new look and to rename them Jolyon (pronounced Jo-lee-on) restaurants. The name Jolyon, which had been registered before the start of the Second World War, had been chosen because it reflected the famous name of Joe Lyons while suggesting a distinctive new image. Further, the name had been given worldwide publicity by the hugely popular television adaptation in the 1960s of John Galsworthy's *Forsyte Saga*, in which 'old Jolyon' was played by the actor Kenneth More. With such omens, success seemed inevitable to Harold Young, the Catering Division's chief executive, who took charge of the transformation. By the end of March 1970 five Jolyon self-service restaurants had been created, the first at Marble Arch in August 1969, the last at London Wall in 1973, seven months behind schedule. Restaurants that had been granted liquor licences were called Jolyon Grills, and these were staffed with waiters and waitresses.

This change of identity, funded by high levels of investment, failed to generate the anticipated interest. Jolyon became a non-entity and the slide in profits continued. By 1977 the inevitable closure programme had started. On 4 January 1981 Lyons teashops passed into history as the last branch closed at Marble Arch. The Piccadilly teashop had closed on 26 September 1976, having provided an unbroken eighty-two-year service to Londoners, through two world wars and the reigns of five monarchs. Meantime other experiments in catering continued.

The imposition of corporation tax, capital gains tax, a new system of investment incentives and a selective employment tax (imposed by the Finance Act of 1966) disadvantaged the catering industry. A weekly employment tax of 25 shillings for male employees over eighteen and 12s. 6d. for women (lower rates applied to those under eighteen) reduced profits from the Corner Houses, although the London Steak House and Wimpy restaurants continued to perform reasonably well. In the twelve months between March 1966 and March 1967 the turnover of the Coventry Street Corner House also fell by £144,000 and the Oxford Corner House by nearly £150,000, forcing the closure of the Oxford Corner House in May 1967, the Coventry Street in August 1969 and the Strand in 1977; surprisingly the Strand Corner House had performed better than the others in its later years. The London Steak Houses, by contrast, increased their turnover by £100,000 in the same period.

Many of the Steak Houses benefited from overseas visitors and in 1970, to encourage this trade, the Catering Division (J. L. Catering Ltd in 1971) purchased a small chain of five travel agencies and placed them under the management of Bill Brickell. For some years he had been promoting and selling a voucher scheme and group party catering to overseas travel agents to encourage them to make more use of Lyons' catering outlets for their travellers. After the chain of travel agents had been acquired, Brickell became eligible to attend the Association of British Travel Agents conferences abroad and was thus able to use the opportunity to promote Lyons' catering and hotel facilities to a wider overseas travel market. These travel agencies were augmented in July 1973 when Lyons paid £123,000 for LSA Young Travellers Ltd and LSA World Travel Service Ltd.

A reversal in company fortunes led to the disposal of the Wimpy business assets in December 1976 to United Biscuits (Holdings) Ltd, whose subsidiary, D.S. Crawford Ltd, had become a principal Wimpy franchisee. The consideration consisted of 6,572,770 fully paid ordinary shares of 25p each in United Biscuits which realised £7 million in cash. This compared with a book value for the business of just over £1 million. The sale of Wimpy assets was confined to the United Kingdom but options to acquire the much smaller operations in Europe were offered for a nominal consideration. The wholly-owned subsidiary of Henry Telfer Ltd continued to supply most of the hamburgers, and the effect of the disposal did not initially have any significant impact on their business.

The Upper Crust

Experimentation in restaurant styles continued throughout the 1970s. In a rush of madness Lyons even tried out the idea of placing a restaurant

An advertising programme and a ticket issued on 27 June 1971 for a tour of London (with meal) on Lyons' Upper Crust bus restaurant.

Not many experiences for the visitor to London can be called unique.

A trip with **The Upper Crust** will be one of them.

7,500,000 people will crowd into Britain's capital city in 1971, and for the privileged few a journey with **The Upper Crust** will be a highlight of their stay.

What is **The Upper Crust?**

Simply, one of the world-famous London red buses coach-built to provide a 24-seat restaurant on the top deck with specially fitted wide-screen windows.

In this restaurant **Upper Crusters** will be able to enjoy a three hour trip and watch a panorama of historic London unfold. As they do so, the very best of food and drink will be served. And, all in the price of the ticket. No extras, no fussing with money or tips.

As our privileged passengers sip champagne they can forget about London's crowded underground railway, leave aside the sheafs of 'how to get there' literature.

That's all taken care of.

Houses of Parliament? (Have another glass of champagne).

Westminster Abbey? (We hope you'll enjoy that smoked salmon).

The Monument? (It marks the spot where the Great London started in 1666), appropriately enough slipping our superb scotch beef steaks under the roll past!

The cabin staff will make sure that those champ keep popping, and that things are running smoo downstairs galley.

There'll be no need for 'request' stops, by the got our own built-in comfort station with a han up' room next door.

Nothing will have been forgotten in our efforts t time with the **Upper Crust** unforgettable.

Upper Crust tours will start from London's V Station. Tickets will cost £10-a-head. Champagne of your choice will be served throughout the trip.

The main meal will consist of four courses and a typical menu is shown on page 4. Reservations may be made through the agents listed or by telephoning 01 (from outside London) 839 3678 or telex 915503 (Tourcater Ldn.).

The bus may be reserved for private parties or day outings and a price will be quoted on request.

Services and Prices subject to alteration without notice.

Printed in England

on the top deck of a London bus. The motorised omnibus had first appeared on the streets of London in 1899, replacing the earlier horse-drawn bus, and one of Londoners' pleasures right up to the start of the Second World War was to sit on the open-top deck and enjoy the ride. The London bus became an icon when tourism returned and Lyons' management decided that their appeal could be exploited by providing tourists with food and drink while they were sightseeing. It seemed an innovative idea and no doubt deflected attention away from the teashops, which were causing great anguish. No projected finance details of this piece of inspiration have survived, but its viability must have been extremely questionable, given the numbers of people one bus could accommodate in comparison to restaurant volumes.

Nevertheless, at a cost of £18,500, British Leyland supplied one of their Atlantean buses, and it was specially adapted for the catering task at a Southampton boat yard. The lower deck contained kitchens and other facilities including toilets, telephone and air-conditioning plant, while the upper deck had been fitted out as a twenty-four-seat restaurant with wide-screen windows. Lyons called this mobile restaurant the Upper Crust, and the first bus went into service in May 1971. According to their advertising material:

Upper Crusters will be able to enjoy a three hour trip and watch a panorama of historic London unfold. As they do, the very best of food and drink will be served. And all in the price of the ticket. No extras, no fussing with money or tips. As our privileged passengers sip champagne they can forget about London's crowded underground railway, leave aside the sheafs of *how to get there* literature. That's all taken care of. Houses of Parliament? (Have another glass of champagne.) Westminster Abbey? (We hope you'll enjoy that smoked salmon.) The Monument? (It marks the spot where the Great Fire of London started in 1666), appropriately enough we'll be slipping our superb Scotch beef steaks under the grill as we roll past! The cabin staff will make sure those champagne corks keep popping, and that things are running smoothly in the downstairs galley. There'll be no need for *request* stops, by the way. We've got our own built-in comfort station with a handy freshen-up room next door.

The tour started and ended at Victoria coach station, and tickets were sold through tour operators at £10 per head. The original intention was to stop the Upper Crust at Blackheath so that the meal could be served while the bus was at a standstill, but legal advice ruled this out: diners must eat while travelling at 15 miles an hour because the licensing authorities pronounced that the bus would be a restaurant if it were stationary. The meal consisted of smoked salmon, Scotch fillet steak and salad, fresh strawberries and cream, cheese, coffee, claret, champagne, brandy and liqueurs – which represented 90 per cent of the £10 ticket cost. Two timings were offered: 12–3 p.m. and 8-11p.m., excluding Mondays.

Despite the detailed planning, the Upper Crust was not a success. Between June 1971 and February 1972 the tour ran for only eighty-eight days and was just breaking even. The most serious problem was the bus's mechanical reliability, as several breakdowns occurred during the first weeks of operation. Lyons were also issued with a police summons for selling alcohol on a public bus and fined £50 with £50 costs. If this were not trouble enough, Lyons soon found themselves in competition with a rival concern run by Frank Morris, a Canadian-born entrepreneur, whose 'Victourama' service provided essentially the same facilities but was based on Queen Victoria's railway carriage, with velvet curtains, engraved glass, leather seats and gas lamps. To add nostalgic atmosphere, a waitress served in period costume. Unlike Lyons, this company planned to operate without the blessing of the Metropolitan Traffic Commissioner by serving a roast beef luncheon for £3.75 taken in Battersea Park while the vehicle was stationary. Frank Morris's company did not, however, survive for very long and went into liquidation.

After the liquor summons fiasco, Lyons introduced an all-charter system to avoid any further clashes with the law, and the Upper Crust was hired out for special occasions. The *Daily Mirror*, for example, hired it to entertain guests at a Varsity rugby match at Twickenham and a private individual spent £260 to hire the bus for his son's bar mitzvah. On one occasion in October 1971 the Hertz organisation chartered it for a fourteen-day return trip to Cannes to attend the Association of British Travel Agents convention there. The journey to and through France was beset by mechanical troubles but the bus eventually arrived after the splendid intervention of the British Consulate – and a plumber to repair the brakes – where it was said that 'the Upper Crust stole the show'. The last reported hiring of the bus was in February 1972 when it was used to entertain journalists during the launch of a new Lyons Harvest Popular Pie.

Nevertheless these public relations exercises did not generate any further interest in the concept of bus restaurants, and quite how management expected to make it work is difficult to comprehend. With hindsight it appears to have been nothing more than an extravagant pipe-dream doomed to failure from the day of its conception.

In the meantime Lyons had more successfully exploited the boom in tourism by modernising, building and acquiring hotels.

Hotel Chains

THE CUMBERLAND, Regent Palace and Strand Palace hotels had survived the war years intact. Unfortunately the Regent Palace Hotel had suffered bomb damage in 1940. On 30 June 1944 it was hit again, this time by a flying bomb which killed a waitress on the top floor and caused injury to guests living in the hotel's annexe. Unlike the three main central London hotels, the Royal Palace Hotel had been requisitioned by the government at the beginning of the war to house Gibraltarian refugees, mainly Maltese in origin, as well as staff from the war ministries, and made no further contribution to Lyons' hotel business. By the time the last of the refugees had departed the Royal Palace had become run down and a buyer was sought. An agreement to sell it to Charles Forte fell through but it was eventually bought in the early 1950s by Maxwell Joseph, of Grand Metropolitan, for £375,000.

In the aftermath of the war, food rationing continued for some time, and price capping on meals tended to constrain hotel catering activities. Strikes became a feature of day-to-day life, including a strike by waiters at some of the leading London hotels including the Strand and Regent Palace hotels between 8 and 15 October 1946. It was called off after the Hotels and Restaurants Association (which in June 1948 merged with the Residential Hotels Association to form the British Hotels and Restaurants Association) – whose members included the Strand and Regent Palace hotels – agreed to recognise the National Union of General and Municipal Workers. In March 1948 the first wages regulations for licensed hotels

and restaurants were enforced by the government. The tipping system, however, baffled the Catering Wages Commission, who advised wages boards to ignore tips when fixing wage rates. Catering wages legislation continued until 1952 and was a burden on hotel and restaurant owners. The *Caterer* demanded drastic amendments to the Catering Wages Act, which it described as 'a hydra-headed nightmare, thwarting and crippling employers at every turn'. It was not until 1959, however, that the Act was abolished and the wages boards were converted into wages councils under the more flexible Wages Councils Act.

Scientific Management

At this time the day-to-day running of each hotel was under the control of a General Manager – a member of or a participant in the Lyons board who was individually accountable directly to the board. Various hotel functions such as buying and management accounting (primarily checking and stock control) had a degree of central co-ordination at the hotel's head office in Sherwood Street near Piccadilly Circus, and it was here too that the financial accounting, company secretarial and legal functions were dealt with by the company's secretariat.

Between 1945 and the late 1950s there was no central co-ordination of marketing within the hotel group. It might well have been argued that, since the three hotels were extremely popular and maintained very high levels of occupancy, virtually throughout the year, there was no need for any marketing policy. Similarly there was no advertising, no seasonal variation in room rates, and no discounting to travel agents or tour operators. Party bookings were not welcome. Price increases usually applied only to individual hotels; in September 1951, for example, the price of single rooms at the Regent Palace and Strand Palace hotels was raised from 20s. 6d. to 22s. (31s. 6d. to 34s. for doubles), whereas the Cumberland rates remained unchanged. However, to ensure that the hotels kept up with the increasing competition – in 1949 television was installed in all rooms of the Strand, Regent Palace and Cumberland hotels – a sales promotion team was established in the late 1950s which gave some degree of co-ordination between the three hotels. But it was not until 1960 that the Hotels Administration, as it became known, was set up, to provide a more structured central management. It comprised a chairman, Douglas Gluckstein (1909–98) who was a grandchild of the firm's co-founder, Montague Gluckstein, the individual General Managers and three representatives from head office. While almost all the day-to-day management of the individual hotels remained the responsibility of the three General Managers, the Hotels Administration decided on policy for the hotel group as a whole – primarily marketing, which included pricing, sales promotion and advertising, but also personnel terms and conditions.

From about 1954 the Strand Hotel Ltd had started to introduce the specialist services which had been utilised in the manufacturing areas of Lyons for many years. Many feared it would not be possible to transpose management techniques from factories into hotels, where personal service was highly rated, but gradual application of these techniques resolved most of the misgivings. By contrast outside observers and hotel trade journals welcomed these advances as essential steps towards improving the industry.

Before long the Strand Hotel Ltd became a model for so-called 'scientific management' largely through its detailed budgeting methods and the production of weekly trading results, based upon actual performance, immediately after the events. This allowed quick action to be taken to remedy any deviation from budgeted costs. Likewise, material and labour costs were

critically examined and applied from the Control Group and Work Study Departments. As office tasks became increasingly mechanised, the Strand Hotel Ltd introduced O & M (organisation and methods) and later electronic data processing, which had so successfully been used within Lyons – in 1968 Digital's largest PDP8/1 computer was in operation at the Strand Palace Hotel for reservations. The first work study observations on room service were carried out at the Regent Palace Hotel in 1954 by John Hutchinson, the hotel group's work study manager.

The new specialists in administration were also available for consultation on the more spasmodic work on developments. Every aspect of every hotel project, whether for existing hotels or for new ones, had to be planned meticulously in advance, with training manuals prepared. All areas were organised to cope with the forecast demand and with the exact materials and plant to be used. This often led to an unconventional but entirely efficient floor plan. This advance preparation became the province of the specialists because operation managers were frequently not appointed until several years after the plans were drawn up.

In later years, and after considerable exposure to the hotel environment, the specialist administrators were able to cut hotel staffing by up to 50 per cent by measuring the work to be done, deploying staff on rotas in accordance with demand, introducing simpler services and taking advantage of convenience foods. The impact of any change was assessed and controlled to ensure that real savings in costs had been made. Experience of running hotels led to the adoption of different methods and hotel layouts in the early phases of new developments. For example, hotel space was calculated by using a model which enabled the size of a new hotel to be determined more accurately, as well as allowing shortcomings in architects' proposals to be identified at the planning stage so that corrections could be made before it was too late.

The construction of new hotels remained frustrated. There was little enthusiasm from the Lyons board, perhaps because of the death in

1940 of Julius Salmon and in 1950 of Harry Salmon, the two most influential figures in the early hotel history. In 1947 Harry Salmon had been appointed one of the twelve board members of the Tourist, Hotel, Catering and Holiday Services Board which the government had set up in January of that year to rehabilitate and expand Britain's tourist and holiday services. Nevertheless, within the hotel group there was awareness of growing competition from rival firms' new hotels, principally in London, which were better able to meet the increasing demand from both the business and burgeoning tourist market. Of constant concern was how long the Regent Palace Hotel, without private bathrooms, could maintain its popularity, especially as its lease was due to expire in 1992. A significant programme of refurbishment was undertaken between 1956 and 1965, not only to modernise the accommodation but to overhaul the catering operations which had become less profitable. By April 1964, in only thirty-two weeks, 292 bathroom suites had been added to the Strand Palace Hotel. However, the incorporation of bathrooms into existing hotel structures is seldom satisfactory, and in time this proved to be the case with the Strand Palace Hotel where, with hindsight, it would have been more expedient to have undertaken this work during the £500,000 extension of 1928–30.

Plans to add bathrooms to the Regent Palace Hotel had been under regular review but the acute planning problems – site, construction and cost – all compounded into a 'let's leave it alone for now' attitude. This was not difficult to

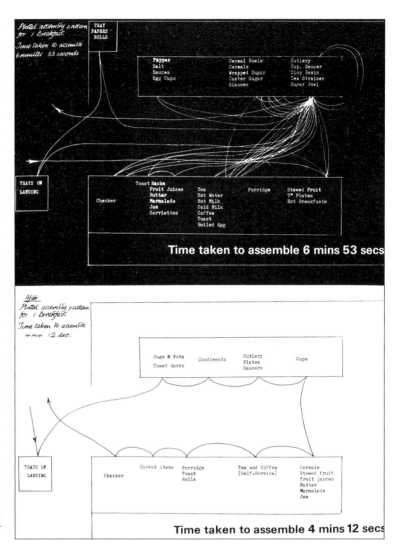

A schematic diagram prepared by the hotels' work study department showing how a simple rearrangement of a breakfast table can save waiters' time. *By kind permission of Ralph Morhaim.*

rationalise when the hotel was virtually full all year, and making a substantial trading profit. Its popularity with Londoners themselves was reinforced when Britain's first carvery restaurant opened on 1 October 1960. Christopher Salmon's father-in-law, a hotelier himself, had come across the idea while on a visit to America and Christopher seized on the idea when hearing of it. The concept of diners carving their own meat from a selection of roasted joints – the vegetables were always carrots and roast potatoes – for a fixed price was unique. With full tables every night, and some diners waiting in line, since tables could not be booked, no time was lost in introducing the idea into other hotels. At one point Lyons even tried to patent the name to prevent others from copying them but without success. The 'carvery' was an immediate and lasting success, and probably the only innovation in catering that has lasted (albeit with many variations) until the present day.

The First New Post-war Hotel: the Ariel at Heathrow

The 'X' Scheme, the development of the Trocadero site for a 1,000-room hotel and ancillary activities, was first considered in 1944 and had taken up much time and effort over a period of some ten to fifteen years. The advantages of the scheme were trivialised by Lyons (it was probably the finest site in London for a new hotel) and the risks exaggerated, although a preliminary costing prepared in 1955 was put at nearly £5 million on the assumption that the new hotel would occupy the whole of the Trocadero and Coventry Street Corner House site. General Management at this time, numbering eighteen, believed the level of investment was too high, even suggesting that the site was totally unsuitable for such development. Barnett Salmon (1895–1965), brother of Felix and Ivor Salmon, and a main-board director closely involved with the hotel operation at this time, was convinced that building new hotels was unwise. He cited the high cost of loans for building the Cumberland Hotel and the insufficient return on capital. He also argued that a new hotel could seriously damage the trade of the Strand and Regent Palace hotels even though a 'Visitor to Britain Study' had concluded that shortage of accommodation was the main impediment to increased booking of visitors to Britain by foreign travel agents. The altercations, which continued into the 1960s, were finally put to rest in 1961 when Sir William Holford, a consultant to London County Council, announced comprehensive plans for the redevelopment of Piccadilly Circus which vitally affected the greater part of the Trocadero site. In the 1960s there was no formal provision for participation in the planning process and when the Piccadilly Circus redevelopment scheme became known there was a torrent of contempt from traditional architects and public bodies. However, careful consideration was given to Holford's proposals by Lyons but there were so many uncertainties that the 'X' Scheme was finally dropped. The Strand Hotel Ltd was more optimistic, as can be seen from the chairman's statement to shareholders in December 1962:

> The trend of expansion which of recent years has been a feature of the industry is continuing and new hotels of varying size are being projected, either alone or as part of mixed development schemes. Openings undoubtedly exist in some parts of the country, and careful study of them may reveal good prospects of a satisfactory return on investment. In principle, therefore, we can consider the present trend a healthy sign of confidence in the future. In relation to the West End of London, however, we venture the opinion that new and projected accommodation at high prices may well have reached the stage of over-estimating the demand perhaps because some estimates are coloured by the conspicuous pressure during certain months of the year.

The catalyst for expansion came in the combination of two events: first, an approach from Watney's the brewers for the construction of a hotel on a site they owned on the Bath Road, close to Heathrow airport; and, second, the sale of the Royal Palace Hotel, with its disposal proceeds providing the bulk of the £500,000 building costs. The initiative for this development was picked up by Julian Salmon (1903–78), younger son of Isidore Salmon. Although at the time a director of Strand Hotel Ltd, Julian Salmon was not directly involved with the day-to-day hotel business, but he did foresee the tremendous growth in air travel and the need for airport hotels. Somehow he was able to persuade his colleagues at Lyons to go ahead with this project.

Planning and construction of the Ariel Hotel, by which name it became known, provided many important, but expensive, lessons for the Strand Hotel Ltd's management. Certain problems were inherited. The contractors, architects and other consultants, who had no previous experience of planning or building large hotels, had already been appointed. The architects had drawn up and had received planning permission for an unconventionally designed circular hotel, the shape being said to deflect noise more effectively. The two-acre site itself was a stone's throw from Heathrow airport runway, requiring the installation not of double glazing but of triple glazing. This had ramifications for the design and durability of the elevational cladding of the building. As for the Strand Hotel Ltd, this was its first hotel since the Cumberland was built in 1933.

Rex Joseph (b.1923), son of Victor Joseph and a grandson of Coleman Joseph and Clara Gluckstein, was put in charge of the development. Regular and *ad hoc* meetings took place almost daily in his office and elsewhere, often attended by up to twenty people. Full-size mock-ups of bedrooms were constructed in the basement of the Regent Palace Hotel. Everyone was invited to comment, and variation orders to the architect and interior designers were scattered like confetti. The interior design of the public areas was entrusted to an American designer based in Chicago – this at a time before the fax machine, let alone e-mail.

Having taken about three years to complete, the Ariel Hotel opened in January 1961, at a final cost of £900,000, approximately three times its original budget. This overrun of expenditure did nothing to enhance the prospects for further hotel building and some in the Lyons hierarchy seized on this issue to argue against future developments. Nevertheless Strand Hotel's first airport hotel was an ambitious venture.

A view of the Ariel Hotel at Heathrow Airport. Exceeding its building budget by three times, it opened in January 1961. Proximity to the airport can be judged by the aircraft standing near the terminal buildings in the top left of the picture. *By kind permission of Ralph Morhaim.*

The Albany Hotels

While the Ariel was still under construction Strand Hotel Ltd received an invitation to participate in another hotel project as part of a substantial redevelopment in Birmingham which was being carried out by John Laing & Sons. Much the same opposition came from the Lyons board as before, coupled with the fact that the Ariel costs were escalating and there was no evidence that it would be profitable. Once again Julian Salmon persuaded his colleagues at Lyons to go ahead. This time, however, the financial terms appeared very favourable to the operator, and, just as important, the construction company would not allow costs to get out of control. Birmingham also was being promoted as a convenient base for visiting historic places, such as Stratford-upon-Avon, which was little more than half an hour away by car. Direct airline flights from France and Germany had begun and more were planned. Birmingham had strong theatrical and musical traditions and was a major centre for conferences, exhibitions and sporting events. More to the point, perhaps, there was no competitor hotel in Birmingham at that time. The Strand Hotel Ltd had learnt, the hard way, the importance of producing a definitive specification of its requirements for the architects and designers; the company had established control procedures with quantity surveyors to ensure costs were maintained within predetermined budgets. Above all, the hotel company knew that the Lyons board had barred the development of any further provincial hotels until the Birmingham Albany, as it became known, had proved itself. The Albany opened with 254 rooms in December 1962 pretty much on time and on budget, the first hotel for the Strand Hotel group in its history outside the London area.

By pre-war standards the Albany Hotel was architecturally bland and built in the rectangular functional style favoured by architects of that period. The lessons learned from the older London hotels were more or less incorporated, chief among which were *en suite* facilities, and built-in wardrobes and cupboards providing generous hanging and drawer space. Room luggage racks were cantilevered and the television sets were placed on pivoting pedestals. Two serious omissions were double-glazing and air-conditioning to guests' rooms. The Birmingham Albany was specifically designed for the businessman who stayed for only one or two nights. On the top floor there were three penthouse suites, each with its own sitting room, bathroom, bedroom and large balcony where guests could view the city. However, it was not until 1976 that banqueting suites were incorporated. Initially there was only one restaurant and the carvery, unlike London's, was not initially a success.

By committing itself to building new hotels at Heathrow airport and Birmingham, the Strand Hotel Ltd had become attractive to many property developers and local authorities who sought them out for their own projects. Many cities and towns in the United Kingdom were planning substantial redevelopment – some to repair war damage and others to revitalise town centres. For its part the Strand Hotel Ltd had always enjoyed a high reputation in its field, as well as having the financial resources and name of the Lyons group behind it. Correspondingly, it was regarded as a strong, able partner for big hotel projects. At the same time many international airlines were seeking partners for hotel development, in the United Kingdom, Europe and elsewhere.

The Strand Hotel company had now begun to promote itself vigorously and set up deals with travel agents, business houses, conference organisers and air and shipping lines. In 1960 a block of rooms was made available in the Strand and Regent Palace hotels for visitors travelling with the Dutch Zeeland Shipping Company. An expanding sales promotion team established contacts overseas and, where practicable, set up offices. A large proportion of visitors came from abroad, and this closer contact paid off handsomely.

Although the hotel company did not have a formal development plan in the 1960s, its executives had a fairly clear idea of the direction they wanted it to go, if allowed to do so by the Lyons board. In general they were interested in big city centre projects along the lines of the Albany concept, and were keen to develop an upmarket motor hotel chain in the United Kingdom, with an eye on the expanding motorway construction.

One new project had been under consideration since 1963, when the Strand Hotel Ltd was approached about an Albany-type hotel in a city centre redevelopment scheme in Nottingham. For several years meetings were held with the local authority, the appointed developer and various architects acting for the developers and the Strand Hotel Ltd. Strand's own architect helped to modify the plans so as to produce a first-rate hotel incorporating extensive banqueting and conference facilities which were missing from the former design. Like Birmingham, Nottingham had no existing or anticipated hotel competition. As icing on the cake there was a 150-year lease on offer with reasonable rent reviews. Approval was given in 1967 and in due course the Nottingham Albany, with 160 rooms, opened in October 1969. Once again it was completed more or less on time and within the £1.5 million budget.

It is perhaps worth reflecting on some of the changes in thinking between the first Albany Hotel in Birmingham and the second in Nottingham. The Birmingham Albany had been designed without any banqueting or conference areas because the norm in London hotels was to provide just enough catering to meet breakfast requirements and the needs of the hotel residents, primarily businessmen. A decision had also been taken not to air-condition or double-glaze the bedrooms of the Birmingham Albany on the grounds that there were not enough hot nights to justify the additional expenditure. These decisions were, with hindsight, wrong. In time both shortcomings were remedied in Birmingham, first when the hotel was doubled-glazed and secondly when the hotel company later acquired an adjoining piece of land in Birmingham and added conference and banqueting facilities. This had been prompted by the development of the new National Exhibition Centre, just outside Birmingham, which opened in February 1976.

Strand Hotels Reorganised and Developed

The 1960s were years of great optimism among Strand's employees at all levels. It was also

gratifying to the hotel group to know that they were so well regarded within the industry. The year 1966 was of great significance to the Strand Hotel Ltd (as indeed to all parts of the Lyons group). For a variety of reasons (discussed in chapter 30) Lyons had set about producing a new 'constitution', setting out policy objectives for the group and then considering the strategic implications. This in turn gave rise to an emerging philosophy of management and an awareness of interrelationships and structures. There was little doubt that the new constitution would have a significant impact on the hotel group, which, although under the ultimate control of Lyons, had nevertheless enjoyed a high degree of autonomy.

From the time of the hotel company's incorporation in 1909 until 1967, the Strand Hotel Ltd remained a public company with some 4,000 shareholders quoted on the London Stock Exchange. Ultimate control, however, had always been in the hands of J. Lyons & Company Ltd through its holding of deferred shares, but, when

Birmingham's Albany Hotel by night. This was the first hotel built by Lyons outside London. *By kind permission of Ralph Morhaim.*

With the same uninspiring architecture as the Birmingham, the Nottingham Albany Hotel nears completion. The lessons learned from building the Birmingham Albany Hotel were incorporated here. *By kind permission of Ralph Morhaim.*

Lyons acquired the whole of the issued share capital of the Strand Hotel Ltd and the Palace Hotel Ltd on 25 and 29 April 1968 respectively, both were turned into wholly owned subsidiaries. The businesses of these two hotel companies were then absorbed by Strand Hotel Ltd, which subsequently changed its name to Strand Hotels Ltd. At the same time Lyons acquired the whole of the share capital of Cumberland Hotels Ltd, formerly a 50 per cent jointly owned company, and this too became a wholly owned subsidiary. These transfers were completed by the end of April 1968 at a total cost of £3,964,500 paid in cash and unsecured loan stock.

In January 1966 Harold Wilson's Labour government introduced an investment incentive scheme. Investment grants largely replaced investment allowances but were not made available to service industries such as the hotel and catering trades. The effect was to deprive hotel companies of a tax concession which had been worth approximately 13 per cent of the cost of investments. In September 1966 selective employment tax, a tax on all employers of labour, was introduced. One of its intentions was to assist manufacturing businesses and thereby promote economic growth, or so it was thought. Until 1 April 1968 this was rebated, with a premium, to firms engaged in manufacturing activities. Selective employment tax was estimated to have constituted some 3.5 to 4.5 per cent of hotel companies' total operating costs. Needless to say, the impact on hotel profits and their return on capital investment was severe. To these measures was added the deflationary action taken by the government in July 1966 – a six-month standstill on wages and dividends, prices frozen for twelve months, increases in purchase tax, cuts in holiday currency allowances and more hire-purchase curbs – to deal with Britain's balance of payments deficit and runaway inflation. In November 1967, in the face of the worst sterling crisis for nearly twenty years, the pound was devalued by over 14 per cent while at the same time the bank rate was hoisted to 8 per cent and £200 million was raised in extra taxes. All this entailed a reversal of government policy during the preceding three years and brought about the resignation of the Chancellor of the Exchequer, James Callaghan.

Following these government measures, the Economic Development Committee for Hotels and Catering was set up under the National Economic Development Council to examine economic performance, prospects and competitiveness, and to assess from time to time the hotel and catering industry's progress in relation to national growth. Along with representatives from government, trade unions and other parts of industry, a representative from each of the larger hotel operators sat on the main committee; for Lyons this was Michael Salmon, grandson of Alfred Salmon.

In August 1968 more democratic management was introduced within the Lyons empire when further control was given to non-family members, partly in order to change management philosophy. The belief that the group depended for its profits solely on catering activities still seemed to be held by some Lyons directors, who underrated the importance of food production which in 1968 accounted for 74 per cent of turnover and 74 per cent of the trading profit. A complete reorganisation subsequently resulted in the formation of three main business units: food products; hotels and catering; and property. All other business activities were consolidated under 'other activities'. In this way the close linking of businesses operating in similar or adjacent markets would be mutually supportive.

The Hotel Sector Management was constituted on 1 January 1969 but this had a short life. Another new organisation came into effect on 1 September 1969 after an earlier decision by the Lyons group to set up 'business areas' for mutually supportive activities. Hence a new Hotels and Catering Business Area, with Brian Salmon as chief executive director, was established. Again there was much reshuffling of personnel and there is little doubt that these changes caused considerable disappointment and distress to certain family and non-family members, for there were both winners and losers in the upheaval. However, this period of transformation coincided with developments that promised a very bright

The Strand Palace Hotel in the 1950s.

future for Strand Hotels. Many projects were already in the pipeline, and so operational staff had no inclination to get preoccupied with organisational charts. There was great enthusiasm throughout the hotel company to get on with the job in hand and to succeed.

In the meantime, tourism was accelerating year on year. Some projections put the number of foreign visitors to the United Kingdom at 10 million by 1975; and this led to an assumption that an extra 40,000 hotel rooms would be needed by the 1970s – about 30,000 of them in London. If Strand Hotels Ltd was to remain competitive it had to participate in this expanding market. Hotel development was given an incentive in 1969 by the Labour government with the introduction of the Development of Tourism Act, which recognised the hotel industry's large contribution to foreign currency earnings and therefore to the balance of payments. The Economic Development Committee for Hotels and Catering reported in 1968 that 'Expenditure on accommodation and catering (£110 M) is the largest item in the total tourist expenditure in the country (£219 M in total).' The Act allowed cash grants to be given to hotels providing new bedroom accommodation, amounting to the lower of £1,000 or 20 per cent (£1,200 or 25 per

cent in development areas) of the eligible expenditure provided work on site started before 31 March 1971 and was completed by 31 March 1973. With hindsight, however, there is little doubt that the grants caused too many new hotel rooms to be supplied in too short a space of time. This over-capacity was destined to have unpleasant repercussions in later years.

On 4 June 1971 Strand Hotels Ltd was the first hotel company to be presented with a Queen's Award to Industry – as an invisible exporter earning foreign currency by providing a service to overseas visitors. The award was seen as recognition that the hotel industry warranted as much serious consideration as manufacturing industry selling goods abroad. It was a great morale booster to hotel employees, notably those working at the three large London hotels where the larger foreign earnings had been made.

Glasgow and Crick: City Centre and Motor Hotels

By the end of 1969 Strand Hotels had obtained authority from the Lyons board to proceed with three new projects: an Albany Hotel in Glasgow to continue the city centre brand; a motor hotel at Crick, Rugby, on a site very close to the intersection between the M1 and proposed M6 motorways as a trial for a possible chain; and a 600-bedroom hotel on the outskirts of Amsterdam. When complete the new hotels would provide an additional 950 bedrooms.

The Glasgow Albany Hotel was part of a city centre redevelopment scheme, which had been awarded to Myton Ltd, a subsidiary of the Taylor Woodrow group. Myton, which had also built the Ariel Hotel, had already appointed its various consultants. The architect was Richard Seifert & Partners – probably at the time Britain's best-known firm of commercial architects – whose practice had designed the much criticised Centre Point office block in London's West End and the Royal Garden Hotel. The unenviable task of persuading Richard Seifert to withdraw from the hotel development fell on Ralph Morhaim, of Strand Hotels' board. Strand was then able to bring in its own nominated architect (James A. Roberts), quantity surveyors (Geoffrey & Burgess)

and interior designer (Peter Glyn-Smith & Partners) and thus to continue working with a team the company knew and respected.

At the end of the 1960s Glasgow did not have a new city centre hotel. Most of the business clientele and the big functions and conferences were accommodated in the old railway hotels. In order to secure this trade, the entire hotel was to be air-conditioned and double-glazed, and the finest catering, banqueting and conference facilities were to be provided.

The 256-bedroom hotel, built in a similar rectangular style to the Birmingham and Nottingham Albany hotels and costing £3 million, was officially opened on 13 February 1973. Brian Beardsmore, of Dennis Lennon and Partners, who designed the hotel's interiors, remarked in the *Lyons Mail* of March 1973: 'We acknowledge the influence of Charles Rennie Mackintosh. The design of the screens in the lobby of the hotel is derived from the high back chair in the Directors' Room at the Glasgow School of Art, and the dark stained timber ceiling, stone floor, simple plaster and brick walls have for us an affinity with the work of Mackintosh and give the hotel a strong identity with the City of Glasgow.' The price for a single room, including continental breakfast, was £8.25 per night. A twin- or double-bedded room was £12.50.

The Rugby Albany Inn site at Crick was offered to Strand Hotels by a local developer who had already obtained outline planning permission and wanted to retain an involvement in the scheme. The site appeared to meet the required criteria; it was just off a motorway junction and within three miles of the intersection between the M1 and M6, which was under construction. Although it was a greenfield site it was nevertheless close to several large towns and to various commercial sites, both existing and planned, and all with potential for further development. Once again it was necessary to negotiate the withdrawal of the original developer and to introduce the Strand development team.

The Hotel in Amsterdam

In 1967 an approach regarding a hotel in Amsterdam was made to Strand Hotels by General

Kruls on behalf of the Dutch national airline, Koninkluke Luchtvaart Maatschappu (KLM). General Kruls had been the Chief of Staff of the Royal Dutch Air Force during the Second World War, had spent much time in London and knew the Cumberland Hotel well. He was to remain involved with the project and be supportive of the development team. KLM, in common with many other national airlines, was at this time planning for the arrival of jumbo jets, each carrying hundreds of visitors. Amsterdam, with its famous canals and art galleries, attracted enormous numbers of tourists as well as businessmen. It was therefore regarded as a target European city by Strand Hotels.

KLM had already identified a possible site a few kilometres outside the city centre, in a pleasant residential area on the way to Schiphol airport. New road and railway connections were in place, and the site was close to the main exhibition and conference centre in Amsterdam, a sports stadium, an open area intended for botanical gardens and a vast garden centre. KLM's own research findings suggested a 600-bedroom hotel (1,200 beds), to be built as quickly and as economically as possible. Rooms should be well equipped but with few luxuries. Catering should be based on visitors' requirements and no function or conference facilities would be provided.

After carrying out its own research Strand Hotels found little to disagree with in KLM's proposals. The size of the hotel posed some concern, however. The largest existing hotel in Amsterdam was much smaller. Nevertheless, KLM firmly believed that their customer projections warranted their proposal, and, of course, they were prepared to provide 25 per cent of the equity. Although the support of KLM and all the Dutch team was notable, there was no doubt the project was a significant challenge to Strand Hotels. This was its first overseas project and it was a large one. Currency exchange control was still in force in the United Kingdom; therefore the Bank of England's permission was required for all monies transferred to Holland and for any financial liabilities incurred by Strand Hotels Ltd in Holland. Once budgets had been approved,

the Bank of England would not look kindly on requests for additional funds. In fact the Bank of England's displeasure was often used as a weapon to fend off claims for extras by the contractors and the suppliers. The Dutch contractor and architect had been selected by KLM, but Strand was able to use its own architects and quantity surveyors as consultants. Again interior design was to be in the hands of Peter Glyn-Smith & Partners.

The Strand Hotels project team worked in a totally foreign environment. The Dutch legal system – finance, property law, personnel law and practice, contract law and accounting require-ments – was different. Strangely, there was hardly any support from Lyons' central functions (except for insurance and pension schemes). Members of the project team felt very lonely and exposed but they received great support and guidance from the Dutch consultants. As virtually all the Dutch professionals spoke and understood English well, there was rarely any need for interpreters. It is interesting that one of the Dutch accounting firm's partners visited the United Kingdom on several occasions to familiarise Strand Hotels executives with the intricacies of value added tax (VAT) prior to its imposition in the United Kingdom. The Dutch had been operating their version (BZT) for some years. This small example of co-operation was to stand the Strand Hotels group in good stead.

Financing of the project was advantageous – again probably through the involvement of KLM. The site benefited from a long lease held by the city of Amsterdam with a moderate ground rent. The total cost of the project was split three ways: a ten-year fixed-rate first mortgage with the Dutch Coal Miners' Pension Fund; a twenty-five-year fixed-rate loan from the National Investment Bank; and 75 per cent of equity capital provided by Strand Hotels, 25 per cent by KLM. Neither mortgager had rights of recourse against Lyons in the event of default by its subsidiary, Strand Hotels Ltd.

The Dutch contractor and architect both had considerable experience of designing and building low-cost, high-rise domestic accommo-dation, using a large degree of prefabrication.

The advantages were speed and economy. Although never mentioned officially, the design concept was believed to have incorporated an alternative residential use, should such a need ever arise. The hotel building had two wings, fourteen and sixteen floors respectively, off a central core. At the appropriate stage of construction, all the side elevations, possibly up to 200 feet high, were hoisted up off the ground and locked into position in a matter of hours. When the building was completed, the clean external lines gave an effect of horizontal stripes. It was named the Alpha Hotel. Each twin-bedded room had an *en suite* bathroom and a striking interior design. The restaurant claimed to be one of Amsterdam's top eating spots but the publicity was more than generous, since Amsterdam, with its myriad of excellent small restaurants, is renowned for its cosmopolitan cuisine. The design of the hotel's Falstaff Restaurant took the theme of old Elizabethan London. It was decorated in rich colours of red, brown, purple and blue, with oak tables and chairs and a carpet displaying the emblem of a large Tudor rose. By contrast the coffee shop was strictly Dutch, with a blue and white Delft theme. The Alpha Hotel also incorporated a pub called The Grenadier, named after the Dutch as well as the British grenadiers.

The Alpha Hotel was opened to the public on 5 April 1971 by HRH Prince Bernhard of the Netherlands. After an initial rush of interest, however, it failed to attract enough tourists, who seemed to prefer the traditional city centre hotels which were close to Amsterdam's chief attractions. In addition, its main foyer was so vast that it lacked warmth. For many years the Alpha Hotel struggled to make profits. Being nearer to the airport than to Amsterdam's centre, the hotel did profit from the encampment of airline passengers when flights were delayed. Since Schiphol is one of Europe's main interconnecting airports, these delays were fairly commonplace.

New Hotel Chains

In addition to the three projects in Glasgow, Crick and Amsterdam there was further hotel activity on many fronts. Between 1970 and 1974, for reasons which are not especially clear, other than the wish to expand quickly, Lyons/Strand acquired the Kingsley-Windsor group and Park Court hotels. The original Kingsley Hotel had opened in 1906 as a temperance hotel and is said to have been named after Charles Kingsley, author of *Westward Ho!* and *The Water Babies*. It came as a shock to Lyons/Strand, after they had renovated the new bar with photographs of the author, to learn that Charles Kingsley was a teetotaller.

Most of Kingsley-Windsor properties were in London but Kingsley-Windsor also owned three hotels in Eastbourne and three in the Republic of Ireland, two of which were in Dublin. Thus Strand Hotels again found itself operating outside the UK and in another capital city. Further smaller hotel acquisitions followed, mostly in rural areas; they included Whitly Inns Ltd, White's Hotel, Bowness Hotels Ltd, the Keswick Hotel Company Ltd, the Crown Hotel, Harrogate, Whately Hall Hotel Ltd, Craiglands Hotel Ltd, the Strathclyde Hotel and the Park Hotel, Siena, which had come into the group through a European subsidiary.

The Kingsley-Windsor and Park Court hotels in London were mainly concentrated in what was originally a Victorian terrace of town houses in Lancaster Gate. At one stage it was planned to demolish the hotels in order to build a much larger one as a replacement for the Regent Palace Hotel. Environmental and planning restrictions prevented Strand Hotels from doing this because of the terrace's architectural and historic interest, so eventually the company settled for a conversion which involved gutting all the contiguous but separate buildings, while leaving the external façade intact. Then the site was replanned and rebuilt internally as a whole building with some 450 bedrooms. This scheme, which had cost more than £2 million, was completed in October 1973, and the new hotel which resulted was named the Park Court Hotel. A garden running the length of the hotel was retained as a showpiece.

The extent and the complexity of the expansion programme, both current and planned, during 1969–71 prompted a further change in the management organisation. In June 1971 a new department called the Hotel and Catering Development Function was established and headed by Christopher Salmon (1926–1985), son of Julius Salmon and brother to Anthony, Brian and Neil. Patrick Salmon, grandson of Julius Salmon and a nephew of Christopher Salmon, was made development manager for leisure catering and a group called Falcon Inns. Formed as an umbrella company, Falcon Inns operated the variety of smaller provincial hotels which were being acquired throughout the UK. They appeared to have little in common with the large city centre hotels and again the rationale, other than expansion for its own sake, is difficult to understand. The first Falcon Inn, Brandon Hall near Coventry, was taken over and modernised in 1970. Frimley Hall, near Camberley in Surrey, was the second Falcon Inn. It was refurbished in 1971 with the aim of creating the atmosphere of a country house. This was a far cry from Lyons' usual bold schemes. Falcon Inns had run a total of nineteen hotels before being merged into Strand Hotels Ltd in September 1976.

February 1972 saw another organisational change in the Lyons group. This was prompted by a change of chairman from Geoffrey Salmon (who retired) to Brian Salmon; the need to pay more attention to group strategic planning; the need to allocate management resources to enable the Lyons group to transform itself from a UK business to a European one; and the need to provide appropriate management organisation for large-scale property development which was in the planning stage. The effect on Strand Hotels Ltd was that Len Badham (group assistant managing director) became responsible for all hotels and catering and became chairman of Strand Hotels Ltd, J.L. Catering Ltd and Falcon Inns Ltd. The three managing directors of these companies – Rex Joseph, Harold Young and Patrick Salmon – became responsible to Len Badham, one of the first non-family directors (excluding employee directors) to make it to the board from starting as a Lyons graduate management trainee. Property development, which included the creation and construction of new hotels, became the responsibility of Christopher Salmon, who was accountable to his brother Anthony Salmon. This last-mentioned change effectively moved Christopher Salmon from the Hotel Sector into the Lyons Estates Function. Ralph Morhaim moved with Christopher Salmon, but retained the position of non-executive director (property liaison) with Strand Hotels. This reorganisation lasted just one year. In February 1973 responsibility for planning and construction of hotels was transferred to the managing directors of Strand Hotels Ltd and Falcon Inns Ltd.

The Hotel in Paris

Meanwhile Strand Hotels Ltd continued with its development programme. It included two further motor hotels, the Wakefield Albany Inn, which opened in May 1972 with 96 bedrooms, and the Havant Albany Inn at Hayling Island, which opened in April 1973 with 96 bedrooms. The Havant Albany did not fit the original motor hotel criteria, but experimented with a combination of leisure and commercial business. Then came the acquisition in October 1973 of the four-star 170-bedroom Hôtel Commodore on the Boulevard Haussmann in Paris and the construction of the 826-bedroom Tower Hotel in the St Katharine's Dock redevelopment scheme alongside the Tower of London.

Before Strand Hotels acquired the Hôtel Commodore in Paris, there had been an exhausting search for a city centre site on which to build a new hotel. Planning controls in Paris were at this time extremely rigid. There was little or no likelihood of obtaining permission to erect any building with more than five to six floors within the city centre. In any case there were no sites large enough for building a new hotel combining commercial facilities such as offices and shops which were needed to make a redevelopment scheme viable.

The French town planners were anxious to push new hotel developments to the outer suburbs where massive redevelopment schemes were in progress or planned – for example, La Défense to the west of the city and Bercy to the east. There was, however, one site in the Montparnasse area to the south-west, where a large hotel was planned, and where Air France had already located their own vast new head office. The city of Paris put the hotel project out to competition. In due course Strand Hotels submitted its plans and was eventually awarded second place; the winner was the American Sheraton group. No doubt their pulling power with the American tourist market influenced the judges' final choice. As it turned out, the work undertaken in preparing the submission proved a worthwhile learning experience for Strand Hotels in that it demonstrated the difficulties for a British company in undertaking such projects, not least of which was the huge financial risk.

Having failed to win the Montparnasse project, Strand Hotels decided to acquire an existing business and the search for a large four-star hotel was started. There were many, almost all privately owned, but because of the intense competition between several hotel groups – French, British and American – Paris hoteliers continually increased their selling prices. During the course of the searches, Strand Hotels was approached by the son of the Hôtel Commodore's proprietor. The proprietor, a refugee from Romania where he had been an eminent tax lawyer, had arrived in Paris after the Second World War and had acquired the lease on the Hôtel Commodore. A rectangular building on nine floors with a central courtyard, the Commodore had been built as a hotel in 1922. Since the hotel provided the proprietor with both a home and a comfortable income he was disinclined to move out. Discussions between Strand Hotels, their lawyers and their bankers on the one hand, and the owner, his family and their lawyers on the other, went on intermittently for two years. Eventually agreement was reached and a large group of people representing both sides met in a banker's office in Paris to exchange contracts, but the proprietor failed to appear. After a while a message was received to say that his wife had just died. There ensued a delay of many months before contracts were exchanged. The final details were completed on 19 October 1973, when Strand Hotels Ltd acquired the shares held by the proprietor and his family in the Société Anonyme de l'Hôtel Commodore.

The first task was to modernise the public, restaurant and kitchen areas on the ground floor. At the same time fire precautions had to be installed for the whole hotel. In the light of the hotel's location on the Boulevard Haussmann, Strand Hotels hoped that a carvery restaurant might be attractive and profitable, but it was to be adapted for French tastes. Although the Commodore's carvery retained the principle that diners should carve the roast meat themselves, the variety of other food was greatly increased. As the French take pride in their own cuisine and the typical roast dinner is a very English concept, it took some time for them to be convinced. Strand also began to plan for the refurbishment of the hotel's bedrooms, but by then the renewal of the building's lease was under discussion. The negotiations progressed so slowly that they were overtaken by events at the end of 1976, and this effectively brought about the end of Strand's involvement. From then on the emphasis changed to disposal of assets and the Hôtel Commodore was sold to Aer Lingus some twelve to eighteen months later.

The Tower Hotel

The final hotel phase for Lyons began in 1970 and Strand's involvement came about through a fortunate coincidence. The St Katharine's Docks site development, then owned by London County Council, included a hotel, as well as a marina, a World Trade Centre, office buildings and domestic accommodation. The development had been put out to competitive tender. On the day in the summer of 1970 when it was made public that the Taylor Woodrow group had won the competition, the Strand Hotels director, Ralph Morhaim, had previously arranged to meet Edward North, a director of Taylor Woodrow, to discuss matters concerning the construction of the Glasgow Albany Hotel. Ralph Morhaim had seen the announcement in the morning papers and raised the matter with Edward North later that day. In a matter of days, a meeting was set up between representatives of Strand Hotels and of Taylor Woodrow, including their chairman Frank Taylor. Taylor Woodrow had apparently intended to put the hotel site out for sub-tender to principal hotel groups, but the hotel was the first stage of the development scheme and there was pressure on Taylor Woodrow to get the work started quickly. The presence of the hotel would provide an incentive for the development of the other stages.

This single meeting resulted in a consensus between the two groups to go ahead, subject only to the exchange of heads of agreement within a very limited period to enable both groups to study each other's proposals and assess their viability. Despite this, work on clearing the site and preparing foundations went ahead. Plans had already been prepared by the Renton Howard Wood Partnership. For Strand Hotels the task of exchanging contracts presented a formidable challenge. Although the site was unique, facing the river Thames and alongside the Tower of London, many believed it was too far outside central London to attract tourists. There was also pressure for work on the hotel to be started and completed within the period set out in the Development of Tourism Act. In other words, it had to begin before the end of March 1971 and be finished within two years. Many argued that a hotel with almost 1,000 rooms and ancillary conference and banqueting areas could not be completed inside such a tight programme. It was to be a huge building on a small piece of land surrounded on three sides by water, and with difficult access. Without the personal assurance of Frank Taylor that the hotel would be finished on time, it is doubtful whether Strand Hotels would have proceeded with the project. During the short exploratory period Strand produced its own projections and commissioned market research. This came together in January 1971, although work on site had begun four months earlier.

The funding of the project was complicated. As the ground lessee, Taylor Woodrow required a rent; and because the cost of the structure and the mechanical services was being met by an insurance company it too had to be paid a rent. Both parties insisted that their rentals had to be related to profits, and this involved making detailed profit projections from 1973–4 to 1976–7 as well as agreeing a definition of 'profit' – not a simple task. Strand Hotels would bear the cost of fitting out the hotel and provide working capital.

Negotiations between Strand Hotels and Taylor Woodrow on the ground lease took several months. One of the biggest problems was road access to and from the hotel, and access to and from the Thames for the marina. Taylor Woodrow were anxious to ensure maximum flexibility for users of the marina, but equally Strand Hotels was concerned that hotel guests should not be delayed. Access to the marina from the Thames was provided through an interconnecting lock, with a footbridge at one end and a vehicular bridge at the other. Motor traffic on the hotel site was one-way, so that traffic leaving the hotel had to go over the vehicular bridge before it could enter the main traffic stream. If the bridge was out of use for any length of time when river craft were passing through the lock, congestion would

The Tower Hotel (now the Thistle Tower Hotel), with its magnificent views of Tower Bridge, has probably some of the finest views of any London hotel. *By kind permission of Ronald Kingston, Thistle Tower Hotel.*

tion, enough pumping plant to deal with such a flood was installed in the hotel's basement which housed the garage and most of the equipment for the mechanical services.

The cruciform shape of the hotel, with its floors progressively set back, was described in *Lyons Mail* as 'giving a rugged, almost cliff-like quality to the building which, though completely contemporary, in no way conflicts with its surroundings'. From a tourist point of view it could not have occupied a finer site, with the Tower of London next door and many of the 826 rooms overlooking Tower Bridge. Bedroom furniture and decoration were designed to give the rooms a nautical feel appropriate to a riverside setting. The Princess Room restaurant (overlooking Tower Bridge) with its dark stained timber panelling, smoke silk walls, brown velvet carpet, rose linen tablecloths and rose-coloured upholstered chairs, was situated on the upper foyer level. In the evenings diners were entertained by a harpist. On the same level as the Princess Room was a carvery decorated in brilliant reds to reflect meat off the bone. The all-inclusive charge for the carvery was £2.20 per head, and diners could look out on to the marina at the rear and side of the hotel. The Tower Hotel was opened on 19 September 1973 by Field Marshal Sir Richard Hull, Constable of the Tower of London, and the many guests being entertained to lunch were greeted by music of the band of the Grenadier Guards, who played on the hotel's riverside esplanade.

With the completion of the Tower Hotel, the Lyons hotel subsidiaries were operating some 6,900 rooms in the United Kingdom, Ireland, France and Holland. In the UK Strand Hotels Ltd ranked as the third largest after Trusthouse Forte and Grand Metropolitan, and in London second to Grand Metropolitan. Strand Hotels Ltd had increased its number of rooms by some 4,000 in a period of about fourteen years.

The Sell-off

After 1973 there followed a period of consolidation. The hotel construction boom had more or less ended, and hoteliers were hoping that the expected increase in tourism would

be inevitable. Many hours were spent in discussing the priority rights of both parties.

Work on the £7 million project started on 15 October 1970 and enough of the hotel had been completed to allow it to open in September 1973, six months later than stipulated by the Development of Tourism Act. However, the English Tourist Board, who administered the hotel grant scheme, accepted that the delays which had occurred were beyond the control of Strand Hotels Ltd and in due course paid the appropriate grant. An interesting facet of the Tower Hotel development was the prediction, at the start of the project, that the Thames was likely to flood at least once during the next sixty years. (This was of course before the construction of the Thames Barrier at Woolwich.) As a precau-

materialise, to take up the extra accommodation. This did not happen. The Yom Kippur War in the Middle East in October 1973 had a disastrous and immediate impact on trade and tourism. The United Kingdom suffered a drastic fall in the number of foreign visitors as well as massive increases in the price of oil. Electricity was rationed by means of power cuts – as a result of a strike by miners, railwaymen and power workers – and the 'three-day week' was introduced by Edward Heath's Conservative government. Hotel occupancy rates dropped significantly, compounding the problem of low occupancy which the new hotels had created.

The impact of the subsequent economic recession was felt by the whole of the Lyons group. The parent company had been investing large sums in Europe and the United States in expanding the food and drink business. Much of Lyons' expansion had been funded by borrowings from abroad. The whole group was under pressure to try to avoid financial collapse by conserving and generating cash to pay its bank interests. Despite some success, several company disposals were inevitable if Lyons was to survive. At this stage the hotel group could do little to help, since it had always been accepted that new hotels were unlikely to contribute to profitability in their early years of operation. However, interest on loans and rental commitments still had to be met in full. It might well have been argued that the development programme which Strand Hotels had undertaken during the period 1970–3 had been too big and too rapid and therefore somewhat rash. In response it would be fair to say that, with the exception of the Tower Hotel, each project had been carefully researched. So far as the Tower was concerned, Strand Hotels relied on its unique experience of the London market, in which it had successfully operated three of the largest hotels in Europe for many years. In retrospect, events showed that there were no real defects in Strand's assessments regarding its new hotels. The subsequent owners were to enjoy the benefits of Strand's planning.

The UK economy continued to deteriorate in 1974 and 1975, with adverse effects on the Lyons group as a whole. Further organisational changes took place in December 1975 at group level. Responsibility for Strand Hotels passed from Len Badham, who was appointed deputy group managing director, to Frank Merry, with Rex Joseph continuing as managing director. In September 1976 the Lyons group decided that all the activities of Strand Hotels Ltd and Falcon Inns Ltd should come under the unified management of Strand Hotels Ltd, with Rex Joseph as managing director of the unified hotel group, and the integration was structured primarily on a regional basis.

During the years 1974–6 it had become apparent that the Lyons group would have to dispose of some of its assets including hotels, and it was under strong pressure to do so by its financial advisers. From time to time Strand Hotels Ltd was asked to produce information about its operation which could be distributed to any prospective buyer. Many rumours were circulating. At first Lyons had hoped that an American company might consider buying the hotel business, but interest was lukewarm. Likewise Grand Metropolitan Hotels either were not interested, or else could not raise the cash. In the event, towards the end of 1976, the hotel group executive was informed that the buyer was to be Trusthouse Forte Ltd. Few details of the financial settlement were given in the 1977 statement of accounts, which included the brief comment: 'On 27 January 1977 the company's Hotel interests in the United Kingdom and Eire (with the exception of the Tower Hotel, London) were sold to subsidiaries of Trust Houses Forte Limited.'

In his 1986 autobiography Charles Forte records that Lyons had asked for £35 million for their hotel business, but he was not prepared to pay so much, because some of the properties were in need of refurbishment and repair. He offered £25 million, £5 million in cash and the balance in tranches of £5 million over four years. Lyons insisted that the down-payment should be £8 million, with interest on the outstanding balance. Interest rates on the London market were high, at 15 per cent, and Lyons were looking for something more than a £5 million down-payment to compensate. The parties finally agreed on a down-payment of £7.2 million in cash together with promissory notes totalling £20.7 million bearing interest of 5 per cent per annum.

By negotiating the payment for the business over eight years on what amounted to credit from Lyons, at 10 per cent below business borrowing rates, Forte had secured the hotels for less than £27.9 million. The true price has been put at nearer £18.5 million, and in the event Charles Forte did not refurbish the hotels for many years. In his autobiography Charles Forte commented:

> I must pay tribute to them [Lyons]. They had influenced everything in our business for the good. They had nurtured the trade association, their public relations were excellent. They had influenced the hygiene standards of catering, how kitchens should be planned, and the training of staff. They did great things for the industry, and in particular the provision of good food for millions of people at a popular price. I have always had great respect for them.

There was no doubt that Charles Forte was aware of the property adage 'Sell companies but buy assets'. With the exception of the Tower Hotel in London, the Alpha Hotel in Amsterdam, the Hôtel Commodore in Paris and the Park Hotel in Siena, all the individual hotels were transferred to Trusthouse Forte on 27 January 1977. The handover period was conducted with speed and efficiency. Despite the usual disclosure warranties in the sale contract, no irregularities came to light.

Virtually all the operational staff were re-employed by Trusthouse Forte – the bulk of the 150 redundancies which did result fell on the head office staff of Strand Hotels Ltd. The sale had come at a most fortunate time for Charles Forte, for in the Queen's Jubilee year of 1977 hoteliers could have filled their rooms many times over. For all those in Strand Hotels, however, it was a tragic event, a black day in the history of Lyons.

All that remained was the disposal of the Tower Hotel, the Alpha Hotel and the Hôtel Commodore. First the Tower Hotel was sold to EMI on 15 July 1977 for £6.5 million. Then the Alpha Hotel was transferred to Novotel Nederland BV on 2 January 1978 through the sale of the shares of Strand Hotels (Nederland) BV and Alpha Hotel BV. Last of all to be sold was the Hôtel Commodore in Paris. It took almost as long to sell it as it had taken to buy.

Despite the distressing sell-off, the spirit of Strand Hotels has endured. Since 1977, on 27 January every year, a reunion of up to a hundred former employees from the hotels, their head office and the service departments takes place. Many of those who attend are now retired, many have achieved high positions in other hotel groups, and some have gone into other businesses or are self-employed. Sometimes, on special occasions, former professional consultants and friends turn up. It is not surprising that so many should still feel loyalty towards a hotel company which had lasted, in one form or another, for seventy years, and had built some of the most palatial hotels of the early twentieth century.

Chapter 19

TEA-BAGS AND INSTANT COFFEE

IN THE YEAR leading up to the Second World War Lyons' net profit for packet tea and coffee was £429,000. Although no figures are available, profits from tea continued to rise during the war years but they were, in part, illusory. The savings made on advertising, distribution and other overheads had artificially inflated tea profits, thus masking the true state of the tea business, which had actually halved mainly at the expense of Brooke Bond and Ty·phoo. In the first year of trading after the war the net profit of the Tea Department was £616,000. Early in 1952 the tea subsidy was withdrawn and the ration was increased; then tea rationing ceased altogether in October. Kenneth Gluckstein continued as General Manager but the philosophy of the Tea Department continued to be heavily influenced by Harry Salmon, whose insistence on maintaining links with the small retailers prevailed. This close association had started early in the 1900s when George Pollard had cultivated what he called the 'tea agents'.

Labour costs and the price of auction tea had risen steeply by the mid-1950s, and unexpectedly consumers turned to cheaper products. More importantly there was a market trend towards quick-infusion teas for which Lyons were unprepared. Sales of Horniman's Dividend Tea remained buoyant. After a slow start Black & Green's Family Tea improved but then later suffered from a poor image, having been the means by which Lyons disposed of its cheap tea allocations during the war. The overall performance of the Lyons tea business was nevertheless sound, but because the larger-leaf blends – broken orange pekoe, for example – were not as profitable as the small-leaf blends tea management were disappointed and unprepared for the consumer change.

Christopher Salmon joined the Tea Department in 1954 at the time when Lyons belatedly launched their first quick-infusion tea. In the same year tea management turned down an opportunity to acquire Ty·phoo on the ground that it would be difficult to integrate the Lyons van-selling operation with Ty·phoo's wholesale business, a decision which must have later been regretted. Instead, Lyons invested heavily in advertising their new quick-infusion tea. They called it Quick Brew, deliberately leaving the name Lyons off the packet for the first time. Two years later Premium Tea made its debut – its name capitalising on the publicity then being given to government Premium Bonds, which had first been issued on 1 November 1956. The Premium Tea packet carried a dividend stamp equal in value to a staggering 3d. Stamps could be stuck on a Premium Tea savings card which, when full, could be redeemed for 15s. from any stockist. Brooke Bond immediately responded by introducing an even larger dividend to protect their market.

Quick-infusion and dividend teas marked a change in policy for Lyons. This brought a frisson of excitement in sales circles, but because management had been so dilatory on this matter in years past Lyons never did regain their once dominant position in the packaged tea market. By 1960 Lyons accounted for just 14 per cent compared with Brooke Bond's and Ty·phoo's 29 and 18 per cent respectively. The overheads of blending, packing, selling and distribution meant that Lyons were having to allocate proportionally higher resources to these functions, leaving less for profit. In other words they had to run faster just to stand still.

With hindsight, the unsatisfactory perform-ance of post-war tea can be directly attributed to the trading philosophy of tea management in the inter-war period and during the difficult years of the Second World War. First, the loss of market share was partly due to the high standards and principles adopted by management, who refused to sacrifice the quality of their tea and become involved in a vicious price war. During and after the war the Tea Department insisted that their best blends in the retail market – Orange, Green and even the mid-range Blue Label – were better than competitors' at the same price. Second, the decision to promote Red Label rather than develop a quick-infusion tea delayed any effort to regain markets lost to the cheaper blends. Third, no fewer than eighteen disparate blends continued to be sold without proper advertising support. Finally, the decision to turn down the purchase of Ty·phoo – which would have catapulted Lyons to market leader with 32 per cent of the packet tea market – was a huge error of judgement. With the benefit of hindsight these all seem to have been fundamental failures in strategy. Tea management appeared completely unaware of consumer trends, or the growing field of market research, or the importance of branding – a complex mixture of taste positioning, advertising, packaging, pricing, trade and promotional terms in order to develop a differentiated product. They seemed instead to prefer to cling to the old doctrinal philosophy of 'we know best'.

Realising these deficiencies Kenneth Gluckstein, the son of Major Montague Gluck-stein, appointed Michael Lovatt, a marketing specialist, to the Tea Division in 1957 to address the issues. Sadly, he did not live to see how Lovatt transformed the business. He died of cancer in 1959, when only forty-seven years old, soon after Lovatt had introduced brand managers and brought his own marketing talents to bear on the business. On Kenneth Gluckstein's death, Christopher Salmon assumed responsibility for the Tea Division and on Lovatt's recommendation immediately set about integrating the Horniman tea business, which accounted for only a small share of the total packet tea market.

Death of the Van Sales

In the mid-1950s Lyons were faced with a dilemma. Some wholesalers were selling Lyons tea and ground coffee to small grocers at prices lower than those charged by Lyons' van salesmen. Since the wholesalers refused to stop undercutting the van salesmen, Lyons cut off their supplies and ceased trading with them. Lyons could ill afford to run an expensive van sales operation if it was losing volume to wholesalers to whom a discount had been paid. At the same time the entire pattern of retailing and wholesaling was changing. Supermarkets and grocery chains were developing rapidly, and by 1963 the 1,000 supermarkets then operating accounted for 70 per cent of all grocery turnover; this was expected soon to increase to 85 per cent. Wholesaler-sponsored groups formed and became organised in such a way that they resembled chains. Only by dealing with sellers as a group could Lyons expect to obtain price parity or price advantage in respect of competition, and to receive their full merchandising support. Collectively these changing trading patterns caused management to recognise that the time had come to discon-tinue their cherished van sales system.

Christopher Salmon argued that van salesmen could not be trained to deal effectively with supermarket managers; the buyers for the large supermarket chains would have less confidence in Lyons if their sales staff were not of equal status and in a position to provide more informed advice. Experience had shown that van salesmen were increasingly disadvantaged when dealing with the new breed of buyer whose overall knowledge of marketing, manufacturing pro-cesses, pricing and consumer trends far outstripped the wisdom of the traditional van salesman. Christopher Salmon believed that successful marketing was evolving into a two-pronged attack, coercing the consumer into buying the product on the one hand by sophisticated media advertising and on the other by follow-up displays in supermarkets, pack reductions, coupons and send-away offers. He, and others, felt that the small shops could not display Lyons products adequately enough to cause impulse buying, or buying as the result of an advertising campaign. Lyons were also finding it progressively more difficult to fight for shelf space in the larger supermarkets, not just with their old tea competitors, but with manufacturers such as Heinz, Campbell and Lever Brothers, who were selling their own non-tea goods. Although Lyons had for many years built a substantial business on van selling, costing £1 million in 1963, the changing retail market exposed three inherent weaknesses in this approach. First, the physical handling not only of a van but, more important, of the goods was tiring to the extent that it blunted the salesman's enthusiasm for the task of selling. Second, supermarket managers earned high salaries and were accorded such high status that they resented dealing with someone they regarded as a delivery man; this resentment in turn affected the salesman's self-confidence and thus his ability to sell. Third, it had become increasingly difficult to recruit good van salesmen, and some complained that those under forty years of age were 'inferior to their forefathers'. Good recruits were soon lost to other organisations that could offer more responsible work, increasingly with company cars.

Having come to the conclusion that van selling must end, at least in the grocery sector, the prospect of bringing this about seemed daunting. Generations of salesmen had traipsed the United Kingdom, building up huge sales, and were now part of Lyons' folk history; their traditions, like those of the teashops, were deeply rooted, and many people were strongly opposed to change. Christopher Salmon, however, was convinced that change must occur, if only to maintain current sales, which had already begun to falter. As the cost of van selling accelerated and sales volume fell, by January 1964 he had enough support to replace 476 van salesmen with 190 retrained sales representatives who exchanged their vans for Ford Anglia estate cars.

Working from their own homes, they were organised on an area basis, with approximately eight in each area team. In charge of the twenty-three areas (and two van sales areas in Scotland) was the area manager. Areas were grouped into nine regions with their own regional managers.

The original plan called for nine regional managers to report to the sales manager, but, since this was an unwieldy structure, three divisional managers were appointed instead, responsible for roughly one-third of the country and liaising between the regions and the sales manager. It was at this point that the idea was born of making the three divisional managers responsible not for geographical areas but for specific types of sales outlets. These then became a 'multiple channels' manager, who liaised with supermarkets; a 'wholesaler and independent channels' manager, who dealt with wholesalers and small retail groups such as Spar; and, lastly, a field sales manager, who was in charge of the organisation and deployment of the sales force, its training and methods and the development of area managers and salesmen. This structure deviated from conventional reporting hierarchy in that regional managers reported to two bosses. Essentially they were responsible to the channel managers for *what* they did in the respective channels, and to the field sales managers for *how* they did it. Although this change was not a financial exercise, Christopher Salmon was nevertheless pleasantly surprised that the conversion showed a small saving, after having allowed for modified distribution, trade discounts and other set-up expenditure.

Following the restructuring, every retailing chain, independent retailer, co-operative and independent wholesaler was visited weekly, fortnightly or monthly, depending on their trading needs, with twenty-four-hour follow-up delivery. Independent retailers ordering goods of less than 36 shillings in value per week would not receive a personal call from a Lyons sales representative but instead would be serviced by a wholesaler. Independent outlets at this time numbered 75,000 and generated turnover of £2.5 million, but Christopher Salmon had calculated that losses from these 'non-worthwhile' accounts,

Miscellaneous tea
and coffee labels.

as he put it, would be more than compensated by increased volume from larger groups. No records exist to prove or disprove his analysis; it seems, however, an extraordinary attitude to have taken. For many years opinion remained divided about the wisdom of abolishing van sales and there is no doubt it created varying degrees of unrest between managers of sales, marketing and tea-buying departments who had previously enjoyed considerable influence in how teas were marketed.

Experimentation: Ready Brek and Instant Tea

After the abolition of rationing, the Tea Division became more autonomous. It began to experiment with items other than tea, in particular with developing a cereal mix. During the war, Lyons had transferred manufacture of the sugar substitute Malogel from the Cadby Hall ice-cream factory to Greenford, where it continued until sugar rationing ended in the early 1950s. Walter Pitts, a factory manager in charge of Malogel, started to experiment with a liquid made from oatflakes. After passing this through the roller driers used in the making of Malogel he found that the resulting dried mixture could be reconstituted with milk to form a highly acceptable porridge substitute. Large-scale manufacture initially proved difficult but with Kenneth Gluckstein's encouragement and through Lyons' engineering innovations the problems were eventually overcome. The new product was launched in 1957 as Ready Brek, advertised as an instant porridge. It was made from rolled oats, oat flour and malt extract, and consumers simply had to add hot milk (and sugar if desired).

At first, Ready Brek sales were very promising, but after five years they reached a plateau. After extensive market research, and to their utter surprise, Lyons found that people who ate traditional porridge did not buy Ready Brek at all. Half the consumption was accounted for by children, of whom 70 per cent were under the age of fifteen. The idea that instant porridge was in itself attractive was therefore false, and Lyons decided to reposition Ready Brek to a children's market. Using clever advertising aimed at mothers

and their children, Lyons succeeded in matching the product with its market. By 1964 Ready Brek was the largest single contributor to the Tea Division's profits, apart from tea itself. Television commercials used the slogan 'Ready Brek – central heating for kids' and depicted children supposedly glowing in winter weather after eating the hot breakfast cereal. By the mid-1970s Ready Brek was established in third place in the UK cereal market, taking an even greater share of business in the autumn and winter months.

The breakfast cereal market was further exploited by the introduction of '8 till 1' which, after test marketing, was expanded nationally in April 1972. A mixture of oats, wheat, raisins, hazelnuts and demerara sugar, the new packet cereal was aimed at the growing muesli market but cost slightly less. As its name suggests, '8 till 1' was marketed as a health food which prevented 'mid-morning hunger pangs'. It was introduced to 300 trade guests, including Sir John Cohen of Tesco, at a cocktail party on 4 February 1972.

In 1967 management attention again turned to instant tea, although Nestlé's Nestea brand had been a resounding failure because it did not compare with conventional tea in any way. Lyons too had been unsuccessful for much the same reason but continued to experiment anyway, believing that in time it could be sufficiently improved. Brooke Bond, similarly, were taking the study of instant tea seriously and in partnership with the Canadian instant coffee company, Tenco, had built a freeze-drying plant in South Wales which was able to produce, from concentrated liquid coffee or tea, instant coffee or instant tea. Freeze-drying is a technique in which foodstuffs or liquids are first frozen on a moving conveyor belt. The frozen slab is then broken into pieces and ground to the required particle size. Frozen coffee granules are transferred to a chamber where under vacuum and low heat the ice sublimes, leaving behind dry granules of coffee. The texture and flavour of freeze-dried coffee and other foods is much better, but the process is more expensive than spray-drying and its capital cost much higher.

Lyons believed that Brooke Bond's new freeze-drying plant had been designed for the

Checking the weight of Ready Brek on a production line at the Greenford factory. *By kind permission of Waldegrave Films.*

company to switch from instant coffee to instant tea, thereby gaining some eighteen months' lead over their competitors. The success of freeze-dried coffee, Lyons management thought, might well hasten the marketability of a satisfactory instant tea. Not all the management, however, were convinced that Lyons should take the road of instant tea if a competitor were to prove successful in this. John Gluckstein (b. 1936), great-grandson of Samuel Gluckstein, argued that Lyons should perhaps instead replace their traditional tea and instant coffee with some other, unspecified, grocery product. Quite how he expected to achieve this, and what the product might be, remains puzzling.

W.S. Atkins & Partners, engineering and management consultants, were nevertheless commissioned in July 1967 to carry out a planning study to determine the cost and viability of introducing a new instant tea, based on the freeze-drying method. The estimated cost was £1.25 million but the consultants' report raised many issues concerning the project's objectives, goals, conditions and limitations. It seems that the

project had risen out of crisis management in the face of a perceived threat from a competitor's launching a satisfactory instant tea. If there had been no threat it is unlikely that any study would have been carried out at all. Lyons' own management had also just completed a practical study of the emerging instant tea technology. Spray-drying was considered the cheapest method of producing instant tea but the result was inferior to the more costly freeze-dried version. Not only was this study inconclusive, it proved expensive. The problem was that Lyons at this time were having to compete with other strong brands in a declining tea market. In any case, the public were beginning to show interest in tea-bags, not instant tea.

Tetley's Tea-Bags

The origin of the tea-bag is lost in time; some say it was invented, accidentally, by the Chinese, who sent their samples to London in small silk bags. Apart from at least one patent being filed in 1928, it is known that Peter Norman, a Lyons chemist, visited Dresden in 1937 to conduct tests on tea-bags being developed by a German firm. Made of Cellophane, the bags were shaped like modern ones and perforated with hundreds of tiny pin-holes through which the tea infusion leached. However, the tiny holes let through too much tea dust to make the infusion palatable. Around 1943, when tea-bags were starting to make an impact in the UK, as a result of their introduction by American forces stationed here during the war, the tea tasters at Greenford found that the paper and glue used in their manufacture tended to taint the flavour of the tea blends. A more satisfactory version had in fact been introduced into Britain from America by Tetley Ironside Tetley-Jones just before the Second World War. Because of tea rationing tea-bags did not to appear again in the UK until the early 1950s, by which time the Americans were using them extensively. Ironically, the tea-bag is also claimed to have been invented by an Englishman, Sandy Fowler, while working on a tea plantation in Sri Lanka in 1945. Unfortunately for him he did not patent the idea but instead took £150 for his invention. Thomas Sullivan, a New York wholesaler, is also said to have invented tea-bags since he sent his samples to customers in small fabric bags in much the same way as the earlier Chinese merchants.

In Britain, where tea was still the national drink and tea-making a respected ritual, tea-bags were relatively slow to catch on. Lyons' management had in any case always refused to compromise on quality, and there was a strong belief that tea made from tea-bags could never match the taste of 'proper' tea. It was not until the late 1960s that the tea-bag market was so great that it could no longer be ignored by Lyons. In the meantime, in keeping with General Management policy, a new structure was introduced in 1970 which gave more autonomy to tea management. To reinforce this change the Tea Division became a fully owned subsidiary of Lyons under the title of Lyons Groceries Ltd; the 'groceries' in its title referred to the cereals, slimming biscuits and other products which had progressively been introduced. The relatively new private-label and contract-selling businesses were transferred to the subsidiary W.H. & F.J. Horni-

man & Co. Ltd under the management of Barry Silverman, former Tea Division marketing manager. The new company adopted the title of Horniman because the name had a good reputation in the grocery industry. Horniman's was to increase sales in both private-label trade and contract selling.

Branded tea and grocery products remained with Lyons Groceries Ltd under the management of John Gluckstein (managing director) and Frank Merry (chairman). Keith Jamieson joined in March 1970 as marketing director, having been recruited from Bulmer's, the cider manufacturers. He was supported by a team of 370 marketing and sales staff. John Gluckstein's involvement, however, was short-lived, since a further top management reshuffle was occasioned by the retirement of the Lyons chairman, Geoffrey Salmon, in February 1972. John Gluckstein then became European development co-ordinator responsible for planning and managing new businesses in Europe, and his place at Lyons Groceries Ltd was taken by J.L. Massarella, who before the Spillers/French bread and flour merger in 1971 had been managing director of J.W. French (Milling & Baking) Ltd, in which Lyons had a substantial share, and who had earlier managed the Massarella ice-cream business.

In August 1971 senior Lyons Groceries management and marketing staff, hitherto occupying offices at Cadby Hall, were moved into a new office development at Greenford, where they shared space with Sol Café staff. With packet tea declining – and the tea-bag market doubling in 1971 – the new Lyons Groceries management raised the whole scale of their tea operations by purchasing the American Tetley Tea Company from Beech-Nut Incorporated in December 1972. Tetley's history can be traced to Huddersfield where they started trading as tea merchants in 1837; they expanded into America in 1913 to help support poor UK sales. The formidable task of merging the two tea companies to compete in the £130 million tea market was completed in April 1973. It resulted in a change of company name to Lyons Tetley Ltd, to reflect both companies' interests. With a combined workforce of 3,000, the business was based at three main centres, Greenford (Lyons Groceries), Bletchley (formerly Tetley's UK head office and factory where all Tetley's export brands and tagged tea-bags were produced) and Eaglescliffe (Tetley). At the time of the merger more than 20 per cent of Tetley's total production in the United Kingdom was exported.

As well as giving them a share in the tea-bag market, the acquisition of Tetley brought into the Lyons group two American speciality coffee brands, Matinsons and Bustelo. For the first time this took Lyons into Australia, through Tetley's subsidiary, Robert Timms Proprietary Ltd, which in addition to the Tetley tea business there also had the largest coffee business. (Robert Timms was eventually sold to Unilever but in 1986–7 the tea brands were bought back into the Lyons group.) At the time of purchase the Tetley company had begun expanding its tea-bag market into the United Kingdom and had just built the largest tea-bag factory in the world at Eaglescliffe, on Teesside, with the help of generous regional grants. The machinery was the most modern available, with pneumatic packing replacing a manual operation.

With an aggregate turnover of £45 million Tetley had cost Lyons £23 million but by 1980 the much enlarged business enabled Tetley to dominate the UK tea-bag market. Their position was further consolidated in May 1989 when, after five years of planning and research, Tetley introduced the world's first round tea-bag. Round tea-bags were introduced into Canada and Ireland in 1991, by which time Tetley claimed to be market leader, having spent £360 million on brand advertising and promotion.

Instant Coffee

Following the disappointing decline of Bev coffee essence after the war, the Greenford 'technicians' had developed a new coffee product which they called Quoffy. Conceptually similar to Bev, Quoffy differed in that it was an instant dried coffee powder, with a glucose additive, packed in airtight containers. Launched in 1950, Quoffy was supplemented one year later with a lower-priced instant coffee called Chico, but both failed dismally. Until the 1970s Britain had a strongly established tea-drinking culture favoured by an older generation. A Monopolies and Mergers Commission (MMC) report into soluble coffee in 1991 claimed that 'Whereas in 1970 3.7 cups of tea were drunk for every cup of coffee, that ratio had fallen to 2.5:1 by 1980. In 1986 the value of the United Kingdom coffee market overtook that of the tea market.' However, this is partly due to the relative prices of tea and coffee, a factor which had perhaps prevented coffee from catching on earlier when an older generation had less disposable income.

Spray-dried soluble coffee is claimed to have been invented by a Swiss employee of the Nestlé food manufacturer in 1939. This had followed an approach by the Brazilian Coffee Institute who were looking for some method of dealing with Brazil's coffee surpluses. By the start of the Second World War instant coffee was being manufactured in Switzerland, America and the UK. The 1991 MMC's report remarks: 'During the Second World War, the United States government encouraged the use of new methods of manufacture of soluble coffee by all coffee processors. Nestlé believes that as a result its newly patented spray-drying process was used by others without its consent, consequently the technology of soluble coffee manufacture became much more widely and freely available by the end of the war.'

In spray-drying, coffee is brewed in large containers and then sprayed into the top of a tall tower through fine atomising nozzles. At the same time hot air is blown into the tower and mixes with the particles of liquid coffee extract as they fall. By the time these particles reach the bottom they have turned into a fine powder. Two big companies used this method in the early 1950s, the Swiss firm Nestlé and the American Maxwell House. Believing that this new process would eventually kill off the traditional ground coffee market, Christopher Salmon felt that Lyons should enter the soluble coffee market in a big way. The process was so simple that he was convinced the coffee-growing countries would introduce their own spray-drying systems and sell coffee powder to the rest of the world, who would then act as mere packing agents and no longer be able to make profits from manufacturing. His co-directors reigned back his enthusiasm, since they not only considered the huge investment unjustified but did not share his belief that the coffee-growing countries would invest heavily in spray-drying equipment; eventually, however, some capital was authorised for a spray-drying coffee plant to be installed at Greenford in 1959. With Nestlé and Maxwell House now national brand leaders, Christopher Salmon believed that the market for soluble coffee – commonly referred to as instant coffee – was large enough to accommodate another manufacturer, and studies made between 1950 and 1958 confirmed this. Yet Lyons' instant coffee never lived up to expectations, mainly because the quality was mediocre and the advertising budget was inadequate. Nevertheless management were surprised that the additional trade they had created, while not being taken up by their own Lyons' brand, was being absorbed by the supermarket chains' own labels, which Lyons had begun manufacturing under licence.

Meanwhile Lyons' chocolate and sugar-confectionery lines, the marketing of which had been transferred to their subsidiary, Rolls Confectionery Ltd, in 1959, continued to perform badly. As the lines had such a small share of the market, management decided to withdraw completely from the confectionery trade. Accordingly they came to an agreement with Callard & Bowser Ltd, a subsidiary of Arthur Guinness Sons & Company Ltd, who acquired the goodwill, trade names and manufacturing facilities of Lyons' sugar-confectionery and chocolate bar business from 1 July 1961. The couverture and Maison Lyons range of chocolates, which were hand-dipped and of higher quality, were not affected by this transaction.

Although the ground coffee business remained robust and profitable, the failure of the instant coffee venture was viewed as far more devastating than the confectionery disappointment. It was worse because the popularity of instant coffee was causing a decline in tea drinking in Britain. As share of the instant coffee market seemed imperative, if only as security against further falling tea sales, Lyons decided to use the instant coffee facilities at Greenford

to target the contract private-label business of the supermarkets. Their energetic campaign utilised the Horniman subsidiary as the manufacturing vehicle for their private-label business, which in the first year yielded a profit of £150,000. By April 1965 a second spray-drying plant had been commissioned and this too was quickly brought up to full capacity. The early returns on investment looked promising and before the second plant had become fully operational Lyons had forged a relationship with an American company, Chock Full O'Nuts Corporation of America, which was in a similar line of business.

This improbably named firm produced instant and ground coffee, tea-bags and nuts, and owned restaurants. Their net sales had grown from $24.5 million in 1958 to $43.25 million in 1964, but the growth between 1963 and 1964 had been only $1 million compared with $6 million a year earlier. Lyons had formed its relationship with the American company before it reported its near-disastrous year in 1964. The main reason for the stagnant profits was a misplaced judgement not to forward-buy Brazilian coffee because Brazil's excesses indicated that prices would fall during 1964. In the event coffee prices increased enormously, making it necessary to buy at high rates. Competitors who had bought futures had avoided the price increases, and to maintain market share Chock Full O'Nuts had to sell their coffee at a loss.

In July 1964 the American corporation had decided to acquire three other coffee manufacturers: the Old Judge Coffee Company (based in St Louis, Missouri), Nash's (in St Paul, Minnesota) and Boscul (in Camden, New Jersey). With these acquisitions, Chock Full O'Nuts now traded in a total of thirty American states. Old Judge had the highest coffee sales in the St Louis area, and, since all its coffees were priced in the middle range, it complemented the premium-priced coffee bearing the Chock Full O'Nuts brand name. In addition to coffee and tea-bags the company owned forty-eight restaurants in New York and New Jersey with several more under construction. On 1 April 1965, with a share capital of £100,000, Lyons and Chock Full O'Nuts formed Sol Café Ltd, with Lyons holding 51 per cent and the Americans 49 per cent of the equity. In 1969 Lyons acquired the remaining 49 per cent from Chock Full O'Nuts, making Sol Café Ltd a wholly owned Lyons subsidiary.

By 1970 Lyons had captured 80 per cent of the UK market in private-label instant coffee, which itself comprised 20 per cent of the whole instant coffee market in the UK. Remarkably, the contingent measures adopted to remedy the initial failure of branded instant coffee resulted in success. Indeed, the situation was turned to positive advantage, since Lyons, unlike their competitors, could improve the quality of their private-label coffee without fearing it might damage their own branded line, which was insignificant.

Sol-Tenco

The grocery sector of the Lyons group now operated under three main British companies. First, there was Sole Café Ltd under Simon Kester for the production of instant coffee. Second, under Christopher Brooks, there was Lyons Catering Supplies Ltd, which had been formed in July 1966 to carry on and develop the business previously managed by the Catering Industries Department, selling special blends of tea and coffee to caterers. To Lyons Catering Supplies Ltd was later added W. Symington & Co. Ltd, which supplied dried food (mainly soup, sauces, gravy, custard powder and dessert mixes) to the catering trade and had been acquired in February 1969. Margetts Ltd, a preserves company founded by James Margetts in 1869 at a shop in Hackney, was also brought into Lyons Catering Supplies. Third, there was Lyons Tetley Ltd under J.L. Massarella which concentrated on developing the tea-bag trade.

By 1976 the growth of the grocery business, principally breakfast cereals and tea-bags, 'continued to be impressive', as the report to the shareholders noted. In 1974 coffee-bags – containing ground coffee for quick infusion – had been introduced into Britain by Lyons Tetley, and within ten months sales reached £2 million. As well as pioneering a new type of product, Lyons Coffee Bags stimulated consumption of packaged ground coffee, because they were bought mainly by people who had previously drunk only instant coffee and who, discovering the new taste and aroma, were converted to real ground coffee. Other grocery items produced by Lyons Tetley were instant pastry, cake and batter mixes, and in September 1975 mixes for brown and white bread, and for doughnuts, were launched. In 1976, to take advantage of the synergistic benefits of combined operations, Lyons Tetley and Lyons Catering Supplies were merged under common management. In this way they could avoid duplication of product range and distribution and make the relevant technology more readily available for wider application. After Allied Breweries Ltd acquired J. Lyons & Co. Ltd in September 1978, sales of tea, ground coffee and Ready Brek continued to improve, but Ready Brek, along with Cluster cereal bars, was eventually sold to Weetabix Ltd on 29 June 1990. Production continued at Greenford, by agreement, for a further twelve months.

In March 1982 Lyons acquired from the Coca-Cola Company of Atlanta the issued share capital of Ibenco (Great Britain) Ltd, subsequently named Tenco (UK) Ltd. With headquarters in Linden, New Jersey, the Tenco Division reported to the Coca-Cola Foods Division and had manufacturing, warehousing and distribution facilities at six locations in North America. It was the largest supplier of private-label instant coffee and tea in the United States and had one of only four factories producing high-margin decaffeinated coffee. The Tenco Division of the Coca-Cola Company (UK branch) was managed by Charles Druce, who continued as managing director of Tenco (UK) Ltd. An uncomplicated business, Tenco purchased spray-dried coffee powder from countries of origin and packaged it in jars and cartons (labelled in accordance with customers' requirements) from an unpretentious factory in Ilderton Road, Peckham. Spray-dried powder was sometimes agglomerated by moistening a falling curtain of milled powder with steam, then drying it so that it stuck together in lumps. This practice did nothing for its quality but made it look like freeze-dried coffee, which was a superior product commanding a higher mark-up. During periods when the cost of coffee was high, chicory was blended in as a cheap substitute. The linchpin of Tenco UK's operation was the exclusive supply of packaged coffee to the Co-operative Wholesale Society (CWS), a contract which had existed since the late 1960s and which accounted for 60 per cent of packaging volume (the Peckham factory also packed and sold a non-dairy creamer which was supplied by Premier Brands Ltd). At the time of purchase Tenco UK had been expected to lose part of its business, since the CWS had declared its intention to do its own packaging, although substantial business had been budgeted throughout 1982.

In the United Kingdom the Lyons board were unsure whether there would be synergistic benefits from merging Tenco UK and Sol Café. They planned to operate the two companies separately for a while, to gain insight from an exchange of know-how between the two, for it appeared that Tenco UK was achieving a higher margin of profit than Sol Café. The two businesses did, however, complement each other in that Sol Café was focusing increasingly on agglomerated and freeze-dried coffee, while Tenco concentrated on powdered coffee. During the five years immediately preceding the sale to Lyons a pre-tax return on assets of over 50 per cent was the norm within Tenco UK. Lyons had paid $34.8 million for the Tenco business. The Tenco portfolio was completely at odds with Coca-Cola's philosophy. Own-label products with no marketing input did not sit well with the best-known brand name in the world. In any case, the rich returns of the previous five years in the UK, when the pre-tax profits exceeded £15 million, were destined to cease once packaging for the CWS labels finally ended in March 1983.

Developments in producing instant coffee were restricted to the search for methods which least distorted the taste of freshly brewed ground coffee. Market leaders tended to install their own facilities for processing raw beans, since local operations were not always strictly controlled. Tenco was an extremely efficient packaging business, with modern equipment and a flexible, non-unionised, workforce. There is little doubt that it would have succeeded in replacing much of the lost CWS volume, largely at the expense

of Sol Café's bought-in powder packaging trade. Tenco management, however, found it difficult to adapt to the management ethos within Lyons, which was described by a former employee as a culture shock and vastly different from that of Coca-Cola: 'rather like stepping back forty years in terms of management philosophy and employee relationships'. A lack of strategic planning had allowed a multi-layered structure to develop, with little regard for business needs. The questioning of total manning levels in comparison to competitors invariably led to confrontation and acrimony, as individual managers at various levels defended their vested interests.

By now there was a growing demand from principal private-label customers for better products, generally in the image of Nescafé coffees. Sol Café had built up a processing capability over several years and, although the firm tended to buy coffee powder, in the years immediately before the Tenco acquisition the basic equipment and expertise were retained at Greenford. Techniques developed by Sol Café increasingly produced soluble coffees at least equal to the brand leaders; this enabled the company to expand its market share to about 18 per cent by 1984. Instant coffee production was supported by a vastly improved packaging facility at Greenford. One of the benefits of acquiring Tenco UK was the injection of capital plant into the production area at an economic cost and over a short time-scale. For example, one renovated fast jar-filling line was commissioned at Greenford in 1982 at a cost of £500,000. It was supplemented by two further lines from the Tenco site at Peckham in mid-1982. Acquisition of these lines and other plant made the operation flexible enough to handle packaging orders within a single-shift working pattern. There were associated cuts in the workforce within the production area, with no loss of output; and direct packaging labour per unit of throughput was reduced by 40 per cent.

Tenco UK had roughly 440 customers and 260 labels, whereas Sol Café had only 90 customers and 120 labels. The immediate benefits of the acquisition were, as foreseen, the avoidance of a painful conflict between two major suppliers of private-label instant coffee in Britain and a revitalising of the newly named Food Division's instant coffee business. However, the revitalisation was not wholly apparent in the financial results of the combined business for the years after acquisition. In the absence of the CWS business, Tenco UK and Sol Café sold 8,352 tons of packed coffee in 1980–1 and produced pre-tax profits of £1.6 million. The sales force of the two companies covered the entire market: Sol Café tended to concentrate on the larger retailers handled from head office, whereas Tenco UK employed a field sales team to handle numerous smaller accounts.

In 1982 the Sol Café and Tenco UK businesses were brought together in a new company called Sol-Tenco Ltd, with Charles Druce of Tenco installed as managing director and Simon Kester of Sol Café taking on the role of chairman until his retirement. The upheaval of transferring all operations to the Greenford site, coupled with the adverse reaction of customers to the discovery that two leading suppliers were now one, caused profits for 1983–4 to fall to a mere £155,000. Competitors took full advantage of customers' nervousness about dealing with a sole supplier, and employees' efforts were somewhat dissipated by uncertainty regarding their future employment. This period witnessed a resurgence of activity by brand leaders, and it was they who benefited from the volume loss by Sol-Tenco rather than private-label competition.

Sol-Tenco's instant coffee trade continued to lie mainly in own-label products, but small amounts of its Gold Roast brand were sold through 'cash and carry' outlets. Green coffee was bought from European Community traders or from representatives of traders in the country of origin. Ready-made spray-dried or powdered coffee was also bought from Brazil, Columbia, India and Salvador. Decaffeinated beans for instant coffee manufacture were obtained from France or Germany by a German company, Coffein Compagnie. Sol-Tenco also bought small quantities of decaffeinated coffee powder from Brazil and supplies of freeze-dried coffee from Germany.

Although the new business was reported to be 'healthy and efficient' in November 1984 (who would want to hear otherwise?), it was not. Nevertheless, against all odds, record profits were announced for the years ending March 1986 (£7.6 million) and March 1987 (£6 million). Thereafter the private-label coffee business went into slow decline. Instant tea, which had been fairly successful in America, never took off in the UK. In the coffee market customers were able to grind down selling prices and use a firmer voice in demanding improved product, packaging and service – added-value elements on which it was more difficult to gain returns. Some business was lost (Argyll/Safeway, Linfood) as a result of business mergers and reorganisations. Yet new business was won with Asda, Marks & Spencer and Tesco. Lyons had hoped to develop export markets, principally Australia, which showed an increase in quality coffees where competition was between Nestlé and private-label coffee. By 1990, however, all tea and coffee businesses, including the tea business on Jersey where up to 250 different packages were supplied to forty countries throughout the world, were brought together under the single company of Lyons Tetley Ltd.

By February 1994, after Allied-Lyons had acquired the Pedro Domecq sherry group for £739 million, the instant coffee business, which had fallen to 11 per cent of the UK market, was sold for £20 million to Kraft Jacobs Suchard, part of the Philip Morris empire. Lyons' ground coffee business, which had over 17 per cent of the market and a loyal customer base, was sold for a similar amount to the British subsidiary of the Finnish, family-owned Paulig group, Finland's largest food company. The Tetley tea business was the last to go. In July 1995 it was bought by a management team, headed by Leon Allen, and backed by Prudential Venture Managers Ltd after unsuccessful talks with others. With an initial price tag of £400 million, Allied Domecq reportedly turned down a £300 million offer from Nestlé in the hope that more could be raised. It soon became apparent, however, that Allied Domecq's expectations were too high, and the Tetley tea business, excluding the Irish tea company based in Dublin, was eventually sold for £190 million.

Chapter

LYONS MAID

ETWEEN OCTOBER 1942 and November 1944 the manufacture of ice-cream in any form had been banned by the government. The justification for this was twofold: first, there was a shortage of raw materials (milk, fats and sugar) and, second, the transportation of ice-cream placed an unnecessary demand on fuel supplies. Although shortages of milk, fats and sugar did occur from time to time, in the matter of transportation the government's reasoning seems to have been perverse. Since other food deliveries were allowed, it would not have been impossible for Lyons to use the same vehicles for the distribution of ice-cream. Long-distance deliveries were in any case sent by the railways, which did not place a drain on the country's dwindling petrol supplies, even though the trains may have been less reliable than before the war. The government's motivation for banning the production of ice-cream during the war is more likely that it was regarded as a luxury and consequently – in the view of civil servants anyway – may have been seen by the public as an unnecessary extravagance, given the harsh controls applied to other food items at the time. This idea is partly borne out by the expeditious removal of the ice-cream controls in 1945, allowing consumers unrationed supplies when the nation's food stocks were still in a perilous plight. In other words, the ban seems to have related more to public opinion than to savings, which in the case of ice-cream would have been small, given that it was a seasonal item.

Rebuilding Ice-Cream Manufacture

In December 1944 ice-cream controls were partially lifted, but the shortage of milk, fats, sugar and other ingredients made the task of restarting manufacture forbidding. Experienced workers remained scarce, and this further limited what could be accomplished with the meagre allowances. However, additional raw materials were obtained through the endeavours of William Brown, who had so successfully introduced the use of rail transport to take bakery products to a wider area in the 1920s and 1930s, and who by now was in charge of ice-cream operations. In Lyons' laboratories the chemists too had been striving to formulate alternatives for all food products including ice-cream. Dextrinised wheat flour had been employed as a substitute for milk solids, and margarine replaced butter. Food substitutes continued after the war, and the extensive use of vegetable fats led to arguments over product definition, especially of ice-cream and chocolate.

After controls were lifted altogether in 1945, ice-cream sales accelerated rapidly and small producers again prospered. Their fortunes were short-lived, however, for in 1947 the government introduced heat treatment regulations to ensure that ice-cream was manufactured in the most hygienic manner, and it became illegal to make ice-cream unless it had been pasteurised by a prescribed method. As many small manufacturers were unable to afford the expensive pasteurising technology, large manufacturers such as Lyons were able to expand their markets relentlessly at the expense of others.

Shortly after the war Lyons recruited George Handelman, from the building contractor Bovis, to develop the overseas ice-cream market. In this he was extremely successful – partly because he was fluent in several languages – and markets were soon established in the Middle East (Kuwait, Dubai), the West Indies, Malta, Cyprus and South Africa. These additional markets demanded an increase in production, and the Cadby Hall factory was almost at full stretch, even though most food was still rationed. To improve distribution, Handelman had introduced cold storage depots, using refrigerated cold boxes on railway sites, and this made it easier to satisfy local demand which depended largely on the weather. When it was hot, ice-cream sales soared; when it was cold, there was a corresponding trough. These climatic cycles plagued the industry, and all manufacturers made great efforts to introduce alternative markets and products so as to smooth out demand.

Neil Salmon, whose radical if insensitive ideas were to transform the Corner Houses in the 1950s, joined the ice-cream division in 1946 at the age of twenty-five. Production was constantly being interrupted by equipment breakdowns, and Neil Salmon was determined to modernise the factory. Wartime closures, from September 1942, had left plant without proper maintenance, and corrosion had taken its toll. Spare parts for machinery were in short supply if not unobtainable, since most post-war machine manufacturers preferred to make new equipment rather than provide spare parts for old pre-war machinery. Once travel restrictions had been lifted, Neil Salmon led a small team to the United States in 1948 primarily to visit the Ice-cream Exposition in Atlantic City. While in the States the team took the opportunity of visiting the Hershey Creamery in Harrisburg, Pennsylvania, where a High Temperature Short Time (HTST) unit was on trial. On a later visit to a Kraft margarine plant they studied an automatic weighing, measuring and proportioning device, designed by Yale & Towne. This impressed them so much that they decided to combine the two processes and set up a HTST unit. On their return home Neil Salmon immediately began to organise

a collaboration between Lyons' laboratory staff and production engineers and the APV Company (until 1948 known as Aluminium Plant & Vessel Co. Ltd), specialists in the design and manufacture of processing, heat transfer and refrigeration equipment in the brewery, chemical, food and petroleum industries. When the Ministry of Health accepted the HTST process, agreeing that it conformed to the heat treatment regulations, Lyons gained a lead before the system became universally available to other firms.

Ice Lollies

With the need for more production capacity as well as rising transport costs, Lyons successfully negotiated the purchase of Walker's Dairies Ltd in September 1947 after protracted discussions. A business relationship had already been formed as long ago as 1930 when, under contract, Walker's, a Liverpool firm, had agreed to distribute Pola-Maid to Woolworth's branches in the north of England. The Walker's ice-cream acquisition cost Lyons £335,000 but it enabled them to manufacture ice-cream in Liverpool as well as Cadby Hall and to reach markets in the north without expensive transport costs.

Ice lollies started to appear in the United States during the 1920s with names like Popsicle, Creamsicle and Fudgicle. At the same time the first foil-wrapped choc ice on a stick appeared as a Good Humour Sucker. Ice lollies first arrived in the UK at the beginning of the Second World War but no progress was made until 1944, when the ban on frozen commodities was lifted. Initially intended for the children's market, they soon became popular with adults too, as flavours and styles became more sophisticated. After the war, sales of ice lollies grew so well that they began to threaten the traditional ice-cream market. Some companies specialised in ice lollies to the exclusion of ice-cream; others, such as Lyons and Wall's, were contemptuous of the ice lolly market and at first refused to become involved. Post-war shortages of milk and fats may have encouraged this trade to continue but by now the ice lolly was popular in its own right among young people. The emergence of teenagers as a social group is generally agreed to have started in the 1940s, when some parents were absent or distracted by problems relating to the war. Adolescents found themselves with new freedoms and responsibilities, and a specific 'youth culture' began to flourish, leading to a new market. Many other factors caused this social group to burgeon, but what is beyond doubt is teenagers' influence on British eating habits, some of which continued into adulthood.

Lyons failed to recognise the cultural change, and rejected the offer to purchase Glacier Foods (an ice lolly manufacturer) in the late 1940s because of a misplaced view of the product. However, an opportunity presented itself again in 1951 when Julian Salmon met Glacier Foods' owner Guy Lawrence (b. 1914), whom he had known in RAF Bomber Command during the war. Salmon raised the question of a possible acquisition and after preliminary discussions it was agreed that Lyons should buy the business and that Lawrence should continue to run it. The agreed price of £71,000 was raised by issuing preference shares in Lyons.

As a young man Guy Lawrence had been a champion skier. He also owned and flew his own aeroplane and at the outbreak of war joined Bomber Command, flying over fifty missions into Germany and occupied territories, and winning the DSO and DFC. During the last year of the war he was a group captain on the staff of Bomber Command headquarters and for these services was awarded an OBE. In the 1945 general election Lawrence stood as Liberal candidate for the Colne Valley constituency but was beaten by the Labour candidate. Afterwards he started an aircraft-engineering and freight-carrying business in Buckinghamshire but sold it after four years and bought the ice lolly factory in Maidenhead.

Guy Lawrence's factory was one of the most successful in exploiting the ice lolly market. In 1951 Lawrence was supplying the wholesale trade. He had bought what was then called the Koola Fruta Company from two bankrupt entrepreneurial speculators while it was in receivership. After he renamed it Glacier Foods Ltd, he continued to specialise in making ice lollies and retained the Koola Fruta range, which later included Koola Kreems, lollies containing milk

solids. In 1954 the Orange Maid ice lolly was launched as 'a drink on a stick'; made from frozen fresh orange juice, it was wrapped in foil and sold at the then high price of 6d. Guy Lawrence, who continued to run Glacier Foods after Lyons had bought it from him, went on to make important contributions to Lyons' ice-cream business in the years following, becoming a main board director in 1966 and deputy chairman. He was knighted in 1976.

In 1953 the Yorkshire firm, Massarella Ice-cream Co. Ltd, was bought by Lyons, bringing into the group a factory at Doncaster which was used primarily to make ice lollies for the growing youth market. John and Dominic Massarella had arrived in Britain in the 1890s from Cassino in Italy; one settled in Doncaster, the other in Leicester, and both established independent ice-cream businesses. Later, John Massarella's four sons – Carmen, Andrew, Vincent and Lewis – in turn started their own ice-cream businesses in Doncaster, and much the same happened in the Leicester branch of the family. When large capital expenditure was required for new manufacturing plant after the war, the various branches of the family decided to pool their resources, with Rebori & Company of Rotherham and J. Carolis of Sheffield, and to have a combined manufacturing centre in Doncaster. Thus in October 1945 the new company, Massarella Supplies Ltd, came into being. A new factory was built in a former skating rink, just released by the army, in Hunt Lane, Doncaster. Impressive modern ice-cream processing and packing equipment was provided by Cherry-Burrell Ltd. Work was begun in 1945 and by Easter 1949 ice-cream production had started with a capacity of 5,000 gallons per day.

By 1956 sales of Orange Maid had increased by 375 per cent – a large proportion of which was attributed to adult consumers. Manufacturers were increasingly directing their advertising of ice lollies towards cinema audiences, in order to boost ice-cream sales during the winter. Cinema was still enjoying its heyday, when people of all ages visited the cinema as often as twice a week. Following the success of Orange Maid a rectangular ice-cream on a stick was introduced and this was further developed by surrounding the ice-cream with a frozen strawberry-juice shell, shaped like a tongue, which Lyons sold as the Mivvi. It became their biggest-selling product up to that date. Mivvy is cockney slang for 'marvellous', but why Lyons chose this name is perplexing. It was fortunate for Lyons that they decided after all to enter the ice lolly trade, since this was to influence the entire ice-cream business.

Bridge Park Ice-Cream Factory

By the early 1950s production at Cadby Hall had again outgrown its food-manufacturing space and as in 1920 it became necessary to consider moving out to a primary factory. New refrigeration methods and automatic packing machines, which required large spaces for the conveyor systems, made it essential to relocate the ice-cream factory. In 1954 a committee headed by Neil Salmon was set up to plan a new factory on land adjacent to the tea factory at Greenford. This site, alongside the Grand Union Canal, which was no more than a wheatfield in 1954, became known as Bridge Park. The first pilot operations started in 1956–7 and by May 1958 it had been brought into full operation when it was officially opened by HRH The Princess Margaret.

Designed by the architects Harrison, Stevens, Ashby & Partners, the Bridge Park factory was on two levels and from the outset was planned with potential expansion. All the heavy manufacturing equipment was placed on the upper floor while the ground floor was given over to the engine rooms, cold stores, raw material storage tanks and a staff restaurant. The main contractors were G. Percy Trentham & Co. Ltd; the electrical, mechanical engineering and interior design were carried out by Lyons' own Works Department. Because the factory was so specialised, over seventy engineering, seventeen electrical and forty-five building sub-contractors were used.

The layout of the Bridge Park factory was crucial, since the aim was to avoid any possibility of contamination. Therefore the pipes did not come down through the ceiling to the various machines because they could form dust traps; instead, pipelines for ingredients, water, refrigeration, electricity and other services were led up through a specially built upper floor which was totally waterproof. The result was a clear uncluttered space. Lighting and ventilation (which was set at a higher air pressure inside than outside to prevent the ingress of dust, insects and so on) were flush with the ceiling. The production lines were laid out symmetrically and the whole was controlled from a central computerised control panel from which an operator could direct the flow of the various ingredients to the requisite points.

Bridge Park produced many flavours of bulk ice-cream, choc ices, 'family bricks', Pola-Maid (only two machines were installed supplying almost exclusively the catering and hospital trade with strawberry and vanilla flavour) and Zippy. Zippy was a form of brick ice-cream which had been sliced and prepared for wafer portions. It had been developed, and patented, by Harold Boon and was an entirely new process for treating and wrapping the ice-cream as it emerged from the freezer. Zippy reached the retailer in cartons containing individual rectangular portions, each enclosed in a cardboard collar so that it could be placed between two wafers and the wrapping removed in a second or two without anyone touching the ice-cream itself. The process had been discovered almost by accident when Lyons were working on a method of cutting and storing ice-cream for sale in this way. When the boxed bricks were cut, it was found that the cut surfaces did not freeze together when they were placed in cold storage. After ice-cream has been cut it shrinks fractionally while the outer frame remains proud, and the protruding edges of the frame prevent the ice-cream from refreezing to itself at the cut faces.

Late in 1958, Glacier Foods' ice-cream and lolly production at Maidenhead closed; part of its production moved to Bridge Park and part to Doncaster. Extensions to Bridge Park were made, and continued for years until a total of sixteen bays were in operation. These housed not only increased manufacturing, hardening and holding cold stores, but also centralised product and process development departments, an engineering design department, marketing and sales outfits, an overseas division and head office administration. Much of the engineering for plant and service design was undertaken by Lyons themselves. The last major development at Bridge Park, around 1989, was the installation of a large Danish Høyer machine – after the Danish engineer Oluf Gudmund Høyer – consisting of automatic freezers, extruders, a hardening tunnel, enrobers, and wrapping and boxing machines for various types of choc ices.

Frozen Desserts for the Catering Trade

Although most of Cadby Hall's ice-cream production had now transferred to Bridge Park, speciality ice-cream continued to be made at the former factory. Here special-order ice-cream gateaux and sweets were handmade for parties and banquets. Fanciful creations that sometimes took weeks to prepare were no doubt demolished in minutes. In addition to the one-off creations the Cadby factory produced a range of specialities available all the year round but particularly at Christmas. They included Yule logs decorated with holly, fluffy snowballs with robins on them, teddy bears and pompadour dolls. These so-called miniatures could only be kept in perfect condition for a few weeks and so there was a considerable build-up towards Christmas when more than sixty women were employed in their manufacture.

It was here in 1950 that the famous Wonder Cake made its debut. The brainchild of factory manager Frank Theobold, it was made by hand and consisted of layers of ice-cream with discs of sponge cake. The recipe had been formulated to withstand temperatures to which the product was subjected while creating a suitable blend of flavour and texture to complement the ice-cream. Sponge cake, made by the bakery department, was sliced horizontally and then sandwiched together with alternate layers of pistachio, strawberry and vanilla ice-cream. The whole confection was decorated with creamy scrolls and glacé cherries and encircled with a gold band. Originally produced for the restaurant trade, it was made available to the public, through Lyons' dealers, in 1952.

By the end of 1967 Lyons Maid were making a range of eighty ice-cream desserts for the catering trade. They included Peach Slice, which consisted of layers of vanilla and raspberry ice-cream with a peach sorbet centre. Egg Caramel was made from triangles of French and vanilla ice-cream surrounded by caramel ice-cream. French ice-cream, sometimes wrongly referred to as egg ice-cream, was made from milk, cream, sugar, egg yolk and flavouring. Tutti-Frutti Whirl contained tutti-frutti and strawberry ice-cream blended together in a serving cup, and Orange Gateau was made of layers of orange and vanilla ice-cream decorated with candied orange slices and chocolate whirls.

The Great Competition with Wall's

While ice-cream production and sales accelerated rapidly after the war, Lyons were faced with many challenges. Foremost was a decision by Wall's to abandon tricycle selling and instead build a network of agents to compete directly with Lyons. With rising labour costs, Wall's tricycle operation had become prohibitively expensive and in any case was unsuitable for winter sales. The move from selling from 8,500 tricycles asking 'Stop me and buy one' to setting up a nationwide agency network presented such a hurdle to Wall's that Lyons seemed in an unassailable position to steal yet a greater lead over their main rival. The circumstances of rationing, however, prevented this from happening, since the allocation of raw materials favoured Wall's and, whereas Lyons had many agents and smaller allocations, Wall's had fewer agents to satisfy with their larger allocations. Wall's therefore cherry-picked some of the larger agents, especially the growing retail chains, whose demand Lyons could not fully satisfy. In this way Wall's secured valuable summer contracts at seaside resorts. This process continued well into the 1950s and seriously eroded Lyons' trade.

At the same time many of the refrigerated cabinets which Lyons had installed in their agents' premises before the war were faulty, after six or seven years of neglect, and prevented Lyons from making deliveries. Spare parts were in short supply but so were skilled refrigeration engineers, and it became necessary to establish a training school, under Lyons' refrigeration engineer Reginald Guy, before the task of repairing equipment could be started. Eventually a refrigeration service department, which covered the whole of England and Scotland, was set up with almost 100 engineers, operating with their own vehicles from regional offices.

Rail transport, which had served the company well for many years, was becoming unreliable and costly. In 1951 it cost 1s. 4d. to send a gallon of ice-cream by road, compared with 2s. 7d. by rail. Four years later the respective costs were 1s. 10d. and 6s. 5d. Drikold (ICI's branded dry ice) costs also increased, adding to the expense of rail distribution. This drastic rise in rail transport charges caused Lyons to introduce their own road network based around a series of cold depots. Two depots, Greenwich and Tottenham, had been established before the war, and another was opened in Chelsea in 1950. By 1955 thirty-six depots were operating around the country and sales increased from 1.5 million gallons in 1945 to almost 14 million gallons in 1959.

Although ice-cream sales remained buoyant throughout the 1950s, Lyons faced increasing competition from Wall's, whose effective marketing and advertising campaigns were building brand loyalty. Wall's had also developed a highly efficient distribution system based on 100 depots. By the 1960s and 1970s the ice-cream market was more or less dominated by Lyons and Wall's, with Lyons having approximately 40 per cent to Wall's 45 per cent. For years Lyons and Wall's had remained friendly competitors and after the war had a rather cosy relationship. It was not unknown, for example, for one to help the other make ice-cream in their respective factories at times of difficulties. They also shared ideas on technology, primarily through Mark Bogod (ice-cream director) and Cecil Rodd (the Maurice Salmon of Wall's), since they were good friends and prominent members of the associations and advisers to the industry. After Bogod's retirement in 1964, Lyons and Wall's maintained frequent contact, mainly to discuss and agree a common strategy regarding government legislation which became onerous when purchase tax, decimalisation and VAT were introduced. Contrary to statements made by both companies during studies of the industry, they did, from time to time, fix prices. For example,

following clandestine meetings prior to the imposition of purchase tax, both agreed not to use halfpennies in their pricing but rather to round up. Similar agreements were made at the time of decimalisation. Both companies, however, remained strong competitors, even though sometimes they imitated each other's products. There is no evidence, however, that the two companies 'fixed' territories, as was frequently claimed. The fact that most kiosks on Brighton beach were selling Lyons ice-cream, for example, was not due to a fixing arrangement but to local councillors' preference for catering contracts to be made with single suppliers. Both companies provided ice-cream cabinets for their respective retail outlets and for reasons of economy shared the maintenance cost of these by way of a jointly owned company, Total Refrigeration Ltd.

Apart from the competition with Wall's, by the late 1950s the ice-cream businesses of Associated Business Foods (Neilson's) and Union International (Eldorado) were also beginning to make inroads into Lyons' traditional market, each company having approximately 10 per cent of the ice-cream market. This made it difficult for Lyons to generate more growth, since Neilson and Eldorado were causing over-capacity, exacerbated by the growing trade from ice-cream vans (an updated version of the tricycle) and static sites where soft ice-cream was sold from special dispensers. Lyons could no longer depend on its production competence, product range (which lacked effective branding) and customer loyalty. Therefore, under Guy Lawrence, who as chairman of Lyons Maid by now had overall responsibility for the ice-cream business, a major reorganisation of the division was carried out between 1957 and 1963. With little scope to reduce costs further, Lyons decided they had no alternative but to increase their market share by acquisition.

Lyons Maid Ltd: Mergers and Acquisitions

Guy Lawrence and Neil Salmon had analysed the UK ice-cream market during 1961–2 and came to the conclusion that it was growing by about 1.5 per cent a year. Lawrence and Salmon felt that the market would not support four big manufacturers. Accordingly, they submitted their analysis to the management of United International and Associated British Foods with the recommendation that they merge their companies. Such a consortium would be large enough to compete with Wall's and would create opportunities for rationalisation especially in manufacturing resource with all the attendant savings. There was, however, a business risk attached to such an approach but surprisingly the Lawrence/Salmon proposals were received very favourably and there was an unexpected bonus when Associated British Foods decided to sell their interests in Neilson Holdings Ltd and withdraw from ice-cream manufacturing completely.

In 1962, therefore, Lyons Maid acquired Neilsons Holdings Ltd from the parent company, then acquired Eldorado from the Union International Company Ltd, and merged their own ice-cream operation with the purchased businesses. Glacier Foods Ltd had been set up as a holding company to take over the interests of the Lyons Maid ice-cream division, to acquire Eldorado ice-cream from Union International for 25 per cent of the equity in Glacier Foods and to purchase Neilson's from Associated British Foods for £3 million. At the same time Glacier Foods Ltd acquired the refrigerated distribution business in the north of England from W.D. Mark & Sons Ltd. Following the consolidation of the companies, the ice-cream business became known as Lyons Maid Eldorado Neilson Ltd, which subsequently changed its name to the less cumbersome Lyons Maid Ltd on 1 January 1964. After the merger, ice-cream production centred mainly on four factories located at Bridge Park, Barking, Liverpool and, briefly, Cadby Hall. The number of products was rationalised to eliminate overlapping lines formerly sold by the three separate companies, and the inevitable redundancies followed. Marketing became concentrated on new lines.

The merger of Union International and Lyons also created an opportunity for both companies to combine their frozen food interests, and these activities are covered in chapter 23. These mergers brought about the rationalisation

of refrigerated transport, when Alpine Refrigerated Deliveries Ltd was incorporated to handle all ice-cream and frozen food products for the respective companies. Jack Silverman, previously distribution manager for Glacier Foods, became its chief executive and it was largely under his direction that substantial economies were made. The rationalisation also enabled Glacier Foods to reduce staffing levels in its factory, depot, administration and van fleet by roughly a half and to cut the capital employed by a third.

In the first full year after the mergers, sales dropped by 22 per cent and Lyons' loss in Glacier Foods amounted to £266,539. This was said to be due to the cost of reorganisation, bad weather (a recurring excuse in the accounts) and the burden of purchase tax, which had been applied to food for the first time by Harold Macmillan's Conservative government in the 1962 budget. The imposition of purchase tax is calculated to have cost Glacier Foods over £1.5 million in lost sales and took the price of ice-cream beyond what some consumers were prepared to pay. In the second full year after reorganisation Glacier Foods made a profit of £194,741. This was welcome, but insignificant when measured against investment. It can be largely attributed to the wide difference between the below-average weather in 1963 and the above-average weather of 1964. Clearly the new Glacier Foods business – in common with the ice-cream industry generally – was not operating profitably enough to service the capital employed or to maintain progressive growth. As the food-manufacturing business did not receive investment grants for improved factory and distribution systems, it cost as much (on average) to distribute and sell ice-cream as it did to manufacture it. These factors all contributed to the continuing poor performance of ice-cream – as did the weather, if the accounts are to be believed!

Children's Market: Zoom and Fab

By the 1960s sales of ice-cream were stagnant, but ice lollies – known in the trade as 'frozen confectionery' – were not only selling well but reaching entirely new markets. With the birth of commercial television in 1955, TV advertising

Zoom ice-cream competition featuring Thunderbirds,
August 1966.

became crucial to the launch of any new product. It was in fact television itself that provided the inspiration for the revolutionary new type of ice lolly which was to transform the ice-cream industry from the 1960s onwards.

At the end of the 1950s a British producer, Gerry Anderson, and his wife Sylvia developed an innovative technique for using puppets in children's television science-fiction adventures. Dubbed 'Supermarionation', this method was first employed in the series *Supercar* in 1959 and culminated in the mid-1960s with *Thunderbirds*, which became a classic. The best-known series were accompanied by a huge merchandising trade, including bubble gum cards, sweet cigarette boxes and cards, biscuit tins, board games, jigsaws, model-making kits and toy cars.

With the extraordinary success of the Mivvi, Lyons Maid decided to make similar experiments in the children's market, and the new TV science-fiction craze was ideal for their purpose. Zoom was launched in May 1963, as Lyons Maid's first 6d. ice lolly. Shaped like a rocket, with lime, lemon

and strawberry flavours placed in horizontal stripes of colour, it was originally designed to tie in with Gerry Anderson's 1961 series, *Fireball XL5*, although later it was linked to *Thunderbirds*. Fireball was a spacecraft piloted by Colonel Steve Zodiac which zoomed around the galaxy, patrolling against alien invaders in the year 2062. The launch of Zoom was supported by large quantities of display material featuring picture cards and Steve Zodiac. In 1963 the idea of putting picture cards into the lolly bags was another first. It had already been done on a small scale in the United States but never in Britain. After months of experimenting, a way was found of placing a card in a separate waterproof compartment inside the lolly bag. Children could collect a set of fifty different cards, and, for the price of postage only, a free album could be obtained in which to stick them. A firm called Comet Miniatures produced a plastic kit (Kitmaster) for building a replica of the rocket, and Lyons Maid used it as part of their promotion for Zoom. According to the *Lyons Mail* of July

1963, 'The model's normal price was 9s. but it was made available for 4s. 6d. plus two Zoom wrappers.' Lyons Maid had estimated that 100,000 sets would be bought, each month, in the two months after Zoom's launch.

Then Sea Jet ice lollies were introduced to tie in with the series *Stingray*, in which Captain Troy Tempest was the pilot of an underwater vessel. Sea Jets, priced at only 4d., were available in four flavours – vanilla, strawberry, lemon and orange. The Super Sea Jet (which cost 2d. more) had three flavours in one – mint and vanilla dipped in chocolate. Children who collected Sea Jet wrappers could obtain the Airfix Stingray plastic model kit.

Not surprisingly, these rocket-shaped lollies linked with male action heroes and model-making were bought mainly by boys. Since there was no specific children's product for girls, the development team set about creating one. As part of their research the team came up with twenty-one three-flavour combinations, all theoretically acceptable to girls and all feasible for large-scale manufacture. The twenty-one combinations were sent to Lyons Maid's psychologist, Ray Brown, who assembled a taste panel of 300 girls aged between five and fifteen. After the girls had tasted and selected their preferences, the number of flavour combinations was reduced to three. These were then submitted to the panel, who chose a combination of strawberry fruit ice and vanilla cream ice, with the top dipped in chocolate and coated with 'hundreds and thousands'.

Marketing of the new ice lolly for girls was based on the formula used for Zoom and Sea Jet; this time Lyons Maid chose Gerry Anderson's phenomenally successful *Thunderbirds* television series (and films). As well as the usual male heroes in the form of Scott Tracy and his family, who piloted the Thunderbird vehicles of the International Rescue organisation, these programmes included a heroine – Lady Penelope Creighton-Ward. She owned a specially adapted pink Rolls-Royce which bore the registration number FAB 1, and her radio call sign was F.A.B. This provided the name Fab for the new ice lolly for girls, which went on sale in May 1967, priced at 6d., and shaped like a cross between the Mivvi

and the Zoom. Like Lady Penelope, it was supposed to suggest luxury, modern style and adventure. The word 'fab', in *Thunderbirds* as well as in general usage, was the fashionable word of the 1960s; short for 'fabulous', it was used by young people to describe anything regarded as outstandingly good, including the Beatles pop group (the 'Fab Four'). Like the Beatles, the Fab ice lolly was an immediate success; by August 1967 sales had reached 1.5 million per week. Fab's launch had been followed by TV advertising transmitted nationally five times a week during children's peak viewing times. Over a ten-week period 10 million Fabs were sold – 77 per cent more than expected. It was the most successful launch, in terms of sales, in Lyons Maid's history.

Lyons Maid went on to make Orbit, another rocket-shaped lolly, linked to the next Anderson television production, *Captain Scarlet and the Mysterons*. Priced at 9d., it much resembled the Zoom, and was flavoured chocolate and orange. The Supermarionation team also produced TV and cinema commercials for Lyons Maid between 1962 and 1968 featuring the four linked series and a later one, *Joe 90*, which was also depicted on Zoom wrappers.

Meanwhile other products were being targeted at the youth market. On 17 June 1963 an ice lolly called Pick of the Pops was launched. Priced at 8d., it had a combination of coffee and advocaat flavours and was coated in milk chocolate with biscuit pieces. Pick of the Pops was supported by a television advertising campaign which ran from 30 June for eight weeks. Then on 12 May 1969 Lyons Maid launched Luv, a lolly similar to Fab (three-quarters covered in chocolate and hundreds and thousands) but at 9d. costing 3d. more, and aimed at girls aged ten to fifteen. Luv was backed by TV advertising and a promotion offering the chance to collect a set of picture cards of pop stars (such as the Beatles, the Rolling Stones, Cliff Richard and Cilla Black) included in the wrappers.

Ice lolly manufacture, requiring multi-flavoured confections in complex shapes, had become increasingly sophisticated. This made it necessary for Lyons Maid to invest in an ultra-fast automatic frozen-confectionery unit (the

Ice-cream poster featuring the popular ice-creams of the 1930s. By kind permission of John Bishop.

Marcialine 1400) towards the end of 1969. Costing £30,000, and made by Vanmar Products of Richmond, the unit could produce well over half a million ice lollies a day and was one of three ordered to keep pace with the demand for Zooms, Pick of the Pops, Fabs, Sea Jets, Orbits and Luvs for children and teenagers.

Frozen Yoghurt and Soft Ice-Cream

In November 1968 Lyons Maid test-marketed what they described as 'evening ice-cream', an entirely new product made from frozen yoghurt. Three different lines were launched. Battenburg consisted of chequered vanilla and strawberry frozen yoghurt surrounded by coffee ice-cream and it sold for 3s. 6d. for a five-portion pack. Strawberry Ripple Roll, vanilla yoghurt rippled with a sauce made from crushed strawberries and wrapped in a soft chocolate sponge, was priced at 3s. for four portions. Finally Partners was a twin pack of strawberry and vanilla yoghurt topped with chocolate sugar whirls. At this time frozen yoghurt was virtually unknown in Britain, although on the continent it had scored a huge success. Initial marketing took place in London and the Home Counties only, with advertising in serial form in the London *Evening News* and *Evening Standard* newspapers which had a combined circulation in the target area of two million. Nevertheless the 'evening ice-cream' did not succeed. Little market research had been undertaken and the advertising was badly focused. Despite their experience with Zoom and Fab, Lyons had still not understood that bringing a new product to the market required a massive marketing effort with a corresponding budget. They could no longer depend on their new product managers dreaming up new ideas and expecting the Lyons name alone to compel consumers to buy.

Another 1960s development was soft ice-cream, which was popularised by sales from vans equipped with special dispensing machines. The vans travelled around housing estates and other strategic locations where their trade depended largely on impulse buying mainly by children, who rushed from all directions when hearing their familiar ding-dong tunes. The Tonibell Manufacturing Company Ltd, a subsidiary of the British American Tobacco Company Ltd, operated 500 purpose-built vans, many franchised, from which they sold ice-cream direct to the public across the whole country. In 1969 Lyons paid £1.75 million to acquire them.

Supported by eighteen depots and a factory in Borehamwood, Hertfordshire, Tonibell had been started in 1937 by the Italian-born Toni Pignatelli and his Scottish-born wife. Their business, known as Toni's, consisted of a small shop in Burnt Oak High Street in North London where ice-cream was sold from the shop's front window. Twelve years later the couple's son

Hostess ice-cream production line at the Bridge Park factory, Greenford, 1986.

Ronald, who had changed his surname to Peters, began to develop the business and bought a second shop nearby. A tricycle was obtained in 1951 and the first adapted van, complete with chimes, was introduced a year later. By 1953 six vans were operating in the area and in 1955 the production centre was moved to Barnet Way. The company name was changed to Tonibell in 1960 because competitors started to use the Toni's name and van livery, and the vans were all repainted in light blue with a picture of a cow. In 1961 soft ice-cream was introduced and all vans were converted to enable them to handle this new product as well as the standard ranges of ice-cream. In 1964 the British American Tobacco Company bought Tonibell, introduced a more varied selection of ice-cream and continued to sell it from vans.

Lyons were well acquainted with soft ice-cream, which had been available since before the war. Soft ice-cream, sold as if it were 'Italian' ice-cream, was in many respects inferior to hard ice-cream, having a slimy texture and leaving a strange aftertaste. The powdered ingredients were made from dried milk, fat, sugar flavouring and normally a stabiliser. Many people found the taste quite awful, and this was probably because the gums used in the stabiliser contained a derivative of moss or seaweed (carageenan). Many Woolworth's stores sold it during the summer but the mix had to be kept chilled.

In 1952 the Lyons laboratories were closely studying the development of a process for making ultra-heat-treated milk products by the Swiss Bernese Alps Milk Company. The following year the process, known as uperisation, was demonstrated in Bernese Alps Milk's dairy in Konolfingen, Switzerland, to a team from Lyons headed by Dr Jack Bushill, the laboratory's expert on milk and its use in large-scale food manufacture. Interest was focused on a small transportable unit, manufactured by Sultzer in Winterthur, which treated 1,000 litres of milk per hour and was coupled to a Martin aseptic canning machine made in San Francisco by the James Dole Company. This 'uperiser' was subsequently sold to Lyons, who used it to convince the Ministry of Health that the process could be used to sterilise

ice-cream mix for aseptic canning and storage for long periods without refrigeration. It was installed in 1956. Two larger uperisers, manufactured by the APV Company under licence, were installed at the Bridge Park factory, and the treated milk was made into soft ice-cream which could travel around in vans and be sold from such outlets as kiosks and small shops or cafés without being refrigerated. The machines were in full operation when the factory closed. The trade in this ice-cream became so successful that Lyons formed an association with Tastee Freeze Ltd to sell the new product from Lyons' Wimpy bars and other static sites. At the same time Lyons acquired a 39 per cent stake in the equity of Mister Softee Ltd and formed a mobile franchising company to sell soft ice-cream from vans.

The Three Dancing Children

Despite a number of successful experiments, by the end of the 1960s Lyons' ice-cream business as a whole was disappointing. With the market share of hard ice-cream reduced to only 37 per cent and annual sales persistently meagre, in 1971 Lyons decided to create a new 'fun food' image. As part of the ice-cream offensive, and in keeping with the trend of other Lyons products, Lyons Maid introduced a logo in the form of a slab of cake on ice-cream packaging. The larger cartons displayed cheerful pictures of figures and scenes drawn in children's story-book style. Many promotions were planned and an extensive television campaign ran continuously from April to September with the slogan: 'Enjoy yesterday today – with Lyons Maid'. Despite the huge costs of repackaging, advertising and consultancy fees, Lyons Maid failed to increase their market. According to the 1972 accounts, 'Lyons Maid achieved reasonable results in spite of the weather being somewhat below average.' Such a dismal comment from the chairman suggests the 1971 sales campaign had failed.

The 1972 and 1973 seasons showed a slight improvement, helped largely by their 85 per cent acquisition of Midland Counties Dairy Ltd on 1 January 1973. The additional large manufacturing plant and good weather of 1973 enabled Lyons Maid to gain substantial sales, prompting

Brian Salmon, the chairman, to report 'an excellent year, additionally fortified by good summer weather'. However, he noted, 'value added tax has now been imposed – a retrogressive step which is deplored by most commentators and greatly deprecated by consumers, especially families with limited means and those with young children. There is, moreover, ample evidence that the imposition of indirect taxes has an adverse effect on ice-cream consumption.'

Whether the new packaging played a part in the brief recovery of ice-cream sales is not known, but in any case the product images were changed in January 1973 for what became known as the three dancing children. They were first used on Neilson's vans but the new logo bore such a strong resemblance to a logo which had appeared on Horniman vans in 1936 that the 1973 design was probably based on the earlier one. Subsequently the 'dancing children' logo was extended to all ice-cream advertising, partly because it was less expensive but, more importantly, because it branded all Lyons Maid's products under one logo.

An American Acquisition: Baskin-Robbins

On 31 December 1973 J. Lyons (US Holdings) Inc., a wholly owned American subsidiary of the company, acquired from a subsidiary of United Brands Company the Baskin-Robbins Ice Cream Company. The purchase price was $35.5 million paid partly in cash, partly by way of three promissory notes at each anniversary in 1974, 1975 and 1976.

Irvine Robbins opened his first Snowbird store in December 1945 in Glendale, California offering twenty-one flavours and a wooden spoon for his customers to taste samples before buying. Burt Baskin, Robbins brother-in-law, also opened ice-cream parlours but it was not until 1949 that they merged their forty-three parlours thus forming Baskin-Robbins Ice Cream Company. Selling in many countries throughout the world, they provided 'portioned' ice-cream – that is to say scooped for each customer – from display cabinets holding up to thirty-one different flavours. Sixteen flavours were standard and fifteen were changed every day.

As part of the settlement terms the American management remained in place and no attempt was made to combine the American and British ice-cream businesses, which were run quite differently. Baskin-Robbins operated by way of franchises; the management had built up a good relationship with these and interference from outside was seen as unnecessary. Lyons Maid, on the other hand, sold their products through retailers. Some attempts have been made to introduce Baskin-Robbins to the United Kingdom but without much success. By contrast with America, the British ice-cream market tends to be seasonal and subject to the vagaries of the British climate, despite the growth of home freezer ownership.

Baskin-Robbins had and still has an enviable reputation for high-quality ice-cream which it manufactured and sold under its famous 'Baskin-Robbins 31' symbol. In 1974, its ice-cream was sold in over 1,300 Baskin-Robbins stores located in all major cities of the United States. As the ice-cream business in the United States was more advanced and sophisticated than anywhere else in the world, the acquisition was seen as a valuable investment with attractive growth prospects. Unlike Lyons Maid, Baskin-Robbins regularly recorded good profits and its popularity spread to many countries worldwide. This was by far the most important ice-cream acquisition made. Whereas Lyons Maid in the UK continued to report the handicaps of the imposition of VAT and an explosion in material costs, Baskin-Robbins' performance was reported to have surpassed expectations. When the manufacturing resources of the Ideal Milk Company in Indiana were acquired soon afterwards the production franchise for much of the mid-west was regained and integrated with the existing Baskin-Robbins installations in other states. Year on year the business continued to perform well, alongside the increasing growth of its franchise outlets both in the United States and abroad.

The growth of the consumer market after the Second World War had just as much impact on the ice-cream trade as on other areas of the food industry. While the range of ice-cream products had remained almost static before 1939, the 1950s, 1960s and 1970s were characterised by innovation in product type, packaging and marketing styles. This created a need for display designers, graphic artists, design engineers and even psychologists. More importantly marketing departments became key players in deciding what products to launch after having carried out exhaustive market research. Their research, however, was not infallible: in 1967 the Lyons Maid marketing department underestimated sales of Fab by 77 per cent; it was fortunate that Lyons had the production capacity to cope.

During this period a whole range of ice-cream categories developed: desserts with exotic flavours, 'space age' shapes and innovative mixtures, bulk ice-cream for supermarkets and the take-home trade, ices for cinemagoers and what seemed to be an endless cycle of hand-held ice-creams from lollies to King Cone cornets. As sales for home consumption were fuelled by the growth of supermarkets and affordable home freezers, own-label brands started to appear. Since ice-cream manufacture is relatively simple, however, other companies producing higher-quality, larger-volume packs and few flavours began to satisfy the supermarket trade. On the other hand, Loseley Dairy Products were successful in selling 'real' ice-cream to the supermarkets; other brands followed, and before long American brands began to challenge these and the traditional ice-cream makers such as Lyons and Wall's. Recent changes in consumer trends have seen expensive luxury ice-cream in large tubs become popular as home desserts – pioneered by such firms as Häagen-Dazs and Ben & Jerry's.

A recurring theme in Lyons, over many years, was the complaint that product was frequently in the wrong place at the wrong time, and a poor distribution system did nothing to alleviate this. Product which could have been sold in the south, for example, was located in the north. Until 1964 Lyons were responsible for their own ice-cream deliveries but in 1964, when the interests of Union International were acquired, a joint distribution company was established under Alpine Refrigerated Deliveries. When Findus frozen foods began to be carried by Alpine, Lyons suffered from a second-class service. This, however, is not the final chapter in the story of Lyons ice-cream; the events of more recent years are recounted in the concluding part of this book.

LET THEM EAT CAKE

THE LYONS BAKERY had come through the war in a reasonably healthy state, largely because of its mass-production capability, and its ability to innovate and seize upon speculative opportunities. However, the country's food stocks were in a critical condition, worse than in the gloomiest period of the war. The stimulus of competition and the freedom to utilise expertise could not be fully exploited. Shortages of all kinds also made it intensely difficult to obtain factory equipment for a much-needed reconstruction and modernisation programme.

Bread Rationing

In July 1946 bread was rationed for the first time in British history, even though Europe had been at peace for over a year. This followed a disastrous shortage of world grain: the United Kingdom's import of wheat was reduced by 250,000 tons in the first half of 1946. It was also necessary to feed 30 million Germans, for whom famine loomed after the collapse of their agriculture. Bread supplies were not rigorously controlled, but its quality was adversely affected by the progressive restrictions that had been imposed during the war years. As time passed, rationing became nominal; none the less it caused average consumption per head to be reduced by 19 lb a year compared to that of 1945. The extremely cold weather which followed the war diminished livestock populations and in November 1947 the severe frosts brought about the rationing of potatoes. During the 1946–7 season families had been eating more potatoes, probably because the lack of other foodstuffs such as meat, fish and

sugar forced them to keep up their calorie intake by consuming more of what was available in the shops.

Despite these problems, Lyons' manufacturing divisions gradually improved their performance to the extent that a new bread plant opened at Tottenham in 1951. Other new bread factories followed – at Bristol, Crawley in Sussex, Chessington in Surrey and Eastleigh, Hampshire. The Brighton factory too became a provincial bakery which by the 1960s had diversified into manufacturing own-label cake, including Nippy Fancies, for the Marks & Spencer stores. The opening of these bakeries provoked a violent reaction from some quarters of the trade, since local bakers felt their own markets might be threatened; the National Association of Master Bakers, for example, organised a series of mass protest meetings.

At this time the heavy costs of reconstruction, which most industries had to undertake, continued to rise. Increased petrol taxation and the new railway freight charges, which were indiscriminately imposed, added well over £100,000 a year to the direct cost of distributing the finished food products. Inevitably, these additional overheads were reflected in the price of manufactured food which households had to bear. Indirect taxation accounted for about one-half of Britain's total taxation, and most of this, in one form or another, entered into the food chain, ultimately reaching the customer. Tax, in theory at least, had previously been levied on consumer goods but, since it was charged on many items of equipment as well, it was regarded by many manufacturers as a tax on the tools of the trade. Between 1945 and 1950 approximately one-third of Lyons' machinery had been replaced at an average cost of over two and a half times that of pre-war days.

Some opportunities occasionally did arise for management to minimise raw material expenditure. In 1950, for reasons now unknown, the government had offered a large discount to catering firms to buy more than 100 tons of contaminated frozen whole egg on condition they had facilities for pasteurising it. Few firms had the expertise to deal with such a consignment but Lyons enthusiastically took up the challenge, treating the whole shipment in their ice-cream department under strict laboratory control, and under the watchful eyes of the Ministry of Health and food inspectors. The process was so successful that it was adopted by the bakery department, which made use of the technique whenever other contaminated shipments were identified by government officials.

Government control of the milling industry ended at midnight on 29 August 1953, freeing the baking industry from all restraints and allowing white bread to be produced after thirteen years of control. The National Association of Master Bakers announced that the recommended price for the new 14oz white loaf was to be 5½d. in London and 6d. in most other parts of the country – a small increase due to the withdrawal of government subsidy.

Baking Monopolies

By 1953 Lyons were classified as the third largest producer of bread in the UK, while Allied Bakeries and the Co-operative Wholesale Society enjoyed a huge lead. With the demise of the small craft baker, the bread and cake industry began to consolidate into a few large producers. Concerned that their margins might be threatened by the bakeries, the milling industry sought to secure their markets. Rank and Spillers – the two largest flour suppliers – began diversifying by forming their own baking companies, which became known as British Bakeries and United Bakeries respectively. In response, between 1954 and 1957 Garfield

Weston's Associated British Foods spent more than £10 million acquiring milling and bakery interests; by 1960 it owned thirty-one milling companies, eighty bread plants and thousands of bakery shops, and created Sunblest as its national loaf. As mentioned earlier, one of his most stunning acquisitions was the ABC teashops. Rank, on the other hand, spent £20 million buying into bakery businesses and merged with Hovis-McDougall in 1962; its national bread was Mother's Pride.

Before the war Lyons had gained a good reputation with its Puriti Wrapped Bread. With no artificial ingredients, just flour, yeast, lard, salt and water, it was highly popular, especially since it could be conveniently bought in all teashops. After the war, Lyons' national brand was Superbread. During the 1950s, competition from Mother's Pride and Sunblest became so intense that by 1960 Lyons' bread-making position had slipped to fifth place, accounting for only 1 per cent of the national market, although its share in London and Bristol, where the main bread factories were situated, was higher. Traditionally Lyons had favoured the cake market, not only because of its longer shelf life but because there was greater scope for innovation, allowing higher profit margins. From the table it can be seen that profits from cake outstripped bread profits enormously between 1949 and 1964.

Pre-tax profits of bread and cake 1949–1964 (£000's)

Year	Bread	Cake	Year	Bread	Cake
1949	42	342	1957	119	983
1950	59	433	1958	55	857
1951	64	436	1959	33	560
1952	37	601	1960	12	638
1953	103	743	1961	109	502
1954	76	843	1962	135	573
1955	71	860	1963	293	646
1956	58	888	1964	454	835

Lyons' loss of market share in bread was due not only to competition but to a number of factors. Unlike some of their rivals Lyons objected to paying the vast sums of money that were needed to acquire regional bread bakeries in order to boost market share. Lyons had already invested heavily in a new bread plant, and in any case were reluctant to enter into the retail bread trade for fear it might alienate their wholesale traders. Closure of some of the teashops had also reduced the volume of bread being sold through the front shops. With Lyons' stranglehold on the more profitable cake market, the effort expended in increasing bread sales had diminishing returns. As to milling, Lyons had always preferred to buy their flour from a diversity of suppliers because their vast consumption helped them obtain the keenest price.

In 1957 the Bakery Division was formed. This was part of a general process of decentralising large manufacturing units so as to give management greater control over important functions such as accounting. As a result, marketing departments were established in the hopes they would match Lyons' skill in mass production, on which the company had depended hitherto. Responsibility for financial targets and new product development was transferred from production management to marketing management. New products were now evaluated within an overall marketing strategy which took account of market research and advertising budget. Historically the manufacturing philosophy at Cadby Hall, largely through the influence of Maurice Salmon, had been to produce large volumes as a way of keeping prices down and maintaining market share. This had been a perfectly balanced policy until bakery competitors emerged in the 1950s and 1960s when the British cake market first exceeded £100 million. There were signs that the markets were being invaded by more specialised producers who could use the same technology as Lyons. Consumers too were changing, and 'Mr Kipling' cakes took an increasing share of the cake market. The increasing power of the supermarket chains, with their low prices, own labels, frozen food and wider range of goods, began to have an impact on the high street. Unfortunately the Lyons management did not fully recognise this transformation, or if they did they chose to ignore it, continuing instead to maintain their links with retailers and wholesalers who were becoming an extinct species.

When Rank and Spillers became part of the baking industry in 1962 – and also began to absorb small milling companies – management's thinking was transformed. They realised the importance of securing flour supplies, especially as they had just bought Galbraith's bakery in Glasgow to improve their distribution in the north, which appeared to be under increasing threat by the integration of millers (flour producers) and bakers. For Lyons it became imperative to obtain supplies of a range of flours on acceptable terms, and so in September 1963 they invested nearly £1 million in the milling firm of J.W. French & Co. Ltd by securing 50 per of Celebrity Holdings Ltd, the holding company. The French business had been formed by the merger of three companies, J.W. French & Company Ltd (Frenlite Flour Mills), Chelsea Flour Mills Ltd and H. Cohen & Company Ltd.

The bread-manufacturing department of Lyons formally became the Bread Division in 1963 under Brian Salmon. He continued the process, started in 1962 to improve profitability, of decentralising some of the new bread factories which had opened in Bristol, Crawley and elsewhere by giving the management control of their own production, distribution and accounting. Some were given additional cake-producing facilities. Later, departments for 'morning goods' (a bakery term used to describe small items of dough such as rolls and buns) were added to each of these plants, enabling them to produce a full range of speciality lines. In May 1963, in a joint venture with Kitchens of Sara Lee Inc., a subsidiary of the American Consolidated Foods Inc., Lyons formed a new company, Sara Lee Ltd, and started producing, under licence, a new line of pre-packaged luxury cakes from their Cadby Hall bakery. First made by Charlie Lubin in Chicago in 1950, the American cakes, which were made with fresh milk, eggs and natural flavourings, were baked in individual aluminium foil containers and many were quick frozen after baking to extend shelf life. Others were sold fresh, some under the brand name of Sally Brown, and among the most popular were the New England, cinnamon, chocolate fudge and fresh fruit banana cakes.

In 1965, on becoming a wholly owned subsidiary, Sara Lee Ltd changed its name to Morning Bakeries Ltd.

Distribution

The rapid pre-war growth of Lyons' bakery business had been largely due to the railway system of distribution, pioneered by William Brown, when Lyons could guarantee delivery of goods, anywhere in the country, within twenty-four hours of order. After the war the railways slowly improved their services and at midnight on 1 January 1948 they were nationalised. In just two years the increase in rail freight charges, together with increases in petrol tax, had added well over £100,000 to the direct cost of distributing goods. Nevertheless over 26,000 orders per week continued to be dispatched by rail from Addison Road station right up to July 1954. However, distribution by rail became increasingly expensive, the railways became less reliable and many branch lines began to be closed, preventing the delivery of goods to some of the more remote areas of the country. This process had started in June 1957 when British Railways reported a loss of £16.5 million; by May 1959 they had closed 230 stations. It culminated when the Conservative government in 1963 accepted a report by British Railways chairman Dr Richard Beeching which advocated closing many rural and branch lines. The government then announced the closure of 280 passenger lines, 1,850 stations (26 per cent), hundreds of branch lines and uneconomic freight services. With the railways undergoing such an immense closure programme, Lyons were forced to develop an extensive alternative system of distribution by road which not only proved to be expensive but was not completed until 1965, by which time nearly 3,500 railway miles had been lost.

Lyons first had to establish regional depots from which local deliveries could be made, and the first phase was to open depots at Chessington, Hemel Hempstead, Hammersmith, Crawley and Romford. Provincial depots and sub-depots in large areas were added to complete the national network. Once all the road depots had been set up, only 1,000 orders were dispatched by rail, with the balance going from forty distribution centres. The depot network was supplied largely from the massive baking capacity at Cadby Hall by their 'trunker' lorries (a term denoting Lyons' large freight distribution vehicles). Other manufacturing plants around the country, notably at Wakefield and Bristol, also fed the distribution depots and helped to relieve pressure on the Cadby Hall bakeries which for many years had run at full capacity. These additional plants had been extensively modernised after the war, making use of automatic raw material handling, continuous mixing and new cake processes. At Cadby Hall changes had been made to the jam tart plant in 1956 and a layer cake plant in 1959; in 1961 new ovens were installed in Cadby Hall's 'V' block. Known as Turboradiat ovens, they were capable of operating at higher speeds on more product lines than the ovens they replaced, which had been installed some thirty years earlier.

Despite the difficulties Lyons continued to maintain their position as brand leaders in cake, and the Bread Division did manage to increase its market marginally by the introduction of a larger range of bread rolls and other traditional products such as crumpets. Nevertheless cake competition was fierce and during the 1950s there was little growth in the British cake market as a whole.

Lyons Bakery

The first significant change occurred in 1964–5, when the Bakery Division adopted the house name of Lyons Bakery. Although expansion in the cake market in the UK slowed, Lyons continued to grow faster than the national average. Bread sales, however, were now only modest in volume, just about meeting budgeted forecasts. While the national consumption of bread remained static, Lyons could increase its share of the total market only by relentlessly pursuing efficiency in production and distribution. The quality of bread had improved enormously since the 1950s, but this did not stop consumers from complaining that it was not as good as bread in the past. Management, on the other hand, were convinced that the public had never enjoyed such a wide choice and such a high standard of bread.

There were also big improvements in bakery workers' pay and conditions during the mid-1960s. Wages of production workers increased by 11 per cent, partly because of a two-hour reduction in the working week and the change from a five-and-a-half-day week to a five-day week. An even higher wages rise of 16 per cent was awarded to workers in bread distribution, where there was also a move towards a five-day week, resulting in substantial bonus and overtime payments because bread had to be distributed and sold six days a week. This additional operating expenditure and the high initial cost of automating and mechanising operations within the bakery sector led to a temporary reduction in the net return on capital in 1965.

Nevertheless Lyons Bakery's strength in the cake market continued to grow, encouraging management to allocate further capital expenditure. A new bakery opened in the summer of 1965 in Wakefield, while further installations and modifications were carried out at the bakeries in Glasgow, Bristol, Brighton and London.

After a long period of virtually full employment, the mid-1960s saw a return to unemployment, which reached half a million in October 1966. In the same month the government invoked a prices and wages freeze under the new Prices and Incomes Act. As a result, even allowing for the 1d. increase in the price of bread in January 1966, the return on capital earned by bakeries was low. The Prices and Incomes Board tended to think of productivity in the bread industry in terms of output per man, which was an oversimplification. It is true that a vastly greater output of bread per man-hour can be achieved in a modern automated bread plant than in the old-style hand bakery. But the output of each bread factory was strictly limited to the capacity for which the plant was designed – it was not possible to improve productivity by working the plant faster or more efficiently. In any event the industry's problem was not simply how to produce more bread with fewer men in less time. Bread is highly perishable (it should be sold within twenty-four hours of baking) and stocks could not be built up to deal with fluctuations in demand. Both daily production and distribution were delicately balanced so that exactly the right amount of bread was efficiently produced at the right interval before sale, and delivered to the outlets at exactly the right time.

The normal weekly pattern of demand for bread indicated sharp variations from one day to the next, with a peak at the weekend. This pattern was further complicated by sudden and unpredictable changes in weather, and by the heavy demand prior to bank holiday weekends. So as to meet retailers' individual requirements, and yet comply with restrictions on unloading in busy streets, bread deliveries had to be timed with precision, and journeys had to be carefully planned so as not to make distribution uneconomic. The bread industry remained under the close surveillance of the government, and state intervention restricted the operation of market forces until the second half of the 1960s. This occurred during the worst sterling crisis for twenty years, when the pound was devalued by 14.3 per cent and international credit reached £250 million.

By 1967 Lyons Bakery was producing over fifty varieties of bread and continuing to diversify. In a foray into the developing slimmers' market, the Bread Division brought out a high-protein, low-calorie loaf called Slim-Vita, which was made from stoneground wholemeal flour and baked at a lower temperature than other bread. In March 1968 at Cadby Hall, under the Bakery Sector chairman Christopher Salmon and the Bread Division chief executive Robin Salmon (second cousins), a new bread roll plant came on stream. Costing £250,000, it was capable of producing up to 18,000 rolls or buns every hour. Just two hours after the dough entered the dividers, where it was divided and moulded into shape, it left the factory in a delivery van as a bakery product. This could be a plain, fruit or Bath bun, a Wimpy burger bun, a finger roll or a soft round roll, or a speciality Vienna roll, as market needs dictated. Later that year a similar plant was installed at the Eastleigh bread depot, which made a variety of bread rolls and buns, but specialised in Vienna rolls and other types of crusty bread which had become popular in southern England.

However, as Lyons Bakery had such a tiny share of the UK bread market as a whole, in June 1969 management decided to hand over its bread-making business to J.W. French and at the same time reinforce Lyons' influence in Celebrity Holdings by acquiring the outside shareholders' interests. Thus J. W. French & Co. Ltd became a fully owned subsidiary into which Lyons transferred its Bread Division for £2.5 million on 31 March 1969.

'Think about a Lyons cake ...'

Post-war competition in cake manufacture was not as intense as for bread. For a decade after 1950 the cake market continued to grow, with manufacturers able to sell everything they could produce. While the milling and baking firms had to sell their cakes through their recently acquired bakery retailers, Lyons were able to preserve their leading position by selling cakes through their traditional grocery outlets. They were estimated to have over 20 per cent of the total packaged cake market, and Lyons remained market leaders until 1960, when they were challenged by Marks & Spencer, for whom, paradoxically, Lyons had been a significant supplier.

In the late 1960s, as the cakes market suddenly became fiercely competitive, Lyons Bakery established itself as the biggest packaged cakes firm in Britain. In particular, Lyons led the field in product development, introducing three new ranges during eighteen months, and promoting these aggressively. Backed by television advertising and other promotions costing half a million pounds, Souflette sponge cakes and Hostess Swiss rolls were launched in 1967. The chocolate-covered Hostess was intended to revolutionise the Swiss roll market, as the product manager Pat Morrissey explained in the *Lyons Mail*: 'Up till now, the Swiss roll has been regarded by the consumer as a rather humble product, for which she was not prepared to pay more than 1s. 9d. For the Hostess we have had to carry out a campaign aimed at raising the status of the Swiss roll.' At the first of many sales conferences, a 'jet-age' atmosphere was created at Heathrow airport, where marketing and sales management teams wearing aircrew uniforms and models in mini-skirted 'air hostess' outfits addressed 300 salesmen against a background of simulated aircraft noises and departure announcements.

The most significant new product was launched in April 1968. This was a dessert range known as Harvest Fruit Pies, aimed at opening a new convenience food market through grocery stores. Lyons had invested more than £1 million in plant and machinery at Cadby Hall and in Glasgow. Ranking among the most technically advanced baking systems in the world, the plant was fully automatic. Machinery at Cadby Hall occupied all seven floors of 'Y' block as well as a 'penthouse' addition at the top for large storage tanks. Some of the pies were also made in the Glasgow factory. The Harvest Pie project was the result of three years of intensive research by Lyons Bakery's management and two major equipment suppliers, Baker-Perkins and Jahn. Available to the public in two sizes, priced at 2s. 6d. and 3s. 5d., the pies were made with a variety of fillings to meet regional preferences. Hailed as the most revolutionary development in the baking business for many years, Harvest Pies became an instant success. It was claimed in the *Lyons Mail* that they 'come closer than any other pie on the market to the quality standards achieved by the housewife in her own kitchen'. The pastry was rolled to give it a light, short texture instead of being sheeted as was usual in large-scale baking, and 'The fresh fruit is baked in the pastry, just as it is in the home, instead of being pre-boiled.' Ingredients for both pastry and filling were pumped to the top floor, where the dough and fruit were separately and automatically mixed in sealed containers, then channelled through pie make-up machines, ovens, coolers and conveyors to the packaging and loading bays on the ground floor.

In addition to the Souflette sponge, the Hostess Swiss roll and the Harvest Pie, Lyons Bakery also produced such popular lines as Kup Kakes, Jolyrols, Jersey Slices, trifle sponges, Battenberg, Eccles Puffs and fruit flan cases. Even though Lyons claimed its share in the grocery cakes market was larger than that of the next three next biggest manufacturers combined, the firm did not rest on its laurels. September 1968 saw the start of the most extensive promotion ever in the cake industry: an eight-week national bingo competition with cash prizes totalling £40,000. Over 25 million entry forms were printed for distribution in groceries, on the backs of Souflette and Harvest Pie boxes and as coupons in the press; and the competition was advertised on television and in women's magazines. In addition, all store managers and owners of grocery outlets served by Lyons Bakery's sales force were given trade bingo cards and invited to play for prizes worth £3,500 in total. Vic Steel, Lyons Bakery's marketing manager, remarked in *Lyons Mail* in October 1968, 'Putting it simply, it's a show of strength. We're demonstrating to both the trade and the consumer why we are brand leaders in the cake market, emphasising the wide range of our products and the formidable marketing effort we are able to put behind them.' A month later the journal reported the launch of yet another cake product in the Southern Television region. Named Lyons Bakery Gateau, it consisted of a rectangular sponge cake layered with a cream filling, covered with chocolate- or coffee-flavoured coating and topped with an elaborate decoration. At 2s. 11d., it was cheaper than similar products from competitors, and Vic Steel declared: 'This is the sort of cake that the housewife cannot bake at home unless she has a good deal of skill, time and equipment. We have been able to meet the market demand for a high-quality product at a price which competitors will find hard to beat, lacking as they do Lyons' knowledge and experience of volume cake production.'

Lyons Bakery had now explored two ways of growing: by applying modern marketing techniques to packaging, branding and merchandising in order to increase sales of existing products; and by investing in research and development to introduce new products and open up new markets – for example, the highly successful Harvest Pie project. By late 1968 management was planning its first big step along a third path to growth: acquisition. A £5.5 million share of the cake market was obtained in March 1969 when Lyons acquired the interests of the Scribbans-Kemp group – which included Scribbans-Kemp (Bakeries) Ltd, Oliver & Gurden

Ltd and Kunzle (Products) Ltd – for an undisclosed sum. Properties in London and other provincial cities were sold to raise £5 million for these bakery companies as well as other food acquisitions such as W. Symington & Co. Ltd (soups and sauces) and Margetts (preserves, jams, etc.). On 24 March 1969 Lyons Bakery Ltd was formed and the recent acquisitions became its subsidiaries.

Some £30 million per year was to be spent on products made by the Scribbans-Kemp bakeries. The firm of C. Kunzle Ltd (which was taken over by Fullers in 1964 and acquired as Fullers-Kunzle by Scribbans-Kemp in 1968) had been set up in the early 1920s by Christian Kunzle, a Swiss chef who worked for a time at the House of Commons. On behalf of Lyons Bakery, Kunzle's factory in Birmingham continued to specialise in making small cakes – such as mint meringues, macaroons, Fondant Fancies and Home-Made Crackle Cakes – as well as producing own-label cakes for Marks & Spencer, British Home Stores and Tesco. Kunzle's best-selling line was the Showboat, a chocolate shell containing a sponge filling, topped with butter cream and decorated by hand; 40,000 were made every week. Another part of Scribbans-Kemp, Oliver & Gurden, specialised in Christmas puddings, which they produced at their factory in Oxford. The puddings were made to a traditional recipe which the company's founders, William and Aubrey Gurden, had developed when they were chefs at Keble College before the First World War. About 10 per cent of their Christmas puddings were exported, mainly to the United States and France. They also produced mince pies, Yule logs and Christmas cakes. By autumn 1973, however, it was decided to change the name of Oliver & Gurden to Fullers Cakes Ltd, after market research found more consumers were familiar with that name and associated it with being 'good value', 'high quality' and 'suitable for special occasions'. Fullers, of course, had been acquired by Lyons as part of Scribbans-Kemp, having been founded at the turn of the century with bakeries in Dublin and Hammersmith, London. Nevertheless the name Oliver & Gurden was retained on some specialised lines such as shortbread and luxury cake, and for overseas marketing.

Meanwhile Lyons Bakery continued with their big promotions. 'Diddymania' started in June 1969 and ran for six weeks to coincide with several changes to products and packaging. The comedian Ken Dodd, with his Diddymen, was signed up to take part in a sales briefing film and make personal appearances during the campaign. All major bakery lines were packaged with Diddymania flashes and applications for special offers relating to Ken Dodd's comic inventions in his stage and television shows – including an inflatable Diddyman for 13s. 11d. plus two proofs of purchase, and an Idendiddy Kit containing Diddy badges, a 'tickling stick' and mask for 6s. 6d. plus two proofs of purchase. Packaging of twelve brands carried cut-outs on the back: Diddymobiles (model cars powered by marbles), Tattifaces (cut-outs to stick on potatoes and make Diddymen faces) and Diddy Games (the Knotty Ash Grand Prix and Diddymystify).

During the second half of the year a television advertising campaign costing more than half a million pounds was launched. A long-running series of commercials invited viewers to 'Think about a Lyons cake ...' and aimed to make them recognise a Lyons Bakery product by its visual image. Each commercial featured a leading product. For example, for four weeks in the summer of 1970 television viewers were urged to 'Think about a Harvest Pie'. Frames showing images of fruit and pastry were accompanied by a voice-over saying 'Think about something fresh – like an apple, a blackcurrant, an apricot ... You're thinking about a Lyons Harvest Pie ... Every season's freshest fruit ... packed in short golden pastry ... There's a Harvest Pie to suit everyone.' This supposedly hypnotic style of television advertising was virtually a new concept in its day, and was intended to prepare potential consumers for the product launches of 1969–70, such as the Double Delight and Princess Angel cakes, Blackcurrant Puffs and new 'heat and serve' sponge puddings. Lyons Bakery Nines, chocolate-covered sponge fingers with Jaffa orange and vanilla filling, were developed by the marketing and R&D departments after intensive

market research. In the summer of 1970 Nines were advertised on television in the now familiar way: 'You're thinking about brand-new Lyons cakes ... called Nines ... Nine more delicious reasons to ... think about a Lyons cake tomorrow.'

Another marketing idea was for Lyons Bakery and Nestlé to undertake a joint promotion whereby purchasers of Lyons cakes obtained money-off coupons for Nescafé instant coffee (one wonders why this promotion could not have been undertaken with Lyons' own coffee products). A joint television commercial was broadcast in February 1970 showing cakes and coffee as a perfect pair, with the inevitable words: 'Think about a Lyons cake and the great taste of Nescafé tomorrow – and save sixpence.' An even bigger joint promotion – '£10,000 Race to the 70s' – involved the *Daily Express* and began in October 1970, running for eight weeks. This was a competition with a hundred £100 prizes, and everyone who entered received a free souvenir – six miniature editions of the *Daily Express*, each covering one of six 'great days' in twentieth-century history. These were VE Day in 1945, Queen Elizabeth's coronation in 1953, the first moon walk in 1969, the abdication of Edward VIII in 1936 (an issue including an advertisement for Lyons cakes), the first transatlantic flight by Alcock and Brown in 1919 and the news of the relief of Mafeking in 1900. The promotion, coinciding with the seventieth anniversary of the *Express* newspaper, was 'flashed' on some 22 million packages of Lyons cakes as well as being advertised on television.

The following year Lyons Bakery decided to redesign their packaging with new logos, since it had been found that customers did not identify individual products with each other as being made by the same manufacturer. The repackaging was supported by a television advertising campaign claiming that 'Lyons make more of a cake'. In September 1972, Lyons Bakery promoted Harvest Dessert Pies, treacle tarts and Bakewell tarts by means of a competition in which the first prize was a 9½-acre orchard. This unusual prize, it was believed, was another first for Lyons.

By then the packaged cakes business was at its peak, and there was a need for new production facilities to meet the increased demand. Lyons' decision to build a new factory, however, led the company down a road strewn with obstacles, as will be seen later in this chapter. In the meantime the Lyons group were planning further acquisitions and mergers.

Consolidation of Baking and Milling

Once J.W. French had established itself as a Lyons subsidiary, management entered into discussions with the Co-operative Wholesale Society Ltd (CWS) with a view to merging common flour milling and bread interests. The two businesses complemented each other, since their respective strengths were in different parts of the country. In February 1971, after successful negotiations, French transferred their milling and baking interests to a new wholly owned subsidiary called J.W. French (Milling & Baking Holdings) Ltd, for an aggregate consideration of £5.5 million satisfied by the allotment to the vendor companies of fully paid equity shares in the new company. The holding company had two chairmen, Guy Lawrence of Lyons and R.G. Wilson of CWS. The other two directors from the Lyons group on the six-man board were Len Badham and Dr M.C. Schaul, chairman of the original J.W. French & Co., which continued to control a number of non-baking and milling operations. On 10 February 1971 the new subsidiary acquired from the CWS its flour milling and baking interests, comprising its wholly owned subsidiary company CWS (Milling & Baking) Ltd, for a sum of £8.8 million. After the merger the J.W. French (Milling & Baking Holdings) group consisted initially of seven flour mills and twenty-four bakeries and employed 9,000 staff. With this additional national coverage the company was able to benefit from the economies of large-scale production.

Another merger followed in January 1972, when a new company called Spillers-French Holdings Ltd was set up. To this were transferred the flour-milling, baking and animal food interests of Spillers Ltd and the flour-milling and baking businesses comprised in J.W. French (Milling & Baking Holdings) Ltd. Spillers-French Holdings Ltd had 75.1 per cent of the equity of the joint company and J.W. French (Milling & Baking

Holdings) Ltd had 24.9 per cent. As a result of this merger Spillers-French became one of the largest baking and milling companies in Britain alongside Rank Hovis McDougall and Associated British Foods.

Meanwhile, in April 1970, Lyons had taken over the bakery business of International Stores Ltd, thereby substantially increasing the turnover of bakery products through over 1,000 International Stores. In July they consolidated their position by acquiring Gateaux Ltd, a high-class cake manufacturer incorporated in the Irish Republic, for £300,000. Gateaux's famous Molly O'Rourke brand, with its generous Irish whiskey content, sold throughout the world in air-tight tins with a large export business to Australia. Later the company made expensive cakes for Marks & Spencer, who tried to persuade Gateaux, unsuccessfully, not to supply similar products to other parts of the trade.

In reviewing the wholesaling business carried out by the subsidiary F.J. French (Wholesalers) Ltd – an associated company controlled by Frenlite Flour Mills Ltd and not to be confused with J.W. French – Lyons decided that it was not large enough to make any meaningful contribution to group profits. When in 1972 Lyons bought Patrick Grainger and Hutleys Ltd, a leading Cambridge-based supplier in the cash-and-carry provisions trade, management decided to merge the two businesses to form Patrick Grainger & French Ltd.

Expansion into Europe

Having now consolidated a number of small baking and milling businesses into the group at home, Lyons turned its attentions to continental Europe. While food consumption was high in other European countries, individual businesses in the food industry tended to be smaller than their counterparts in the United Kingdom. Lyons believed that transferring their large-scale operations to Europe would be fruitful. However, the differences in diet and taste were reflected in different product ranges and types. Accordingly Lyons decided to enter the European market by acquiring local firms, staffed by their own nationals. The first bakery acquisition had already occurred in June 1969, when 51 per cent of the Dutch firm Ulrich NV (later Lyons Bakkerijen NV), a subsidiary of Holland's largest bakery and confectionery group, Sitos (in turn owned by a large milling concern), had been bought by the subsidiary J. Lyons Netherlands Holdings BV, which had been established some time earlier specifically as a Dutch holding company. It was not until 1972, however, that any large-scale expansion took place.

In accordance with the policy of entering established local markets, the acquisitions in cakes and biscuits concentrated on a particular speciality of the country concerned. Thus in 1972 Lyons bought the Italian company Riunite del Panforte di Sienna SpA (Sapori), which produced spiced Siena cake as well as other Italian cakes and confectionery; this later brought into the group the Park Hotel Marzocchi in Siena.

In March 1973 a 99 per cent stake was obtained in A. Hooimeijer en Zonen NV in Barendrecht on the outskirts of Rotterdam. This rusk-making company had been established in 1905 by A. Hooimeijer in the south of Rotterdam but in the 1930s the business had been expanded, with the help of four sons, and relocated to Barendrecht. During the war, production at Hooimeijer all but ceased because of a lack of raw materials; however, in 1953 a new rusk factory was built just in time to be destroyed by the serious flooding of the region in that year. By 1959 Hooimeijer had recovered and were exporting such large quantities of rusks to the United Kingdom that they acquired another Dutch rusk company called Hille, whose subsidiary, Haust, became the brand name for the Hooimeijer products. Soon after this the Dutch Stereo company was added to the group. After Lyons took control of Hooimeijer it continued to develop its business by acquiring Galema, a melba toast factory, in 1974, Brink BV and Baartrams BV (biscuits) in 1985, Tércribel NV in Belgium (rice wafers) in 1988 and A. Krombach & Söhne (biscuits), Germany, in 1993. All these companies were managed by Hooimeijer.

On 24 May 1973 Lyons acquired Jb. Bussink Koninklijke Deventer Koekfabrieken BV (Bussink), the oldest independent family business in the Netherlands, established in 1593 and renowned for its rye honey cake. As well as satisfying home consumption, Bussink's honey cake had been exported to the Baltic countries for many centuries; by 1973, 50,000 cakes were produced every day in their Deventer factory. Bussink and the Dutch business of AHO (spiced cookies), which was bought at the same time, both came under the management of Hooimeijer. In quick succession the German cake company Marina Kuchen GmbH. (May 1973) and Hale-Trent (Holdings) Ltd (April 1974) were acquired at a time when the packaged cakes market was declining in the wake of severe price increases caused by raw material costs said to be 'unprecedented' in the industry.

A New 'Home of Cakes': the Yorkshire Factory

In the early 1970s management decided to build a new cake factory which would provide more modern production resources. The bakery at Cadby Hall, traditionally the 'home of cakes', and the provincial factories had been designed to accommodate the needs of the first half of the twentieth century. For twenty or more years, however, they had imposed physical and technical constraints on efficiency. With Lyons still leaders in the packaged cakes market, new facilities were urgently required if the company was to stay ahead. As own-label business gradually took more of the cake market, production management needed to have greater control over the manufacturing process. This meant highly flexible production facilities to deal with short- and long-run orders, for different labels or not, all within a purpose-built hygienic environment and in an almost fully automated operation. Bakery management knew what they wanted: it had to be a single-storey modern factory with long flow-lines and all the necessary power supplies, raw material storage and distribution requirements. It also had to be large enough to meet all the current bakery needs with room for expansion. Such construction would not be possible at Cadby Hall or indeed anywhere else in the London area. After extensive studies it was decided to build a new factory on a 62-acre site at the village of Carlton, a few miles from Barnsley, South

Yorkshire, and transfer all primary cake baking there. This would free up 10 acres at Cadby Hall, where Lyons planned a new development comprising a hotel, an apartment block and office buildings. As the company cherished its long association with Hammersmith, the development included a new corporate headquarters, thus perpetuating the name of Cadby Hall.

Not only cake manufacture but also meat pie production was moving from Cadby Hall. The two new factories required capital in excess of £30 million and it took eight years to complete the transfer from London. In December 1972 Woodall-Duckham applied for permission to develop land at Carlton for a 500,000-sq. ft. building housing plant, food-manufacturing equipment and offices; the layout of land, roads and sewers had been approved one year earlier. The factory plan incorporated parking for 400 cars, and it was expected that 160 lorry movements would be made daily for delivering raw materials and taking manufactured goods away. Government relocation grants, which were not available in the south of England, were one of the main attractions of Yorkshire. Another advantage was the proximity of the Wakefield bakery, which had been established for many years as a profitable efficient factory and was only ten minutes away by car from Carlton. Further, there was a local abundance of potential labour, especially female. In London the ratio of male to female workers in the Cadby Hall bakery was 50:50; the plan was to reduce this to 20:80 in Yorkshire, with a consequent saving in labour costs. Despite the Equal Pay Act of 1970 which in theory guaranteed women equal pay for equal work, employers still exploited the many loopholes.

Geographically, the choice of site could not have been worse. Carlton had previously been a mining village and contained all the scars of the coal industry, with slag heaps and a water course looping through the centre of the site. In a massive redevelopment scheme, undertaken by the Coal Board and Barnsley Council, the derelict mine buildings were demolished and the mountainous slag heaps contoured and landscaped. Nevertheless research had indicated

that most cakes sales were made in southern Britain and, since much of the factory's output travelled by road, it is curious that the factory was built so far away from the principal markets. Transportation costs, which were already high, were exacerbated in 1973 when the oil-producing Arab states of the Middle East increased oil prices by 70 per cent following US support for Israel against Egypt and Syria during the Yom Kippur war in October that year. Other problems were the concerns voiced by key staff who were reluctant to relocate to Yorkshire, particularly those with children at school. Among these dissenters were Lyons Bakery directors and their support staff in the sales, marketing, personnel and finance departments, who preferred to travel to Barnsley on Monday and return to London on Friday. This practice, which continued after the factory was fully operational in 1977, added considerable hotel and travelling expenditure to the project and its eventual running costs. Production and engineering management had, on the other hand, relocated during 1974–6 as plants came on stream. The full commissioning process took many months – in fact a new plant was being commissioned every six to eight weeks and management had to ensure that existing factories were able to produce all the varieties of cake until the new plants became productive. During the whole planning stage Lyons Bakery management refused all help from the group's Estates Department – which had years of building experience – and because they tried to manage the project themselves they ran into elementary problems of design, construction and fitting out.

Much of the local male labour in the Barnsley district had previously been employed in the coalmining industry where there was a tradition of militant trade-unionism. Absenteeism frequently made it difficult to staff full shifts on Mondays and Fridays, when many workers reported in sick. The Carlton factory, claiming to be the most modern bakery in the world, never did fulfil Lyons' aspirations, according to its senior management. While the first two plants came on stream in late 1974, full commissioning was not achieved until 1977 and even then it took months to achieve planned levels of productivity. Some

The new bakery factory at Carlton, South Yorkshire, after Cadby Hall closed. Coal mining scars are still in evidence. This view is taken from the rear of the factory with the administration block facing Fish Dam Lane on the other side. *By kind permission of Waldegrave Films.*

of the buildings needed to be modified or repaired, and remedial action took many months after long disputes and litigation. Disappointing as all this may have been, the market for cakes and biscuits strengthened in the late 1970s. By 1980 consumers were spending more on health foods, and to benefit from this Lyons installed a new plant at Carlton producing 'Krispen' crispbread, to complement the rusks and similar continental products manufactured by Hooimeijer in Rotterdam.

From Allied Breweries to Manor Bakeries

The 1980s were mixed years for the bakery sector, partly because of the sudden takeover of Lyons by Allied Breweries Ltd in 1978. As fortunes fluctuated, European companies generally performed better than those in the UK. To strengthen the group's baking companies and to co-ordinate presentation in brands, Hale-Trent merged their sales, marketing and distribution functions with those of Lyons Bakeries in 1985, forcing the closure of their Clevedon factory three years later. Since 1974, when Hale-Trent first came into the group (along with their Far Famed Cake Company), they had retained a measure of independence from Lyons Bakery.

Allied Breweries wasted no time in reorganising the enlarged business, which they categorised into three distinct divisions – the Beer Division, Wines and Spirits Division and Food Division – incorporating all the food companies in the Lyons group. The Food Division was reorganised in January 1988, and Jack Silverman became sector chairman for the European cake, biscuit and confectionery companies, before his deputy, Gordon Jenkins, took over on his retirement at the end of the year. Then in November 1989 the European bakery businesses were divided; Ian Gazzard became the managing director of an enlarged British bakery business incorporating frozen cakes and biscuits, while the European companies came under the control of Frans Fontein, the group export director for Hooimeijer. Some tinkering with rebranding followed and various new products were introduced to meet consumer demands for healthier eating. When all manufacturing had

The cake cooling tower in the new bakery at Carlton. *By kind permission of Waldegrave Films.*

finally been centred on the Carlton and Wakefield bakeries in 1988–9 after the integration of Hale-Trent into Lyons Bakery, an aggressive product development programme followed, with more than fifty new lines launched in a single year.

In December 1989, for the sum of £196 million, Lyons acquired Dunkin' Donuts Inc., a dedicated franchise group running 1,850 stores throughout the world. Of these 1,600 were in the United States; total gross sales from all stores were $800 million. The acquisition of Dunkin' Donuts brought an important international brand leader into the Lyons Bakery portfolio. When Dunkin' Donuts' main rival, the Mister Donut chain, was bought from International Multifoods Inc. in April 1990, a further 550 outlets were added in the USA and Canada. The purchase was delayed by a temporary restraining order issued by the US District Court in Philadelphia at the request of a group of Mister Donut franchisees seeking an injunction against the sale. However, in a ruling of 27 March 1990, the US District Court of Eastern Pennsylvania denied the motion for the preliminary injunction and allowed the sale to proceed.

At the end of the 1980s the Spanish and Dutch bakery businesses were still in far better shape than their British counterparts. The Food Division's largest bakery business was in Spain, where the joint-venture company Panrico went from strength to strength, achieving a notable 35 per cent compound increase in profits over five years. By 1991 Panrico was the bakery sector's main source of profit; Panrico's doughnuts had 85 per cent of the Spanish market and Bollycao (a bread roll with chocolate filling) 90 per cent. So great was demand that a new bread-making plant had to be installed in Madrid and Barcelona while another opened in Portugal. Spanish sales were in stark contrast to the British market which, badly affected by recession, was in decline.

After the new Allied-Lyons consortium purchased the Spanish Pedro Domecq group in February 1994, less and less importance was placed on the food and brewing businesses of Allied-Lyons and just twelve months later the baking business was sold. Manor Bakeries – part of the Tomkins group, which had taken over Rank Hovis McDougall with their 'Mr Kipling' brand and Cadbury's Cakes – bought Lyons Bakery for £35 million in February 1995. At the time Lyons' cakes had just under 10 per cent of the UK market.

SOFT DRINKS

The Early Soft Drinks Trade

THE HEALING EFFECT of mineral waters, long established in Europe from Roman times, was at first achieved by bathing in them. The practice of drinking mineral waters did not start until the Middle Ages, when many thought they possessed medicinal qualities. As a consequence some spring sources were named after saints, such as St Ann's Well and St John's Well in the Malvern Hills. During the seventeenth century chemists found a way of replicating naturally carbonated waters but it was not until 1767 that Richard Bewley of Great Massingham, Norfolk, created the first soda water beverage. Douglas Simmons (in *Schweppes – The First 200 Years*) describes Bewley's method in the chemists' language of the day: 'dissolve three drams of fossil alkali in each quart of water and throw in streams of fixed air'. Simmons goes on to say that 'Thomas Henry, chemist and apothecary of Manchester, is attributed the honour of being the first to manufacture artificial mineral waters for sale commercially' in about 1776. It is not known how successful this business was.

Jean Jacob Schweppe (1740–1821), founder of the famous firm of Schweppes, was one of the first entrepreneurs to capitalise on the growing belief that mineral waters were good for health. Born in Germany into an agricultural family, Jacob Schweppe was attracted to Geneva, where he studied the watchmaker's craft. In 1788 he became interested in the new chemical technology of producing mineral waters and in ten years had created a profitable mineral waters business. Two years later he joined forces with

two rivals, Nicholas Paul and Henry Gosse, who had blatantly copied his technique. Schweppe thought it better to amalgamate the businesses than to compete. This relationship was not ideal, but it endured, and in 1792 Schweppe travelled to England and opened a mineral water factory at 141 Drury Lane, London. Despite the enlargement of the business, the acrimonious partnership with Paul and Gosse continued and in 1795 Jacob Schweppe decided to end it. By mutual agreement Paul and Gosse kept the Geneva operation and Jacob Schweppe the London business. By the 1800s Schweppes had become a sizeable company, and, with a desire to retire early, Jacob Schweppe sold three-quarters of his business to three Channel Islanders, Henry and Francis Lauzun and Robert Brohier. The three Jerseymen were initiated into the arts and secrets of mineral water manufacture and agreed to continue trading as Schweppe and Company. Their products were extended throughout the country and Schweppes eventually became one of the leading soft drinks suppliers in the world.

In 1825 Dr F. Struve (later Hooper, Struve) challenged Schweppes when he started importing and selling German seltzer water. Struve, a medical man of Dresden, Germany, had the idea of dispensing 'health-giving' mineral waters to those not living in, or able to visit, the spa towns. After opening dispensing centres in the non-spa resorts of Dresden, Leipzig and Berlin, Struve decided to take his idea to England and he set up a dispensing centre at Brighton, Sussex. His centre became hugely popular with fashionable society and after King George IV became a client

Struve advertised his business as the Royal German Spa. The vogue for taking spa water continued to grow until the middle of the century, when it declined in favour of squashes and lemonade, which some believed prevented obesity. Anthelme Brillat-Savarin, French politician, gastronome and writer, wrote in 1825, 'There is a current opinion among women which every year causes the death of many young women, – that acids, especially vinegar, are preventatives of obesity. Beyond all doubt, acids have the effect of destroying obesity; but they also destroy health and freshness. Lemonade is, of all acids, the most harmless; but few stomachs can resist it long.'

By the 1900s the firm of Schweppes dominated the mineral drinks business in the UK and was continually opening new factories to satisfy demand. When the premises at 64 Hammersmith Road, formally known as the Kensington Co-operative Stores, became available in 1901, Schweppes decided to take them over from the liquidator and build another production centre to help offset the cost of transporting drinks from their Hendon factory to markets in the south of England and West London. Surveys had shown they could sink a well on the property to satisfy their need for 10,000 gallons of water a day. During this period Lyons, who were already occupying a large estate adjacent to the new Schweppes works (Lyons' head office was known as 66 Hammersmith Road), became business neighbours. After ten years Schweppes increased their output by 50 per cent and, because Lyons had bought up most of the available property in the immediate vicinity, they could not expand. More important, the well was beginning to run dry and its quality deteriorated, making it necessary to ship water from the Hendon works in 400-gallon consignments. These difficulties prompted them to vacate the Hammersmith factory in 1911 and move to the Albert Embankment, where a new factory was built. Meanwhile Lyons acquired the Schweppes property some time between 1911 and 1916 to expand their food production. Thus by 1916 virtually the whole length of Hammersmith Road between Blythe Road and Brook Green was now owned by Lyons.

When Lyons built their new A2 block in 1935 (immediately behind Cadby Hall), construction workers came across the original Schweppes well, which was reported to have been 300-500 feet deep. It had to be filled with concrete before construction could proceed.

The UK soft drinks market continued to grow and many new names entered the fray including Idris Mineral Waters, R. White & Sons, L. Rose & Co., W. & J. Burrow of Great Malvern and Kia-Ora Ltd. Kia-Ora, which is a Maori word for 'good health', was started in 1896 by an Australian farmer, John Dixon, who decided to leave the land to make and sell ice in Sydney, New South Wales. He branched out into lemonade and ginger beer but his greatest achievement was the creation of a hot and spicy chilli punch which he sold as 'OT'. In 1909 he brought his company to England where his 'OT' sold chiefly to the licensed trade, who added it to beer and spirits to give extra zest. In 1930 Schweppes acquired a 51 per cent interest in Kia-Ora Ltd, securing full ownership in 1946. L. Rose & Co. was until 1957, when it was bought by Schweppes, an old-established Leith company founded in 1865 by Lauchlan Rose for the sole purpose of importing limes and lemons. Rose's main business was supplying lime juice to the shipping industry, primarily to the mercantile marine, as a prevention against scurvy on long sea voyages (from which derives the 'Limey' nickname for British seamen).

The soft drinks trade appears to have diversified in about 1908, when companies started to make concentrated fruit juices known as cordials or squashes. Flavoured with orange, lemon, lime and peppermint, they only required the addition of water to make a refreshing drink. Not only was their success due to their convenience, but they were also priced low enough for all but the poor to afford them. However, the First World War intervened, and the squash trade did not pick up again until 1919.

It is not known when Lyons first entered the soft drinks business but almost certainly they were making some form of soft drink before the First World War, mainly for use in the teashops; larger-scale manufacturing is believed to have started in the 1930s. Although soft drinks in teashops were regularly available from in-house sources, mineral waters and other carbonated drinks were supplied by the traditional manufacturers such as Schweppes and White's.

Sunkap and Sunfresh

In 1937 Lyons became interested in an American machine known as a Freshway Converter, which was used in an extraction process called comminution. Leonard Greenaway, resident chemist of the soft drinks division, went to California to collect information. The machine's rotary blades finely grated (or shrived) small pieces of whole citrus fruits. The shredded fruit was then mixed with a sugared solution, colouring and a preservative. In the comminution process the natural fruit oils and extracts were retained and the small particles of fruit made the drink more distinctive, with a better flavour and aroma. Most of the juice from the fruit was extracted, along with some of the cells and oils, a little of the membrane or 'rag' and much of the peel. The preserving agent was benzoic acid, a substance occurring naturally in some plants, which is chemically less reliable than sulphur dioxide but has the advantage of being virtually tasteless. It was bottled at a ready-to-drink strength in one-third pint containers and was more appealing than those made from crudely concentrated juices which had been preserved with sulphur dioxide. It became an instant success.

With a view to using the process in the Corner Houses, Lyons obtained the franchise rights to the machine in the United Kingdom and introduced the first comminuted drinks in 1937. In 1938 Wallace Hill of Glendale, California, took out a British patent for his Freshway Converter invention. In January 1937 Lyons had changed the name of their 1925-registered subsidiary, Real Cones Ltd, to O.R. Groves Ltd, to market the new product through a chain of licensees. However, the start of the Second World War, with rationing and closures of soft drinks factories, caused the idea to be temporarily shelved.

During the whole period of the war the soft drinks industry was left very much to run its own affairs under the close supervision of the Ministry

of Food. In 1940 the industry was asked to reduce its production from 116 million gallons to 85 million gallons to conserve sugar supplies and reduce fuel usage associated with distribution. By May 1942, under the direction of the government, 160 members of the industry had met and approved what became known as the Soft Drinks Industry (War Time) Association, or the SDI. This association, in collaboration with Ministry officials, set rules for the industry. One contentious issue agreed upon in 1943, under the emergency laws, was the abandonment of individual labels as a means of economy. The imposed national label stated only the name of the drink, the letters SDI and a code number to identify the production factory. Many of the well-established brands felt their image might be tarnished by such devices, and members of the public did not know what brand they were drinking. This led some people to joke that the letters SDI stood for 'some die instantly'. The SDI had draconian powers and as the war proceeded the association closed factories, took control of distribution, commandeered transport fleets, and gave priority to ships' stores, canteens, hospitals and to the Canadian and US troops stationed in the UK. This situation prevailed until 1948, when the SDI was disbanded and the industry returned to normal.

In 1952 Freshway Converters were again licensed to a number of dairies, which sold the orange drink from their milk rounds under the trade name of Sunkap. As Sunkap quickly became very popular, soon O.R. Groves began receiving royalty payments from a number of dairies up and down the country. Sugar restrictions were further eased in 1954, and new government classifications of soft drinks required that 27.5 lb of oranges be used to make 10 gallons of concentrated drink. Lyons then introduced Sunfresh, a comminuted orange drink in concentrated form, to be diluted by adding four parts water to one part squash. Licences were granted to approximately twenty soft drinks companies to manufacture and sell Sunfresh. Each was allocated an area of the country and O.R. Groves, a wholly owned subsidiary of Lyons, curiously licensed Lyons to sell Sunfresh in the

A comminuter, used in the production of citrus drinks, in use at Rannoch Road, Fulham.

London area. Leonard Gluckstein (1907–70), son of Barnett Gluckstein and grandson of one of the original founders, Isidore Gluckstein, became chairman of O.R. Groves in the 1950s. He had joined Lyons after coming down from Cambridge in 1929 and throughout his career was recognised for his innovative abilities. His first managerial responsibilities were for the Coventry Street Corner House but in 1941 he was made a Lyons director and during the early part of the war was catering adviser to Anti-Aircraft Command. Towards the end of the war, after leaving the army, he led a team experimenting with frozen food (covered later) and played an important role in the establishment of the Lyons pension fund.

Freshway Converters came in two sizes, one holding about five gallons, used by most dairies, and a larger unit holding about twenty-five gallons. As both were too small for mass production of Sunfresh, a factory-sized machine was developed. One of the main obstacles to increased production at this time was the difficulty of obtaining a constant supply of good-quality oranges at economic prices. The original patent of the Freshway Converter had been held by the

Californian, Wallace Hill, and when his patent expired in 1957 Lyons were free to develop or modify his process. Leonard Gluckstein suggested it might be more economic to transfer the extraction process to the countries where oranges were widely grown. After initial technical difficulties, Lyons developed machines that were capable of producing a concentrated fruit base which could then be supplied to the licensees for making Sunfresh. In 1961 the equipment was first sent to Spain, followed by Israel, South Africa and Cyprus, where an orange base was made; a lemon base was later produced in all locations and a grapefruit base in Cyprus. The Lyons invention was so successful that a patent was taken out in 1963 under the inventors Leonard Gluckstein and William Tom Everington, the factory manager. In order to economise on packaging and freight costs Lyons also developed methods for extracting much of the water content, before shipment, thereby concentrating the fruit base by up to three times. At a much later date this was improved to four times.

Sunfresh appeared on the market at a time when soft drinks manufacture was starting to flourish after the end of wartime rationing. Between 1954 and 1957 soft drinks production in the United Kingdom doubled and showed no signs of faltering. Sunfresh, the only comminuted drink available in Britain, dominated the market after Lyons acquired the Coventry-based firm of W. Lant & Co. Ltd in 1956 specifically to improve their sales in the Midlands. At the same time they introduced a new tonic water and lemon juice drink followed by a lemon and glucose drink which sold under the name of Citroze. The introduction of the tonic water drink surprised Schweppes' management who reacted by introducing their own now famous Bitter Lemon drink. Sales of other products, however, rose from 3 million to 18 million bottles per annum and by 1960 Sunfresh accounted for 25 per cent of the soft drinks market. Sales were further boosted by the introduction of a carbonated blend of Sunfresh which had been launched in 1956 as 'sparkling Sunfresh' in a sub-section of the soft drinks market. Thus by the end of the 1950s the Lyons Soft Drinks Division were marketing diluted, concentrated and carbonated orange and lemon drinks.

The Merger with Schweppes: Rose Kia-Ora and Groves

Other established soft drinks manufacturers, notably Schweppes, had to meet the challenge of developing comminuted drinks, although with slightly different methods from those used by Lyons. Schweppes' product, Suncrush, was also made in Spain, and a fierce struggle for market dominance ensued. With the aid of an expensive advertising campaign using television commercials, Schweppes rapidly expanded their market share to the detriment of Lyons. Despite a lack of enthusiasm for advertising in those days, Lyons nevertheless had to follow Schweppes' example but soon found that the cost of promoting Sunfresh in this way eroded profits. In their efforts to gain an advantage, Schweppes, Beecham's – who had recently entered the market – and Lyons allowed retailers to force down prices, with the result that each manufacturer offered bonuses to try to increase sales. Around 1960 it was not uncommon for retailers to be offered one free

bottle of drink for every dozen bought. Such tactics proved disadvantageous to Lyons, whose dominance of the market began to decline and with it the profits that Sunfresh once enjoyed. Unlike the other main competitors, who had highly organised marketing teams with strong branded products, Lyons were in the hands of over twenty licensees who each had to be consulted by O.R. Groves before any change could be made to marketing strategy. This led to a lack of co-ordination between Lyons and Groves.

In 1954 Leonard Gluckstein had stolen a lead in the citrus drinks market. He had also shown a keen interest in technical matters, had introduced new bottling plants and was always seeking ways of improving processes at the soft drinks factory at Rannoch Road in Hammersmith. Although Leonard Gluckstein showed frequent flashes of brilliance, he is said to have had an 'unpredictable temperament', not always patient and consistent in dealing with the licensees. By the early 1960s he had alienated so many that some did not participate in the bonus schemes he introduced in 1960 and sales of Sunfresh slumped. Once they had lost confidence in him, Leonard Gluckstein found himself in the situation of having to fight off strong competition from other manufacturers while at the same time engaging in arguments with his franchisees.

Matters were eventually resolved in January 1962 when Schweppes and Lyons decided to merge their soft drinks businesses by forming a new marketing company, the Rose Kia-Ora Sales Co. Ltd. Both parent companies took legal advice to ensure that their marketing arrangements did not fall foul of the Restrictive Trade Practices legislation. The Registrar of Restrictive Trading Agreements thought otherwise and there followed a twelve-year legal wrangle. Meanwhile the new sales company continued to market both Sunfresh and sparkling Sunfresh (Lyons) and Suncrush and Kia-Ora squash (Schweppes). Schweppes held 51 per cent of the equity in the new company and also acquired a 49 per cent interest in O.R. Groves Ltd, but both Lyons and Schweppes remained in control of their respective production, with Schweppes responsible for overall sales. All licences for the production of Sunfresh in

England were terminated; instead Lyons manufactured and bottled all Sunfresh drinks at the Rannoch Road factory. On 1 June 1962 W. Lant & Co. Ltd was sold to a subsidiary of the lemonade manufacturer, R. White & Sons Ltd.

After the formation of the Rose Kia-Ora Sales Co., Groves played a declining role in the soft drinks story, since its main function, the licensing of Freshway Converters, had been removed. Some royalties continued to flow from the dairies but their business had been harmed by the emergence of Schweppes and other manufacturers, and the dairies' contribution to Lyons' soft drinks profits gradually became less. At one time it was even suggested that O.R. Groves should be liquidated. Within a year of the Schweppes/Lyons agreement, however, Groves were developing a private-label business in the orange comminuted drinks market. Freed from the ties of franchises and branded products, it was soon selling more private-label bottles than the Rose Kia-Ora operation. Private-label customers included Sainsbury, Marks & Spencer, Express Dairy, Waitrose and Safeway.

The success of O.R. Groves, both before and after the Schweppes sales merger, must be credited to Leonard Gluckstein, but again he caused conflict – this time with the Schweppes management. When Rose Kia-Ora sales, principally those of Sunfresh, began to fall, Gluckstein accused Schweppes of promoting their brand to the detriment of Sunfresh. When, on the other hand, O.R. Groves' own-label sales improved, Schweppes blamed Leonard Gluckstein for their loss of market to the private label. Although the misunderstandings continued, Lyons did not favour a break with Schweppes, since Kia-Ora drinks were produced at Rannoch Road, alongside Lyons' Sunfresh and Groves' private-label concentrates, and this arrangement helped to lessen the unit production costs.

In 1965 Leonard Gluckstein was replaced by Richard Charles after Gluckstein had been made a director of Strand Hotel Ltd. Leonard Gluckstein died in January 1970 and in March of that year Lyons bought the factory and plant of KC Developments Ltd, Wigan, with a view to expanding into the north of England and at the same time rationalising distribution costs. Its acquisition also brought into the group a cooking oil product, not previously made by any Lyons company or division, and this was added to the division's private-label products. By 1971 the Rannoch Road factory had become one of the largest production centres for concentrated fruit drinks in the country, despite a sudden official ban in 1970 on the use of cyclamate sweeteners which caused a temporary trough in production. Until this time the main sweetener had been sugar, and this was followed by saccharin and then a combination of the two. In the late sixties the intense sweetener cyclamate had a far better taste profile than saccharin, with none of the metallic, bitter aftertaste. Good-character, low-calorie and lower-cost products could be produced. Such was the success of cyclamate in soft drinks that it threatened virtually to eliminate saccharin and sugar usage, but cyclamate was banned in 1970 when research in the USA indicated that it caused tumours in laboratory rats (a piece of research subsequently discredited in the main). After the acquisition of KC Developments Lyons' Soft Drinks Division increased its production capacity by 25 million bottles a year.

Another small acquisition was made in October 1970 when Lyons bought the East London firm of Orange Grove Fruit Drinks Ltd. Based in Hackney, they were supplying 2.5 million sealed cartons of ready-to-drink orange squash a year to West End cinemas. Orange Grove was started in 1946 by two brothers, Frank and Lou Marino, to supply cinemas with ice-cream, but this trade was swept aside by Lyons and Wall's in the 1950s and the firm switched to supplying soft drinks in cartons instead. Their business flourished until the 1960s, when television began to cause cinema audiences to decline and many cinemas closed. By 1964, however, the Marino brothers managed to supply the West End cinemas but did not have the capital to extend their trade nationwide until Lyons became involved.

Because the private-label business was based solely on concentrated drinks – now including a lime juice cordial and a blackcurrant health drink – it was vulnerable. Efforts were made to establish businesses overseas, either by franchise or by direct sales, but none proved profitable. The only successful diversification was into fruit juices. Traditionally the only citrus juices available in the UK were imported canned concentrates. Advances in technology made it possible to import frozen orange and grapefruit juice, reconstitute it and package it in retail containers. Lyons was one of the first companies to adopt this method, initially using 1-litre jars, later using aseptic packing in cartons. There was, however, an embarrassment after the 1-litre bottles had been introduced when several weeks' worth of orange juice production was found to have a bad taste. Lyons' chemists discovered that diluted orange juice had been left standing overnight, or longer, in bulk tanks, where some bacterial growth had occurred, very slightly affecting the flavour. The bacteria had entered the juice via the pump used to transfer the juice concentrate. Although the micro-organisms were killed off by pasteurisation, by then they had done their damage. The unpleasant flavour could not be detected until the orange juice in the bottle had been standing for some time. Only orange was affected because it was of lower acidity than grapefruit. After a lengthy investigation the laboratories were both castigated for not advising on the process initially (in truth they were never asked) and praised for resolving a potential calamity.

By the mid-1970s the Registrar of Restrictive Trading Practices was concluding its enquiry into the marketing arrangements between Lyons and Schweppes to discover whether Lyons had an unfair production advantage. In 1973, prior to any ruling, Schweppes and Lyons decided to disentangle their joint operation for commercial reasons. Schweppes sold their interests in O.R. Groves to Lyons and Lyons sold their interests in Rose Kia-Ora to Schweppes, but Lyons continued producing Sunfresh under a contract packing agreement with Schweppes for five years. When the Restrictive Practices Court reported in 1975, it found there was no case to answer.

Private-Label Drinks

After the break with Schweppes, O.R. Groves effectively ceased to exist, since Lyons became the manufacturing and sales organisation for what was then a wholly private-label business. Although Lyons remained the leading supplier of private-label citrus products to the retail trade, a small quantity of branded goods were produced for those companies which did not want private-label drinks. In fact a new branded product was launched in September 1979 based on Roger Hargreaves's 'Mr Men' characters, which were highly popular with children. With bottles packed in boxes of twelve and only eleven Mr Men created so far, Lyons persuaded Roger Hargreaves to introduce a twelfth character, Mr Thirsty, thus enabling Lyons to box twelve different characters in a carton. The brand failed within a few weeks through lack of advertising or other promotions. Now that the grocery retail business was concentrated in the hands of very few large multiple companies (mainly Sainsbury, Tesco, Waitrose, Safeway, Asda and the Co-op) and many of the smaller retailers had formed themselves into buying groups like Spar, intense competition developed. The price of all private-label products, including soft drinks, was forced down to uneconomic levels.

After VAT was imposed and the bad summer of 1974 caused a drop in sales, the comminuted citrus drinks business was merged with the private-label coffee business in 1975 under a unified managed company, JL Private Label Ltd. The new company was supposed to reflect a common purpose and similar customer profiles but apart from having a common board both companies continued to trade as if they were separate. Two salesmen continued calling on each customer, one for coffee and one for juice, there were two marketing managers, and so on. Both products initially sold well, however, coffee because it was positioned at the less vulnerable end of the price spectrum and drinks because of the hot summer of 1976 and the growing market for natural fruit juice. Manufacturers tended to create a more sophisticated image for natural fruit juice by selling it in more expensive glass bottles. As far as Lyons was concerned, management took months to decide whether to invest in a new glass production line, and when they eventually made a decision to go ahead it was too late. There were

This view of the Rannoch Road soft drinks factory illustrates its close proximity to residential properties. In earlier times the factory made jam and frozen food. At one time it housed a large Works Department and consignments of timber were discharged on to its quayside. *By kind permission of Peter Murch.*

already signs that the soft drinks industry was changing from glass to the new Tetra-packs – which were easier to handle and did not break – with the result that there was less call for glass. In any event, engineers failed to make the new glass production line work consistently and it was finally written off in 1984.

The Rannoch Road factory had formed part of Lyons' West London estate as long ago as 1928 when it was first described in the statement of accounts as 'Construction and Engineering Works'. In times past it had been used to produce jam, mincemeat, beef suet, canned fruit, puree and other food-related products as well as providing space for a large joinery department. With its riverside wharf it was a convenient transit centre for raw materials, brought by barge from London's docks, much of which was destined for the food factories at Cadby Hall. It had been the centre of soft drinks production since before the Second World War, but it was becoming increasingly difficult to operate a factory in the middle of a built-up residential area – especially a factory that dealt in high-volume, low-value products. In effect empty bottles or cartons were shipped into the factory, filled with liquid and then shipped out. The concentrated bases from which the juice was made, 1,200 tons per annum, came from five different countries at a cost of £1 million. From this some 8 million litre packs were produced, 75 per cent of which were orange. To cope with seasonal fluctuations it was necessary to work night shifts, with all the associated disturbance to local residents. It was common for lorries to be queuing for half a mile, waiting to be loaded or unloaded, and this became a source of irritation among local residents. These problems were resolved after Allied Breweries acquired Lyons. The soft drinks business was merged with Britvic, an associated Allied Breweries soft drinks company, but, on the formation of Britannia Soft Drinks, Britvic ceased to be a wholly owned subsidiary of Allied Breweries and there was a huge reorganisation of manufacturing operations. This resulted in the closure of the Rannoch Road factory in March 1988.

Chapter

THE BIRTH OF FROZEN FOOD

FOOD PRESERVATION has always been essential to the well-being and existence of mankind. The idea of freezing food to preserve it had been practised by the Innuit and others living in the frozen wastes of the northern hemisphere as long ago as prehistoric times. The animals and fish they killed could be kept for many months in frozen form, until ready for consumption. This method of freezing is known as weather freezing. When Julius Caesar ruled over much of Europe in the first century BC, fish caught in the Rhine, the North Sea and the Baltic were immediately packed in ice and sent off to the markets of the Roman empire where they arrived still frozen under layers of ice and insulating furs. In the Middle Ages special underground ice-houses were constructed for refrigeration, and these were still used in Europe in the nineteenth century, especially in grand country houses.

Early Refrigeration Technology

Food preservation by refrigeration was advanced enormously in the nineteenth century by two French engineers, Ferdinand Carré (1824–1900) and Charles Tellier (1828–1913). Carré is credited with having invented the first ice-cube-making machine, which he exhibited at the Great Exhibition in London in 1859. His rival, Tellier, in 1876 wagered that he could send a leg of mutton undamaged across the Atlantic to South America, a journey which took three and a half months. He fitted out a ship, renamed it the *Frigorifique*, a French word meaning 'cooling' (later refrigeration), filled it with meat frozen by his new method, and sent it off to Buenos

Aires. As the meat arrived in perfect condition, Ferdinand Carré persuaded the Argentine government to fit out another ship, the *Paraguay*, which landed 80 tons of meat at Le Havre in good condition. So started South America's trade with Europe in frozen meat.

The world's first freezing works were set up in Sydney, New South Wales, in 1861 by Thomas Mort. However, the trade developed rapidly when William Vestey (1859–1940) and his brother Edmund (1866–1953) built freezing works in Argentina and in 1909 formed the Blue Star Line Ltd to transport South American meat to the UK. Uruguay too became a major meat supplier, processor and shipper; one of its ports on the Uruguay River was given the name Fray Bentos (believed to be the name of a local monk) after a brand of corned beef. The Union Cold Storage Company made the Vestey family a fortune and when William was made a baron and became the first Lord Vestey the family crest included an iceberg representing their frozen food business.

The Union Cold Storage Company entered into the ice-cream business in 1925 with their Eldorado company, which was acquired by Lyons in 1962 from what was by then the Union International Company. In 1948 the company bought Fropax of Ware and entered the frozen food trade; in 1953 a frozen vegetable business was started in New Zealand and in 1956 production of frozen vegetables and fruit began in South Africa. By 1962 Fropax was combining its interests with those of Lyons, as this chapter later recounts. In this way Lyons' links with frozen food go back to its earliest development.

However, the early refrigeration processes had limitations, and it was not until the 1920s that frozen food became commercially viable. The American fur trapper and scientist, Clarence Birdseye (1886–1956), is credited with the technological innovation of fast-freezing food, specifically fish, and making it more readily available to the public. The idea had first come to him while on a fishing trip to Labrador in 1912. He had observed how a fish that he had placed on the ice had quickly frozen but after it thawed it had lost none of its flavour when eaten. When he returned home he sought to replicate this effect.

Both vegetable and animal foodstuffs consist of cell tissues containing water. The water makes up the greater part of their weight and volume (a beefsteak, for instance, is approximately 74 per cent water). When food is exposed to a temperature of between -1°C and -5°C the water freezes, but only on the surface. If the food is to freeze all the way through, the temperature must drop to -18°C; but the meat frozen by Carré and Tellier in their experiments in shipping it across the Atlantic was frozen to only -8°C. If the threshold temperature of -18°C is reached only gradually, the water freezes slowly and forms large crystals which expand and break up the cell structure. When the food is defrosted the damage cannot be undone: serum and mineral salts all drain out. The answer lies in quick-freezing food by plunging it into a temperature of -40°C to -50°C, thereby freezing it instantly, before there is time for the cells to be destroyed by large ice crystals. Clarence Birdseye experimented for several years until he discovered a method of fast-freezing the food (fish) by placing it between two intensely cold metal plates. In 1924 he co-founded the General Sea Foods Company to market his frozen food, which first went on sale in a store in Springfield, Massachusetts, on 6 March 1930. His was not the only process, but his idea was a good one, although expensive. As he was more concerned with innovation than marketing, Birdseye's business was slow to develop and so he sold his company and patents to the Postum Company, which later became part of Lever Brothers and the Anglo-Dutch Unilever Corporation. His name now forms the trademark – Birds Eye – of their frozen food business.

Lyons' Frood

Lyons had first been alerted to Birdseye's process in 1930 by a director of Baker Perkins, prompting Maurice Salmon to make a special visit to the USA to learn more about it. However, although he had enthusiastically embraced other American food technology, Maurice Salmon did not decide to develop food freezing, perhaps through lack of funds. After all, in 1925 Lyons had invested heavily in a new ice-cream factory and by 1931 had installed American Vogt ice-cream machines. Massive expenditure had also been laid out on the Cumberland Hotel, which opened in 1933.

In the late 1930s Lyons' interests were revived when they began experimenting with frozen food themselves, supplying some of their teashops with frozen rice pudding, custard, waffles and soup. These experiments were accelerated at the onset of war, when road and rail distribution deteriorated and Lyons found themselves with a large ice-cream plant which could not be fully employed because of government legislation preventing ice-cream manufacture. By 1941 teashops and other catering outlets were being supplied with experimental frozen food which by 1945 included whole frozen meals. Some frozen food was supplied during the war to American forces who used the teashop at 37 Duke Street as a canteen because it was near to their Duke Street headquarters and the US embassy in Grosvenor Square. In the early 1950s, when rationing was still very much part of everyday life, the Duke Street teashop was converted to a frozen food restaurant. By 1954 frozen meals were being supplied to other parts of the retail trade.

Immediately after the war Leonard Gluckstein had led a small experimental team, which set out to develop and market frozen meals for the shipping companies and especially for the growing airline industry including Pan American Airways, Trans-Canadian Airways, the British Overseas Airline Corporation and British South American Airways. A wartime Horsa glider, of the type used at Arnhem, was modified so it could be used for displaying products at Cadby Hall and, later, for teaching air stewards how to prepare frozen meals. The converted glider, which had a capacity similar to that of a 28-seat Douglas Dakota airliner, incorporated a small but compact galley with a small sink and a specially designed air-circulating oven, manufactured by the General Electric Company; fuselage work was done by Airwork Ltd. The oven held nine trays, three for entrée dishes, three for potatoes and three for other vegetables. There was enough food to serve twenty-four guests within thirty minutes (very fast in the 1940s, but not compared with today's microwave oven heating). In March 1947 the Réunion des Gastronomes sampled their first frozen food when they were entertained at Cadby Hall for a lunch of soup, turbot, veal, vegetables and a sweet. At the first post-war Hotelympia (an annual exhibition for the hotel and catering trades first held in November 1935) in January 1948 frozen cooked food was shown to the public for the first time; it was also served daily in a special restaurant at the exhibition.

Marketed under the brand name Frood, Lyons' frozen food quickly became popular with the airlines, which could specify particular recipes, combinations of food and packaging. All frozen meals were pre-cooked and pre-packaged on aluminium trays covered with foil. Air travel in the 1950s and early 1960s was expensive and long-haul journeys were lengthy. A flight from London to Japan, for example, might take up to three days, stopping overnight at least once. The frozen food supplied to the airlines at this time was of a very high standard. It was reheated on the journey in air-circulation ovens similar to those used in the converted Horsa glider at Cadby Hall. Airlines held stocks of Frood in cold stores at airports around the world, at strategic points for drawing what they needed for either onward or return flights to London. The arrangements came to an end after two or three years, mainly because the flights became so much shorter that food could be put on to planes and kept hot until served. Some larger airlines also started to produce their own frozen dishes, over which they had greater control. As food shortages receded across Europe, airlines established in-flight catering units at other airports, allowing them

to collect and replenish en route instead of taking everything with them for long hauls.

When the restrictions on ice-cream manufacture were lifted at the end of the war there was little spare capacity for the production of frozen meals in the ice-cream factory at Cadby Hall. Therefore a freezing tunnel was built in the kitchen block, where meat products had previously been kept until they were dispatched to the teashops; yet capacity was still limited and in 1954 the Kitchens Department transferred to the Rannoch Road factory. Rannoch Road was already supporting the frozen meals production line at Cadby Hall making soup, mousse and sandwiches. The soup plant was a scaled-up version of the one at Cadby Hall and the mousse plant similar to an ice-cream plant. In the manufacture of sandwiches, special equipment was used for slicing bread and spreading on fillings; the bread was supplied by the Lyons Bakery and delivered three times a day by a freighter from Cadby Hall.

In August 1953 an order for frozen food was received from a most unusual source: an American services club in Frankfurt, Germany. Lyons were instructed to prepare 100 frozen dinners consisting of chicken and mushroom vol-

Top. The teashop in Duke Street, London, which became the first frozen food restaurant. During the Second World War it was used by US staff billeted nearby.

au-vents, barbecued spare ribs, potato puffles (croquette potatoes), broiled mushrooms and deep-dish blackcurrant pie. These were a forerunner of thousands of frozen meals sold to American troops and their families stationed in Germany who were accustomed to frozen meals back home in America.

The growth of the market in frozen, preserved or processed foods has been one of the major socio-economic phenomena of the twentieth century. It was fuelled by the development of the home refrigerator, although in 1968 only 50 per cent of British households had a refrigerator and only 1 per cent a home freezer. To take the frozen food market alone, in 1955 it was worth only £7.5 million but by 1963 it had increased tenfold to £75 million. The particular appeal of the so-called convenience foods was to working women, who could save time and effort in return for the increased cost of frozen food. From 1951 the owners of Birds Eye embarked on a massive advertising campaign with an initial budget of £30,000 increasing to £1.5 million in 1961. More than 75 per cent of the budget was spent on television advertising after the advent of commercial television in 1955, and sales of Birds Eye frozen food rose during this period from £1 million to £37.5 million.

By 1959 frozen food accounted for nearly one-fifth of total household expenditure in Britain, but in those days far fewer married women were in paid employment. Therefore the higher cost of frozen food was not worth the saving in labour, and a survey carried out in 1952 showed that 38 per cent of married women still cooked three meals a day. Since fresh food was more readily available in the 1950s, and since most working-class households still did not have a refrigerator, consumers were unwilling to experiment with novelty. Frozen food was also thought not to be as nutritious as fresh food, as well as being inferior to most home cooking.

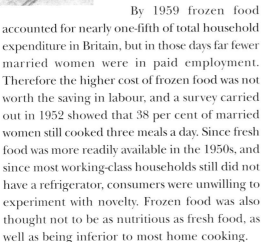

Above. Frood being loaded onto a ship from an ice-cream refrigerated van in 1950.

In 1954 the Frood Division was established under Leonard Gluckstein to target the catering and retail trades. The advantages to caterers were that frozen food eliminated waste and could be prepared by unskilled staff. However, it was expensive, and few retailers had proper storage facilities, although Birds Eye products were being stocked by 900 stores by 1948. The teashops, which were less than enthusiastic about frozen food, were in any case becoming less dependent on Cadby Hall and buying in their own supplies from other firms. Thus the Frood Division was faced with three main difficulties: as turnover was low, overheads were high; retailers were deterred by the high price and the lack of refrigeration in most homes at this time; and, lastly, the best sales came from single frozen food items such as peas (a market dominated by Birds Eye) and not from the frozen meals on which Lyons had concentrated. Ironically, fish fingers had been one of Lyons' earlier successful products long before Birds Eye started marketing them in this country. Lyons' fish fingers were totally unlike the majority of today's versions, being made from high-quality fish cut from whole cod, with no fillers or additives.

After an encouraging start, Frood profits began to deteriorate: by 1962 losses of £150,000 were being recorded. One reason for caterers' lack of interest in frozen meals was the high cost of microwave ovens – or cooking by radar as some newspapers described it. Although frozen food cooking was not dependent on them, microwave ovens had been in existence since 1948 but they were expensive and unreliable; the public too feared that radiation from these ovens might be detrimental to health. In an effort to improve sales to the catering market Lyons entered into an agreement with Microtronic, a Swiss-owned German company, which were marketing a microwave oven for £250, when the cheapest unit then available cost £500. The German oven also had a unit for browning food as well as reheating and cooking it. These ovens were rented out on the condition that caterers bought a minimum quantity of Frood per year. No records have survived to show whether or not this project was successful.

Undeterred by their losses, Lyons continued instructing their chemists to experiment with other frozen food alternatives and soon introduced a new product called Flavour Seal. By this method the food was cooked and then quick-frozen in a plastic bag which only needed to be immersed and heated in boiling water by the consumer – hence the usual name of 'boil-in-the-bag'. This process was said to retain more of the food's flavour. Again, however, Lyons' inadequate advertising budget probably accounts for the fact that the product never really took off, and again it was left to other firms to exploit the technology.

Frozen Food Mergers

When in 1962 Lyons Maid acquired Eldorado ice-cream from Union International and Neilsons Holdings from Associated British Foods, the resultant ice-cream merger led to a similar combination of frozen food interests. Fropax Ltd, a subsidiary of Union International with 6 per cent of the frozen food market, took over the Frood Division of Lyons, which was allocated 49 per cent of shares in Fropax; at the same time Union International increased its holdings in Glacier Foods to 49 per cent. In 1963–4 Eskimo Foods Ltd, a subsidiary of Associated Fisheries Ltd, joined this consortium; the equity of Fropax Ltd was redistributed, so that Lyons and Union International owned just under 39 per cent each and Associated Fisheries just under 21 per cent. The interests of Lyons and Union International were held in such a way that that Glacier Foods was a subsidiary of Lyons but Fropax was not.

It was hoped that in the rapidly expanding and highly competitive frozen food market a larger unit would be better placed to make progress against the strong competition. Because the ice-cream and frozen food businesses were in many ways complementary, the companies were able to share a number of facilities (such as refrigerated transport and depots). Each partner was to have a stake in both enterprises and the three partners' respective interests were to be of the same proportionate size. By the time the mergers were complete, the combined group, named Fropax Eskimo Frood, controlled about

12 per cent of the British frozen food market. Its chairman was Guy Lawrence, who was also chairman of Lyons Maid. However, many policy differences soon manifested themselves between Union International and Lyons. Senior managers were unable to agree, and serious personality rifts developed to the point where some found it impossible to work together. The day-to-day working relationship between managers was described as 'abysmal' and the merger as a whole as 'disastrous'. In any case, Birds Eye still dominated the frozen food sector. In 1968, therefore, Union International and Lyons decided to merge their frozen food business with that of Nestlé (Findus Ltd), thus creating Findus Eskimo Frood Ltd. This was now the second largest frozen food company in the UK with approximately 22 per cent of the £110 million frozen food market. At the same time Lyons acquired an additional 5.25 per cent of the equity capital of Glacier Foods Ltd, as a result of which they owned directly or indirectly just over 24 per cent of Fropax Ltd (the holding company for Findus Eskimo Frood Ltd) and 44.5 per cent of Glacier Foods Ltd. With Lyons holding just over 24 per cent of the new frozen food business, the larger group was able to increase frozen food sales by 18 per cent during 1968, but the UK market was still sluggish; consumption per capita was only 11 lb compared with 60 lb in the United States. Nevertheless, the relationship with Nestlé (Findus) was a good one and continued to go smoothly for the next six years. The main task from 1968 onwards was to expand the business.

'Findus the Fishermen'

Before the formation of Findus Eskimo Frood Ltd, Findus had established factories on Humberside, but in 1970 its Grimsby factory was redeveloped as part of a programme costing £18 million. Vegetable production was moved to nearby Cleethorpes, to create more room for making beefburgers. Findus had recently introduced a new beefburger to replace the former Findus Frood 'steakburger'; and the launch was backed up with the heaviest advertising campaign ever given to a single Findus product. At this time beefburgers were the third

Meals being cooked at Cadby Hall which will be frozen as Frood.

fastest-selling frozen food item after peas and fish fingers.

Despite the diversification, Findus remained best known for their frozen fish products, and in 1970 exported over £150,000-worth of fish fingers, breaded haddock and plaice to Australia. Exports increased by 20 per cent that year, as orders were received from as far afield as Greece, the West Indies and Singapore. Refrigerated ships were regularly sailing out of Grimsby to ports all around the world. A consignment of fish cakes, fish fingers, shepherd's pies and vegetables was even sent by boat 2,000 miles up the Amazon to Iquitos in Peru.

By the spring of 1972 Findus had introduced cod and haddock portions in batter, Savoury Fish Fiesta, Fish Bake Bordelaise, Savoury Pancakes (filled with smoked haddock or steak and kidney) and Fisherman's Pie. To promote the new fish products, a vast advertising campaign was mounted under the slogan 'Findus the Fishermen'. Television commercials focused on the sea and the lives of fishermen to revitalise Findus' image; posters and magazine advertisements showed a trawler at sea with the caption 'Gone Fishing'. Throughout that year Findus launched further varieties such as frozen lasagne, cod in sauce, sirloin steaks, individual chicken and mushroom pies, faggots in gravy, potato croquettes flavoured with egg and bacon or cheese and bacon, the Goldenburger (a beefburger in breadcrumbs) and individual blackcurrant turnovers. Frozen curries had already been introduced two years before. Peas were still the most popular frozen product in the UK, accounting for about 20 per cent of the total retail business. In November 1971 a vegetable-packaging plant costing £1 million was opened at Cleethorpes, close to the vegetable-processing and freezing factory. Two years later the frozen vegetable range had been extended to include whole young carrots, Country Mix vegetables (peas, cut beans, fluted carrots and cauliflower) and Spanish Mix (peas, savoury rice, sweetcorn and red peppers). Other products launched in 1973 included sliced roast pork in gravy, chicken curry, beef and vegetable casserole, whole roasting chickens and Country Style sausage rolls.

In the October 1972 issue of *Lyons Mail*, the product development manager for Findus, Peter Trimingham, explained how new ones were devised. The firm might introduce a line that was popular abroad and adapt it to British tastes (the filled savoury pancake); or they could exploit the popularity of an existing line (beefburgers) by making a small change to turn it into something new (the Goldenburger); or they might simply produce a modified version of a competitor's successful product (Birds Eye's Cod in Butter Sauce was copied by Findus but using onion sauce instead); or they could take a favourite foreign dish (lasagne) and prepare a frozen version that could be served up at home without the bother of learning how to make it. By the beginning of 1973 the frozen food retail industry in the UK was worth £180 million, but Findus, with 20 per cent of the market, still lagged far behind Birds Eye, with 58 per cent. Findus' share of the market in frozen food for catering was slightly larger; overseas too, the Findus brand was much stronger. Consumption of frozen food in the UK had increased from 11 lb per head in 1968 to 16 lb in 1973, while 67 per cent of households now had a refrigerator, though only 5 per cent had freezers.

According to the *Lyons Mail* in October 1972, Findus believed that the next great wave of expansion within the frozen food market would come about through the introduction of new convenience foods. Lyons, however, did not wait to find out whether the Findus management would prove to be correct, since they disposed of their stockholding in Findus less than two years later, in August 1974. The shareholder accounts merely stated: 'On 2 August 1974, the Company disposed of its 49.94% holding in the equity share capital of Findus (UK) Limited.' No reason was given for the sell-off but it may well have been necessary to help fund other food acquisitions being made around that time.

The Decline of Food Manufacture

Henry Telfer's Struggle to Survive

THE LATE 1940s had seen a trebling of both profits and turnover at Henry Telfer Ltd, as the firm took advantage of Lord Woolton's Rural Pie Scheme during the post-war reconstruction. Cessation of the scheme in the early 1950s, however, left Telfer's much weaker than before it was introduced. With hindsight it can be seen that too much attention was paid to satisfying the enormous demand which everyone knew would eventually cease. As minds stayed focused on exploitation of the short-lived scheme, plans for the long-term future of the business had been neglected.

When meat rationing ended on 3 July 1954 Telfer's faced severe competition in the meat pie market from Thomas Wall & Sons. Formed in 1840, Wall's became a household name with their sausages and pies and by 1951 their turnover was over £2 million. When meat supplies returned after rationing, turnover increased to £4 million; by 1965 Wall's business was worth an amazing £40 million. This astonishing growth had been partly achieved with the co-operation of the farmers and agricultural scientists who devised the most efficient ways of breeding pigs. The methods involved selective breeding from high-producing sows, greater care of litters to reduce mortality, some measure of factory farming to obtain the fastest growth, and a controlled diet to produce leaner meat.

Ivor Salmon (b. 1911), who had taken over from his cousin Geoffrey in 1945, had the unenviable task of downsizing Henry Telfer Ltd which by then had a turnover of about £400,000

a year. He was the youngest of three sons born to Alfred Salmon and was therefore a grandson of one of the firm's founding members, Barnett Salmon. He too had started his career with Lyons, at the age of eighteen, in the Trocadero kitchens, but unlike many of his family was educated at Tonbridge School and not the City of London. After joining the Territorial Army, following the Munich crisis of 1938, he served as a major in the Catering Corps during the whole of the war. At the time of Ivor Salmon's appointment in 1945 the former sales manager, Arthur Lyons (no relation to Joseph Lyons), had just been succeeded by Jim Hall, a famous ex-motorcycling champion who had joined from Firestone Tyres and had an extraordinary network of contacts (he also wrote a regular article in the *Tatler* under the byline of Bickerstaff). Hall's appointment helped to secure the royal warrant which Telfer's received in 1955.

Telfer's, after having had contracts with the big department stores such as Selfridge's, the Army and Navy Stores, John Barker and others, found itself relegated to supplying works canteens, hospitals and working-class restaurants. For the next five years the business stagnated and little effort was made to improve its image and retail market. By contrast, Wall's continued to break new ground, supplying the increasing number of supermarket chains and creating branded goods.

Telfer's nevertheless still had a strong presence in the market for meat pies but had less success with sausages. In February 1958 they bought part of the Excel Meat Company, which had a substantial trade in sausages but not in meat pies. The two businesses appeared to complement each other. Telfer's meagre sausage production moved to Stratford in East London and Excel's pie production to Fulham. The acquisition brought almost instant benefits and turnover began to improve, but G. Brazil & Co. Ltd suddenly broke into the market with extensive advertising and superior products, creaming off much of Telfer's business. George Brazil had established himself as a sausage-maker in 1949. From his Amersham-based factory in Buckinghamshire he rapidly built up a substantial retail trade with high-quality sausages and pork pies. In two or three years his company had captured much of the Greater London sausage and meat pie trade but eventually it was absorbed by Bowyer's Ltd of Wiltshire.

Some of Telfer's products were unknown or lacked appeal to consumers, since there was no advertising and the firm produced no branded goods, had a downmarket image and was still run as a family concern. Moreover it had not adapted to the need for hygiene and quality control. Lyons commissioned Stuart Dorizzi, one of their marketing consultants, to carry out a thorough survey of Telfer's operation. Dorizzi recommended the appointment of a marketing director and other marketing personnel. He also suggested that the company concentrate on creating a distinctive brand and make efforts to change its image. In essence this amounted to introducing modern management techniques such as work study and quality control, developing new products and changing van livery again. As a result of Dorizzi's recommendations, there was a temporary transformation, and by 1962 both turnover and profits had doubled, but Lyons had not taken up the idea of building up a brand. Frank Merry, Telfer's marketing director, who had been appointed in 1960 following Dorizzi's report, believed that the business could not survive if it failed to break into the retail sector. He continually championed the development of a brand but his views were not shared. Lyons had neither the money nor the enthusiasm to embark on such a speculative if not expensive scheme. In 1964, however, Lyons did acquire the Salmon

family's 49 per cent interest in Henry Telfer Ltd for £389,550, making Telfer's a fully owned Lyons subsidiary.

Since Telfer's had insufficient capital to create their own retail pie brand, they concentrated their effort into supplying the catering trade and geared up accordingly. In 1966, however, Frank Merry – concerned at losing the retail market – suggested a merger. Merry argued that companies already supplying the retail trade could, without incurring any additional cost, turn their attention to the catering trade and thus undermine the whole of Telfer's business. The idea of a merger to protect their pie market did not appeal to the Lyons management, who must have felt this was a back-door attempt to secure established brand names. They had after all embarked on a process of restructuring the catering, coffee, ice-cream and bakery businesses, with all the attendant cost, and a meat pie partner was never seriously considered.

Supplying the Catering Trade

Frank Merry's team nevertheless pushed ahead with new plans, and frozen pies, sausage rolls and scotch eggs were introduced in late 1967, when Telfer's salesmen began calling on cafés, fish and chip shops, bakers, butchers and self-service stores to sell the idea of in-store baking, to install equipment and to begin supplying what was largely a new and so far untapped area of catering. The process was dubbed 'before your very eyes cooking' – employed so successfully by the Wimpy Bars and Steak Houses. The Telfer's services were provided with the backing of Bake-o-Mat (ovens and heated display cabinets) and Total Refrigeration (freezer cabinets) at specially negotiated prices. Customers buying the equipment were provided with £20-worth of pies, Cornish pasties and sausage rolls free of charge. By the late 1960s, with Guy Lawrence now in charge, Telfer's had also secured contracts to supply hamburgers to the Lyons subsidiary Wimpy Restaurants and both hamburgers and other food products to the franchising business of Pleasure Foods.

Early in 1969 Telfer's began supplying cash-and-carry warehouses with frozen meat products, including smaller pack sizes for the small caterers who frequented these outlets. A new catering range was launched in September 1970 at a series of presentations across the country. Giant 6 lb frozen steak and kidney pies, beef and vegetable pies and 5 lb cottage pies were put on the market after extensive research and development. Using shortcrust pastry (rather than puff pastry) for the first time, Telfer's promoted the new range as 'home made' in style and flavour. With just a pastry crust on top, and no pastry at the sides or bottom, they contained more meat than usual, and the beef and vegetable version was seasoned with Worcester sauce.

For many years Telfer's had supplied pubs with hot and cold snacks – such as sausage rolls and sandwiches – and in 1969 they developed a range of frozen main course dishes to meet the growing demand for pub food. In association with a number of large breweries, Telfer's launched the Good Food Corner service, which offered pubs frozen food which could be used in preparing simple meals quickly; the items included chicken fricassee, cottage pie, chicken and beef curry, steak and kidney pie filling and bolognese sauce, and they were intended to be served with rice, potato, pastry or spaghetti. Delivered at least once a week, the frozen blocks were designed to be kept for several weeks in a deep freeze.

In an arrangement almost reminiscent of the old days of Lyons' outdoor catering, Telfer's were asked in 1969 to supply food for the Isle of Wight pop festival, held annually at August Bank Holiday. By the festival's second year the order had doubled in value to around £10,000. Operating from their depot in Portsmouth, in August 1970 Telfer's sent nearly half a million food items in a refrigerated van, supplied by British Rail, which carried the goods across to the Isle of Wight on the car ferry. The order included 216,000 hamburgers, 105,000 king frankfurters, 24,000 steak and kidney pies, 6,000 apple pies, 15,600 sausage rolls, 9,000 pork pies, 12,000 Cornish pasties and 53,760 or 2 tons of sausages.

Although the new frozen food outlets had increased Telfer's profits by approximately 25 per cent, the improvement was short-lived. In the 1970s, prices, including meat prices, began to rise steeply. Computerised recipe techniques were utilised to experiment with alternative ingredients, with the aim of cutting production costs, and the quality of products deteriorated – chicken skin, gristle, and pulverised bone and feathers were no substitute for meat. To reduce costs, the Fulham factory was closed on 8 September 1968 and production then centred on Stratford and Cadby Hall, both units operating to capacity. Until this time no effort had been made to exploit Lyons' sophisticated expertise in food technology. Even at this late stage it was it was used reluctantly, and only because the large supermarket chains, such as Sainsbury's, began to impose their own high standards. By the late 1960s Telfer's were Britain's largest manufacturer of meat products for the catering trade, with 20 per cent of the market. Between 1973 and 1978 turnover doubled from £13 million to £26 million per year. Profits, on the other hand, were most unsatisfactory. From a modest loss of £14,000 in 1973, losses escalated and by 1978 the company accounts record an accumulative loss of nearly £5 million.

Although the number of administrative staff had grown, the service departments were unsatisfactorily billeted in separate buildings close to the factory. Building regulations precluded extensions to the factory and it became more urgent to provide modern facilities for both production and administration. There were only two alternatives. Either the meat pie factory together with its administration must be transferred to another location – probably out of London – or extra space would have to be made for it at Cadby Hall by moving other units. Eventually, since attractive relocation incentives were being offered by development area agencies, it was decided to build a new meat products factory on 20 acres at Moulton Park Estate, Northampton.

The factory opened fully in 1974 at a cost of £3 million and was hailed as the most modern in Europe. However, production management continued to have difficulty in coming to terms with quality control, as supermarkets insisted on ever higher levels of hygiene and their representatives made frequent, and unannounced, visits to inspect the production lines and packaging departments. These inspections, which some staff considered were a distraction, did not rest here, since many supermarket companies established their own laboratories where their chemical analysis of food became more sophisticated. Increasingly, they made random tests for microbiological deterioration of food supplied to them, as well as checking that it contained what it was supposed to. More importantly perhaps, as techniques advanced, the chemists were able to detect banned substances sometimes used as preservatives.

The Northampton factory had been a drain on funds and Telfer's continued to trade unprofitably. In January 1980 Henry Telfer Ltd changed its name to J. Lyons Products Ltd before its disposal, on 15 February, with those of the French meat business Société Nouvelle des Établissements Reybier SA, to the Unigate Group.

Turn of the Tide

After the Second World War, Lyons were ideally placed to meet growing consumer demand and in retrospect it can now be seen that it was a turning point for the food industry generally. The Lyons teashops which had dominated high streets before the war were now in some disrepair. Little or no refurbishment had been possible during the austere years of war other than the introduction of an 'ugly' self-service which replaced the much-loved Nippy. Social fashions too had changed, and Lyons were challenged by a new breed of caterers more attuned to consumers' needs. The Lyons catering management found they were having to reform their own catering methods to match competition; ironically, while revenues from Lyons' teashops declined, small competitors' profits increased. In other words management found themselves, for the first time, in a reactive rather than a proactive mode. In most of the company's divisions too, pressure was mounting from smaller but more adaptable businesses. Ice-cream, bakery, tea, meat pies and soft drinks all came under pressure from medium-sized companies which like Lyons were able to adopt modern machinery

to minimise production costs. Lyons too were coming under increasing strain from larger multinationals such as Unilever who not only adopted a management style more democratic than that of Lyons but excelled in marketing and branding. These large multinationals were not averse to spending huge sums of money to promote the brands of their individual trading subsidiaries.

With the exception of cake, Lyons increasingly found that their market share of products was declining. This came at a time when supermarkets began replacing the proverbial corner shop into which Lyons had traditionally sold. The supermarkets' combined buying power not only forced down the price of many foodstuffs but their growth removed the main outlet for many of Lyons' food items. Lyons could no longer depend on the loyalty of Britain's shopkeepers, who soon found it necessary to create their own buying groups to counteract the supermarket onslaught. Now, at the end of the twentieth century, the process is complete and the supermarket companies dominate food retailing to the extent that they now commission their own brands from food manufacturers who are the subordinate partner.

Faced with strong competition from multinationals, declining market share for many of its products and reduced returns on manufactured goods, Lyons embarked on an aggressive period of acquisitions to create size and volume in order to compete with the multinationals. During this period there was increased legislation affecting taxation, prices and employment, as well as rising raw material costs and a fuel crisis. At the same time management had to come to terms with budgeting for new marketing methods, repackaging and better distribution of goods.

The expansion of the Lyons food empire between 1950 and the 1970s occupied much of management's time, coming as it did when senior management had no real long-term objectives other than to expand into Europe and become multinational. The logistical process of achieving those objectives were hasty and not well studied. Some success was achieved in own-label brands, particularly coffee and soft drinks. Mass production, however, was not the recipe for success that it once was. Marketing, in which Lyons was inherently weak, now became more important to business success. These changes were occurring when the whole industrialised economy of the United Kingdom was going through a fundamental transformation. Whereas Britain once commanded industrial leadership, occupying a dominant position in a great empire, this gradually declined after 1945 when other countries became more industrialised (and competitive) and the British empire began to disintegrate.

For most of the post-war period Lyons' entrenched management styles remained fixed in the early part of the century and whereas many of their competitors were able to readjust to changing business patterns Lyons arrogantly continued to depend on their reputation to turn matters around. Indecisiveness, poor decision-making, massive borrowings to fund the expansion programme and poor leadership had brought Lyons to the brink of insolvency. It was a position from which the company could not recover.

Part 4
THE SUPPORT SERVICES

FROM HORSE-DRAWN VANS TO MOTOR MANUFACTURE

THE TRANSFORMATION of Lyons from an exhibition catering company into a leading food manufacturer must rank as one of the business success stories of the twentieth century. The multiplicity of food-manufacturing departments – such as bakeries, kitchens, grocery and ice-cream – had been formed to serve the original catering needs but it had soon become logical to supply to the public through retailers for home consumption. In time some of the individual food-manufacturing departments had become main subsidiary companies, forming the most important elements of the business, in terms of both profit and investment, while catering grew less significant. The Tea Department was the first expansion beyond catering, when a packet tea business developed nationally. Then the bakery developed, and more perishable products and fluctuations in demand led to a separate system of selling and distribution quite apart from that best suited to tea and coffee. Other food-manufacturing businesses had individual production and distribution needs. These large manufacturing units, together with restaurants and hotels, required the support of substantial service departments.

Lyons' service departments were vertically integrated to serve the needs of the various parts of the company and included transport, laboratories, printing, carton making, and building and engineering workshops. It was preferable to manufacture, as well as to design, some of the specialised food production machinery and catering equipment. The history of each of these service departments reveals a recurrent tendency for them to become revenue-earning by undertaking work for others as well as providing services to the company. Many branched out into other areas of business. The first support service to be set up was transport, which rapidly developed into the Lyons subsidiary, Normand Ltd.

Handcarts and Horse-Drawn Vans

For over thirty years after its formation, Lyons' delivery systems were based on the ubiquitous horse-drawn van. Products manufactured at Cadby Hall – initially bread and pastry goods but later tea, coffee and cocoa – were all sold from handcarts and horse-drawn vehicles.

The stabling facilities at Cadby Hall were extensive, and as the business grew so more space was allocated in the north-west part of the factory in what was known as Sackville House. The stables here, accessed from Brook Green Place, were on two levels, with ramps leading up to the higher level. On their return from their rounds, sometimes late in the evening, salesmen were responsible for the care of their own animals. Early records reveal that the overall cost of keeping the horses was higher than the cost of employing salesmen. Some of the expenditure – forage, harness repairs, veterinary fees, shoeing, bedding, and so on – was offset by the sale of manure to local market gardeners. At one time over 1,000 horses were used by Lyons, operating from Cadby Hall and depots up and down the country, and the company had horse-van repair shops at London, Birmingham and Liverpool. As the combustion engine gradually took over from the horse, many of the horse-van bodies were converted into motor bodies.

Distribution by Road, Rail and Canal

The years immediately following the First World War were revolutionary for Lyons, and nowhere more so than in the Transport Department. In 1919 Walter Henry Gaunt, formerly a distribution superintendent for the Board of Trade, was recruited as distribution manager. Gaunt was both acclaimed and influential in transport circles and in his work for Lyons he is credited with having facilitated much of the evolution from horse-drawn to motor transport. Before his arrival Lyons had been using steam tractors from as early as 1912 for towing vans carrying tea and cocoa from London Docks, or Hammersmith Wharf, where it had been off-loaded from Lyons' barges.

Once the Greenford factory was fully operational, the manufacture of non-perishable products at a 30-acre site outside London had tremendous advantages, although management were concerned about whether removing the centre for so large a tonnage away from London Docks and the Greater London distribution networks would cause problems. However, the efficient use of local road, rail and canal distribution systems enabled the Greenford factory to be well served.

Most of the raw materials imported from abroad were dutiable and therefore under the control of HM Customs and Excise until duty had been paid. Consignments of tea purchased overseas arrived in London Docks by freighter and were transferred in 30-50-ton loads into barges, which were towed, three at a time, to the Brentford Dock by steam tug. The eleven barges in use were owned by George Henry Collier Ltd, a wholly owned subsidiary of Lyons. From Brentford Dock the barges were pulled first by steam tug and then by horse along the Grand Union Canal before entering Greenford's own gated dock where the resident customs officer accepted delivery into the bonded warehouse. Cocoa and coffee beans, sugar and canned fruit were transported in the same way. The tea-chests and sacks of coffee or cocoa beans were transferred from the barges by overhead conveyor

and allocated to their different parts of the bonded warehouse, where up to 30,000 tea-chests or equivalent quantities of other goods could be stored before weighing and examination.

Each of Lyons' factories had its own area in which daily production was assembled before dispatch, which normally contained up to three days' output to allow for the fluctuations of orders and weather. Bread was stored on a daily basis. Salesmen sent their orders to the Distribution or Dispatch Departments, not to the factory. Goods were date coded so that distribution could be undertaken in rotation, thus avoiding stock becoming stale. With the exception of northern Scotland and the west of Ireland, every village and town in Britain was served by Lyons' local cash sales delivery vans. By the mid-1920s there were several hundred horse-drawn and motor vans with a capacity from 7 cwt to 1 ton. They were stationed singly in a small town like Hitchin, or in pairs in a medium-sized town such as Peterborough, or in groups of ten to twenty in a big city like Birmingham.

The drivers of the sales vans were not only good salesmen but had to be taught to drive and to keep their accounts for paying cash into local banks. They were organised into groups under fourteen district supervisors. Among the hundreds of journeys made every year, some consisted of a few square miles in a city, while others might extend to several hundred square miles in a larger territory like Scotland; in 1954, 60,000 journeys were made. Every trip was planned to a strict timetable, not only for orderly management but to ensure that the shopkeeper would be in his shop, with cash available, and knowing when to expect the next delivery. Salesmen could replenish their stock at the various depots around the country or they could order from Greenford and collect the goods from a local railway station, or at some point on the trunk-road system.

Much of the product manufactured by Lyons was sent as railway freight categorised into three classes: skip, chest and loose. The skips, or containers, were of 3-ton, 2-ton or 25-cwt capacity. Until 1921 all skips were wooden and their tare – or weight to be deducted from gross weight in ascertaining net weight – was reckoned to be about 33 per cent of their contents; the container was charged at the same rate as contents, and at half-rate as empty returns. That meant that on a consignment of 3 tons net, charged at £6 per ton, an extra £9 was spent on getting the skip out and back again. To reduce this expenditure, Lyons developed a 'duralumin' metal skip of half the weight, and this created a saving of £117 per annum per skip, based on twenty-six journeys per year. The metal skips were found to be more durable and could be sealed to prevent pilferage. Moreover, they could be handled automatically by electric hoists at the Greenford dispatch dock. On certain days of the week train wagons were loaded for delivery at particular junctions or important towns and travelled practically direct over any of the railway companies' networks.

Within the London area vehicle maintenance was carried out at the Normand Garage at Shepherd's Bush. In other parts of the country maintenance was undertaken in Manchester. Random inspections were made of motor transport and no one was allowed to drive a vehicle until it had passed scrutiny at the garage.

Sentinel Waggons and Motor Vans

When Walter Gaunt joined Lyons in 1919, the triangular estate at Greenford had just been bought. On one side was the Great Western Railway, on the other the Grand Union Canal and to the south Oldfield Lane, which connected to the arterial road systems being built westward out of London. When Greenford became fully operational a more flexible means of transport was required and a 6-ton steam wagon, a Sentinel Waggon (the Sentinel Waggon works at Shrewsbury always used this spelling), was purchased to gauge its usefulness to the company. It must have proved its worth, because Lyons took delivery of twenty-seven Sentinel Waggons between 1919 and 1923, the first at a cost of £1,265.

Before the First World War, Lyons had experimented with a variety of small internal combustion vehicles produced by Renault, Guy, Buick, Vulcan and with Model-T Fords, as well

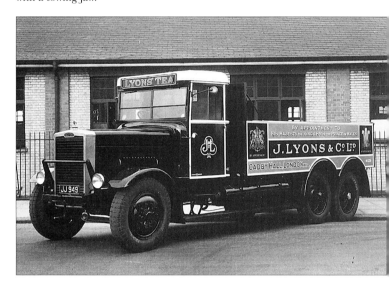

A Pagefield of 1932 built for carrying lift-vans and fitted with a towing jaw.

This Pagefield Pompian of 1936 vintage is in the livery of Horniman's tea. The three dancing children on the panel on the side of the cab door is thought to have inspired the logo introduced by Lyons Maid in 1973.

as small battery vans made by GV and Edison. One of their first acquisitions was a Lacre, which was fired by low-tension igniters and driven by a chain transmission. It was used by a tea salesman who had answered an advertisement in 1908 for 'Pioneer Motor Salesmen'. He reported to George Pollard of the Tea Agents Department and operated from the Clerkenwell depot. Having

A small van advertising Lyons' Staff Stores.

This Pagefield lorry has been fitted with a large box-like carrying body. It is photographed in Brook Green in about 1935.

served an apprenticeship with Vauxhall Engineering Company, he eventually became a senior buyer for Normand Garage.

By 1911 sixty small motor vans were in use, Renault being the salemen's favourite. Some were fitted with non-skid tyres, and all included Automobile Association membership. In the 1920s, however, the Tea Division was provided

with Ford vans driven by bowler-hatted salesmen who penetrated to the smallest villages in Britain. Yet the horse-drawn vehicle still dominated the roads and in 1923 The *Sentinel Transport News* estimated that horses still outnumbered motors by twelve to one in London, perhaps because of traffic congestion.

During the 1920s some vehicle manufacturers, notably Shelvoke & Drewry, began using small-diameter rubber-tyred wheels on their 2- and 3-ton models, enabling them to reduce platform heights. Some of these were used as mobile promotional shops but they were also useful for transporting insulated boxes from the ice-cream factory at Cadby Hall to the Addison Road station where they were loaded on to railway wagons for shipment to the depots. The first vehicle embodying its own compressor refrigeration unit was introduced in 1929, when it carried its own refrigeration unit on the front of the body – as is still the practice today.

The Road Traffic Acts of 1930 restricted the total gross weight for a four-wheeled vehicle to 12 tons, 19 tons for a six-wheeled vehicle and 22 tons for an eight-wheeler. The Act also limited steam wagons on solid tyres to a maximum of 16 miles per hour; this was increased to 20 miles per hour if the wagons were fitted with pneumatic tyres. These regulations had a disastrous effect on heavily constructed vehicles – such as steam Sentinels – because their maximum carrying capacity was greatly reduced. Some changes were made in the 1931 Motor Vehicles (Construction and Use) Regulations to help makers of steam-driven transport overcome these difficulties but the days of steam road vehicles were numbered.

Normand Ltd

The first vehicle workshop was set up at Cadby Hall in about 1905 to service Lyons' growing fleet of combustion-engine cars. This later moved to another Lyons location in the Hammersmith Road, known as Spike House, and from there to the Normand Garage repair shop in Normand Road, Fulham. On 7 February 1921 this repair shop operation was transformed into a wholly owned subsidiary under the title Normand Garage Ltd, which soon afterwards acquired the specialist engineering company Hydraulic Gears Ltd. Under the directors Samuel Gluckstein, Conrad Thorne (engineer) and George Biles (accountant) the company retained its registered office at Normand Road. A second workshop was soon established in Lots Road, Fulham, where the company's motor cars were serviced until the Second World War.

As Greenford played a more important part in the distribution network, in 1925 Normand Garage Ltd (which became Normand Ltd on 19 June 1941) moved to new premises at Cumberland Avenue, Park Royal, where it could service both Cadby Hall and Greenford and where there was sufficient capacity to build more distribution vehicle bodies in-house. By 1935 the growing business made it necessary to find other workshops for the engineering department and 3½ acres of freehold premises were purchased at Abbey Road, Park Royal, adjacent to the former property. Most of the engineering works moved to the enlarged premises but the registered office remained at Cumberland Avenue until 13 March 1969, when it too moved to Abbey Road. The factory tackled between 5,000 and 6,000 jobs a year. Like most engineering works of the period, Normand employed many apprentices who were engaged in various crafts, from engineering to vehicle body-building and sign-writing. At the start of the war Gaunt himself was made transport adviser to the Ministry of Food.

Normand established its first modern car park in November 1934. Called the Cumberland Garage and Car Park, it was opened by Leslie Hore-Belisha, then Minister of Transport, who described it as the 'garage of tomorrow'. Situated near Marble Arch, with its entrance in Bryanston Street, it was 1.25 million cubic feet in size and

One of the entrances to an underground car park near Marble Arch which was operated by Lyons' subsidiary Normand Garage Ltd. It was designed to double as a shelter should the need arise.

had been designed by Sir Owen Williams, who had used reinforced concrete throughout. The ceiling of each of the five parking floors was striped with a distinctive colour and there was one-way traffic control. A so-called 'car-clinic' was located on the ground floor, where every kind of valeting service was available; cars were washed over a large grid and dried off with compressed air. An 'invisible ray' checked each car's height and a klaxon was sounded if it was too high to negotiate the ramps. There were dressing rooms, bathrooms and lounges for male and female motorists and for the chauffeurs a rest and recreation room. Luggage could be deposited in a cloakroom and shoppers could have their

The Lyons Mail   *June, 1923*

NORMAND GARAGE LIMITED
Automobile Agents and Engineers,
OLAF STREET, W.11
'Phone : Park 897   'Phone : Park 1289

RADIO
Western Electric

Crystal Set	£4	2	6
Crystal and Amplifier Set ...	£13 15	0
Valve Detector and Tuner ...	£11 10	0

(The above include Headphones)

Three-valve Detector & Tuner	£19 0 0
Single-stage Amplifier	£10 0 0
Two-stage Amplifier	£13 10 0
Small Loud Speaker	£2 10 0
Head Receivers, 4000 ohms ...	£1 12 0

SPECIAL TERMS TO
MEMBERS OF THE LYONS CLUB

CARS
Any make of car supplied

7 H.P. Austin	£165
10 H.P. Trojan	£175
8 H.P. Rover	...From £180
10 H.P. B.S.A.	...From £205
11.9 H.P. Lagonda ...	...From £275
11.9 H.P. Bean	...From £335
18.2 H.P. Buick	...From £355
12 H.P. Austin	...From £450
20 H.P. Austin	...From £595

DEFERRED PAYMENTS
CARS TAKEN IN PART EXCHANGE

HOW TO BUY A CAR OUT OF INCOME

1/4th DOWN		1/4th DOWN	
11.9 BEAN		**10 H.P. TROJAN**	
Cost of Car	£335 0 0	Cost of Car	£175 0 0
Interest at 4%	13 8 0	Interest at 4%	7 0 0
TOTAL ...	£348 8 0	TOTAL ...	£182 0 0
Against Delivery ...	87 2 0	Against Delivery ...	45 10 0
Balance	£261 6 0	Balance ... '	£136 10 0
By 12 Instalments of ...	21 15 6	By 12 Instalments of ...	11 7 6

WRITE FOR FULL PARTICULARS
SPECIAL FACILITIES TO MEMBERS OF THE LYONS CLUB

ANY MAKE OF MOTOR CYCLE SUPPLIED

432

Some of the vehicles sold by Normand Garage Ltd in 1923. 'In-car entertainment' was costly.

purchases delivered to the garage and thence to their specific car location. Associated with the garage was a twelve-pump filling station with a capacity of 12,000 gallons. During the Second World War the building was modified and equipment installed to enable armoured-car parts to be manufactured.

By 1957 the Lyons transport fleet had grown to 2,750 vehicles of all shapes and sizes, from small 8-cwt runabouts to the big articulated lorries carrying 10-ton loads or 2,500 gallons of ice-cream, and 400 cars for commercial travellers and executives. Heavy steam transport had been replaced by diesel power, pioneered in the United Kingdom by Foden, whose ERF vehicles were

legendary. Initially powered by a Gardner boat diesel, the engines were low-revving, reliable and able to haul huge loads over great distances. For the driver too they were easier to handle than steam wagons, although power steering had not yet been introduced and so they required considerable strength when turning in small spaces. Diesel wagon manufacturing was started by many other companies including the London bus manufacturer AEC, which developed their very successful Mammoth Major. Traffic speed restrictions, however, still limited these vehicles to 20 miles per hour right up to 1950, when the restrictions were relaxed.

Van Liveries

When Lyons' main trading divisions decentralised in the 1960s, the responsibility for transport livery fell on the respective boards. A precedent for change had been set in the 1950s when the ice-cream department had adopted a predominantly white van with a wide band of grey and dark blue on the lower third. Otherwise the Lyons transport livery was based on the traditional combination of dark blue and grey with gold lettering – a design immediately recognised by many members of the public and almost as commonly seen as the red Post Office vans. However, the new management boards wanted to break away from tradition by creating individual identities for their own businesses, and leading this movement was the Bakery Division's marketing manager John Ramsden, who favoured a complete change of image for all bakery commercial vehicles. Nevertheless, Ramsden felt that there were three related issues which needed to be addressed: the Lyons image; the allocation of responsibility for the evolution and maintenance of a satisfactory image; and the delivery van as a vehicle for the communication of the ideas and associations which add up to that image. Given the total 1,466 Lyons delivery vehicles then in service he calculated that an impact of advertising worth £46,720 could be achieved by better use of van design.

Before the 1960s no brand advertising had been displayed on any Lyons vehicles. The chairman of Lyons at this time, Brian Salmon, had already recognised that most competitors in the bread and cake market had adopted new liveries. Among these were Hale-Trent (not yet acquired by Lyons), whose design symbolised cleanliness and hygiene, the Royal Arsenal Co-operative Society and Cadbury. Wall's too were considering using different van design for their separate divisions handling ice-cream, meat and convenience foods, and they solved the problem by adopting an individual colour scheme for each division, while maintaining a standard logo for the name 'Walls'. With trading sectors already responsible for their own transport fleets, there was a groundswell of opinion within the Bakery Division favouring change. For over sixty years the well-recognised blue and gold livery of the Lyons vans had been a familiar sight to Londoners, and any change would obviously be resisted by traditionalists.

The issue was so important that all twenty-seven members of the Lyons board discussed it on 11 October 1962. Although there were many who were appalled at the idea of change, the principle of divisional autonomy was respected. It was therefore agreed that individual trading divisions would, if they felt the need, be allowed to design their own liveries; these started to appear in the mid-1960s. For the Bakery Division a white van with oatmeal-coloured lettering displaying an egg whisk and basin was adopted. When it appeared, most thought it was an uninspired, vulgar design concocted by the Lyons Bakery marketing department which did little for the image of Lyons or, for that matter, of Lyons Bakery.

Below. This 1929 Leyland Tiger was used to deliver food to London and provincial teashops. Its side shutters had been designed to make the unloading of trays easier in London's busy streets.

Diversification and Expansion

Formed originally to service and repair the company's own motor vehicles, Normand rapidly developed into retail activities, including public garaging and the operation of petrol and service stations. It achieved a position of some importance within the retail motor trade and in time acquired several subsidiary companies of its own. One of its main engineering activities was commercial body-building, both for the Lyons group and for outside sales. On one occasion in the early 1950s Normand was commissioned to build a mobile bank for the Maharaja of Patiala, in the Punjab state of India. Built on a chassis of a Guy Otter and weighing just over 6 tons, it

Above. Built in collaboration with Western Electric, this 1931 open air daylight cinema toured the country, screening advertising cartoons for Lyons tea, at fairs and carnivals.

had bullet-proof windows and was heavily armour-plated with 7-mm steel side-panels.

Travelling workshops and 10-ton semi-trailer photographic units for the Royal Air Force were also produced at the Park Royal workshops. Children's roundabouts, cinema vans from which Lyons showed promotional films, three-wheeled parcel vans and product display vehicles were all part of Normand's vehicle-building activities. One of their most unusual contracts required the construction of a caravan trailer for exhibitions. It had been ordered in the early 1960s by Greville Wynne, the British businessman, as part of his equipment when travelling to eastern Europe and it was designed to conceal a British Leyland Mini. He was arrested in Hungary in November 1962, accused of being a spy and was sentenced to eight years' imprisonment. In April 1964 he was exchanged for the spy Gordon Lonsdale but

Colonel Oleg Penkovsky, Wynne's go-between in Russia, was executed.

Normand and its subsidiaries also negotiated agreements to become distributors and dealers for many leading motor vehicle manufacturers, and from its fifteen establishments in 1966 Normand retailed a substantial number of new and used vehicles. To take advantage of the growing demand for off-street car parks, Normand also acquired a 50 per cent interest in Europark Holdings Ltd, which operated car parks in both the United Kingdom and western Europe. After the partnership had been officially registered, Normand transferred their 1,000-car Park Lane Garage, built under Hyde Park, to the new company and in January 1965 a new 'mechanical' car park opened in Old Burlington Street, London. Towards the end of 1969 an offer was made by the controlling shareholders of National Car Parks Ltd to acquire Europark Holdings Ltd and its associated companies and Normand disposed of its 50 per cent holding for £280,000 in cash.

During the next twenty years Normand concentrated on their retail motor business and became one of the most important dealerships for continental cars in Britain – Mercedes-Benz, BMW, Audi and Citroën being the major ones – as well as being suppliers for Ford, General Motors and others. From their sales outlets in 1980 Normand were selling 6,000 cars a year, new and second-hand, with a turnover of £28 million. They also developed a sizeable trucking business, but profits from this and the car dealerships were mediocre and the parent company accounts seldom mentioned the motor subsidiary activities.

With a declining market share, and lacking high profit performance, Normand was eventually sold to a management team, headed by Struan Wiley and funded by NMG, on 2 February 1990. The management buyout was badly timed, since the car industry went into deep recession and sales of new luxury models, with which Normand were associated, collapsed. With cash-flow difficulties caused by insufficient turnover, Normand were unable to compete with their larger rivals. Management disposed of the business to European Motor Holdings on 12 July 1994.

THE FOOD LABORATORY

FROM LYONS' EARLIEST BEGINNINGS, individual managers had been responsible for the strict control of their own departments, upon which the whole company depended. This practice, which had started with the first catering assignments, permeated the entire company and encompassed every department, notably the food-manufacturing units. Maurice Salmon, director in charge of all food production at Cadby Hall between the wars, was acutely aware that successful manufacturing depended on standardisation. Moreover, he recognised at an early stage the need for quality in the increasingly sophisticated manufacture of food and he set high standards for his production management. After the First World War he became convinced that greater automation in food manufacturing would improve hygiene, especially in the production of ice-cream, which during the years 1890–1905 had suffered several scandals.

Food Adulteration

During the late eighteenth and nineteenth centuries food adulteration had been widespread and reached its peak in the late eighteenth century, by which time it had attained alarming proportions. Bread, the mainstay of the poor, was the worst affected. Many small bakers used potato flour, rice flour and even whitened sawdust to eke out their flour supplies. Sometimes they undercooked the adulterated dough because the excess moisture content gave the loaf extra weight. Milk, which was used in other preparations such as confectionery, was often watered down. In 1783 a committee of the House of Commons reported:

> The quantity of fictitious tea, which is annually manufactured from sloe and ash-tree leaves, in different parts of England, to be mixed with genuine teas, is computed at more than four millions of pounds, and this, too, at a time when the whole quantity of genuine teas sold by the East India Company did not amount to more than six million pounds annually. Verdigris and other copper salts were used to produce a bloom on the tea-leaf, sugar of lead was applied in the improvement of wines, vinegar was adulterated with sulphuric acid and alum, gypsum, chalk and pipe clay were incorporated with the materials of bread.

The modern pure food movement in Britain started in about 1850, with a campaign in *The Lancet* which resulted in the first Food and Drink Act of 1860. In 1875 all the Food Acts then in force were repealed and replaced by the Sale of Food and Drugs Act, which has since been progressively strengthened, but, unlike the USA and Australia, the UK did not legislate for the production of ice-cream until the 1930s. In many cases the public authorities who were entrusted with the administration of these Acts did not enforce them. In 1898 a Local Government Board report found that in six areas of London where 699 samples of milk were tested no fewer than 40 per cent were found to have been adulterated. In Manchester, where the Acts were vigorously administered, 1,600 samples were taken and the

The new purpose built laboratory in Hammersmith Road. Only very senior staff were allowed to use the front entrance; others entered by a side door.

percentage of adulteration was less than 3 per cent.

The Grocers' Company were vitriolic in their fight against food adulteration and felt that the government was not doing enough to control food imports. Many foodstuffs were imported on the basis that they were genuine, but the weight of the law fell on the man selling them. Many thought that the government should take steps occasionally to inspect all food at the port of entry, as they did with tea. Grocers also criticised the inadequacy of fines imposed on persistent adulterators. In some cases the fines imposed for second and third offences were lower than those for the first, and the size of the fine often depended on which magistrate was sitting.

Legislation against food adulteration was only made effective by progress in the detection of fraud by the chemist. Most prominent among

these was the versatile Frederick Accum (who played a leading part in the introduction of gas lighting in England). In the early nineteenth century Accum helped to increase awareness of the dangers of food adulteration, not only by his chemistry lectures but by his publication in 1820 of *A Treatise on Adulterations of Food, and Culinary Poisons*, in which he observed:

> Of all possible nefarious traffic and deception, practised by mercenary dealers, that of adulterating the articles intended for human food with ingredients deleterious to health, is the most criminal, and, in the mind of every honest man, must excite feelings of regret and disgust.

Leslie Lampitt and the Bio-Chemical Department

From Lyons' point of view, the idea of applying science to food manufacture for monitoring the purity of raw materials and for controlling all food production processes had germinated in the trenches in Flanders, when Samuel Gluckstein first met Dr Leslie Lampitt and learned of his pre-war experiences. Leslie Herbert Lampitt (1887–1957) had gained a Priestley Scholarship to Birmingham University where he was a distinguished student between 1906 and 1911. He obtained a general BSc in 1909 at a time when specific degrees were only awarded in engineering, metallurgy or mining. In the same year he was awarded a MSc and in 1910 a Diploma in Malting and Brewing. His doctoral thesis was on 'Nitrogen Metabolism in Saccharomyces Cereuiseae', and he obtained his doctorate in 1919. Saccharomyces is a generic name for many varieties of yeasts, all of which have the capacity to ferment food; *Cereuiseae* denotes baker's, rather than brewer's, yeast. Lampitt was chief chemist at La Meunerie Bruxelloise, the largest flour mill in Belgium, when the First World War broke out, but he managed to escape to England. He volunteered for the Warwickshire Regiment but because of a long wait joined the Royal Army Service Corps and returned to France, where most of his time was spent on the supply side in Dunkirk and Le Havre. He attained the rank of major, at which time Samuel Gluckstein, who subsequently won a Military Cross for bravery, served under him as a subaltern.

After the war Lampitt and his wife Edith, also a graduate chemist, casually met Samuel Gluckstein when they were boarding a train for Brighton. Apart from the normal pleasantries exchanged on such occasions, the conversation inevitably centred on food production and Gluckstein invited the Lampitts to visit Cadby Hall to see Maurice Salmon's factory. Having been given a thorough tour, Leslie Lampitt suggested to Maurice Salmon that he should consider employing a chemist to utilise the growing knowledge of science in food production. It did not take long for Maurice to realise the importance of Lampitt's idea and in his indefatigable style convinced his co-directors likewise. Shortly afterwards Gluckstein wrote to Lampitt offering him a job as a food chemist, but to Gluckstein's surprise Lampitt turned the offer down. From his days at La Meunerie Bruxelloise, Lampitt was well aware of the problems experienced by a chemist in a food factory and he preferred instead to pursue some less troublesome career. In any case he had his mind set on joining the Indian Army, where he had been offered a commission, and both he and his wife were looking forward to travelling. Unaccustomed to being turned down, Samuel Gluckstein wrote back to Lampitt suggesting he might name his conditions if he reconsidered the offer. After long discussions with his wife, Lampitt decided to write and accept the offer, setting out what both he and his wife believed would be desirable but probably unacceptable terms. One of his conditions, upon which he was convinced Lyons would be unable to agree, was that he should have total independence in running the laboratory (no other Lyons department had such independence) with a generous budget to fund qualified staff and purchase equipment. Leslie Lampitt had reckoned that a salary of £500 a year would be justified if rather high, but Edith Lampitt suggested that he double this to £1,000. Having posted his letter, Lampitt did not think for one moment that Lyons would accede to his

The complete laboratory staff in 1926 taken outside St Mary's College in Brook Green.

extravagant demands and he continued to make plans to accept the Indian Army commission. Within a few days, however, and to his utter surprise, his conditions were accepted and after some preliminary horse-trading Lampitt started work in July 1919. Thus Leslie Lampitt had filled what was almost a self-created job and the application of science to food manufacturing had begun at Lyons.

Lampitt established his initial 3,000-sq. ft. laboratory, known as the Bio-Chemical Department, in a building near Cadby Hall at 46 Brook Green, formally known as Sackville House. By 1925 the increasing number of

Dr Leslie Lampitt, Chief Chemist. *By kind permission of John Lampitt.*

company who feared a dilution of their responsibilities, especially at factory management levels. Service departments too felt uneasy about the creation of a laboratory run by a young upstart chemist. His antagonists used a number of delaying tactics to slow the progress of negotiations for laboratory space. More important, perhaps, were the conditions of Lampitt's employment. Despite the payroll department's probity (this salary level was handled by a few trusted employees), the size of his salary must have leaked out and soured relations with many of the production managers with whom he had to work. However, during these difficult early months Lampitt was given unwavering support from Maurice Salmon and other Lyons board directors, and his talents as a chemist, administrator and publicist gradually won over most of his many adversaries.

Shortly after his appointment Lampitt engaged Dr Edwin Hughes to act as his deputy and later employed Dr Jack Bushill, a distant relative. Their equipment consisted initially of a few test-tubes, flasks, beakers and Bunsen burners. Few records of the laboratory's early work have survived but it is known that the first experimental essence-distilling department was created in 1921. Citrus fruit flavours were difficult for chemists to replicate at that time but they did provide the strongest essences. Much work centred on flavours produced from highly purified materials. More success was achieved with vanilla essence, obtained from the pods of the climbing orchid *Vanilla planifolia*. An industrial chemist, Walter Messenger, was engaged to manage this aspect of the work, but he died in May 1943, having apparently committed suicide by drinking ammonia at his home while on remand for allegedly stealing postage stamps from an auction.

From just three in 1919, laboratory staff numbers increased to nearly forty by 1924, and it is obvious from this that their work and influence were becoming more important within Lyons. The teams were divided into small groups comprising two categories: the first would be responsible for a business function such as bread baking, while the second would undertake more

chemists and support staff had outgrown their accommodation and they were moved into St Mary's College, a former Catholic seminary in Brook Green, when that property also became part of the Cadby Hall estate, Lyons having paid £190,000 for the buildings and freehold.

The laboratory, the first of its kind in the European food industry, set about analysing the changes that occurred during the manufacture of food and during its subsequent storage before sale. The founding of the laboratory alone had been a significant achievement, since Lampitt had faced considerable resentment, suspicion and downright hostility from many within the

general tasks such as bacteriology. In this way research and routine analysis were carried out in parallel.

Soon after Dr Lampitt joined the company, Lyons purchased the first milk spray-drying plant in England. Up until then dried milk was produced by roller-drying, which seriously impaired its quality. The spray-drying plant was American and was installed in a dairy at Hemyock, near Taunton. Lampitt and the chief engineer, José Manuel Sierra, were involved in its installation and commissioning. However, it did not function properly and it was left to Lyons to solve the problem. In view of the technical nature of the drying operation, a laboratory was built and staffed in the dairy. The chemist appointed to manage it was Dr Edward Bertram Anderson (1895–1971), an expert on alpine and rock plants and former president of the Alpine Gardeners Society, who wrote several books on the subject. The milk powders produced were called Milkal and Kookal – the former a soluble full-cream milk powder, the latter a skimmed milk powder. Both were used internally in Lyons for food manufacture. The attempt at selling these products in catering and retail packs was unsuccessful and eventually the operation was sold to United Dairies Ltd. Dr Anderson then became the chief chemist of United Dairies.

The Hammersmith Road Laboratory

As their work became more important, Lampitt persuaded the directors that a new laboratory should be built, incorporating all the modern scientific apparatus available at that time. Of modern design, this laboratory opened in 1928 on a plot of land along the Hammersmith Road at a point facing Brook Green. With 35,000 square feet of space, it was set out on seven floors, and employed ninety staff, who analysed 40,000 food samples per year. Every conceivable facility had been provided and at each work-bench water, gas, steam, compressed air, vacuum and AC and DC power were supplied. One room was specially built for photographic and microphotographic work, and there were two constant-temperature rooms, one kept at 77°F and the other at 86°F. The laboratory represented the united efforts of the

The bakery technical laboratory in the early 1950s.

A view of the main laboratory. Seated at the desk is Dr Brooks.

chemists (Lampitt himself scrutinised the plans thoroughly), construction and engineering staff, who were responsible for design, layout, erection and equipment of the building as well as some of the special apparatus.

In the basement was technical laboratory no. 1, where small-scale factory plant and machines were used for research and development and to evaluate large-scale factory problems. The basement also contained the boiler house, hot water generator, machine shop and a bulk chemical store. On the ground floor was the main entrance hall with waiting room, samples room and goods entrance. The ground floor also housed a cocoa and chocolate laboratory and an edible oil and fat laboratory with a combustion room for incinerating food samples as a preliminary step to many analytical procedures. A balance room on the ground floor contained delicate weighing apparatus. There was also a distillation room for the recovery of inflammable solvents; there, in spite of every conceivable precaution (all steam heating and no electrical switches), a disastrous fire occurred some years later.

The first floor housed a laboratory for all work of a general nature, with combustion, furnace, balance, polarimeter and wash-up room. It also contained an area used for the preparation and issue of reagents and a general store for apparatus and chemicals. On the second floor, in addition to laboratories devoted to milk products and ice-cream, bakery products (bread, cakes and flour), fuel oils and lubricants, there was an important and to some extent secret section dealing with flavours, essences and colours. It was run by Walter Messenger and employed chemists who had exceptionally sensitive noses and palates. A high proportion of all colouring and flavouring materials were formulated here and were manufactured and dispensed in a small factory unit outside Cadby Hall. Every formulation was a closely guarded secret and the other laboratory staff were not encouraged to enter this section.

The third floor contained the physical chemistry laboratory, which included a flourishing photographic section used for recording progress in research work and evidence of product faults or of factories in need of attention. It also included the microbiochemical section where living bacteria, yeasts and moulds could be safely cultivated and stored. Among the equipment were numerous small incubators at various temperatures. This section was the main user of the constant-temperature rooms for storage tests to determine the shelf life of various products. It was from this section that Lyons pioneered work on the strict hygiene control of food handling.

The offices of the chief chemist, the statisticians and administrators were located on the fourth floor, together with the library and textile laboratory for the examination of materials, wrapping papers and laundry research. In the library, in addition to standard works of reference and specialised volumes, ninety journals were regularly filed, classified under pure science (twenty-one), applied science (fifty-seven) and trade journals (twelve). The top floor of the laboratory was given over to research, with combustion, inoculation, balance and polarimeter rooms for special research. Finally there was a building materials laboratory for testing, among other commodities, cement and plaster used by the company's building department.

A novel feature introduced by Lampitt, of some disquiet to factory management, was the fee he charged for all work carried out on the factories' behalf, thus making the laboratory self-financing. This was carried one stage further: when Lampitt's staff invented or developed a new process, they sold it to the appropriate department of Lyons. Lampitt's charging system was resented by many but the idea took hold and soon other parts of the business were charging each other for work – including departments under the general umbrella of administration.

Individual chemists had to account for time spent on each project so that the correct amount was charged and the laboratory recovered its costs. Work carried either a sample or a job number, and time-sheets recorded the time spent on any of the separate accounts. It was the laboratory statisticians' task to analyse these time-sheets and ascertain an appropriate fee.

The laboratory became involved in all aspects of food production. Its objectives can be summarised in four main categories:

1. To ensure the chemical and bacteriological purity of food supplied either through the teashops and restaurants or through the wholesale trade. This included setting up a comprehensive hygiene service which eventually affected nearly every manufacturing department.
2. To check the efficiency of all processes of food manufacture employed by the company.
3. To study new processes, new machinery and new materials, both raw and processed.
4. To investigate complaints, sometimes trivial, sometimes even fraudulent and sometimes so serious as to involve the closure of a whole department.

The Development of Food Technology

It must be remembered that in the 1920s most food manufacture was based on the craft knowledge handed down through the various branches. With the growth of large-scale manufacture, such as the production of packaged cakes, it was essential to have a scientific understanding of what was going on. As laboratories investigated these matters, much of their work was published to the general benefit of all involved in similar trades. Detailed analyses of naturally occurring raw materials were published. Analytical techniques were developed to measure the composition of raw and finished goods. In the course of time every manufacturing process was covered by a 'laboratory formula instruction' (LFI). Scientists sought to determine the effect of composition and storage conditions on the growth of micro-organisms which affected the shelf life of the finished goods, or was a health hazard in catering outlets. In order to understand, and therefore control, some processes, it was necessary to investigate such fundamentals as the basic structure of starch and proteins. In later years this in turn necessitated trying out new methods such as X-ray crystallography. In order to provide on-the-spot analyses for the control of factory operations, sub-laboratories were set

up in the factories. The largest of these was at Greenford but there were smaller ones in most production locations. All were staffed and managed by the central laboratory.

Under the guidance of Dr Lampitt, who was highly respected in his day, the laboratory set exemplary standards and became nationally known, attracting many graduates from Birmingham, Oxford and Cambridge universities, all believing this was the place to gain maximum exposure to food technology. In common with most organisations at that time, there was a rigid hierarchical structure for the laboratory staff which extended to all aspects of life in the workplace. There was a canteen where all chemists had lunch (service staff ate in the Cadby Hall canteens), but male and female chemists ate at separate tables, and the graduate staff, called seniors, sat apart from non-graduates, or juniors. Bushill and Messenger had their own table. Such was the culture in Lyons at this time that ordinary staff were forbidden to use the main laboratory entrance, which was reserved exclusively for the most senior chemists, while the rest had to use a side door. Similar rules applied to the toilets. Whenever Lampitt arrived at the lift, anyone inside it had to get out so that he could rise up in solitary splendour. Juniors, or unqualified staff, were expected to undertake extramural studies leading to a professional qualification; then their status changed and they could eat with the qualified staff. Another rule required female staff to be referred to by their maiden names if they happened to be married. This perhaps is not so unusual, since many obtained their degrees and wrote theses under their maiden names and it was felt proper that their work, and any papers they subsequently published, should continue under the same name so as to avoid confusion. Today such regulations are almost beyond belief, but from the 1920s to the 1950s they were rigidly applied and accepted by all.

Lampitt's own workload was enormous, but so was his ability to read and absorb a vast amount of paperwork. He worked fast and after the war kept two secretaries fully occupied. Every memorandum, letter and report was signed by him before it left the laboratory. All research papers were submitted by him and a credit was given to the researcher(s). After a full day's work, which frequently included lunchtime meetings with other academics and professionals, he took home the letters and reports which had been prepared by his chemists that day, working into the night reading and making any necessary corrections for the following day. When satisfied he would sign the work and it was dispatched. Lampitt ruled the laboratory as an autocrat and was devastating in his criticism of his staff, at all levels, when they failed to perform to his expectations. In relation to the rest of the company and the directors, however, he took full responsibility for everything done by his staff. He was also helpful to members of his staff who had personal problems. In this he was much assisted by the prevailing paternalistic attitude of the Lyons directors.

It was in June 1949, after graduating in chemistry from Somerville College, Oxford, that a young research chemist, Margaret Roberts, joined other laboratory staff working in the physical chemistry section. She remained there until her marriage in 1951 to a wealthy businessman, Denis Thatcher, when she left to study law, becoming a barrister in 1954. In 1959 she was elected Member of Parliament for Finchley and twenty years later became, of course, Britain's first woman Prime Minister. Even in 1949, while still working at Lyons, her laboratory colleagues recall that Margaret Roberts was highly motivated politically and stood unsuccessfully as the Conservative candidate for Parliament in Dartford, Kent, in the general election of February 1950, while still working with Lyons. Colleagues remembered her as hard-working but they believed that her time with Lyons had very little influence on her subsequent development. At the time of her departure she was working on a project to determine vitamin C in cabbage.

A whole range of research papers were produced by the laboratory staff, some in the course of attaining qualifications. One such researcher was Dr Winifred Wright, who became a UK expert on crystallography. She had read natural sciences at Girton College, Cambridge, where she obtained her doctorate before joining the physical chemistry section of the Lyons laboratory. In the physical chemistry laboratory the interaction of raw materials and changes due to processing were analysed to determine, among other matters, the stability, taste, texture and appearance of the final product. Crystallography was one of several techniques used in this analysis. Crystallography could also be used to check for contamination of raw materials, and it could help predict flow properties of powders and liquids in bulk handling systems. Winifred Wright, who was a quiet, unassuming but respected researcher, was a senior chemist in the physical chemistry laboratory when Margaret Roberts joined it as a junior member of staff. Winifred Wright retired after spending her total career with Lyons; she never married and died in 1993 at the age of seventy-six.

During the Second World War the 300 or so laboratory staff spent much of their time trying to overcome shortages of food and other materials and collaborated with various governmental departments in resolving important nutritional problems. One activity during the war, not generally known, was the feeding of the American Army Headquarters staff based in the Selfridges building in London. The opportunity was taken to use this contact as a large-scale trial of frozen ready cooked meals (Frood). Shortly before the war Lyons had started experimental mass production of frozen ready-to-eat meals. The technical problems associated with changing the scale (from six chef-produced portions to several hundred portions) without loss of quality necessitated close collaboration between the chemists and the chefs.

In the large-scale trial the dishes were prepared and frozen at Coventry Street Corner House, then transported to, reheated and served at a converted teashop in Duke Street. A member of the laboratory staff was employed full-time to monitor the whole process with particular attention to hygiene. The experiment was considered highly successful and had almost run its course when it was abruptly terminated by a night-time bomb which fell on the teashop.

Transformation of Laboratory Management

When Leslie Lampitt died in June 1957 he was succeeded by Dr Edwin Hughes. Although a first-rate chemist, Hughes did not have the creative genius of Dr Lampitt and ran the laboratories in a rather formal style, sticking to rigid principles rather than adapting to the changing world of the 1960s. As a consequence many of Lampitt's idealistic beliefs – that laboratory statements could not be disputed – and cultural idiosyncrasies were perpetuated far longer than necessary. He did not have the same warmth as Lampitt nor the ability to exchange ideas with his colleagues. Hughes retired in 1963, and Dr Jack Bushill took charge. His appointment came at a time when the central laboratory's management were being scrutinised by Lyons. Management of the laboratories had its origins in the degree of autonomy granted to Lampitt by Maurice Salmon as part of his employment terms and was compounded by Lampitt's own style: extremely autocratic, with little or no delegation of authority. His system of job numbers and time-sheets was not conducive to innovative research. The creation of a food laboratory had been a pioneering venture in 1928 but in the 1950s Lyons paid the price. The individual sections dealing with specific topics were very small compared with the dedicated laboratories of large manufacturers of specific products like coffee, fruit or confectionery, and could not compete with their competitors' research and development budgets and activities. The problem was aggravated by the fact that Lampitt's policy was that everyone's time should be distributed between routine analysis and research, with priority for routine analysis.

The tactic adopted by the management consultants brought in to advise on these problems was to select about a dozen of the senior chemists and dispatch them to a hotel for several days until they had thrashed out an acceptable scheme for ongoing management of the laboratories. The scheme that finally evolved worked reasonably well, with a few modifications, for the next ten years or so and was very different from that in place during the previous three decades.

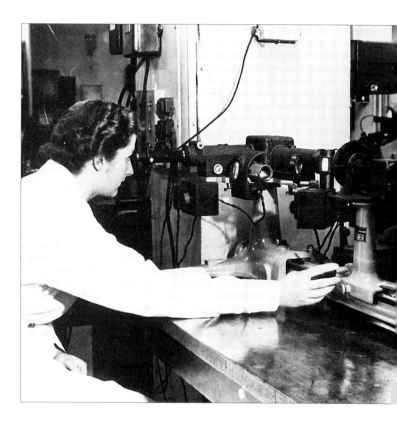

Top left. Margaret Thatcher (née Roberts) photographed in the 1950s using equipment in the Lyons' laboratory.

Below left. These two laboratory staff are using high speed Farinograph (water absorption) apparatus.

Right. Laboratory reporting structure.

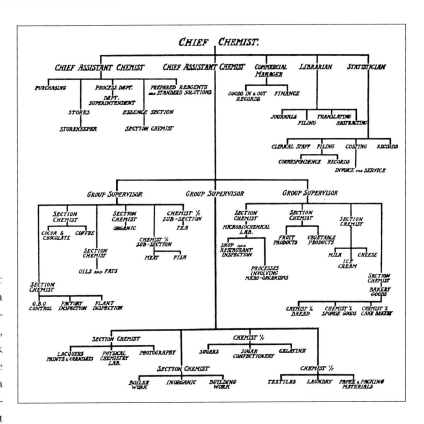

Instead of an autocratic chief chemist, there was a management committee consisting of a group of chemists, each responsible for the work carried out for a section of the company or responsible for a service section such as microbiology. Each manager-chemist was not only responsible for the scientific work but had to sell his or her services to the 'customers' (the departments) and budget for the numbers and salaries of the required staff. With the increasing autonomy of the operating divisions, however, many of the functions of the central laboratory were taken over by the divisions. The management committee was headed in succession by Dr John Wren and Harry Benson, who had Kurt Berger and Dr Winifred Wright in support.

After Lampitt's death in 1957, and his successors' brief tenures of office, major research continued right up until the early 1970s. However, in March 1979 Sir Alex Alexander was appointed Lyons' new chairman following Allied Breweries' acquisition of the Lyons group a year earlier. He too was autocratic. Soon after he was appointed a major restructuring of directors' responsibilities was carried out to reinforce the process, already started, of decentralising operating companies. They had gradually been achieving their independence and their managers had a healthy desire to take control of all their business functions including laboratory research. Work which had previously been undertaken by the celebrated central laboratories was now being transferred to these new autonomous units, thus exposing the cost of research and other work covered by these charges. As the board of directors were not prepared to fund this work, the ultimate closure of the laboratories was inevitable.

For nearly sixty years it had been an important department in Lyons, and in its heyday – the years between the wars – was widely known as a pioneer in food technology. Members of its staff, and particularly its founder, Dr Leslie Lampitt, contributed significant papers to the scientific journals on original work in their specialised fields. In those days staff numbered about 300 and all the research and the evaluation and testing of raw materials used in products was their sole responsibility, as well as the supervision of quality control in the factories. Many who trained there subsequently became well known in the world of food technology, including Nathaniel Goldenberg, who left to set up the Marks & Spencer food laboratory which he based on the principles of Lyons' central laboratories.

THE BIGGEST LAUNDRY IN EUROPE

JAMES HAYES SET UP his first laundry at Rushey Green, near Lewisham, in 1868. He advertised it as a power laundry as distinct from a hand laundry. His machines largely conformed to principles set out by Henry Sidgier in a patent he had taken out in 1783, a reproduction of which forms part of the Master's Jewel of the Company of Launderers of the City of London. Despite the availability of mechanical washing machines, the laundering trade continued to do the washing mainly by hand. It was Manlove Alliott of Nottingham, Isaac Braithwaite of Kendal, Thomas Bradford of Manchester and James Lane of London who were among the first pioneers in the field of laundry machines.

By the second half of the nineteenth century, hotels, hospitals and institutions of various kinds were experiencing the need for their laundering to be carried out away from their premises. James Hayes was one of the first to see the commercial possibilities of meeting this need. The laundry that he opened at Rushey Green, which he named The Royal, specialised at the outset in providing contract services. In this he was a notable pioneer. Although he had equipped his laundry with washing machines, centrifugal hydro-extractors and decoudun ironers (the name derived from a French inventor), he still had to employ many laundresses to do hand ironing using the incongruously named Glad Iron. One of his first corporate customers was the London Stock Exchange; 100 years later Hayes laundry were still providing that institution with laundry services. When Hayes' premises at Rushey Green became too small for his expanding business, he

The Coldharbour Lane laundry of James Hayes & Sons.
By kind permission of Tony Hawthorne.

moved to a building in Culmore Road, Peckham, which he leased from the brewers Whitbread.

In 1900 the laundry was renamed James Hayes & Sons Ltd and in the same year a business relationship began with Lyons, who already owned the Belgrave Laundry in Pimlico, which they had bought in 1894. Recognising the greater efficiency of the Hayes laundry, Lyons transferred their work and the Belgrave Laundry to Hayes' new premises in Peckham. The main contract consisted of laundering tablecloths and napkins for the teashops and restaurants. Business grew

rapidly and in 1908 James Hayes bought a plot of land in Coldharbour Lane, Camberwell, designing for himself a building that would provide the best possible working conditions for his staff and installing the best laundry equipment available at that time. Acting as his own architect

and utilising the knowledge of his own laundry staff, he built what was acknowledged to be one of the most modern and best-equipped businesses of its kind in Britain.

By the start of the First World War James Hayes' sons, James junior and Sydney, began to take a prominent part in the business. As a result of unexpected levels of growth the Hayes family needed large-scale capital expenditure, and this was secured when Lyons acquired a financial interest in 1921. By then James Hayes' health was failing and he died in 1922. His sons continued with the business, introducing comprehensive welfare measures for their staff and making it a leader in its field. In 1926 Lyons made an offer to acquire all the equity in Hayes laundry, at which point it became a full subsidiary of Lyons. James and Sydney Hayes remained active directors supported by Samuel Salmon, Leonard Gluckstein, Harry Bennett and William Gray. Gray was a Lyons business efficiency expert who speedily made his mark in the laundry world. He gained his place on the councils of the laundry industry's employers' organisation and its associated research organisation. During the Second World War he is described as having been a 'tower of strength both to Lyons and the laundry business as a whole', playing a very active part in keeping the laundry businesses operating under severe operational difficulties. At the height of his power in 1949 he was struck down by a heart attack. Partially recovering, he became president of the trade association in 1950 but died suddenly during a national congress in 1955.

The introduction of the float-roll ironing machine from America in the early 1920s resulted in a boom in the mass-produced family laundry service. The Hayes board was quick to take advantage of this development. Their intro-duction of the 'Ful£worth' (full pound's worth) domestic service in 1926 became so popular that additional depots had to be opened to meet the demand in London. Unlike other laundries, Hayes had recognised that the catchment area for this type of work was within a seven-mile radius of the works, and for their deliveries and collections they used horse transport right up until 1931, when motorisation gradually took over.

The laundry business fell into three main areas of activity. First, there was the work for Lyons and its associated hotel and catering businesses. Then there was the contract work for outside organisations such as civil and military hospitals, hotels, restaurants and so on. Finally there was the Ful£worth service, brought in either by house-to-house collection or through the receiving depots. Directors introduced a bonus scheme based on the American time-and-motion study plans of Charles Bedeaux (this system was introduced into most of Lyons' factories but was intensely disliked by the staff – apart from anything else it could not be easily understood). By 1938 James Hayes & Sons Ltd had grown into one of the world's largest laundry businesses, employing over 1,000 staff who processed some 250 tons of work each week, collected and delivered by a large fleet of vehicles supplied by the Normand vehicle subsidiary.

At the outbreak of war in 1939 there was a tenfold decrease in commercial and domestic laundry work. This, however, was compensated for by the additional work generated by the War Office and other government departments. The movement of female labour from laundries to munitions and other factory work and the evacuation of mothers and their children to safe areas caused considerable difficulties for the management at this time. Difficult though the labour shortages were, they were minor compared with the damage caused by bombs on 13 September 1940, when the main laundry was hit and much of its plant destroyed. Under the direction of William Gray a scheme had already been devised whereby other laundries came to the aid of those damaged in raids. While the Camberwell factory was being repaired, the Hayes staff carried out their work in various other laundries which had spare capacity. The bombing of 13 September 1940 was the first of many to damage the Coldharbour Lane factory during the war.

When peace returned to war-weary London, Hayes faced the need for a complete review of rehabilitation. Buildings, plant, staff and trade all had to be renewed, and there were problems in every area except trade. Although at first there was still plenty of work available, machinery and

staff were in short supply and rebuilding was a tiresome affair of permits, shortages and frustration.

Management recognised that the shortage of suitable staff was not just a passing phase but was likely to become a permanent feature of the labour market. Consequently management introduced as much reliable labour-saving machinery as possible, but the work level was less than half of its pre-war peak so expenditure was difficult to justify. Moreover, an increasing number of domestic washing machines were being installed in the homes of the better-off – those very people who had previously used laundry services. With domestic laundry declining, Hayes turned their attention to linen hire, which had become the fastest-growing service in the laundry trade.

Hayes' linen hire was named Haylin. It began in earnest in 1962 and its expansion was so fast that it soon accounted for 50 per cent of the Hayes

Top left. Linen folding at James Hayes laundry.

Top right. The washing department of James Hayes laundry in about 1920.

operatives. The creation of the Haylin linen hire plant was part of a unitisation programme for the Hayes organisation, which was carried a stage further in 1965 with the opening of the newly equipped household unit in the Coldharbour Lane factory. This had been followed by self-contained hotel and miscellaneous laundry units to complete the programme.

In 1966 Jack Pennell and his fellow directors decided to make a trial installation of the continuous flatwork processor. This machine, derived from an invention by the British Launderers' Research Association and developed by J. Stone & Co. (Deptford) Ltd, was formally set in motion by the then Miss World on 15 November 1966. Linked to a complete automatic flatwork ironing and folding complex and, subsequently, to a computer, the unit completely laundered a sheet in 45 seconds. Moreover, the whole concept was so revolutionary in its planning and scope that linen supply operators and launderers from many parts of the world flocked to Camberwell to see it in action.

In the 1970s a complete range of workwear garments, available for customers of the Haylin Garment Hire Service, was introduced. Both serviceability and fashion had been the design criteria. Manufactured in Terylene and cotton and finished in the laundry on a new unit, the garments were claimed to represent a break-through in the design and processing technique of industrial apparel. To promote their services, Hayes introduced a mobile showroom and a cinema which toured factories and factory estates throughout the country. At each stop, key executives were invited aboard the vehicle for their own private fashion show.

In 1979, after the Lyons group had passed into the ownership of Allied Breweries, James Hayes & Sons Ltd was sold to Johnson Group Cleaners for £2.1 million. This transfer had been expected ever since the disposal two and a half years earlier of the hotel business with which James Hayes did a sizeable part of its business. It was the hotel, with their vast requirements for laundering, which had been largely responsible for Lyons buying James Hayes in 1926.

Above. Early ironing apparatus (1923) at James Hayes laundry.

business. John (Jack) Pennell, who had joined Hayes in 1948, played a leading role in this development. Haylin's rapid progress resulted in a need for additional processing space and plant, which in turn led to a new laundry being established in a former ice-cream factory at West Norwood in 1964. This new linen plant was designed as a complete entity, with 60,000 pieces per week being processed by just eleven

Chapter 28

OFFICE TECHNOLOGY AND COMPUTER MANUFACTURE

I N 1895 LYONS were employing 200 workers at their Cadby Hall factory at a cost of some £75,000 per annum. As the business expanded, the numbers increased so rapidly that by the 1930s there were approximately 30,000, of whom 1,500 were support clerks and statisticians, and this remained the same for the next thirty years. Most of these workers were employed in food-manufacturing and sales, but the catering businesses employed large numbers including a high proportion of female workers (up to 10,000 waitresses at any one time), some of them part-time. Every business transaction was meticulously recorded and written up in ledgers, mainly by male clerks; the first female clerks were not employed until 1915. Little or no technology was employed until the 1920s.

By the early 1920s the 200 teashops and the large restaurants, together with the teashops' associated retail counters, were generating thousands of small transactions. It was calculated that only a farthing profit was made on each of the 150 million meals sold annually from all teashops, and that only a decimal of a penny profit was made on the 75,000 tons per week of other goods sold through front shops. As management wished to control costs to fractions of a penny, the volume of paperwork and the consequent flood of dull routine processing of business transactions was becoming an accounting nightmare. More worrying was that a small error in cost accounting could have a disastrous effect on profits.

One of the earliest typewriters used by Lyons. Made by the American Hammond Company and designated No. 12, it had an unusual – non qwerty – curved keyboard with three shift positions.

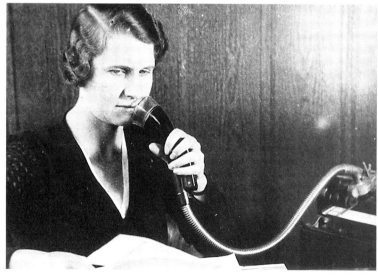

The mouth-piece of an office Dictaphone being used by Miss B. Joerin, an assistant to Nell Bacon.

The Stock Department in 1934 using Burroughs decimal accounting machines. The noise from these machines was almost deafening. The picture was taken in Spike House, an annex to Cadby Hall.

Comprising two papier-mâché and one brass cylinder this Fuller's Spiral Rule gave a working length of over 41 feet. It was used by Lyons' Statisticians in the 1920s.

Dictaphone typists at work in Elms House (Cadby Hall) in the early 1950s still using equipment of an earlier era.

Simmons and Thompson: Development of O & M

Lyons realised that the phenomenal business growth and the attendant copious minutiae of clerical work could, if not controlled, overwhelm them. In 1923, therefore, they appointed five university graduates as management trainees to study this problem. It was Lyons' policy at this time to recruit graduates for fast-stream management training before this practice was fully accepted by other parts of industry. Among the appointees was a Cambridge mathematics graduate named John Richardson Mainwaring Simmons (1902–85). Reporting to George Booth, the company secretary, Simmons had the responsibility for developing new accounting and office procedures to enable the business to run more efficiently. Simmons would eventually become chief comptroller (a title then used in Lyons to identify the person in charge of management accounts and other economic information) and later, in 1950, an employee director.

Soon after Simmons joined Lyons he recruited another mathematics graduate, Thomas Raymond Thompson (1907–76), who began work on 1 June 1931. Thompson had started his career with Owen & Owen Ltd in Liverpool, where he had been an assistant secretary. During the next thirty-five years these two brilliant mathematicians together transformed Lyons' office procedures; in doing so they placed Lyons at the forefront of expertise in clerical methods.

By 1935 Simmons and Thompson had replaced isolated groups of clerks in various factories, teashops and elsewhere by three main centralised clerical offices which handled the trading and accounting records of the whole Lyons business and which were highly mechanised, with dictating and calculating machines. The first office established was the Checking Department, where 450 clerks were in charge of cash control and checked the catering establishments' records, including every waitress's bill produced. Each shop's receipts were sorted into numerical and alphabetical order, normally by school-leavers, and then passed to another section where the more senior staff worked out the totals on Burroughs adding machines. The totals were checked against teashop banking and discrepancies were investigated. Since waitresses' stubs were also retained, it was possible to trace every transaction undertaken by a waitress in every teashop. Clearly, this was a labour-intensive task.

The second office, known as the Stock Department (after the Second World War renamed the Statistical Office), employed 400 clerks. It maintained the stock records of the different Lyons departments, such as raw materials and equipment. Later, more elaborate departmental records were kept and the function that is now generally known as management accounting developed. In June 1943 the Checking Department and the catering section of the Stock Department amalgamated under the name of the Catering Office.

The third and largest office was the Accounts Department, where 600 clerks kept Lyons' trading accounts (sales and purchase ledgers) and prepared the payroll. After the war, the payroll office functioned as a separate entity in which particular groups were responsible for particular payroll units – for example, bakery, clerical, tea, works services. This centralised clerical function was crucial in identifying accounting problems, as well as creating an environment in which research into their solution could take place. Having created these three main offices by 1936, Simmons was able to provide consolidated financial information to members of the board in weekly (later quarterly) summaries known as White Books, which helped management to understand Lyons' trading patterns relatively soon after the event.

By 1934 the Checking Department had over 100 calculating machines at its disposal, and an additional 150 adding and bookkeeping machines were in use elsewhere. Simmons judged that mechanisation was the only long-term solution to the costly and depressing employment of the human beings in this kind of work. In his view, 'The curse of routine clerical work is that, without exercising the intellect, it demands accuracy and concentration.'

As early as 1928, Simmons had introduced a form of decimal notation for Lyons' internal accounting procedures. This had probably been forced on him, since the majority of accounting machines then were American and would not handle UK currency. In 1936 Sir Isidore Salmon, then managing director, became president of the Decimal Association, a body which advocated the introduction of decimal coinage and the metric system of weights and measures. He considered this to be an issue of national importance and used the shareholders meeting of June 1937 to launch a £50,000 fighting fund so that the Decimal Association could carry out a programme of education, campaign for public support and convince the government of the need for change. Salmon and the more enlightened of his fellow champions believed that decimalisation would save the nation millions of pounds annually.

By the end of the Second World War Lyons had developed some of the most advanced office systems in Britain, and Simmons' reputation in office management methods continued to grow. From his power base at Lyons he carried out further clerical research, leading eventually to large-scale automation that had huge implications not only for Lyons but for all businesses. Without the detailed analysis and experience of Lyons' clerical operations, the development of automated clerical procedures in the United Kingdom might have been delayed for many years

and British industry might have turned to American technology.

Clerical Automation: the Building of LEO

Clerical efficiency had been of concern to management for many years, but Simmons realised that the use of electromechanical machines and improvements in document design would not be a panacea. As the business grew, more and more documents were generated to be handled by more and more staff, and this in turn required more and more space, thus increasing overheads. Simmons had realised that the most efficient method of processing business data was to have it recorded at the outset in a form that could be understood by a machine. These ideas were radical and far-reaching, but it was not until the Second World War, which created acute staff shortages, that he was able to take them further.

With their eagerness to automate clerical operations, it is hardly surprising that Lyons displayed a keen interest in the work being undertaken in the USA after the Second World War on electromechanical calculators, though they had little enthusiasm for the punched card technology then being developed. In 1947 Thompson together with Oliver Standingford (1913–80), a senior office manager, went on a

Part of the completed LEO I computer in 1954.

tour of the United States and Canada to look at the latest work on electronic calculators. It was during this visit that Thompson and Standingford first heard of an advanced project being undertaken by Cambridge University. After their return, copies of their report were submitted to members of the Lyons board on 20 October 1947, with a covering memorandum in which it was declared:

> We believe that we have been able to get a glimpse of a development which will, in a few years' time, have a profound effect on the way in which cleri-cal work (at least) is performed. Here, for the first time, there is a possibility of a machine which will be able to cope, at almost incredible speed, with any variation of clerical procedure, provided the conditions which govern the variations can be predetermined. What effect such machines could have on the semi-repetitive work of the office needs only the slightest effort of imagination. The possible saving from such a machine should be at least £50,000 a year. The capital cost would be of the order of £100,000.

> We feel, therefore, that the company might well wish to take a lead in the development of the machine and indeed that, unless organisations such as ours, the potential users, are prepared to do so, the time at which they be-come commercially available will be unnecessarily postponed for many years.

Although the proposal that Simmons and his team submitted was radical, and even apparently lacked a full cost analysis, they managed to convince the Lyons board. After all, they had considerable reputations in office management techniques with impressive past successes, and when they approached the board with this notion to build an electronic brain they took it very seriously and regarded it as a perfectly reasonable proposition. In retrospect, it seems an extremely casual, but far-sighted, decision for a catering and food-manufacturing organisation to have taken during this difficult post-war period, but,

Wynne Simmons (standing), wiring supervisor, instructing Jean Astiss how to wire a computer component at the computer factory in Minerva Road, Acton. Ms Simmons was a wages clerk before being trained as a 'wirewoman'. *By kind permission of Wynn Simmons.*

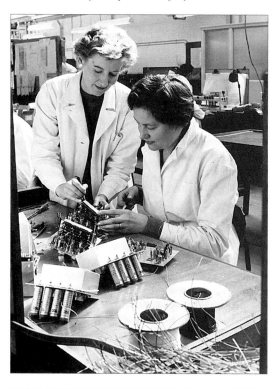

Anthony Barnes, Managing Director of Leo Computers Ltd, escorting HRH Prince Philip on a tour of the computer factory, Minerva Road, Acton, on 22 March 1960.

The operators console of LEO II installed in Elms House. From left to right: Peter Townsend, Mike Randolph and Chuck Knowles.

computer design was given to John Pinkerton (1919–97). He had graduated from Cambridge with a degree in natural sciences just after the outbreak of the Second World War. During the war he had worked on radar research in Swanage and returned to Cambridge after the war to study for his doctorate. It was there that he heard of Lyons' plan to build their own computer, and he answered their advertisement for an electronic engineer when it appeared in the scientific journal *Nature* during October 1948. He assembled a team of engineers, no more than half a dozen, and proceeded to accomplish almost the impossible. By 1954, after many setbacks and an expenditure of £150,000, the first working device, dubbed LEO (Lyons Electronic Office), carried out its first full clerical task, the processing of Lyons Bakery's staff payroll. An earlier application had been run in September 1951 and was successfully completed each week thereafter, but Lyons did not consider it to be a full clerical task. It was, nevertheless, the first clerical task to be carried out on an electronic computer using programmed instructions. Some Americans may dispute this but the facts are clear.

Reliable as LEO was (actually it was fairly unreliable in the early days), Simmons prudently decided that full loading should not commence without a second machine in place to act as standby. As Simmons commented at the time, 'They could not be kept waiting because an interesting experiment had failed.'

Leo Computers Ltd

To maximise the commercial opportunities, which became increasingly obvious to the Lyons board, it was soon decided to form a company to manufacture, sell and lease electronic computers and to provide other associated services. This was a significant departure from the firm's core business of catering and food manufacture, but a natural decision for Lyons to take. They had, after all, previously diversified into other non-food activities such as vehicle assembly, carton manufacture, printing and laundries, to avoid being dependent on others for their supplies, and the decision to create a computer-manufacturing subsidiary was seen as an

surprisingly, there was no resistance from any board member to this revolutionary idea.

Following the board's approval George Booth, the company secretary, along with Thompson and Harry Bennett (1891–1978), an assistant secretary and employee director, visited Cambridge in November 1947. Without too many preliminaries they offered to donate £3,000 to the university and assign a Lyons employee to the Cambridge computer project if the university in turn could give guidance to Lyons on how to develop their own computer. By providing the donation Lyons hoped to accelerate the Cambridge research, from which they might benefit, and their own assistant would glean valuable training in computer technology.

Lyons' early system designers were chosen from the clerical departments, and the software team was led by David Caminer, who had started work at Lyons in 1936 and was now manager of the System Research Office. Caminer was joined by Derek Hemy, who had served his time in the Checking Department. Overall responsibility for

opportunity to exploit their unique office expertise and make money. Leo Computers Ltd was incorporated on 4 November 1954 and the event received wide newspaper publicity.

At the start of the 1960s British industry had been less eager than some of its competitors in the United States and Europe to adopt the electronic computer as an aid to commerce or production. By the summer of 1960 only about 250 computers were in use in the United Kingdom compared with over 1,000 in Europe and many more in the United States. Added to this, Lyons found themselves with several operational problems. First, they were finding it increasingly difficult to fund, from the reserves of their core catering and food businesses, the research and development of their computer subsidiary. The revenues from the limited sales of their machines were barely covering the production and marketing costs, and any scant profit was totally inadequate for the continuing research budget. An operating loss had been made on six of the eleven LEO II computers manufactured between 1957 and 1961. The *Journal of the Office Management Association* reported in 1957, perhaps unfairly, that 'A potential computer user needs to have some confidence in his own judgement if he is to buy his computer from a teashop.'

More serious, perhaps, was the threat from America, where great advances had been made in computer technology. American research and development budgets had been on a scale far in excess of those in the UK. As a result, their products were well engineered, well packaged, superbly marketed and supported by huge advertising budgets – a field in which Lyons had been traditionally weak. The Americans' strong domestic base enabled them to enter the UK market effortlessly. Not only were the American systems technically superior, many of them were cheaper to buy. Although some of their computers were inferior in performance, their lower price made it easier for British management to justify capital expenditure. Perhaps the most fundamental mistake which British industry made at this time was to underestimate the American challenge. There was a sense of arrogance in some

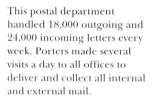

This postal department handled 18,000 outgoing and 24,000 incoming letters every week. Porters made several visits a day to all offices to deliver and collect all internal and external mail.

The general office of the Treasury (Cadby Hall) in 1950 where some 30,000 payslips were made up for weekly paid staff.

quarters, and developments in laboratories and universities did not find their way into the world of commerce quickly enough. Lyons, clearly, did not have the resources for expensive research and marketing follow-through. By the late 1950s they only had half a dozen researchers working on their computers, whereas IBM's research and development staff were numbered in hundreds.

Disposal of Computer Interests

By 1962, the main board directors had already embarked on other business plans more in keeping with their traditional food and catering businesses, and had realised that Leo Computers Ltd could not survive as an independent manufacturer. Management also recognised that they had seriously underestimated the pitfalls of becoming involved in high-technology products and were clearly unable to compete on equal grounds with the electronics giants. They decided, therefore, to merge their computer-manufacturing business with one or more similar British operations.

This theme was echoed by Lazard Brothers, Lyons' merchant bankers, who coincidently were talking to the English Electric Company at the time about partnerships to enlarge their own data-processing division. Lazard's advised both English Electric and Lyons to put together a consortium of companies to fight off the challenge from the American firm of IBM – rhetoric which was also beginning to be heard in political circles. Anthony Salmon and Sir Gordon Radley (1898–1970), an English Electric director, jointly toured Europe and had preliminary talks with Olivetti, Phillips, Siemens and Bull with a view to encouraging them to join a computer consortium, but these talks were unsuccessful. Lyons did not believe that Leo Computers and English Electric alone were big enough to mount a challenge to the Americans and were reluctant to proceed on this basis, but expediency, and the lack of alternatives, made it necessary to seriously consider a merger. Discussions were friendly and both companies worked hard together, but both were conscious that the business community might assume that Leo Computers was failing, and that would undermine the client base and jeopardise any

Above. This 1951 telephone exchange at Cadby Hall had 20 operator positions and handed 14,000 calls every day. There were two supervisors and an enquiry station. *By kind permission of Denis Toombs (deceased).*

Right. The main arrangement of clerical offices in 1951. Booth and Simmons had ultimate control of all.

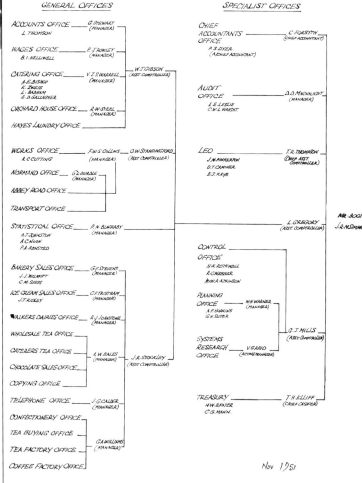

This LEO III computer, ordered by Rand Mines in Johannesburg, is seen here in the Acton factory under test before its despatch in May 1962. *By kind permission of Tony Morgan.*

potential business in the pipeline. English Electric asked for a statement to the effect that Lyons would remain associated with the new undertaking, that each would have three directors on the board of the new company and that Anthony Salmon would continue to serve as a director. At all times it was understood that the changes would take the form of a merger and Lyons would be committed to a new manufacturing consortium. This arrangement was adopted and on 8 February 1963 Lyons announced they had agreed with the English Electric Company to merge their computer businesses at home and abroad.

The price Lyons received (£1,856,250) was less than had been expected; they had hoped for £2 million to fend off any allegations from stockbrokers that they had lost money on their investment. The investment of £150,000 to build LEO I had, by 1964, turned into a total investment of £2 million. At the outset, Lyons had not contemplated manufacturing computers for sale outside the group, but once LEO I came into operation in 1954 the market potential had become apparent. In the words of one executive, 'We deluded ourselves that this could be a money-spinner.' Nevertheless where other companies with the technical and marketing resources waited on events, Lyons, with a small but passionately dedicated team, demonstrated what could be achieved and helped to lay the foundations of a world-wide industry that has caused a revolution in information processing.

Chapter 29

WELFARE AND EMPLOYMENT

THE INDUSTRIAL WELFARE facilities at Lyons were widely respected and for the first sixty years of the twentieth century were viewed by other firms as a model. They had started in an unusual way. It was during the First World War that Lena Salmon (1882–1953), wife of managing director Harry Salmon, and daughter of Isidore Gluckstein, voluntarily took on the task of helping the wives and dependants of employees who were serving in the armed forces. One of her first assignments was to visit the wife of an employee who was reported missing on the Flanders front. Lena Salmon ventured to ask the young wife the nature of the husband's former employment with Lyons. The young wife was aghast, replying, 'You really mean to tell me that you do not know my husband's work?' After due apologies the young wife told Lena Salmon that her husband was the 'royal bread deliverer' – in other words, he drove the Lyons van that took the bread to Buckingham Palace every morning. This incident – minor though it was in the scheme of things, except perhaps to the distraught wife – taught Lena Salmon that she should learn something of the background of families she was to visit.

Lyons' Staff Stores

When women began replacing men in the factories during the First World War, Lena Salmon opened a crèche that could accommodate fifty children, and within a short time it was enlarged to take a hundred. It was a huge success. Then she found that the poor quality of clothing and the high price of material during the war, not to mention rationing, prompted her to form what was known as the Drapery Club, where employees could obtain clothing for themselves and their children at reasonable prices, if necessary by paying in flexible instalments. This proved so successful that Lena Salmon persuaded the directors to open a Staff Stores in 1915 for the convenience of staff working at Cadby Hall. It soon became apparent that people living in the area would use Lyons' Staff Stores if they could, and so the shop was later opened to the public, though the name remained unchanged until 1956, when it was converted into a self-service shop – and called Lyons Supermarket – under the leadership of Rex Joseph. By today's standards the range of goods in the new 'supermarket' was small, being just 6,000. The items stocked, however, did include fresh meat and fish, wine, spirits and stationery as well as grocery and other foodstuffs.

The Lyons 'supermarket' was not the first self-service shop in Britain, as many in Lyons believed. Jack Cohen had opened his Tesco Stores nearly nine years earlier in 1947 but it was not until 1950 that he greatly expanded his business by opening another twenty stores. Cohen had started his business in a modest way, after the First World War, by buying surplus food, mainly tinned food from the NAAFI, and reselling it at a profit from a market stall. T.E. Stockwell, of the tea firm Torring & Stockwell, sold him a few chests of blended tea which Cohen packaged and sold as own-label. When deciding what to call his tea, Cohen used the initials of T.E. Stockwell and the first two letters of his own surname, thus

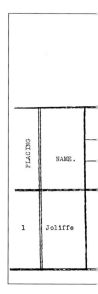

J. LYONS & COMPANY
are attacking
TRADE UNIONISM

Since April 21st. ELECTRICIANS employed by Messrs. J. LYONS & COMPANY have been on strike to maintain 100% TRADE UNION organisation at the Greenford factory.

In an endeavour to obtain a mutually satisfactory settlement discussions have taken place and despite reasonable proposals put forward by the UNION the talks have been abortive.

J. LYONS & COMPANY
will settle only
ON THEIR TERMS

We therefore appeal to all TRADE UNIONISTS and the GENERAL PUBLIC to support the UNION on this fundamental TRADE UNION principle.

DO NOT
ENTER ANY LYONS SHOP
BUY ANY LYONS PRODUCTS

THE ELECTRICAL TRADES UNION

Published by the Electrical Trades Union, Hayes Court, Bromley, Kent

Issued by the Electrical Trades Union in the 1950s, this poster urged members and the public to boycott Lyons' products. Unions were most militant at Greenford during the 1950s, '60s and '70s.

...ION OF STAR APPRENTICE FOR 1936 (Session 1935-1936)

ENGINEERS DEPARTMENT.

...N 1935-1936						PRACTICAL to 30.9.36. (Foreman's Reports)			TRADE (ORAL)EXAMINATION		TOTAL	YEAR OF APPRENTICE-SHIP.
...eral duct	Principals Report	Total				Poss:	Obtained:	%	Poss:	Obtained.	%.	
...s:Act:	Poss:Act:	Poss:Act:										
15	60	55	100	95	1200	1200	100.0	100	100	98.3	Final Year (4th)

This record is the final examination of a four-year apprenticeship served in the Engineers Department. Mr Jolliffe (whose name is misspelled) gained first place under the Star Apprenticeship Scheme in this final year and achieved a similar success in his third year. *By kind permission of Jack Jolliffe.*

conceiving one of the best-known names in retail trading, TESCO.

Health and Education Welfare

In parallel with these developments a first aid department was gradually established, staffed with nurses and furnished with all the equipment necessary for dealing with any unexpected injury within the large factory complex at Cadby Hall. The department, staffed twenty-four hours a day, had its own ambulance on constant standby to transport seriously ill or injured employees to hospital. The first full-time medical officer was Dr John Lockhart-Mummery, who took up his duties around 1926. Although he worked at Lyons for ten years, his management style has been described by some as ill-mannered. In 1936 he was succeeded by Dr William Blood, a general practitioner from Essex, whose personality was in stark contrast. Under Dr Blood's guidance the medical department developed rapidly and eventually provided full dentistry, massage and manicure, chiropody and eye care facilities. Lyons' health-care department became a model for other industrial firms all over Britain. Dr Blood (who was somewhat unfortunately named) was a pioneer in industrial medicine. Disabled during the First World War, he worked tirelessly for the employment of disabled people, and for this he was awarded an OBE.

Lena Salmon visited prisons and assisted in the rehabilitation of offenders by persuading Lyons managers to provide jobs when prisoners were paroled or released from their custodial sentences. She persuaded her family to establish welfare administrators specialising in such matters as financial help and loans, illness of dependants, hospital treatment, convalescent homes, health advice and payments for treatment, since the National Health Service had not yet come into existence. Sick visiting was also considered a vital part of the firm's welfare work: several experienced visitors were employed full-time to call upon staff in every part of London and sometimes delivered baskets of fruit and other items. During 1926 the number of visits to sick or injured staff exceeded 350 per month; some viewed these visits as ways of snooping on staff who might be malingering. Despite such criticism, Lena Salmon, who was a compassionate woman, is remembered for her positive achievements. Lyons' medical and other welfare services were provided at her instigation by quiet but forceful diplomacy – and, it must be said, without her seeking any credit or limelight.

The Athletic and Social Club

On 10 March 1913 members and friends of the Cadby Hall Athletic Club met to celebrate the close of the tenth year of its existence. In introducing the toast the club president also delivered its 'funeral' oration; for he then announced the complete success of his earlier appeal to the staff of Lyons that every man and boy in the company's service – women were not yet emancipated – should join in forming a new Athletic and Social Club. In April 1913 they published their first house journal, the *Lyons Mail,* to report their sporting activities, and it became the 'Official Organ of Lyons Athletic Club'. The first issue published the rules of the club, stating that their colours were to be light and dark blue, like those of Oxbridge. The *Lyons Mail,* just twelve A5 pages in length, included sections on gossip, provincial news, tennis, swimming, rifle shooting, rowing, cricket, football and town gardening.

The earliest sports ground of the Athletic Club was situated in Gunnersbury Lane, near Acton Hospital, where on Empire Day 1903 the first sports day was held. Joseph Lyons and his wife, Psyche, were among the 2,000 spectators. After 1904 the club moved to a more spacious area at the corner of Gunnersbury Lane where they remained until 1919. These sporting activities were vigorously encouraged by Lyons directors, who in November 1913 bought Linden House, a large property by the river Thames in Beavor Lane, the Upper Mall, Hammersmith, and converted it into a clubhouse for use by the staff. In 1924 Linden House Estate, an adjacent piece of land bought from Isabel Pembroke de Clare Arter for £7,500, was added. This enabled an indoor rowing tank and shooting range to be built; these pursuits had been highly popular with Cadby Hall staff well before 1913. Soon afterwards further rowing facilities were made available on

Lyons Staff Stores in the 1950s. Self service was tried out in 1949 and in 1956 it became a supermarket. It closed in the 1980s.

the river itself, because both male and female employees particularly enjoyed this exercise.

The *Lyons Mail* was suspended for most of the First World War, although one or two issues were printed naming those employees who had volunteered or been killed in action. Publication resumed in September 1919 as a New Series. Its two centre pages were given over to a roll of honour for all those who had lost their lives in the war. Apart from temporary interruptions during the First World War the *Lyons Mail* ran from 1913 until June 1995 making it Britain's longest running house journal.

The *Lyons Mail* (New Series) and the 66 acres of land that Lyons had recently bought from the John Lewis Partnership at Sudbury Hill (near

Greenford, Middlesex) were intended to serve as a permanent memorial to those members of staff who lost their lives in the war. At the inaugural opening of the new grounds on 2 August 1919 Montague Gluckstein announced:

> The Club is intended to serve as a memorial to those noble fellows who at the bidding of their country left our service, went forth to the Great War and laid down their precious lives in the defence of freedom of the World and of our hearths and homes. It was also designed to commemorate the gallant deeds performed by those others of our staff who had happily escaped making the great sacrifice, but who had suffered permanent injury in the discharge of their duties on land and on sea. It was felt that the establishing of the Club was the greatest tribute from the heart, marking the directors' deep sympathy with those who had suffered. I am sure that we are one in the opinion that the greatest homage we can pay to the memory and deeds of those heroes is by our earnest endeavours to make this dear country of ours greater, stronger, happier and more prosperous than before....Today our staff number 15,000, a splendid record of 32 years existence.

To reinforce the company's commitment to honour the Sudbury sports grounds as a memorial, a granite obelisk, designed by Lyons' own architect Charles Oatley, was erected near the entrance. The unveiling by General the Lord Horne took place on Saturday 7 October 1922, one month after Oatley had died, and it was followed by a service conducted by the Reverend Walsh, vicar and rural dean of Hammersmith.

Above right. The staff hairdressing salon which opened at the Cumberland Hotel in 1946.

Right. Some of the 'extraordinary bargains' available in the Staff Stores in 1928.

Of the total fit for military service in the firm's employ at this time 95 per cent had served with the allied forces and of these the names of 227 who lost their lives were inscribed on the obelisk (the true number was 238). A memorial was added in 1947 to commemorate those who died in the Second World War. Designed by Robert Bryson, of the Lyons Works Department, it consisted of an arc of Portland stone, and the names of 247 employees who had died were inscribed in gold letters. This memorial was officially opened on Armistice Sunday, 9 November 1947. (A full list of all the names inscribed on both memorials is contained in Appendix 5 with explanatory notes for discrepancies.)

The sporting activities of the Lyons Athletic and Social Club grew to phenomenal proportions. By 1921 no less than 80 per cent of the staff were members with subscriptions totalling £6,500 a year. The scale of the club activities, however, demanded substantial subsidies from Lyons – 'an outlay made with the greatest pleasure by the board'. Ten years later a further 22 acres of land were added, by which time the club boasted forty championship tennis courts and a bowling green – unsurpassed in the south of England – where the Middlesex county matches were played. A large open-air swimming pool was opened on 2 June 1935, by Lady (Kate) Salmon, wife of the managing director Sir Isidore Salmon. There were several football and rugby pitches and well-tended cricket grounds. Lyons' annual Sport Carnival days were legendary and attracted wide interest; in 1946 the official attendance was recorded as 29,513 – mainly staff and their families – and events were so popular that foreign as well as British newspapers reported them. The Sudbury sports ground was for many years the finest set of sports facilities of any company in the country. The clubhouse provided a complimentary venue for the club's less physically active pursuits such as dramatics, photography, chess, literary and debating societies, table tennis, snooker and many more.

The Pension Fund

Saving for old age is a relatively recent development that began in earnest in the nineteenth

The Club House of the Lyons Athletic Club in November 1913.

century. Before then public authorities were supposed to provide the poor with the means of subsistence as far back as Elizabethan times, when the Poor Relief Act was passed in 1601. Concerned with giving relief to the sick, unemployed and orphaned children, the legislation made no special provision for the elderly, but by the sheer weight of their numbers they posed the greatest problem to the authorities. Although there were many changes in the poor relief structures, the so-called Poor Laws were not finally abolished until the National Assistance Act of 1948. Some would say that the stigma of poverty still exists within society and that the introduction of benefit, from whatever source, has not eliminated this.

Towards the end of the 1930s it was becoming clear that the piecemeal growth of social security in Britain was leading to some confusion. Benefits overlapped, many separate bodies were receiving contributions and paying benefits, and there were four different means tests for non-contributory pensions. With these anomalies in mind, the wartime coalition government in 1941 appointed Lord Beveridge (then Sir William Beveridge) to

Camping holidays at the Sunbury Sports Ground in the 1940s.

conduct a survey of the existing social security schemes and make recommendations. The *Beveridge Report*, as it became known, was presented to Parliament in November 1942 and recommended a comprehensive system of social insurance covering the whole population. A single weekly contribution would cover sickness, unemployment benefit, industrial injury benefit, funeral expenses, widow's pension, retirement pensions and maternity grants. Pensions were set at £1 6s. per week for a single man and £2 2s. for a married couple.

It was not until 1946 that Lyons officially introduced their own pension (or superannuation) scheme. Prior to this *ex gratia* pensions, based on a combination of service and remuneration, had been paid to employees who had worked at Lyons for at least twenty-five years. *Ex gratia* payments continued to be made after 1946; by 1973 £3.75 million *ex gratia* payments had been made compared with pensions from the new fund of nearly £4 million in the same period. Some of the *ex gratia* payments had been borne annually as a charge against the Lyons group's profit, others were secured by the group transferring properties or rents from properties into special trust funds, with the effect that Lyons did not receive profit on the capital sums involved.

The earliest documentary evidence of a deed of trust for the benefit of employees who had retired and/or their dependants is dated 20 December 1932. The deed of trust was made between the company on the one part and Barnett Alfred Salmon and Harry Bennett on the other, acting as trustees. The numbers receiving such payments ran into several hundred, and many were well over what is now recognised as normal retirement age before they received any payment. Each candidate had to be personally submitted to Harry Bennett, secretary and director of Lyons, for calculation and approval of the pension. Catering workers such as teashop assistants, cleaners and ladies' room attendants suffered badly because of their low basic pay. The *ex gratia* pension awarded was regularly £2 5s. 6d. per month, the minimum payable.

The Lyons pension fund was constituted and established by a deed of trust dated 25 March

In this Issue—
EDGAR WALLACE, EDWARD CECIL, H. C. BAILEY, Etc.

The **Lyons Mail**

VOL. VII Nº 1 *(New Series)*   OCTOBER 1922.

Price 2d.   SUBSCRIPTION, 4/-

The front cover of *Lyons Mail* in October 1922 with Edgar Wallace as one of the contributors.

1946, made between the company and the trustees, with commencement of the fund being 1 July 1946. At first the company began by contributing more to the fund than employees, so that the fund could be quickly established. It was intended that contributions should, in the course of time, become equal. The first adjustment was made in 1961, when the company's contribution was fixed at five-sixths of that of staff, with credit taken each year for four-fifths of the company's contribution in respect of staff who had left and withdrawn their own contributions. A further adjustment occurred in 1966 when part of the fund's surplus was used to reduce the company's contribution by £167,000 a year, and balance of the surplus was used to increase all

The Lyons Club first football eleven of 1928. Lyons had two categories of soccer teams; the Lyons Club, where eight teams could be fielded, and the departmental teams of which there were 29. Before the wars the Lyons Club played in the Spartan League.

pensions by 7.5 per cent. By 1971 Lyons' contributions since the start of the pension fund totalled £5.63 million compared with staff contributions of £5.46 million. This ratio had reversed by 1972, when staff contributions overtook the company's by £50,000.

Those who entered employment after 1946 were required to join the Lyons pension fund on completing two years' continuous service. The amount of pension paid depended upon the years of membership and earnings throughout an employee's career with the company. The fund did not make provision for past service, nor for future service of employees who were already beyond the age limit; in this respect management were conscious that the scheme did not achieve all they would have wished. They did, however, endeavour to make provision outside the fund for retiring employees of long-pensionable service, although, because of the uncertain prospects for trade and industry at the time, they made no definite promises. Nevertheless Lyons did make *ex gratia* payments to retired employees, in addition to those paid by the company's pension fund. These payments were recorded as

£186,678 in 1967 and £141,917 in 1969. Trust funds were established for the appropriate years and Lyons injected £1,369,000 into the 1967 trust fund and £2,040,795 in the 1970 trust fund, the actuarial sum computed to cover the *ex gratia* pensions.

The first batch of retirements under the terms of the fund (those having completed ten years' membership) occurred in July 1956. Men aged sixty-five and women aged sixty had one common retirement date: 1 July. This meant that some retired before reaching their sixty-fifth or sixtieth birthday. Nevertheless, the event was considered most important, and Harry Bennett handled each case personally. For each employee on the list who had at least twenty-five years' service a calculation was made, based on earnings and length of service, to determine the level of *ex gratia* payment.

Running in parallel with the pension fund, from 1949 onwards, was the supplementary pension scheme No. 1, the cost of which was met entirely by the company. Its intention was to top up the pensions of certain categories of managers and specialists (men or women) with a promise of 50 per cent of final salary, which in that context meant the average annual salary over five years before normal retirement date. With a salary criterion of £2,000 per annum, the promised 50 per cent pension was scaled down according to age on entering employment. By the early 1960s, supplementary pension scheme no. 2 was set up; at the same time the salary criterion was raised to £3,500 (soon raised again to £5,000) and the proportion adjusted to one-third. For expatriate employees working in the foreign companies (Africa in particular) special pension arrangements were funded through an insurance company. There was also a policy to pay for children's education for managers working abroad.

The first medical officer, Dr Lockhart-Mummery, in his surgery during the 1930s.

On retirement every male pensioner was given the opportunity to provide a pension for a widow or dependant in the event of his death occurring first. If this option was exercised, the pensioner had to forfeit part of the pension, and this was dependent on the age of the spouse. Not too many could afford this sacrifice but some did. Under this scheme there were no automatic payment increases other than those following a five-yearly valuation of the fund which in the 1970s became three-yearly.

An additional death benefit scheme was introduced on 1 July 1965 in association with the Legal and General Assurance Society; the full cost of the insurance policy was borne by the company. The death in service benefit depended on the employee's salary at time of death. All employees were entitled to at least twice their annual salary. For those earning over £2,500 a year, the death benefit was equal to three times the salary and for those whose annual salary was over £3,000 it was four and a half times the salary. The pension fund also allowed employees to contribute additional voluntary contributions fixed at 1s. per week (4s. 4d. per month), a facility not introduced into other pension funds until much later.

A Pensions Retirement Committee was formed in 1965. It met weekly and included Felix Salmon, Neil Salmon, Leonard Salmon, Peter Blackaby, Geoffrey Mills and Robert Cook; guest members were invited from personnel departments. Apart from adjudicating on every early retirement occurrence, the committee discussed variations, innovations and pension policy, particularly the well-being of those retiring on medical grounds or through redundancy.

In the early 1970s the 'Top Management Retirement Policy' was introduced. The policy, which covered relatively few senior managers or executives, enabled them to retire at an earlier date (sixty years for men) – not always, it must be said, to the individual's liking. As their promised benefits were being paid earlier, extra provision had to be made for them.

A fundamental change was made to the pension fund in 1973 when, under the leadership

A typical clerical office at Cadby Hall in the 1950s. The windows in this building (Elms House) were opaque glass to prevent staff from idly looking out. Window ledges were angled to prevent files and other items from being placed thereon. Heating was underfloor.

widow's benefit, equal to half the member's pension at the time of death, at no loss to the member; the opportunity to exchange part of the pension for a tax-free lump sum; the prospect of a more substantial death benefit in the event of death in employment; automatic annual increases in pensions (minimum 3 per cent) to moderate the effects of inflation and improved terms for deferred pensions when members left service for whatever reason. Regrettably, the general pension improvements did little to benefit the lower-paid catering workers.

One further benefit introduced with the 1973 changes was that all employees who were current members of the fund on 30 June 1973 had the whole of their service recognised as 'pensionable service'. This was introduced to overcome the two-year waiting period and it greatly increased some employees' pensionable service.

of Neil Salmon and after much debate, it was reconstituted. Once in the forefront of industrial schemes, it had fallen short of the standards expected of a large group. Consideration had been given to the views expressed by members of staff or their representatives, by pensioners themselves and by consulting actuary, R. Watson & Son. The main benefits from the new arrangements were: the pension was to be related to earnings in the five years before retirement and, when added to the state retirement pension, to provide after a full career in the Lyons group a total retirement income equal to two-thirds of such earnings; the provision of an automatic

The Management share Purchase Scheme

Under a scheme approved by shareholders in 1968 a limited number of senior employees, including directors, were the first to benefit from the allocation of Lyons' shares which were officially described as 'employee convertible loan notes'. Under the scheme, participating employees acquired loan notes which would, five years after allotment, be converted automatically to 'A' (non-voting) shares. Intended to run for five years, the scheme was superseded by a share purchase scheme because changes in tax laws made it unattractive after only one issue.

In 1969, therefore, the company, pursuant

to sanction given at an extraordinary general meeting, introduced a management share purchase scheme to a wider management participation. It was formulated under section 54 of the Companies Act of 1948, and the National Westminster Bank Ltd, as trustees, purchased 'A' (non-voting) ordinary shares issued to them by Lyons at current market value, the necessary funds being lent to the trustees by the company. The shares were resold to participating employees at the same price, on condition that their obligation to pay would not arise unless they died or left the service of the company, if the cost had not been met previously. As long as the price remained unpaid by the employee, no dividend accrued.

The share purchase scheme was implemented in 1969, 1970 and 1971 and under the scheme the total nominal amount of shares issued amounted to £343,488. Managers with a full twelve months' service on 31 March qualified for the maximum entitlement, being shares costing 25 per cent of their annual salary at 30 June. Entitlement of managers with less than twelve months' service was proportionally less.

These schemes provided participating employees with a direct financial interest in the company, with the intention of cultivating a sense of corporate identity, even though a relatively low number of employees benefited. Lyons had intended to continue issuing shares up to an aggregate amount of £700,000, which had been authorised under the scheme, but the Finance Act of 1972 would have disadvantaged many participants. The Act provided that, unless a scheme complied with the various conditions set out in it, was approved by the Inland Revenue and received the sanction of those members of the company who were entitled to attend and vote at general meetings, the participants would be subject to income tax on benefits derived under the scheme. Participants would in any event have been subject to capital gains tax made on disposal of the shares.

Therefore in 1973 a new scheme, the Lyons stock option scheme, was formulated and conformed with the requirements of the Act, enabling the company to grant options to acquire shares by senior employees, including executive directors, employed in the United Kingdom. The scheme, being widely based, extended to approximately 1,000 employees. The amount payable in respect of each option was set at 1p for each £1 share granted; this was taken into account when the shares were exercised. All options had to be held for three years before they could be exercised and no option could be exercised more than seven years after it was granted. However, because of the government's counter-inflation measures at this time, it was not possible to grant shares under the new scheme, although shareholders' approval had been obtained on 24 July 1973. With the slide in company profits, shares in this scheme were never issued and share options did not become available again to Lyons staff until after the merger with Allied Breweries Ltd in 1978.

Part 5
FALL OF THE LYONS EMPIRE

1979   Sir Alex Alexander becomes Lyons Chief Executive (29 March).
        Lyons' Laboratory closed (October).
        James Hayes & Sons Ltd sold to Johnson Group Cleaners (June).
        Midland Counties ice-cream brand discontinued (December).
1980   Henry Telfer meat business sold.
1981   Last teashop closed, Marble Arch (January).
        Lyons Tetley Eaglescliffe factory sold to Golden Wonder Ltd.
        New revived Corner House in Strand opened (22 June).
        Allied-Lyons plc registered (30 October).
1982   Tenco (UK) Ltd bought from the Coca Cola Company (March).
        Sir Keith Showering dies (23 March).
1983   Lyons supermarket closes (4 March).
1984   Demolition of Cadby Hall factories completed (April).
1985   Elders IXL hostile bid for Allied-Lyons plc (October).
        Allied-Lyons plc buys into Hiram Walker-Gooderham & Worts.
        Dutch firm of Brink BV acquired (May).
1986   New Cadby Hall Head Office occupied (14 July).
1987   Lyons win catering contract for Gatwick Airport North Terminal
            (October).
1988   Lyons pull out from high street catering (June).
1989   Lyons buys the American Dunkin' Donuts business (December).
1990   Normand Ltd sold to management buyout team (2 February).
1990   Cadby Hall, Hammersmith closes (24 August).
1991   Foreign currency speculation fiasco (March).
1992   Lyons Maid sold to Clarke Foods (UK) Ltd (February).
        Ready-Brek cereal sold to Weetabix (29 June).
        Nestlé buys Clarke Foods (November).
1994   Allied-Lyons plc buys Pedro Domecq of Spain (February).
        Lyons' coffee businesses sold (February).
        DCA and Margetts Foods businesses sold (November).
        Normand Ltd sold to European Motor Holdings (12 July).
        Allied-Lyons changes name to Allied Domecq plc (19 September).
        Lyons Sea Foods sold (November).
        Lyons Biscuits (Symbol) sold to Hillsdown Holdings (December).
1995   Lyons Bakery sold to Manor Bakeries (Tomkins Group)
            (February).
        Lyons Tetley sold to management buyout team (June).
        Last Statement of Accounts for Lyons filed, their 101st year
            (19 August).
        Sir Christopher Hogg appointed chairman Allied Domecq plc
            (December).
2000   Tetley (GB) Ltd sold to the Indian conglomerate, Tata (March).
        Allied Domecq plc drops out of FTSE top 100 (March).

Chapter

WIND OF CHANGE

URING THE EIGHTEENTH and nineteenth centuries most industrial expansion was undertaken by the one-man or family partnerships funding their business expansions largely from current earnings. Such partnerships did not have corporate existence, and partners were individually liable for all debts of the firm. Towards the end of the seventeenth century the joint-stock company emerged, but this fell into disfavour with the legislature, largely because of the activities of fraudulent promoters and share dealers. After an Act of 1720 prohibited the formation of joint-stock companies, for over a century it was only possible to raise public funds by means of a parliamentary private bill.

Until this time London's commercial élite were members of the three main money-lending institutions: the Bank of England, the East India Company and the South Sea Company. The South Sea Company, founded in 1711, had a monopoly of trade with South America. In 1719 it offered to take over more than half the national debt in return for huge concessions from the government. There was little legislation to protect investors from the dishonest practices of the South Sea Company – such as bribes, directors' dishonest dealings in their own stock and scam promotions – and its stock rose tenfold in two months, as speculators clambered to secure a stake in fishing, foreign trade and land development. To halt the proliferation of imprudent investors, the Whig government passed the so-called Bubble Act on 9 June 1720, which made it illegal for joint-stock companies to trade without a charter. With the drying up of new money, South Sea Company

investors took what profit they could, causing a collapse of confidence, and the legendary South Sea Bubble burst. After the 1720 Act was passed, investors lost their taste for high-risk speculation, preferring to take the 3 or 4 per cent fixed returns on government securities. More important, parliamentary private bills became enormously expensive to enact and had no chance of success except where the proposed stock-holding company intended to undertake some public duty such as supplying a town with gas or water. Investors therefore had fewer opportunities and many reinstated their funds in the few stock-holding companies still trading, such as the Bank of England, the Hudson Bay Company and the powerful East India Company, which had survived the investment débâcle.

In 1825 the Act prohibiting the formation of joint-stock companies was repealed in the case of small businesses only. Parliament and, to a greater extent, the public viewed limited liability as a dishonest device to evade payment of debt. Politicians were also reluctant to grant general limited liability, since they feared it would divert capital from government stock and the railway companies in which, no doubt, some had invested. Small businessmen voiced their objections loudly, complaining that if the public could invest in railways and other infrastructure projects they should be allowed to invest in manufacturing industry. Their protestations resulted in Parliament legalising limited liability in 1855 and 1856 for companies engaged in any form of manufacture or trade, and in 1862 a General Consolidating Act greatly simplified registration procedure. Then the Directors' Liability Act of 1890 introduced the principle of the liability of the directors to pay compensation to persons who had been induced to take shares in a company on the strength of false statements in a prospectus.

Limited liability, however, remained under a cloud of suspicion. With trade booming and profits high, many private companies were reluctant to share their gains with others, partly through their management's tendency to be conservative. Many company owners were not only resistant to change but ignorant of social, economic and technological advancement. Such companies did not see the need for long-term plans and tended to react to events instead of adopting a proactive approach. Fierce foreign competition and depression did eventually force many companies to register for limited liability, with shareholders forcing change in management style. Families began to lose control of 'their' companies as more innovative administration bought, sold and merged with other organisations, and greatly improved investors' returns. It is now generally accepted that industrial expansion in the last quarter of the nineteenth century would have been greatly restricted if companies had had to rely on their own earnings alone to fund growth. There is no doubt that joint-stock enterprise played an important role in business evolution in the United Kingdom.

Family Control of Lyons

The Salmon & Gluckstein tobacco business, which had started from modest means, was one of those family enterprises which took advantage of the Limited Liability Acts. Unable to expand their tobacco business as quickly as they wished, the Salmon and Gluckstein families obtained a stock flotation in 1895 to raise £400,000. With such a large influx of new investors, the families, like most private owners, did not want to lose control of their company and therefore arranged the share structure so as to prevent any other party from obtaining a controlling interest. The new shareholders were content with the arrangement, provided of course they continued to receive an acceptable return on their investment. Everyone was delighted and understood the rules under which the company traded.

The structure of Lyons closely resembled that of Salmon & Gluckstein, in that a number of individual investors took shares in the company but the controlling voting shares remained in the hands of the founding members: Isidore and Montague Gluckstein, Barnett Salmon, Joseph Lyons and other lesser family investors. Thus the voting shares of Lyons were held by the Salmon and Gluckstein families or their trust fund, enabling them to control ownership of Lyons for many years. The first non-voting shares – classified as 'A' ordinary – were issued in 1918 when numbers stood at 80,410, rising to almost 30 million by 1976.

With its ownership secured by the share structure, J. Lyons & Co was still very much a family concern. Management passed from father to son, and many believed their directorship an inherited right, irrespective of their individual capabilities or talents. Non-family employees did occasionally make it to the board – Joseph Martin-Browne was appointed a director in the first year, for example – but the appointment of employee directors, as they were known, was 'recognition of services rendered'; they played little or no part in company policy or decision making. Within Lyons the real power rested not with the board but with 'General Management', an exclusive body of family directors (almost exclusively bearing the name of Salmon or Gluckstein) which made policy and influenced all important decisions within the company. The board structure was a formality, a necessary legal requirement under the Companies Act. Every male family member taking a career in Lyons – and most were urged to do so – could expect to become a director, *by right*, and gain a seat in General Management within a few years. General Management was organised by seniority; thus the eldest assumed the most senior role but all had equal rights, and decisions had to be unanimous. This is in stark contrast to accepted practice, where collective responsibility by the board of a company is avoided at all times and every member is assigned an area of responsibility for which he or she alone is liable. Peter Drucker, the widely acclaimed American scholar of management structures, politics, economics and society, puts it unambiguously: 'deliberation should be joint; decision single'. The Lyons structure, on the other hand, enabled a nepotistic culture to flourish at the highest levels of management, from the company's incorporation until the 1960s and beyond. In his book, *User-Driven Innovation* (McGraw-Hill, 1996), David Caminer observes:

> It was sometimes said in Lyons that expansion took place mainly to match the growth in the family as sons and daughters married and had children of their own to be placed in the business. … The Salmons and Glucksteins were like a government that did not change. Beneath them was a civil service, a very capable body that paid testimony to the family's ability to choose and delegate.

Young male family members entered the business as junior managers after having undertaken a period of 'basic catering training', frequently carried out in the Trocadero restaurant kitchens. They learned to prepare food and later moved into the grill room for a spell as waiters. They also learned something of the buying operation, visiting Smithfield, Billingsgate and Covent Garden markets before gaining another three years' experience in one of the catering or food-manufacturing units. Practical ability alone was taught; no formal business training was considered necessary. Instead the young manager, who sometimes did not have a university education, was expected to develop his own business expertise during his training period. After a period of some five years, the new man would become a General Manager, taking his place at the bottom of a list of some twenty other family members. Sometimes he would work under the direction of another member of his family, or he might be given responsibility for a small division or unit or in some cases a subsidiary company.

While no single person had responsibility for the company, the egalitarian family system adopted during the tobacco era ensured that each member received an equal share of the profit.

The Salmons and Glucksteins had been bred to believe that the business was a natural extension of the family. Since they forged strong family bonds – such as marriage – they saw no reason why this principle should not be applied to the business. Indeed, the family adopted the 'bundle of sticks' as their emblem, after the bitter dissolution of the first tobacco business in 1870, which is still used on the letter-headed stationery of S&G Administration Ltd, the moral being that a bundle of sticks cannot be broken but separated out individually they can, implying 'unity is strength'.

Since any male family member who had completed his training was quickly appointed to a senior position within the company regardless of his merits, it was possible for a non-family manager or director, of long standing and exceptional talent, to find himself reporting to a younger, less experienced person. Some managers who discovered that promotion was barred to them left the organisation. Although most males were expected to enter the business at some time, some chose not to: Cyril Salmon (son of Montague Salmon), for example, had a most distinguished career in law and became Lord of Appeal in 1972. A few family managers did feel uneasy about being appointed over more experienced men, but, since this had been the practice for so long, their reservations soon evaporated.

There is no doubt that the early success of Lyons had been dependent on the extraordinary talents of Isidore and Montague Gluckstein and Joseph Lyons, and later by Harry, Maurice and Julius Salmon. All had particular talents which were used to great effect in building the business into one of the largest catering and food-manufacturing empires in the world. They had recruited and nurtured high-calibre staff who were able to run, on a day-to-day basis, some of the Lyons departments with exceptional competence. During the period after the Second World War, deprived of its brilliant leaders and faced with strong competition, General Management stubbornly believed that the business could be revitalised while continuing to be managed in the same manner as before the war. However, not only did General Management find it increasingly difficult to make decisions on key issues but senior managers who felt they were being deprived of career prospects left to take up jobs outside the company. With General Managers' dual role – as departmental head and as member of General Management – there was no separation of responsibilities and thus no real accountability. This structure also made it increasingly difficult for quick business adjustments to be made; more seriously, it prevented long-term business planning. Whereas the first two generations had produced outstanding leaders who could generate the momentum needed to drive the business forward, the post-war generations entered a period of indecision, when there were not enough radical ideas to aid forward planning in the face of changing markets. The most fundamental flaw was that decisions for action were taken without proper objective analysis or input from management councils or other impartial contributors.

It would be wrong, however, to create the impression that all the Lyons' difficulties in the immediate post-war period were due to management deficiencies. The economic problems of the period were acute, and much rebuilding of the firm's production and catering businesses had to be undertaken in a climate where industry generally was converting from war production to consumer needs. Some small investment had been made in North America during 1951, when Lyons bought the E. C. Rich Company, based in New York, and delegated Kenneth Gluckstein as director of operations there. With its eighty-year reputation for crystallised Canton ginger, E. C. Rich distributed Lyons' tea, marmalade, candies, biscuits, Dundee cakes and Christmas puddings. The end of food rationing and the removal of building restrictions left Lyons free to make the most of the post-war period. Effort and money poured into new development and by 1958 £2 million had been spent on the Corner Houses alone. Nevertheless, a company's success depends on the quality of its management and the profit it can return on shareholders' investment. During the period 1934–40 net profits of over £1 million per annum

had been achieved. Profits, understandably, fell during the war years, but on the whole shareholders did not see an improvement in dividends over a thirty-year period and high levels of net profit were not achieved again until 1958, when the £1 million barrier was again exceeded. Between 1946 and 1956 dividend payments were fixed at 22.5 per cent and apart from one year continued to fall until 1978, when company losses were reported at over £9 million and shareholders' dividend was fractionally over 2 per cent (see Appendix 6).

Adapting any business to changing circumstances requires management dexterity, but in Lyons personal feelings and prestige seemed more important than sound commercial reasoning. One example was the indecision about the future of teashops, whose popularity waned after the war. Because teashops had been part of the original company business and had played such an important role in the Lyons story, management were reluctant to dispose of them, even though their contribution to business profits was insignificant. Some divisions of the business did improve after the war, most notably the bakery sector, which became fully productive again in 1954. Soft drinks (as a result of more plentiful supplies of citrus fruits), the new Wimpy hamburger business and frozen foods all did well. The traditional engines of profit – catering, ice-cream and groceries (tea and coffee) – did not recover to pre-war levels and suffered badly from competition, with ice-cream the most erratic.

The poor trading results of the 1950s were reflected in the depressed value of the company's shares. Expenditure on the post-war replacement of plant and machinery had been high, with over £1 million allocated to capital expenditure in 1951 alone. Raw material costs increased, as did labour costs, but these were not properly reflected in the price charged for finished products. As a result insufficient profit was made on individual items and the company retained its policy of running on razor-thin margins. This policy continued into the 1960s, by which time there was a further fall in Lyons' equity.

Lyons' management style had remained almost unchanged since 1894, when the supply and manufacture of food, for both retail sale and catering, were under the control of a single family director. Yet the Lyons business had become diverse, with some subsidiary companies operating independently while others operated as part of a main department. There were two hotel companies, Strand Hotel Ltd and Cumberland Hotels Ltd. The management of Cumberland Hotels was also responsible for Maison Lyons at Marble Arch and it operated, surprisingly, independently from the other catering establishments. Added to this disparate business was a computer-manufacturing subsidiary, a carton company, a meat company, a printing company, a motor company, a laundry company, a wine company and many other business activities. The decision to develop an electronic computer was seen at the time as praiseworthy, but there was no proper control of the project's finances. Tens of thousands of pounds were frittered away, and development expenditure was posted to dubious accounts within the business to hide the losses. Originally it was intended to make eight series-two computers a year to sell to outside organisations, but the numbers only reached three in 1958, two in 1959, three in 1960 and two in 1961. Technology, too, was advancing rapidly and thousands of pounds of stock, such as valves, was frequently written off.

As the business developed in size and diversity, severe strains were placed on management, whose style and structure had still not fundamentally changed throughout the company's history. With profits and growth depressed, at a time when the nation was experiencing higher prosperity, bold reform seemed essential to secure the continuance of the firm – which could only be achieved by improving its profitability. The acute difficulties of the late 1950s brought home to General Management the desperate need to rethink their traditional role.

Decentralisation and Relaxation of Family Control

The first manifestation of change occurred between 1958 and 1962. These subtle changes are officially unrecorded but amounted to a decentralisation of the manufacturing businesses. In the 1958 company accounts, the business units were referred to as Departments, a name by which they had always been known, but by 1962 the terminology of Divisions had been substituted and by 1964 the Bakery Division, Bread Division, Catering Division and Tea Division were all listed and reported upon separately in the company accounts; but management made no attempt to separate out singular trading details. The divisionalisation process varied significantly depending on the departments' particular complexity and function. For some the transformation was relatively quick and clean. For others the process became drawn out and complicated, as in the case of the Works Department, but in many instances subsidiary companies were formed with their own director structures. The intention was that new management, who were close to the trading operations, should play a greater role in the running of the businesses. However, their accountability continued to be to an appropriate General Manager and the new management did not have full command of their Divisions. To a large extent the changes amounted to no more than an exercise on paper.

The Transport Department, which so far had provided a centralised service for all production areas, was completely disbanded and the newly created Divisions became responsible for conveying their own materials. Many introduced their own transport livery in order to help create individual company images, but the traditional dark blue vans with their distinctive gold lettering and coloured royal warrants regrettably disappeared.

As well as changes to transport, many of the new production divisions set up their own laboratories, and then became responsible for their own quality control and product development – tasks hitherto undertaken by the central laboratories. This not only duplicated the central service departments – ice-cream, bakery and groceries all had separate laboratories – with the attendant high costs, but exposed them so that eventually they closed, and their expertise was lost. The central laboratories, which had achieved no less than a revolution by bringing science to food manufacture and had played a crucial role during the war, continued until the late 1960s, when a Food Science Research Committee considered their future.

Recruitment and personnel functions did not escape the change. Differing personnel and remuneration policies quickly emerged and caused problems when staff were transferred from one division to another within the Lyons group. At the time of these changes a large part of the Comptrollers Department transferred to the separate operating divisions, with the loss of yet another standard method of working.

Brian and Neil Salmon, who both had responsibility for large divisions (bakery and ice-cream), realised that divisionalisation had brought little benefit and seized the opportunity to persuade the younger members of General Management that a change in management philosophy was essential to ensure long-term stability. In this they were advised by John Simmons, an acknowledged expert on organisational structures both within Lyons and at the Institute of Office Management. Other members of the family supported change, but some became recalcitrant and resisted the appointment of non-family members to senior positions, even though fewer male heirs threatened the future management of an expanding family business. Surprisingly, many also resented the introduction of a management training scheme, which they perceived would help non-family managers to improve their proficiency and thus become a greater threat to the families. A turning point occurred in 1958, when Mark Bogod's name was put forward by Neil Salmon as chief executive of Ice-Cream Division. Neil Salmon assured the families that 'he did not think the appointment would interfere with or undermine our central control'. Ice-cream had originally been the responsibility of Maurice Salmon, as was all Cadby Hall production; this passed from him to Isidore Howard Gluckstein (1903–1933) and after his untimely death to Julian, and finally Neil Salmon. Mark Bogod had worked in the laboratories, and after Julian Salmon had taken charge of the ice-cream

department he appointed Bogod and Frank Theobold as joint managers until Theobold's retirement some years later. Neil Salmon recognised Bogod's qualities and pressed for him to assume full control of the ice-cream business as well as to be appointed to the main Lyons board as an employee director. Mark Bogod still reported to Neil Salmon on ice-cream matters. This contentious appointment nevertheless caused much resentment in family circles; many argued it was a withdrawal of family responsibility, favoured rights and privilege. Despite these setbacks Brian and Neil Salmon did not shirk from what they considered responsible changes, but contentious appointments were made only when circumstances became critical, and the process of moving from family to non-family control was fraught with difficulty.

In 1964 John Simmons, Leonard Gluckstein, Julian, Felix, Brian and Neil Salmon formed a study group to examine how the management structure of Lyons could be transformed. They were aided in this by the American management consultant Peter Drucker, who as we have heard had a legendary reputation. Having examined the changes to Lyons and the tensions these placed on General Management, he noted that the ice-cream business had gone through many mergers and acquisitions and frozen food was faced with stiff competition from Birds Eye. He also observed that the computer subsidiary had consumed vast sums of capital which would have been better directed towards food-manufacturing. Drucker confirmed Lyons' worse fears: he concluded that it was the inadequacy of its management style which was responsible for the company's under-performance, bearing in mind the enormous opportunities of the British consumer market between 1954 and 1964. In his report of December 1964 he said:

> To remain competitive Lyons must be able to attract, use and hold professional managers as good as those of any other company in the United Kingdom ... Lyons must therefore be able to offer this kind of manager recognition, rewards and opportunities equal to those he finds elsewhere.

As a result of this report, the study group recommended to General Management that the business be reorganised into sectors, where analogous businesses, irrespective of their size, could be brought together under a single director. In some cases this meant combining subsidiary companies with smaller divisional departments. The Catering Sector, for example, included teashops, Corner Houses, restaurants, public houses and the subsidiaries engaged in catering franchise operations. Shareholders were advised that the many advantages of integrating own-managed and franchised-managed catering activities was that each division would be better placed to learn from the experience of the other. The companies or divisions within each sector would be headed largely by non-family members, each reporting to a Sector chairman who was also a member of General Management. Hence control by the family was preserved – which in any case had been a prerequisite of any initial restructuring. Most other senior managers within Lyons regarded the so-called restructuring as an exercise, nothing more.

As so many independent 'companies' began to take on separate identities, the Lyons group lost its corporate image. Customers and suppliers began to drive hard bargains, to the detriment of the group. No division knew what business another was doing, with the same customer, and sometimes higher discounts were unjustifiably agreed. Line management also tended to focus on turnover and gave less emphasis to unit profit. Many managers were now faced for the first time with real competition. They could no longer rely on other parts of the group to support them financially but instead had their own targets and objectives, which some found hard to achieve. The quality of many traditional products deteriorated and markets became harder to sustain against fierce competition.

Lyons' profits remained dismally low, partly as a result of not being able to generate sufficient volume of business to provide the profitability of large-scale operation. The necessary volume could have been achieved by promoting growth from within; by merger; or by the purchase of another company engaged in a similar or complementary line of business. Meanwhile catering steadily expanded into the 1970s, so that by 1973 JL Catering had over 20,000 seats spread throughout its various restaurants in the United Kingdom which had to be filled several times each day. A Sales Promotion Office of eight staff, based in the Strand Corner House, worked tirelessly to help meet this need.

Family management continued into the mid-1960s but the promotion of non-family staff to key positions in the new trading sectors was not a success; the new structures did not work entirely satisfactorily with old foundations. At this stage behavioural science, which had been used with mixed results in the tea, ice-cream and bakery businesses to help management adapt to a decentralised company, was introduced. Behavioural methods were used to teach management how to solve their own problems and create an atmosphere of open criticism. Some managers cracked under the strain. This led some family members to believe they were being persecuted when they were only being judged. These behavioural sessions were assisted by the Tavistock Institute of Human Relations and started from the premise that Lyons needed a high level of skilled professionals and that the family was unable to provide this. The Tavistock Institute formally registered the need for managers to be given genuine opportunities for career development to the highest levels of the company:

> If owners insist on retaining rights of unrestricted access and detailed control, they will not attract the most capable and self-respecting agents, or perhaps even agents of sufficient capacity to carry the responsibility that must inevitably be delegated. Such men will not accept this degree of servant definition of their roles. They require a professional management culture, not an owner culture.

Faced with these blunt options, Neil Salmon again expressed his fears for the future of the business if the family persisted in resisting changes to management style. He reminded his colleagues that the family's wealth, as well as their very jobs, depended on the success of Lyons, but many were reluctant to subordinate the interests of the family, believing that some apparatus could be introduced which would not only give greater responsibility to non-family management but would preserve family control as well. A series of meetings composed of family members were held at the Cumberland Hotel during the first quarter of 1966 to examine all attitudes. By the middle of the year a draft constitution had been published. In essence it stated that decisions within the company should be based on commercial considerations rather than on family or personal feelings with all authority vested in the Lyons board, to which all directors were accountable. Reporting to the main board, a small committee known as the Lyons Group Planning Executive undertook preliminary studies to establish objectives and strategies. This committee, comprising Neil, Brian, Geoffrey and Felix Salmon, assisted by Len Badham, began its work immediately, undertook a comprehensive review of the main operating divisions/departments and by December 1967, with its work completed, it was dissolved.

In 1969 changes occurred at the highest levels of management. Neil and Brian Salmon remained joint managing directors, positions appointed in 1968, with Guy Lawrence becoming chief executive director responsible for food products, and Len Badham as technical and commercial director. Sir Julian Salmon, deputy chairman, retired from the company's service in July and at the same time Brian Salmon relinquished his appointment as joint managing director when he was appointed deputy chairman in succession to Sir Julian. After these changes, voting became an accepted procedure and retirement ages were gradually introduced. The family maintained control of the shares but those family members who chose to work in Lyons were promoted on merit and not on the basis of inherited right. The most fundamental change in Lyons' management structure since its incorporation in 1894 had been completed, with senior employees having equality with the highest managerial ranks.

Having been recruited for fast-stream management, Len Badham had eventually made

it to the top. More important, he liaised between family and non-family directors, some of whom found the new regime difficult to accept. Having also been a member of the Group Planning Executive, as well as being appointed commercial director, Badham played an important role in the future direction of the company, whose first priority was to improve profits and increase the value of Lyons' shares. The Group Planning Executive study had stipulated that capital employed should have a return of 14.4 per cent. Investment in hotel property became a source of contention; some hotel management believed this could not be compared with factory or similar investments. Three-year divisional budgets were prepared to reflect these objectives, and operations unable to fulfil the requirements were closed down. Within fifteen months loss-making activities of £1 million were closed or disposed of and there began a period of rapid acquisitions with the objective of improving profit and the asset value of shares.

Race for Growth

The process of enlarging the Lyons empire to meet competition started in 1967 and accelerated rapidly under the new management. In 1967 arrangements were made with the Union International Company and the Nestlé Company to merge joint frozen food businesses. In 1968 the Tonibell Manufacturing Company represented a significant contribution to the ice-cream trade while Chalmar Holdings and Symington Ltd strengthened the catering supply businesses. Bakery interests were consolidated with the acquisitions of Allied Bakeries (Cake) Ltd, Scribbans-Kemp Ltd, Celebrity Holdings Ltd and for the first time a Dutch company, Ulrich NV. Likewise the Grocery Sector benefited from the Sol Café instant coffee business. Hotels, too, expanded quickly both by acquisition and by the building of new ones in city centres and elsewhere.

In 1970, and for the first time in its history, net profits exceeded £3 million, up 33 per cent from the previous year, but managers could take little comfort from these results, as shareholder dividends fell from 14.33 per cent to 6.83 per cent in the same period. If Lyons were to survive, it had to increase its size faster than the home market would allow, and attention turned to Europe. As the original European Economic Community (EEC) market was four times that of the United Kingdom, it was essential to establish a foothold on the continent. While consumption levels were high there, the individual businesses in the food industry tended to be smaller than in the United Kingdom. The differences in diet and palate were reflected in product ranges and types. The markets in Europe in which Lyons had strong expertise (such as tea and packaged cake) were undeveloped, and management decided that in embarking on European development Lyons should do so through products which were already being consumed there rather than through products which were traditionally sold in the United Kingdom – while awaiting the opportunity to introduce British products where and when appropriate. Research had also shown that the processed meat market in Europe was largely in the hands of family-run businesses and, with some knowledge of meat processing themselves, Lyons acquired the family business of Homburg NV.

Situated at Cuyk in south-eastern Holland, Homburg was one of the largest processors of pig meat in western Europe and it became Lyons' first significant European purchase when they took control in 1972 by securing 99.8 per cent of the issued share capital. Lyons had previously established a holding company in the Netherlands under the management of Christopher Salmon, and Homburg, and later other Dutch companies, were consolidated here. Homburg had developed a sophisticated pig-breeding operation, Fomeva, subcontracting local farmers to rear the animals up to their slaughter ages. With a range of products from sausages to quality Parma ham, and markets in eastern and western Europe as well as the United States, the business had suffered badly from lack of investment. Its management style was in many ways reminiscent of that of Lyons, and Homburg's management did not take kindly to the new ownership and the aggressive style of Christopher Salmon.

The Homburg acquisition was followed and complemented by the acquisition of Vleeswaren-

fabriek Beckers NV, the largest Dutch manufacturer of speciality products for the catering trade, notably frikadellen (meat balls). In France, Lyons acquired the majority interests in the Reybier group in Lyon, one of the leading branded meat and charcuterie businesses in France, and Le Rosemont in Besançon, the leading charcuterie firm of its region. The total consideration for these acquisitions was £21 million.

In accordance with the policy of entering established local markets, the purchase of companies in the cake and biscuit field concentrated on a particular speciality of the country concerned. Thus Sapori, producers of the famous spiced Siena cake (Panforte) in Italy, opened new markets to Lyons. By procuring Hooimeijer in Rotterdam, Lyons secured the predominant rusk business in Holland and in Bussink in Deventer the leading honey cake manufacturer. These additional bakery businesses were to cost Lyons a further £4 million.

Despite the poor performance of the Alpha Hotel in Amsterdam, where the build-up of business was slower than expected, Lyons continued their search for properties. Through the Italian subsidiary Sapori, the Park Hotel in Siena became the first country hotel on the continent, followed by the Hôtel Commodore in Paris.

By 1974 Lyons could be described as a trans-European business but realised that the successful companies were increasingly being dominated by international conglomerates. Lyons had so far restricted their European expansion to countries within the EEC, but managers became impressed with the rate of industrial growth and commercial prospects in Spain (Portugal and Spain were not admitted to the EEC until 1 January 1986) with its population of nearly 40 million, and subsequently bought into the Panrico and Panificio companies. In the United States important tea, ice-cream and cereal interests were bought, and although there was a downturn in the economy during the mid-1970s it remained the largest economy in the world – one in which Lyons had to be strongly represented.

In 1968 almost all of the Lyons' turnover

(£125 million) and profit (£5,563) were derived from its activities in the United Kingdom, with food manufacture and distribution accounting for 74 per cent. By 1974 turnover of overseas food operations surpassed that of the United Kingdom by £27 million, with a corresponding increase in profit from overseas operations (see Appendix 7). The financial improvement achieved between 1968 and 1974 was testimony to the company's new strategy and in 1973 the report to shareholders stated:

> This has been a significant year in the history of the company. It was the year in which we had previously envisaged the United Kingdom being sufficiently secure to enable us to embark on a large-scale expansion overseas, particularly Continental Europe.
>
> Accordingly the company has greatly extended the geographical span of its operations during the year and whilst overseas turnover represented 8 per cent of the group total in the previous year it accounted for 23 per cent in the year under review and is expected to account for 41 per cent in the current year. However, the improvement in net earnings stems almost entirely from our UK businesses. This is for two reasons: first that many of our acquisitions took place in the latter half of the year and, second, that overseas companies tend to favour financial years ending in December and, insofar as this practice applies, we have no profits to set against the interest cost for the March quarter of our own financial year in which the acquisition is made.

Recession, Crisis and Takeover

The euphoria caused by the international growth was short-lived. Britain went into a recession, which started with the oil crisis in the autumn of 1973 and deepened in 1975 after inflation had soared to 20 per cent at the end of 1974 with no signs of abating. The high level of borrowing, mainly from American investors, to pay for the aggressive expansion programme severely impacted on the profit and loss account, because of the punitive level of world-wide interest rates which prevailed throughout 1974. In May 1975 the pound lost over 25 per cent of its value against the dollar and the year was described by Brian Salmon, the Lyons chairman, in his statement to shareholders as 'the most difficult year in the company's post-war history'. The priority switched from expansion to containment, and every effort was made to reduce borrowings. A £20 million loan from the Finance Corporation for Industry was taken up in August 1975 and used to repay short-maturity debt and reduce overdrafts. Arrangements were also made with bankers for the repayment dates of some other short-term debts to be extended, thereby improving the general maturity plan. Sterling continued to decline during 1976, but the Lyons group did manage to protect its position marginally by switching some foreign currency debt into sterling. This created a significant interest rate penalty but the group's reserves were better insulated against any further fall in the value of sterling. By the end of 1977, $69.5 million had been converted to £40.5 million.

With hindsight it can be seen that the company had adopted an expansionist programme which it was unable to afford. Worse still, by borrowing in foreign currency to fund the British and European acquisitions it had acted recklessly. However, Lyons' acquisitions in the early 1970s were principally to improve its international position as a food manufacturer and, simultaneously, to reduce its dependence on the UK economy. At the same time Lyons began moving its meat and baking operations from Cadby Hall and these large capital programmes exacerbated the reliance on borrowings. The constraints imposed by exchange control and the financial marketplace at that time required that the new acquisitions be for the most part financed by foreign currency borrowings, and with unconstrained availability management did not think through all the consequences of their actions. Several companies, especially the European ones, had been acquired with undue haste and without a proper in-depth analysis of their circumstances. The French meat businesses were in a bad shape, aggravated by expensive litigation in fighting the French tax authorities, which claimed FF19.3 million of tax liability alleged to have arisen as a result of the creation of Reynier (previously a subsidiary of Reybier), prior to Lyons' acquisition of its interests in Reybier. The business also suffered badly from the price control in that country. Reybier was also investigated by the Italian authorities for allegedly exporting Parma-labelled ham to Italy. A private anti-trust action was also started in the United States against Baskin-Robbins in connection with unlawful tying arrangements. Wimpy International too became embroiled with its auditors in South Africa with regard to the accounts ending 31 March 1975, while at home Lyons began to formulate substantial claims in respect of the construction of the new bakery at Carlton, South Yorkshire. The period was also characterised by a drop in consumer spending at home as a result of fierce competition between food retailers, which impacted on manufacturers' margins. A further factor was the serious dislocation of tea and coffee price movements, said to have been unprecedented since 1900. With hindsight Lyons should have adopted a more measured approach by integrating the earlier acquisitions before embarking on other significant appropriations.

From 1976 there followed a period of disposals in a desperate attempt to reduce the company's borrowings. The most significant of these was that of the hotel business in January 1977, when the total group borrowings had risen to nearly £243 million. Ironically, the hotels began to enjoy a substantial upturn in business in the mid-1970s which was led by a strong recovery in tourism, fuelled by an exchange rate increasingly favourable to visitors. This made it possible to negotiate their sale on 'an acceptable basis' but in reality it was a give-away. The sale of the hotel business, the jewel in the Lyons crown, chronicled the darkest day in the company's history when many directors were reported to have been brought to tears. It became a turning point from which the company would not recover.

Brian Salmon relinquished his chairmanship of Lyons in April 1977 after forty-two years'

service. During his five years as chairman he had the unenviable task of guiding the company through its turbulent vicissitudes. He was succeeded by his brother Neil Salmon, who appointed Sir Alec Ogilvie and Austin Bide as non-executive directors under pressure from City bankers and institutional shareholders. The following year Sir Alex Page, chairman of Metal Box Ltd, joined the Lyons board as a third non-executive director.

On the day after the annual general meeting of Lyons, which took place on 27 July 1978, Allied Breweries Ltd approached the Lyons board with a proposal to buy the company. It is difficult to believe that this had been the first approach, since

Demolition of
Cadby Hall in 1983.
A war-time fire
watch position relic
sits precariously on
top of a building
just behind old
Cadby Hall.

The new Cadby
Hall in 1986.

the terms of the sale were agreed by 4 August 1978 and on 31 August 1978 Samuel Montague & Co. Ltd, bankers acting for Allied Breweries Ltd, circulated their recommended offer to shareholders. This offered eleven shares in Allied Breweries for every six shares in Lyons. The practical consequence of acceptance to Lyons' shareholders were that a holder of sixty Lyons ordinary shares who accepted the ordinary offer received 110 new Allied Breweries ordinary shares which had the following effect:

Capital

110 new Allied ordinary shares at 82.5p	£90.75
60 Lyons ordinary shares at 98p	£58.80

This represented an increase of approximately 54 per cent.

Income

Gross dividend of 6.552p per share on 110 new Allied shares	£ 7.21
Gross dividend of 3.133p per share on 60 Lyons ordinary shares	£1.88

This represented an increase of approximately 283 per cent.

The Allied Breweries group had interests in the United Kingdom, the Netherlands and Belgium embracing the brewing of beer, production of British wine, cider, fruit juice, perry, port, Scotch whisky, sherry and soft drinks, and wholesaling and retailing of alcoholic and non-alcoholic drinks and tobacco. The group's products included the well-established brands of Double Diamond, Skol Lager and Long Life, the regional beers of Ansells, Ind Coope and Tetley, Babycham, Harvey's sherry, Cockburn's port, Whiteway's and VP British wine, Coates and Gaymer's cider, Teacher's and Stewarts whisky, Britvic fruit juice, Warninks advocaat and Appleford health foods. The acquisition became effective on 13 November 1978, when the Lyons shares were transferred to Allied Breweries Ltd.

After the acquisition of Lyons, Allied Breweries became the tenth largest company in Britain with an exceptionally wide range of interests across the world. Annual turnover in the home market alone was £1.5 billion and the overseas interests were worth a further £641 million. With a capitalisation of £600 million, the company employed 90,000 people and had extended their traditional markets of beer, wines and spirits into tea, coffee, cakes, ice-cream and catering. Allied Breweries could provide additional outlets for Lyons' products and vice versa, each exchanging much complementary experience and expertise. One exception to this was probably the Baskin-Robbins chain of ice-cream parlours in the United States, where over 2,000 were operating from coast to coast; Allied Breweries were weak in the United States at this time, apart from one or two branded spirits such as Teacher's whisky and Harvey's Bristol Cream sherry. With the financial support of Allied Breweries, Lyons would be free to concentrate on improving the performance of their acquisitions. It was Allied Breweries' intention that Lyons should be operated as a new separate Food Division of the Allied group and to reflect this the group was renamed Allied-Lyons plc.

The City's reaction to the merger – as it was described – was enthusiastic. Most knew it was a takeover but the Lyons board must have viewed Allied Breweries as a white knight, given the perilous state of Lyons' finances. This then marked the end of Lyons' autonomy. Five Victorian entrepreneurs had started the business in 1887 by selling tea and cake to visitors to the Newcastle Exhibition. Over ninety years later they could not have anticipated their company becoming a food empire – the first food empire – whose operations touched every family in the United Kingdom. It is ironic that the company bore the name of a lesser contributor to the original consortium throughout its whole independent history. The man, of course, was Joseph Lyons and the company which bears his name is now part of our commercial history. This is not quite the finish, however, and the next chapter describes the break up and the eventual end of the Lyons empire.

FROM ALLIED-LYONS TO ALLIED DOMECQ

THE LAST INDEPENDENT financial trading year of Lyons (1977–8) had been a difficult one, with reduced consumer spending, fierce price competition, bad summer weather and price controls both in Britain and overseas. Although world-wide turnover increased from £769 to £790 million, trading profit fell by nearly £10 million, despite the sale of the hotels, the Lujeri tea estates and Wimpy Overseas. Nevertheless the chairman, Neil Salmon, remained convinced there had been no fundamental adverse change in the underlying strength of the group's trading position. Therefore it came as a shock when Allied Breweries Ltd approached him on 28 July 1978, one day after the annual general meeting of Lyons shareholders, with a proposal to buy his business. Even with disastrous trading profits and huge debts the Lyons board still felt the group could prosper as an independent company, but the board had a fiduciary duty to shareholders to consider the terms.

At the time there seemed to be no way of using revenues to reduce the heavy borrowings. Accordingly, Lyons' bankers and consultants, Morgan Grenfell & Co. Ltd and N.M. Rothschild & Sons Ltd, advised that the offer should be accepted. Shareholders subsequently and overwhelmingly endorsed the recommended offer as did Neil Salmon, who held nearly two million ordinary shares in Lyons. Allied's shareholders had also met in September 1978 and similarly gave their wholehearted approval to the arrangements.

Keith Showering, Allied's chairman, passionately believed that the purchase of Lyons was an outstandingly good investment. He was impressed by Lyons' customers' loyalty to its great tradition and to its brand names. Now that Allied Breweries were no longer just a drinks company, he recommended to shareholders that the name of the combined group be changed to Allied-Lyons plc to reflect the larger group interests. The new name was registered on 30 October 1981.

By the end of September 1978 Keith Showering, John Clemes (finance director) and Derrick Holden-Brown (vice-chairman) had joined the Lyons board, while Austin Bide, Sir Alec Ogilvie and Sir Alexander Page resigned their non-executive directorships in October. Sir Alex Alexander had joined on 29 March 1979 as Lyons' chairman and chief executive. His appointment to the Lyons board provoked some hostility from staff who found his management style abrasive, and some regarded him initially as a hatchet man. Nevertheless, his energy and imagination probably helped Lyons to make a modest recovery in the years immediately following the Allied Breweries takeover.

During the 1979–80 fiscal year Lyons acquired the entire issued share capital of Embassy Hotels Ltd from Allied Breweries. The 42 hotels then became part of the Food Division under its new management. Other small acquisitions made by Lyons or its subsidiaries included that of Pepi SpA, which was bought by the Italian subsidiary Industrie Riunite del Panforte di Siena SpA on 3 March 1980. Interests in Spillers-French Holdings were disposed of to the majority shareholder, Dalgety, severing links with all flour milling within Lyons. The former Lyons Tetley factory at Market

Harborough was sold to Golden Wonder Ltd during 1980–1 together with the Symington trademarks and the Galbraith factory in Glasgow closed. In the Netherlands several plants were closed and jobs were cut. Henry Telfer and Reybier were sold with losses of £16.6 million; in 1981 a further £8 million loss was sustained in disposing of other parts of the business. With Lyons' debts now largely cleared or renegotiated, and limited rationalisation measures undertaken, pre-tax profits returned in 1981 when £29.3 million was recorded followed by £33 million in 1982.

Before the full trading results for 1982 could be announced, Sir Keith Showering, who had been knighted in 1981, suddenly died on 23 March 1982 at the age of fifty-one. He had been chairman of Allied Breweries for seven years. A bold innovative thinker, he had played an important part in bringing Lyons into a wider group and making Allied-Lyons one of the largest international food and drinks empires in the world. Without his vision it is likely that Lyons would eventually have gone into receivership or been absorbed by another group or company or survived only in part. After Sir Keith Showering's death Sir Derrick Holden-Brown became chairman and chief executive of Allied-Lyons plc, with Sir Alex Alexander as one of two vice-chairmen.

Under the leadership of Holden-Brown, Allied-Lyons continued to develop and prosper and several modest food-related acquisitions were made. Domestic trade, however, remained sluggish. Embassy Hotels began to suffer not only from a decline in business conference activity but from the effects of reduced summer tourism and bad winter weather in 1983. Lyons Bakery too was affected by bad weather, despite the introduction of new product lines.

By April 1984 the old Cadby Hall factories had been demolished, with only the administration block remaining. Having sold most of the property to developers, Alexander decided to have a new Cadby Hall built on a small, landscaped island site bordered by Blythe Road and Hammersmith Road. Designed by Ove Arup and constructed by Sir Robert McAlpine & Sons, the new five-storey, bow-shaped Cadby Hall building provided 64,000 square feet of office space as well as two sub-levels of underground car parking. Top floors were given over to restaurants where directors kept up their class-dividing tradition of having separate dining facilities. On 14 July 1986 staff moved into the new Cadby Hall and demolition of the old head office began.

In October 1985 the United Kingdom's first highly leveraged buyout – a process in which investors use huge pools of borrowed money to buy giant companies with little of their own cash – occurred when John Elliott, using a little-known Australian company named Elders IXL, launched a £1.8 billion bid for Allied-Lyons plc. It was an unusual bid in every respect. First, the 255p offered in floating loan notes or cash was 23p below the shares' market price. Secondly, shareholders would not be entitled to retain the 3.25p interim dividend already authorised for payment by the board. Thirdly, the IXL company concealed a curious financial ruse. Fourthly, John Elliott had secured £1.23 billion of dubious finance from a consortium of banks led by Citicorp with the intention of dismembering a highly respected international company without any meaningful assurances to employees. Placing a price of £800 million on the Lyons food business alone – which Elliott hoped to break up and sell – he had unsuccessfully tried to bring on board another consortium both to massage his own finance and to give credibility to his proposals. Fortunately for Allied-Lyons, their share price had been consistently higher than 300p and City editors were not impressed with Elders' tactics. Allied-Lyons defended the hostile bid with a spirited press campaign culminating on 6 December 1985 when the Secretary of State for Trade and Industry referred the Elders bid to the Monopolies and Mergers Commission, because of anxiety about Elders' financing. In March 1986 Elders, realising their predatory campaign had failed, disposed of all their shares in Allied-Lyons. Nevertheless the Monopolies and Mergers Commission continued their investigation. Elders IXL were eventually given permission to renew their bid but by 18 September 1986 they had reached agreement with Hanson Trust to acquire the Courage brewery and did not renew their bid for Allied-Lyons. Thus ended an episode that lasted nearly eighteen months and caused a defence cost of £14.3 million to Allied-Lyons, as well as wasting management's time.

Meanwhile an opportunity arose to acquire a substantial stake in the Canadian firm, Hiram Walker-Gooderham & Worts Company, with Gulf Canada Corporation as partners holding the lesser stake of 49 per cent. Hiram Walker Resources Ltd, parent of Hiram Walker-Gooderham & Worts, were themselves taken over by Gulf Canada Corporation on 23 April 1986 and the contract Allied-Lyons had secured – $2.6 billion Canadian – was challenged in the Canadian courts by Gulf Canada's parent, Olympia & York Enterprises Ltd. The resulting litigation turned in Allied-Lyons' favour and in March 1988, following a reorganisation of Gulf Canada Corporation, Allied-Lyons acquired their 49 per cent equity in Hiram Walker for £202 million in cash and £370 million by way of 81 million new cumulative convertible preference shares of 25p. To cement the importance of this merger, Clifford Hatch Jr, a descendant of the Hatch family which was involved in supplying liquor to the American market during prohibition, joined Allied-Lyons as finance director from Hiram Walker in 1987.

Rationalisation within Lyons continued throughout the mid-1980s, by which time the Food Division were contributing 37.3 per cent to total group turnover, which in turn accounted for 24.5 per cent of pre-tax profits, much of it coming from the American businesses. In January 1985 a new tea-packing line was installed at Greenford at the cost of £3 million. In May 1985 Hooimeijer acquired the Dutch company Brink BV, whose annual sales amounted to £8 million, 80 per of which went to export. During this period some modest acquisitions were also made including the Dutch meat snack manufacturer, Tappaz Beheer BV, a frozen gateaux company with the unlikely name of CDL 44 (later changed to Lyons Patisserie Ltd), Tuckfield Teas Pty Ltd in Australia, and Tecribel NV in Belgium, a manufacturer and distributor of rice cakes

throughout western Europe. The principal disposal at this time was the Homburg pig meat business. It had been part of Lyons since 1972 and was sold to a management buyout team headed by two former executives of Homburg, P.M.J. van Loosbroek and G. Mol, for a loss of £15.5 million. The business suffered another blow in 1993 when it went into liquidation and its meat activities were taken over by Bovleco.

In June 1988 Lyons announced it was pulling out from high street catering. The six remaining restaurants were the Southfork at Harrow, Choices in Windsor, the Fisherman's Wharf in Croydon and Baker Street and the Steak Houses at Wimbledon and Dulwich. When the Southfork had opened in 1986 with the theme of the TV soap opera *Dallas*, it had been seen as an indication that Lyons might develop a presence in branded restaurants. Others, however, had regarded it as a strategic withdrawal, allowing the firm to concentrate on contract catering. The subsidiary Town & County Catering had won the catering contract for Gatwick's North Terminal in October 1987 and for Terminal 4 at Heathrow in March 1988. Catering contracts had also been won for the National Railway Museum in York, the Royal Botanical Gardens at Kew and in November 1988 the Theatr Clwyd at Mold in North Wales. Plans were also in hand for diversification into leisure, with contracts for three projects in Portsmouth, Deal and Sheringham. All combined water attractions with extensive bar and catering facilities. In effect the company was returning to the catering activities of its historical past.

The confectionery company Mars decided to enter the ice-cream market in 1990. In the first year Mars claimed at least £75 million of sales, which had been achieved by an intensive advertising campaign, and demonstrated that consumers were prepared to pay premium prices for known brands in whatever guise they came. Lyons Maid was caught between the Mars onslaught and the response of Wall's, which by 1990 had 50 per cent of the ice-cream market, with their Bonanza, Sky and Dream ice-creams undercutting the Mars ice-cream bars by 10 pence. This proved too much for Lyons, which during the twelve months up to March 1990 had made a loss of £2.5 million on sales of £44 million compared to profits in the immediately previous years of approximately £1 million. Lyons Maid still controlled 9 per cent of the ice-cream market, with a strong presence in confectioners across the country, but concentrated in the high-volume, low-margin sector. Lyons Maid was not an international name and the new Allied-Lyons management were eager to expand the Baskin-Robbins business. In February 1992 Lyons Maid Ltd was sold for £12 million to Henry Clarke (Clarke Foods (UK) Ltd), a high-profile American entrepreneur, who immediately embarked on a rapid expansion programme by acquiring three ice-cream factories from Hillsdown Holdings. It is not difficult to understand why Lyons disposed of its ice-cream business. In the last two full years of trading it had made an accumulated loss of £11.5 million on a turnover of £107.5 million (see Appendix 8).

Early in 1989 Sir Alex Alexander announced his retirement, fuelling speculation on the future of the Food Division. Tony Hales – from Ansells Ltd, the Midlands trading company of Allied Breweries – took over as chief executive on 12 June 1989. By mid-year yet another strategic review of the Food Division had recommended that the division concentrate on food-manufacturing and distribution, with special focus on a number of core product sectors where the company could compete internationally. These changes resulted in the closure of the corporate offices in North America and of Cadby Hall itself, which closed on Friday 24 August 1990. Those staff not made redundant were transferred to Greenford, where the offices had been refurbished.

With hindsight, business historians might argue that the sectoring of the Food Division made it easier for disposal. As events turned out, this is roughly what happened, although by the 1990s a recession had set in and disposal took longer than anticipated. Perhaps another subtle indicator that the Food Division's days were numbered was the exclusion of any reference to Lyons by the chairman in his statement to shareholders in the 1989 report and accounts.

In the period before Lyons became part of Allied Breweries, management dealt on the foreign exchange markets to hedge currency exposure, with any profits treated as a bonus. Utilising computer technology the treasury department became able to forecast, with some moderate reliability, when the exchange rates might alter and were thus able to buy or sell currency on the best terms. These systems transferred to Allied in 1979 and in common with other international groups they continued to speculate in foreign currency. In a news release of May 1991 Sir Derrick Holden-Brown claimed that profits of £10 million per annum were made from these activities. From June 1989 the treasury department diversified into trading in foreign currency options in the volatile derivatives market – a high-risk activity. The scale of trading, notably in put-options, grew substantially during 1990 and became increasingly disproportionate to foreign currency cash-flow requirements. As one journalist wrote, 'The billion pound positions taken by Allied had nothing to do with prudent hedging and everything to do with speculation.' The group finance director, Clifford Hatch, received warnings from external and internal sources that exposure limits had been breached and he attempted to trade out of these during February 1991 with minimum cost. This failed, and the resulting unbalanced exposures at a time when the US dollar was rapidly strengthening gave rise to substantial losses of £147 million, representing nearly 20 per cent of the trading profit in 1992, the year in which the loss was taken. It was believed at the time to have been the largest loss of its kind in British corporate history and prompted a fall of 25p in the company's share price.

Holden-Brown, who had been alerted to the situation in the summer of 1990, had instructed National Westminster Bank to take action to close out the positions on 14 March 1991, when exposure stood at £1.5 billion, three times its limit, but the strengthening dollar had moved against the positions before action could be taken and added a further £40 million to the £100 million loss already suffered. National Westminster Bank's prompt action saved the company from even further losses as the dollar continued in an upward direction for some time thereafter and were absolved from any blame. It was axiomatic that Allied-Lyons' treasury management were dealing in foreign currency instruments in which they lacked expertise, and their scale of trading was excessive. Clifford Hatch, who had been appointed finance director of Allied-Lyons in 1986 after the acquisition of Hiram Walker, where he had been president and chief executive, accepted departmental responsibility for the débâcle and resigned on 28 June 1991. The disastrous excursion into foreign trading also claimed the early retirements of Sir Derrick Holden-Brown and Richard Martin, both of whom had previously been regarded in the City as cautious.

Michael Jackaman succeeded Holden-Brown as chairman of Allied-Lyons, with Tony Hales as chief executive. Between 1991 and 1992 the trading performance of Lyons remained buoyant. Trading profits increased by 35 per cent, with impressive growth from Tetley, Baskin-Robbins and Dunkin' Donuts. The round tea-bag had captured 30 per cent of the Canadian market, and in the Republic of Ireland and Northern Ireland, where Lyons had over 55 per cent of the total package tea market with their famous Green Label blend, they did particularly well – according to the International Tea Trade Statistics, the Republic of Ireland has the highest tea consumption per capita in the world.

During the early 1990s recession the United Kingdom, United States, Canada and Australia became increasingly difficult markets as a result of price competition. The group's strategy focused on the higher-growth economies, in particular Mexico and the Pacific Rim countries. Some seed-corn investment was made in eastern Europe (Tetley set up a tea factory in Budapest and Margetts a joint fruit-processing venture in Poland) and in China as long-term prospects.

In 1992 Allied-Lyons sold its Harvey's brandy and distribution interests in Spain to Pedro Domecq SA in exchange for cash and additional shares in Domecq. In March 1994 Allied-Lyons created the world's second largest spirits company in a bold move to acquire the whole Pedro Domecq group, a Spanish sherry and spirits

business founded around 1730. Allied-Lyons had owned 32 per cent of Domecq prior to acquisition, 5 per cent directly and 27 per cent indirectly through its 50 per cent Hiram Walker Europa joint venture, which owned 54 per cent of Domecq. The £739 million payable for the business was made up by: £283 million for the share capital of Domecq not already owned by Hiram Walker Europa; £74 million for the minority shareholding in Destilerias y Crianza del Whisky SA; £102 million for the minority shareholders in Pedro Domecq Mexico SA de CV, Domecq Importers Inc. and Tequila Sauza SA de CV; and £280 million for the 27 per cent minority holdings of the Mora-Figueroa family owned through its holding in Hiram Walker Europa on the exercise of a put-option granted by Allied-Lyons. This consideration was to be reduced by the amount of any dividends paid in respect of the 27 per cent holding prior to the exercise of the put-option. The put-option remained exerciseable at any time up to 18 May 2000.

Shares in Hiram Walker Europa were held in a new company, Spain Alecq BV. Unless and until the put-option had been exercised, Allied-Lyons owned 73 per cent of Spain Alecq and therefore had control of the Domecq group. Exercise of the put-option gave 100 per cent ownership to Allied-Lyons. In addition to the £739 million consideration, Allied-Lyons assumed the net debt of the Domecq group and Hiram Walker Europa. At 31 January 1994 this amounted to £191 million. The Domecq and Hiram Walker companies remained organisationally distinct but there was close commercial co-operation.

The Domecq deal came about when a minority group of the Mora-Figueroa family shareholders indicated a desire to sell out, while the majority of the family wished to remain in charge of the business. Pedro Domecq is one of the oldest-established sherry companies in Jerez and had been bought by the present family in 1816. Since then the business had expanded into Latin America, with an exceptionally strong presence in Mexico, where it was the largest spirits producer owning the second largest tequila distillery. Its Presidente brandy is claimed to be the world's best-selling brandy.

The purchase of Domecq confirmed to all that the group were now embarked on reshaping the business – away from food manufacture and distribution (and from the brewing of beer) towards its core spirits and retailing businesses (Baskin-Robbins and Dunkin' Donuts ice-cream and donut franchises in the case of Lyons). All the food-manufacturing operations were earmarked for sale. The Lyons name disappeared from the group's title on 19 September 1994 when it became known as Allied Domecq plc. In a *Times* advertisement Michael Jackaman reported:

> Allied Domecq is now a truly international business with an impressive range of premium brands and an attitude to its customers which places enjoyment high on the agenda. Under this new banner we will increase our strategic emphasis in international spirits and wine and seek further development opportunities internationally in our retailing and franchising businesses.

There followed a hasty disposal programme of the Lyons food businesses (the coffee business had already gone in February 1994 and ice-cream in 1992) as the drinks sector suffered from the recession and the economy of Mexico collapsed. Shares plunged in November 1994 after lacklustre interim figures emphasised the difficulties in the international drinks market. Turnover and operating profit remained flat, rising by just £4 million over the comparative 28-week period of the previous year. Michael Jackaman described the circumstances as 'short-term turbulence' in the Mexican market, with volumes down by 5 per cent. The shares fell by 19.5p to 555.5p and in December fell by a further 8p to 544p amid stockholders' fears concerning the worsening financial crisis in Mexico. This crisis had also affected the private company of Ramon Mora-Figueroa (an Allied Domecq board member since September 1994), a dominant shareholder (27 per cent) of Spain Alecq and £280 million of put-options. The decision to sell had come just six months after the Allied Domecq business was formed and the reasons given for exercising now were reported to be personal. Purchase of the Mora-Figueroa family's shareholding was financed by borrowings raising the company's gearing substantially from 70 to 80 per cent.

As the sale of food businesses continued, in November 1994 Allied Domecq received an unexpectedly higher offer for its food ingredients business (DCA), which was mostly American-based but included Margetts Foods, the fruit flavour and products maker based in the United Kingdom. Kerry group, an Irish dairy combine, emerged to pay £402 million in cash and thereby thwarted Dalgety's offer, which was some £20 million less. Lyons Seafoods (a Wiltshire-based company bought in 1985 and formally known as Flying Goose Ltd), which dominated the market for own-brand frozen prawns, with sales of £55 million per year, sold for just over £20 million to a management buyout team in December 1994. Lyons Biscuits (Symbol Biscuits) was sold in December 1994 to Hillsdown Holdings for an undisclosed sum, believed to be worth £20 million. Based in Blackpool, its main business was in own-name labels; Maryland Cookies was its brand leader. In April 1995 Lyons Cakes went to Manor Bakeries, a subsidiary of the Tomkins group. Manor Bakeries had already acquired Mr Kipling and Cadbury Cakes as part of the RHM deal in 1992 and now for only £35 million added one of the most famous names in cakes to its portfolio.

Uncertainties over the Mexican market continued into 1995 and shares continued to lose ground. A profits warning came in March 1995, then another in July 1995, when Michael Jackaman painted a gloomy picture of the international drinks and retailing prospects in the short term:

> The necessary reshaping to reach our objective of concentrating on those parts of the business where we are, or can become, world leaders, will result in some short-term cost which will for a time overshadow continued sound performance in our mainstream businesses.
>
> … Our food disposals will dilute earnings until we can reinvest the proceeds in our

mainstream businesses. Our remaining food businesses are trading in very competitive markets.

The previous week Allied had disposed of its last significant food business, Lyons Tetley, for a reported sum of £190 million to a management buyout team. After renaming the company Tetley (GB) Ltd, the new owners subsequently sold it on, in March 2000, to the Indian conglomerate, Tata, who reportedly paid £271 million for the business.

The disposal of the tea business marked the end of the Lyons empire, although one or two other European subsidiaries took longer to sell. It is impossible to say precisely on what date the empire ceased to exist; there was no lowering of flags or firing of guns. Why it ended in the way it did is difficult to comprehend. When Keith Showering bought Lyons in 1978 it was his intention to bring good management and financial discipline to the struggling food business. In just three years Lyons achieved a fivefold increase in profits, confirming his expectations. It must also be remembered that Allied Breweries had largely depended on its beer sales from a home market and the acquisition of Lyons had the effect of catapulting it into a global company. Keith Showering's death on 23 March 1982 shocked everyone and senior management were unprepared for the rapid change in stewardship which his death created. Nevertheless, under the management of Sir Derrick Holden-Brown and Sir Alex Alexander, for several years the enlarged company continued to make headway in three main business areas: Beer Division; Wines Spirits and Soft Drinks Division; and the Food Division. After Alexander's retirement in 1989, however, less interest was shown in the Lyons companies and in 1994, after the acquisition of Pedro Domecq, senior management began an investment programme centred on spirits and retailing. This was said to be 'a more logical and profitable response to the trading environment of the 1980s and 1990s'. By now several enterprises had been given purchasing rights to use the Lyons name and so began the asset-stripping of Lyons to help fund the purchase of spirits-based companies. One by one the old-established food brands were sold to pay for the expansion into spirits and retailing. Thus in 1995, when the process of selling Lyons' subsidiaries was virtually complete, the chairman, Michael Jackaman, informed shareholders that: 'We aim to be the world's leading spirits marketer by the ownership of standard and premium brands, and the breadth of our regional and category coverage. We aim to be a world-beating retailer as measured by the quality and success of our offerings, in pubs and off-licences in Great Britain and in franchised ice cream and donut stores world-wide.'

Five years on from this confident statement one has to ask whether the decision to realign the business towards spirits and retailing was sound. Since then shares have under-performed – they fell by a third between 1998 and 1999 – provoking angry outbursts from investors and City analysts. Some drinks brands have been sold and the pub retailing business was bought by Punch Taverns and Bass in September 1999. As we enter a new millennium, Allied Domecq plc has become no more than a spirits company, a mere shell of its previous existence. This is a tragic and sadly ignominious end to the Lyons empire – an empire founded in a spirit of enterprise, showmanship and courage during the closing years of the nineteenth century. Now deprived of the jewels in their crown, and pushed out of the *Financial Times*-Stock Exchange Index of the 100 biggest stocks, many speculate that Allied Domecq plc will not survive as an independent firm much beyond the year 2000, unless they acquire, or merge with, another spirits business.

APPENDICES

Appendix 1: Teashop Waitress Pay Scales 11 November 1895

Total Number of Waitresses Employed in Teashop	Number of Waitresses in Teashop paid 15s.	Number of Waitresses in Teashop paid 12s. 6d.	Number of Waitresses in Teashop paid 10s.
6	1	2	3
7	1	2	4
8	1	3	4
9	1	3	5
10	1	4	5
11	1	5	5
12	2	5	5
13	2	5	6
14	2	6	6
15	2	6	7
16	2	7	7
17	2	7	8
18	2	8	8
19	2	8	9
20	2	9	9
21	2	9	10
22	2	10	10
23	2	10	11

Meals: No dinner will be provided but all other meals will be served as usual.

Source: J. Lyons & Co. Ltd.

Appendix 2: Factory Output Statistics for Tea, Coffee, Cocoa and Drinking Chocolate

Year	Tea (tons)	Coffee (tons)	Cocoa (tons)	Chocolate (tons)
1903	279.48	117.25	-	-
1904	539.34	140.72	-	-
1905	1,095.34	182.28	-	-
1906	2,090.86	214.97	-	-
1907	3,133.67	258.38	-	-
1908	4,466.98	308.59	-	-
1909	6,437.15	332.05	98.89	12.98
1910	8,257.19	390.01	353.59	33.58
1911	10,086.09	550.97	489.58	45.44
1912	11,276.04	460.15	784.29	38.07
1913	13,159.07	494.45	871.38	32.34
1914	13,926.37	557.37	958.41	35.90
1915	13,632.94	581.35	1,047.38	40.34
1916	10,553.87	507.96	1,082.92	38.96
1917	8,643.21	533.01	1,065.15	25.06
1918	8,858.66	708.59	1,462.24	-
1919	14,118.60	659.86	1,161.05	-
1920	15,174.37	687.66	697.48	-
1921	16,650.28	701.62	642.61	-
1922	17,482.55	782.29	-	-
1923	20,043.65	948.27	-	-
1924	22,572.91	-	-	-

General Notes:
The Greenford tea factory opened on 18 July 1921.
The Cadby Hall tea factory closed on 21 October 1921.
Cocoa and drinking chocolate manufacture moved from Cadby Hall to Clerkenwell in 1910–1 and thence to Greenford in March 1922.
Cocoa sales out-performed coffee between 1912–20.

Source: J. Lyons & Co. Ltd. Production Statistics.

Appendix 3: London Hotels – Gross Income, Net Profit & Dividend Payments 1914–1919

Hotel Company	*1913–1914* Gross Income £	Net Profit £	*1917–1918* Gross Income £	Net Profit £	*1918–1919* Gross Income £	Net Profit £
Burlington Hotels	44,285	1,750	47,962	10,212	61,145	14,092
Carlton Hotel	75,797	35,441	61,785	26,083	76,390	97,410
Frederick Hotels	339,549	31,906	107,604	67,368	119,640	79,380
Gordon Hotels	161,665	81,890	107,110	26,533	174,543	94,576
Holborn & Frascati	171,068	39,348	134,974	22,361	192,055	47,690
Hotel Cecil	237,595	39,881	123,369	64,715	63,121	37,598
Piccadilly Hotel	246,492	22,220	357,068	38,416	459,339	33,521
Romano's	23,460	5,065	24,436	8,942	35,108	14,953
Savoy Hotel	182,891	42,239	178,057	108,041	201,116	131,276
Smedley's Hydro	50,938	10,072	69,495	10,559	74,786	9,199
Strand Hotel	69,507	28,376	111,787	64,527	121,405	68,544
Waldorf Hotel	36,512	17,165	45,892	19,642	56,551	23,273

Percentage Dividends for Years

Hotel Company	*1910-11*	*1911-12*	*1912-13*	*1913-14*	*1914-15*	*1915-16*	*1916-17*	*1917-18*	*1918-19*
Burlington Hotels	nil	nil	nil	nil	nil	nil	nil	nil	nil
Carlton Hotel	7	7	8	6	nil	nil	nil	nil	nil
Frederick Hotels	nil	nil	2½	nil	nil	nil	nil	nil	nil
Gordon Hotels	3	2	3	3	nil	nil	nil	nil	nil
Holborn & Frascati	10	10	11	11	8	2½	2½	8	11
Hotel Cecil	5	3	5	7	nil	1	nil	9	5
Piccadilly Hotel	-	-	193	50	25	75	133	150	150
Romano's	10	10	10	5	nil	5	6	7½	7½
Savoy Hotel	5	5	5	5	nil	nil	nil	nil	nil
Smedley's Hydro	12½	17½	15	12½	17½	12½	12½	17½	12½
Strand Hotel pref ord	9	9	9	9	9	9	9	9	10
Waldorf Hotel	6	6	6	6	3	nil	nil	nil	6

Source: *The Caterer and Hotel Keepers' Gazette.* January 1920

Appendix 4: Teashops and Other Restaurants of J. Lyons & Co. Ltd

This list identifies all teashops, which were opened between 1894–1969; secondary restaurant uses (Steak Houses etc.) after teashop permanent closure have been ignored. Some teashops only opened for a short period of time probably because they were badly sited or too small. Many closed for modernisation or street improvements and reopened. In these circumstances the period of closure has been ignored if the teashop code remained the same on reopening. During the Second World War many London teashops closed due to bomb damage or food shortages. Some were commandeered by the government and used as forces post offices where mail was censored. For security reasons precise wartime closing dates were never published. Some teashops occupied corner sites and were thus confusingly known under two different addresses. Where these are known the lesser address is shown in brackets after the main address. Additional teashop notes following the main listings.

Date Opened	Date Closed	Teashop Code	Address
Sep. 1894	Sep. 1976	A	213 Piccadilly, London.
Oct. 1894	Nov. 1938	B	17 Queen Victoria Street, London.
Nov. 1894	Sep. 1901	C	76a Chancery Lane, London. (see TT 1901)
Jan. 1895	Jun. 1974	D	5 Ludgate Circus (Bride Lane), London.
Feb. 1895	Jun. 1975	E	152 Bishopsgate, London.
Mar. 1895	Dec. 1940	F	19-20 Cannon Street, London.
Mar. 1895	Dec. 1940	G	68 Aldersgate Street, London.
Mar. 1895	Sep. 1905	H	14 Great Chapel Street, London.
Apr. 1895	Dec. 1940	I	54 Fore Street, London.
May 1895	May 1895	J	31 Fenchurch Street, London. (see S3 1903 & Q9 1928)
May 1895	1943	K	154 Strand, London.
May 1895	Oct. 1915	L	23 Cheapside, London.
Jun. 1895	Feb. 1933	M	73 Gracechurch Street, London.
Jul. 1895	Dec. 1940	N	58-60 Pasternoster Row (61 St Paul's Churchyard), London.
Sep. 1895	1913	O	168 Regent Street, London.
Mar. 1896	Sep. 1968	P	185 Oxford Street, London.
Feb. 1898	Mar. 1918	Q	23 Lime Street, London.
Feb. 1898	Jul. 1935	R	47 Oxford Street, London.
May 1898	Apr. 1916	S	17 Telegraph Street, London.
May 1898	1943	T	3 Westbourne Grove, London.
May 1898	Mar. 1972	U	52 Old Broad Street (Wormwood Street), London.
Jul. 1898	Nov. 1918	V	7 Ludgate Broadway, London.
Sep. 1898	May 1925	W	21 Ludgate Hill, London.
Sep. 1898	May 1919	X	29 & 30 Basinghall Street, London.
Apr. 1899	Mar. 1974	Y	46 Gresham Street, London.
May 1899	Aug. 1972	Z	290 Pentonville Road, London.
Jun. 1899	Mar. 1904	AA	21 Borough High Street, London.
Jul. 1899	Dec. 1912	BB	50 King William Street, London.
Oct. 1899	Aug. 1928	CC	33 & 34 Bow Street, London.
Nov. 1899	1939	DD	51 Brompton Road, London.
Feb. 1900	Dec. 1975	EE	123 Tottenham Court Road, London.
Mar. 1900	Aug. 1929	FF	92 Victoria Street, London.
Apr. 1900	Dec. 1935	PA	45 High Street, Sheffield. *
May 1900	1939	GG	75 Bishopsgate, London.
Jul. 1900	1955	HH	35 Strand, London. (Rebuilt as B11).
Oct. 1900	1950	II	490 Brixton Road, London.
Oct. 1900	Nov. 1963	JJ	61 Fleet Street, London.
Jan. 1901	May 1931	KK	266 (later 274) Edgware Road, London.
Feb. 1901	Feb. 1969	LL	11 Borough High Street, London.
Mar. 1901	Dec. 1928	MM	Crown Court, Old Broad Street, London.
Mar. 1901	Dec. 1940	NN	4 Walbrook, London.
Mar. 1901	1940	OO	254 Upper Street, London.
Mar. 1901	Jan. 1973	PP	3 George Street, Croydon. (Round Trip from July 1972)
Jun. 1901	1940	QQ	159 Newington Causeway, London.

Jul. 1901	Feb. 1937	RR	123 High Holborn, London.
Aug. 1901	Jan. 1925	SS	31 Poultry, London.
Sep. 1901	Sep. 1965	TT	88 Chancery Lane, London.
Oct. 1901	May 1969	UU	244 Great Portland Street, London.
Nov. 1901	Feb. 1922	VV	8 City Road, London.
Nov. 1901	Jul. 1932	WW	121 Kensington High Street, London.
Nov. 1901	Feb. 1973	XX	474 Oxford Street, London.
Dec. 1901	Feb. 1929	YY	143 Queen Victoria Street, London.
Jan. 1902	Dec. 1922	ZZ	25 Wood Street, London.
Jan. 1902	May 1933	A3	193 Aldersgate Street, London.
Jan. 1902	Oct. 1936	B3	31 Leicester Square, London.
Mar. 1902	Aug. 1915	C3	173 Fleet Street, London.
Mar. 1902	Mar. 1911	D3	25 Cockspur Street, London.
Mar. 1902	Jan. 1929	E3	35 Bucklesbury, London.
Apr. 1902	Jan. 1941	F3	112 Moorgate (Finsbury Pavement Hse), London.
May 1902	May 1919	G3	49 St. Mary Axe, London.
May 1902	Oct. 1915	H3	4 Honey Lane Market, London.
May 1902	Dec. 1969	I3	101 Finsbury Pavement, London.
May 1902	Feb. 1930	PB	87 Lord Street, Liverpool. *
Jul. 1902	Mar. 1969	J3	35 Eastcheap, London.
Aug. 1902	Dec. 1936	K3	87 Newgate Street, London.
Dec. 1902	Mar. 1963	L3	97-99 City Road, London.
Dec. 1902	Apr. 1937	M3	10 Queen Street, London.
Jan. 1903	May 1937	N3	53 Parliament Street, London.
Feb. 1903	1913	O3	34 King William Street, London.
Feb. 1903	Dec. 1940	P3	17 Fore Street, London.
Mar. 1903	1940	Q3	150 Southampton Row, London.
Mar. 1903	Mar. 1966	R3	23 Fleet Street, London.
Mar. 1903	Dec. 1972	S3	4 Railway Place, Fenchurch Street, London.
Apr. 1903	Nov. 1923	T3	14 Holborn Viaduct, London.
May 1903	May 1964	PC	14 Cook Street, Liverpool. *
Jun. 1903	Jun. 1936	U3	114 Charing Cross Road, London.
Jul. 1903	Jan. 1920	V3	61 King William Street, London.
Aug. 1903	Feb. 1975	W3	147 Holborn, London.
Oct. 1903	1940	X3	51-52 Carey Street, London.
Oct. 1903	1953?	Y3	Cadby Hall, Hammersmith Road, London.
Oct. 1903	Mar. 1967	Z3	11 Whitehall, London.
Oct. 1903	Dec. 1960	PD	53 London Road, Liverpool. *
Nov. 1903	Apr. 1927	A4	13 New Bridge Street, London.
Oct. 1903	Jul. 1938	PE	County Arcade, Leeds. (Originally Arcade Café)
Jan. 1904	Dec. 1940	B4	9 Jewin Street, London.
Jan. 1904	Jan. 1930	C4	106 Oxford Street, London.
Feb. 1904	Dec. 1966	D4	277-279 Oxford Street, London.
Feb. 1904	Jul. 1929	E4	445 Strand, London.
Mar. 1904	Jul. 1920	F4	Eldon Buildings, Eldon Street, London.
Mar. 1904	Jun. 1939	G4	9 Lower Regent Street, London.
Mar. 1904	Jun. 1932	H4	230 High Holborn, London.
May 1904	Dec. 1962	I4	94 Oxford Street (Newman Street), London.
Sep. 1904	Mar. 1976	J4	30 St Martin's Lane (William IV Street), London.
Nov. 1904	1940	K4	Baltic Street, London.
Oct. 1904	Nov. 1938	L4	74 Great Tower Street, London.
Oct. 1904	Dec. 1964	PF	35 Market Street, Manchester. *
Jan. 1906	Jul. 1928	M4	396 Strand, London.
Jan. 1906	Feb. 1967	N4	85 Victoria Street, London.
Apr. 1906	Jan. 1969	O4	7 Brompton Road, London.
Aug. 1906	Jul. 1940	P4	215 Brompton Road, London.
Aug. 1906	1913	Q4	64 Leadenhall Street. London.
Aug. 1906	Jun. 1929	PG	44 Deansgate, Manchester. *
Sep. 1906	Mar. 1964	PH	77 Piccadilly, Manchester. *
Oct. 1906	Nov. 1965	R4	396 Strand (Adelphi), London.
Oct. 1906	1946	S4	96 Hatton Garden. London.
Oct. 1906	Apr. 1965	PI	1 Princes Street, Manchester. *

Nov. 1906	Jun. 1975	T4	124 Victoria Street, London.
Dec. 1906	Mar. 1935	U4	80 St. Paul's Churchyard, London.
Dec. 1906	Feb. 1967	V4	375 Oxford Street, London.
Jan. 1907	May 1975	W4	Hammersmith Broadway, London.
Jan. 1907	Dec. 1966	X4	321 Oxford Street, London.
Jan. 1907	1940	Y4	4-6 Theobalds Road, London.
Mar. 1907	Feb. 1929	Z4	51 Gracechurch Street, London.
May 1907	Mar. 1928	PM	57 Market Street, Bradford. *
Mar. 1907	Jul. 1934	PK	74 Mosely Street, Manchester. *
Mar. 1907	Mar. 1928	PL	2 Pinstone Street, Sheffield. *
Jun. 1907	Dec. 1940	A5	Blackfriars Station, London.
Jul. 1907	1939	B5	2 Newgate Street, London.
Aug. 1907	Aug. 1969	C5	10-12 Copthall Avenue, London.
Oct. 1907	1939	PN	74 Market Street, Manchester. *
Oct. 1907	Apr. 1975	D5	47 London Wall, London.
Oct. 1907	Aug. 1915	E5	70 Westbourne Grove, London.
Oct. 1907	May 1975	F5	215 Oxford Street, London.
Nov. 1907	Jul. 1967	G5	316 High Holborn, London.
Nov. 1907	Sep. 1975	H5	47 George Street, Richmond.
Dec. 1907	Sep. 1968	I5	54 Uxbridge Road, London.
Jan. 1908	Sep. 1966	PO	24 Bond Street, Leeds. *
Feb. 1908	May 1941	J5	10-12 Ludgate Hill (Ave Maria Lane), London.
Mar. 1908	Jan. 1969	K5	128 Cheapside, London.
Mar. 1908	May 1924	L5	99 Powis Street, London.
Mar. 1908	Jan. 1967	M5	6 Leadenhall Street, London.
May 1908	1955	N5	24 Leadenhall Street, London.
Jun. 1908	Aug. 1940	O5	80-81 Mark Lane (14 London Street), London.
Jul. 1908	Mar. 1967	P5	124 New Bond Street, London.
Jul. 1908	Dec. 1975	Q5	Westminster Bridge Station, London.
Jul. 1908	Mar. 1967	R5	287 Whitechapel Road, London.
Jul. 1908	May 1963	PQ	City Buildings, Old Hall Street, Liverpool. *
Sep. 1908	1950	S5	24 Aldgate (Station), London.
Oct. 1908	1939	T5	57a West Smithfield, London.
Jan. 1909	Mar. 1930	U5	558 Oxford Street (Marble Arch), London.
Feb. 1909	Jan. 1975	V5	26 Rye Lane, London.
Mar. 1909	Feb. 1975	W5	134 Gloucester Road (Station), London.
Mar. 1909	Oct. 1936	X5	9 Redcross Street, London.
Jun. 1909	Oct. 1922	Y5	74 Ludgate Hill, London.
Jul. 1909	Mar. 1926	Z5	29 Charing Cross Road, London.
Aug. 1909	Aug. 1920	A6	3 Eastcheap, London.
Sep. 1909	Jul. 1962	B6	29 St. James's Street (27 Bury Street), London.
Sep. 1909	Feb. 1936	C6	376 Holloway Road, London.
Oct. 1909	Jun. 1940	D6	102 Euston Road, London.
Nov. 1909	Jan. 1934	E6	99 Cannon Street, London.
Nov. 1909	Jul. 1933	PR	25 Old Haymarket, Liverpool.
Dec. 1909	Jan. 1969	F6	182-184 Clapham High Street, London.
Dec. 1909	Jul. 1966	G6	44 Cannon Street, London.
Jan. 1910	Feb. 1931	H6	450 Strand, London.
Feb. 1910	1910	PS	Lord Street, Southport.
Feb. 1910	Feb. 1960	I6	37 Moorgate Street, London.
Mar. 1910	Jul. 1939	J6	287 High Holborn, London.
Mar. 1910	Jan. 1966	K6	48 Kilburn High Road, London.
Apr. 1910	Aug. 1927	PT	53 New Street, Birmingham.
May 1910	Jun. 1940	L6	49 Cheapside, London.
May 1910	Sep. 1959	M6	258-262 Westminster Bridge Road, London.
May 1910	1941	N6	211 Shoreditch High Street, London.
May 1910	Dec. 1964	O6	49a Lincoln's Inn Fields, London.
Jun. 1910	Sep. 1937	PU	34 Long Row, Nottingham.
Jun. 1910	Aug. 1975	P6	24 St. John's Road, London.
Jul. 1910	1956	Q6	8 Charterhouse Buildings, Goswell Road, London.
Jul. 1910	1939	R6	7 Blackfriars Road, London.
Jul. 1910	Aug. 1965	PV	51 Lime Street, Liverpool.

Jul. 1910	Jan. 1975	S6	Mark Lane Station (now Tower Hill), London.
Jul. 1910	Nov. 1937	T6	49 Cannon Street, London.
Aug. 1910	Jun. 1960	U6	Walham Green Station (now Fulham Broadway), London.
Aug. 1910	Aug. 1966	V6	161-3 Bishopsgate, London.
Sep. 1910	Mar. 1976	W6	202 Streatham High Road, London.
Sep. 1910	Mar. 1967	X6	88 Notting Hill Gate (4 Pembridge Road), London.
Oct. 1910	Dec. 1975	Y6	253 Kensington High Street, London.
Nov. 1910	Sep. 1975	SA	14 North Street, Brighton.
Dec. 1910	1940	Z6	37 Piccadilly, London.
Jan. 1911	Nov. 1972	A7	101 Putney High Street, London. (Round Trip from June)
Feb. 1911	May 1972	SB	72 Western Road, Brighton.
Feb. 1911	Nov. 1936	B7	8-10 Broadway, Stratford, London.
Feb. 1911	Sep. 1974	C7	88-90 North End, Croydon.
Mar. 1911	Dec. 1928	PW	59 Church Street, Liverpool.
Mar. 1911	Oct. 1968	D7	143 Strand, London.
Apr. 1911	Jul. 1926	PX	2 New Street, Birmingham.
May 1911	Nov. 1940	SC	45 Wine Street, Bristol.
May 1911	Jan. 1975	SD	140 Terminus Road, Eastbourne.
Jun. 1911	Jun. 1958	PY	74 Bull Street, Birmingham.
Jul. 1911	Sep. 1967	E7	32-33 & 40 Ealing Broadway, London.
Sep. 1911	Jun. 1963	F7	10 Westminster Broadway, London.
Oct. 1911	Dec. 1961	PZ	36 Oxford Street, Manchester.
Feb. 1912	Aug. 1970	G7	175 Camden High Street, London.
Sep. 1912	Jun. 1975	H7	62-64 Lewisham High Street, London.
Jul. 1913	Feb. 1976	I7	10 Oxford Street, London.
Nov. 1913	1950	J7	51 King William Street, London.
Apr. 1914	Jun. 1937	K7	53 Deptford Broadway, London.
May 1914	Feb. 1969	L7	Praed Street Station, London.
Jun. 1914	Mar. 1975	M7	3 Wimbledon Hill Road, London.
Feb. 1915	Apr. 1938	N7	23 Thames Street, Kingston-on-Thames.
Aug. 1915	1950	O7	359 Mare Street, London.
Aug. 1915	Jan. 1970	SE	7-8 Victoria Square, Birmingham.
Jan. 1916	Dec. 1971	P7	100 Wood Green High Road, London.
Jan. 1920	May 1941	SF	10 James Street, Liverpool.
Jun. 1921	Dec. 1965	Q7	133 Rye Lane, London.
Aug. 1921	Jul. 1969	R7	114d High Street, Watford.
Sep. 1921	1955	S7	150 Balham High Road, London.
Dec. 1921	May 1933	T7	265 Finchley Road, London.
Jan. 1922	Jan. 1966	U7	45 Harlesden High Street, London.
Mar. 1922	Feb. 1967	V7	147a Stoke Newington High Street, London.
Oct. 1922	Dec. 1967	W7	268 Seven Sisters Road (11 Rock Street), London.
Nov. 1922	Feb. 1939	X7	26 High Holborn, London.
Jan. 1923	1941	SG	17 Colemore Row, Birmingham.
Jan. 1923	Mar. 1976	Y7	18 Buckingham Palace Rd (Victoria St), London.
Jan. 1923	Aug. 1962	Z7	4 Princes Parade, Muswell Hill, London.
Feb. 1923	Sep. 1968	A8	254 Green Lanes, London.
Mar. 1923	Jul. 1966	B8	21-22 Camberwell Green, London.
Mar. 1923	Dec. 1971	C8	506-508 Brixton Road, London.
Mar. 1923	Dec. 1972	D8	76 High Street, Sutton.
Mar. 1923	May 1967	E8	361 Station Road, Harrow, London.
May 1923	May 1975	F8	300 Regent Street, London.
May 1923	1942	G8	299 Kentish Town Road, London.
Jun. 1923	Jan. 1963	H8	161 Cricklewood Broadway, London.
Jun. 1923	Aug. 1972	I8	342 Chiswick High Road, London.
Jun. 1923	Aug. 1973	J8	118-120 Acton High Street, London.
Aug. 1923	Nov. 1974	K8	20 Powis Street, London.

Sep.	1923	Feb.	1975	L8	61-63 Tooting High Street, London.
Oct.	1923		1939	M8	295 Euston Road, London.
Nov.	1923	Jan.	1975	SH	51-52 North Street, Brighton.
Nov.	1923	Sep.	1928	SI	101 Bull Street, Birmingham.
Dec.	1923	Oct.	1968	SJ	15-16 Queen's Square, Wolverhampton.
Dec.	1923	Aug.	1962	N8	1 Crouch End Broadway, London.
Dec.	1923	Feb.	1962	O8	486 Harrow Road, London.
Jan.	1924	Mar.	1975	P8	28-30 Sloane Square, London.
Apr.	1924	Nov.	1940	SK	4a Castle Street, Bristol.
Jun.	1924	Nov.	1926	SL	41 Temple Street, Birmingham.
Jun.	1924	Jan.	1963	Q8	226 East Ham High Street, London.
Aug.	1924	Mar.	1970	R8	158-160 High Street, Bromley.
Sep.	1924	Jan.	1973	S8	7 High Street, St. Albans.
Sep.	1924	Jun.	1966	SM	36 Oldham Street (Hilton Street), Manchester.
Sep.	1924		1958	T8	810 Holloway Road, London.
Oct.	1924	May	1967	U8	38 King Street, Hammersmith, London.
Oct.	1924	Aug.	1938	SN	223 High Street, West Bromwich.
Dec.	1924	Nov.	1940	SO	5 Wine Street, Bristol.
Mar.	1925		1939	V8	346 Walworth Road, London.
Mar.	1925	May	1975	W8	167 Ilford High Road, London.
Apr.	1925	Aug.	1957	SP	45-46 Briggate, Leeds. *
Jun.	1925	Dec.	1940	X8	21-23 Farringdon Road, London.
Jul.	1925	Aug.	1973	Y8	8 Stratford Broadway, London.
Oct.	1925	May	1975	Z8	258-260 Hoe Street, London.
Oct.	1925	Aug.	1969	A9	33-37 North End, Croydon.
Dec.	1925		1958	B9	25-27 Woodgrange Road, London.
Feb.	1926		1956	C9	299 East India Dock Road, London.
Apr.	1926	Jun.	1940	D9	36-38 New Oxford Street, London.
Jun.	1926	Feb.	1960	E9	31 Beak Street, London.
Jun.	1926	Jan.	1975	SQ	16 Marine Drive (42 High Street), Margate.
Jul.	1926		1941	SR	6 New Street, Birmingham.
Sep.	1926	Dec.	1972	F9	Aldgate Station, London.
Sep.	1926	Jul.	1962	G9	52 Baker Street, London.
Dec.	1926	Jun.	1962	H9	83-84 Long Acre, London.
Jan.	1927	Aug.	1966	I9	86 West Ealing Broadway, London.
Feb.	1927	Jun.	1960	J9	315 Commercial Road, London.
Feb.	1927		1941	ST	164 Commercial Road, Portsmouth.
Mar.	1927	Jul.	1966	K9	119 Kingsway, London.
Mar.	1927	Dec.	1975	SU	19 Above Bar, Southampton, Hants.
Apr.	1927	May	1974	SV	19 Broadgate, Coventry.
May	1927	Sep.	1962	SW	38 Harbour Street, Ramsgate.
Jun.	1927	Aug.	1963	L9	56-58 Wardour Street, London.
Jul.	1927	Aug.	1975	M9	Empire House, St.Martin-le-Grand, London.
Jul.	1927	Sep.	1963	N9	42 Poultry (Old Jewry), London.
Jul.	1927	Feb.	1975	SX	96 Maidstone High Street, Kent.
Aug.	1927	Jan.	1975	SY	61-62 New Street, Birmingham.
Sep.	1927	Jan.	1968	O9	8-9 Great Newport Street, London.
Dec.	1927	Mar.	1972	P9	23 Kingsland High Street, London.
Apr.	1928	Apr.	1974	Q9	152 Fenchurch Street, London.
Apr.	1928	Mar.	1975	SZ	13a Old Steine (1 St James Street), Brighton.
May	1928	Jan.	1975	HA	74(was 27)High Street, Weston-Super-Mare.
Jun.	1928		1950	R9	336-338 Green Street, London.
Jun.	1928	Jun.	1963	S9	24 Russell Street, London.
Aug.	1928	Jun.	1968	T9	841 Leytonstone High Road, London.
Aug.	1928	Aug.	1975	HB	13 Tavern Street, Ipswich.
Nov.	1928	Apr.	1966	HC	13 Gentlemen's Walk, Norwich.
Apr.	1929	Feb.	1976	HD	72-74 High Street, Southend-on-Sea.
May	1929	Jan.	1975	HE	14 Commercial Road, Bournemouth.
May	1929	Apr.	1941	HF	174 King Street, Great Yarmouth.
Sep.	1929	Jan.	1970	U9	138 Rushey Green, London.

Oct. 1929	Feb. 1975	HG	14 The Parade, Canterbury.
Dec. 1929	1955	V9	37 Duke Street, London.
Jan. 1930	1939	W9	177 Wandsworth High Street, London.
Mar. 1930	Jan. 1981	X9	4 Marble Arch, London. (Last teashop closed)
Apr. 1930	1953?	HI	72-76 Church Street, Blackpool.
Nov. 1930	Jul. 1975	HJ	50 High Street, Guildford.
Dec. 1930	Jun. 1975	Y9	108 New Oxford Street, London.
Feb. 1931	May 1967	Z9	35 Golders Green Road, London.
Mar. 1931	Feb. 1969	A10	49 Albemarle Street (6 Dover Street), London.
Mar. 1931	May 1975	B10	10 Central Parade, Wembley, London.
Mar. 1931	Apr. 1975	C10	43 Thurloe Street, London.
May 1931	Dec. 1962	D10	274 Edgware Road, London.
Jul. 1931	Dec. 1940	HK	8 St. Mary's Gate, Manchester.
Aug. 1931	Mar. 1974	HL	54-56 George Street, Luton.
Sep. 1931	May 1975	E10	9 Cranbrook Road, London.
Dec. 1931	Mar. 1974	HM	30-31 Petty Cury, Cambridge.
Jan. 1932	Dec. 1980	F10	450 Strand, London. (Opp. Charing X Station)
Mar. 1932	Feb. 1973	HN	13 Church Street, High Wycombe.
May 1932	Sep. 1965	G10	8 Clifford Street, London.
May 1932	Feb. 1975	H10	10 The Town, Enfield, London.
Jun. 1932	May 1975	I10	226 High Holborn (Kingsway), London.
Jun. 1932	1941	J10	87 Berwick Street, London.
Jul. 1932	May 1975	K10	105 Kensington High Street, London.
Aug. 1932	Mar. 1970	L10	172 Kilburn High Road, London.
Nov. 1932	Jun. 1974	HO	40 Broad Street, Reading.
Jan. 1933	Mar. 1976	HP	229 High Street, Exeter, Devon.
Feb. 1933	Nov. 1969	M10	82 Gracechurch Street (1 Bull's Head Passage), London.
May 1933	Oct. 1971	N10	17 South Street (25 Quadrant Arcade), Romford.
Dec. 1933	Feb. 1975	HQ	48 South Street, Worthing.
Oct. 1934	Mar. 1941	HR	18 Bedford Street, Plymouth.
Oct. 1934	Dec. 1974	HS	3 Cornmarket Street, Oxford.
Dec. 1934	Dec. 1975	O10	3 Horseferry Road, London.
Jan. 1935	Mar. 1967	HT	16-17 Union Street, Bath.
Mar. 1935	Jan. 1975	P10	Hyde Park Corner, London.
Aug. 1935	1940	Q10	24-26 Maddox Street, London.
Oct. 1935	Jun. 1967	HU	10 Northgate Street, Gloucester.
Nov. 1935	Feb. 1975	HV	16 Whitefriargate, Hull.
Nov. 1935	Oct. 1972	HW	15 Wellington Place, Hastings.
Feb. 1936	Jun. 1967	R10	448-450 Holloway Road, London.
Aug. 1936	Aug. 1975	HX	109 High Street, Chatham.
Sep. 1936	1940	S10	393 Mile End, London.
Sep. 1936	Apr. 1965	T10	122-124 Charing Cross Road, London.
Feb. 1937	Jun. 1975	U10	15-16 New Burlington Street, London.
Feb. 1937	Mar. 1967	V10	3 Southampton Row, London.
Jul. 1937	Apr. 1974	HY	60 High Street, Bedford.
Sep. 1937	Apr. 1972	HZ	33 Long Row, Nottingham.
Sep. 1937	Sep. 1972	KA	13 Pride Hill, Shrewsbury.
Apr. 1938	Mar. 1975	W10	27 Thames Street, Kingston. (Replaced N7)
1946	May 1975	KB	220 Commercial Road, Portsmouth. (Replaced ST)
1951	Mar. 1976	X10	9 Regent Street, London. (Replaced G4)
1955	Sep. 1975	KC	42 New George Street, Plymouth. (Replaced HR)
Mar. 1957	Jan. 1975	KE	20-21 Peascod Street, Windsor.

May	1958	May	1975	Z10	9 Walbrook (Bucklesbury House), London.
Jun.	1958	Nov.	1975	KF	New Street, Birmingham.
Dec.	1958	Aug.	1975	A11	Duke Street, London.
	1958	Aug.	1975	Y10	26 Leadenhall Street (53 Lime Street), London.
Aug.	1959	Sep.	1975	B11	35 Strand (Villiers Street), London. (Replaced HH)
Feb.	1960	Jun.	1963	KG	Church Street, Liverpool.
Apr.	1960	Dec.	1972	KH	Bull Street, Birmingham. (Replaced PY)
Sep.	1960	Feb.	1966	C11	47a Gresham Street, London.
Jun.	1961	Jan.	1966	KI	16 High Street, Colchester.
Oct.	1961	Sep.	1975	KL	24-25 High Street, Chelmsford.
Mar.	1962	Feb.	1967	N4	85 Victoria Street, London.
Sep.	1962	Aug.	1966	I9	86 West Ealing Broadway, London.
May	1963	Mar.	1975	M6	258-262 Westminster Bridge Road, London.
Jul.	1963	May	1969	D11	77 Clarence Street, Kingston.
Feb.	1964	Feb.	1966	JJ	61 Fleet Street, London. (Reopened)
Feb.	1964	Mar.	1967	E11	Kensington High Street, London.
		Jul.	1967	F11	Holborn, London.
Feb.	1964	Jul.	1967	G11	Clifford Street, London.
Mar.	1964	Feb.	1968	I4	94 Oxford Street, London. (Reopened)
Mar.	1964	Apr.	1967	SS1	Tolworth, Surrey.
Mar.	1969	Jan.	1973	SS2	12 Broad Walk, Dunstable.

* Until 1909 these teashops were owned by the Ceylon Café Company Ltd. The County Arcade teashop in Leeds had a five-piece orchestra.

General Notes

Most London teashops and those in major cities suffered minor war damage of one sort or another but this damage seldom caused the shops to close for long. The teashop situated at 54 Fore Street (off London Wall) was damaged by the first bomb which was dropped on the City of London in the Second World War. This happened at 00.15 on 25 August 1940 when number 38 Fore Street took a direct hit and many properties in the area were either destroyed or damaged. The damaged teashop was temporarily reopened but was bombed and gutted by fire in 1941 after which it closed and never reopened. After the war some teashops were closed for long periods during rebuilding and road improvement schemes such as the teashop in East India Dock Road; the fittings of this teashop were left in place for the workers building the new Blackwall Tunnel.

The first teashop opened on 20 September 1894, the last one closed in 1981. The Duke Street teashop (V9) was the first experimental frozen food (Frood) restaurant. The teashop at 396 Strand, London (R4) was the original waitress training school in 1913.

The teashop at 450 Strand, London was first opened on 25 January 1910 and was the fifth teashop to be located on the Strand thoroughfare. It was closed on 11 February 1931 and reopened in January 1932 after the site was rebuilt. It was closed again in December 1980, and reopened to the public after refurbishment, on Monday 22 June 1981, as a 'revived' Corner House. It was small (just under 300 seats compared with 1,500 or more in the previous Corner Houses) having been completely restructured to an interior and exterior design of Dennis Lennon CBE, interior design co-ordinator for RMS *Queen Elizabeth II*. Whilst queues formed soon after opening the nostalgia soon waned and the Corner House revival was not a success. The restaurant ceased trading in June 1988.

The teashop at 42 Poultry (N9) opened the first Buffet Bar in London. Here customers could order sandwiches cut from York Hams displayed on the counter.

The teashop at Notting Hill Gate (X6) was converted to a higher spending restaurant in 1965 and was called the Notting Hill Gate Corner House. It was not, however, on the same scale as the Coventry, Strand and Oxford Corner Houses. It closed on 4 March 1967.

The Lyons publicity department occupied part of 61 Fleet Street (JJ).

The dressmaking department, which was first located in St John Street, Clerkenwell, relocated to the fifth floor of Orchard House, Oxford Street, in 1930 and thence to the teashop at 182-4 Clapham High Street (F6) in about 1956.

The two premises that opened in 1965 and 1969 respectively departed from the original teashop nomenclature coding. The restaurant abbreviations of SS represented Sugar & Spice, the name of a new look experimental restaurant.

Lyons opened their so-called 'mechanical shop' at the Camberwell Green (B8) teashop on 30 June 1932.

Some teashops were converted into Cup & Platter restaurants during the 1960s and 1970s. These formed a small chain of restaurants (about twelve) which were less expensive than the London Steak Houses.

Other Restaurants Operated	Opened	Closed
Trocadero Restaurant, London	05.10.1896	13.02.1965
Throgmorton Restaurant, London	15.10.1900	still open under new owners.
Victoria Mansions Restaurant, Manchester	05.10.1903	30.03.1922
Blenheim Café, New Bond Street	05.09.1904	05.08.1921
Popular Café, Piccadilly, London	10.10.1904	15.09.1939
State Restaurant, Liverpool	09.01.1905	14.07.1949
Popular Café, Manchester	16.01.1906	13.07.1938
Coventry Street Corner House, London	04.01.1909	13.06.1970
Birkbeck Café, Holborn London	09.06.1904	29.03.1923
Maison Lyons Liverpool (first)	02.03.1911	24.12.1928
Maison Lyons, Oxford Street (first)	21.11.1912	17.09.1916
Strand Corner House	08.04.1915	28.02.1977
Maison Lyons, Shaftesbury Avenue	16.08.1915	14.11.1940
Maison Riche, Regent Street, London	23.11.1915	05.04.1924
Maison Lyons, Oxford Street, (second)	18.09.1916	22.10.1933
Angel Café Restaurant, Islington, London	21.02.1922	1959
Oxford Corner House (Tottenham Court Road)	03.05.1928	05.1967
Maison Lyons Liverpool (second)	14.03.1929	08.1939
Maison Lyons (Marble Arch)	23.10.1933	27.01.1977
Diplomat, Mount Street, London	06.08.1965	24.02.1967
Restaurant Sebastian (Dukes), Wimbledon	1964	converted to fish restaurant.
Restaurant Belvedere, Holland Park	05.1966	still open under new owners.
Strand Corner House (revived one)	22.06.1981	14.06.1988
Upper Crust (Double Decker bus)	04.06.1971	02.02.1972

General Notes

The Restaurant Sebastian at Wimbledon Village, known initially as Club Sebastian when acquired by Lyons in 1964, was renamed Dukes Restaurant after the Diplomat Restaurant closed in 1967. This was done so that the expensive monogrammed china from the Diplomat could be used in Dukes. The Diplomat Restaurant had been designed to replace the Trocadero Restaurant but opened just as the tax restriction on business entertaining was enacted and it failed to attract the high-spending business customers and was not a success. After its closure Scotts took over the premises. Dukes was subsequently converted into a fish restaurant (Fisherman's Wharf) in September 1970. It suffered a serious fire on 2 August 1976, was rebuilt and opened again on 11 October 1976.

The Upper Crust was a restaurant on a double-decker bus. With a restaurant upstairs (kitchens below) it drove visitors around London pausing at Blackheath for lunch of smoked salmon, Scotch fillet steak, strawberries and cream with wine, champagne and brandy priced at £10. The vehicle had been supplied by British Leyland for a cost of £18,500 and it had air conditioning, toilets and a telephone. The venture was not a success; apart from the occasional breakdown, the police issued a summons in October 1971 for selling alcohol on a public bus and Lyons were fined £50 with £50 costs. As a result Lyons changed to an all-charter system to avoid further trouble and a number of charters were secured, one from Hertz for a fourteen-day return journey to Cannes and Nice.

In addition to the above restaurants J. Lyons & Co. Ltd, and/or its subsidiaries, owned or managed a number of other restaurants at varying times. Some of these came into the Group when the interests of the Ceylon Tea Company (1909) and the Robley Group Limited (1962) were acquired. Some underwent further changes to name and style and some catering contracts were lost.

Arcade Café, Leeds	Golden Fleece, Chelmsford	Pen & Wig, Liverpool
Arlington (The), Brighton	Greyhound (The), Bromley	Red Lion Inn, Goostrey
Barons Keep, Solihull	Grosvenor Arms (The), Aldford	Rembrandt Restaurant, Liverpool
Barons Keep, Cheltenham	Hanbury Restaurant, Liverpool	Royal Restaurant, Liverpool
Barons Keep, Bournemouth	Hayworthe, Haywards Heath, Sussex	Shakespeare Theatre, Liverpool
Bull & Bear, Liverpool	Jenny's Seafood Restaurant, Liverpool	Star & Garter Hotel, Andover
Bull's Head Inn, Macclesfield	La Broche, Liverpool	Tap Grill, Fleet Street, London
Camellia Restaurant, Syon Park	La Bussola, Manchester	Tavern in the Sky, Heathrow
Carlton Restaurant, Manchester	La Bussola, Liverpool	Three Maypoles (The), Shirley
Casey's Bar, Liverpool	Leadenhall Grill, London	Three Stags, Bebington
Christopher (The), Bath	Lion & Lamb Hotel, Brentwood	Town Hall Tavern, Manchester
Cornmarket Hotel, Liverpool	Lutine Room, Empire House, London	Triple Choice, London
Dog & Partridge, Tutbury, Staffs.	Meads Restaurant, Purfleet	Victoria Mansions Restaurant, London
Dolphin (The), Romsey	Palace Restaurant, Manchester	Victoria Station Restaurant, London
Garrick (The), Manchester	Panorama Restaurant, Gatwick	Wheelhouse (The), Nottingham

London Steak Houses

Several London Steak House restaurants had previously been Lyons teashops. After having being run as Steak Houses some were later turned into more fashionable fish restaurants under the names of Fisherman's Wharf and Hook Line & Sinker. Some also became Lyons' Grills. The Steak House at Northwood, Hillingdon opened as an Italian restaurant in April 1977, named Il Mondo Cane (It's a Dog's World).

Baker Street, London W1
Basil Street, London SW3
Blackheath, London SW3
Brighton, East Sussex
Bristol, Avon
Brompton Road, London SW3
Buckingham Palace Road, London
Chislehurst, Kent
Clifford Street, London W1
Croydon, Surrey
Davies Street, London W1
Dulwich Village, London. SE21
Eastbourne, East Sussex
Ebury Street, London SW1
Epsom, Surrey
Esher, Surrey

Gerrards Cross, Buckinghamshire
Gloucester, Gloucestershire
Guildford, Surrey
Harrow-on-the-Hill, Middlesex
Highgate, London N6
Kendal Street, London W8
Kensington High Street, London W8
Kings Road, London SW3
Kingston, Surrey
Lincoln's Inn, London WC2
Northwood, Middlesex
Norwich, Norfolk
Old Brompton Road, London SW7
Southampton, Hampshire
Southgate, London
Streatham, London SW16

Swiss Cottage, London
Tunbridge Wells, Kent
Upper Brook Street, London
Wardour Street, London
Watford, Hertfordshire
Westminster, London SW1
Weybridge, Surrey
Whitehall, London
Wimbledon, Surrey
Winchmore Hill, London
Windsor Hill, London

Private Catering Contracts (1936–1960) not necessarily held concurrently

Aldwych Club
Alliance Assurance Company
Colonel Aster's Cruises
Athenaeum Club
Balfour Services Club
Bank of England
Barclays Bank Luncheon Club
Beaver Club
Bloomsbury House
Boulton & Paul Limited
Bovis Limited
Brooklands Club
Buckingham Palace Garden & Staff Parties
Cable & Wireless Limited
Carlise State Management Scheme
Cecil House Inc.
City University Club
Constitutional Club
Corpus Christi College, Oxford
Devonshire Club
Dulwich College
Dunlop & Company
Earls Court
Emmanuel College, Cambridge
Eton College
E.M. Industries
Fire Services College, Dorking
Goodwood Races
Government Communications Headquarters
Gresham Club
Guards Club
Home & Hospital for Jewish Incurables
King Edward VII Sanatorium, Midhurst
Knebworth
Knights of Columbus
Lincoln's Inn
Lloyds Bank Luncheon Club

L.M.S. Luncheon Club, Manchester
London Hospital
London School of Economics
Lords Cricket Club
Malvern College
Marlborough College
Middle Temple
Orient Steamship Line
Oxford & Cambridge University Club
Phoenix Telephone Company
Police Staff College, Myton
Police Training College, Warrington
Police Training College, Witney
Polytechnic, Regent Street
Priory Nursing home, Roehampton
Queen Mary's Hospital, Roehampton
Royal Cancer Hospital
Royal Empire Society
Royal Holloway College
Royal Horticultural Society, Wisley
Royal Marine Barracks, Chatham
St Catherine's College, Cambridge
St Mary's Hospital, Paddington
Shenley Military Hospital
Skefee Company
Union Club
United Services Club
Wellington College, Crowthorne
Westminster Hospital
Wiggins-Sankey & Company
Wimbledon Borough Council
Wimbledon Lawn Tennis Club
Winchester College
Windsor Castle, Staff Parties
Windsor Safari Park
Woburn
Y.W.C.A.

Appendix 5: Lyons War Memorial Inscriptions

On 2 August 1919 the Lyons Club grounds at Sudbury were dedicated by the Lyons chairman, Montague Gluckstein, as a memorial to those employees who gave their lives in the Great War. To reinforce this inspiration a granite obelisk, designed by Charles Oatley – architect and designer of the first teashop – and bearing the names of those employees killed, was unveiled there on 7 October 1922.

Twenty-five years later, on 9 November 1947, an arc-shaped memorial of Portland stone, designed by Lyons' architect Robert Bryson, was dedicated to those members of staff who lost their lives in the 1939–45 war. Both memorials were moved to the Greenford factory site when Lyons disposed of the Sudbury Club grounds in 1968.

Secondly, two separate war memorials, in the form of wall tablets, were erected in the entrance lobby of Head Office, Cadby Hall, some time after the Sudbury memorials had been dedicated. When the old Head Office was demolished in 1984 it was not possible to remove these tablets without damage and so a *Book of Remembrance* was created therefrom and displayed in a glass cabinet in the new Head Office atrium until 1990 when the offices moved to Greenford.

Research has identified a number of misspellings and ambiguities between this book and the memorials. In compiling the following lists all names from the *Book of Remembrance* and the memorials are recorded for completeness. The anomalies, which cannot be explained, are identified in the notes at the end of the appendix. The redevelopment of the Greenford factory site requires the memorials be moved again in 2000 to, an as yet, unknown location.

A Roll of Honour was published in the *Lyons Mail* journal in September 1919 but there are many discrepancies with the stone memorial erected three years later. To avoid confusion the *Lyons Mail* list of 1919 has been disregarded but historians can view this (which lists regiments) at the London Metropolitan Archives, item reference ACC/3527/268 and 269.

'Erected by J. Lyons & Company Limited
In Memory Of The Staff Who Fell In The Great War 1914–1918'

Abecasis A.	Burgin A.	Dyer C.	Hillman R.
Aley E. J.	Burrell C.	Entwistle J.	Hipworth A. E.
Ashley H. R. see note 1	Burton R. W.	Exworthy A.	Holland W. J.
Astill G.	Cade W. see note 1	Fendall S.	Holmes F.
Austin W.	Carpenter W.	Field E. V.	Holmes H.
Avery W.	Carswell J. A.	Fife M.	Houghton M. N.
Avril E. R. see note 1	Casey S.	Fishwick E. A.	Houston J.
Bailey F.	Chamberlain A.	Fletcher B.	Humphreys E.J. see note 1
Baker F. A.	Chamberlain F. G.	Forrester R.	Hurst J.
Barnard E.	Chamberlain W.	Fox H.	Hutton C. A.
Barnes A. G.	Chart B.	Frost W. E.	Ings F. H.
Barnes F.	Chesher A. J.	Fuller H.	Ireland W.
Barrett P.	Chesworth T.	Fyfield G. see note 1	Jacobs A. see note 1
Baxter H. F.	Christian E.	Gardiner A.	Janson W. F.
Baxter W. S see note 1	Christopher B.	Gigg R.	Jardine A. M.
Beard C. E.	Clarkson C. T.	Gibert G. see note 4	Jennings C. H.
Belshaw H.	Clayton C.	Gilbert G. E.	Johnson C.
Bird L. P.	Clegg A.	Giles J.	Johnson W. E.
Bispham F.	Clements C. see note 1	Godby T. S.	Johnson W. J.
Bitmead A.	Cobble F. see note 1	Goddard J.	Jonas J.
Blandon T.	Conquest A.	Godfrey F.	Jones T.
Bodington R. see note 2	Conway W.	Gooding J. W.	Kasper M.
Boetius E. A.	Cook T. W.	Gordon G.	Kattle C. W.
Boissy E.	Cook R. G.	Grange W.	Kearney A.
Boocock C.	Cornier E.	Greatorex R. N.	Kemp C. H.
Boothby H. C.	Cox E.	Hadaway C. H.	Kenny W. T.
Boother W. E.	Craven E.	Hammond A.	King R.
Bourne F.	Crispin A. see note 3	Hargrave L.	Kingston A.
Bower C.	Croft T.	Harmsworth F.	Kirk N.
Breden W.	Crowhurst H.	Harris W.	Leeson W. J.
Bridges A.	Curl J.	Hart R. D.	Levy A. I.
Brooker L.	Death A. S.	Hawley E.	Lewin A.
Brooker L. V. G.	Dighton H.	Hazelwood R.	Lidbetter F.
Bubear A. G.	Dobson R.	Heafield H. C.	Lilly W. G.
Buck J. T.	Donatz C.	Herring P.	Lloyd G.
Burgess E.	Dudley J. W.	Hillier H. F.	Lodge R.

Long R.
Mackay W.
Marsh H.
Martin J. H.
Mathews F.
Mathies A. J. [see note 1]
Maziere A.
McEnery J.
McNotty W. S.
Meinke W.
Miller M. J.
Mills J.
Mills S. A.
Moodie D.
Moore A.
Moore H.
Morris C. D.
Morris E. C.
Mott C. F.
Mungeam E. C.
Mungeam R. G.
Munson W.
Naylor H. C.
Nevill S.

Noble H. W.
Norman W. H.
Nyburg B. S.
O'Brien W.
O'Neill E.
Palmer A.
Parkinson T.
Partridge H.
Perlmann D. W.
Phipps T.
Pinn F. J.
Polley E.
Pollock D. G. [see note 5]
Porter W. G.
Potts F.
Poujol J. L.
Pownall E. [see note 3]
Pownall H. [see note 3]
Prior A. E.
Pritchard G.
Pulman P.
Purnell W.
Ramage C.
Raynor E. G.

Reid W.
Reuter H.
Rickets W.
Riglin T. E.
Rixon E.C.
Roscoe G. I.
Ross W. G.
Scott S. D.
Shaw F.
Shepperson H. W.
Simonet H. K.
Slade F.
Slater T.
Smith H.
Snelling R.
Stacey G.
Stevens F.
Stone L. E.
Stone W.
Summers G. F.
Summers W.
Taylor T. H.
Taylor W.
Tery A.

Thrush C.
Timberlake H.
Tompkinson A.
Townsend W.
Uglow T.
Vicars S. E.
Walters J.
Ward G. F.
Warman T.
Wass M. E.
Weathersby H.
West C. T.
White A. J.
White F. S.
White J.
Wilkinson H. E.
Willy W.
Wilson A. J.
Wilson C.
Winter T.
Wood A. J.
Woodman R. A.
Wyman W.

1939–1945

'At The Going Down Of The Sun And In The Morning We Shall Remember Them
And In Memory Of The Men And Women Who Fell Defending The Home Front'

Allcoat P. S.
Anderson F. [see note 6]
Andrews L. V.
Ascott E. E. [see note 6]
Atwell R.
Bachegalup L.
Barker M.
Barley H. G.
Barnes E.
Barnfather C. C. [see note 6]
Barter C. J. R.
Baughurst W. J.
Beament W. H.
Beaufort P. [see note 6]
Beck A.
Behan D. J.
Bell D. R.
Bell N. [see note 6]
Bewsey A. A.
Bishop H. E.
Blandon C. G.
Bolton W. F. [see note 6]
Boreman A. C.
Bradley P. G.
Brady P. A.
Bramley W. J.
Brand J. R.
Brand W.
Bressloff S. I.
Bromhead D. T.
Brook D. E. M.
Brown J. R.
Brown P. F. C.
Browning A. C.

Bryant F. W.
Budd T. A. [see note 6]
Bull J. W.
Burgess A.
Burne J. A.
Burnall J. R. [see note 6]
Burtwell M. G.
Busby A. J. [see note 6]
Butler J.
Callan J.
Camm P. A.
Campbell A. J. [see note 6]
Campbell T. J. [see note 7]
Case G.
Carr T. F. [see note 6]
Chambers S.
Chandler J. H.
Cheeseman R. E.
Clayton J.
Collett T. W.
Collier V.
Collins H. H.
Conway W. [see note 6]
Copeland C. F. G. W.
Costis S. C. S.
Coulling A. W.
Coulthard W. [see note 3]
Crawley F. W. [see note 6]
Crockett A. W.
Crowley D. A.
Danks E. W.
Davis S.
Davison J. L. [see note 6]
Day F. W. R.

Dee P. S.
Denford F. V.
Dicker J. S. [see note 6]
Dillnutt G. W.
Diplock H.
Dixon J.
Double C. [see note 6]
Dray C. G.
Drury C. A.
Dunn G. B.
Dyson K. W.
Eatwell S.
Edkins D. R.
Elliott J. A.
Essery R. C.
Evans G. [see note 6]
Excel R. O. [see note 6]
Ferrarone D.
Fewings R. E.
Firth D. W.
Floyd P. J.
Fox E. J.
Frew H.
Furby S.
Gathercole C. F.
Gibbons A. E. [see note 6]
Goodman D. [see note 6]
Goom D. G.
Gowlett G. A.
Grayson G. W.
Grimmond J. R. [see note 6]
Grist F. R. [see note 6]
Hale F. G. E.
Hall J. R.

Harcourt S.
Harding B. L. [see note 6]
Hardy G. F.
Harmer W.
Harris W. A.
Harsum D. A. [see note 3]
Hatton W. [see note 6]
Hayman J. W.
Hayselden L.
Helyer R. K. [see note 6]
Henbrey H.
Herratt J.
Hill W. H.
Hobbs A. C.
Hocking D. C. E.
Holben R. J.
Hood G. L.
Hook J. B. J.
Horney E.
Hough E.
Impey H. [see note 6]
Isaacs B. R. S.
Jackson C. [see note 6]
Jarman A. [see note 6]
Jenkin F. N.
Jenkins H. H.
Johnson K. [see note 6]
Johnson K. W. [see note 6]
Jones L. S.
Jones L. W. [see note 6]
Jordon P. J.
Joslin O. G.
Kennewell E. W.
Kerr E. E.

1939–1945 (continued)

Kilby W. H.	Moody E. J. *see note 6*	Rose H.	Verrent C. *see note 6*
King W. G. H.	Moore D. P.	Rothwell H. K.	Vickery S. G. T. *see note 6*
Kingsley W. J.	Moore L. H.	Saunders J. H. *see note 6*	Vine G. D.
Knights E. H. *see note 8*	Morbey R. F.	Sawyer W. C.	Walker C. F. *see note 6*
Kuflick P.	Morris S. W.	Schmitt L.	Wallace C. *see note 11*
Lague G. D.	Murdock A. H. F.	Seex R. D. J.	Wallace S.
Landing H.	Murphy J.	Sharp E. T.	Wardell D. M. *see note 6*
Laurence W.	Myers J. L.	Sharkey T. C.	Ward K.C.
Lee W. J.	Naylor J. L.	Sharpley M. I.	Warner P.
Levack S. J.	Ness R.	Simpson G. *see note 6*	Waterhouse E. *see note 6*
Lewis W. M.	Nixon C. W.	Sims G. R.	Watson R.
Limb W. F. *see note 6*	Norris C. *see note 6*	Skudder E. J.	Webb F. C.
Long A. F.	O'Mahoney J.	Smith A. O. *see note 10*	Webb G. W.
Luckett F. J. *see note 6*	O'Shaughnessy E.	Smith G. A.	Webb R. C. H. *see note 6*
Mabbot L. E. *see note 6*	Perkins G. A.	Smythson L. *see note 6*	Welchman E. R. *see note 6*
McSweeney J.	Perrett R.	Spencer N.F. *see note 6*	West W.
McCormick J. *see note 6*	Perriam H. R.	Spriggs A. *see note 6*	Westlake G. E.
McIvor C. *see note 6*	Pitts W. N.	Steel L. F.	Whittle T.
McWade E.	Povey R. W.	Stephens H. A.	Wickham A.
Malin F. G.	Powell E. J.	Stone L. S.	Wilkinson W. J.
Mason F. W.	Preedy S. G. *see note 6*	Tais S.	Willans H.
Mayhew M. S.	Ramsden A.	Tarrant A. W.	Willetts F. H.
Mead F. *see note 6*	Reason L. J. *see note 6*	Thomas F. C. *see note 6*	Wilson F.
Meldrum G. *see note 9*	Reynolds T.	Tucker B. C. *see note 6*	Wood L. J.
Menniss C. *see note 6*	Richardson A .C.	Tuvey F. A.	Wright J. F.
Mills W. S.	Richardson E. J.	Tyson V. R.	Younger W. S. *see note 11*
Mitchell H. A.	Riches A. G.	Upperton J. R. *see note 6*	

War Memorial Notes

Note 1. These names appear in the *Book of Remembrance* but not on the WW I memorial.

Note 2. Bodington's initial appears as 'T' in the *Book of Remembrance* and 'R' on the WW I memorial.

Note 3. On the WW I memorial Crispin but in *Book of Remembrance* Crispen. Likewise Pownall/Pownhall. On the WW II memorial Coulthard/Couthard, Harsum/Harsom.

Note 4. Records show that a Mrs Gibert (no 'L') was awarded the Croix de Guerre with Star in 1920 earned by her late husband whilst serving with the French Army during WW I. Both Mr and Mrs Gibert worked in the Throgmorton Restaurant.

Note 5. Pollock's name wrongly appears on the WW I memorial. He was captured on the Somme and returned home to his parents in Norwich. Consequently his name does not appear in the *Book of Remembrance*.

Note 6. These names appear on the WW II memorial but are not listed in the *Book of Remembrance*.

Note 7. Both Campbells are listed on the WW II memorial and it must be assumed they are different persons. See note 6 for A.J. Campbell.

Note 8. On the WW II memorial Knights' initials are listed as 'E.H'. In the *Book of Remembrance* they are 'F. H'.

Note 9. On the WW II memorial Meldrum's initial is listed as 'G'. In the *Book of Remembrance* it is listed as 'C'.

Note 10. On the WW II memorial Smith's initials are listed as 'A. O.' In the *Book of Remembrance* they are 'A. Q'.

Note 11. Wallace's and Younger's names are listed in the *Book of Remembrance* under WW I but they appear on the WW II memorial.

Source: J. Lyons & Co. Ltd *Book of Remembrance, Lyons Mail* and War Memorials.

Appendix 6: Issued Share Capital, Net Profits & Dividends 1895–1978

Year End	Ordinary £1 shares	5% First Cumulative Preference Stock	6% First Preferred Ordinary Stock	'A' Ordinary (Non-voting) £1 shares	Proportional Profit £1 Preference Stock	7% Second Cumulative Preference Stock	8% Third Cumulative Preference Stock	Proportional Profit 10s. Loan Stock	5½% Unsecured Loan Stock	7¾% Unsecured Loan Stock	Employees 'A' £1 Ordinary Shares	Net Profit (Loss)	Shareholder Dividend %
1895	150,000	nil	nil	nil	nil	nil	nil	nil	nil	nil	nil	9,404	10.00
1896	150,000	nil	nil	nil	nil	nil	nil	nil	nil	nil	nil	15,004	nil
1897	165,000	nil	nil	nil	nil	nil	nil	nil	nil	nil	nil	30,014	8.00
1898	165,000	nil	nil	nil	nil	nil	nil	nil	nil	nil	nil	44,322	15.00
1899	200,000	nil	nil	nil	nil	nil	nil	nil	nil	nil	nil	57,776	17.50
1900	240,000	nil	nil	nil	nil	nil	nil	nil	nil	nil	nil	77,745	23.75
1901	270,000	nil	nil	nil	nil	nil	nil	nil	nil	nil	nil	95,676	26.25
1902	300,000	nil	nil	nil	nil	nil	nil	nil	nil	nil	nil	121,423	28.75
1903	310,000	nil	nil	nil	nil	nil	nil	nil	nil	nil	nil	137,815	30.00
1904	320,333	250,000	nil	nil	nil	nil	nil	nil	nil	nil	nil	156,895	30.00
1905	331,000	250,000	nil	nil	nil	nil	nil	nil	nil	nil	nil	176,011	30.00
1906	331,000	250,000	nil	nil	nil	nil	nil	nil	nil	nil	nil	192,646	30.00 +2 for 5 bonus
1907	331,000	500,000	nil	nil	nil	nil	nil	nil	nil	nil	nil	231,849	32.50
1908	331,000	500,000	nil	nil	nil	nil	nil	nil	nil	nil	nil	248,825	32.50
1909	331,000	500,000	33,100	nil	nil	nil	nil	nil	nil	nil	nil	287,852	32.50 +1 for 10 bonus
1910	356,000	500,000	68,700	nil	nil	nil	nil	nil	nil	nil	nil	288,069	32.50 +1 for 10 bonus
1911	356,000	500,000	400,000	nil	nil	nil	nil	nil	nil	nil	nil	302,390	45.50
1912	356,000	500,000	400,000	nil	nil	nil	nil	nil	nil	nil	nil	321,059	45.50
1913	356,000	500,000	400,000	nil	nil	nil	nil	nil	nil	nil	nil	339,518	42.50
1914	356,000	500,000	400,000	nil	nil	nil	nil	nil	nil	nil	nil	356,303	42.50
1915	400,000	500,000	400,000	nil	nil	nil	nil	nil	nil	nil	nil	276,403	32.50
1916	400,000	500,000	400,000	nil	nil	nil	nil	nil	nil	nil	nil	278,293	25.00
1917	400,000	500,000	400,000	nil	nil	nil	nil	nil	nil	nil	nil	268,475	25.00
1918	400,000	500,000	400,000	nil	nil	nil	nil	nil	nil	nil	nil	316,212	25.00
1919	400,000	646,840	400,000	80,410	500,000	nil	nil	nil	nil	nil	nil	258,076	35.00
1920	400,000	647,065	400,000	80,410	500,000	1,000,000	nil	nil	nil	nil	nil	396,683	42.50
1921	400,000	647,065	400,000	87,910	500,000	1,000,000	1,000,000	nil	nil	nil	nil	503,000	42.50
1922	400,000	647,065	400,000	87,910	500,000	1,000,000	1,000,000	nil	nil	nil	nil	595,615	25.00
1923	400,000	647,065	400,000	681,820	500,000	1,000,000	1,000,000	225,000	nil	nil	nil	631,816	25.00
1924	400,000	647,065	400,000	694,580	500,000	2,000,000	1,000,000	225,000	nil	nil	nil	665,376	25.00
1925	400,000	647,065	400,000	700,580	500,000	2,000,000	1,000,000	225,000	nil	nil	nil	718,581	25.00
1926	400,000	647,065	400,000	1,173,773	500,000	2,000,000	1,000,000	225,000	nil	nil	nil	754,960	21.25
1927	400,000	647,065	400,000	1,181,273	500,000	2,000,000	1,000,000	225,000	nil	nil	nil	757,159	21.25
1928	400,000	647,065	400,000	1,188,773	500,000	3,000,000	1,000,000	225,000	nil	nil	nil	832,515	22.50
1929	400,000	647,065	400,000	1,196,273	500,000	4,000,000	1,000,000	225,000	nil	nil	nil	908,950	22.50
1930	400,000	647,065	400,000	1,203,773	500,000	4,000,000	1,000,000	225,000	nil	nil	nil	935,870	22.50
1931	400,000	647,065	466,667	1,216,273	500,000	4,000,000	1,000,000	225,000	nil	nil	nil	942,320	22.50
1932	400,000	647,065	466,667	1,228,773	500,000	5,000,000	1,000,000	225,000	nil	nil	nil	942,000	22.50
1933	400,000	647,065	466,667	1,241,273	500,000	5,000,000	1,000,000	225,000	nil	nil	nil	972,389	22.50
1934	400,000	647,065	466,667	1,253,773	500,000	5,000,000	1,000,000	225,000	nil	nil	nil	1,008,341	22.50
1935	400,000	647,065	466,667	1,266,273	500,000	5,000,000	1,000,000	225,000	nil	nil	nil	1,009,272	22.50
1936	400,000	647,065	466,667	1,266,273	500,000	5,000,000	1,000,000	225,000	nil	nil	nil	1,010,753	22.50
1937	400,000	647,065	466,667	1,226,273	500,000	5,000,000	1,000,000	225,000	nil	nil	nil	1,010,887	22.50
1938	400,000	647,065	466,667	1,226,273	500,000	5,000,000	1,000,000	225,000	nil	nil	nil	1,011,000	22.50 note 1

Year												
1939	400,000	647,065	466,667	1,226,273	500,000	5,000,000	1,000,000	nil	nil	nil	1,011,980	22.50
1940	400,000	647,065	466,667	1,226,273	500,000	5,000,000	1,000,000	nil	nil	nil	1,011,452	20.00
1941	400,000	647,065	466,667	1,226,273	500,000	5,000,000	1,000,000	nil	nil	nil	883,600	20.00
1942	400,000	647,065	466,667	1,226,273	500,000	5,000,000	1,000,000	nil	nil	nil	896,500	20.00
1943	400,000	647,065	466,667	1,226,273	500,000	5,000,000	1,000,000	nil	nil	nil	905,305	20.00
1944	400,000	647,065	466,667	1,226,273	500,000	5,000,000	1,000,000	nil	nil	nil	905,890	20.00
1945	400,000	647,065	466,667	1,266,273	500,000	5,000,000	1,000,000	nil	nil	nil	907,090	20.00
1946	400,000	647,065	466,667	1,266,273	500,000	5,000,000	1,000,000	nil	nil	nil	970,130	22.50
1947	400,000	647,065	466,667	1,266,273	500,000	5,000,000	1,000,000	nil	nil	nil	985,425	22.50
1948	400,000	647,065	466,667	1,266,273	500,000	5,000,000	1,000,000	nil	nil	nil	591,631	22.50 note 2
1949	400,000	647,065	493,829	1,266,273	500,000	5,000,000	1,000,000	nil	nil	nil	566,234	22.50
1950	400,000	647,065	493,829	1,266,273	500,000	5,000,000	1,000,000	nil	nil	nil	578,063	22.50
1951	400,000	647,065	493,829	1,266,273	500,000	5,000,000	1,000,000	nil	nil	nil	610,262	22.50
1952	400,000	647,065	564,846	1,926,273	500,000	5,000,000	1,000,000	nil	nil	nil	615,075	22.50
1953	400,000	647,065	564,846	1,926,273	500,000	5,000,000	1,000,000	nil	nil	nil	689,451	22.50
1954	400,000	647,065	564,846	2,555,342	500,000	5,000,000	1,000,000	nil	nil	nil	686,914	22.50
1955	400,000	647,065	564,846	2,555,342	500,000	5,000,000	1,000,000	nil	nil	nil	728,336	22.50
1956	400,000	647,065	650,000	2,555,342	500,000	5,000,000	1,000,000	nil	nil	nil	762,261	22.50
1957	400,000	647,065	650,000	2,555,342	500,000	5,000,000	1,000,000	nil	nil	nil	871,767	25.00
1958	400,000	647,065	650,000	2,555,342	500,000	5,000,000	1,000,000	nil	nil	nil	1,143,111	14.17
1959	400,000	647,065	650,000	5,700,684	500,000	5,000,000	1,000,000	nil	nil	nil	905,256	14.17
1960	400,000	647,065	650,000	5,700,684	500,000	5,206,939	1,000,000	nil	nil	nil	1,399,255	15.83
1961	400,000	647,065	650,000	5,700,684	500,000	5,206,939	1,000,000	nil	nil	nil	1,036,907	15.83
1962	400,000	647,065	650,000	5,700,684	500,000	5,206,939	1,000,000	nil	nil	nil	1,070,104	15.83
1963	400,000	647,065	650,000	5,757,882	500,000	5,206,939	1,000,000	nil	nil	nil	1,078,475	15.83
1964	400,000	647,065	650,000	5,757,882	500,000	5,206,939	1,000,000	nil	nil	nil	1,794,354	17.50
1965	400,000	647,065	650,000	8,931,823	500,000	5,206,939	1,000,000	nil	nil	nil	2,240,621	13.33 +1 for 2 bonus
1966	400,000	647,065	650,000	8,931,823	500,000	5,206,939	1,000,000	nil	nil	nil	1,822,960	13.33
1967	400,000	55,108	34,001	8,931,823	500,000	784,874	92,087	899,956	5,765,086	nil	1,595,388	13.33
1968	400,000	55,108	34,001	8,931,823	500,000	784,874	92,087	899,956	8,059,870	nil	1,782,207	13.75
1969	400,000	55,108	34,001	9,181,823	500,000	784,874	92,087	899,956	8,059,870	nil	2,312,327	14.33 +1 for 3 bonus
1970	400,000	55,000	34,000	12,976,000	500,000	785,000	92,000	900,000	8,060,000	115,000	3,098,000	6.83 note 3
1971	400,000	55,000	34,000	13,266,000	500,000	785,000	92,000	900,000	8,635,000	226,000	3,601,000	7.69
1972	400,000	55,000	34,000	13,293,000	500,000	785,000	92,000	900,000	8,635,000	333,000	4,635,000	9.05
1973	400,000	55,000	34,000	28,719,000	500,000	785,000	92,000	900,000	8,635,000	298,000	7,157,000	7.27 note 3
1974	400,000	55,000	34,000	29,326,000	500,000	785,000	92,000	900,000	8,635,000	283,000	5,727,000	7.63
1975	400,000	55,000	34,000	40,394,000	500,000	785,000	92,000	900,000	8,635,000	283,000	8,335,000	7.38
1976	400,000	55,000	34,000	29,695,000	500,000	785,000	92,000	839,000	8,635,000	283,000	6,166,000	7.57 note 3
1977	41,173,000	55,000	34,000	nil	nil	785,000	92,000	706,000	7,320,000	282,662	(5,402,000)	7.57
1978	41,279,000	55,000	34,000	nil	nil	785,000	92,000	706,000	7,320,000	282,662	(9,002,000)	2.07

Source: J. Lyons & Co. Ltd Annual Report and Accounts.

Notes

Note 1. Accounts first produced in decimal. General Decimalisation was not introduced until 15 February 1971.

Note 2. In 1948 the Companies Act required new accounting methods which came into effect on 1 July. For comparison the 1947 adjusted figure is £590,806.

Note 3. Adjusted for Script and Rights issues.

General Notes:

The net profit reported in the official accounts for 1895 shows £11,404. In the figures here, £2,000 has been deducted for depreciation as pointed out by the auditors. In 1894 the original authorised share capital for the company was £120,000. It was increased by £30,000 during the first year.

In 1967 a restructuring of share capital was carried out. A 'Scheme of Arrangement' dated 9 January 1967 relating to the company's Preferential capital was approved by stockholders on 1 February 1967 and became effective with the sanction of the High Court of Justice on 8 February 1967. In accordance with the provisions of the Scheme, the issued share capital of the company was reduced by the cancellation of:

> £591,957 5% Preference stock   £907,913 8% Preference stock
> £4,422,065 7% Preference stock   £615,999 6% Preferred Ordinary stock.

In substitution for the foregoing, £899,956 5½% Unsecured Loan stock 1987/97 and £5,765,086 7¾% Unsecured Loan stock 1987/97 was issued in proportions laid down in the Scheme. In accordance with the Scheme the authorised capital of the company was restored to £19,244,283 by the creation of 6,540,869 additional unclassified shares of £1 each. The remaining Preferential stocks and the Preferred Ordinary stock were redesignated as:

> £55,108 5% First Cumulative Preference Stock   £92,087 8% Third Cumulative Preference Stock.
> £784,874 7% Second Cumulative Preference Stock   £34,001 6% First Preferred Ordinary Stock.

So in 1967 the authorised share capital of the company was £18,278,213 and the issued £10,056,823.

In 1970 some stock was rounded in the accounts to the nearest thousand.

On 29 July 1976 the authorised share capital of the company was increased to £70,000,000 by the creation of 8,500,000 new unclassified shares of £1 each. On the same date each class of stock comprised in the issue share capital of the company was re-converted into shares of the same class. During 1976 the company issued 148,350 Ordinary shares of £1 on conversion of 296,700 7% Convertible Redeemable Preference shares of £1.

Additional, Incomplete, Financial Data.

Year	Number of Employees	Salaries Paid £
1895	200 (Cadby Hall)	
1896		73,908
1897		82,308
1898		114,263
1899		132,530
1900		180,416
1901		204,430
1902		231,640
1903		304,361
1904		327,116
1905		369,705
1906		474,808
1907		503,244
1908		548,766
1909		681,454
1910		827,811
1911		920,979
1912		1,360,997
1913		1,117,450
1914		1,224,755
1915		1,254,755
1916		1,314,873
1917		
1918		

Year	Number of Employees	Salaries Paid £
1919		15,000
1921		20,000
1922		22,000
1928		30,000
1933		30,000
1936		30,000
1957		31,000
1958		31,000
1966		31,000
1968	32,636	27,352,000
1969	31,734	29,131,000
1970	34,229	33,998,000
1971	33,977	37,450,000
1972	31,262	38,353,000
1973	31,389	42,191,000
1974	33,521	50,984,000
1975	33,751	64,007,000
1976	29,138	72,191,000
1977	26,573	70,843,000
1978	19,985	61,123,000
1979	22 weeks 19,570	43,200,000
1993	5,887	90,766,000
1994	52 weeks 5,560	93,667,000
1995	76 weeks 2,843	95,912,000

Source: J. Lyons & Co. Ltd Annual Report and Accounts.

Appendix 7: Principal Trading Sectors of the company and its Subsidiaries showing Turnover & Trading Profit 1968–1978.

| Year | TURNOVER £M | | | | | | TRADING PROFIT £1000s | | | | | |
	UK Food	Overseas Food	UK Hotel Catering	Overseas Hotel Catering	Property	Non-food	UK Food	Overseas Food	UK Hotel Catering	Overseas Hotel Catering	Property	Non-food
1968	93	-	21	-	-	11	4,097	-	833	-	512	121
1969*	91	-	27	-	-	11	4,706	-	1,378	-	912	24
1970*	113	-	29	-	-	13	5,394	-	1,792	-	1,094	12
1971*	122	-	33	-	-	13	5,864	-	2,542	-	1,037	384
1972	119	12	35	3	-	20	6,328	856	2,775	-308	1,176	406
1973	133	57	40	3	3	23	6,300	2,539	3,194	-244	2,348	541
1974	174	201	44	4	4	21	7,769	8,276	887	63	3,478	211
1975	224	264	51	6	11	21	8,919	12,767	-661	55	4,554	40
1976	229	339	55	7	3	18	11,645	17,355	-1,187	-695	511	-546
1977	275	407	19	6	1	18	13,031	18,612	244	-178	-219	-112
1978**	309	436	14	1	2	22	5,707	16,513	521	-154	1,339	249

* The overseas turnover and trading profit for 1968, 1969, 1970 and 1971 were not shown separately in the accounts and are left blank above.

** The UK hotel and catering figures for 1978 reflect catering profits only since the UK hotels were sold in 1977. The Alpha Hotel Amsterdam was sold in January 1978.

Source: J. Lyons & Co. Ltd Annual Report and Accounts.

Appendix 8: Lyons Maid Limited – Profit & Loss Account 1971–1991

Financial Year End	Turnover £1000s	Profit/(Loss) £1000s
1971	24,401	397
1972	25,212	257
1973	31,196	1,289
1974	33,812	666
1975	45,210	1,426
1976	51,820	2,505
1977	52,798	308
1978	not available	not available
1979	65,407	(1,495)
1980	65,984	(120)
1981	70,020	402*
1982	50,920	(1,865)
1983	51,958	(946)
1984	52,243	(1,140)
1985	51,809	642
1986	42,732	513
1987	42,979	856
1988	42,780	1,100
1989	44,001	(551)
1990	53,784	(2,408)
1991	53,644	(9,182)

* The retained (profit) at the end of this period should have shown a loss of £120,000. It was incorrectly entered as a profit.

The turnover and profit/loss figures in following year accounts are sometimes adjusted. These adjustments have been ignored and year of reporting figures have been used.

Source: Lyons Maid Ltd Accounts filed at Companies House, Cardiff.

Appendix 9: Directors 1894–1978

Name	Directorship Term	Date of Birth	Date of Death	Business Occupation
LYONS, Sir Joseph Nathaniel Kt 1911 DL	1894–1917	29.12.1847	22.06.1917	Chairman
GLUCKSTEIN, Montague Isidore	1894–1922	18.07.1854	07.10.1922	Chairman
GLUCKSTEIN, Isidore	1894–1920	13.08.1851	10.12.1920	Director
SALMON, Alfred	1894–1928	20.07.1868	11.10.1928	Managing Director
LEVY, Edwin	1894–1895	29.08.1840	26.02.1895	Director
BROWNE-MARTIN, Joseph	1894–1925	1835	20.01.1926	Gentleman
OATLEY, Charles Wake	1898–1922	11.12.1857	20.09.1922	Architect/Surveyor
BOOTH, George William	1898–1959	12.02.1869	19.09.1959	Secretary
MARKS, Albert Morris	1899–1914	01.03.1864	16.09 1914	Colonial Merchant
SALMON, Sir Isidore, Kt 1933	1903–1941	10.02.1876	16.09.1941	Managing Director
SALMON, Harry, JP	1909–1950	23.08.1881	13.10.1950	Chairman
GLUCKSTEIN, Samuel Montague, MC	1914–1928	21.02.1886	29.08.1928	Director
JOSEPH, John (Jack) Before 9.7.1918 Isiah Joseph	1914–1929	06.05.1881	05.05.1929	Director
SALMON, Maurice	1918–1947	09.12.1885	08.06.1947	Managing Director
SALMON, Julius	1918–1940	06.04.1888	09.01.1940	Managing Director
POLLARD, George Arthur	1918–1939	18.01.1863	20.03.1939	Manager Tea Dept.
GLUCKSTEIN, Maj. Montague, OBE	1919–1956	13.10.1886	25.12.1958	Chairman
DEE, George Silver	1919–1936	24.06.1868	23.02.1938	Accountant
WATKINS, Alfred Charles	1922–1933	09.10.1866	11.01.1934	Employee Director
GLUCKSTEIN, Isidore Montague	1925–1966	02.11.1890	16.01.1975	Managing Director
GLUCKSTEIN, Barnett Salmon	1926–1941	25.03.1879	09.07.1941	Director
SALMON, Barnett Alfred	1927–1965	10.11.1895	30.05.1965	Managing Director
SALMON, Sir Samuel Isidore Kt 1960, CBE, JP MP	1933–1968	18.10.1900	10.11.1980	Chairman
EDWARDS, Henry Lane	1934–1935	16.02.1871	24.07.1935	Manager
BENNETT, Harry Herbert Gladstone	1935–1966	12.03.1891	01.11.1978	Director/Secretary
LAMPITT, Dr Leslie Herbert	1936–1957	30.09.1887	03.06.1957	Doctor of Science
SALMON, Sir Julian, Kt 1969, OBE	1938–1969	29.08.1903	22.12.1978	Deputy Chairman
SALMON, Alfred Harry Barnett	1938–1960	08.05.1905	22.07.1960	Director
SIERRA, José Manuel Ernest	1939–1942	21.12.1889	27.05.1942	Chief Engineer
GLUCKSTEIN, Leonard	1941–1970	18.06.1907	17.01.1970	Director
GAUNT, Walter Henry, CBE, JP	1942–1951	13.01.1874	31.10.1951	Distribution Manager
SALMON, Geoffry Isidore Hamilton, CBE	1945–1972	14.01.1908	29.04.1990	Chairman
SALMON, Felix Addison	1946–1969	16.07.1908	25.08.1969	Director
COYTE, William Arthur	1946–1951	29.01.1886	19.07.1968	Chief Engineer
JENKINS, Alan James	1946–1959	21.09.1892	08.11.1966	Manager
BROWN, William Isaac	1946–1966	01.09.1888	19.11.1976	Director
JOSEPH, Sir Norman Samuel, Kt 1964, KCVO, CBE	1947–1973	12.12.1908	17.11.1974	Director
GLUCKSTEIN, Douglas Montague, DL	1950–1976	25.03.1909	02.10.1998	Director
GLUCKSTEIN, Kenneth Montague	1950–1959	04.10.1911	23.09.1959	Director
SIMMONS, John Richard Mainwaring	1951–1968	19.03.1902	14.01.1985	Comptroller
SALMON, Ivor Francis	1951–1977	24.08.1911		Director
GLUCKSTEIN, Guy Ferdinand Montague	1952–1971	20.01.1912	14.02.1986	Director
CROSSLÉ, Cecil A	1952–1969	08.02.1904	06.11.1985	Tea buyer
SALMON, Anthony Montague Lawson	1955–1978	05.05.1916		Director
BOGOD, Mark	1958–1964	10.11.1898	19.03.1968	Department Manager
SCOTT, Henry Joseph	1960–1965	03.10.1901	30.06.1991	Engineer
SALMON, Brian Lawson, CBE	1960–1977	17.06.1917		Chairman
SALMON, Neil Lawson	1965–1981	17.02.1921	08.08.1989	Chairman
BADHAM, Leonard	1965–1987	10.06.1923	11.06.1992	Managing Director
DYER, Philip S	1965–1972	19.05.1909		Director
YOUNG, Harold George	1965–1981	24.06.1921	20.11.1989	Director
SALMON, Christopher Robin Lawson	1966–1979	21.12.1926	28.11.1985	Operations Director
LAWRENCE, Sir Guy Kempton, Kt 1976, DSO, DFC, OBE	1966–1975	05.11.1914		Deputy Chairman
MERRY, Frank	1967–1988	14.03.1927		Corp. Development Director
SILVERMAN, Jacob Barnett	1971–1988	29.02.1928		Asst. Managing Director
GLUCKSTEIN, John Michael Howard	1972–1977	17.01.1936		Operations Director
MENDELSSOHN, John Nigel	1975–1982	19.04.1929		Finance/Property Director
OGILVIE, Sir Alec Drummond, Kt 1965	1977–1978	17.05.1913	13.11.1997	Non-executive Director
BIDE, Austin Ernest	1977–1978	11.09.1915		Non-executive Director
PAGE, Sir Alexander Warren, Kt 1977	1978–1978	01.07.1914		Non-executive Director
MOLLETT, Philip Thomas Wetherall	1978–1982	14.05.1928	28.02.2000	Personnel Director

Prior to 1 July 1837 births, marriages and deaths were recorded in parish registers only and are therefore not available at the Office for National Statistics (births, marriages & deaths).

Source: Office for National Statistics, Companies House and S&G Trust Limited.

Appendix 10: Hotels Operated by the Strand, Cumberland & Lyons Group Companies

Hotel Name	Year Opened (O) or Acquired (A)	Number of Rooms*	Room Price* (1976) single	double	Remarks
Albany Hotel Group					
Albany Hotel, Birmingham	1962 (O)	250	£15.90	£21.00	
Albany Hotel, Glasgow	1973 (O)	250	£16.90	£24.50	
Albany Hotel, Nottingham	1969 (O)	160	£15.90	£21.90	
Havant Albany Inn, Hayling Island	1973 (O)	100	£13.00	£16.75	
Rugby Albany Inn, Crick	1971 (O)	100	£13.50	£16.00	
Wakefield Albany Inn, Ossett	1972 (O)	100	£13.00	£16.00	
European Hotels					
Alpha Hotel, Amsterdam	1971 (O)	600	G80.00	G110	
Hôtel Commodore, Paris	1973 (A)	170	F185	F250	Note 1
Park Hotel, Siena	1973 (A)				Note 2
Strand Hotel Group					
Ariel Hotel, Heathrow Airport	1961 (O)	180	£13.30	£18.00	
Cavendish Hotel, Lancaster Gate, London	1971 (A)	60	n/a	n/a	Note 3
Clifton Hotel, Eastbourne	1970 (A)	150	£ 9.50	£16.00	
Dominion Hotel, Lancaster Gate, London	1971 (A)	90	n/a	n/a	Note 3
International Hotel, Lancaster Gate, London	1971 (A)		n/a	n/a	Note 3
Kingsley Hotel, Bloomsbury, London	1970 (A)	180	£ 9.50	£14.00	
Mansion Hotel, Eastbourne	1970 (A)	100	£..9.00	£16.00	Note 4
Park Court Hotel, Lancaster Gate, London	1971 (A)	450	£11.90	£17.00	Note 3
Regent Palace Hotel, Piccadilly, London	1915 (O)	1,130	£ 8.50	£14.60	Note 5
Strand Palace Hotel, Strand, London	1909 (O)	780	£13.50	£19.60	Note 6
Tower Hotel, London	1973 (O)	830	£19.50	£26.00	
White's Hotel, Lancaster Gate, London	1970 (A)	60	£14.50	£20.00	
Windsor Hotel, Lancaster Gate, London	1971 (A)	100	£ 9.00	£14.00	
Wish Tower Hotel, Eastbourne	1970 (A)	80	£ 9.00	£16.00	Note 4
Royal Palace Hotel Group					
Royal Palace Hotel, Kensington, London	1919 (A)				Note 7
Cumberland Hotel Group					
Cumberland Hotel, Marble Arch, London	1933 (O)	900	£19.00	£26.00	
Maison Lyons, Marble Arch, London	1933 (O)	n/a	n/a	n/a	Note 8
Falcon Inns Hotel Group					
Atholl Palace Hotel, Pitlochry	1973 (A)	120	£13.00	£20.50	Note 4
Belsfield Hotel, Bowness-on-Windermere	1971 (A)	90	£17.00	£26.50	Note 4
Brandon Hall Hotel, Coventry	1972 (A)	70	£15.50	£21.00	Note 4
Burnside Hotel, Bowness-on-Windermere	1971 (A)	30	£14.50	£23.00	Note 4 & 9
Cally Hotel, Gatehouse of Fleet	1973 (A)	90	£13.00	£20.50	Note 4
Chester Curzon Hotel, Chester	1973 (A)	60	£14.00	£17.50	Note 4
Craiglands Hotel, Ilkley	1973 (A)	70	£14.00	£21.00	Note 4
Crown Hotel, Harrogate	1972 (A)	120	£13.00	£22.50	Note 4
Frimley Hall Hotel, Camberley	1972 (A)	70	£16.00	£22.00	Note 4
Glenborrodale Castle, Ardnamurchan	1973 (A)	30	£14.00	£22.00	Note 4
Ivy Bush Royal Hotel, Carmarthen	1975 (A)	100	£12.00	£19.00	Note 4
Keswick Hotel, Keswick	1972 (A)	80	£12.50	£19.50	Note 4
Marine Hotel, North Berwick	1973 (A)	100	£12.00	£19.00	Note 4
Stradey Park Hotel, Llanelli	1975 (A)	80	£12.50	£19.00	Note 4
Swans Nest Hotel, Stratford-on-Avon	1972 (A)	80	£12.50	£23.00	Note 4
Whately Hall Hotel, Banbury	1972 (A)	70	£13.50	£22.00	Note 4
Ye Olde Bell Hotel, near Retford	1973 (A)	60	£12.50	£18.00	Note 4
Royal Hibernian Group					
Old Ground, Ennis, County Clare (Eire)	1970 (A)	70	£10.85	£13.45	
Hotel Russell, Dublin	1970 (A)	60			Note 10
Royal Hibernian Hotel, Dublin	1970 (A)	110	£12.40	£15.50	

*Hotel rooms have been rounded to nearest ten. Room numbers varied from time to time as modifications and hotel improvements were made. Prices too were subject to variation depending on room size, outlook and other features. The above should be taken as average.

Hotel Notes

Note 1. The Hôtel Commodore was sold to Aer Lingus.

Note 2. The Park Hotel Marzocchi, Siena (Italy) came into the group when the subsidiary Industrie Riunite del Panforte di Sienna S.p.A. acquired it. It did not feature in the main hotel operations being of a small country type. It was refurbished in 1975 and sold to Villa Cipriana S.p.A. in 1978.

Note 3. After acquiring the Park Court Hotel several adjacent hotels (Cavendish, Dominion and International) were acquired and under a major £2 million development scheme were converted into one hotel, the Park Court.

Note 4. Prices are 1978 rates. All have private bathrooms. Rooms without *en suite* facilities were typically £2-4 less expensive. In some cases breakfast was not included. The Swans Nest was owned by Whitly Inns, a 50-50 joint company formed with Whitbread the brewers but operated by Falcon Inns.

Note 5. An annexe to the Regent Palace Hotel opened in 1934 adding 102 rooms to the previous total.

Note 6. When the Strand Palace Hotel opened in 1909 it had 450 bedrooms. A large addition was added in 1928–1930 providing a further 458 bedrooms making 908. Bedroom-bathroom suites were added in 1960 which reduced bedroom numbers to 776. Strand Hotel Limited changed its name to Strand Hotels Limited in 1967.

Note 7. Sold to Grand Metropolitan in the early 1950s.

Note 8. Maison Lyons was a Corner House with a number of restaurants and a retail front shop forming part of the Cumberland Hotel complex and, unlike the other three Corner Houses, was operated by Cumberland Hotels Limited.

Note 9. Lyons acquired the Burnside Hotel, originally known as the Burnside Private Hotel, when they purchased Chateau Hotels of Europe Limited for £37,402 in 1971. In March 1975 several acres of the hotel grounds were sold to Lyons by Chateau Hotels and a number of self-catering cottages and apartments were built.

Note 10. The Hotel Russell in Dublin closed in 1973 in order that the site, including some neighbouring properties, could be redeveloped.

Small Public House Hotels some of which were owned by the subsidiary, The Robley Group Limited.

Lion & Lamb Hotel, Brentwood	Master Builder's House, Beaulieu	The George, Slough
Golden Fleece, Chelmsford	The Angel Hotel, Midhurst	
Greyhound, Bromley	The Three Maypoles, Shirley, Birmingham	
The Hayworthe Arms, Haywards Heath	The Wheelhouse, Nottingham	
Star & Garter, Andover	The Christopher, Bath	
Red Lion Hotel, Petersfield	The Arlington, Brighton	
The Dolphin Hotel, Romsey	The Magpie, Sunbury-on-Thames	

Source: J. Lyons & Co. Ltd Annual Report and Accounts, Strand Hotel marketing literature.

Appendix 11: Royal Warrants Bestowed

May 1899 J. Lyons & Company Ltd His Royal Highness The Prince of Wales bestowed the Warrant of Appointment.
April 1902. J. Lyons & Company Ltd appointed Bakers to His Royal Highness The Prince of Wales.
01.02.1904. J. Lyons & Company Ltd appointed as refreshment contractors to King Edward VII.
10.12.1910. J. Lyons & Company Ltd appointed refreshment contractors to King George V.
01.12.1948. J. Lyons & Company Ltd appointed caterers to King George VI.
15.07.1955. J. Lyons & Company Ltd appointed caterers to HM Queen Elizabeth II.
15.07.1955. Henry Telfer Ltd by appointment to HM Queen Elizabeth II purveyors of pork pies.
01.03.1956. J. Lyons & Company Ltd appointed caterers to Queen Elizabeth the Queen Mother.
01 02. 1967. Symbol Biscuits Ltd appointed supplier of biscuits to HM Queen Elizabeth the Queen Mother.
10.01.1971. Lyons Bakery Ltd appointed manufacturers of cakes to HM Queen Elizabeth II.
01.02.1978. Lyons Maid Ltd appointed manufacturers of ice-cream to HM Queen Elizabeth II.
01.01.1985. J. Lyons & Company Ltd appointed caterers to HRH Prince of Wales.

Notes

Lyons first established a Buckingham Palace liaison representative ('Jack' Goodden) in 1903. They catered for a garden party at Windsor Castle in 1905 and in the same year for a gala performance at the opera. However, they did not start catering for the royal garden parties at Buckingham Palace until 1919 and in that year catered for a party on 27 June. There were five garden parties held altogether in 1919, the largest being for 10,000 people. Before the Second World War up to 15,000 people were catered for at Buckingham Palace's garden parties.

Appendix 12: The Gluckstein Family Tree

Lehmann Meyer Gluckstein = Helena, daughter of Samuel Nathan Horn & Bina Suss Spiro
1794–1859
b.Jenver
1797–1854
b.Reinberg

Samuel Gluckstein = Hannah, daughter of Coleman Joseph & Judic Marcus Neeter
1821–1873
b.Reinberg
1819–1885
b.Amsterdam

Meyer
1822–
b.Lippe

Nathan
1824–
b.Reinberg

Solomon
1830–

Naphtali
1832–
b.Arnhem

Bincha
1834–

Gershom
1836–
b.Rotterdam

Benjamin
1843–

Julia G.
1846–1891
married
Abraham
Abrahams
1838–1925

Helena G.
1846–1907
married
Barnett
Salmon
1829–1897

Bertha G.
1848–1921
married
Julius
Koppenhagen
1854–1930

Catherine G. *
1850–1911
married
Samuel
Joseph
1851–1936

Isidore G.
1851–1920
married
Rose
Cohen
1851–1908

Montague G.
1854–1922
married
Matilda
Franks
1861–1950

Joseph G. *
1856–1930
married
Kate
Joseph
1853–1889
m. secondly
Francesca Hallé
1874–1958

Henry G. *
1857–1914
married
Emma
Joseph
1854–1930

Sarah G. *
1859–1929
married
Abraham
Joseph
1858–1930

Clara G. *
1862–1918
married
Coleman
Joseph
1856–1930

Hannah S. m. Samuel Abrahams*
Alfred S. m. Frances Abrahams*
Isidore S. m. Kate Abrahams*
Montague S. m. Marian Abrahams
Joseph S. m. Rachel Mandel
Harry S. m. Lena Gluckstein*
Rose S. m. Barnett Gluckstein*
Maurice S. m. Katie Joseph*
Julius S. m. Emma Gluckstein*

Celia J. m. Harry Schneiders
John J. m. Deborah Halle
Hannah J. m. John Trevor
Julia J. m. Samuel Gluckstein*

Samuel G. m. Johanna Koppenhagen*
Isidore G. m. Rosalind Adler
Emma G. m. Julius Salmon*

Samuel G. m. Caroline Schneiders
Sidney G. m. Clair Vos
Isidore G. m. Esme Frischer

Isiah (Victor) J. m. Rose Atwel
Nancy J. m. Montague Gluckstein*

Hannah G.
(assumed name Gluck)
Louis G. m. Doreen Klean

Hannah G. m. Henry Atwell
Barnett G. m. Rose Salmon*
Samuel G. m. Julia Joseph*
Lena G. m. Harry Salmon*
Julia G. m. Frederick Lever
Montague G. m. Nancy Joseph*
Matilda G. died 8 yrs

Bertie J.
Katie J. m. Maurice Salmon*
Samuel J. m. Edna Cicely

Johanna K. m. Samuel Gluckstein*
Samuel K. m. Madge Mitchell
Lena K. m. John Moss
Mayer K.
Julia K. m. Percival Sharp

John A. m. Amy Benjamin
Samuel A. m. Hannah Salmon
Frances A. m. Alfred Salmon*
Barnett A.
Maurice A. m. Caroline Bronet
dissolved 1926
m. secondly Eve Bailey
Hannah A. m. Arthur Salmon
Kate A. m. Isidore Salmon*
Montague A. m. Miriam Simmons
Sarah A. m. Herbert Wolf

* Signifies marriage to a first cousin

Appendix 13: The Salmon Family Tree

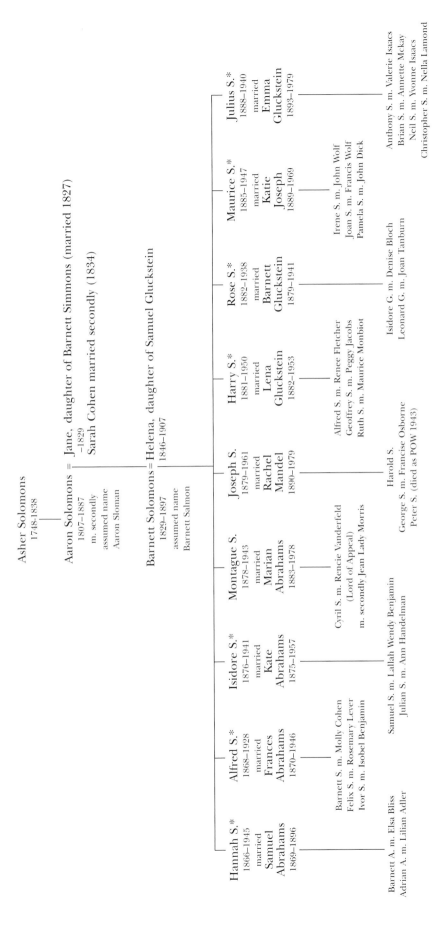

Asher Solomons
1748–1838

Aaron Solomons = Jane, daughter of Barnett Simmons (married 1827)
1807–1887   –1829
m. secondly   Sarah Cohen married secondly (1834)
assumed name
Aaron Sloman

Barnett Solomons = Helena, daughter of Samuel Gluckstein
1829–1897   1846–1907
assumed name
Barnett Salmon

Hannah S.*
1866–1945
married
Samuel
Abrahams
1869–1896

Alfred S.*
1868–1928
married
Frances
Abrahams
1870–1946

Isidore S.*
1876–1941
married
Kate
Abrahams
1875–1957

Montague S.
1878–1943
married
Marian
Abrahams
1883–1978

Joseph S.
1879–1961
married
Rachel
Mandel
1890–1979

Harry S.*
1881–1950
married
Lena
Gluckstein
1882–1953

Rose S.*
1882–1938
married
Barnett
Gluckstein
1879–1941

Maurice S.*
1885–1947
married
Katie
Joseph
1889–1969

Julius S.*
1888–1940
married
Emma
Gluckstein
1893–1979

Barnett S. m. Molly Cohen
Felix S. m. Rosemary Lever
Ivor S. m. Isobel Benjamin

Cyril S. m. Rencie Vanderfeld
(Lord of Appeal)
m. secondly Jean Lady Morris

Samuel S. m. Lallah Wendy Benjamin
Julian S. m. Ann Handelman

Harold S.
George S. m. Francise Osborne
Peter S. (died as POW 1943)

Alfred S. m. Renee Fletcher
Geoffrey S. m. Peggy Jacobs
Ruth S. m. Maurice Monbiot

Isidore G. m. Denise Bloch
Leonard G. m. Joan Tanburn

Irene S. m. John Wolf
Joan S. m. Francis Wolf
Pamela S. m. John Dick

Anthony S. m. Valerie Isaacs
Brian S. m. Annette Mckay
Neil S. m. Yvonne Isaacs
Christopher S. m. Nella Lamond

Barnett A. m. Elsa Bliss
Adrian A. m. Lilian Adler

* Signifies marriage to a first cousin

Appendix 14: Allied-Lyons and Allied Domecq trading profit by sector 1979–1995 (£millions)

Year	*Total	Food	Wines	Beer	Retail
1979	137.1	33.0	48.2	55.9	-
1980	137.5	28.8	58.3	50.4	-
1981	136.9	31.5	58.6	46.8	-
1982	153.4	33.1	67.7	52.6	-
1983	171.9	38.5	65.1	68.3	-
1984	195.8	53.2	66.9	77.3	-
1985	218.0	63.5	66.9	87.6	-
1986	261.6	74.8	76.1	110.7	-
1987	368.1	100.5	120.4	149.6	-
1988	519.8	106.8	249.7	176.5	-
1989	569.0	97.0	271.0	203.0	-
1990	656.0	108.0	318.0	232.0	-
1991	798.0	139.0	403.0	256.0	-
1992	813.0	147.0	410.0	258.0	-
1993	683.0	64.0	401.0	64.0	195.0
1994	720.0	71.0	365.0	90.0	204.0
1995	**959.0	22.0	514.0	103.0	320.0

* The trading profit ignores those activities listed as central companies. It includes only those activities listed as continuing operations and disregards restructuring costs, acquired operations or associated undertakings. Totals were rounded to whole numbers from 1989.

** 18 months.

Source: Allied-Lyons plc and Allied Domecq plc Annual Report and Accounts.

BIBLIOGRAPHY

First Report on the Royal Commission on Food Prices. Vol 1. (HMSO, 1925)
Advertising Labelling & Composition of Food (Ministry of Food, 1949)
ALFORD, B.W.E., *W. D. & H. O. Wills* (Methuen & Co., 1973)
ANONYMOUS, *Facts About British Railways in Wartime* (Railways' Press Office, 1943)
AUSTRIAN, Geoffrey, *Hollerith-Forgotten Giant of Information Processing* (Columbia Univ. Press, 1982)
BATES, H.E., *The Tinkers of Elstow* (not known)
BESANT, Walter, *London* (Chatto & Windus, 1894)
BIRCH, G. Gordon *et al*, *Food Science* (Pergamon Press, 1978)
BIRD, Peter John, *LEO-The First Business Computer* (Hasler Publishing Ltd, 1994)
BLAKE, George, *Lloyd's Register of Shipping 1760–1960* (Lloyd's Register of Shipping, 1960)
BRADWELL, Cyril, *Fight the Good Fight* (The Salvation Army)
BRAMAH, Edward, *Tea & Coffee* (Hutchinson, 1972)
BREARS, Peter *et al*, *A Taste of History* (British Museum Press, 1993)
BRIGGS, M. & JORDAN P., *Economic History of England* (Univ. Tutorial Press, 1978)
BUTLER Robert, *Sandwich Haven and Richborough Port* (Sandwich History Society, 1966)
CARETER, Oliver, *British Railway Hotels 1838–1983* (Silver Link Publishing, 1990)
CENTRAL STATISTICAL OFFICE, *Fighting with Figures* (Central Statistical Office, 1995)
CHALKEY, Brian *et al* (ed.), *Plymouth: Maritime City in Transition* (David & Charles, 1991)
COLE, Howard N., *The Story of the Army Catering Corps* (Army Catering Corps Ass., 1984)
COOK, Chris & STEVENSON J., *Handbook of Modern British History 1714–1980* (Longman Group Ltd, 1983)
DIXON, R. & MUTHESIUS, S., *Victorian Architecture* (Thames & Hudson Ltd, 1978)
DRUCKER, Peter F., *The Practice of Management* (Butterworth-Heineman, 1989)
DUVAL, G.R., *Presentation Aircraft of the Two World Wars* (D. Bradford Barton Ltd, 1976)
FENELON, K.G., *Britain's Food Supplies* (Methuen & Co., 1952)
FIENE, Dr. F. & BLUMENTHAL S., *Handbook of Food Manufacture* (Chapman & Hall Ltd, 1939)
FLOUD, Roderick *et al*, *The Economic History of Britain vol. 2 1860–1970* (Cambridge Univ. Press, 1988)
FORREST, Denys, *Tea for the British* (Chatto & Windus, 1973)
FORTE, Charles, *The Autobiography of Charles Forte* (Sidgwick & Jackson, 1986)
GERRARD, Frank, *Sausage & Small Goods Production* (Leonard Hill Ltd, 1955)
GIACOMI, R. De (ed.), *Food Processing & Packaging Industry Directory* (Tothill Press Ltd, 1965)
GILLING-SMITH, G.D., *The Complete Guide to Pensions & Superannuation* (Penguin Books, 1967)
GLUCKSTEIN, Joseph, *Family Trees* (Private publication, 1954)
GREEN, Daniel, *A Family of Food Companies* (Hodder & Stoughton)
HAMMOND, R.J., *Food Vol III Studies in Administration & Control* (HMSO, 1962)
HANNAH, Leslie, *Inventing Retirement* (CUP, 1986)
HARBURY, Colin & LIPSEY R., *An Introduction to the UK Economy* (Pitman Publishing Ltd, 1986)
HARTLEY, Harold, *Eighty-Eight Not Out* (Frederick Muller Ltd, 1939)
HAY, Donald & Morris, Derek J., *Unquoted Companies* (The Macmillan Press Ltd, 1984)
HEWLETT, Geoffrey, *History of Wembley* (Brent Library, 1979)
HOBSBAWM, E.J., *Industry and Empire* (Penguin Books Ltd, 1969)
HONEYCOMBE, Gordon, *The Murders of the Black Museum 1870–1970* (Hutchinson & Co.)
HOUGHTON, H.W. (ed.), *Developments in Soft Drinks Technology – Vol 3* (Elsevier App. Science Pub., 1984)
HUGHES, W. & THOMAS, J., *The Sentinel. Volume 1 1875–1930* (David & Charles, 1973)
INWOOD, Stephen, *A History of London* (Macmillan Publishers Ltd, 1998)

IRONS, J.R., *Breadcraft* (Virtue & Co. Ltd, 1948)
JENKINS, Alan, *The Twenties* (Book Club Associates, 1974)
KEAY, John, *The Honourable Company* (HarperCollins, 1991)
KERRIGAN, Colm, *A History of Tower Hamlets* (London Borough of TH, 1982)
KNIGHT, Donald, *The Lion Roars at Wembley* (Private Publication, 1984)
KYNASTON, David, *The City of London. Vol II 1890–1914* (Chatto & Windus, 1995)
LAPPING, Brian, *End of Empire* (Paladin Grafton Books, 1989)
LLOYD'S of LONDON, *Lloyd's Register of British and Foreign Shipping* (Lloyd's, 1884)
LLOYD'S of LONDON, *Lloyd's Weekly Shipping Index* (Lloyd's, 1883–4)
MACINTOSH, R.W.D., *Frozen Foods. The Growth of an Industry* (Refrigeration Press)
MATHIAS, Peter, *Retailing Revolution* (Longmans, Green & Co., 1967)
MIDDLEBROOK M. & EVERITT C., *The Bomber Command War Diaries* (Midland Publishing Ltd, 1996)
MINISTRY of INFORMATION, *Transport Goes to War* (HMSO, 1942)
MITCHELL, B.R., *British Historical Statistics* (CUP, 1988)
OLDFIELD, Maurice, *Understanding Pension Schemes*, 3rd edition (Fourmat Publishing, 1987)
OLSEN, Donald J., *The Growth of Victorian London* (B. T. Batsford Ltd, 1976)
POPE, Wm. J. (Sir), *The People's Food* (unknown)
PRIESTLEY, J.B., *Man Power: The Story of Britain's Mobilisation for War* (HMSO, 1944)
RAWLINGS, John D.R., *Fighter Squadrons of the RAF & Their Aircraft* (Crecy Books Ltd, 1993)
READER, W.J., *50 Years of Unilever* (Heinemann, 1980)
REINDERS, Pim, *Licks, Sticks & Bricks. A World History of Ice Cream* (Unilever, Rotterdam, 1999)
ROCQUE, J. *et al*, *The A-Z of Georgian London* (The British Library)
ROSE, Douglas, *The London Underground-A Diagrammatic History* (Douglas Rose, London, 1990)
SHEPPARD, R. & NEWTON, E., *The Story of Bread* (Routledge & Kegan, 1957)
SIMMONS, Douglas A., *Schweppes – The First 200 Years* (Springwood Books, 1983)
SIMMONS, J. & BIDDLE G. (eds.), *The Oxford Companion to British Railway History* (Oxford University Press, 1997)
SIMMONS, John R.M., *Management of Change – The Role of Information* (Gee & Co (publishers) Ltd, 1970)
SIMMONS, John R.M., *Leo and the Managers* (Macdonald, 1962)
SMALES, Bernard J., *Economic History Made Simple* (W.H. Allen, London, 1975)
SOUHAMI, Diana, *Gluck-Her Biography* (Pandora Press, 1988)
SPENCER, Michael, *Food Science* (Pergamon Press, 1972)
STONER, R. & ROWE, D., *Measurement of Consumer Expenditure in the United Kingdom. 1920–1930* (CUP, 1954)
SWALLOW, William *et al*, *Investment in Hotels & Catering* (HMSO, 1968)
THE TIMES (comp.), *British War Production 1939–1945 a Record* (The Times Publishing Co., 1945)
TOUSSAINT-SAMAT, Maguelonne, *A History of Food* (Blackwell, Camb. MA, 1992)
TRENCH, Richard, *London Before The Blitz* (Weidenfeld & Nicholson, 1989)
WALFORD, Edward M.A., *Village London Vol 1 Story of Greater London* (The Alderman Press, 1983)
WHITTING, Philip D., *A History of Hammersmith* (Local History Group, 1965)
WILLIAMS, Ken, *The Story of Ty-phoo* (Quiller Press, 1990)
WILSON, Charles, *Unilever 1945–1965* (Cassell, 1954)
WYLD, Ross, *The War Over Walthamstow* (Walthamstow Borough Council, 1945)
ZIEGLER, Philip, *London at War 1939–1945* (Sinclair-Stevenson, 1995)

Index

Lyons' Wedding Cakes

'CERES'
design

A superb cake, fashioned with consummate artistry and in dignified keeping with the spirit of the ceremony. This design is iced a delicate parchment, but is also available in white. Lyons' wedding cake mixture, almond iced.

Approx. overall height - 28"
Approx. diameter - 15"
Approx. weight from 27 lbs.
Price from - £5 5s. 0d

£5-12-0

The standard colour of this cake is PARCHMENT which will be sent unless otherwise specified.

J. LYONS & Co. Ltd. Cadby Hall, London, W. 14.